Respectfully Quoted

Courteous Reader,

I have heard that nothing gives an Author so great Pleasure, as to find his Works respectfully quoted by other learned Authors. This Pleasure I have seldom enjoyed; for tho' I have been, if I may say it without Vanity, an *eminent Author* of Almanacks annually now a full Quarter of a Century, my Brother Authors in the same Way, for what Reason I know not, have ever been very sparing in their Applauses; and no other Author has taken the least Notice of me, so that did not my Writings produce me some solid *Pudding,* the great Deficiency of *Praise* would have quite discouraged me.

BENJAMIN FRANKLIN, Preface, *Poor Richard Improved: Being an Almanack and Ephemeris . . . for the Year of Our Lord, 1758,* in *The Papers of Benjamin Franklin,* ed. Leonard W. Labaree, vol. 7, p. 340 (1963).

Respectfully Quoted

A Dictionary of Quotations from the Library of Congress

edited by **Suzy Platt**
Congressional Research Service

Congressional Quarterly Inc.
Washington, D.C.

1414 22nd St. N.W., Washington, D.C. 20037

Printed in the United States of America

Fourth Printing

Book design by Adrianne Onderdonk Dudden
Cover design by Paula Anderson

This book was first published in 1989 by the Library of Congress under the title *Respectfully Quoted: A Dictionary of Quotations Requested from the Congressional Research Service.*

Library of Congress Cataloging-in-Publication Data

Respectfully quoted : a dictionary of quotations from the Library of
Congress / edited by Suzy Platt, Congressional Research Service.
p. cm.
Includes indexes.
ISBN 0-87187-687-6 (cloth). -- ISBN 0-87187-674-4 (paper)
1. Quotations, English. I. Platt, Suzy. II. Library of
Congress. Congressional Research Service.
[PN6081.R435 1992]
808.8'2--dc20 91-45490
CIP

Contents

Foreword

I have heard that someone once asked Woodrow Wilson how long it took him to write a speech. He replied, "It depends. If I am to speak ten minutes, I need a week for preparation. If fifteen minutes, three days. If half an hour, two days. If an hour, I am ready now."

We would like to think that with the quotations in this book, we would all be "ready now" for the long ones, but that these quotations would make even our ten-minute versions more precise, more thoughtful, and more perfectly shaped to express our intentions.

The Congressional Research Service has been responding to Congressional inquiries about quotations for nearly seventy-five years now, and during this time we have searched out many of the most popular statements many times over. But we have tracked down many others that had never been identified before but which had a pith and point equal to the more traditional thoughts. The 2100 statements included in this book are the best of the latter.

We hope they will be helpful to the Members of Congress in their task of expressing our national purpose and in their debating the public issues before the Legislature. Having been requested by a Member or his staff, and then having been located by the librarians of the Congressional Research Service, we believe they have a wide usefulness and should be shared with successive generations of legislators—and, in turn, with the broadest possible audience.

We hope you will find them of value.

GILBERT GUDE
Director, Congressional Research Service
1977–1986

Preface

A great many people have had a hand in this project over the years. Numerous staff members of the Congressional Research Service have searched for quotations wanted by Members of Congress and have made cards for the Congressional Reading Room quote file. Many a harried librarian has breathed a sigh of relief and thankfulness when finding right at hand in the quote file just what was being sought for a speech *right now.*

Kenton Kilmer we think translated the Latin, often more elegantly than we could find in printed sources. Harvey Baugh, long-time evening and weekend supervisor of the Reading Room and equally long-time searcher for elusive quotations, made his presence known during this project when I received from the stacks a dusty volume and found in it, marking the desired paragraph, a bookmark with Harvey's distinctive handwriting.

Thanks are due in great measure to Teresa S. Blackwelder, Deborah C. Brudno, Adriana P. Orr, Carolyn A. Larson, and Barbara V. Fontana, who did the research with imagination, energy, perseverance, and devotion. The topical arrangement and the author and keyword indexes were prepared by Victoria P. Agee with skill and enthusiasm. LeeEllen Friedland proofread and provided editorial guidance. Thanks are also due to the individuals and organizations who helped us track down the sources of quotations.

This book is yet another cooperative effort of the entire staff of the Congressional Reference Division of CRS—those who worked on the quotes directly and those who provided administrative, technical, clerical, and backup support and services—and all are entitled to feel pride of accomplishment in its appearance. Among the present and former members of the Division who have contributed greatly are Margaret E. Melun, F. Anne Ritchings (who spearheaded the project), Victoria C. Hill, Mary Nell Bryant, and Robert Newlen. Basil T. Owens, former assistant director of CRS for assignment, reference, and special services, and Catherine A. Jones, chief, Congressional Reference Division, provided administrative leadership.

We are librarians, not scholars, and this works reflects it. We were also using the collections of a very large, busy library. The volumes wanted were not always available, or if available once, not always later. We have in many instances used the first edition or an early edition of a work, but in some cases we have deliberately used twentieth-century editions, which are generally much more readily available in libraries. We have provided an exact citation to a printed work, except for Shakespeare and the Bible, and we have tried to make it easy for others to find the same item by giving chapters, paragraphs, sections, and so on, where appropriate. Many dictionaries of quotations only give the name of the work or the chapter, and it can take a great deal of reading in a chapter of seventy to one hundred pages to find the desired paragraph or sentence. We have sometimes used the best-known translations, other times not, because we tried to get as close to the translations in the quote file as we could.

Not surprisingly, many of the persons quoted in this book were Members of Congress, if not when quoted then at some other time in their careers. We have identified them by using "Representative" or "Senator" before the name if the individual was a Member of Congress at the time the remark was made. If the individual was a Member of Congress at some other time, a note to that effect appears.

We have given the context of the quotations in many cases, along with notes as appropriate, necessary, or interesting. As the compilers of *The Oxford Dictionary of Quotations* expressed it: "In many places more of the context of the actual familiar phrase has been given than is strictly necessary; but this has been a practice throughout the book, and one which it was thought would add to its value and charm" (2d ed., p. ix, 1956).

Where we have been able to identify the published source of the quotation, we have given it. Where we have searched an author's works without finding the quotation, we have added "unverified." We would be happy to receive information giving sources as exactly as may be possible. However, it will not help to point out that such-and-such a work also attributes this quotation to, say, Disraeli, if it does not give a source. Information and queries may be sent to Quotations Editor, Congressional Reference Division, CRS, Library of Congress, Washington, D.C. 20540.

SUZY PLATT
Congressional Reference Division

Introduction

This is a different kind of quotation book. Most quotation books are compiled by learned literateurs who sit in silent rooms reading thc words of wise people and asking, "I wonder if that thought might be useful to somebody?" These quotations have already answered that question. They have already been used by somebody, and others have already heard them, have already decided they want to use them again, and that they want to be sure they have got them exactly right for further public consumption.

How This Quotation Book Came To Be

For nearly seventy-five years, Members of Congress and their staffs have been calling the Congressional Research Service of the Library of Congress to verify quotations that they wanted to use in public debate. They wished to be certain that these quotations were both accurate and armored against challenge. In most cases the quotes they sought were ones they had heard someone else use, but in some cases they were ones that had been flung at them by the opposition, and the Members were sufficiently irritated that they hoped the quote could be refuted, labelled spurious, and buried once and for all. Either way, they turned to the CRS for authentication and the Service in turn turned to the almost limitless resources of the Library of Congress.

Through the years, this matter of quotation verification became big business. The quotations increased from the tens to the hundreds and have now reached thousands each year. (The CRS, incidentally, now receives congressional inquiries of *all* varieties in excess of 1500 queries a *day*!)

Most of the "quote questions" were handled by the staff of a unit called the Congressional Reading Room, and after some twenty years of this reference work, the staff began to detect three kinds of citations that seemed to stand apart from the routine traffic: the hard ones, the repetitive ones, and the impossible ones. All of these consumed an unusual amount of research time, and ultimately—now almost fifty years ago—the "CRR Quote File" was created to prevent staff from wasting time on citations that had already been found and to identify those items which had proved to be either "spurious" or "unidentifiable" after reasonable, professional search. The 2100 quotations in this book are the cumulated result of fifty years of such insertions into that Congressional Reading Room Quotation File.

Savage Politics

These quotations come from the real world of cut and thrust politics. They show the combination of spirit and humor that represents American political activity at its best. Recalling that each of these quotations was requested specifically by some Member or his staff, it is intriguing to speculate on what situation was occurring that precipitated the need for such items as the following:

> If you give me six lines written by the hand of the most honest of men, I will find something in them which will hang him.—Cardinal Richelieu
>
> Democracy is the theory that the common people know what they want, and deserve to get it good and hard.—H. L. Mencken
>
> Never explain; your friends do not need it and your enemies will not believe you anyway.—Elbert Hubbard
>
> Politicians are the same all over. They promise to build a bridge even where there is no river.—Nikita Khrushchev
>
> He has been called a mediocre man; but this is unwarranted flattery. He was a politician of monumental littleness.—Theodore Roosevelt (speaking of President John Tyler)
>
> In order to act, you must be somewhat insane. A reasonably sensible man is satisfied with thinking.—Georges Clemenceau
>
> It is a sin to believe evil of others, but it is seldom a mistake.—H. L. Mencken
>
> There is no credit in being a comedian, when you have the whole Government working for you. All you have to do is to report the facts. I don't even have to exaggerate.—Will Rogers (in 1935)
>
> I didn't say that I didn't say it. I said that I didn't say that I said it. I want to make that very clear.—George Romney
>
> You have to pursue the ideals of a Joan of Arc with the political prowess of an Adam Clayton Powell. Whatever you say about Joan, her purpose was noble. And whatever you say about Adam, his politics is effective; it gets things done he wants done.—Bill Moyers (in 1965)
>
> Remember, democracy never lasts long. It soon wastes, exhausts, and murders itself. There never was a democracy yet that did not commit suicide.—John Adams

Magnificent Politics

You wonder what was happening to the Member that he needed that John Adams quote—and indeed, what happened to Adams the day he said it! But for every frustration that served up the bitter remarks above, the CRR Quote File reveals marvelous statements of the American purpose like those that follow. The first, incidentally, is the quotation the Congressional Reading Room staff reports is the one most frequently supplied at the present time:

> Senator Hubert H. Humphrey at the dedication of the Humphrey Building in 1977: "It was once said that the moral test of government is how that government treats those who are in the dawn of life, the children; those who are in the twilight of life, the elderly; and those who are in the shadows of life—the sick, the needy and the handicapped."
>
> George Washington, speaking as the presiding officer of the Constitutional Convention, 1787: "It is too probable that no plan we propose will be adopted. Perhaps another dreadful conflict is to be sustained. If to please the people, we offer what we ourselves disapprove, how can we afterwards defend our work? Let us raise a standard to which the wise and the honest can repair. The event is in the hand of God."
>
> Adlai Stevenson in 1952: "When an American says that he loves his country, he means not only that he loves the New England hills, the prairies glistening in the sun, the wide and rising plains, the great mountains, and the sea. He means that he loves an inner air, an inner light in which freedom lives and in which a man can draw the breath of self-respect."
>
> Walter Lippmann in 1955: "Yet this corporate being, though so insubstantial to our senses, binds, in Burke's words, a man to his country with 'ties which though light as air, are as strong as links of iron.' That is why young men die in battle for their country's sake and why old men plant trees they will never sit under."
>
> Benjamin Franklin in 1789: "God grant, that not only the Love of Liberty, but a thorough knowledge of the Rights of Man, may pervade all the Nations of the Earth, so that a Philosopher may set his Foot Anywhere on its Surface, and say, 'This is my Country.' "
>
> Carl Sandburg speaking of Abraham Lincoln before a joint session of the Congress: "Not often in the story of mankind does a man arrive on earth who is both steel and velvet, and who is as hard as rock and soft as drifting fog, who holds in his heart and mind the paradox of terrible storm and peace unspeakable and perfect."

Words We've All Heard—But Were Never Said

There are a surprisingly large number of Americanisms which never passed the lips of those to whom they are attributed. How this manages to occur is always slightly inexplicable. The words do indeed strike a chord of truth with many of their audiences (regardless of who said them first), but without the cachet of the national figure, lose some of their impact in the dialogue. Some, like the following Mark Twain, are essentially trivial and little is lost without the imprimatur.

> "When I was a boy of 14, my father was so ignorant I could hardly stand to have the old man around. But when I got to be 21, I was astonished at how much the old man had learned in seven years."

No Twain scholar has even been able to find that Twain said this. The Twain Museums in Maine and Connecticut cannot identify it, nor can the Twain Papers staff at Berkeley find it in anything he wrote. It is frequently traced back to a *Reader's Digest* item of September 1937.

But of much greater significance is the problem of Lincoln's Ten Points. The familiar

> 1. You cannot bring about prosperity by discouraging thrift.
> 2. You cannot strengthen the weak by weakening the strong.
>
> (et cetera; the full list appears as quotation No. 1117)

has never been connected to a known Lincoln writing or statement. Lincoln scholars all over the country have been pursuing these maxims for three decades now, but have never found the list earlier than the 1940s when it was printed in various advertisements and on motto cards.

Indeed, the mottoes and broadside printings seem to reinforce each other as one author passes a quotation on from his predecessor. The more impressive the presswork, the more legitimate we assume the source to be. The familiar "Desiderata" seems to be a classic example of this. ("Go placidly amid the noise and the haste . . . be cheerful. Strive to be happy . . ." The full text appears as quotation No. 1114.) This was, in fact, written by Max Ehrmann and published in 1927. But the story of its antecedents has acquired a drama all its own. In trying to trace its history, the Congressional Reading Room researchers found the following:

> In 1956, the rector of St. Paul's Church in Baltimore used the poem in a collection of mimeographed inspirational material for his congregation. Someone printing it later said it was found in Old St. Paul's Church, Baltimore, dated 1692. The year 1692 is the founding date of the church and has nothing to do with the poem, which was written in 1927. It was widely distributed with the 1692 date. A copy of it was found on the bedside table in Adlai Stevenson's New York apartment after his death in 1965. He has been planning to use it on his Christmas cards, identifying it as an ancient poem.

Lincoln's "You can fool all of the people some of the time, and some of the people all of the time . . ." (No. 609) has never been verified; Marie Antoinette's "Let them eat cake" (No. 1347) is considered spurious; and there are many quotations which are quite accurate—but were in fact said by someone else:

> Winning isn't everything, it's the only thing

was first said by Red Sanders at Vanderbilt around 1948, and, surprisingly, Vince Lombardi always stated he had not said it at all.

It is better that one hundred guilty Persons escape than one innocent Person should suffer

was used by Benjamin Franklin in the 1700s, not begun by Justice Holmes or Brandeis.

Politics is the art of the possible

was first said by Chancellor Otto von Bismarck, not Mr. Dooley.

many things in life that are not fair

was indeed said by Jimmy Carter, but John F. Kennedy had said, "life is unfair" fifteen years earlier.

And do you recognize the following?

Are you a politician asking what your country can do for you or a zealous one asking what you can do for your country? If you are the first, then you are a parasite; if the second, then you are an oasis in the desert.—Kahlil Gibran, written in Arabic after the First World War

Finally, scattered among the 2100 quotations that accumulated in the file, there are several the CRS has been unable to prove one way or the other, and they are deliberately included in this collection—labelled as unverified—in the hope that some reader will be able to fasten them to a source. An amusing example of one of these is the following, written by Leonard Harman Robbins:

How a minority
Reaching a majority
Seizing authority
Hates a minority!

Have you seen it in print? Send the citation to the Congressional Reading Room at the Library!

Advice On How To Govern

As might be expected, the fifty-year accumulation has acquired many hundreds of thoughts on how to govern effectively. They run from humorous irony to sensitive truths. A sample of the spectrum:

The great art of governing consists in not letting men grow old in their jobs.—Napoleon Bonaparte

There is no Democratic or Republican way of cleaning the streets.—Fiorello La Guardia

"My country, right or wrong," is a thing no patriot would think of saying except in a desperate case. It is like saying, "My mother, drunk or sober."—G. K. Chesterton

A government which robs Peter to pay Paul can always depend on the support of Paul.—George Bernard Shaw

Take things always by their smooth handle.—Thomas Jefferson

Human nature being what it is, all men prefer a false promise to a flat refusal. At the worst the man to whom you have lied may be angry. That risk, if you make a promise, is uncertain and deferred, and it affects only a few. But if you refuse you are sure to offend many, and that at once.—Quintus Tullius Cicero

Harold Cox tells a story of his life as a young man in India. He quoted some statistics to a Judge, an Englishman and a very good fellow. His friend said, "Cox, when you are a bit older, you will not quote Indian statistics with that assurance. The Government are very keen on amassing statistics—they collect them, add them, raise them to the nth power, take the cube root and prepare wonderful diagrams. But what you must never forget is that every one of those figures comes in the first instance from the *chowty dar* [village watchman], who just puts down what he damn pleases.—Josiah Stamp (in 1929)

There is no merit in putting off a war for a year if, when it comes, it is far worse or one much harder to win.—Winston Churchill

We think that for a general to fight an enemy, it is important to know the enemy's numbers, but still more important to know the enemy's philosophy.—G. K. Chesterton

If we desire to avoid insult, we must be able to repel it; if we desire to secure peace, one of the most powerful instruments of our rising prosperity, it must be known, that we are at all times ready for War.—George Washington

The true rule, in determining to embrace, or reject any thing, is not whether it have *any* evil in it, but whether it have more of evil, than of good. There are few things *wholly* evil, or wholly good. Almost every thing, especially of governmental policy, is an inseparable compound of the two; so that our best judgment of the preponderance between them is continually demanded.—Abraham Lincoln (in the House of Representatives, 1848)

Words and the Congress

It is both fitting and proper that Congress should be so sensitive to words that their inquiries about precise speech have produced the rich reservoir we find here. This collection of "perfect words" celebrates the 200th anniversary of the founding of the Legislature. This is singularly appropriate, since throughout the life of the nation, the Congress has been the temple of great oratory in our country led by such figures as Webster, Clay, Calhoun, Lincoln, the Breckinridges, Borah, and La Follette. The Members through the years have carried the double role of expressing the views of their personal constituencies and of distilling the national issues, choices, and concerns. To hear these speeches was, as Rufus Choate said about Daniel Webster's, to hear "a national consciousness—a national era, a mood, a hope, a dread, a despair—in which you listen to the spoken history of the time."

Political oratory is an honorable art, which has made the practice of democracy work for two centuries. But it has changed rather dramatically during those years. Its purposes have remained the same, but the rules and practices have shifted sharply in our own time.

The scholars tell us that what came to be known as political oratory stemmed from the speaking style of the eighteenth-century American pulpit. The cadences of John Calvin, John Knox, and Martin Luther were read out by early divines, and then built on by the passionate preaching of Jonathan Edwards, George Whitefield, and Francis Asbury. The golden age of Revolutionary oratory started with Patrick Henry and James Otis twenty years before the War itself, and flowed toward the high water mark of political speech up to the outbreak of the Civil War—the days of Clay, Calhoun, and Webster. All of these had a florid grandeur which could hold the attention of a hall of people with persuasive eloquence. We read of incredibly long addresses successfully presented under what to us sound like impossible conditions. Webster's impassioned reply to Haynes—which still reads with excitement to this day—was given for three hours of extemporaneous analysis, and then the Senator, noting that most of his audience had been standing through the dinner hour, suggested that they all return the next day—when he talked for three more hours to complete his thought. Senator Edward Everett talked to a standing audience for one hour and fifty-seven minutes from a wind-swept platform at Gettysburg—after having rehearsed the same memorized speech the day before to test his time and to practice the level of shouting necessary to be heard across the field.

Each of these great speakers has unusual mannerisms that were a part of his style and image. Contemporaries describe Lincoln's voice at Gettysburg as metallic, "clear, ringing, very penetrating and it reached everybody on the outskirts of the throng." In his earlier speeches, Lincoln used the traditional oratorical device of letting his voice sink very low and then rising as he made his points—accompanied by dramatic gestures. By the time he was president, he stood very quietly and rarely moved his hands at all. (Lincoln had several eccentricities of pronunciation that attracted attention at the time: he always said "America" as if it were spelled "Amerikay," "chairman" was "cheerman," and when he spoke in the House he attracted attention by saying all his "tos" as "toes." When he gave his first speech in the House, he wrote home to Herndon, "I find speaking here and elsewhere almost the same thing. I was about as badly scared and no more than when I speak in court.")

Webster could speak for hours at such a pitch that his voice filled the Senate and newsmen complained that no one could conduct side conversations, even in the galleries.

Patrick Henry is described as always starting out as if he were ill, unprepared, and had not intended to speak on the occasion, but as he talked his voice rose, the tempo increased, so that by the time he had reached the important matter, his words were pouring out like a "torrent of strong, ringing sentences and pictorial paragraphs, words tumbling over words like a cataract . . . he would storm and persuade, berate and beg, threaten and cajole, argue and amuse, convince and convulse," totally dominating both the room and the occasion.

According to Edgar Dewitt Jones, Henry Clay's voice "was sweet and soft, as a mother's to her babe. It could be made to float into the chambers of the air, as gently as descending snowflakes on the sea; and again it shook the Senate, strong, brain-shaking, filling the air with its absolute thunder." It is frightening to consider what these giants could have done with a public address system.

But it seems to have been the appearance of the electrical devices that clipped the length of political discourse and lowered the histrionics. Amplification in halls reduced the need for over-sized gestures; radio and the motion picture newsreel pulled the listener close to the speaker so it became in both of their eyes a person-to-person dialogue. But as important as any aspect of the oratorical tradition was the effect of such twentieth-century figures as Hitler and Mussolini who brought oratory into disrepute by using the device to whip their audiences into emotional frenzies. By the time television arrived, political dialogues demanded a me-and-thee style, low-keyed and distilled to a twenty-minute maximum—which in turn would be reduced to sixty seconds on the evening news. Even formal speeches on the floors of the legislature now tend toward the conversational, "sincere," "thinking-on-their feet" style of delivery.

This is where the quotation continues to prove its worth. At first, citations to the great classical thinkers were called on to affirm the validity of the oratorical assertions. Then the quotations began to be used to provide humor and variety to long stretches of narrative. Now, with the style more intimate and the length diminished, the quotations become a form of shorthand, a distillation of a grander—longer—thought. The only difficulty is that today's audiences bring a much narrower set of mental references to the hall than did those of a few generations back. Reference to the Greek and Roman authors are almost useless, Biblical allusions are increasingly less effective, literary quotations carry ever more limited images. Motion picture and television references seem to generate the broadest recognition from the audience—but their half-lives seem barely to last through a thirteen-week season. In short, the challenge of the modern political speaker has never been greater. We would hope the attached storehouse will therefore be doubly useful.

Not a Dry Eye

Note should be taken of the great classic texts, the congressional folklore of certain speeches that have become so much a part of congressional tradition that to long-standing members of the two houses only the words "Senator Vest and his dog" are needed to bring smiles of recognition and delight. The text of Senator Vest's eulogy is found as Quotation No. 446. Here he rises to the final peroration:

> And when the last scene of all comes, and death takes the master in its embrace, and his body is laid away in the cold ground, no matter if all other friends pursue their way, there by his graveside will the noble dog be found, his head between his paws, his eyes sad but open in alert watchfulness, faithful and true even in death.

In no way to be outdone is Adlai Stevenson's "Cat Bill Veto" (No. 163). Here he concludes his negation of a cat leash law with the judgment:

> The problem of cat versus bird is as old as time. If we attempt to resolve it by legislation who knows but what we may be called upon to take sides as well in the age old problems of dog versus cat, bird versus bird, or even bird versus worm. In my opinion, the State of Illinois and its local governing bodies already have enough to do without trying to control feline delinquency.

In the same vein of rich, congressional oratory, you find Senator John Sharp Williams's "Mocking Bird Speech" as he contemplates returning to his beloved Mississippi at the end of twenty-eight years on Capitol Hill. With the full text appearing as Quotation No. 295, he concludes:

> And as night and the time for bed approaches, I will listen to the greatest chorus of voices that man ever heard, music that will charm me and make me ready for repose—the voices of my mocking birds, trilling from the trees. In that way I want to live the rest of my life. And when the end comes, I hope to be carried out of the house by my neighbors and laid to rest among my people.

Congressman Billy Matthews's report of a Member's reply to a constituent's query, "Where do you stand on whiskey?" appears as Quotation No. 38.

> If, when you say whiskey you mean the Devil's brew, the poison scourge, the bloody monster that defiles innocence, destroys the home, creates misery and poverty [he goes on for 42 more words], then certainly I am against it with all of my power.
>
> But, if, when you say whiskey, you mean the oil of conversation, the philosophic wine . . . that puts a song in their hearts and laughter on their lips . . . Christmas cheer . . . the drink that enables a man to magnify his joy and his happiness and to forget, if only for a little while, life's great tragedies, and the heartbreaks and sorrows [ultimately 140 laudatory words], then certainly I am in favor of it.

Great Thoughts From the Ages

As can be seen from the above, while these quotations were primarily used on political occasions and in public meetings, the topics run far more broadly than the simple aspects of governing. The war between the sexes is well represented, while some of the most unlikely topics appear among those requested for verification and attribution. Again, a sample:

> Men marry because they are tired;
> Women because they are curious.
> Both are disappointed.—Oscar Wilde

Also Wilde:

> One should never trust a woman who tells you her real age. A woman who would tell one that would tell one anything.

Benjamin Franklin answers a letter to the editor:

I am about courting a girl I have had but little acquaintance with. How shall I come to a knowledge of her faults, and whether she has the virtues I imagine she has?
Answer: Commend her among her female acquaintances.

A reflective Mark Twain:

We have not the reverent feeling for the rainbow that a savage has, because we know how it is made. We have lost as much as we gained by prying into the matter.

Whenever possible, the CRS researchers have attempted to express the context in which a quotation is found. Through the years this has served to protect an inquiring Congressman from using a quotation where the context would be antithetical to his own views or purpose, or it frequently enriches the more familiar part of the quote. Several examples of these "broader citations" have been noted above; the following is a charming, if not particularly significant elaboration:

When I die, my epitaph or whatever you call those signs on gravestones is going to read: "I joked about every prominent man of my time, but I never met a man I dident like." I am so proud of that I can hardly wait to die so it can be carved. And when you come to my grave you will find me sitting there, proudly reading it.—Will Rogers

Incidentally, apropos only of the sameness of things, there is an unlikely set of headlines a Member heard described which, when finally run down, turned out to be a skit from a French theater piece written in 1815:

What news? Ma foi!
The tiger has broken out of his den.
The monster was three days at sea.
The wretch has landed at Frejus.
The brigand has arrived at Antibes.
The invader has reached Grenoble.
The General has entered Lyons.
Napoleon slept last night at Fontainbleau.
The Emperor proceeds to the Tuileries today.
His Imperial Majesty will address his loyal subjects tomorrow.

Or Disraeli reporting to the Commons in 1864 on the latest international conference:

The Conference lasted six weeks. It wasted six weeks. It lasted as long as a Carnival, and, like a Carnival, it was an affair of masks and mystification. Our Ministers went to it as men in distressed circumstances go to a place of amusement—to while away the time, with a consciousness of impending failure.

Candidates For a Trivia Card

In conclusion, you might be amused by a quick quiz of some fragments from the CRR quote trays. How many of these can you recall "who said and in what context?"

"like two scorpions in a bottle"

[Robert Oppenheimer, No. 237]

"till a shrimp learns to whistle"

[Nikita Khrushchev, No. 244]

"not one cent for scenery"

[Joseph Cannon, No. 308]

"the moral equivalent of war"

[William James, No. 526]

"lives of quiet desperation"

[Henry David Thoreau, No. 1124]

"the silent majority"

[Richard Nixon, No. 1140]

"Have you no sense of decency, sir . . ."

[Joseph Welch, No. 1171]

"Catch-22"

[Joseph Heller, No. 1179]

"electrical energy too cheap to meter"

[Lewis Strauss, No. 1256]

"nail a drop of water to the wall"

[George Danielson, No. 1394]

"a splendid misery"

[Thomas Jefferson, No. 1493]

"The *Eagle* has landed"

[Neil Armstrong, No. 1737]

"Because it's there"

[George Mallory, No. 1741]

"dooth with youre owene thyng"

[Geoffrey Chaucer, No. 447]

How To Use This Book

Quotation books, surprisingly enough, are a rather recent invention. The classic Bartlett's *Familiar Quotations* started the tradition in this country and was begun in 1855 by the owner of the University Book Store in Cambridge, Massachusetts. Burton Stevenson's massive *Home Book of Quotations* started in 1934, and the dignified *Oxford Dictionary of Quotations* did not appear until 1941. Each of these is organized in a different way, depending on the primary purpose of the author. Some are alphabetical lists by the source of the quotation, others are arranged chronologically, and in others the quotations are clustered by subject content.

Since this present collection was accumulated through the years on the traditional library three-by-five cards, the cards could have been sorted by any of the three traditional sequences, but it was thought that inasmuch as the primary use of the collection would be in the preparation of public speeches, the material would be most useful in subject categories which could be browsed for apt statements in the construction of speech texts. Thus, the materials can be found in one of three ways:

By Subject

The list of Subjects, with appropriate "see" and "see also" references, follows this introduction; and there is also a subject index. Using them will be the best approach if you are looking for an appropriate quotation without having a specific one in mind before you start.

By Keyword

If you are searching for a specific "half-remembered, almost forgotten" quotation, and can only recall a word or phrase, this alphabetical index of keywords will be the most efficient approach. This index refers you to the number of the specific citation.

By Author

If you can recall who said the quotation you seek, all items included in this collection by that author can be found in the alphabetical author index. Again, the reference is to the number of the various citations included from that speaker.

Good Hunting!

CHARLES A. GOODRUM
Assistant Director, Congressional Research Service
1970–1976

List of Subjects

List of Subjects

Injustice
See also Justice
Isolationism
Israel
Italy

J

Jails
See Prisons
Jesus Christ
See also Christianity
Joy
Judges
Judgment
Judiciary
Justice
See also Injustice

K

Kentucky
Kings
Knowledge
See also Education; Thought; Wisdom

L

Labor
See also Unemployment; Work
Labor unions
See also Strike
Last words
Law
Lawyers
Leadership
League of Nations
Legislators
See also Congress; Congressmen; Politicians
Legislature
See also Congress
Liberals
Liberty
See also Civil rights; Democracy; Freedom; Human rights
Lies
Life
See also Living
Lincoln, Abraham (1809–1865)
Living
See also Life
Lobbyists
Loneliness
Losing
See Winning and losing
Love

M

Majority
Man
Marriage
See also Wives
McCarthyism
Mediocrity
Memory
Military affairs
See also Soldiers; War
Military service
See also Soldiers; War
Mind
Moderation
Money
Morality
Mortality
See also Death
Mothers
Motives
Murphy's Law

N

Nation
See also America; Country; Patriotism; Republic
Natural resources
See Conservation; Earth; Environment
Needs
New England
News
Newspapers
See also Press
Nobility
North Carolina
Nuclear energy
Nuclear war
See also Bombs and bombing; War

O

Oath of office
Obscenity
See also Censorship
Opinions
See also Point of view; Public opinion
Optimism
See Positive thinking
Oratory
See also Speaking out
Order

P

Parliament
See Legislature
Parties, political
See Democratic party; Political parties; Republican party
Past
See also History
Past and future
See also Future; History
Past and present
See also History
Patriotism
See also America; Country; Freedom
Patronage
Peace
See also War and peace
People
See also American people; Government—by the people
People's Republic of China
See China
Perfection
Perseverance
Perverseness
Plans
Pledge of Allegiance
Point of view
See also Belief; Opinions
Policy
See also Foreign policy
Political parties
See also Democratic party; Republican party
Politicians
See also Congress; Congressmen; Legislators; Statesman
Politics
See also Government
Positive thinking
Postal Service
Poverty
Power
Praise
Prayers
Prejudice
Presidency
Press
See also Newspapers
Prisons
Privacy
Progress
Promise
Promises
Property
Public affairs
Public opinion
See also Opinions
Public service
Public speaking
See Oratory
Publicity
Puritans

R

Race
  See also Blacks; Slavery
Reading
  See also Books; Censorship
Reasons
Reform
Regulation
  See also Government; Law
Relevance
Representation
  See also Congress; Legislature
Republic
  See also America; Country; Nation
Republican party
Responsibility
Retribution
Revolution
Revolutionary war (1775–1783)
Rich
Right
Right and wrong
Rights
  See also Civil rights; Equality; Human rights
River
Rome
Rules
Running
Russia

S

Sacrifice
Santa Claus
Science
Sea
Secrecy
Security
Self
Self-deception
Self-examination
Self-importance
Self-pity
Self-respect
Separation of powers
  See Government—separation of powers
Sex
Shakespeare, William (1564–1616)
Ships and shipping
Silence
Sincerity
Sins
Slavery
  See also Blacks; Race
Sleep
Smile
Smithsonian Institution
Socialism
Society
  See also Civilization
Soldiers
  See also Military service; war
Solution
  See also Decision
Soviet Union
  See Russia
Space exploration
Speaking out
  See also Belief; Oratory
Spirit
State
  See also Government
States rights
Statesman
  See also Diplomacy; Foreign policy
Statistics
Statue of Liberty
Strength
Strike
Success
  See also Failure

T

Taxation
Teachers
  See also Colleges and universities; Education
Television
Ten Commandments
Theory
Thought
  See also Education; Knowledge; Wisdom
Three-mile limit
Time
Times
Timing
Today
Treason
Trust
Truth
Trying
Tyranny

U

Unemployment
  See also Labor; Strike; Work
Union
  See also America; Democracy; Government; Labor unions; Nation; Republic
Union of Soviet Socialist Republics
  See Russia
United Nations
Unity

V

Values
Victory
  See also Winning and losing
Vietnam War
  See also Bombs and bombing; War; War in Asia
Violence
  See also Campus violence
Voters and voting
  See also Elections

W

War
  See also Civil War (1861–1865); Cold war; Military service; Revolutionary war (1775–1783); Vietnam War; World War I (1914–1918); World War II (1939–1945)
War and peace
  See also Peace
War in Asia
  See also Vietnam War
Washington, D.C.
  See also Capitol building, Washington, D.C.
Washington, George (1732–1799)
Water
Watergate affair
Weather
Welfare
Westward movement
Winning
  See also Victory
Winning and losing
  See also Defeat
Wisdom
  See also Education; Knowledge; Thought
Wives
  See also Marriage
Women
Words
  See also Last words
Work
  See also Labor; Strike; Unemployment
World
  See also Earth
World domination
  See also Communism
World War I (1914–1918)
World War II (1939–1945)
Worth
Writers and writing

Y

Youth
  See also Children

Respectfully Quoted

1 I do not believe in a fate that falls on men however they act; but I do believe in a fate that falls on them unless they act.

G. K. CHESTERTON, *Generally Speaking,* chapter 20, p. 137 (1929).

2 A man who waits to believe in action before acting is anything you like, but he's not a man of action. It is as if a tennis player before returning a ball stopped to think about his views of the physical and mental advantages of tennis. You must act as you breathe.

GEORGES CLEMENCEAU, conversation with Jean Martet, December 18, 1927.—*Clemenceau, The Events of His Life as Told by Himself to His Former Secretary, Jean Martet,* trans. Milton Waldman, chapter 11, p. 67 (1930).

3 When a man asks himself what is meant by action he proves that he isn't a man of action. Action is a lack of balance. In order to act you must be somewhat insane. A reasonably sensible man is satisfied with thinking.

GEORGES CLEMENCEAU, conversation with Jean Martet, January 1, 1928.—*Clemenceau, The Events of His Life as Told by Himself to His Former Secretary, Jean Martet,* trans. Milton Waldman, chapter 12, p. 78 (1930).

4 Come! Let us lay a lance in rest,
And tilt at windmills under a wild sky!
For who would live so petty and unblest
That dare not tilt at something ere he die;
Rather than, screened by safe majority,
Preserve his little life to little end,
And never raise a rebel cry!

JOHN GALSWORTHY, "Errantry," stanza 1, *The Collected Poems of John Galsworthy,* p. 1 (1934).

5 I find the great thing in this world is not so much where we stand, as in what direction we are moving: To reach the port of heaven, we must sail sometimes with the wind and sometimes against it,—but we must sail, and not drift, nor lie at anchor.

OLIVER WENDELL HOLMES, *The Autocrat of the Breakfast-Table,* p. 93 (1891).

Josephus Daniels, ambassador to Mexico, sent this quotation to President Franklin D. Roosevelt, January 1, 1936, in a note of New Year greetings, with this comment: "Here is an expression from Holmes which, if it has missed you, is so good you may find a use for it in one of your 'fireside' talks."—*Roosevelt and Daniels,* ed. Carroll Kilpatrick, p. 159 (1952).

6 The point I wish to make is this: [President William] McKinley gave Rowan a letter to be delivered to Garcia; Rowan took the letter & did not ask, "Where is he at?" By the Eternal! there is a man whose form should be cast in deathless bronze & the statue placed in every college of the land. It is not book-learning young men need, nor instruction about this and that, but a stiffening of the vertebrae which will cause them to be loyal to a trust, to act promptly, concentrate their energies: do the thing—"Carry a message to Garcia!"

ELBERT HUBBARD, "A Message to Garcia," originally published without title in Hubbard's magazine, *The Philistine,* March 1899, p. 110, and later widely reprinted and distributed.

The message "asked the Cuban insurgent general how much coöperation our army could hope for from his forces in the forthcoming campaign against the Spaniards in Cuba. His reply, with its accompanying plans and military information, was of the greatest information to Major-General Miles. This information Lieutenant Rowan secured and delivered safely to his general at the risk of his life."—R. W. G. Vail, *"A Message to Garcia," A Bibliographical Puzzle*, p. 11 (1930).

7 With a good conscience our only sure reward, with history the final judge of our deeds, let us go forth to lead the land we love, asking His blessing and His help, but knowing that here on earth God's work must truly be our own.

President JOHN F. KENNEDY, inaugural address, January 20, 1961.—*The Public Papers of the Presidents of the United States: John F. Kennedy, 1961*, p. 3.

This is one of seven inscriptions carved on the walls at the gravesite of John F. Kennedy, Arlington National Cemetery.

8 It is from numberless diverse acts of courage and belief that human history is shaped. Each time a man stands up for an ideal, or acts to improve the lot of others, or strikes out against injustice, he sends forth a tiny ripple of hope, and crossing each other from a million different centers of energy and daring those ripples build a current which can sweep down the mightiest walls of oppression and resistance.

Senator ROBERT F. KENNEDY, "Day of Affirmation," address at the University of Capetown, South Africa, June 6, 1966.—*Congressional Record*, vol. 112, June 6, 1966, p. 12430.

This quotation is an inscription on the Robert F. Kennedy gravesite at Arlington National Cemetery.

9 You will be better advised to watch what we do instead of what we say.

JOHN N. MITCHELL, U.S. attorney general, remarks (overheard by reporters) in July 1969 after meeting with a group of black civil rights workers, who protested the Administration's action on the Voting Rights Act of 1965.—*The Washington Post*, "Watch What We Do," editorial, July 7, 1969, p. A22.

10 It is not the critic who counts; not the man who points out how the strong man stumbles, or where the doer of deeds could have done them better. The credit belongs to the man who is actually in the arena, whose face is marred by dust and sweat and blood; who strives valiantly; who errs, and comes short again and again, because there is no effort without error and shortcoming; but who does actually strive to do the deeds; who knows the great enthusiasms, the great devotions; who spends himself in a worthy cause; who at the best knows in the end the triumph of high achievement, and who at the worst, if he fails, at least fails while daring greatly, so that his place shall never be with those cold and timid souls who know neither victory nor defeat.

THEODORE ROOSEVELT, address at the Sorbonne, Paris, France, April 23, 1910.—"Citizenship in a Republic," *The Strenuous Life* (vol. 13 of *The Works of Theodore Roosevelt*, national ed.), chapter 21, p. 510 (1926).

11 We are face to face with our destiny and we must meet it with a high and resolute courage. For us is the life of action, of strenuous performance of duty; let us live in the harness, striving mightily; let us rather run the risk of wearing out than rusting out.

THEODORE ROOSEVELT, address at the opening of the gubernatorial campaign, New York City, October 5, 1898.—"The Duties of a Great Nation," *Campaigns and Controversies* (vol. 14 of *The Works of Theodore Roosevelt*, national ed.), chapter 45, p. 291 (1926).

See also Nos. 575 and 1118.

12 Things won are done, joy's soul lies in the doing.

WILLIAM SHAKESPEARE, *Troilus and Cressida,* act I, scene ii, line 313. Cressida is speaking.

13 Let us develop the resources of our land, call forth its powers, build up its institutions, promote all its great interests, and see whether we also, in our day and generation, may not perform something worthy to be remembered.

Representative DANIEL WEBSTER, address at the laying of the cornerstone of the Bunker Hill Monument, Charlestown, Massachusetts, June 17, 1825.—*The Writings and Speeches of Daniel Webster,* vol. 1, p. 254 (1903).

These words are also incised in marble on the wall of the U.S. House of Representatives chamber, directly behind the Speaker's chair. The word "develop" is spelled there with a final "e."

14 Bullfight critics row on row
Crowd the vast arena full
But only one man's there who knows
And he's the man who fights the bull.

Author unknown. These lines were quoted in a letter to the editor by Representative F. Edward Hébert, chairman of the House Committee on Armed Services, who said, "President Kennedy was fond of quoting some lines from the Spanish poet García Lorca."—*The Washington Post,* April 11, 1971, p. C7. These lines are believed not to be García Lorca's.

Affluence

15 We are stripped bare by the curse of plenty.

WINSTON CHURCHILL, lecture, Cleveland, Ohio, February 3, 1932.—*Winston S. Churchill: His Complete Speeches, 1897–1963,* ed. Robert Rhodes James, vol. 5, p. 5130 (1974).

Churchill was referring to the theory that over-production caused the Depression.

16 More and more Americans feel threatened by runaway technology, by large-scale organization, by overcrowding. More and more Americans are appalled by the ravages of industrial progress, by the defacement of nature, by man-made ugliness. If our society continues at its present rate to become less livable as it becomes more affluent, we promise all to end up in sumptuous misery.

JOHN W. GARDNER, *No Easy Victories,* ed. Helen Rowan, p. 57 (1968).

Gardner was secretary of health, education, and welfare 1965–1968.

17 Tax reduction has an almost irresistible appeal to the politician, and it is no doubt also gratifying to the citizen. It means more dollars in his pocket, dollars that he can spend if inflation doesn't consume them first. But dollars in his pocket won't buy him clean streets or an adequate police force or good schools or clean air and water. Handing money back to the private sector in tax cuts and starving the public sector is a formula for producing richer and richer consumers in filthier and filthier communities. If we stick to that formula we shall end up in affluent misery.

JOHN W. GARDNER, *The Recovery of Confidence,* p. 152 (1970).

He was secretary of health, education, and welfare 1965–1968.

Affluence

18 With breathtaking rapidity, we are destroying all that was lovely to look at and turning America into a prison house of the spirit. The affluent society, with relentless single-minded energy, is turning our cities, most of suburbia and most of our roadways into the most affluent slum on earth.

Attributed to ERIC SEVAREID. Unverified.

Aged

19 Yet somehow our society must make it right and possible for old people not to fear the young or be deserted by them, for the test of a civilization is in the way that it cares for its helpless members.

PEARL S. BUCK, *My Several Worlds*, p. 337 (1954).

20 Old age isn't so bad when you consider the alternative.

Attributed to MAURICE CHEVALIER.—James B. Simpson, *Contemporary Quotations*, p. 295 (1964), citing *The New York Times*, Sunday, October 9, 1960. Unverified.

21 As I give thought to the matter, I find four causes for the apparent misery of old age; first, it withdraws us from active accomplishments; second, it renders the body less powerful; third, it deprives us of almost all forms of enjoyment; fourth, it stands not far from death.

MARCUS TULLIUS CICERO, *De Senectute (Of Old Age)*, book 5, section 15.—Herbert N. Couch, *Cicero on the Art of Growing Old*, p. 21 (1959).

22 This increase in the life span and in the number of our senior citizens presents this Nation with increased opportunities: the opportunity to draw upon their skill and sagacity—and the opportunity to provide the respect and recognition they have earned. It is not enough for a great nation merely to have added new years to life—our objective must also be to add new life to those years.

President JOHN F. KENNEDY, special message to the Congress on the needs of the nation's senior citizens, February 21, 1963.—*Public Papers of the Presidents of the United States: John F. Kennedy, 1963*, p. 189.

23 As one grows older, one becomes wiser and more foolish.

FRANÇOIS DE LA ROCHEFOUCAULD. The maxim, "En vieillissant, on devient plus fou et plus sage," was first published in his *Réflexions ou Sentences et Maximes Morales*, 1655. There are various English translations, including that above from his *Selected Maxims and Reflections*, trans. Edward M. Stack, p. 26 (1956).

24 Between the years of ninety-two and a hundred and two, however, we shall be the ribald, useless, drunken, outcast person we have always wished to be. We shall have a long white beard and long white hair; we shall not walk at all, but recline in a wheel chair and bellow for alcoholic beverages; in the winter we shall sit before the fire with our feet in a bucket of hot water, a decanter of corn whiskey near at hand, and write ribald songs against organized society; strapped to one arm of our chair will be a forty-five calibre revolver, and we shall shoot out the lights when we want to go to sleep, instead of turning them off; when we want air we shall throw a silver candlestick through the front window and be damned to it; we shall address public meetings (to which we have been invited because of our wisdom) in a vein of jocund malice. We shall . . . but we don't wish to make any one envious of the good time that is coming to us . . . We look forward to a disreputable, vigorous, unhonoured, and disorderly old age.

DON MARQUIS, *The Almost Perfect State*, pp. 183–84 (1927).

25 Growing old is no more than a bad habit which a busy man has no time to form.

ANDRÉ MAUROIS, *The Art of Living*, trans. James Whitall, chapter 8, pp. 282–83 (1940).

26 To hold the same views at forty as we held at twenty is to have been stupefied for a score of years, and take rank, not as a prophet, but as an unteachable brat, well birched and none the wiser.

ROBERT LOUIS STEVENSON, "Crabbed Age and Youth," *Virginibus Puerisque and Later Essays*, p. 67 (1969). Written between 1874–1879.

Agriculture

27 Burn down your cities and leave our farms, and your cities will spring up again as if by magic; but destroy our farms and the grass will grow in the streets of every city in the country. . . . We will answer their demand for a gold standard by saying to them: You shall not press down upon the brow of labor this crown of thorns, you shall not crucify mankind upon a cross of gold.

WILLIAM JENNINGS BRYAN, speech at the Democratic national convention, Chicago, Illinois, July 8, 1896.—*Speeches of William Jennings Bryan*, rev., vol. 1, pp. 248–49 (1911).

Often referred to as the "Cross of Gold" speech because of its widely-quoted concluding sentence, above. He served in Congress 1891–1895.

28 For of all gainful professions, nothing is better, nothing more pleasing, nothing more delightful, nothing better becomes a well-bred man than agriculture.

MARCUS TULLIUS CICERO, *De Officiis*, book 1, chapter 42, *Cicero's Three Books of Offices, or Moral Duties*, trans. Cyrus R. Edmonds, p. 73 (1873).

29 Cultivators of the earth are the most valuable citizens. They are the most vigorous, the most independant, the most virtuous, and they are tied to their country and wedded to it's liberty and interests by the most lasting bands. As long therefore as they can find emploiment in this line, I would not convert them into mariners, artisans, or any thing else. But our citizens will find emploiment in this line till their numbers, and of course their productions, become too great for the demand both internal and foreign.

THOMAS JEFFERSON, letter to John Jay, August 23, 1785.—*The Papers of Thomas Jefferson*, ed. Julian P. Boyd, vol. 8, p. 426 (1953).

30 And, he gave it for his Opinion; that whoever could make two Ears of Corn, or two Blades of Grass to grow upon a Spot of Ground where only one grew before; would deserve better of Mankind, and do more essential Service to his Country, than the whole Race of Politicians put together.

JONATHAN SWIFT, "A Voyage to Brobdingnag," *Gulliver's Travels*, part 2, pp. 119–20, in *The Prose Works of Jonathan Swift*, ed. Herbert Davis, vol. 11 (1941).

Agriculture

31 Man has only a thin layer of soil between himself and starvation.

Attributed to Bard of Cincinnati. Unverified.

Alamo

32 Thermopylae had her messenger of defeat—the Alamo had none.

Attributed to THOMAS JEFFERSON GREEN.

Green is said to have included the sentence in a speech he helped Edward Burleson prepare. While Burleson has often been credited with originating the sentence as well as using it, he lacked the classical education necessary to have made the allusion. The sentence became popular after it was engraved on the first monument to the Alamo, which is located in Austin, Texas. The 10-foot-high statue, made of stones from the Alamo, was destroyed by fire when the Capitol at Austin burned. Another monument subsequently erected on the Capitol grounds also included the sentence.—J. Frank Dobie, "The Alamo's Immortalization of Words," *Southwest Review*, summer 1942, pp. 406–10.

Alaska

33 I wanted the gold, and I sought it;
I scrabbled and mucked like a slave.
Was it famine or scurvy—I fought it;
I hurled my youth into a grave.
I wanted the gold, and I got it—
Came out with a fortune last fall,—
Yet somehow life's not what I thought it,
And somehow the gold isn't all.

No! There's the land. (Have you seen it?)
It's the cussedest land that I know,
From the big, dizzy mountains that screen it
To the deep, deathlike valleys below.
Some say God was tired when He made it;
Some say it's a fine land to shun;
Maybe; but there's some as would trade it
For no land on earth—and I'm one.

ROBERT W. SERVICE, "The Spell of the Yukon," stanzas 1 and 2, *The Spell of the Yukon*, p. 15 (1961).

Alcohol

34 At the third cup, wine drinks the man.

Hokekyō Sho, a Buddhist Sanskrit text. From *Kojikotowaza Jiten (Dictionary of Tradition and Proverbs)*.

Several commentators in the 1500s wrote about this; however, the earliest commentary was around the 12th century. The translation is literally: "Man drinks wine. Wine drinks wine. Wine drinks man."

35 Were I to commence my administration again, . . . the first question I would ask respecting a candidate would be, "Does he use ardent spirits?"

Attributed to THOMAS JEFFERSON in both Samuel Austin Worcester, *Cherokee Almanac*, p. 36 (1850), and Charles Noel Douglas, *Forty Thousand Quotations*, p. 544 (1925). Unverified in Jefferson's writings. Possibly spurious.

36 I believe, if we take habitual drunkards as a class, their heads and their hearts will bear an advantageous comparison with those of any other class.

ABRAHAM LINCOLN, address before the Springfield [Illinois] Washingtonian Temperance Society, February 22, 1842.—*The Collected Works of Abraham Lincoln*, ed. Roy P. Basler, vol. 1, p. 278 (1953).

37 There is as much of a chance of repealing the eighteenth amendment as there is for a humming bird to fly to the planet Mars with the Washington Monument tied to its tail. This country is for temperance and prohibition and it is going to continue to elect members of Congress who believe in that.

Senator MORRIS SHEPPARD, as reported by *The Washington Post*, September 25, 1930, p. 5.

38 Dear Friend:

I had not intended to discuss this controversial subject at this particular time. However, I want you to know that I do not shun a controversy. On the contrary, I will take a stand on any issue at any time, regardless of how fraught with controversy it may be. You have asked me how I feel about whiskey. Here is how I stand on the question.

If, when you say whiskey you mean the Devil's brew, the poison scourge, the bloody monster that defiles innocence, dethrones reason, destroys the home, creates misery and poverty . . . takes the bread from the mouths of little children; if you mean the evil drink that topples the Christian man and woman from the pinnacles of righteous, gracious living into the bottomless pit of degradation and despair, shame and helplessness and hopelessness, then certainly I am against it with all of my power.

But, if, when you say whiskey, you mean the oil of conversation, the philosophic wine, the ale that is consumed when good fellows get together, that puts a song in their hearts and laughter on their lips and the warm glow of contentment in their eyes; if you mean Christmas cheer; if you mean the stimulating drink that puts the spring in the old gentleman's step on a frosty morning; if you mean the drink that enables a man to magnify his joy and his happiness and to forget, if only for a little while, life's great tragedies, and the heartbreaks and sorrows; if you mean that drink, the sale of which pours into our treasuries untold millions of dollars, which are used to provide tender care for our little crippled children, our blind, our deaf, our dumb, our pitiful aged and infirm, to build highways, hospitals, and schools, then certainly I am in favor of it.

Author unknown. According to former Representative D. R. Billy Matthews, this story was told in the early 1960s by another member of Congress, who did not know the author. It purports to be the reply of a congressman to a constituent who had written the congressman to ask, "Where do you stand on whiskey?"

Alliance for Progress

39 The Alliance for Progress is an alliance between one millionaire and many beggars.

FIDEL CASTRO, interview with C. L. Sulzberger, *The New York Times*, November 7, 1964, p. 26.

Allies

40 I am most anxious that in dealing with matters which every Member knows are extremely delicate matters, I should not use any phrase or expression which would cause offence to our friends and Allies on the Continent or across the Atlantic Ocean.

WINSTON CHURCHILL, chancellor of the exchequer, remarks, House of Commons, December 10, 1924.—*Parliamentary Debates (Commons)*, 5th series, vol. 179, col. 259 (1925).

The subject was inter-Allied debts.

41 It is not given to us to peer into the mysteries of the future. Still, I avow my hope and faith, sure and inviolate, that in the days to come the British and American peoples will for their own safety and for the good of all walk together side by side in majesty, in justice, and in peace.

Prime Minister WINSTON CHURCHILL, speech to a joint session of Congress, Washington, D.C., December 26, 1941.—*Winston S. Churchill: His Complete Speeches, 1897–1963*, ed. Robert Rhodes James, vol. 6, p. 6541 (1974).

These words, the conclusion of Churchill's speech, were followed by "Prolonged applause, the Members of the Senate and their guests rising," according to the *Congressional Record*, vol. 87, p. 10119.

42 We have no eternal allies, and we have no perpetual enemies. Our interests are eternal and perpetual, and those interests it is our duty to follow.

LORD PALMERSTON, remarks in the House of Commons defending his foreign policy, March 1, 1848.—*Hansard's Parliamentary Debates*, 3d series, vol. 97, col. 122.

America

43 It may be that without a vision men shall die. It is no less true that, without hard practical sense, they shall also die. Without Jefferson the new nation might have lost its soul. Without Hamilton it would assuredly have been killed in body.

JAMES TRUSLOW ADAMS, *Jeffersonian Principles and Hamiltonian Principles*, p. xvii (1932).

See also No. 1331.

44 But America is a great, unwieldy Body. Its Progress must be slow. It is like a large Fleet sailing under Convoy. The fleetest Sailors must wait for the dullest and slowest. Like a Coach and six—the swiftest Horses must be slackened and the slowest quickened, that all may keep an even Pace.

JOHN ADAMS, letter to Abigail Adams, June 11/June 17, 1775.—*Adams Family Correspondence*, ed. L. H. Butterfield, vol. 1, p. 216 (1963).

45 Of America it would ill beseem any Englishman, and me perhaps as little as another, to speak unkindly, to speak *unpatriotically*, if any of us even felt so. Sure enough, America is a great, and in many respects a blessed and hopeful phenomenon. Sure enough, these hardy millions of Anglosaxon men prove themselves worthy of their genealogy. . . . But as to a Model Republic, or a model anything, the wise among themselves know too well that there is nothing to be said. . . . Their Constitution, such as it may be, was made here, not there. . . . Cease to brag to me of America, and its model institutions and constitutions.

THOMAS CARLYLE, *Latter-Day Pamphlets*, no. 1, pp. 23, 24 (1850).

46 Nothing that we could say could add to the impressiveness of the lesson furnished by the events of the past year, as to the needs and the dangerous condition of the neglected classes in our city. Those terrible days in July—the sudden appearance, as if from the bosom of the earth, of a most infuriated and degraded mob; the helplessness of property holders and the better classes; . . . immense destruction of property—were the first dreadful revelations to many of our people of the existence among us of a great, ignorant, irresponsible class who were growing up here without any permanent interest in the welfare of the community or the success of the government. . . . It should be remembered that there are no dangers to the value of property, or to the permanency of our institutions, so great as those from the existence of such a class of vagabond, ignorant, and ungoverned children. This "dangerous class" has not begun to show itself as it will in eight or ten years when these boys and girls are matured. Those who were too negligent or too selfish to notice them as children, will be fully aware of them as men. They will vote. They will have the same rights as we ourselves, though they have grown up ignorant of moral principle. . . . They will poison society. They will perhaps be embittered at the wealth and the luxuries they never share. Then let society beware, when the outcasts, vicious, reckless multitude . . . swarming now in every foul alley and low street, come to know their power and use it.

CHILDREN'S AID SOCIETY, 11th *Annual Report*, "written in the aftermath of the draft riots of 1864," according to Senator Robert F. Kennedy, who quoted from it August 25, 1966.—*Federal Role in Urban Affairs*, hearings before the Subcommittee on Executive Reorganization of the Committee on Government Operations, United States Senate, 89th Congress, 2d session, part 4, p. 919 (1966).

47 America is the only nation in history which miraculously has gone directly from barbarism to degeneration without the usual interval of civilization.

Attributed to GEORGES CLEMENCEAU.—Hans Bendix, "Merry Christmas, America!" *The Saturday Review of Literature*, December 1, 1945, p. 9.

48 What then is the American, this new man? He is either an European, or the descendant of an European, hence that strange mixture of blood, which you will find in no other country.

J. HECTOR ST. JOHN CRÈVECOEUR, "What Is an American," *Letters from an American Farmer*, p. 54 (1782, reprinted 1925).

49 The metaphor of the melting pot is unfortunate and misleading. A more accurate analogy would be a salad bowl, for, though the salad is an entity, the lettuce can still be distinguished from the chicory, the tomatoes from the cabbage.

CARL N. DEGLER, *Out of Our Past: The Forces That Shaped Modern America*, rev. ed., chapter 10, section 4, p. 296 (1970).

50 To me, the irony of this involvement with size, as I observed earlier, is the unwillingness or inability of so many Americans to identify themselves with something as vast as the United States. Bigger cars, bigger parking lots, bigger corporate structures, bigger farms, bigger drug stores, bigger supermarkets, bigger motion-picture screens. The tangible and the functional expand, while the intangible and the beautiful shrink. Left to wither is the national purpose, national educational needs, literature and theater, and our critical faculties. The national dialogue is gradually being lost in a froth of misleading self-congratulation and cliché. National needs and interests are slowly being submerged by the national preoccupation with the irrelevant.

Senator J. WILLIAM FULBRIGHT, "In Need of a Consensus," Penrose Memorial Lecture, delivered to the American Philosophical Society, Philadelphia, Pennsylvania, April 20, 1961.—*Proceedings* of the Society, August 1961, p. 352.

51 I cannot say that I am in the slightest degree impressed by your bigness, or your material resources, as such. Size is not grandeur, and territory does not make a nation. The great issue, about which hangs true sublimity, and the terror of overhanging fate, is what are you going to do with all these things?

THOMAS HENRY HUXLEY, address on university education delivered at the formal opening of Johns Hopkins University, Baltimore, Maryland, September 12, 1876.—Huxley, *American Addresses,* p. 125 (1877).

Vice President Hubert H. Humphrey used the same words in a commencement address at the Holton-Arms School, Bethesda, Maryland, June 1967.—*The Washington Post,* June 11, 1967, p. K3.

52 We cannot expect that everyone, to use the phrase of a decade ago, will "talk sense to the American people." But we can hope that fewer people will listen to nonsense. And the notion that this Nation is headed for defeat through deficit, or that strength is but a matter of slogans, is nothing but just plain nonsense.

President JOHN F. KENNEDY, remarks prepared for delivery at the Trade Mart in Dallas, Texas, November 22, 1963.—*Public Papers of the Presidents of the United States: John F. Kennedy, 1963,* p. 891.

This speech was never delivered. President Kennedy was on his way to the Trade Mart when he was assassinated.

Kennedy referred to Adlai E. Stevenson's slogan from the 1952 presidential election campaign, No. 85.

53 We have been the recipients of the choicest bounties of Heaven. We have been preserved, these many years, in peace and prosperity. We have grown in numbers, wealth and power, as no other nation has ever grown. But we have forgotten God. We have forgotten the gracious hand which preserved us in peace, and multiplied and enriched and strengthened us; and we have vainly imagined, in the deceitfulness of our hearts, that all these blessings were produced by some superior wisdom and virtue of our own. Intoxicated with unbroken success, we have become too self-sufficient to feel the necessity of redeeming and preserving grace, too proud to pray to the God that made us!

President ABRAHAM LINCOLN, proclamation appointing a National Fast Day, March 30, 1863.—*The Collected Works of Abraham Lincoln,* ed. Roy P. Basler, vol. 6, p. 156 (1953).

54 To make it possible for our children, and for our children's children, to live in a world of peace. To make this country be more than ever a land of opportunity—of equal opportunity, full opportunity for every American. To provide jobs for all who can work, and generous help for those who cannot work. To establish a climate of decency and civility, in which each person respects the feelings and the dignity and the God-given rights of his neighbor. To make this a land in which each person can dare to dream, can live his dreams—not in fear, but in hope—proud of his community, proud of his country, proud of what America has meant to himself and to the world.

President RICHARD M. NIXON, address to the nation about the Watergate investigations, April 30, 1973.—*Public Papers of the Presidents of the United States: Richard Nixon, 1973,* p. 332.

Nixon listed "some of my goals for my second term as President."

55 Religion, morality, and knowledge, being necessary to good government and the happiness of mankind, schools and the means of education shall forever be encouraged. The utmost good faith shall always be observed towards the Indians; their lands and property shall never be taken from them without their consent; and, in their property, rights, and liberty, they shall never be invaded or disturbed, unless in just and lawful wars authorized by Congress; but laws founded in justice and humanity, shall from time to time be made for preventing wrongs being done to them, and for preserving peace and friendship with them.

NORTHWEST ORDINANCE, 1787, article 3.—Henry Steele Commager, ed., *Documents of American History*, p. 131 (1934).

56 We defend and we build a way of life, not for America alone, but for all mankind.

President FRANKLIN D. ROOSEVELT, fireside chat on national defense, May 26, 1940.—*The Public Papers and Addresses of Franklin D. Roosevelt, 1940*, p. 240 (1941).

This sentence is one of many quotations inscribed on Cox Corridor II, a first floor House corridor, U.S. Capitol.

57 Every man among us is more fit to meet the duties and responsibilities of citizenship because of the perils over which, in the past, the nation has triumphed; because of the blood and sweat and tears, the labor and the anguish, through which, in the days that have gone, our forefathers moved on to triumph.

THEODORE ROOSEVELT, assistant secretary of the Navy, speech before the Naval War College, Newport, Rhode Island, June 1897.—"Washington's Forgotten Maxim," *American Ideals* (vol. 13 of *The Works of Theodore Roosevelt*, national ed.), chapter 12, p. 198 (1926).

See No. 411 for the maxim Roosevelt felt had been forgotten.

58 Americanism means the virtues of courage, honor, justice, truth, sincerity, and hardihood—the virtues that made America. The things that will destroy America are prosperity-at-any-price, peace-at-any-price, safety-first instead of duty-first, the love of soft living and the get-rich-quick theory of life.

THEODORE ROOSEVELT, letter to S. Stanwood Menken, chairman, committee on Congress of Constructive Patriotism, January 10, 1917. Roosevelt's sister, Mrs. Douglas Robinson, read the letter to a national meeting, January 26, 1917.—*Proceedings of the Congress of Constructive Patriotism*, Washington, D.C., January 25–27, 1917, p. 172 (1917).

59 I see America, not in the setting sun of a black night of despair ahead of us, I see America in the crimson light of a rising sun fresh from the burning, creative hand of God. I see great days ahead, great days possible to men and women of will and vision . . .

CARL SANDBURG, interview with Frederick Van Ryn, *This Week Magazine*, January 4, 1953, p. 11.

Sandburg had used these words previously at a rally at Madison Square Garden, New York City, October 28, 1952, praising Adlai E. Stevenson during his 1952 presidential campaign.—*The Papers of Adlai E. Stevenson*, vol. 4, p. 175 (1955).

A similar prediction was made by Benjamin Franklin nearly two centuries earlier in a letter to George Washington, March 5, 1780: "I must soon quit the Scene, but you may live to see our Country flourish, as it will amazingly and rapidly after the War is over. Like a Field of young Indian Corn, which long Fair weather and Sunshine had enfeebled and discolored, and which in that weak State, by a Thunder Gust, of violent Wind, Hail, and Rain, seem'd to be threaten'd with absolute Destruction; yet the Storm being past, it recovers fresh Verdure, shoots up with double Vigour, and delights the Eye, not of its

Owner only, but of every observing Traveller."—*The Writings of Benjamin Franklin,* ed. Albert H. Smyth, vol. 8, p. 29 (1907).

60 If she [America] forgets where she came from, if the people lose sight of what brought them along, if she listens to the deniers and mockers, then will begin the rot and dissolution.

CARL SANDBURG, *Remembrance Rock,* epilogue, chapter 2, p. 1001 (1948).

61 Those of us who shout the loudest about Americanism in making character assassinations are all too frequently those who, by our own words and acts, ignore some of the basic principles of Americanism—

The right to criticize.
The right to hold unpopular beliefs.
The right to protest.
The right of independent thought.

Senator MARGARET CHASE SMITH, remarks in the Senate, June 1, 1950, *Congressional Record,* vol. 96, p. 7894.

She added, "The American people are sick and tired of being afraid to speak their minds lest they be politically smeared as Communists or Fascists by their opponents." These and other remarks preceded the Declaration of Conscience (p. 7895), which she drafted and in which she was joined by six other Republican Senators.

62 Our nation stands at a fork in the political road. In one direction lies a land of slander and scare; the land of sly innuendo, the poison pen, the anonymous phone call and hustling, pushing, shoving; the land of smash and grab and anything to win. This is Nixonland. But I say to you that it is not America.

ADLAI E. STEVENSON, *The New America,* ed. Seymour E. Harris, John B. Martin, and Arthur Schlesinger, Jr., p. 249 (1971).

These words were written in 1956 during Stevenson's second presidential campaign.

63 If these Commentaries shall but inspire in the rising generation a more ardent love of their country, an unquenchable thirst for liberty, and a profound reverence for the constitution and the union, then they will have accomplished all that their author ought to desire. Let the American youth never forget that they possess a noble inheritance, bought by the toils, and sufferings, and blood of their ancestors; and capable, if wisely improved, and faithfully guarded, of transmitting to their latest posterity all the substantial blessings of life, the peaceful enjoyment of liberty, property, religion, and independence. The structure has been erected by architects of consummate skill and fidelity; its foundations are solid; its compartments are beautiful as well as useful; its arrangements are full of wisdom and order; and its defences are impregnable from without. It has been reared for immortality, if the work of man may justly aspire to such a title. It may, nevertheless, perish in an hour by the folly, or corruption, or negligence of its only keepers, THE PEOPLE. Republics are created by the virtue, public spirit, and intelligence of the citizens. They fall, when the wise are banished from the public councils, because they dare to be honest, and the profligate are rewarded, because they flatter the people in order to betray them.

JOSEPH STORY, *Commentaries on the Constitution of the United States,* 2d ed., vol. 2, chapter 45, p. 617 (1851). This passage was not in the first edition, but in all later editions.

Justice Story served in Congress 1808–1809.

64 The surface of American society is covered with a layer of democratic paint, but from time to time one can see the old aristocratic colors breaking through.

ALEXIS DE TOCQUEVILLE, *Democracy in America*, ed. J. P. Mayer, trans. George Lawrence, vol. 1, part 1, chapter 2, p. 49 (1969). Originally published in 1835–1840.

65 I was born on July 4, 1776, and the Declaration of Independence is my birth certificate. The bloodlines of the world run in my veins, because I offered freedom to the oppressed. I am many things, and many people. *I am the nation.*

I am 213 million living souls—and the ghost of millions who have lived and died for me.

I am Nathan Hale and Paul Revere. I stood at Lexington and fired the shot heard around the world. I am Washington, Jefferson and Patrick Henry. I am John Paul Jones, the Green Mountain Boys and Davy Crockett. I am Lee and Grant and Abe Lincoln.

I remember the Alamo, the Maine and Pearl Harbor. When freedom called I answered and stayed until it was over, over there. I left my heroic dead in Flanders Fields, on the rock of Corregidor, on the bleak slopes of Korea and in the steaming jungle of Vietnam.

I am the Brooklyn Bridge, the wheat lands of Kansas and the granite hills of Vermont. I am the coalfields of the Virginias and Pennsylvania, the fertile lands of the West, the Golden Gate and the Grand Canyon. I am Independence Hall, the Monitor and the Merrimac.

I am big. I sprawl from the Atlantic to the Pacific . . . my arms reach out to embrace Alaska and Hawaii . . . 3 million square miles throbbing with industry. I am more than 5 million farms. I am forest, field, mountain and desert. I am quiet villages—and cities that never sleep.

You can look at me and see Ben Franklin walking down the streets of Philadelphia with his breadloaf under his arm. You can see Betsy Ross with her needle. You can see the lights of Christmas, and hear the strains of "Auld Lang Syne" as the calendar turns.

I am Babe Ruth and the World Series. I am 110,000 schools and colleges, and 330,000 churches where my people worship God as they think best. I am a ballot dropped in a box, the roar of a crowd in a stadium and the voice of a choir in a cathedral. I am an editorial in a newspaper and a letter to a Congressman.

I am Eli Whitney and Stephen Foster. I am Tom Edison, Albert Einstein and Billy Graham. I am Horace Greeley, Will Rogers and the Wright brothers. I am George Washington Carver, Jonas Salk, and Martin Luther King.

I am Longfellow, Harriet Beecher Stowe, Walt Whitman and Thomas Paine.

Yes, I am the nation, and these are the things that I am. I was conceived in freedom and, God willing, in freedom I will spend the rest of my days.

May I possess always the integrity, the courage and the strength to keep myself unshackled, to remain a citadel of freedom and a beacon of hope to the world.

This is my wish, my goal, my prayer in this year of 1976—two hundred years after I was born.

OTTO WHITTAKER, "I Am the Nation," *Norfolk and Western Railway Company Magazine*, January 15, 1976, front cover.

This was originally written in 1955 as a public relations advertisement for the Norfolk and Western Railway, now the Norfolk Southern Corporation, and did not contain the phrase, "the steaming jungle of Vietnam." It has been widely reprinted, generally without attribution, has been set to music, is reprinted by some newspapers every Independence Day, and has been read into the *Congressional Record* several times. Ellipses in original.

America

66 The great voice of America does not come from the seats of learning, but in a murmur from the hills and the woods and the farms and the factories and the mills, rolling on and gaining volume until it comes to us the voice from the homes of the common men. Do these murmurs come into the corridors of the university? I have not heard them.

WOODROW WILSON, president of Princeton, address to Princeton University alumni, Pittsburgh, Pennsylvania, April 17, 1910.—*The Papers of Woodrow Wilson,* ed. Arthur S. Link, vol. 20, p. 365 (1975).

67 I believe that we are lost here in America, but I believe we shall be found. And this belief, which mounts now to the catharsis of knowledge and conviction, is for me—and I think for all of us—not only our own hope, but America's everlasting, living dream.

THOMAS WOLFE, *You Can't Go Home Again,* chapter 48, p. 741 (1940).

68 So, then, to every man his chance—to every man, regardless of his birth, his shining, golden opportunity—to every man the right to live, to work, to be himself, and to become whatever thing his manhood and his vision can combine to make him—this, seeker, is the promise of America.

THOMAS WOLFE, *You Can't Go Home Again,* chapter 31, p. 508 (1940).

69 America . . . . It is a fabulous country, the only fabulous country; it is the only place where miracles not only happen, but where they happen all the time.

THOMAS WOLFE, *Of Time and the River,* book 2, chapter 14, p. 155 (1935).

70 When God made the oyster, he guaranteed his absolute economic and social security. He built the oyster a house, his shell, to shelter and protect him from his enemies. . . . But when God made the Eagle, He declared, "The blue sky is the limit—build your own house!". . . . The Eagle, not the oyster, is the emblem of America.

Author unknown.—Jacob M. Braude, *Braude's Source Book for Speakers and Writers,* p. 14 (1968).

American people

71 I do not choose to be a common man. It is my right to be uncommon—if I can. I seek opportunity—not security. I do not wish to be a kept citizen, humbled and dulled by having the state look after me. I want to take the calculated risk; to dream and to build, to fail and to succeed. I refuse to barter incentive for a dole. I prefer the challenges of life to the guaranteed existence; the thrill of fulfillment to the stale calm of utopia. I will not trade freedom for beneficence nor my dignity for a handout. I will never cower before any master nor bend to any threat. It is my heritage to stand erect, proud and unafraid; to think and act for myself, enjoy the benefit of my creations, and to face the world boldly and say, this I have done. All this is what it means to be an American.

DEAN ALFANGE, creed.—*Who's Who in America, 1984–85,* vol. 1, p. 42. These words have appeared at the end of his entry in several successive editions.

Originally published in *This Week Magazine.* Later reprinted in *The Reader's Digest,* October 1952, p. 10, and January 1954, p. 122, lacking these words: "I will never cower before any master nor bend to any threat" and "to stand erect, proud and unafraid."

72 Sir, since the debate opened months ago those of us who have stood against this proposition have been taunted many times with being little Americans. Leave us the word American, keep that in your presumptuous impeachment, and no taunt can disturb us, no gibe discompose our purposes. Call us little Americans if you will, but leave us the consolation and the pride which the term American, however modified, still imparts.

Senator WILLIAM E. BORAH, remarks in the Senate, November 19, 1919, *Congressional Record,* vol. 58, p. 8783.

This speech, known as the "Little American" speech, referred to the treaty to ratify the League of Nations proposed after World War I.

73 Parties do not maintain themselves. They are maintained by effort. The government is not self-existent. It is maintained by the effort of those who believe in it. The people of America believe in American institutions, the American form of government and the American method of transacting business.

CALVIN COOLIDGE, governor of Massachusetts, speech before the Republican Commercial Travelers' Club, Boston, Massachusetts, April 10, 1920.—Massachusetts State Library, George Fingold Library, Boston. Manuscripts: speeches and messages of Calvin Coolidge, 1895–1924.

74 I do not want a honeymoon with you. I want a good marriage. I want progress, and I want problemsolving which requires my best efforts and also your best efforts. I have no need to learn how Congress speaks for the people. As President, I intend to listen. But I also intend to listen to the people themselves—all the people—as I promised last Friday. I want to be sure that we are all tuned in to the real voice of America.

President GERALD R. FORD, address to a joint session of Congress, August 12, 1974.—*Public Papers of the Presidents of the United States: Gerald R. Ford, 1974,* p. 7.

75 Good Americans, when they die, go to Paris.

OLIVER WENDELL HOLMES, *The Autocrat of the Breakfast-Table,* chapter 6, p. 143 (1868), originally published 1858, attributing this remark to "one of the wittiest of men."

Later writers have attributed the saying to Thomas Gold Appleton, a friend of Holmes's and a fellow member of the Saturday Club. In 1859, Ralph Waldo Emerson, also a member of that club, recorded in one of his journals, "T. Appleton says, that he thinks all Bostonians, when they die, if they are good, go to Paris."—*Emerson in His Journals,* ed. Joel Porte, p. 486 (1982). Although neither sentence has been found in the published writings of Appleton, the remark was probably made in the presence of Holmes and Emerson.

Oscar Wilde used Holmes's version of the statement in two of his works, *The Picture of Dorian Gray,* p. 75 (*Complete Works,* vol. 4, 1923), originally published 1890, and *A Woman of No Importance,* p. 180 (*Complete Works,* vol. 7, 1923), originally published 1893.

76 They are damn good projects—excellent projects. That goes for all the projects up there. You know some people make fun of people who speak a foreign language, and dumb people criticize something they do not understand, and that is what is going on up there—God damn it!

HARRY L. HOPKINS, head of the Works Progress Administration, in a statement defending the Federal Arts Project at a press conference, April 4, 1935.—Robert E. Sherwood, *Roosevelt and Hopkins,* p. 60 (1948).

Sherwood says, "The reports of this conference quoted Hopkins as saying that 'the people are too damned dumb,' and this phrase was given plenty of circulation in the press" (p. 61). He adds in a footnote that "it will be seen from the transcript of his remarks that this particular statement was directed not at the people but at the critical orators" (p. 938).

77 Let the word go forth from this time and place, to friend and foe alike, that the torch has been passed to a new generation of Americans.

President JOHN F. KENNEDY, inaugural address, January 20, 1961.—*The Public Papers of the Presidents of the United States: John F. Kennedy, 1961*, p. 1.

This is one of seven inscriptions carved on the walls at the gravesite of John F. Kennedy, Arlington National Cemetery.

78 Has it [popular sovereignty] not got down as thin as the homeopathic soup that was made by boiling the shadow of a pigeon that had starved to death?

ABRAHAM LINCOLN, rejoinder in the sixth debate with Senator Stephen A. Douglas, October 13, 1858.—*The Collected Works of Abraham Lincoln*, ed. Roy P. Basler, vol. 3, p. 279 (1953).

79 I think very much of the people, as an old friend said he thought of woman. He said when he lost his first wife, who had been a great help to him in his business, he thought he was ruined—that he could never find another to fill her place. At length, however, he married another, who he found did quite as well as the first, and that his opinion now was that any woman would do well who was well done by. So I think of the whole people of this nation—they will ever do well if well done by. We will try to do well by them in all parts of the country, North and South, with entire confidence that all will be well with all of us.

President-elect ABRAHAM LINCOLN, remarks at Bloomington, Illinois, November 21, 1860.—*The Collected Works of Abraham Lincoln*, ed. Roy P. Basler, vol. 4, pp. 143–44 (1953).

80 Americans never quit.

General DOUGLAS MACARTHUR, president of the American Olympic committee, comment when the manager of the American boxing team in the 1928 Olympic games wanted to withdraw the team because of what he thought was an unfair decision against an American boxer.—*The New York Times*, August 9, 1928, p. 13.

81 Races didn't bother the Americans. They were something a lot better than any race. They were a People. They were the first self-constituted, self-declared, self-created People in the history of the world. And their manners were their own business. And so were their politics. And so, but ten times so, were their souls.

ARCHIBALD MACLEISH, Librarian of Congress, "The American Cause," address delivered at Faneuil Hall, Boston, Massachusetts, November 20, 1940.—MacLeish, *A Time to Act; Selected Addresses*, p. 115 (1943).

82 Is it not the glory of the people of America, that, whilst they have paid a decent regard to the opinions of former times and other nations, they have not suffered a blind veneration for antiquity, for custom, or for names, to overrule the suggestions of their own good sense, the knowledge of their own situation, and the lessons of their own experience? To this manly spirit, posterity will be indebted for the possession, and the world for the example, of the numerous innovations displayed on the American theatre, in favor of private rights and public happiness.

JAMES MADISON, *The Federalist*, ed. Benjamin F. Wright, no. 14, p. 154 (1961).

This quotation was used on the official invitations to the 1985 presidential inaugural of President Ronald Reagan.

83 The average American is just like the child in the family. You give him some responsibility and he is going to amount to something. He is going to do something. If, on the other hand, you make him completely dependent and pamper him and cater to him too much, you are going to make him soft, spoiled and eventually a very weak individual.

President RICHARD M. NIXON, interview with Garnett D. Horner following election to a second presidential term, *The Washington Star-News*, November 9, 1972, p. 1.

84 For the American people are a very generous people and will forgive almost any weakness, with the possible exception of stupidity.

WILL ROGERS, *The Illiterate Digest*, p. 228 (1924).

85 Let's face it. Let's talk sense to the American people. Let's tell them the truth, that there are no gains without pains, that we are now on the eve of great decisions, not easy decisions, like resistance when you're attacked, but a long, patient, costly struggle which alone can assure triumph over the great enemies of man—war, poverty and tyranny—and the assaults upon human dignity which are the most grievous consequences of each.

ADLAI E. STEVENSON, governor of Illinois, speech accepting presidential nomination, Democratic national convention, Chicago, Illinois, July 26, 1952.—*Speeches of Adlai Stevenson*, pp. 20–21 (1952).

86 Americans cleave to the things of this world as if assured that they will never die, . . . They clutch everything but hold nothing fast, and so lose grip as they hurry after some new delight. An American will build a house in which to pass his old age and sell it before the roof is on; he will plant a garden and rent it just as the trees are coming into bearing; he will clear a field and leave others to reap the harvest; he will take up a profession and leave it, settle in one place and soon go off elsewhere with his changing desires. If his private business allows him a moment's relaxation, he will plunge at once into the whirlpool of politics. Then, if at the end of a year crammed with work he has a little spare leisure, his restless curiosity goes with him traveling up and down the vast territories of the United States. Thus he will travel five hundred miles in a few days as a distraction from his happiness. Death steps in in the end and stops him before he has grown tired of this futile pursuit of that complete felicity which always escapes him. At first sight there is something astonishing in this spectacle of so many lucky men restless in the midst of abundance. But it is a spectacle as old as the world; all that is new is to see a whole people performing in it.

ALEXIS DE TOCQUEVILLE, *Democracy in America*, ed. J. P. Mayer, trans. George Lawrence, vol. 2, part 2, chapter 13, p. 536 (1969). Originally published in 1835–1840.

87 The people reign over the American political world as God rules over the universe. It is the cause and the end of all things; everything rises out of it and is absorbed back into it.

ALEXIS DE TOCQUEVILLE, *Democracy in America*, ed. J. P. Mayer, trans. George Lawrence, vol. 1, part 1, chapter 4, concluding sentences, p. 60 (1969). Originally published in 1835–1840.

American people

88 The people of those foreign countries are very, very ignorant. They looked curiously at the costumes we had brought from the wilds of America. They observed that we talked loudly at table sometimes. They noticed that we looked out for expenses and got what we conveniently could out of a franc, and wondered where in the mischief we came from. In Paris they just simply opened their eyes and stared when we spoke to them in French! We never did succeed in making those idiots understand their own language.

MARK TWAIN (Samuel L. Clemens), letter appearing in the *New York Herald*, November 20, 1867, the day after he arrived in New York on the steamer *Quaker City*.—*Traveling with the Innocents Abroad; Mark Twain's Original Reports from Europe and the Holy Land*, ed. Daniel M. McKeithan, p. 316 (1958).

Twain later revised the 58 letters written on the trip and turned them into *The Innocents Abroad*, where this quotation appears in "A Newspaper Valedictory," vol. 2 of *The Writings of Mark Twain*, p. 437 (1897, reprinted 1968).

Animals

89 And for these also, Dear Lord, the humble beasts, who with us bear the burden and heat of the day, and offer their guileless lives for the well-being of their country, we supplicate Thy great tenderness of heart, for Thou hast promised to save both man and beast. And great is Thy loving kindness, Oh Master, Savior of the world.

Attributed to ST. BASIL of Caesarea, prayer, A.D. 370.—*The Washington Daily News*, April 16, 1971, p. 23. Unverified.

90 To my way of thinking there's something wrong, or missing, with any person who hasn't got a soft spot in their heart for an animal of some kind. With most folks the dog stands highest as man's friend, then comes the horse, with others the cat is liked best as a pet, or a monkey is fussed over; but whatever kind of animal it is a person likes, it's all hunkydory so long as there's a place in the heart for one or a few of them.

WILL JAMES, *Smoky, the Cow Horse*, Preface, p. v (1929).

Architecture

91 The stone which the builders refused is become the head stone of the corner.

The Bible, Psalms 118:22.

92 Architecture worth great attention. As we double our numbers every 20 years we must double our houses. Besides we build of such perishable materials that one half of our houses must be rebuilt in every space of 20 years. So that in that term, houses are to be built for three fourths of our inhabitants. It is then among the most important arts: and it is desireable to introduce taste into an art which shews so much.

THOMAS JEFFERSON, hints to Americans travelling in Europe, letter to John Rutledge, Jr., June 19, 1788.—*The Papers of Thomas Jefferson*, ed. Julian P. Boyd, vol. 13, p. 269 (1956).

93 Architecture has its political Use; publick Buildings being the Ornament of a Country; it establishes a Nation, draws People and Commerce; makes the People love their native Country, which Passion is the Original of all great Actions in a Common-wealth. . . . Architecture aims at Eternity.

SIR CHRISTOPHER WREN, "Of Architecture," *Parentalia; or Memoirs of the Family of the Wrens*, comp. by his son Christopher, Appendix, p. 351 (1750, reprinted 1965).

94 Bridges are America's cathedrals.

Author unknown.

Arts

95 The more minimal the art, the more maximum the explanation.

HILTON KRAMER, *The New York Times* art critic, in the late 1960s when the term "minimal art" was in vogue.

96 I look forward to an America which will reward achievement in the arts as we reward achievement in business or statecraft. I look forward to an America which will steadily raise the standards of artistic accomplishment and which will steadily enlarge cultural opportunities for all of our citizens. And I look forward to an America which commands respect throughout the world not only for its strength but for its civilization as well.

President JOHN F. KENNEDY, remarks upon receiving an honorary degree, Amherst College, Amherst, Massachusetts, October 26, 1963.—*Public Papers of the Presidents of the United States: John F. Kennedy, 1963*, p. 817.

Inscription on the John F. Kennedy Center for the Performing Arts, Washington, D.C.

97 There is a connection, hard to explain logically but easy to feel, between achievement in public life and progress in the arts. The age of Pericles was also the age of Phidias. The age of Lorenzo de Medici was also the age of Leonardo da Vinci. The age of Elizabeth was also the age of Shakespeare. And the New Frontier for which I campaign in public life, can also be a New Frontier for American art.

Senator JOHN F. KENNEDY, letter to Miss Theodate Johnson, publisher of *Musical America*, September 13, 1960.—*Musical America*, October 1960, p. 11.

Inscription on the John F. Kennedy Center for the Performing Arts, Washington, D.C.

98 To further the appreciation of culture among all the people, to increase respect for the creative individual, to widen participation by all the processes and fulfillments of art—this is one of the fascinating challenges of these days.

President JOHN F. KENNEDY, "The Arts in America," *Look*, December 18, 1962, p. 110. Also *Public Papers of the Presidents of the United States: John F. Kennedy, 1962*, p. 907.

Inscription on the John F. Kennedy Center for the Performing Arts, Washington, D.C.

Associations

99 Americans combine to give fêtes, found seminaries, build churches, distribute books, and send missionaries to the antipodes. Hospitals, prisons, and schools take shape in that way. Finally, if they want to proclaim a truth or propagate some feeling by the encouragement of a great example, they form an association. In every case, at the head of any new undertaking, where in France you would find the government or in England some territorial magnate, in the United States you are sure to find an association. I have come across several types of association in America of which, I confess, I had not previously the slightest conception, and I have often admired the extreme skill they show in proposing a common object for the exertions of very many and in inducing them voluntarily to pursue it.

ALEXIS DE TOCQUEVILLE, *Democracy in America*, ed. J. P. Mayer, trans. George Lawrence, vol. 2, part 2, chapter 5, pp. 513–14 (1969). Originally published in 1835–1840.

Athenian oath

100 I will not disgrace my sacred arms
Nor desert my comrade, wherever
I am stationed.
I will fight for things sacred
And things profane.
And both alone and with all to help me.
I will transmit my fatherland not diminished
But greater and better than before.
I will obey the ruling magistrates
Who rule reasonably
And I will observe the established laws
And whatever laws in the future
May be reasonably established.
If any person seek to overturn the laws,
Both alone and with all to help me,
I will oppose him.
I will honor the religion of my fathers.
I call to witness the Gods . . .
The borders of my fatherland,
The wheat, the barley, the vines,
And the trees of the olive and the fig.

Athenian Ephebic Oath, trans. Clarence A. Forbes.—Fletcher Harper Swift, *The Athenian Ephebic Oath of Allegiance in American Schools and Colleges*, University of California Publications in Education, vol. 11, no. 1, p. 4 (1947).

"The true and exact text of the Athenian ephebic oath is no longer in doubt. In 1932, L'École Française d'Athènes discovered in the ancient Athenian deme (township) of Archarnae a fourth-century stele on which was engraved 'in dubitable letters of stone the true, ancient, authentic and official wording of the oath.' " (pp. 2–3)

"Less widely known [than the Oath of Hippocrates] but of equally surpassing nobility is the ancient Athenian oath of citizenship, dating probably from 'very early times.' Later, it was adopted as the oath to be taken by ephebi, young men of eighteen to twenty years, enrolled in the Ephebic College established in 335–334 B.C. to implement a state-supported system of military training. . . . every legitimate son of pure Athenian parentage who had reached the age of eighteen must, in order to be admitted to citizenship, be enrolled therein and undergo its two-year course of rigorous training in military and civic duties and activities." At the end of the first year each ephebus was given a spear and a shield; after receiving these arms, the ephebi took their oath. (pp. 1–2)

Adaptations of the oath, with varying translations, have been used by American colleges and universities.

Banks and banking

101 The bank mania is one of the most threatening of these imitations. It is raising up a monied aristocracy in our country which has already set the government at defiance, and although forced at length to yield a little on this first essay of their strength, their principles are unyielded and unyielding.

THOMAS JEFFERSON, letter to Josephus B. Stuart, May 10, 1817.—*The Writings of Thomas Jefferson,* ed. Andrew A. Lipscomb, vol. 15, p. 112 (1904).

The Beatitudes

102 Blessed are the poor in spirit: for theirs is the kingdom of heaven.
Blessed are they that mourn: for they shall be comforted.
Blessed are the meek: for they shall inherit the earth.
Blessed are they which do hunger and thirst after righteousness: for they shall be filled.
Blessed are the merciful: for they shall obtain mercy.
Blessed are the pure in heart: for they shall see God.
Blessed are the peacemakers: for they shall be called the children of God.
Blessed are they which are persecuted for righteousness' sake: for theirs is the kingdom of heaven.
Blessed are ye, when men shall revile you, and persecute you, and shall say all manner of evil against you falsely, for my sake.
Rejoice, and be exceeding glad: for great is your reward in heaven; for so persecuted they the prophets which were before you.

The Bible, Matthew 5:3–12.

These verses are called the Beatitudes. Some scholars do not include verse 12 because it does not begin with the word *blessed.*

Beauty

103 [On vanity:] The nose of Cleopatra: if it had been shorter, the face of the earth would have changed.

BLAISE PASCAL, *Pascal's Pensées,* trans. Martin Turnell, part 1, section 6, p. 133 (1962).

104 I look forward to an America which will not be afraid of grace and beauty.

President JOHN F. KENNEDY, remarks upon receiving an honorary degree, Amherst College, Amherst, Massachusetts, October 26, 1963.—*Public Papers of the Presidents of the United States: John F. Kennedy, 1963,* p. 817.

Inscription on the John F. Kennedy Center for the Performing Arts, Washington, D.C.

Belief

105 Believe nothing, O monks, merely because you have been told it . . . or because it is traditional, or because you yourselves have imagined it. Do not believe what your teacher tells you merely out of respect for the teacher. But whatsoever, after due examination and analysis, you find to be conducive to the good, the benefit, the welfare of all beings—that doctrine believe and cling to, and take it as your guide.

Attributed to BUDDHA.—*Life,* March 7, 1955, p. 102. Unverified in his writings.

Belief

106 Give to us clear vision that we may know where to stand and what to stand for—because unless we stand for something, we shall fall for anything.

PETER MARSHALL, Senate chaplain, prayer offered at the opening of the session, April 18, 1947.—*Prayers Offered by the Chaplain, the Rev. Peter Marshall . . . 1947–1948*, p. 20 (1949). Senate Doc. 80–170.

107 What counts now is not just what we are against, but what we are for. Who leads us is less important than what leads us—what convictions, what courage, what faith—win or lose. A man doesn't save a century, or a civilization, but a militant party wedded to a principle can.

ADLAI E. STEVENSON, governor of Illinois, welcoming address before the Democratic national convention, Chicago, Illinois, July 21, 1952.—*Speeches of Adlai Stevenson*, p. 17 (1952).

Bermuda

108 We, the undersigned, visitors to Bermuda, venture respectfully to express the opinion that the admission of automobiles to the island would alter the whole character of the place, in a way which would seem to us very serious indeed. The island now attracts visitors in considerable numbers because of the quiet and dignified simplicity of its life. . . . It would, in our opinion, be a fatal error to attract to Bermuda the extravagant and sporting set who have made so many other places of pleasure entirely intolerable to persons of taste and cultivation.

WOODROW WILSON, president of Princeton, petition to the Bermuda Legislature, c. February 1, 1908.—*The Papers of Woodrow Wilson*, ed. Arthur S. Link, vol. 17, pp. 609–10 (1974).

Wilson drafted this petition, which had a total of 111 signers, including Samuel L. Clemens. The Bermuda Legislature did ban all motor cars.

Best

109 He has called on the best that was in us. There was no such thing as half-trying. Whether it was running a race or catching a football, competing in school—we were to try. And we were to try harder than anyone else. We might not be the best, and none of us were, but we were to make the effort to be the best. "After you have done the best you can," he used to say, "the hell with it."

Senator ROBERT F. KENNEDY, tribute to his father, Joseph P. Kennedy. Read at Joseph Kennedy's funeral by Senator Edward M. Kennedy, November 20, 1969.—*Congressional Record*, November 25, 1969, vol. 115, p. 35877.

110 I do the very best I know how—the very best I can; and I mean to keep doing so until the end. If the end brings me out all right, what is said against me won't amount to anything. If the end brings me out wrong, ten angels swearing I was right would make no difference.

President ABRAHAM LINCOLN.—Francis Carpenter, *Six Months at the White House*, pp. 258–59 (1867).

See note at No. 731 about Carpenter's stay at the White House.

President Richard M. Nixon used similar words about his plan for peace in an address to the nation on the war in Vietnam, November 3, 1969: "If it does succeed, what the critics say now won't matter. If it does not succeed, anything I say then won't matter."—*Public Papers of the Presidents of the United States: Richard Nixon, 1969,* p. 909.

111 That what is true of business and politics is gloriously true of the professions, the arts and crafts, the sciences, the sports. That the best picture has not yet been painted; the greatest poem is still unsung; the mightiest novel remains to be written; the divinest music has not been conceived even by Bach. In science, probably ninety-nine percent of the knowable has to be discovered. We know only a few streaks about astronomy. We are only beginning to imagine the force and composition of the atom. Physics has not yet found any indivisible matter, or psychology a sensible soul.

LINCOLN STEFFENS, "This World Depression of Ours is Chock-full of Good News," *Hearst's International Combined with Cosmopolitan,* October 1932, p. 26. This is reprinted in his *The World of Lincoln Steffens,* ed. Ella Winter and Herbert Shapiro, p. 216 (1962).

112 In this best of all possible worlds, My Lord the Baron's castle was the finest of castles, and My Lady the best of all possible Baronesses. "It is demonstrated," he [Pangloss] said, "that things cannot be otherwise, for, everything being made for an end, everything is necessarily for the best end."

(Dans ce meilleur des mondes possibles, le château de monseigneur le baron était le plus beau des châteaux, et madame la meilleure des baronnes possibles. "Il est démontré, disait-il, que les choses ne peuvent être autrement: car tout étant fait pour une fin, tout est nécessairement pour la meilleure fin.")

VOLTAIRE (François Marie Arouet), *Candide,* chapter 1.—*Voltaire's Candide, Zadig, and Selected Stories,* trans. Donald M. Frame, p. 4 (1961).

With judicious omissions and elisions, and by reversing phrases, the above can be made into the often-quoted, "Everything is for the best in this best of all possible worlds," an aphorism popularized in the 1960s by the musical, *Candide,* words by Lillian Hellman and music by Leonard Bernstein.

Betrayal

113 On this tenth day of June, 1940, the hand that held the dagger has struck it into the back of its neighbor.

President FRANKLIN D. ROOSEVELT, commencement address at the University of Virginia, Charlottesville, June 10, 1940.—*The Public Papers and Addresses of Franklin D. Roosevelt, 1940,* p. 263 (1941).

On June 10 Italy declared war against France.

114 I am in blood
Stepp'd in so far that, should I wade no more,
Returning were as tedious as go o'er.

WILLIAM SHAKESPEARE, *Macbeth,* act III, scene iv, lines 136–38. Macbeth is speaking.

Blacklist

115 I would rather quit public life at seventy, and quit it forever, than to retain public life at a sacrifice to my own self-respect. I will not vote for any law which will make fair for me and foul for another. The blacklist is the most cruel form of oppression ever devised by man for the infliction of suffering upon his weaker fellows.

Speaker of the House JOSEPH G. CANNON, speech opposing the Pearre Injunction Bill, 1906.—L. White Busby, *Uncle Joe Cannon*, p. 278 (1927).

Cannon noted that Samuel Gompers blacklisted him for opposing the legislation. "Uncle Joe" Cannon, who was Speaker of the House 1903–1911, served in the House for 46 years.

Cannon expanded this passage in a speech in Lewiston, Maine, September 5, 1906, while successfully campaigning for Representative Charles Littlefield, to counter efforts of Gompers and his labor forces to defeat Littlefield. Here, he said, ". . . any law which will make fish of one and fowl of another."—Joseph G. Cannon papers, box 1, Illinois State Historical Library, Springfield, Illinois.

Blacks

116 In my judgment, the slogan "black power" and what has been associated with it has set the civil rights movement back considerably in the United States over the period of the last several months.

Senator ROBERT F. KENNEDY, remark during testimony of Floyd McKissick before a Senate subcommittee of which Kennedy was a member, December 8, 1966.—*Federal Role in Urban Affairs*, hearings before the Subcommittee on Executive Reorganization of the Committee on Government Operations, United States Senate, 89th Congress, 2d session, part 11, p. 2312 (1967).

117 None of these strictures, however, should inhibit any one of us, in his individual capacity, from declaring himself on the issues of the trial and its fairness . . . So in spite of my insistence on the limits of my official capacity, I personally want to say that I am appalled and ashamed that things should have come to such a pass in this country that I am skeptical of the ability of black revolutionaries to achieve a fair trial anywhere in the United States. In large part this atmosphere has been created by police actions and prosecutions against the Panthers in many parts of the country. It is also one more inheritance from centuries of racial discrimination and oppression. . . . The first contribution to the fairness of the trial which anyone can make is to cool rather than heat up the atmosphere in which the trial will be held.

KINGMAN BREWSTER, president of Yale, statement to a closed meeting of the faculty of Yale College, explaining why the university could not use its funds to help the defendants in the Black Panther murder trial.—*The Washington Post*, editorial, May 5, 1970, p. A16.

118 Beware of Greeks bearing gifts, colored men looking for loans and whites who "understand the Negro."

ADAM CLAYTON POWELL, JR., "The Soapbox," *The New York Amsterdam News*, June 6, 1936, p. 12.

Powell wrote a weekly column, "The Soapbox."

119 Now, Mr. Chairman, before concluding my remarks I want to submit a brief recipe for the solution of the so-called American negro problem. He asks no special favors, but simply demands that he be given the same chance for existence, for earning a livelihood, for raising himself in the scales of manhood and womanhood that are accorded to kindred nationalities. Treat him as a man; go into his home and learn of his social conditions; learn of his cares, his troubles, and his hopes for the future; gain his confidence; open the doors of industry to him; let the word "negro," "colored," and "black" be stricken from all the organizations enumerated in the federation of labor.

Help him to overcome his weaknesses, punish the crime-committing class by the courts of the land, measure the standard of the race by its best material, cease to mold prejudicial and unjust public sentiment against him, and my word for it, he will learn to support, hold up the hands of, and join in with that political party, that institution, whether secular or religious, in every community where he lives, which is destined to do the greatest good for the greatest number. Obliterate race hatred, party prejudice, and help us to achieve nobler ends, greater results, and become more satisfactory citizens to our brother in white.

This, Mr. Chairman, is perhaps the negroes' temporary farewell to the American Congress; but let me say, Phoenix-like he will rise up some day and come again. These parting words are in behalf of an outraged, heart-broken, bruised, and bleeding, but God-fearing people, faithful, industrious, loyal people—rising people, full of potential force.

Mr. Chairman, in the trial of Lord Bacon, when the court disturbed the counsel for the defendant, Sir Walter Raleigh raised himself up to his full height and, addressing the court, said: "Sir, I am pleading for the life of a human being."

The only apology that I have to make for the earnestness with which I have spoken is that I am pleading for the life, the liberty, the future happiness, and manhood suffrage for one-eighth of the entire population of the United States.

Representative GEORGE H. WHITE, remarks in the House, January 29, 1901, *Congressional Record,* vol. 34, p. 1638.

He was the only black in the 55th and 56th Congresses (1897–1901).

Blood

120 A conscientious man would be cautious how he dealt in blood.

EDMUND BURKE, letter to the Sheriffs of Bristol, April 3, 1777.—*The Works of the Right Honorable Edmund Burke,* vol. 2, p. 206 (1899).

121 i
have often noticed that
ancestors never boast
of the descendants who boast
of ancestors i would
rather start a family than
finish one blood will tell but often
it tells too much

DON MARQUIS, "A Roach of the Taverns," *Archy and Mehitabel,* pp. 156–57 (1927, reprinted 1930).

Bohemia

122 Who is master of Bohemia is master of Europe.

Attributed to OTTO VON BISMARCK. Unverified.

While this statement has frequently been quoted, it cannot be found in the official writings and pronouncements of Bismarck. It is possible that he said it, and it was passed on orally rather than being recorded, or that he expressed the sentiment in other terms and the idea took this form as others tried to quote him.

123 If the radiance of a thousand suns were to burst forth at once in the sky, that would be like the splendour of the Mighty One.

I am mighty, world-destroying Time . . .

Bhagavad Gita. *Bhagavad Gita*, trans. Swami Nikhilananda, chapter 11, sections 12 and 32, pp. 256, 261 (1944).

A variation of this translation flashed through the mind of J. Robert Oppenheimer as he stood in the control room at the explosion of the first atomic bomb at Los Alamos, New Mexico, July 16, 1945: "If the radiance of a thousand suns / were to burst into the sky / that would be like / the splendor of the Mighty One" and "I am become Death, the shatterer of worlds."—*Current Biography Yearbook, 1964*, p. 331.

124 Some recent work by E. Fermi and L. Szilard, which has been communicated to me in manuscript, leads me to expect that the element uranium may be turned into a new and important source of energy in the immediate future. Certain aspects of the situation seem to call for watchfulness and, if necessary, quick action on the part of the Administration. . . .

This new phenomenon would also lead to the construction of bombs, and it is conceivable—though much less certain—that extremely powerful bombs of a new type may thus be constructed. A single bomb of this type, carried by boat or exploded in a port, might very well destroy the whole port together with some of the surrounding territory. However, such bombs might very well prove to be too heavy for transportation by air.

ALBERT EINSTEIN, letter to President Franklin D. Roosevelt, August 2, 1939, delivered October 11, 1939.—*Einstein on Peace*, ed. Otto Nathan and Heinz Norden, pp. 294–95 (1960, reprinted 1981).

125 What a curious picture it is to find man, homo sapiens, of divine origin, we are told, seriously considering going underground to escape the consequences of his own folly. With a little wisdom and foresight, surely it is not yet necessary to forsake life in the fresh air and in the warmth of the sunlight. What a paradox if our own cleverness in science should force us to live underground with the moles.

Senator J. WILLIAM FULBRIGHT, "The Effect of the Atomic Bomb on American Foreign Policy," address to the Foreign Policy Association, New York City, October 20, 1945.—*Congressional Record*, November 2, 1945, vol. 91, Appendix, p. A4654.

126 I happened to read recently a remark by the American nuclear physicist W. Davidson, who noted that the explosion of one hydrogen bomb releases a greater amount of energy than all the explosions set off by all countries in all wars known in the entire history of mankind. And he, apparently, is right.

NIKITA S. KHRUSHCHEV, address at the United Nations, New York City, September 18, 1959, as reported by *The New York Times*, September 19, 1959, p. 8.

The physicist quoted was eventually found to be William Davidon, associate physicist at Argonne National Laboratory, Lemont, Illinois.

127 My solution to the problem [of North Vietnam] would be to tell them frankly that they've got to draw in their horns and stop their aggression, or we're going to bomb them back into the Stone Age. And we would shove them back into the Stone Age with Air power or Naval power—not with ground forces.

General CURTIS E. LEMAY, *Mission with LeMay: My Story*, p. 565 (1965).

In an interview two years after the publication of this book, General LeMay said, "I never said we should bomb them back to the Stone Age. I said we had the capability to do it. I want to save lives on both sides."—*The Washington Post*, October 4, 1968, p. A8.

128 I'd rather be Red than dead.

Author unknown. Slogan of Britain's Campaign for Nuclear Disarmament supporters.—*Time*, September 15, 1961, p. 30.

Books

129 The world of books is the most remarkable creation of man. Nothing else that he builds ever lasts. Monuments fall; nations perish; civilizations grow old and die out; and, after an era of darkness, new races build others. But in the world of books are volumes that have seen this happen again and again, and yet live on, still young, still as fresh as the day they were written, still telling men's hearts of the hearts of men centuries dead.

And even the books that do not last long, penetrate their own times at least, sailing farther than Ulysses even dreamed of, like ships on the seas. It is the author's part to call into being their cargoes and passengers,—living thoughts and rich bales of study and jeweled ideas. And as for the publishers, it is they who build the fleet, plan the voyage, and sail on, facing wreck, till they find every possible harbor that will value their burden.

CLARENCE S. DAY, *The Story of the Yale University Press Told by a Friend*, pp. 7–8 (1920).

130 Books are the quietest and most constant of friends; they are the most accessible and wisest of counsellors, and the most patient of teachers.

CHARLES W. ELIOT, "The Happy Life," *The Durable Satisfactions of Life*, p. 37 (1910, reprinted 1969).

Eliot, president of Harvard, 1869–1909, first read this before Phillips Exeter Academy, Exeter, New Hampshire, but it was later rewritten.

131 All good books are alike in that they are truer than if they had really happened and after you are finished reading one you will feel that all that happened to you and afterwards it all belongs to you; the good and the bad, the ecstacy, the remorse and sorrow, the people and the places and how the weather was.

ERNEST HEMINGWAY, "Old Newsman Writes," *Esquire*, December 1934, p. 26.

132 If this nation is to be wise as well as strong, if we are to achieve our destiny, then we need more new ideas for more wise men reading more good books in more public libraries. These libraries should be open to all—except the censor. We must know all the facts and hear all the alternatives and listen to all the criticisms. Let us welcome controversial books and controversial authors. For the Bill of Rights is the guardian of our security as well as our liberty.

Senator JOHN F. KENNEDY, response to questionnaire, *Saturday Review*, October 29, 1960, p. 44.

133 Books are good enough in their own way, but they are a mighty bloodless substitute for life.

ROBERT LOUIS STEVENSON, "An Apology for Idlers," *Virginibus Puerisque and Later Essays*, p. 80 (1969). Written between 1874–1879.

Brotherhood

134 No man is an island, entire of itself; every man is a piece of the continent, a part of the main. If a clod be washed away by the sea, Europe is the less, as well as if a promontory were, as well as if a manor of thy friend's or of thine own were: any man's death diminishes me, because I am involved in mankind, and therefore never send to know for whom the bells tolls; it tolls for thee.

JOHN DONNE, *Devotions upon Emergent Occasions,* no. 17, pp. 108–9 (1959). Originally published in 1624.

Although the phrase is widely quoted as "for whom the bell tolls" and appears that way in Donne's *Selected Prose,* sel. Evelyn Simpson, ed. Helen Gardner and Timothy Healy, p. 101 (1967), most editions give the wording above.

135 Speak not too well of one who scarce will know
Himself transfigured in its roseate glow;
Say kindly of him what is, chiefly, true,
Remembering always he belongs to you;
Deal with him as a truant, if you will,
But claim him, keep him, call him brother still!

OLIVER WENDELL HOLMES, "Poem," read at a dinner given for the author by the medical profession of the City of New York, April 12, 1883.—*The Poetical Works of Oliver Wendell Holmes,* ed. Eleanor M. Tilton, p. 71 (1895, rev. 1975).

136 There is a destiny that makes us brothers:
None goes his way alone:
All that we send into the lives of others
Comes back onto our own.

EDWIN MARKHAM, "A Creed," stanza 1, *Poems of Edwin Markham,* p. 18 (1950).

Business

137 Bigness is still the curse.

Justice LOUIS D. BRANDEIS, conversation with Alfred Lief, December 7, 1940.—*The Brandeis Guide to the Modern World,* ed. Alfred Lief, p. 20 (1941).

The Curse of Bigness is the title of a collection of Brandeis's papers published in 1934.

138 The substance of the eminent Socialist gentleman's speech is that making a profit is a sin, but it is my belief that the real sin is taking a loss.

WINSTON CHURCHILL, remarks in the House of Commons responding to a Laborite speech on the evils of free enterprise.—James C. Humes, *Speaker's Treasury of Anecdotes About the Famous,* p. 45 (1978). Unverified.

139 The trusts and combinations—the communism of pelf—whose machinations have prevented us from reaching the success we deserved, should not be forgotten nor forgiven.

President GROVER CLEVELAND, letter to Representative Thomas C. Catchings, August 27, 1894.—*Letters of Grover Cleveland, 1850–1908,* ed. Allan Nevins, p. 365 (1933).

140 After all, the chief business of the American people is business.

President CALVIN COOLIDGE, address before the American Society of Newspaper Editors, Washington, D.C., January 17, 1925.—Coolidge, *Foundations of the Republic*, p. 187 (1926).

Usually misquoted as: "The business of America is business."

141 One aspect of modern life which has gone far to stifle men is the rapid growth of tremendous corporations. Enormous spiritual sacrifices are made in the transformation of shopkeepers into employees. . . . The disappearance of free enterprise has led to a submergence of the individual in the impersonal corporation in much the same manner as he has been submerged in the state in other lands.

WILLIAM O. DOUGLAS, chairman, Securities and Exchange Commission, speech at annual dinner of Fordham University Alumni Association, New York City, February 9, 1939.—James Allen, *Democracy and Finance*, p. 291 (1940, reprinted 1969).

This was Douglas's last speech before his appointment to the Supreme Court.

142 We believe that there is one economic lesson which our twentieth century experience has demonstrated conclusively—that America can no more survive and grow without big business than it can survive and grow without small business. . . . the two are interdependent. You cannot strengthen one by weakening the other, and you cannot add to the stature of a dwarf by cutting off the legs of a giant.

BENJAMIN FRANKLIN FAIRLESS, president of United States Steel Corporation, testimony, April 26, 1950.—*Study of Monopoly Power*, hearings before the Subcommittee on Study of Monopoly Power of the Committee on the Judiciary, House of Representatives, 81st Congress, 2d session, part 4A, "Steel," p. 466 (1950).

143 So the question is, do *corporate executives*, provided they stay within the law, have responsibilities in their business activities other than to make as much money for their stockholders as possible? And my answer to that is, no they do not.

MILTON FRIEDMAN, interview with John McClaughry, contributing editor of *Business and Society Review*, on the topic of corporate social responsibility.—"Milton Friedman Responds," *Chemtech*, February 1974, p. 72.

144 We are obviously all hurt by inflation. Everybody is hurt by inflation. If you really wanted to examine who percentage-wise is hurt the most in their incomes, it is the Wall Street brokers. I mean their incomes have gone down the most.

ALAN GREENSPAN, chairman of the Council of Economic Advisers, at a conference on inflation, Washington, D.C., September 19, 1974.—*Report* of the Health, Education, and Welfare, Income Security, Social Services Conference on Inflation, pp. 804–5 (1974).

145 This administration is not sympathetic to corporations, it is indentured to corporations.

RALPH NADER, quoted in a news conference, October 3, 1972, speaking about the Nixon Administration, as reported by *The Washington Post*, October 4, 1972, p. A2.

146 *Method* goes far to prevent Trouble in Business: For it makes the Task easy, hinders Confusion, saves abundance of Time, and instructs those that have Business depending, both what to do and what to hope.

WILLIAM PENN, *Some Fruits of Solitude in Reflections & Maxims*, no. 403, p. 70 (1903, reprinted 1976).

Business

147 Most of those who say so easily that this is our way out do not, I am convinced, understand that fundamental changes of attitude, new disciplines, revised legal structures, unaccustomed limitations on activity, are all necessary if we are to plan. This amounts, in fact, to the abandonment, finally, of laissez faire. It amounts, practically, to the abolition of "business."

REXFORD G. TUGWELL, "The Principle of Planning and the Institution of Laissez Faire," paper presented at the 44th annual meeting of the American Economic Association.—*The American Economic Review,* vol. 22, no. 1, supplement, March 1932, p. 76.

California

148 What was the use of my having come from Oakland it was not natural to have come from there yes write about it if I like or anything if I like but not there, there is no there there.

GERTRUDE STEIN, *Everybody's Autobiography,* p. 289 (1937, reprinted 1971).

149 The Senator says the territory of California is three times greater than the average extent of the new States of the Union. Well, Sir, suppose it is. We all know that it has more than three times as many mountains, inaccessible and rocky hills, and sandy wastes, as are possessed by any State of the Union. But how much is there of useful land? how much that may be made to contribute to the support of man and of society? These ought to be the questions. Well, with respect to that, I am sure that everybody has become satisfied that, although California may have a very great sea-board, and a large city or two, yet that the agricultural products of the whole surface now are not, and never will be, equal to one half part of those of the State of Illinois; no, nor yet a fourth, or perhaps a tenth part.

Senator DANIEL WEBSTER, remarks in the Senate on admitting California into the Union, June 27, 1850.—*The Writings and Speeches of Daniel Webster,* vol. 10, p. 130 (1903).

Campaign funds

150 Groups like ours are potentially very dangerous to the political process. We could be a menace, yes. Ten independent expenditure groups, for example, could amass this great amount of money and defeat the point of accountability in politics. We could say whatever we want about an opponent of a Senator Smith and the senator wouldn't have to say anything. A group like ours could lie through its teeth and the candidate it helps stays clean.

JOHN TERRY DOLAN, as reported by *The Washington Post,* August 10, 1980, p. F1.

Dolan, chairman of the National Conservative Political Action Committee (NCPAC), later claimed this remark was taken out of context, since he was speaking of a hypothetical situation.

151 I am deeply touched—not as deeply touched as you have been coming to this dinner, but nevertheless it is a sentimental occasion.

Senator JOHN F. KENNEDY, remarks at a fund-raising dinner, Salt Lake City, Utah, September 23, 1960.—*Freedom of Communications,* final report of the Committee on Commerce, United States Senate, part 1, p. 355 (1961). Senate Rept. 87-994.

152 The need for collecting large campaign funds would vanish if Congress provided an appropriation for the proper and legitimate expenses of each of the great national parties, an appropriation ample enough to meet the necessity for thorough organization and machinery, which requires a large expenditure of money. Then the stipulation should be made that no party receiving campaign funds from the Treasury should accept more than a fixed amount from any individual subscriber or donor; and the necessary publicity for receipts and expenditures could without difficulty be provided.

President THEODORE ROOSEVELT, annual message to Congress, December 3, 1907.—*State Papers as Governor and President, 1899–1909* (vol. 17 of *The Works of Theodore Roosevelt*, national ed.), p. 461 (1926).

Campus violence

153 [1.] *The era of appeasement must come to an end.* The political and social demands that dissidents are making of the universities do not flow from sound basic educational criteria, but from strategic considerations on how to radicalize the student body, polarize the campus and extend the privileged enclaves of student power. . . .

[2.] A concise and clear set of rules for campus conduct should be established, transmitted to incoming freshmen, and enforced—with immediate expulsion the penalty for serious violations. . . .

[3.] It is folly for universities confronted with their current crisis in our turbulent times to open their doors to thousands of patently unqualified students. . . .

[4.] No negotiations under threat or coercion. . . .

[5.] No amnesty for lawlessness or violence. . . .

[6.] Any organization which publicly declares its intention to violate the rules of an academic community and which carries out that declaration should be barred from campus. . . .

[7.] We must look to how we are raising our children. . . .

[8.] *We must look to the university that receives those children. Is it prepared to deal with the challenge of the nondemocratic Left?* . . .

[9.] *Let us support those courageous administrators, professors and students on our college campuses who are standing up for the traditional rights of the academic community.*

Vice President SPIRO T. AGNEW, rules to help universities survive the current crisis, speech at Florida Republican dinner, Fort Lauderdale, Florida, April 28, 1970. —*Collected Speeches of Spiro Agnew,* pp. 136, 138–39, 140–41 (1971).

154 This is the criminal left that belongs not in a dormitory, but in a penitentiary. The criminal left is not a problem to be solved by the Department of Philosophy or the Department of English—it is a problem for the Department of Justice. . . . Black or white, the criminal left is interested in power. It is not interested in promoting the renewal and reforms that make democracy work; it is interested in promoting those collisions and conflict that tear democracy apart.

Vice President SPIRO T. AGNEW, speech at a Florida Republican dinner, Fort Lauderdale, Florida, April 28, 1970.—*Collected Speeches of Spiro Agnew,* p. 135 (1971).

155 The streets of our country are in turmoil. The universities are filled with students rebelling and rioting. Communists are seeking to destroy our country. Russia is threatening us with her might and the Republic is in danger. Yes, danger from within and from without. We need law and order. Yes, without law and order our nation cannot survive. Elect us and we shall restore law and order.

Attributed to ADOLF HITLER. Spurious.

Campus violence

This remark was widely used during the early 1970s. Two refutations have appeared in the *Congressional Record*: Lou Hiner, Jr., "Hitler's Phony Quotation on Law and Order," May 21, 1970, vol. 116, pp. 1676–77, reprinted from the *Indianapolis News*; and M. Stanton Evans, "The Hitler Quote," August 11, 1970, vol. 116, p. 28349, reprinted from the *National Review Bulletin*, August 18, 1970.

156 You think of those kids out there. I say "kids." I have seen them. They are the greatest. You see these bums, you know, blowing up the campuses. Listen, the boys that are on the college campuses today are the luckiest people in the world, going to the greatest universities, and here they are burning up the books, I mean storming around about this issue—I mean you name it—get rid of the war; there will be another one. Out there we've got kids who are just doing their duty. I have seen them. They stand tall, and they are proud. I am sure they are scared. I was when I was there. But when it really comes down to it, they stand up and, boy, you have to talk up to those men. And they are going to do fine; we've got to stand back of them.

President RICHARD M. NIXON, informal conversation with one of a group of employees who had gathered in a corridor to greet him at the Pentagon, May 1, 1970.—*The Public Papers of the Presidents of the United States: Richard Nixon, 1970*, p. 417, footnote 1.

157 In several educational institutions during the last few years manifestation of student activity in riots has been exciting the country. To the conservative mind, these riots bode no good. As a matter of fact student riots of one sort or another, protests against the order that is, kicks against college and university management indicate a healthy growth and a normal functioning of the academic mind.

Youth should be radical. Youth should demand change in the world. Youth should not accept the old order if the world is to move on. But the old orders should not be moved easily—certainly not at the mere whim or behest of youth. There must be clash and if youth hasn't enough force or fervor to produce the clash the world grows stale and stagnant and sour in decay. If our colleges and universities do not breed men who riot, who rebel, who attack life with all the youthful vim and vigor, then there is something wrong with our colleges. The more riots that come on college campuses, the better world for tomorrow.

WILLIAM ALLEN WHITE, "Student Riots," editorial, *The Emporia* (Kansas) *Gazette*, April 8, 1932.—White, *Forty Years on Main Street*, comp. Russell H. Fitzgibbon, p. 331 (1937).

Capitalism

158 It is probably true that business corrupts everything it touches. It corrupts politics, sports, literature, art, labor unions and so on. But business also corrupts and undermines monolithic totalitarianism. Capitalism is at its liberating best in a noncapitalist environment.

ERIC HOFFER, "Thoughts of Eric Hoffer, Including: 'Absolute Faith Corrupts Absolutely,' " *The New York Times Magazine*, April 25, 1971, p. 50.

159 You have to choose (as a voter) between trusting to the natural stability of gold and the natural stability of the honesty and intelligence of the members of the Government. And, with due respect for these gentlemen, I advise you, as long as the Capitalist system lasts, to vote for gold.

GEORGE BERNARD SHAW, *The Intelligent Woman's Guide to Socialism and Capitalism*, chapter 55, p. 263 (1928).

In the "Foreword for American Readers" Shaw says, "Finally, I have been asked whether there are any intelligent women in America. There must be; for politically the men there are such futile gossips that the United States could not possibly carry on unless there were some sort of practical intelligence back of them. But I will let you into a secret which bears on this point. By this book I shall get at the American men through the American women" (p. xi).

Capitol building, Washington, D.C.

160 We have built no national temples but the Capitol; we consult no common oracle but the Constitution.

Representative RUFUS CHOATE, "The Importance of Illustrating New-England History by a Series of Romances like the Waverley Novels," lecture delivered at Salem, Massachusetts, 1833.—Samuel Gilman Brown, *The Works of Rufus Choate with a Memoir of His Life*, vol. 1, p. 345 (1862).

161 After much menutial search for an elligible situation, prompted I may say from a fear of being prejudiced in favour of a first opinion I could discover no one so advantageously to greet the congressional building as is that on the west end of Jenkins heights which stand as a pedestal waiting for a monument, and I am confident, were all the wood cleared from the ground no situation could stand in competition with this. some might perhaps require less labour to be rendered agreeable but after all assistance of arts none ever would be made so grand and all other would appear but of secondary nature.

PIERRE CHARLES L'ENFANT, letter to George Washington, June 22, 1791.—*Records of the Columbia Historical Society*, vol. 2, p. 35 (1899).

This letter contained a description of Capitol Hill, then called Jenkins Hill.

162 If people see the Capitol going on, it is a sign we intend the Union shall go on.

President ABRAHAM LINCOLN.—Carl Sandburg, *Abraham Lincoln*, vol. 2, p. 535 (1939).

This remark was made in 1863 to John Eaton of Toledo, Ohio, who had talked to Lincoln about "hoisting the statue of Liberty over the Capitol dome, new marble pillars to be installed on the Senate wing, a massive and richly embellished bronze door being made for the main central portal. People were saying it was an extravagance during wartime" (pp. 534–35).

Cat

163 I cannot agree that it should be the declared public policy of Illinois that a cat visiting a neighbor's yard or crossing the highways is a public nuisance. It is in the nature of cats to do a certain amount of unescorted roaming. Many live with their owners in apartments or other restricted premises, and I doubt if we want to make their every brief foray an opportunity for a small game hunt by zealous citizens—with traps or otherwise. I am afraid this Bill could only create discord, recrimination and enmity. Also consider the owner's dilemma: To escort a cat abroad on a leash is against the nature of the cat, and to permit it to venture forth for exercise unattended into a night of new dangers is against the nature of the owner. Moreover, cats perform useful service, particularly in rural areas, in combating rodents—work they necessarily perform alone and without regard for property lines.

We are all interested in protecting certain varieties of birds. That cats destroy some birds, I well know, but I believe this legislation would further but little the worthy cause to which its proponents give such unselfish effort. The problem of cat versus bird is as old as time. If we attempt to resolve it by legislation who knows but what we may be called upon to take sides as well in the age old problems of dog versus cat, bird versus bird, or even bird versus worm. In my opinion, the State of Illinois and its local governing bodies already have enough to do without trying to control feline delinquency.

ADLAI E. STEVENSON, governor of Illinois, veto message, April 23, 1949.—*The Papers of Adlai E. Stevenson*, ed. Walter Johnson, vol. 3, pp. 73–74 (1973).

This was one of Stevenson's first veto messages. "A small but devoted group of bird-lovers were able to have a bill introduced in the legislature designed to protect birds by restraining cats. In previous years it was passed by one house, only to be turned down by the other. In 1949 it passed both houses and the decision was finally shifted to the Governor. Stevenson's message returning the measure became known as the 'Cat Bill Veto' and received widespread publicity, because of its wit and good humor. On April 27, 1949, the Chicago *Daily News* stated, 'Many Adlaiphiles immediately proclaimed it one of the noble pronouncements of our time, comparable to the boldest state documents from the pen of F.D.R. or Winston Churchill. . . . Mr. Stevenson did no pussyfooting on pussy's perambulations. He did not seek to make a cat's paw out of the Supreme Court by citing decisions of dubious relevancy. He categorically assumed full responsibility for his momentous decision. He did not assert that the bill's effort to restrict felines to lives of sedentary domesticity was a violation of the Constitution. He invoked a higher law—the law of Nature' " (pp. 72–73).

164 Of all God's creatures there is only one that cannot be made the slave of the lash. That one is the cat. If man could be crossed with the cat it would improve man, but it would deteriorate the cat.

MARK TWAIN (Samuel L. Clemens), *Mark Twain's Notebook*, prep. Albert B. Paine, pp. 236–37 (1935, reprinted 1972).

Catholicism

165 And the Generalissimo, the Prime Minister of Russia, leaned on the table, and he pulled his mustache like that, and looked over at Mr. Churchill and said: "Mr. Churchill, Mr. Prime Minister, how many divisions did you say the Pope had?"

JOSEPH STALIN, as quoted by President Harry S. Truman.—*The New York Times*, September 14, 1948, p. 24.

Truman related this while delivering a speech to the American Association for the Advancement of Science, commemorating its 100th anniversary. He described an incident at the Potsdam Conference wherein Churchill had remarked that the Pope would not be happy if the Communists took over the Catholic eastern portion of Poland.

This anecdote was not in the prepared text of the speech, which was used as a press release, and did not appear in the *Public Papers of the Presidents* text, which was taken from the press release, but the Truman Library states that this account is on an audio record in their possession.

C. L. Sulzberger says in his memoirs that Truman told him this story and then added, "That is a true story. I was there." Sulzberger later asked James F. Byrnes, former secretary of state, about it. "Byrnes had heard it and had even mentioned it in his book. He said: 'It is a good story, but it is not true. I know it is not true because I was there.' "—

Sulzberger, *A Long Row of Candles*, pp. 365–66 (1969). Not found in Byrnes's *Speaking Frankly* (1947, reprinted 1974). Byrnes served in Congress 1911–1925 and 1931–1941.

166 Catholic-baiting is the anti-Semitism of the liberals.

PETER VIERECK, *Shame and Glory of the Intellectuals*, chapter 3, p. 45 (1953).

Censorship

167 Any test that turns on what is offensive to the community's standards is too loose, too capricious, too destructive of freedom of expression to be squared with the First Amendment. Under that test, juries can censor, suppress, and punish what they don't like, provided the matter relates to "sexual impurity" or has a tendency "to excite lustful thoughts." This is community censorship in one of its worst forms. It creates a regime where in the battle between the literati and the Philistines, the Philistines are certain to win.

Justice WILLIAM O. DOUGLAS, dissenting, *Roth* v. *United States*, 345 U.S. 512 (1957).

168 Books won't stay banned. They won't burn. Ideas won't go to jail. In the long run of history, the censor and the inquisitor have always lost. The only sure weapon against bad ideas is better ideas. The source of better ideas is wisdom. The surest path to wisdom is a liberal education.

A. WHITNEY GRISWOLD, president of Yale, "A Little Learning," *The Atlantic Monthly*, November 1952, p. 52. Address to students at Phillips Academy, Andover, Mass., spring 1952.

169 The vast number of titles which are published each year—all of them are to the good, even if some of them may annoy or even repel us for a time. For none of us would trade freedom of expression and of ideas for the narrowness of the public censor. America is a free market for people who have something to say, and need not fear to say it.

Vice President HUBERT H. HUMPHREY, as reported by *The New York Times*, March 9, 1967, p. 42.

Humphrey addressed the National Book Awards ceremony in New York City, March 8, 1967, where during his speech more than 50 people walked out to protest the U.S. role in Vietnam.

170 I thought the work would be very innocent, and one which might be confided to the reason of any man; not likely to be much read if let alone, but, if persecuted, it will be generally read. Every man in the United States will think it a duty to buy a copy, in vindication of his right to buy, and to read what he pleases.

THOMAS JEFFERSON, letter to N. G. Dufief, April 19, 1814.—*The Writings of Thomas Jefferson*, ed. Andrew A. Lipscomb, vol. 14, p. 128 (1904).

The letter concerned a new book by M. de Becourt, *Sur la Création du Monde*, which was potentially controversial, as it discussed topics of both a religious and a philosophical nature.

171 I can imagine no greater disservice to the country than to establish a system of censorship that would deny to the people of a free republic like our own their indisputable right to criticise their own public officials. While exercising the great powers of the office I hold, I would regret in a crisis like the one through which we are now passing to lose the benefit of patriotic and intelligent criticism.

President WOODROW WILSON, letter to Arthur Brisbane, April 25, 1917.—Ray Stannard Baker, *Woodrow Wilson, Life and Letters*, vol. 6, p. 36 (1946).

Certainty

172 There is no such uncertainty as a sure thing.

Attributed to ROBERT BURNS. Unverified.

Chance

173 Chance is the pseudonym of God when he did not want to sign.
(Le hasard, c'est peut-être le pseudonyme de Dieu, quant il ne veut pas signer.)

THÉOPHILE GAUTIER.—Théophile Gautier, Jules Sandeau, Mme. de Girardin, and Méry, *La Croix de Berny*, p. 29 (1895).

The four authors used pseudonyms to write the letters which compose the book. Gautier wrote the letters signed Edgard de Meilhan.

174 In the fields of observation chance favors only those minds which are prepared.

LOUIS PASTEUR, inaugural lecture as professor and dean of the faculty of science, University of Lille, Douai, France, December 7, 1854.—*A Treasury of the World's Great Speeches*, ed. Houston Peterson, p. 473 (1954).

Change

175 When it is not *necessary* to change, it is necessary *not* to change.

LUCIUS CARY, VISCOUNT FALKLAND, "A Speech Concerning Episcopacy," delivered in 1641.—Falkland, *A Discourse of Infallibility*, p. 3 (1660).

While the exact date and audience of this speech are uncertain, the speech is known to deal with the Root and Branch Petition, which proposed doing away with bishops in the church (the episcopal system). Some historians consider this issue as the beginning of the definition of parties in Parliament.—J. A. R. Marriott, *The Life and Times of Lucius Cary, Viscount Falkland*, pp. 179–80 (1907).

176 In a progressive country change is constant; . . . change . . . is inevitable.

BENJAMIN DISRAELI, speech on Reform Bill of 1867, Edinburgh, Scotland, October 29, 1867.—*Selected Speeches of the Late Right Honourable the Earl of Beaconsfield*, ed. T. E. Kebbel, vol. 2, part 4, p. 487 (1882).

177 There is a certain relief in change, even though it be from bad to worse! As I have often found in travelling in a stagecoach, that it is often a comfort to shift one's position, and be bruised in a new place.

WASHINGTON IRVING (Geoffrey Crayon, pseud.), *Tales of a Traveller*, Preface, p. 7 (1825? reprinted 1972).

178 I am not an advocate for frequent changes in laws and Constitutions. But laws and institutions must go hand in hand with the progress of the human mind. As that becomes more developed, more enlightened, as new discoveries are made, new truths discovered and manners and opinions change, with the change of circumstances, institutions must advance also to keep pace with the times. We might as well require a man to wear still the coat which fitted him when a boy as civilized society to remain ever under the regimen of their barbarous ancestors.

THOMAS JEFFERSON, letter to Samuel Kercheval, July 12, 1816.—*The Writings of Thomas Jefferson,* ed. Paul L. Ford, vol. 10, pp. 42–43 (1899).

Inscription on the southeast quadrant of the Jefferson Memorial, Washington, D.C. The inscription omits some words without ellipses.

179 Few will have the greatness to bend history itself; but each of us can work to change a small portion of events, and in the total of all those acts will be written the history of this generation.

Senator ROBERT F. KENNEDY, "Day of Affirmation," address delivered at the University of Capetown, South Africa, June 6, 1966.—*Congressional Record,* June 6, 1966, vol. 112, p. 12430.

180 Change alone is eternal, perpetual, immortal.

Attributed to ARTHUR SCHOPENHAUER. Unverified.

181 The older order changeth, yielding place to new,
And God fulfils himself in many ways,
Lest one good custom should corrupt the world.

ALFRED, LORD TENNYSON, "Idylls of the King," line 408, *The Poetic and Dramatic Works of Alfred Lord Tennyson,* p. 574 (1899).

182 Where they [the cultures of Asia and the continent of Africa] resemble each other, however, is that in all cases, it is the Western impact which has stirred up the winds of change and set the processes of modernization in motion. Education brought not only the idea of equality but also another belief which we used to take for granted in the West—the idea of progress, the idea that science and technology can be used to better human conditions. In ancient society, men tended to believe themselves fortunate if tomorrow was not worse than today and anyway, there was little they could do about it. The idea, the revolutionary idea, that tomorrow might be better and that man can do something about it is entirely Western—and all around the world it inspires what Mr. Adlai Stevenson has called "the revolution of rising expectations." If a man has lived in a tradition which tells him that nothing can be done about his human condition, to believe that progress is possible may well be the greatest revolution of all.

BARBARA WARD, lecture, State University of Iowa, Iowa City, April 6, 1961.—Ward, *The Unity of the Free World,* p. 12 (1961).

See No. 1618 for Stevenson's words.

183 It is the first step in sociological wisdom, to recognize that the major advances in civilization are processes which all but wreck the societies in which they occur:—like unto an arrow in the hand of a child. The art of free society consists first in the maintenance of the symbolic code; and secondly in fearlessness of revision, to secure that the code serves those purposes which satisfy an enlightened reason. Those societies which cannot combine reverence to their symbols with freedom of revision, must ultimately decay either from anarchy, or from the slow atrophy of a life stifled by useless shadows.

Change

ALFRED NORTH WHITEHEAD, *Symbolism, Its Meaning and Effect,* chapter 3, p. 88 (1927). This paragraph ends the book.

184 He who rejects change is the architect of decay. The only human institution which rejects progress is the cemetery.

Prime Minister HAROLD WILSON, speech to the Consultative Assembly of the Council of Europe, Strasbourg, France, January 23, 1967.—Text, *The New York Times,* January 24, 1967, p. 12.

Character

185 Of all the properties which belong to honorable men, not one is so highly prized as that of character.

HENRY CLAY.—*The Clay Code, or Text-Book of Eloquence, a Collection of Axioms, Apothegms, Sentiments . . . Gathered from the Public Speeches of Henry Clay,* ed. G. Vandenhoff, p. 93 (1844).

Clay served in the House of Representatives 1811–1814, 1815–1821, and 1823–1825; he was Speaker every year except 1821. He was a senator 1806–1807, 1810–1811, 1831–1842, and 1849–1852.

186 Don't *say* things. What you *are* stands over you the while, and thunders so that I cannot hear what you say to the contrary.

RALPH WALDO EMERSON, "Social Aims," *Letters and Social Aims* (vol. 8 of *The Complete Works of Ralph Waldo Emerson*), p. 96 (1917).

Based on a lecture delivered in Boston, Massachusetts, December 4, 1864.

187 Character is what you are in the dark.

Attributed to DWIGHT L. MOODY by his son, William R. Moody, *D. L. Moody,* chapter 66, p. 503 (1930).

Although both *The Macmillan Book of Proverbs, Maxims, and Famous Phrases,* ed. Burton Stevenson, p. 317 (1948, reprinted 1965), and *The World Treasury of Religious Quotations,* ed. Ralph L. Woods, p. 108 (1966), state that this quotation came from his sermons, Moody scholars have not found it there.

188 An aristocrat in morals as in mind.

OWEN WISTER, describing Justice Oliver Wendell Holmes.—Wister, *Roosevelt: The Story of a Friendship,* p. 130 (1930).

Chesapeake Bay

189 Heaven & earth never agreed better to frame a place for man's habitation; were it fully manured and inhabited by industrious people. Here are mountaines, hil[l]s, plaines, valleyes, rivers, and brookes, all running most pleasantly into a faire Bay, compassed but for the mouth, with fruitfull and delightsome land.

Captain JOHN SMITH, description of countryside around Chesapeake Bay, 1606, *The Generall Historie of Virginia, New England & The Summer Isles,* vol. 2, pp. 44–45 (1907).

190 Perhaps we cannot prevent this world from being a world in which children are tortured. But we can reduce the number of tortured children. And if you don't help us, who else in the world can help us do this?

ALBERT CAMUS, statement made at the Dominican Monastery of Latour-Maubourg in 1948.—Camus, *Resistance, Rebellion and Death,* trans. Justin O'Brien, p. 73 (1961).

191 To be ignorant of what occurred before you were born is to remain always a child.

MARCUS TULLIUS CICERO, *Orator,* chapter 34, section 120.—*Cicero: Brutus, Orator,* trans. H. M. Hubbell, p. 395 (1939).

This work appeared in 46 B.C. and is sometimes confused with his earlier *De Oratore,* which appeared in 55 B.C.

192 Item: And first, I give to good fathers and mothers, but in trust for their children, nevertheless, all good little words of praise and all quaint pet names, and I charge said parents to use them justly, but generously, as the needs of their children shall require.

Item: I leave to children exclusively, but only for the life of their childhood, all and every the dandelions of the fields and the daisies thereof, with the right to play among them freely, according to the custom of children, warning them at the same time against the thistles. And I devise to children the yellow shores of creeks and the golden sands beneath the waters thereof, with the dragon-flies that skim the surface of said waters, and the odors of the willows that dip into said waters, and the white clouds that float high over the giant trees.

And I leave to children the long, long days to be merry in, in a thousand ways, and the Night and the Moon and the train of the Milky Way to wonder at, but subject, nevertheless, to the rights hereinafter given to lovers; and I give to each child the right to choose a star that shall be his, and I direct that the child's father shall tell him the name of it, in order that the child shall always remember the name of that star after he has learned and forgotten astronomy.

Item: I devise to boys jointly all the useful idle fields and commons where ball may be played, and all snow-clad hills where one may coast, and all streams and ponds where one may skate, to have and to hold the same for the period of their boyhood. And all meadows, with the clover blooms and butterflies thereof; and all woods, with their appurtenances of squirrels and whirring birds and echoes and strange noises; and all distant places which may be visited, together with the adventures there found, I do give to said boys to be theirs. And I give to said boys each his own place at the fireside at night, with all pictures that may be seen in the burning wood or coal, to enjoy without let or hindrance and without any incumbrance of cares.

Item: To lovers I devise their imaginary world, with whatever they may need, as the stars of the sky, the red, red roses by the wall, the snow of the hawthorn, the sweet strains of music, or aught else they may desire to figure to each other the lastingness and beauty of their love.

Item: To young men jointly, being joined in a brave, mad crowd, I devise and bequeath all boisterous, inspiring sports of rivalry. I give to them the disdain of weakness and the undaunted confidence in their own strength. Though they are rude and rough, I leave to them alone the power of making lasting friendships and of possessing companions, and to them exclusively I give all merry songs and brave choruses to sing, with smooth voices to troll them forth.

Item: And to those who are no longer children, or youths, or lovers, I leave Memory, and I leave to them the volumes of the poems of Burns and Shakespeare, and of other poets, if there are others, to the end that they may live the old days over again freely and fully, without tithe or diminution; and to those who are no longer children, or youths, or lovers, I leave, too, the knowledge of what a rare, rare world it is.

WILLISTON FISH, *A Last Will*, pp. 12–18 (1908).

This work, also known as *The Hobo's Will* or *The Last Will of Charles Lounsbury*, first appeared in *Harper's Weekly* in 1898. It was reprinted so many times, often in a garbled or "improved" form, that a correct edition was published in 1908.

193 One father is enough to governe one hundred sons, but not a hundred sons one father.

GEORGE HERBERT, *Outlandish Proverbs, Selected by Mr. G. H.*, no. 404 (1640).—*The Works of George Herbert*, ed. F. E. Hutchinson, p. 335 (1941).

194 Give us the child for 8 years and it will be a Bolshevik forever.

Attributed to VLADIMIR ILICH (ULYANOV) LENIN.—*100 Things You Should Know About Communism*, prepared by the Committee on Un-American Activities, U.S. House of Representatives, pp. 46, 48 (1951). House Doc. 82–136. Unverified.

See also No. 199.

195 The children now love luxury; they have bad manners, contempt for authority; they show disrespect for elders and love chatter in place of exercise. Children are now tyrants, not the servants of their households. They no longer rise when elders enter the room. They contradict their parents, chatter before company, gobble up dainties at the table, cross their legs, and tyrannize their teachers.

Attributed to SOCRATES by Plato, according to William L. Patty and Louise S. Johnson, *Personality and Adjustment*, p. 277 (1953).

This passage was very popular in the 1960s and its essence was used by the Mayor of Amsterdam, Gijsbert van Hall, following a street demonstration in 1966, as reported by *The New York Times*, April 3, 1966, p. 16.

This use prompted Malcolm S. Forbes to write an editorial on youth.—*Forbes*, April 15, 1966, p. 11. In that same issue, under the heading "Side Lines," pp. 5–6, is a summary of the efforts of researchers and scholars to confirm the wording of Socrates, or Plato, but without success. Evidently, the quotation is spurious.

196 Know you what it is to be a child? It is to be something very different from the man of to-day. It is to have a spirit yet streaming from the waters of baptism; it is to believe in love, to believe in loveliness, to believe in belief; it is to be so little that the elves can reach to whisper in your ear; it is to turn pumpkins into coaches, and mice into horses, lowness into loftiness, and nothing into everything, for each child has its fairy godmother in its own soul; it is to live in a nutshell and to count yourself the king of infinite space; it is

To see a world in a grain of sand,
And a Heaven in a wild flower,
Hold infinity in the palm of your hand,
And eternity in an hour;

it is to know not as yet that you are under sentence of life, nor petition that it be commuted into death.

FRANCIS THOMPSON, "Shelley," *The Works of Francis Thompson*, vol. 3, pp. 7–8 (1913).

The poem quoted is "Auguries of Innocence" by William Blake.

197 I have found the best way to give advice to your children is to find out what they want and then advise them to do it.

HARRY S. TRUMAN, television interview on "Person to Person," with Margaret Truman as interviewer, May 27, 1955, as reported by *The New York Times*, May 28, 1955, p. 33.

198 Children begin by loving their parents. After a time they judge them. Rarely, if ever, do they forgive them.

OSCAR WILDE, *A Woman of No Importance*, act II, in *The Complete Works of Oscar Wilde*, vol. 7, p. 249 (1923). Lord Illingworth is speaking.

199 Give me a child for the first seven years, and you may do what you like with him afterwards.

Author unknown.—Vincent Stuckey Lean, *Lean's Collectanea*, vol. 3, p. 472 (1903). This source states the quotation is a Jesuit maxim. Unverified.

See also No. 194.

200 Monday's child is fair in face,
Tuesday's child is full of grace,
Wednesday's child is full of woe,
Thursday's child has far to go,
Friday's child is loving and giving,
Saturday's child works hard for its living;
And a child that's born on a Christmas day,
Is fair and wise, good and gay.

Author unknown.—Anna E. K. S. Bray, *Traditions, Legends, Superstitions, and Sketches of Devonshire . . .*, vol. 2, pp. 287–88 (1838).

Later publications of this poetical adage have made minor word changes, including line 7 to read "But a child that's born on the Sabbath day." This is the wording used in *Bartlett's Familiar Quotations*, 15th ed., p. 932 (1980).

China

201 The Chinese said of themselves several thousand years ago: "China is a sea that salts all the waters that flow into it." There's another Chinese saying about their country which is much more modern—it dates only from the fourth century. This is the saying: "The tail of China is large and will not be wagged." I like that one. The British democracy approves the principles of movable party heads and unwaggable national tails. It is due to the working of these important forces that I have the honour to be addressing you at this moment.

WINSTON CHURCHILL, address to a joint session of Congress, Washington, D.C., January 17, 1952.—*Winston S. Churchill: His Complete Speeches, 1897–1963*, ed. Robert Rhodes James, vol. 8, p. 8326 (1974).

202 If I were an Englishman, I should esteem the man who advised a war with China to be the greatest living enemy of my country. You would be beaten in the end, and perhaps a revolution in India would follow.

NAPOLEON.—Unverified except for its publication in *The Mind of Napoleon*, ed. and trans. J. Christopher Herold, p. 249 (1955). In this source the words above were from a conversation, reported in English, in 1817.

China

203 In Sichuan [Szechwan] dogs bark at the sun (because it's a rare sight in that misty region)—an ignorant person makes a fuss about something which he alone finds strange.

A Chinese-English Dictionary, p. 637 (1979).

204 No dogs or Chinese allowed.

Signpost, found in European sections of Shanghai pre-1927. A source at the Mainland China desk, Department of State, said in 1972 that this sign existed in the mid-1920s in the garden of the Bund. This seems to be confirmed by Manley O. Hudson, "The International Settlement at Shanghai," *Foreign Affairs,* October 1927, p. 83: "The question of admitting Chinese to the public parks, maintained out of public funds, has recently become acute. The Land Regulations empower the Council to create and maintain roads and public gardens, 'provided always that such roads and gardens shall be dedicated to the public use, and for the health, amusement and recreation of all persons residing within the Settlement.' This is taken to mean all foreign persons, and the parks are closed to Chinese—old residents say that the prohibition formerly read 'Chinese and dogs.' " A published photograph of such a sign has not been found.

Choice

205 When yu' can't have what you choose, yu' just choose what you have.

OWEN WISTER, *The Virginian,* chapter 13, p. 149 (1929).

Christianity

206 There is no greater drama in human record than the sight of a few Christians, scorned or oppressed by a succession of emperors, bearing all trials with a fierce tenacity, multiplying quietly, building order while their enemies generated chaos, fighting the sword with the word, brutality with hope, and at last defeating the strongest state that history has known. Caesar and Christ had met in the arena, and Christ had won.

WILL DURANT, *The Story of Civilization,* vol. 3, chapter 30, part 1, p. 652 (1944).

207 This is all the Inheritance I can give to my dear Family. The Religion of Christ can give them one which will make them rich indeed.

PATRICK HENRY, from his last will and testament, November 20, 1798.—Moses C. Tyler, *Patrick Henry,* p. 395 (1898, reprinted 1972).

Cigar

208 What this country needs is a really good 5-cent cigar.

Vice President THOMAS R. MARSHALL, a remark reportedly made to Henry M. Rose, the assistant secretary of the Senate, while Marshall was presiding as president of the Senate. The episode is detailed in the *New York Tribune,* January 4, 1920, part 7, p. 1. There are numerous other sources, including Marshall's autobiography, *Recollections of Thomas R. Marshall,* caption facing p. 244 (1925), and Charles M. Thomas, *Thomas Riley Marshall,* p. 175 (1939).

209 When several villages are united in a single complete community, large enough to be nearly or quite self-sufficing, the state comes into existence, originating in the bare needs of life, and continuing in existence for the sake of a good life.

ARISTOTLE, *Politics*, book 1, chapter 2.—*Aristotle's Politics and Poetics*, trans. Benjamin Jowett and Thomas Twining, p. 5 (1952). Jowett translated *Politics*.

210 The American city should be a collection of communities where every member has a right to belong. It should be a place where every man feels safe on his streets and in the house of his friends. It should be a place where each individual's dignity and self-respect is strengthened by the respect and affection of his neighbors. It should be a place where each of us can find the satisfaction and warmth which comes from being a member of the community of man. This is what man sought at the dawn of civilization. It is what we seek today.

President LYNDON B. JOHNSON, special message to the Congress on the nation's cities, March 2, 1965.—*Public Papers of the Presidents of the United States: Lyndon B. Johnson, 1965*, book 1, p. 240.

211 [Solon] being asked, namely, what city was best to live in, "That city," he replied, "in which those who are not wronged, no less than those who are wronged, exert themselves to punish the wrongdoers."

PLUTARCH, *Plutarch's Lives*, trans. Bernadotte Perrin, life of Solon, section 18, vol. 1, p. 455 (1914).

212 We cannot afford merely to sit down and deplore the evils of city life as inevitable, when cities are constantly growing, both absolutely and relatively. We must set ourselves vigorously about the task of improving them; and this task is now well begun.

THEODORE ROOSEVELT, "The City in Modern Life," *Literary Essays* (vol. 12 of *The Works of Theodore Roosevelt*, national ed.), p. 226 (1926). Book review in *The Atlantic Monthly*, April 1895.

213 Cities are the abyss of the human species.
(Les villes sont le gouffre de l'espèce humaine.)

JEAN JACQUES ROUSSEAU, *Émile*, book 1, p. 59 (1979). Originally published in 1762. The word *gouffre* is sometimes translated as sink instead of abyss.

Citizenship

214 Citizenship is no light trifle to be jeopardized any moment Congress decides to do so under the name of one of its general or implied grants of power.

Justice HUGO L. BLACK, *Afroyim* v. *Rusk*, 387 U.S. 267–68 (1967).

215 I am a Roman citizen.
(*Civis Romanus sum.*)

MARCUS TULLIUS CICERO, *Against Verres (In Verrem)*, part 2, book 5, section 57.—Cicero, *The Verrine Orations*, trans. L. H. G. Greenwood, vol. 2, p. 629 (1935).

This was a proud boast when few were citizens. It was enough to stop arbitrary condemnation, bonds and scourging, because Roman citizenship granted the right to be tried in Roman courts.

Citizenship

On June 26, 1963, President John F. Kennedy spoke to the crowd in Berlin, West Germany: "Two thousand years ago the proudest boast was '*civis Romanus sum.*' Today, in the world of freedom, the proudest boast is '*Ich bin ein Berliner*'. . . . All free men, wherever they may live, are citizens of Berlin, and, therefore, as a free man, I take pride in the words '*Ich bin ein Berliner.*' "—*Public Papers of the Presidents of the United States: John F. Kennedy, 1963,* pp. 524, 525.

216 Socrates . . . said he was not an Athenian or a Greek, but a citizen of the world.

PLUTARCH, "On Banishment," *Plutarch's Morals,* rev. William W. Goodwin, vol. 3, p. 19 (1871).

217 Good roads, good schools and good churches are a sure sign of the best citizenship produced by a free republic. How about our roads?

Author unknown. "Sign of Citizenship," *Good Roads, A Monthly Journal Devoted to Our National Highways,* December 1906, p. 176.

Civil rights

218 I hope that you of the IPA will go out into the hinterland and rouse the masses and blow the bugles and tell them that the hour has arrived and their day is here; that we are on the march against the ancient enemies and we are going to be successful.

President LYNDON B. JOHNSON, remarks to the International Platform Association, August 3, 1965.—*Public Papers of the Presidents of the United States: Lyndon B. Johnson, 1965,* book 2, p. 822.

219 This Nation was founded by men of many nations and backgrounds. It was founded on the principle that all men are created equal, and that the rights of every man are diminished when the rights of one man are threatened.

President JOHN F. KENNEDY, radio and television report to the American people on civil rights, June 11, 1963.—*Public Papers of the Presidents of the United States: John F. Kennedy, 1963,* p. 468.

220 Let us therefore continue our triumphal march to the realization of the American dream. . . . for all of us today, the battle is in our hands. . . . The road ahead is not altogether a smooth one. There are no broad highways that lead us easily and inevitably to quick solutions. . . . We are still in for the season of suffering. . . . How long? Not long. Because no lie can live forever. . . . our God is marching on.

MARTIN LUTHER KING, JR., speech on the steps of the State Capitol Building, Montgomery, Alabama, March 25, 1965.—Transcript from tape recording. This speech was not reported in its entirety.

221 Happily for us, students have not tried to overthrow the Government of the United States, but they certainly are making their views felt in public affairs. I think especially of the participation of American students in the great struggle to advance civil and human rights in America. Indeed, even a jail sentence is no longer a dishonor but a proud achievement.

ADLAI E. STEVENSON, U.S. ambassador to the United Nations, commencement address at Colby College, Waterville, Maine, June 7, 1964.—*The Papers of Adlai E. Stevenson*, vol. 8, p. 567 (1979).

Civil war

222 They [the Secessionists] appealed to the Constitution, they appealed to justice, they appealed to fraternity, until the Constitution, justice, and fraternity were no longer listened to in the legislative halls of their country, and then, sir, they prepared for the arbitrament of the sword; and now you see the glittering bayonet, and you hear the tramp of armed men from your capital to the Rio Grande.

Senator ROBERT TOOMBS, remarks in the Senate, January 7, 1861, *Congressional Globe*, vol. 38, p. 267.

223 Here Sunday, April, 9th, 1865, after four years of heroic struggle in defense of the principles believed to be fundamental to the existence of our government, Lee surrendered 9,000 men, the remnant of an army still unconquered in spirit, to 118,000 men under Grant.

Author unknown. Inscription on granite memorial marking site of the original Appomattox Court House, where the Civil War ended, Appomattox Court House National Historical Park, Virginia. When the building burned several decades after the war, the county seat was moved to a new location three miles away.—Mary Louise Gills, *It Happened at Appomattox*, p. 21 (1948).

Civilization

224 But the greatest menace to our civilization today is the conflict between giant organized systems of self-righteousness—each system only too delighted to find that the other is wicked—each only too glad that the sins give it the pretext for still deeper hatred and animosity.

HERBERT BUTTERFIELD, *Christianity, Diplomacy and War*, p. 43 (1953).

225 We must remember that any oppression, any injustice, any hatred, is a wedge designed to attack our civilization.

President FRANKLIN D. ROOSEVELT, letter to Dr. William Allan Neilson, January 9, 1940. The letter was read to the conference of the American Committee for Protection of Foreign-born, Washington, D.C., March 1, 1940.—*The Public Papers and Addresses of Franklin D. Roosevelt, 1940*, p. 36 (1941).

This sentence is one of many quotations inscribed on Cox Corridor II, a first floor House corridor, U.S. Capitol.

226 If we lose the virile, manly qualities, and sink into a nation of mere hucksters, putting gain over national honor, and subordinating everything to mere ease of life, then we shall indeed reach a condition worse than that of the ancient civilizations in the years of their decay.

THEODORE ROOSEVELT, "The Law of Civilization and Decay," *American Ideals* (vol. 13 of *The Works of Theodore Roosevelt*, national ed.), chapter 15, pp. 259–60 (1926). This review of *The Law of Civilization and Decay* by Brooks Adams appeared in *The Forum*, January 1897.

Civilization

227 On this showing, the nature of the breakdowns of civilizations can be summed up in three points: a failure of creative power in the minority, an answering withdrawal of mimesis on the part of the majority, and a consequent loss of social unity in the society as a whole.

ARNOLD J. TOYNBEE, *A Study of History,* vol. 4, part B, p. 6 (1948).

228 Of the twenty or so civilizations known to modern Western historians, all except our own appear to be dead or moribund, and, when we diagnose each case, *in extremis* or *post mortem,* we invariably find that the cause of death has been either War or Class or some combination of the two. To date, these two plagues have been deadly enough, in partnership, to kill off nineteen out of twenty representatives of this recently evolved species of human society; but, up to now, the deadliness of these scourges has had a saving limit.

ARNOLD J. TOYNBEE, *Civilization on Trial,* chapter 2, p. 23 (1948).

229 Now civilizations, I believe, come to birth and proceed to grow by successfully responding to successive challenges. They break down and go to pieces if and when a challenge confronts them which they fail to meet.

ARNOLD J. TOYNBEE, *Civilization on Trial,* chapter 4, p. 56 (1948).

230 The sum of the whole matter is this, that our civilization cannot survive materially unless it be redeemed spiritually.

WOODROW WILSON, "The Road Away from Revolution," article written for *The Atlantic Monthly,* August 1923.—*The Messages and Papers of Woodrow Wilson,* ed. Albert Shaw, vol. 2, p. 1232 (1924).

See also No. 1632.

Clarity

231 "It's very strange," said Mr. Dick . . . "that I never can get that quite right; I never can make that perfectly clear."

CHARLES DICKENS, *David Copperfield,* chapter 14, p. 124 (1950). This novel was originally published serially in 1849–1850.

232 I didn't say that I didn't say it. I said that I didn't say that I said it. I want to make that very clear.

Attributed to GEORGE ROMNEY.—*National Review,* December 12, 1967, cover. Unverified.

Cold war

233 Let us not be deceived—we are today in the midst of a cold war. Our enemies are to be found abroad and at home. Let us never forget this: Our unrest is the heart of their success. The peace of the world is the hope and the goal of our political system; it is the despair and defeat of those who stand against us.

BERNARD M. BARUCH, address at the unveiling of his portrait in the South Carolina legislature, Columbia, South Carolina, April 16, 1947.—*Journal of the House of Representatives of the First Session of the 87th General Assembly of the State of South Carolina,* p. 1085.

The phrase "cold war" was coined by Herbert Bayard Swope, who occasionally wrote speeches for Baruch, and was first used in this speech. It was popularized by, and sometimes mistakenly attributed to, columnist Walter Lippmann, whose 1947 book was titled *The Cold War.*

Baruch used the phrase again on October 24, 1947—"Although the shooting war is over, we are in the midst of a cold war which is getting warmer"—in testimony before the Senate's Special Committee Investigating the National Defense Program, part 42, p. 25740 (1948). William Safire, *Safire's Political Dictionary*, pp. 127–29 (1978), gives an extensive account of the coinage and use of this term, though the date for Baruch's testimony is given there as 1948.

234 A shadow has fallen upon the scenes so lately lighted by the Allied victory. . . . From Stettin in the Baltic to Trieste in the Adriatic, an iron curtain has descended across the Continent.

WINSTON CHURCHILL, "The Sinews of Peace," address at Westminster College, Fulton, Missouri, March 5, 1946.—*Winston S. Churchill: His Complete Speeches, 1897–1963,* ed. Robert Rhodes James, vol. 7, p. 7290 (1974).

The term "iron curtain" was used in this sense as early as 1920, and Churchill had used it earlier in a telegram to President Harry Truman, May 12, 1945: "An iron curtain is drawn down upon their front. We do not know what is going on behind."—Winston Churchill, *Triumph and Tragedy* (vol. 6 of *The Second World War*), p. 573 (1953). It was Churchill's use of the term in this speech, however, which popularized it.

For earlier uses of the phrase see William Safire, *Safire's Political Dictionary*, pp. 339–40 (1978), and *Bartlett's Familiar Quotations*, 15th ed., p. 746, no. 9 (1980).

The same geographic area figures in No. 1654. See note at No. 394 about this speech.

235 The central drama of our age is how the Western nations and the Asian peoples are to find a tolerable basis of co-existence.

WALTER LIPPMANN, "Asia and the West," *New York Herald Tribune* (European edition), September 15, 1965, p. 4.

236 If the estimate of the House Committee on Foreign Affairs is correct, then Russia has lost the cold war in western Europe.

WALTER LIPPMANN, syndicated column, *The Miami Herald,* December 18, 1947, p. 6A.

237 We may be likened to two scorpions in a bottle, each capable of killing the other, but only at the risk of his own life.

J. ROBERT OPPENHEIMER, "Atomic Weapons and American Policy," *Foreign Affairs*, July 1953, p. 529.

Colleges and universities

238 Enter by this gateway and seek the way of honor, the light of truth, the will to work for men

E. A. ALDERMAN, inscription on the archway at the entrance to the medical college, University of Virginia, Charlottesville.

Alderman was the first president of the University, which was administered by a chairman of the faculty until 1905.

239 I would advise no one to send his child where the Holy Scriptures are not supreme. Every institution that does not unceasingly pursue the study of God's word becomes corrupt. Because of this we can see what kind of people they become in the universities and what they are like now. Nobody is to blame for this except the pope, the bishops, and the prelates, who are all charged with training young people. The universities only ought to turn out men who are experts in the Holy Scriptures, men who can become bishops and priests, and stand in the front line against heretics, the devil, and all the world. But where do you find that? I greatly fear that the universities, unless they teach the Holy Scriptures diligently and impress them on the young students, are wide gates to hell.

MARTIN LUTHER, "To the Christian Nobility of the German Nation Concerning the Reform of the Christian Estate, 1520," trans. Charles M. Jacobs, rev. James Atkinson, *The Christian in Society*, I (*Luther's Works*, ed. James Atkinson, vol. 44), p. 207 (1966).

240 It is, Sir, as I have said, a small College, And yet, *there are those who love it.*

DANIEL WEBSTER, arguing the case of Dartmouth College before the Supreme Court, March 1818. These words are not in his formal argument in the official court record. They come from an account Chauncey A. Goodrich, professor at Yale, wrote to Rufus Choate, who quoted at length from it in his eulogy on Daniel Webster, given at Dartmouth College, Hanover, New Hampshire, July 27, 1853.—*The Works of Rufus Choate*, vol. 1, p. 516 (1862).

The *Dictionary of American Biography*, vol. 10, p. 588, notes that "with consummate pathos he presented the case of the small college which he loved as the case of every college in the land. When on Feb. 2, 1819, the Court in its decision completely upheld the college and its counsel . . . Webster became in the opinion of many the foremost lawyer of the time."

Webster served in Congress as a representative from New Hampshire, 1813–1817, and from Massachusetts, 1823–1827, and as a senator from Massachusetts, 1827–1841 and 1845–1850.

Committees

241 A committee is a group of the unwilling, chosen from the unfit, to do the unnecessary.

Author unknown. Attributed to various people.

Communism

242 Just as Marx used to say about the French "Marxists" of the late 'seventies: "All I know is that I am not a Marxist."

FRIEDRICH ENGELS, letter to Conrad Schmidt, August 3, 1890.—Karl Marx and Frederick Engels, *Selected Correspondence, 1846–1895*, trans. Donna Torr, p. 472 (1942).

243 We don't propose to sit here in our rocking chair with our hands folded and let the Communists set up any government in the Western Hemisphere.

President LYNDON B. JOHNSON, remarks to the 10th National Legislative Conference, Building and Construction Trades Department, AFL–CIO, May 3, 1965.—*Public Papers of the Presidents of the United States: Lyndon B. Johnson, 1965*, book 1, p. 480.

244 They say that the Soviet delegates smile. That smile is genuine. It is not artificial. We wish to live in peace, tranquility. But if anyone believes that our smiles involve abandonment of the teaching of Marx, Engels and Lenin he deceives himself poorly. Those who wait for that must wait until a shrimp learns to whistle.

NIKITA S. KHRUSHCHEV, impromptu speech at a dinner for visiting East German dignitaries, Moscow, September 17, 1955, as reported by *The New York Times*, September 18, 1955, p. 19.

245 It is necessary to be able to withstand all this, to agree to any and every sacrifice, and even—if need be—to resort to all sorts of stratagems, manoeuvres and illegal methods, to evasion and subterfuges in order to penetrate the trade unions, to remain in them, and to carry on Communist work in them at all costs.

VLADIMIR ILICH (ULYANOV) LENIN, " 'Left-Wing' Communism, An Infantile Disorder," *V. I. Lenin; Selected Works*, vol. 10, p. 95 (1938).

246 They [capitalists] will furnish credits which will serve us for the support of the Communist Party in their countries and, by supplying us materials and technical equipment which we lack, will restore our military industry necessary for our future attacks against our suppliers. To put it in other words, they will work on the preparation of their own suicide.

VLADIMIR ILICH (ULYANOV) LENIN, as reported by I. U. Annenkov in an article entitled, "Remembrances of Lenin," *Novyi Zhurnal / New Review*, September 1961, p. 147.

Annenkov recounts (pp. 144–47) a visit to the Moscow Institute of V. I. Lenin shortly after Lenin's death, where he examined a number of Lenin manuscripts consisting principally of short and fragmentary notes, some of which were so interesting that he copied them. This Russian-language journal is published in New York City.

The popular and widely-quoted paraphrase, "The capitalists are so hungry for profits that they will sell us the rope to hang them with," has often been considered spurious because it had not been found in Lenin's published works.

247 It seems strangely difficult for some to realize that here in Asia is where the Communist conspirators have elected to make their play for global conquest, and that we have joined the issue thus raised on the battlefield; that here we fight Europe's war with arms while the diplomats there still fight it with words; that if we lose the war to communism in Asia the fall of Europe is inevitable, win it and Europe most probably would avoid war and yet preserve freedom. As you pointed out, we must win. There is no substitute for victory.

DOUGLAS MACARTHUR, letter to Representative Joseph W. Martin, Jr., March 20, 1951.—*Military Situation in the Far East*, hearings before the Committee on Armed Services and the Committee on Foreign Relations, United States Senate, 82d Congress, 1st session, part 1, p. 3544 (1951).

248 [Cold war demonology] is a color word, and I probably should not have used it. It means just sort of interpreting everything in terms of a great communist conspiracy and in terms of communists being supermen who somehow can overcome the great problems of differences between national units, and so on. They are not supermen at all. They are men with feet of clay which extend almost all the way up to their brains.

EDWIN O. REISCHAUER, former U.S. ambassador to Japan, testimony at hearing, January 31, 1967.—*Asia, the Pacific, and the United States,* hearing before the Committee on Foreign Relations, United States Senate, 90th Congress, 1st session, p. 19 (1967).

249 I do not believe in communism any more than you do but there is nothing wrong with the Communists in this country; several of the best friends I have got are Communists.

President FRANKLIN D. ROOSEVELT, conversation with Representative Martin Dies at the White House, as reported by Dies.—*Congressional Record,* September 22, 1950, vol. 96, Appendix, p. A6832.

"The quote is exceedingly dubious; it is most unlikely that FDR would have said anything like it, even flippantly, to the zealous HUAC chairman, though he may have told Dies that he was exaggerating the size of the American communist movement."—Paul F. Boller, Jr., *Quotemanship: The Use and Abuse of Quotations for Polemical and Other Purposes,* chapter 8, p. 361 (1967).

250 People are very much wrought up about the Communist bugaboo.

President HARRY S. TRUMAN, letter to George H. Earle, former governor of Pennsylvania, received February 28, 1947.—*The New York Times,* April 3, 1947, p. 17, quoting Earle.

That same day, in response to a question at his press conference, Truman said, "I am not worried about the Communist Party taking over the Government of the United States, but I am against a person, whose loyalty is not to the Government of the United States, holding a Government job. They are entirely different things. I am not worried about this country ever going Communist. We have too much sense for that."—*Public Papers of the Presidents of the United States: Harry S. Truman, 1947,* p. 191.

Compromise

251 Nearly all legislation is the result of compromise.

Representative JOSEPH G. CANNON, maxim quoted in a tribute to Cannon on his retirement, *The Sun,* Baltimore, Maryland, March 4, 1923.—*Congressional Record,* March 4, 1923, vol. 64, p. 5714.

"Uncle Joe" Cannon, who was Speaker of the House 1903–1911, served in the House for 46 years.

252 Compromise used to mean that half a loaf was better than no bread. Among modern statesmen it really seems to mean that half a loaf is better than a whole loaf.

G. K. CHESTERTON, *What's Wrong with the World,* chapter 3, p. 18 (1910).

253 Those who are prone by temperament and character to seek sharp and clear-cut solutions of difficult and obscure problems, who are ready to fight whenever some challenge comes from a foreign Power, have not always been right. On the other hand, those whose inclination is to bow their heads, to seek patiently and faithfully for peaceful compromise, are not always wrong. On the contrary, in the majority of instances they may be right, not only morally but from a practical standpoint. How many wars have been averted by patience and persisting good will! Religion and virtue alike lend their sanctions to meekness and humility, not only between men but between nations. How many wars have been precipitated by firebrands! How many misunderstandings which led to wars could have been removed by temporising! How often have countries fought cruel wars and then after a few years of peace found themselves not only friends but allies! . . .

But the safety of the State, the lives and freedom of their own fellow countrymen, to whom they owe their position, make it right and imperative in the last resort, or when a final and definite conviction has been reached, that the use of force should not be excluded. If the circumstances are such as to warrant it, force may be used. And if this be so, it should be used under the conditions which are most favourable. There is no merit in putting off a war for a year if, when it comes, it is a far worse war or one much harder to win. These are tormenting dilemmas upon which mankind has throughout its history been so frequently impaled. Final judgment upon them can only be recorded by history in relation to the facts of the case as known to the parties at the time, and also as subsequently proved.

WINSTON CHURCHILL, *The Gathering Storm* (vol. 1 of *The Second World War*), chapter 17, p. 320 (1948).

254 If you are not very clever, you should be conciliatory.

BENJAMIN DISRAELI, *Endymion* (vol. 20 of *The Works of Benjamin Disraeli, Earl of Beaconsfield*), chapter 85, p. 153 (1904, reprinted 1976). Originally published 1880.

255 I believe in friendly compromise. I said over in the Senate hearings that truth is the glue that holds government together. Compromise is the oil that makes governments go.

Representative GERALD R. FORD, remarks during hearings before the House Committee on the Judiciary, November 15, 1973.—*Nomination of Gerald R. Ford to Be the Vice President of the United States*, hearings before the Committee on the Judiciary, House of Representatives, 93d Congress, 1st session (1973).

See also No. 1831.

256 There isn't such a reasonable fellow in the world, to hear him talk. He [Tom Brown] never wants anything but what's right and fair; only when you come to settle what's right and fair, it's everything he wants, and nothing that you want. And that's his idea of a compromise.

THOMAS HUGHES, *Tom Brown's Schooldays*, part 2, chapter 2, pp. 190–91 (1856, reprinted 1971).

257 If you can't lick 'em, jine 'em.

Attributed to Senator JAMES E. WATSON.—Frank R. Kent, "Senator James E. Watson," *The Atlantic Monthly*, February 1932, p. 188, calls this "one of his favorite sayings."

Watson did not use this saying in his memoirs, *As I Knew Them* (1936), but on p. 274 he did say, "All legislation of consequence is a series of compromises, and there are many trades and deals among the senators in order to get important measures through. These trades are not of a sinister nature at all, but are entirely permissible by the highest standards of legislation and morals . . . . Every legislator understands that no measure of importance ever could be passed without this give-and-take policy being practiced to the limit."

The saying has been used by a number of writers, usually with variations in wording. Quentin Reynolds, *The Wounded Don't Cry*, p. 23 (1941), uses the same wording. John Martin, "The Return from Manila," *Ken*, May 18, 1939, p. 15, uses "If you can't beat 'em, join 'em." Niven Busch, *Duel in the Sun*, p. 76 (1944, reprinted 1947), uses "if you can't whip 'em, join 'em."

Compromise

Watson's "long association with politics began at the age of twelve when he accompanied his father to the Republican national convention of 1876. . . . He first won public office in 1894" when he was elected to the U.S. House of Representatives.—*Dictionary of American Biography,* supplement 4, p. 861.

Conformity

258 Our dangers, as it seems to me, are not from the outrageous but from the conforming; not from those who rarely and under the lurid glare of obloquy upset our moral complaisance, or shock us with unaccustomed conduct, but from those, the mass of us, who take their virtues and their tastes, like their shirts and their furniture, from the limited patterns which the market offers.

LEARNED HAND, "The Preservation of Personality," commencement address at Bryn Mawr College, Bryn Mawr, Pennsylvania, June 2, 1927.—Hand, *The Spirit of Liberty,* ed. Irving Dilliard, p. 26 (1959).

Congress

259 The rich, the well-born, and the able, acquire an influence among the people that will soon be too much for simple honesty and plain sense, in a house of representatives. The most illustrious of them must, therefore, be separated from the mass, and placed by themselves in a senate; this is, to all honest and useful intents, an ostracism.

JOHN ADAMS, *A Defence of the Constitutions of Government of the United States of America,* vol. 1 (vol. 4 of *The Works of John Adams,* ed. Charles Francis Adams), Preface, p. 290 (1851). First published in 1787.

260 In legislation we all do a lot of "swapping tobacco across the lines."

Representative JOSEPH G. CANNON, maxim referring to a practice during the Civil War, quoted in a tribute to Cannon on his retirement.

"Mr. Cannon has told how he put through an appropriation for the entertainment of Prince Henry of Prussia when that foreign visitor came over years ago. He prearranged with Oscar W. Underwood, then in the House, that he would propose the appropriation late in the afternoon, when the House attendance was slim. Mr. Underwood, representing objecting Democrats, was to kick strenuously for a time about the cost of entertaining the prince; then Underwood was reluctantly to withdraw his opposition, the chances being no other Democrat would take it up. The 'Swapping of tobacco' across the aisles worked and the appropriation went through."—*The Sun,* Baltimore, Maryland, March 4, 1923; *Congressional Record,* March 4, 1923, vol. 64, p. 5714. "Uncle Joe" Cannon, who was Speaker of the House 1903–1911, served in the House for 46 years.

261 A few years ago Gen. Francis Marion Cockrell, for thirty consecutive years a prominent Senator from Missouri, denominated the United States Senate as "the greatest legislative body in the world," whereupon Senator John C. Spooner, of Wisconsin, an eminent constitutional lawyer and considerable of a wit, said: "The Senate is not the greatest legislative body in the world. It is one of the branches of, I think, perhaps the greatest legislative body in the world, and the Senate may be the greatest part of the greatest legislative body in the world. I am not disposed to dispute that. We all admit that ourselves."

Representative CHAMP CLARK, *My Quarter Century of American Politics*, vol. 1, p. 190 (1920). Unverified.

Clark was Speaker of the House 1911–1919.

262 I am now here in Congress . . . I am at liberty to vote as my conscience and judgment dictates to be right, without the yoke of any party on me, or the driver at my heels, with his whip in hand, commanding me to ge-wo-haw, just at his pleasure.

Representative DAVID CROCKETT, *A Narrative of the Life of David Crockett*, final paragraph, p. 113 (1834).

Earlier (pp. 18–19), he had discussed his lack of formal education: "But it will be a source of astonishment to many, who reflect that I am now a member of the American Congress,—the most enlightened body of men in the world,—that at so advanced an age, the age of fifteen, I did not know the first letter in the book."

263 Too often critics seem more intent on seeking new ways to alter Congress than to truly learn how it functions. They might well profit from the advice of Thomas Huxley, who said a century ago: "Sit down before facts as a little child, be prepared to give up every preconceived notion—or you shall learn nothing."

Representative GERALD R. FORD, address at the University of Florida, Gainesville, November 3, 1966.—*Gerald R. Ford, Selected Speeches*, ed. Michael V. Doyle, p. 114 (1973).

See also No. 583.

264 I know well the coequal role of the Congress in our constitutional process. I love the House of Representatives. I revere the traditions of the Senate despite my too-short internship in that great body. As President, within the limits of basic principles, my motto toward the Congress is communication, conciliation, compromise, and cooperation.

President GERALD R. FORD, address to a joint session of Congress, August 12, 1974.—*Public Papers of the Presidents of the United States: Gerald R. Ford, 1974*, pp. 6–7.

265 Has not the famous political Fable of the Snake, with two Heads and one Body, some useful Instruction contained in it? She was going to a Brook to drink, and in her Way was to pass thro' a Hedge, a Twig of which opposed her direct Course; one Head chose to go on the right side of the Twig, the other on the left, so that time was spent in the Contest, and, before the Decision was completed, the poor Snake died with thirst.

BENJAMIN FRANKLIN "Queries and Remarks Respecting Alterations in the Constitution of Pennsylvania," *The Writings of Benjamin Franklin*, ed. Albert H. Smyth, vol. 10, pp. 57–58 (1907).

266 Congress is so strange. A man gets up to speak and says nothing. Nobody listens—and then everybody disagrees.

BORIS MARSHALOV, a Russian observer, after visiting the House of Representatives.—Senator Alexander Wiley, *Laughing with Congress*, p. 58 (1947).

267 It has always been my ambition since childhood to live such a life that one day my fellow citizens would call me to membership in this popular branch of the greatest lawmaking body in the world. Out of their confidence and partiality they have done this. It is now my sole purpose here to help enact such wise and just laws that our common country will by virtue of these laws be a happier and a more prosperous country. I have always dreamed of a country which I believe this should be and will be, and that is one in which the citizenship is an educated and patriotic people, not swayed by passion and prejudice, and a country that shall know no East, no West, no North, no South, but inhabited by a people liberty loving, patriotic, happy, and prosperous, with its lawmakers having no other purpose than to write such just laws as shall in the years to come be of service to human kind yet unborn. [Applause]

Representative SAM RAYBURN, maiden speech in the House, May 6, 1913, *Congressional Record,* vol. 50, p. 1249.

He was echoing Henry Clay's famous words, "I know no South, no North, no East, no West to which I owe any allegiance. I owe allegiance to two sovereignties, and only two; . . . My allegiance is to this Union and to my State."—Clay, remarks in the Senate, February 14, 1850, *Congressional Globe,* vol. 19, p. 368.

268 A jackass can kick a barn down, but it takes a carpenter to build one.

Representative SAM RAYBURN, during filmed conversation with reporters, c. 1953.—*"Speak, Mister Speaker,"* p. 138 (1978).

269 Too many critics mistake the deliberations of the Congress for its decisions.

Speaker of the House SAM RAYBURN, on the weekly radio broadcast, "Texas Forum of the Air," November 1, 1942.—*Congressional Record,* November 2, 1942, vol. 88, Appendix, p. A3866.

270 And kid Congress and the Senate, dont scold em. They are just children thats never grown up. They dont like to be corrected in company. Dont send messages to em, send candy.

WILL ROGERS, *The Autobiography of Will Rogers,* ed. Donald Day, p. 302 (1949). Advice sent to President-elect Franklin D. Roosevelt, December 2, 1932.

271 So when all the yielding and objections is over, the other Senator said, "I object to the remarks of a professional joker being put into the *Congressional Record.*" Taking a dig at me, see? They didn't want any outside fellow contributing. Well, he had me wrong. Compared to them I'm an amateur, and the thing about my jokes is that they don't hurt anybody. You can say they're not funny or they're terrible or they're good or whatever it is, but they don't do no harm. But with Congress—every time they make a joke it's a law. And every time they make a law it's a joke.

WILL ROGERS.—P. J. O'Brien, *Will Rogers, Ambassador of Good Will, Prince of Wit and Wisdom,* chapter 9, pp. 156–57 (1935).

272 Let me make it clear that I do not assert that a President and the Congress must on all points agree with each other at all times. Many times in history there has been complete disagreement between the two branches of the Government, and in these disagreements sometimes the Congress has won and sometimes the President has won. But during the Administration of the present President we have had neither agreement nor a clear-cut battle.

FRANKLIN D. ROOSEVELT, governor of New York, campaign address before the Republican-for-Roosevelt League, New York City, November 3, 1932.—*The Public Papers and Addresses of Franklin D. Roosevelt, 1928–1932,* p. 857 (1938).

273 I have come to the conclusion that one useless man is called a disgrace, that two are called a law firm, and that three or more become a congress.

PETER STONE, book, and SHERMAN EDWARDS, music and lyrics, *1776, A Musical Play,* scene I. John Adams speaks these lines to open the play.

274 I think I can say, and say with pride, that we have some legislatures that bring higher prices than any in the world.

MARK TWAIN (Samuel L. Clemens), "After-Dinner Speech," *Sketches, New and Old* (vol. 19 of *The Writings of Mark Twain*), p. 235 (1875).

This speech was prepared for a Fourth of July gathering of Americans in London but was not given. General Schenck, the American ambassador, decided to dispense with further oratory after his own speech.

The phrase, "The finest Congress money can buy," has not been found in Twain's writings, and the sentence above is the closest to it that has been identified.

275 It could probably be shown by facts and figures that there is no distinctly native American criminal class except Congress.

MARK TWAIN (Samuel L. Clemens), *Following the Equator,* vol. 1 (vol. 5 of *The Writings of Mark Twain*), chapter 8, epigraph, p. 98 (1897, reprinted 1968).

276 Congress in session is Congress on public exhibition, whilst Congress in its committee-rooms is Congress at work.

WOODROW WILSON, *Congressional Government, A Study in American Politics,* chapter 2, p. 69 (1981). First published in 1885.

277 During the American Revolution, George Washington used to call out for "beef, beef, beef," but the Continental Congress called out for "pork, pork, pork."

Author unknown. Representative Clarence Cannon used to quote this comment of an unknown author. Unverified.

278 One of the standing jokes of Congress is that the new Congressman always spends the first week wondering how he got there and the rest of the time wondering how the other members got there.

Author unknown.—*Saturday Evening Post,* November 4, 1899, p. 356.

Congress—House of Representatives

279 The House is composed of very good men, not shining, but honest and reasonably well-informed, and in time they will be found to improve, and not to be much inferior in eloquence, science, and dignity, to the British Commons. They are patriotic enough, and I believe there are more stupid (as well as more shining) people in the latter, in proportion.

FISHER AMES, letter to George Richard Minot, May 27, 1789.—*Works of Fisher Ames,* ed. Seth Ames, vol. 1, p. 45 (1854).

Ames was a Federalist Representative from Massachusetts at the first Congress, which met in New York City. Representative Hale Boggs quoted Ames at the end of the first session of the 89th Congress: "You know, Mr. Speaker, a long time ago there was a congressman here from the great State of Massachusetts. His name was Fisher Ames. Speaking of the Congress which met in 1789 he wrote a letter to his constituents and this is what he said about his colleagues who served in the Congress of 1789 in describing them. He said: 'On the whole they were very good men, not shining, but honest and reasonably well informed.' I believe it is a very apt description because we come from the people and we are of the people, and, thank God, we have a system that makes that possible."—*Congressional Record*, October 22, 1965, vol. 111, p. 28566.

280 Certainly, Gentlemen, it ought to be the happiness and glory of a representative to live in the strictest union, the closest correspondence, and the most unreserved communication with his constituents. Their wishes ought to have great weight with him; their opinions high respect; their business unremitted attention. It is his duty to sacrifice his repose, his pleasure, his satisfactions, to theirs,—and above all, ever, and in all cases, to prefer their interest to his own.

But his unbiased opinion, his mature judgment, his enlightened conscience, he ought not to sacrifice to you, to any man, or to any set of men living. These he does not derive from your pleasure,—no, nor from the law and the Constitution. They are a trust from Providence, for the abuse of which he is deeply answerable. Your representative owes you, not his industry only, but his judgment; and he betrays, instead of serving you, if he sacrifices it to your opinion.

EDMUND BURKE, speech to the electors of Bristol, November 3, 1774.—*The Works of the Right Honorable Edmund Burke*, vol. 2, p. 95 (1899).

281 The House of Representatives, in some respects, I think, is the most peculiar assemblage in the world, and only a man who has had long experience there can fully know its idiosyncrasies. It is true we engage in fierce combat, we are often intense partisans, sometimes we are unfair, not infrequently unjust, brutal at times, and yet I venture to say that, taken as a whole, the House is sound at heart; nowhere else will you find such a ready appreciation of merit and character, in few gatherings of equal size is there so little jealousy and envy. The House must be considerate of the feelings of its Members; there is a certain courtesy that has to be observed; a man may be voted a bore or shunned as a pest, and yet he must be accorded the rights to which he is entitled by virtue of being a representative of the people. On the other hand, a man may be universally popular, a good fellow, amusing and yet with these engaging qualities never get far. The men who have led the House, whose names have become a splendid tradition to their successors, have gained prominence not through luck or by mere accident. They have had ability, at least in some degree; but more than that, they have had character.

Representative JOSEPH G. CANNON.—L. White Busby, *Uncle Joe Cannon*, p. 260 (1927).

"Uncle Joe" Cannon, who was Speaker of the House from 1903–1911, served in the House for 46 years.

282 It is good to be back in the People's House. But this cannot be a real homecoming. Under the Constitution, I now belong to the executive branch. The Supreme Court has even ruled that I *am* the executive branch—head, heart, and hand.

President GERALD R. FORD, address to a joint session of Congress, August 12, 1974.—*Public Papers of the Presidents of the United States: Gerald R. Ford, 1974*, p. 6.

283 In my many years as a Representative in Congress it is my observation that the district that is best represented is the district that is wise enough to select a man of energy, intelligence, and integrity and reelects him year after year. A man of this type and character serves more efficiently and effectively the longer he is returned by his people.

Speaker of the House SAM RAYBURN, on the weekly radio broadcast, "Texas Forum of the Air," November 1, 1942.—*Congressional Record,* November 2, 1942, vol. 88, Appendix, p. A3866.

284 Don't try to go too fast. Learn your job. Don't ever talk until you know what you're talking about. . . . If you want to get along, go along.

Speaker of the House SAM RAYBURN.—Neil MacNeil, *Forge of Democracy, the House of Representatives,* p. 129 (1963).

"This was Rayburn's traditional advice to freshmen, many times repeated, and reflected his view of the House of Representatives" (note 13 to chapter 6, p. 461).

285 There is only one thing I want to say about Ohio that has a political tinge, and that is that I think a mistake has been made of recent years in Ohio in failing to continue as our representatives the same people term after term. I do not need to tell a Washington audience, among whom there are certainly some who have been interested in legislation, that length of service in the House and in the Senate is what gives influence.

President WILLIAM HOWARD TAFT, speech before the Ohio Society, Washington, D.C.—Quoted in the *Congressional Record,* May 23, 1916, vol. 53, p. 8527.

286 I've said many a time that I think the Un-American Activities Committee in the House of Representatives was the most un-American thing in America!

HARRY S. TRUMAN, third Radner Lecture, Columbia University, New York City, April 29, 1959.—*Truman Speaks,* p. 111 (1960).

Congress—Senate

287 No man, however strong, can serve ten years as schoolmaster, priest, or Senator, and remain fit for anything else.

HENRY ADAMS, *The Education of Henry Adams,* ed. Ernest Samuels, chapter 7, p. 102 (1974). First published in 1906.

Adams was the son of Charles Francis Adams, grandson of John Quincy Adams, and great-grandson of John Adams.

288 We have been through this biennial convulsion four or five different times over the past 10 or 12 years, and now it appears that we are going through this quiet agony all over again.

Senator EVERETT M. DIRKSEN, remarks in the Senate on a resolution to amend Senate Rule 22 (cloture), January 11, 1967, *Congressional Record,* vol. 113, p. 182.

289 "Do you pray for the Senators, Dr. Hale?" someone asked the chaplain. "No, I look at the Senators and pray for the country."

EDWARD EVERETT HALE, Senate chaplain.—Van Wyck Brooks, *New England: Indian Summer, 1865–1915,* p. 418, footnote (1940).

"The celebrated anecdote . . . is not so unambiguous as it appears. . . . There is no reason to doubt the authenticity of Hale's reply, but it should be understood within a framework of respect for the senators as well as concern for the country. He knew every one of them personally and regarded them, as he said in his preface to *Prayers in The Senate*

(1904), as 'intelligent men, in very close daily intimacy with each other, in the discharge of a common duty of the greatest importance.' "—John R. Adams, *Edward Everett Hale*, pp. 100–101 (1977).

290 Two generations ago, Gladstone called the Senate of the United States "that remarkable body, the most remarkable of all the inventions of modern politics."

GEORGE H. HAYNES, *The Senate of the United States, Its History and Practice*, Preface, p. vii (1938). The attribution to William E. Gladstone is unverified.

291 The Senate is a place filled with goodwill and good intentions, and if the road to hell is paved with them, then it's a pretty good detour.

Senator HUBERT H. HUMPHREY, as reported in *Newsweek*, January 23, 1978, p. 23.

292 In order to judge of the form to be given to this institution [the Senate], it will be proper to take a view of the ends to be served by it. These were,—first, to protect the people against their rulers, secondly, to protect the people against the transient impressions into which they themselves might be led.

JAMES MADISON, debates in the Constitutional Convention, Philadelphia, Pennsylvania, June 26, 1787.—Madison, *Journal of the Federal Convention*, ed. E. H. Scott, pp. 241–42 (1893).

293 I fear the vermin that shall undermine
Senate and citadel and school and shrine.

EDWIN MARKHAM, "The Vermin in the Dark," stanza 5, lines 1 and 2, *The Speaker*, vol. 6, no. 3, 1911, p. 249.

294 There is a tradition that, on his return from France, Jefferson called Washington to account at the breakfast-table for having agreed to a second chamber. "Why," asked Washington, "did you pour that coffee into your saucer?" "To cool it," quoth Jefferson. "Even so," said Washington, "we pour legislation into the senatorial saucer to cool it."

MONCURE D. CONWAY, *Omitted Chapters of History Disclosed in the Life and Papers of Edmund Randolph*, p. 91 (1888). This story is probably apocryphal.

295 I am going back to Yazoo City and to my old home on a rural free-delivery route. I want to get up again each morning as I hear the roosters crow. I want to pick flowers while the dew is still on them. Then, I want to come back and have my coffee and breakfast. Later on, if I am so fortunate as to have any left in these days, I want to stir myself a toddy whenever I feel that I would like one.

Through the middle of the day I will read books, putter around the place, and talk to my neighbors. At noon I will leisurely eat my dinner. After dinner I will read some more, and then late in the evening, I will eat supper—and notice that I call it supper, this last meal of the day. That is what we call it in Mississippi.

And as night and the time for bed approaches, I will listen to the greatest chorus of voices that man ever heard, music that will charm me and make me ready for repose—the voices of my mocking birds, trilling from the trees.

In that way I want to live the rest of my life. And when the end comes, I hope to be carried out of the house by my neighbors and laid to rest among my people.

Now some may say that it is not a very wonderful future—all of this I have mapped out for myself—but I say there is merit in calm retirement. Right now I feel that it is more a real life than being a Senator of the United States who serves his people by joining in the petty squabbles that occupy so much time of the Senate today. I may have grown cynical from long service, but this is a tendency I do not like, and I sometimes think I'd rather be a dog and bay at the moon than stay in the Senate another six years and listen to it.

Perhaps it is a sign that I ought to retire. For retirement brings repose, and repose allows a kindly judgment of all things. As for me, it shall also mean a calm in which to make peace with myself and a season to spend in the quiet of my home and in the friendship of my neighbors.

Senator JOHN SHARP WILLIAMS, farewell to his friends, at a dinner organized by the Mississippi Society of Washington, D.C., honoring him shortly before his retirement from the Senate on March 4, 1923. This is sometimes referred to as the "mocking bird speech."—William Norwood Brigance, *Classified Speech Models*, pp. 274–75 (1928).

Sharp's obituary reported an earlier use of the hound dog metaphor. He said to the Senate after it doomed Wilson's League of Nations proposal: "I'd rather be a hound dog and bay at the moon from my Mississippi plantation than remain in the United States Senate."—*The Commercial Appeal*, Memphis, Tennessee, September 29, 1932, p. 2.

296 The Senate of the United States has been both extravagantly praised and unreasonably disparaged, according to the predisposition and temper of its various critics. . . . The truth is, in this case as in so many others, something quite commonplace and practical. The Senate is just what the mode of its election and the conditions of public life in this country make it.

WOODROW WILSON, *Congressional Government, A Study in American Politics*, chapter 4, p. 135 (1981). Originally published in 1885.

Congressmen

297 Had Grant been a Congressman one would have been on one's guard, for one knew the type. One never expected from a Congressman more than good intentions and public spirit. Newspaper-men as a rule had no great respect for the lower House; Senators had less; and Cabinet officers had none at all. Indeed, one day when Adams was pleading with a Cabinet officer for patience and tact in dealing with Representatives, the Secretary impatiently broke out: "You can't use tact with a Congressman! A Congressman is a hog! You must take a stick and hit him on the snout!"

HENRY ADAMS, *The Education of Henry Adams*, ed. Ernest Samuels, chapter 17, p. 261 (1973). Originally published in 1906.

The secretary who made the remark "may well have been Adams's friend, Secretary of the Interior Jacob Dolson Cox," according to note 18 on p. 617.

Adams was the son of Charles Francis Adams, the grandson of John Quincy Adams, and the great-grandson of John Adams.

298 You send me to Washington to represent you in the senate. But you do not send me there because you are interested in grave questions of national or international policy. When I come back to Arizona, you never ask me any questions about such policies; instead you ask me: "What about my pension?" or "What about that job for my son?" I am not in Washington as a statesman. I am there as a very well paid messenger boy doing your errands. My chief occupation is going around with a forked stick picking up little fragments of patronage for my constituents.

Attributed to Senator HENRY FOUNTAIN ASHURST.—Thomas C. Donnelly, *Rocky Mountain Politics*, p. 283 (1940). Unverified.

299 The best legislator is the one who votes for all appropriations and against all taxes.

Attributed to Representative WALTER P. BROWNLOW by his cousin, Louis B. Brownlow. Unverified.

300 I never know what South Carolina thinks of a measure. I never consult her. I act to the best of my judgment, and according to my conscience. If she approves, well and good. If she does not, or wishes any one to take my place, I am ready to vacate. We are even.

JOHN C. CALHOUN, Representative and Senator.—Walter J. Miller, "Calhoun as a Lawyer and Statesman," part 2, *The Green Bag*, June 1899, p. 271. Although Miller states "I will cite his own words," this quotation has not been verified in Calhoun's writings.

301 The truth is being more and more realized by the public that, other things being equal or anywhere near equal, the value of the Representative or Senator increases in proportion to his length of service. A man must learn to be a Representative or Senator, just as he must learn to be a farmer, carpenter, blacksmith, merchant, engineer, lawyer, doctor, preacher, teacher, or anything else. Of course some men learn quicker than others—some of exceptional ability and powers of observation very speedily, and some not at all. The best plan for a constituency to pursue is to select a man of good sense, good habits, and perfect integrity, young enough to learn, and re-elect him so long as he retains his faculties and is faithful to his trust. Such a man grows into power and high position as surely as the sparks fly upward. As a rule, in both House and Senate, the best places go to men of long service, provided they are capable, sober, industrious, vigilant, and punctual in the discharge of their duties. No man should be sent to either House of Congress solely to gratify his own ambition, but because he has qualifications for the position which he seeks—indeed, better qualifications than any of his opponents.

Representative CHAMP CLARK, *My Quarter Century of American Politics*, vol. 1, p. 220 (1920).

Champ Clark was Speaker of the House 1911–1919.

302 One of the countless drawbacks of being in Congress is that I am compelled to receive impertinent letters from a jackass like you in which you say I promised to have the Sierra Madre mountains reforested and I have been in Congress two months and haven't done it. Will you please take two running jumps and go to hell.

Attributed to Representative JOHN STEVEN MCGROARTY.—Senator John F. Kennedy, *Profiles in Courage*, p. 10 (1956).

McGroarty served in Congress 1935–1939.

303 I take the view that equality is equality . . . and that I am a member of Congress as good as anybody else. As long as it is within the law, it's not wrong. . . . If the law is wrong, change the law.

I do not do any more than any other member of the Congress, but by the Grace of God, I'll not do less!

Representative ADAM CLAYTON POWELL, JR., press conference and subsequent interview, February 20, 1963.—Neil Hickey and Ed Edwin, *Adam Clayton Powell and the Politics of Race*, pp. 230–31 (1965).

304 He votes as a Southern man, and votes sectionally; I am also a Southern man, but vote nationally on national questions.

Senator THOMAS HART BENTON.—Theodore Roosevelt, *Thomas Hart Benton,* chapter 15, p. 349 (1897, reprinted 1968).

305 A jay hasn't got any more principle than a Congressman. A jay will lie, a jay will steal, a jay will deceive, a jay will betray; and four times out of five, a jay will go back on his solemnest promise.

MARK TWAIN (Samuel L. Clemens), *A Tramp Abroad,* vol. 1 (vol. 3 of *The Writings of Mark Twain*), chapter 2, pp. 25–26 (1879, reprinted 1968).

306 To my mind Judas Iscariot was nothing but a low, mean, premature Congressman.

MARK TWAIN (Samuel L. Clemens), letter to the editor, March 7, 1873.—*New-York Daily Tribune,* March 10, 1873, p. 5.

307 We have been taught to regard a representative of the people as a sentinel on the watch-tower of liberty.

Senator DANIEL WEBSTER, remarks in the Senate, May 7, 1834.—*The Writings and Speeches of Daniel Webster,* vol. 7, p. 121 (1903).

Conservation

308 Not one cent for scenery.

Representative JOSEPH G. CANNON, squelching a request for funds for some modest Federal undertaking in conservation.—Blair Bolles, *Tyrant from Illinois,* p. 119 (1951).

"Uncle Joe" Cannon, who was Speaker of the House 1903–1911, served in the House for 46 years.

President Lyndon B. Johnson quoted Cannon at the signing ceremony making Assateague Island a national seashore area, September 21, 1965: "Conservation has been in eclipse in this country ever since Theodore Roosevelt's day. It had barely gotten off the ground when Uncle Joe Cannon, the Speaker of the House in those days, issued his ultimatum: 'Not 1 cent for scenery.' Well, today we are repealing Cannon's law. We are declaring a new doctrine of conservation."—*Congressional Record,* September 21, 1965, vol. 111, p. 24540.

309 We may not appreciate the fact; but a fact nevertheless it remains: we are living in a Golden Age, the most gilded Golden Age of human history—not only of past history, but of future history. For, as Sir Charles Darwin and many others before him have pointed out, we are living like drunken sailors, like the irresponsible heirs of a millionaire uncle. At an ever accelerating rate we are now squandering the capital of metallic ores and fossil fuels accumulated in the earth's crust during hundreds of millions of years. How long can this spending spree go on? Estimates vary. But all are agreed that within a few centuries or at most a few millennia, Man will have run through his capital and will be compelled to live, for the remaining nine thousand nine hundred and seventy or eighty centuries of his career as Homo sapiens, strictly on income. Sir Charles is of the opinion that Man will successfully make the transition from rich ores to poor ores and even sea water, from coal, oil, uranium and thorium to solar energy and alcohol derived from plants. About as much energy as is now available can be derived from the new sources—but with a far greater expense in man hours, a much larger capital investment in machinery. And the same holds true of the raw materials on which industrial civilization depends. By doing a great deal more work than they are doing now, men will contrive to extract the diluted dregs of the planet's metallic wealth or will fabricate non-metallic substitutes for the elements they have completely used up. In such an event, some human beings will still live fairly well, but not in the style to which we, the squanderers of planetary capital, are accustomed.

ALDOUS HUXLEY, "Tomorrow and Tomorrow and Tomorrow," *Collected Essays*, pp. 293–94 (1959). First published in *Adonis and the Alphabet* in 1956.

310 The nation behaves well if it treats the natural resources as assets which it must turn over to the next generation increased, and not impaired, in value.

THEODORE ROOSEVELT, speech before the Colorado Live Stock Association, Denver, Colorado, August 29, 1910.—Roosevelt, *The New Nationalism*, p. 52 (1910).

This sentence is one of many quotations inscribed on Cox Corridor II, a first floor House corridor, U.S. Capitol.

311 The idea that our natural resources were inexhaustible still obtained, and there was as yet no real knowledge of their extent and condition. The relation of the conservation of natural resources to the problems of National welfare and National efficiency had not yet dawned on the public mind. The reclamation of arid public lands in the West was still a matter for private enterprise alone; and our magnificent river system, with its superb possibilities for public usefulness, was dealt with by the National Government not as a unit, but as a disconnected series of pork-barrel problems, whose only real interest was in their effect on the reëlection or defeat of a Congressman here and there—a theory which, I regret to say, still obtains.

THEODORE ROOSEVELT, *Theodore Roosevelt, An Autobiography* (vol. 20 of *The Works of Theodore Roosevelt*, national ed.), chapter 11, p. 386 (1926).

312 Conservation and rural-life policies are really two sides of the same policy; and down at bottom this policy rests upon the fundamental law that neither man nor nation can prosper unless, in dealing with the present, thought is steadily taken for the future.

THEODORE ROOSEVELT, "Rural Life," *American Problems* (vol. 16 of *The Works of Theodore Roosevelt*, national ed.), chapter 20, p. 146 (1926). Originally appeared in *The Outlook*, August 27, 1910.

313 Here in the United States we turn our rivers and streams into sewers and dumping-grounds, we pollute the air, we destroy forests, and exterminate fishes, birds, and mammals—not to speak of vulgarizing charming landscapes with hideous advertisements. But at last it looks as if our people were awakening. Many leading men, Americans and Canadians, are doing all they can for the Conservation movement.

THEODORE ROOSEVELT, "Our Vanishing Wildlife," *Literary Essays* (vol. 12 of *The Works of Theodore Roosevelt*, national ed.), chapter 46, p. 420 (1926). Originally appeared in *The Outlook*, January 25, 1913.

Conservatives

314 I am a Conservative to preserve all that is good in our constitution, a Radical to remove all that is bad. I seek to preserve property and to respect order, and I equally decry the appeal to the passions of the many or the prejudices of the few.

BENJAMIN DISRAELI, campaign speech at High Wycombe, England, November 27, 1832.—*Selected Speeches of the Late Right Honourable the Earl of Beaconsfield*, ed. T. E. Kebbel, vol. 1, p. 8 (1882).

315 Is not every man sometimes a radical in politics? Men are conservatives when they are least vigorous, or when they are most luxurious. They are conservatives after dinner, or before taking their rest; when they are sick, or aged. In the morning, or when their intellect or their conscience has been aroused; when they hear music, or when they read poetry, they are radicals.

RALPH WALDO EMERSON, "New England Reformers," lecture read before the Church of the Disciples, Amory Hall, Boston, Massachusetts, March 3, 1844.—*Essays: Second Series* (vol. 3 of *The Complete Works of Ralph Waldo Emerson*), p. 272 (1903).

316 The conservative in financial circles I have often described as a man who thinks nothing new ought ever to be adopted for the first time.

FRANK A. VANDERLIP, *From Farm Boy to Financier*, chapter 25, p. 257 (1935).

Constitution of the United States

317 We have seen that the American Constitution has changed, is changing, and by the law of its existence must continue to change, in its substance and practical working even when its words remain the same.

JAMES BRYCE, *The American Commonwealth*, new ed., vol. 1, chapter 35, p. 401 (1924).

318 Most faults are not in our Constitution, but in ourselves.

RAMSEY CLARK, remarks at meeting sponsored by the Center for the Study of Democratic Institutions, New York City, November 11, 1970, to debate the merits of a new constitution drafted by Rexford Tugwell, as reported by *The Washington Post*, November 12, 1970, p. A2.

Clark was attorney general 1967–1969.

319 The Constitution is the sole source and guaranty of national freedom.

President CALVIN COOLIDGE, address accepting nomination as Republican candidate for president, Washington, D.C., August 4, 1924.—Coolidge, *Address of Acceptance*, p. 15 (1924).

320 To live under the American Constitution is the greatest political privilege that was ever accorded to the human race.

Attributed to CALVIN COOLIDGE, the White House, December 12, 1924. Unverified.

321 I confess that there are several parts of this Constitution which I do not at present approve, but I am not sure I shall never approve them. For having lived long, I have experienced many instances of being obliged by better information, or fuller consideration, to change opinions even on important subjects, which I once thought right, but found to be otherwise.

BENJAMIN FRANKLIN, speech in the Constitutional Convention, Philadelphia, Pennsylvania, September 17, 1787.—James Madison, *Journal of the Federal Convention*, ed. E. H. Scott, p. 741 (1893).

322 In these sentiments, sir, I agree to this Constitution, with all its faults, if they are such; because I think a General Government necessary for us, and there is no form of government, but what may be a blessing to the people if well administered; and believe further, that this is likely to be well administered for a course of years, and can only end in despotism, as other forms have done before it, when the people shall become so corrupted as to need despotic government, being incapable of any other.

BENJAMIN FRANKLIN, debates in the Constitutional Convention, Philadelphia, Pennsylvania, September 17, 1787.—James Madison, *Journal of the Federal Convention*, ed. E. H. Scott, p. 742 (1893).

323 Whilst the last members were signing [the Constitution], Doctor FRANKLIN, looking towards the President's chair, at the back of which a rising sun happened to be painted, observed to a few members near him, that painters had found it difficult to distinguish in their art, a rising, from a setting, sun. I have, said he, often and often, in the course of the session, and the vicissitudes of my hopes and fears as to its issue, looked at that behind the President, without being able to tell whether it was rising or setting; but now at length, I have the happiness to know, that it is a rising, and not a setting sun.

BENJAMIN FRANKLIN, debates in the Constitutional Convention, Philadelphia, Pennsylvania, September 17, 1787.—James Madison, *Journal of the Federal Convention*, ed. E. H. Scott, p. 763 (1893).

324 The principles of a free constitution are irrecoverably lost, when the legislative power is nominated by the executive.

EDWARD GIBBON, *History of the Decline and Fall of the Roman Empire*, chapter 3, third paragraph, p. 33 (1838).

325 As the British Constitution is the most subtile organism which has proceeded from the womb and the long gestation of progressive history, so the American Constitution is, so far as I can see, the most wonderful work ever struck off at a given time by the brain and purpose of man.

WILLIAM E. GLADSTONE, "Kin Beyond Sea," *The North American Review*, September-October 1878, p. 185.

326 The Constitution is not a panacea for every blot upon the public welfare, nor should this Court, ordained as a judicial body, be thought of as a general haven for reform movements.

Justice JOHN MARSHALL HARLAN, dissenting, *Reynolds, Judge, et al.* v. *Sims, et al.*, 377 U.S. 624–25 (1964).

327 I always say, as you know, that if my fellow citizens want to go to Hell I will help them. It's my job.

Justice OLIVER WENDELL HOLMES, letter to Harold J. Laski, March 4, 1920.—*Holmes-Laski Letters*, ed. Mark DeWolfe Howe, vol. 1, p. 249 (1953).

Max Lerner, *The Mind and Faith of Justice Holmes*, p. 222 (1954), said, "Holmes was exacting in construing a statute and latitudinarian in construing powers under the Constitution. He often said that there was nothing in the Constitution that prevented the country from going to hell if it chose to. But once a statute was clearly constitutional and it became a matter of construing it, Holmes put on his most scrupulous spectacles."

328 We are under a Constitution, but the Constitution is what the judges say it is, and the judiciary is the safeguard of our liberty and of our property under the Constitution.

CHARLES EVANS HUGHES, speech before the Chamber of Commerce, Elmira, New York, May 3, 1907.—*Addresses and Papers of Charles Evans Hughes, Governor of New York, 1906–1908*, p. 139 (1908).

"Governor Hughes had prepared a speech for this occasion but Mr. John B. Stanchfield, who spoke before he did, made an attack upon the Public-Service Commissions bill, saying as he did so that he was 'under no retainer from the railroads,' and the Governor abandoned his prepared speech to make an extemporaneous reply to Mr. Stanchfield's arguments" (p. 133, footnote).

329 And lastly, let us provide in our constitution for its revision at stated periods.

THOMAS JEFFERSON, letter to Samuel Kercheval, July 12, 1816.—*The Writings of Thomas Jefferson*, ed. Paul L. Ford, vol. 10, p. 43 (1899).

This letter favored "progressive accomodation to progressive improvement," rather than following the examples of European monarchs, who "clung to old abuses."

330 The constitution, on this hypothesis, is a mere thing of wax in the hands of the judiciary, which they may twist and shape into any form they please.

THOMAS JEFFERSON, letter to Judge Spencer Roane, September 6, 1819.—*The Writings of Thomas Jefferson*, ed. Andrew A. Lipscomb, vol. 15, p. 213 (1904).

331 In questions of power, then, let no more be heard of confidence in man, but bind him down from mischief by the chains of the Constitution.

THOMAS JEFFERSON, from the fair copy of the drafts of the Kentucky Resolutions of 1798.—*The Writings of Thomas Jefferson*, ed. Paul L. Ford, vol. 7, p. 305 (1896).

332 Amendments to the Constitution ought to not be too frequently made; . . . [if] continually tinkered with it would lose all its prestige and dignity, and the old instrument would be lost sight of altogether in a short time.

President ANDREW JOHNSON, speech in front of the White House, February 22, 1866.—Andrew Johnson Papers, Library of Congress.

333 Don't interfere with anything in the Constitution. That must be maintained, for it is the only safeguard of our liberties.

ABRAHAM LINCOLN, speech at Kalamazoo, Michigan, August 27, 1856.—*The Collected Works of Abraham Lincoln*, ed. Roy P. Basler, vol. 2, p. 366 (1953).

334 Your constitution is all sail and no anchor. As I said before, when a society has entered on this downward progress, either civilisation or liberty must perish. Either some Caesar or Napoleon will seize the reins of government with a strong hand; or your republic will be as fearfully plundered and laid waste by barbarians in the twentieth Century as the Roman Empire was in the fifth;—with this difference, that the Huns and Vandals who ravaged the Roman Empire came from without, and that your Huns and Vandals will have been engendered within your own country by your own institutions.

THOMAS BABINGTON MACAULAY, letter to Henry Stephens Randall, May 23, 1857.—*The Letters of Thomas Babington Macaulay*, ed. Thomas Pinney, vol. 6, p. 96 (1981).

"This letter, which naturally aroused great interest in the United States, was published in part as early as 1860 and has frequently been reprinted since, usually in the season of presidential elections or at other time of political crisis; . . . I give *Harper's Magazine* [February 1877] as the place of first full publication so far as I have been able to determine. For detailed history of the letter to 1925 see H. M. Lydenberg, 'What Did Macaulay Say about America?' *Letters, Bulletin of the New York Public Library*, XXIX (July 1925), 459–81" (vol. 6, footnote 1, p. 94).

"In his Journal for 23 May TBM writes: 'wrote an answer to a Yankee who is utterly unable to understand on what ground I can possibly dislike Jefferson's politics' " (footnote 3, p. 94).

335 The danger of disturbing the public tranquillity by interesting too strongly the public passions, is a still more serious objection against a frequent reference of constitutional questions to the decision of the whole society.

JAMES MADISON, *The Federalist*, ed. Benjamin F. Wright, no. 49, p. 349 (1961).

336 Our chief danger arises from the democratic parts of our constitutions.

EDMUND JENNINGS RANDOLPH, governor of Virginia. Attributed to Randolph by James McHenry in his notes of the Constitutional Convention dated May 29, 1787.—*The Records of the Federal Convention of 1787*, rev. ed., ed. Max Farrand, vol. 1, p. 26 (1937).

337 I hope your committee will not permit doubts as to constitutionality, however reasonable, to block the suggested legislation.

President FRANKLIN D. ROOSEVELT, letter to Representative Samuel B. Hill, July 6, 1935.—*The Public Papers and Addresses of Franklin D. Roosevelt, 1935*, p. 298 (1938).

"NOTE: The last paragraph of the foregoing letter to Congressman Hill should, of course, be read as a whole. When it is, it will be seen that the paragraph merely sets forth the traditional rule which the Courts are supposed to follow in determining whether or not a statute is unconstitutional. . . . The letter to Congressman Hill was really an understatement of this rule. During the past two years certain newspaper publishers and columnists have quoted only the last sentence of the letter, taken completely from its text, so as to give a wholly false impression of the letter. It is perhaps typical of methods now prevalent among certain newspaper owners and publishers" (p. 298). This note was written by FDR.

338 However the Court may interpret the provisions of the Constitution, it is still the Constitution which is the law and not the decision of the Court.

CHARLES WARREN, *The Supreme Court in United States History*, vol. 2, chapter 38, pp. 748–49 (1932).

339 If in the opinion of the People, the distribution or modification of the Constitutional powers be in any particular wrong, let it be corrected by an amendment in the way which the Constitution designates. But let there be no change by usurpation; for though this, in one instance, may be the instrument of good, it is the customary weapon by which free governments are destroyed.

President GEORGE WASHINGTON, farewell address, September 19, 1796.—*The Writings of George Washington*, ed. John C. Fitzpatrick, vol. 35, p. 229 (1940).

"The immediate occasion for Washington's Address was the necessity of eliminating himself from the contest for the Presidency. . . . There has been considerable controversy over the question of the authorship of the Address, and Hamilton's admirers claim that he was principally responsible for it."—Henry Steele Commager, ed., *Documents of American History*, 10th ed., vol. 1, p. 169 (1973), where additional details about the authorship may also be found. The farewell address was not delivered by Washington but was published in

Claypoole's *American Daily Advertiser,* Philadelphia, Pennsylvania, September 19, 1796. Fitzpatrick provides a lengthy account (*Writings,* vol. 35, footnote 84, pp. 214–15) of the publication of the address by Claypoole, and dates the address the 19th, from the date of its publication in the *Advertiser,* although Commager and others date it the 17th.

340 It is too probable that no plan we propose will be adopted. Perhaps another dreadful conflict is to be sustained. If to please the people, we offer what we ourselves disapprove, how can we afterwards defend our work? Let us raise a standard to which the wise and the honest can repair. The event is in the hand of God.

GEORGE WASHINGTON, remarks at the first Continental Congress, Philadelphia, Pennsylvania, May 14, 1787.—Max Farrand, *The Framing of the Constitution of the United States,* p. 66 (1934).

Washington was the presiding officer.

341 Should the States reject this excellent Constitution, the probability is, an opportunity will never again offer to cancel another in peace—the next will be drawn in blood.

Attributed to GEORGE WASHINGTON.—*Pennsylvania Journal and Weekly Advertiser,* November 14, 1787, p. 3, col. 1.

Charles Warren, *The Making of the Constitution,* p. 717 (1937, originally published 1928), quotes this, with slight variation in wording, but adds in a footnote: "As Madison does not mention this speech, there is some doubt as to the accuracy of the report."

Contempt

342 Contempt is not a thing to be despised.

EDMUND BURKE, "Letters on a Regicide Peace," letter 3, 1796–1797, *The Works of the Right Honorable Edmund Burke,* vol. 5, p. 436 (1899).

Country

343 Every man has two countries, his own and France.
(Tout homme a deux pays, le sien et puis la France!)

HENRI DE BORNIER, *La Fille de Roland,* act III, scene ii, p. 65 (1909).

Jules Michelet, *Le Peuple,* chapter 6, says "an American philosopher" said "for every man the first country is his native land and the second is France." A translation, however, names Tom Paine as the philosopher.—Michelet, *The People,* trans. John P. McKay, chapter 6, p. 191 (1973). Unverified.

Similarly, Thomas Jefferson in his "Autobiography" said: "Ask the travelled inhabitant of any nation, in what country on earth would you rather live?—Certainly, in my own, where all my friends, my relations, and the earliest and sweetest affections and recollections of my life. Which would be your second choice? France."—*The Writings of Thomas Jefferson,* ed. Paul L. Ford, vol. 1, p. 149 (1892).

344 I cannot conceive how any man can have brought himself to that pitch of presumption, to consider his country as nothing but *carte blanche,* upon which he may scribble whatever he pleases.

EDMUND BURKE, "Reflections on the Revolution in France," 1790, *The Works of the Right Honorable Edmund Burke,* vol. 3, p. 440 (1899).

345 "My country, right or wrong," is a thing that no patriot would think of saying except in a desperate case. It is like saying, "My mother, drunk or sober."

G. K. CHESTERTON, *The Defendant*, p. 166 (1901, reprinted 1972).

346 Our country! In her intercourse with foreign nations, may she always be in the right; but our country, right or wrong.

STEPHEN DECATUR, toast at a dinner in Norfolk, Virginia, April 1816.—Alexander Slidell Mackenzie, *Life of Stephen Decatur*, p. 295 (1848).

Niles' Weekly Register, published in Baltimore, Maryland, gave a slightly different version in its April 20, 1816, issue (p. 136). A number of the toasts at the dinner for Decatur were included, probably reprinted from a Virginia newspaper, and Decatur's appeared as: "*Our country*—In her intercourse with foreign nations may she always be in the *right*, and always *successful*, *right* or *wrong*."

347 God grant, that not only the Love of Liberty, but a thorough Knowledge of the Rights of Man, may pervade all the Nations of the Earth, so that a Philosopher may set his Foot anywhere on its Surface, and say, "This is my Country."

BENJAMIN FRANKLIN, letter to David Hartley, December 4, 1789.—*The Writings of Benjamin Franklin*, ed. Albert H. Smyth, vol. 10, p. 72 (1907).

348 Who saves his country, saves himself, saves all things, and all things saved do bless him! Who lets his country die, lets all things die, dies himself ignobly, and all things dying curse him!

Senator BENJAMIN H. HILL.—Benjamin H. Hill, Jr., *Senator Benjamin H. Hill of Georgia; His Life, Speeches and Writings*, epigraph, p. 594 (1893). From "Notes on the Situation," a series of articles appearing in the *Chronicle and Sentinel*, Atlanta, Georgia.

349 You convey too great a compliment when you say that I have earned the right to the presidential nomination. No man can establish such an obligation upon any part of the American people. My country owes me no debt. It gave me, as it gives every boy and girl, a chance. It gave me schooling, independence of action, opportunity for service and honor. In no other land could a boy from a country village, without inheritance or influential friends, look forward with unbounded hope. My whole life has taught me what America means. I am indebted to my country beyond any human power to repay.

HERBERT HOOVER, letter to Senator George H. Moses, chairman of the Republican national convention, upon learning of his nomination for president, June 14, 1928.—*The Memoirs of Herbert Hoover*, vol. 2, p. 195 (1952).

350 When an American says that he loves his country, he means not only that he loves the New England hills, the prairies glistening in the sun, the wide and rising plains, the great mountains, and the sea. He means that he loves an inner air, an inner light in which freedom lives and in which a man can draw the breath of self-respect.

ADLAI E. STEVENSON, governor of Illinois, speech to the American Legion convention, New York City, August 27, 1952.—*Speeches of Adlai Stevenson*, pp. 83–84 (1952).

351 I would not change my native land
For rich Peru with all her gold

ISAAC WATTS, "Praise for Birth and Education in a Christian Land," song 5, stanza 3, *Divine Songs in Easy Language for the Use of Children*, p. 12 (1975). The first edition of this book was published in 1715, and many editions followed.

352 For years I thought what was good for our country was good for General Motors, and vice versa. The difference did not exist.

CHARLES E. WILSON, confirmation hearing, January 15, 1953.—*Nominations*, hearings before the Committee on Armed Services, United States Senate, 83d Congress, 1st session, p. 26 (1953).

Wilson, who had recently resigned as president of General Motors, was about to become secretary of defense. He was asked if he could make a decision in the interests of the United States government which would be adverse to the interests of General Motors or other companies whose stock he held.

This remark is often misquoted as: "What's good for General Motors is good for the country."

Courage

353 The brave man is not he who feels no fear,
For that were stupid and irrational;
But he, whose noble soul its fears subdues,
And bravely dares the danger nature shrinks from.

JOANNA BAILLIE, "Basil: A Tragedy," *The Complete Poetical Works of Joanna Baillie*, vol. 1, p. 39 (1832).

354 Be scared. You can't help that. But don't be afraid. Ain't nothing in the woods going to hurt you unless you corner it, or it smells that you are afraid. A bear or a deer, too, has got to be scared of a coward the same as a brave man has got to be.

WILLIAM FAULKNER, "The Bear," *Saturday Evening Post*, May 9, 1942, reprinted in *Bear, Man, & God, Seven Approaches to William Faulkner's "The Bear,"* ed. Francis L. Utley, Lynn Z. Bloom, and Arthur F. Kinney, p. 157 (1964). This edition includes (p. 18) the version of "The Bear" in Faulkner's *Go Down, Moses*, where this passage appears with minor variations in wording and punctuation.

355 Without belittling the courage with which men have died, we should not forget those acts of courage with which men . . . have *lived*. The courage of life is often a less dramatic spectacle than the courage of a final moment; but it is no less a magnificent mixture of triumph and tragedy. A man does what he must—in spite of personal consequences, in spite of obstacles and dangers and pressures—and that is the basis of all human morality. . . . In whatever arena of life one may meet the challenge of courage, whatever may be the sacrifices he faces if he follows his conscience—the loss of his friends, his fortune, his contentment, even the esteem of his fellow men—each man must decide for himself the course he will follow. The stories of past courage can define that ingredient—they can teach, they can offer hope, they can provide inspiration. But they cannot supply courage itself. For this each man must look into his own soul.

Senator JOHN F. KENNEDY, *Profiles in Courage*, p. 246 (1956).

356 I love the man that can smile in trouble, that can gather strength from distress, and grow brave by reflection. 'Tis the business of little minds to shrink; but he whose heart is firm, and whose conscience approves his conduct, will pursue his principles unto death.

THOMAS PAINE, "The Crisis," no. 1, *The Writings of Thomas Paine,* ed. Moncure D. Conway, vol. 1, p. 176 (1894).

See note at No. 1821 about this *Crisis.*

Credit

357 Let me remind you that credit is the lifeblood of business, the lifeblood of prices and jobs.

President HERBERT HOOVER, address at Des Moines, Iowa, October 4, 1932.—*The Public Papers of the Presidents of the United States: Herbert Hoover, 1932–1933,* p. 467.

President Hoover referred to "three great perils" that the nation faced. The first of these was the "strangulation of credit through the removal of $3 billions of gold and currency by foreign drains and by the hoarding of our own citizens from the channels of our commerce and business."

358 The maxim of buying nothing without the money in our pocket to pay for it, would make of our country one of the happiest upon earth. Experience during the war proved this; as I think every man will remember that under all the privations it obliged him to submit to during that period he slept sounder, and awaked happier than he can do now. Desperate of finding relief from a free course of justice, I look forward to the abolition of all credit as the only other remedy which can take place.

THOMAS JEFFERSON, letter to Alexander Donald, July 28, 1787.—*The Papers of Thomas Jefferson,* ed. Julian P. Boyd, vol. 11, p. 633 (1955).

359 Credit is the vital air of the system of modern commerce. It has done more, a thousand times, to enrich nations, than all the mines of all the world. It has excited labor, stimulated manufactures, pushed commerce over every sea, and brought every nation, every kingdom, and every small tribe, among the races of men, to be known to all the rest. It has raised armies, equipped navies, and, triumphing over the gross power of mere numbers, it has established national superiority on the foundation of intelligence, wealth, and well-directed industry. Credit is to money what money is to articles of merchandise. As hard money represents property, so credit represents hard money; and it is capable of supplying the place of money so completely, that there are writers of distinction, especially of the Scotch school, who insist that no hard money is necessary for the interests of commerce. I am not of that opinion. I do not think any government can maintain an exclusive paper system, without running to excess, and thereby causing depreciation.

Senator DANIEL WEBSTER, remarks in the Senate in favor of continuing the charter of the Bank of the United States, March 18, 1834.—*The Writings and Speeches of Daniel Webster,* vol. 7, p. 89 (1903).

Criminals

360 There are few better measures of the concern a society has for its individual members and its own well being than the way it handles criminals.

Attorney General RAMSEY CLARK, keynote address, American Correctional Association conference, Miami Beach, Florida, August 20–25, 1967.—*Proceedings* of the Ninety-Seventh Annual Congress of Correction of the American Correctional Association, p. 4 (1968).

361 Let dull critics feed upon the carcases of plays; give me the taste and the dressing.

LORD CHESTERFIELD, letter to Philip Stanhope, his natural son, February 6, 1752.—*The Letters of Philip Dormer Stanhope, 4th Earl of Chesterfield*, vol. 5, p. 1826 (1932).

362 In the proudest nations of the Old World works were published which faithfully portrayed the vices and absurdities of contemporaries; La Bruyère lived in Louis XIV's palace while he wrote his chapter on the great, and Molière criticized the court in plays acted before the courtiers. But the power which dominates in the United States does not understand being mocked like that. The least reproach offends it, and the slightest sting of truth turns it fierce; and one must praise everything, from the turn of its phrases to its most robust virtues. No writer, no matter how famous, can escape from this obligation to sprinkle incense over his fellow citizens. Hence the majority lives in a state of perpetual self-adoration; only strangers or experience may be able to bring certain truths to the Americans' attention.

ALEXIS DE TOCQUEVILLE, *Democracy in America*, ed. J. P. Mayer, trans. George Lawrence, vol. 1, part 2, chapter 7, p. 256 (1969). Originally published in 1835–1840.

Death

363 Show me the manner in which a nation or a community cares for its dead. I will measure exactly the sympathies of its people, their respect for the laws of the land, and their loyalty to high ideals.

Attributed to WILLIAM E. GLADSTONE.—"Successful Cemetery Advertising," *The American Cemetery*, March 1938, p. 13. Unverified.

364 How frighteningly few are the persons whose death would spoil our appetite and make the world seem empty.

ERIC HOFFER, "Thoughts of Eric Hoffer, Including: 'Absolute Faith Corrupts Absolutely,'" *The New York Times Magazine*, April 25, 1971, p. 62.

365 It is not right to glory in the slain.

HOMER, *The Odyssey of Homer*, trans. George H. Palmer, book 22, line 412, p. 288 (1929).

Another translation is: "It isn't right to gloat over the dead."—*Homer's Odyssey*, trans. Denison B. Hull, p. 252 (1978).

366 'Tis after death that we measure men.

JAMES BARRON HOPE, "Our Heroic Dead," *A Wreath of Virginia Bay Leaves*, ed. Janey Hope Marr, p. 71 (1895).

As commander of the camp, he addressed the Confederate veterans on their first decoration day with this poem.—Samuel A. Link, *Pioneers of Southern Literature*, vol. 2, p. 423 (1903).

367 Sweet and glorious it is to die for our country.
(Dulce et decorum est pro patria mori.)

HORACE, *Odes*, book 3, ode 2, line 13.—*The Works of Horace*, trans. J. C. Elgood, p. 58 (1893).

There have been various translations of this sentence, including that in the Modern Library edition, *The Complete Works of Horace*, p. 217 (1936), "For country 'tis a sweet and seemly thing to die." Ernest Hemingway, "Notes on the Next War," *Esquire*, September 1935, p. 156, said, "They wrote in the old days that it is sweet and fitting to die for one's country. But in modern war there is nothing sweet nor fitting in your dying."

368 In the democracy of the dead all men at last are equal. There is neither rank nor station nor prerogative in the republic of the grave.

Senator JOHN JAMES INGALLS, eulogy on the death of Representative James N. Burnes, January 24, 1889.—*A Collection of the Writings of John James Ingalls*, p. 273 (1902).

369 Depend upon it, Sir, when a man knows he is to be hanged in a fortnight, it concentrates his mind wonderfully.

SAMUEL JOHNSON.—James Boswell, *Boswell's Life of Johnson*, ed. George B. Hill, rev. and enl. ed., ed. L. F. Powell, entry for September 19, 1777, vol. 3, p. 167 (1934).

370 Dear Madam,—I have been shown in the files of the War Department a statement of the Adjutant General of Massachusetts, that you are the mother of five sons who have died gloriously on the field of battle.

I feel how weak and fruitless must be any words of mine which should attempt to beguile you from the grief of a loss so overwhelming. But I cannot refrain from tendering to you the consolation that may be found in the thanks of the Republic they died to save.

I pray that our Heavenly Father may assuage the anguish of your bereavement, and leave you only the cherished memory of the loved and lost, and the solemn pride that must be yours, to have laid so costly a sacrifice upon the altar of Freedom. Yours, very sincerely and respectfully.

President ABRAHAM LINCOLN, letter to Mrs. Lydia Bixby, November 21, 1864.—*The Collected Works of Abraham Lincoln*, ed. Roy P. Basler, vol. 8, pp. 116–17 (1953).

The records were later corrected: only two sons died. For information concerning the text, the sons of Mrs. Bixby, and additional sources concerning this letter, see the editor's note on p. 117.

371 Were a star quenched on high,
For ages would its light,
Still travelling downward from the sky,
Shine on our mortal sight.

So when a great man dies,
For years beyond our ken,
The light he leaves behind him lies
Upon the paths of men.

HENRY WADSWORTH LONGFELLOW, "Charles Sumner," stanzas 8 and 9, *The Poetical Works of Longfellow*, p. 324 (1893, reprinted 1975).

372 Earl of Sandwich: 'Pon my honor, Wilkes, I don't know whether you'll die on the gallows or of the pox.

John Wilkes: That must depend my Lord, upon whether I first embrace your Lordship's principles, or your Lordship's mistresses.

Exchange retold by Sir Charles Petrie, *The Four Georges*, p. 133 (1935).

373 I have a rendezvous with Death
At some disputed barricade,
When Spring comes back with rustling shade
And apple-blossoms fill the air—
I have a rendezvous with Death
When Spring brings back blue days and fair.

It may be he shall take my hand
And lead me into his dark land
And close my eyes and quench my breath—
It may be I shall pass him still.
I have a rendezvous with Death
On some scarred slope of battered hill,
When Spring comes round again this year
And the first meadow-flowers appear.

God knows 'twere better to be deep
Pillowed in silk and scented down,
Where Love throbs out in blissful sleep,
Pulse nigh to pulse, and breath to breath,
Where hushed awakenings are dear . . .
But I've a rendezvous with Death
At midnight in some flaming town,
When Spring trips north again this year,
And I to my pledged word am true,
I shall not fail that rendezvous.

ALAN SEEGER, "I Have a Rendezvous with Death . . . ," *Poems*, p. 144 (1917).

374 Your death and my death are mainly of importance to ourselves. The black plumes will be stripped off our hearses within the hour; tears will dry, hurt hearts close again, our graves grow level with the church-yard, and although we are away, the world wags on. It does not miss us; and those who are near us, when the first strangeness of vacancy wears off, will not miss us much either.

ALEXANDER SMITH, "Of Death and the Fear of Dying," *Dreamthorp: A Book of Essays Written in the Country*, pp. 70–71 (1864, reprinted 1972).

375 On the mountains of memory, by the world's wellsprings,
In all men's eyes,
Where the light of the life of him is on all past things,
Death only dies.

ALGERNON C. SWINBURNE, "Super Flumina Babylonis," *The Complete Works of Algernon C. Swinburne*, vol. 2, p. 106 (1925).

376 As for myself, may the "sweet Muses," as Virgil says, bear me away to their holy places where sacred streams do flow, beyond the reach of anxiety and care, and free from the obligation of performing each day some task that goes against the grain. May I no longer have anything to do with the mad racket and the hazards of the forum, or tremble as I try a fall with white-faced Fame. I do not want to be roused from sleep by the clatter of morning callers or by some breathless messenger from the palace; I do not care, in drawing my will, to give a money-pledge for its safe execution through anxiety as to what is to happen afterwards; I wish for no larger estate than I can leave to the heir of my own free choice. Some day or other the last hour will strike also for me, and my prayer is that my effigy may be set up beside my grave, not grim and scowling, but all smiles and garlands, and that no one shall seek to honour my memory either by a motion in the senate or by a petition to the Emperor.

TACITUS, "A Dialogue on Oratory," section 13, *Dialogus, Agricola, Germania*, trans. William Peterson, p. 51 (1914).

Excerpts from this passage, in a different translation, were read at the funeral of Justice Hugo L. Black, September 28, 1971, as they were found underlined in his books and were said to be a favorite passage:

"Let the sweet Muses lead me to their soft retreats, their living fountains, and melodious groves, where I may dwell remote from care, master of myself . . . let me no more be seen in the wrangling forum, a pale and odious candidate for precarious fame . . . let me live free from solicitude . . . and when nature shall give the signal to retire may I possess no more than I may bequeath to whom I will. At my funeral let no token of sorrow be seen, no pompous mockery of woe. Crown me with chaplets; strew flowers on my grave, and let my friends erect no vain memorial to tell where my remains are lodged."—*The Works of Tacitus*, Oxford trans., rev., vol. 2, pp. 408–9 (1854). The printed version differs from the above only in the beginning, "Me let the sweet Muses lead," and in using "anxious" for "odious."

The reference to Virgil is to *The Georgics*, book 2, line 476.

377 Sleep sweetly, tender heart, in peace;
Sleep, holy spirit, blessed soul,
While the stars burn, the moons increase,
And the great ages onward roll.

Sleep till the end, true soul and sweet.
Nothing comes to thee new or strange.
Sleep full of rest from head to feet;
Lie still, dry dust, secure of change.

ALFRED, LORD TENNYSON, "To J. S." [James Spedding], stanzas 18–19, *The Poetic and Dramatic Works of Alfred Lord Tennyson*, p. 78 (1899).

378 Say the report is exaggerated.

MARK TWAIN (Samuel L. Clemens), "The Report of My Death," *Mark Twain in Eruption*, ed. Bernard DeVoto, pp. 252–53 (1940).

In 1897, Twain was living in London where a cousin, Dr. Jim Clemens, fell ill. The newspapers, believing Twain was near death, sent reporters to investigate. Twain made his remark when the correspondent for the *Evening Sun* told him his death had been reported in New York, and asked what he should cable in reply.

Albert Bigelow Paine, *Mark Twain*, vol. 2, chapter 197, p. 1039 (1912), gives a slightly different version of the story, ending, "Just say the report of my death has been grossly exaggerated."

Often heard ". . . greatly exaggerated."

Debt

379 In his first years in the White House, Mr. Roosevelt apologized for each annual deficit. Each new budget message explained that, because of unforeseen circumstances, the promise of the previous year had not been met, but next year things would be better; next year there would be a balanced budget. . . . The 1938 congressional elections were uncomfortably near at hand. . . . it was announced that the President would deliver a Fireside Chat. In it our startled ears caught the opening accents of a grand new liturgy. Spending would be resumed, but let not the heart be troubled. Spending was no longer the rock of unsound finance on which so many liberal governments had been wrecked; it was not danger, but security. Debt, if owed to ourselves, was not debt but investment.

BRUCE BARTON, "A Businessman's Doubts on Government Spending," *Fortune*, February 1943, p. 136.

380 "My other piece of advice, Copperfield," said Mr. Micawber, "you know. Annual income twenty pounds, annual expenditure nineteen nineteen six, result happiness. Annual income twenty pounds, annual expenditure twenty pounds ought and six, result misery. The blossom is blighted, the leaf is withered, the god of day goes down upon the dreary scene, and—and, in short, you are for ever floored. As I am!"

CHARLES DICKENS, *David Copperfield*, chapter 12, p. 185 (1950). First published 1849–1850.

381 And to preserve their independence, we must not let our rulers load us with perpetual debt. We must make our election between *economy and liberty*, or *profusion and servitude*.

THOMAS JEFFERSON, letter to Samuel Kercheval, July 12, 1816.—*The Writings of Thomas Jefferson*, ed. Paul L. Ford, vol. 10, p. 41 (1899).

382 I am for a government rigorously frugal & simple, applying all the possible savings of the public revenue to the discharge of the national debt; and not for a multiplication of officers & salaries merely to make partisans, & for increasing, by every device, the public debt, on the principle of it's being a public blessing.

Vice President THOMAS JEFFERSON, letter to Elbridge Gerry, January 26, 1799.—*The Writings of Thomas Jefferson*, ed. Paul L. Ford, vol. 7, p. 327 (1896).

383 I, however, place economy among the first and most important of republican virtues, and public debt as the greatest of the dangers to be feared.

THOMAS JEFFERSON, letter to William Plumer, July 21, 1816.—*The Writings of Thomas Jefferson*, ed. Andrew A. Lipscomb, vol. 15, p. 47 (1903).

384 I wish it were possible to obtain a single amendment to our constitution. I would be willing to depend on that alone for the reduction of the administration of our government to the genuine principles of it's constitution; I mean an additional article, taking from the federal government the power of borrowing.

Vice President THOMAS JEFFERSON, letter to John Taylor, November 26, 1798.—*The Writings of Thomas Jefferson*, ed. Paul L. Ford, vol. 7, p. 310 (1896).

385 One of the greatest disservices you can do a man is to lend him money that he can't pay back.

JESSE H. JONES, chairman of the Reconstruction Finance Corporation and later secretary of commerce.—*The New York Times Magazine*, July 2, 1939, p. 4.

Debt

386 As an individual who undertakes to live by borrowing, soon finds his original means devoured by interest, and next no one left to borrow from—so must it be with a government.

ABRAHAM LINCOLN, campaign circular from Whig Committee, March 4, 1843.—*The Collected Works of Abraham Lincoln*, ed. Roy P. Basler, vol. 1, p. 311 (1953).

387 Such was the origin of that debt which has since become the greatest prodigy that ever perplexed the sagacity and confounded the pride of statesmen and philosophers. At every stage in the growth of that debt the nation has set up the same cry of anguish and despair. At every stage in the growth of that debt it has been seriously asserted by wise men that bankruptcy and ruin were at hand. Yet still the debt went on growing; and still bankruptcy and ruin were as remote as ever.

THOMAS BABINGTON MACAULAY, *History of England*, vol. 8 (*The Complete Writings of Lord Macaulay*, vol. 8), chapter 19, p. 70 (1899).

388 Our national debt after all is an internal debt owed not only by the Nation but to the Nation. If our children have to pay interest on it they will pay that interest to themselves. A reasonable internal debt will not impoverish our children or put the Nation into bankruptcy.

President FRANKLIN D. ROOSEVELT, address to the American Retail Federation, Washington, D.C., May 22, 1939.—*The Public Papers and Addresses of Franklin D. Roosevelt, 1939*, p. 351 (1941).

Decision

389 Somewhere deep down we know that in the final analysis we *do* decide things and that even our decisions to let someone else decide are really *our* decisions, however pusillanimous.

HARVEY G. COX, *On Not Leaving It to the Snake*, p. viii (1967).

Quoted as "Not to decide is to decide" in *Peter's Quotations* by Laurence J. Peter, p. 297 (1977).

390 Some problems are so complex that you have to be highly intelligent and well informed just to be undecided about them.

LAURENCE J. PETER, *Peter's Almanac*, entry for September 24 (1982).

391 We have a choice: to plow new ground or let the weeds grow.

Attributed to JONATHAN WESTOVER, a fictitious person.

This sentence originally appeared in a Virginia Department of Agriculture report for fiscal year 1958–1959 entitled *Plowed Ground*. When the authors were pushed by a deadline and unable to find the kind of quotation they wanted, they made one up. In January 1970 the sentence was used on the cover of a Virginia Mental Health Commission report, *This Commonwealth's Commitment*. An effort to learn more about Westover after this report appeared uncovered the origin of the sentence.—*Richmond Times-Dispatch*, January 26, 1970, p. B1.

392 I am well aware of the Toil and Blood and Treasure, that it will cost Us to maintain this Declaration, and support and defend these States.—Yet through all the Gloom I can see the Rays of ravishing Light and Glory. I can see that the End is more than worth all the Means. And that Posterity will tryumph in that Days Transaction, even altho We should rue it, which I trust in God We shall not.

JOHN ADAMS, letter to Abigail Adams, July 3, 1776.—*Adams Family Correspondence,* ed. L. H. Butterfield, vol. 2, p. 31 (1963).

393 In 1776, the Americans laid before Europe that noble Declaration, which ought to be hung up in the nursery of every king, and blazoned on the porch of every royal palace.

HENRY THOMAS BUCKLE, *History of Civilization in England,* vol. 2, chapter 7, p. 341 (1903). First published in 1861.

394 We must never cease to proclaim in fearless tones the great principles of freedom and the rights of man which are the joint inheritance of the English-speaking world and which through Magna Carta, the Bill of Rights, the Habeas Corpus, trial by jury, and the English common law find their most famous expression in the American Declaration of Independence.

WINSTON CHURCHILL, "The Sinews of Peace," address at Westminster College, Fulton, Missouri, March 5, 1946.—*Winston S. Churchill: His Complete Speeches, 1897–1963,* ed. Robert Rhodes James, vol. 7, p. 7288 (1974).

Churchill noted at the beginning of his speech that it was unusual for a private visitor to be introduced to an academic audience by the president of the United States, and that he was honored that President Truman had traveled a thousand miles to join them. Churchill and Truman had traveled together from Washington, D.C., by train.

395 We must all hang together, or most assuredly we shall all *hang separately.*

Currently attributed to Benjamin Franklin, at the signing of the Declaration of Independence in 1776, by many dictionaries of quotations. For notes concerning its authenticity, see *Ben Franklin Laughing,* ed. P. M. Zall, p. 154 (1980).

396 We hold these truths to be sacred & undeniable; that all men are created equal & independant, that from that equal creation they derive rights inherent & inalienable, among which are the preservation of life, & liberty, & the pursuit of happiness.

THOMAS JEFFERSON, " 'Original Rough Draught' of the Declaration of Independence," June 1776.—*The Papers of Thomas Jefferson,* ed. Julian P. Boyd, vol. 1, p. 423 (1950).

397 We hold these truths to be self-evident: That all men are created equal, that they are endowed by their creator with certain inalienable rights, among these are life, liberty and the pursuit of happiness, that to secure these rights governments are instituted among men. We . . . solemnly publish and declare, that these colonies are and of right ought to be free and independent states . . . and for the support of this declaration, with a firm reliance on the protection of divine providence, we mutually pledge our lives, our fortunes and our sacred honour.

THOMAS JEFFERSON, "The Declaration of Independence," *The Papers of Thomas Jefferson,* ed. Julian P. Boyd, vol. 1, pp. 429, 432 (1950).

Inscription on the southwest quadrant of the Jefferson Memorial, Washington, D.C. The inscription contains the ellipses above, but it omits other words without ellipses.

Defeat

398 But man is not made for defeat. A man can be destroyed but not defeated.

ERNEST HEMINGWAY, *The Old Man and the Sea,* p. 113 (1952).

399 He said that he felt "like the boy that stumped his toe,—'it hurt too bad to laugh, and he was too big to cry.' "

Attributed to ABRAHAM LINCOLN by John T. Morse, Jr., *Abraham Lincoln,* vol. 1, p. 149 (1893), referring to Lincoln's defeat by Senator Stephen Douglas in the 1858 senatorial campaign in Illinois.

Frank Leslie's Illustrated Newspaper, November 22, 1862, p. 131, attributed this reply to President Lincoln, when asked how he felt about the result of the New York election [where the Democratic candidate won the governorship]: "Somewhat like that boy in Kentucky, who stubbed his toe while running to see his sweetheart. The boy said he was too big to cry, and far too badly hurt to laugh."

Adlai Stevenson told this story in his nationally-televised concession speech after the 1952 presidential election: "Someone asked me, as I came in, down on the street, how I felt, and I was reminded of a story that a fellow-townsman of ours used to tell—Abraham Lincoln. They asked him how he felt once after an unsuccessful election. He said that he was too old to cry, but it hurt too much to laugh."—*The Papers of Adlai E. Stevenson,* ed. Walter Johnson, vol. 4, p. 188 (1974). The speech was delivered at the Leland Hotel, Springfield, Illinois, in the early hours of November 5, 1952.

Defense

400 The Soviets have really been quite single-minded. They increased their defense expenditures as we increased ours. And they increased their defense expenditures as we decreased ours.

HAROLD BROWN, secretary of defense, testimony, January 31, 1979.—*Department of Defense Appropriations for Fiscal Year 1980,* hearings before a Subcommittee of the Committee on Appropriations, United States Senate, 96th Congress, 1st session, p. 278 (1979).

More succinctly, Brown noted, "Soviet spending has shown no response to U.S. restraint—when we build they build; when we cut they build," in a statement before a joint meeting of the House and Senate Budget Committees in early 1979 regarding the fiscal 1980 budget.

401 I do not hold that we should rearm in order to fight. I hold that we should rearm in order to parley.

Prime Minister WINSTON CHURCHILL, radio broadcast, London, October 8, 1951.—*Winston S. Churchill: His Complete Speeches, 1897–1963,* ed. Robert Rhodes James, vol. 8, p. 8257 (1974).

402 Today is Trinity Sunday. Centuries ago words were written to be a call and a spur to the faithful servants of Truth and Justice: "Arm yourselves, and be ye men of valor, and be in readiness for the conflict; for it is better for us to perish in battle than to look upon the outrage of our nation and our altar. As the Will of God is in Heaven, even so let it be."

WINSTON CHURCHILL, first radio address as prime minister, London, May 19, 1940.—*Winston S. Churchill: His Complete Speeches, 1897–1963,* ed. Robert Rhodes James, vol. 6, p. 6223 (1974).

He was referring to the heroism of the biblical Maccabees found in I Maccabees (Apocrypha) 3:58–60.

403 The worst to be feared and the best to be expected can be simply stated.

The *worst* is atomic war.

The *best* would be this: a life of perpetual fear and tension; a burden of arms draining the wealth and the labor of all peoples; a wasting of strength that defies the American system or the Soviet system or any system to achieve true abundance and happiness for the peoples of this earth.

Every gun that is made, every warship launched, every rocket fired signifies, in the final sense, a theft from those who hunger and are not fed, those who are cold and are not clothed.

This world in arms is not spending money alone.

It is spending the sweat of its laborers, the genius of its scientists, the hopes of its children.

The cost of one modern heavy bomber is this: a modern brick school in more than 30 cities.

It is two electric power plants, each serving a town of 60,000 population.

It is two fine, fully equipped hospitals.

It is some 50 miles of concrete highway.

We pay for a single fighter plane with a half million bushels of wheat.

We pay for a single destroyer with new homes that could have housed more than 8,000 people.

This, I repeat, is the best way of life to be found on the road the world has been taking.

This is not a way of life at all, in any true sense. Under the cloud of threatening war, it is humanity hanging from a cross of iron.

President DWIGHT D. EISENHOWER, "The Chance for Peace," address delivered before the American Society of Newspaper Editors, Washington, D.C., April 16, 1953.—*Public Papers of the Presidents of the United States: Dwight D. Eisenhower, 1953*, p. 182.

404 A strong defense is the surest way to peace. Strength makes détente attainable. Weakness invites war, as my generation—my generation—knows from four very bitter experiences. Just as America's will for peace is second to none, so will America's strength be second to none. We cannot rely on the forbearance of others to protect this Nation. The power and diversity of the Armed Forces, active Guard and Reserve, the resolve of our fellow citizens, the flexibility in our command to navigate international waters that remain troubled are all essential to our security.

President GERALD R. FORD, address to a joint session of Congress, August 12, 1974.—*Public Papers of the Presidents of the United States: Gerald R. Ford, 1974*, p. 11.

405 To draw around the whole nation the strength of the General Government, as a barrier against foreign foes, . . . to equalize and moderate the public contributions, that while the requisite services are invited by due renumeration, nothing beyond this may exist to attract the attention of our citizens from the pursuits of useful industry, nor unjustly to burthen those who continue in those pursuits—these are functions of the General Government on which you have a right to call.

President THOMAS JEFFERSON, letter to Amos Marsh, November 20, 1801.—*The Writings of Thomas Jefferson*, ed. Andrew A. Lipscomb, vol. 10, p. 293 (1903).

406 All the armies of Europe, Asia and Africa combined, with all the treasure of the earth (our own excepted) in their military chest; with a Buonaparte for a commander, could not by force take a drink from the Ohio or make a track on the Blue Ridge in a trial of a thousand years.

ABRAHAM LINCOLN, address before the Young Men's Lyceum, Springfield, Illinois, January 27, 1838.—*The Collected Works of Abraham Lincoln,* ed. Roy P. Basler, vol. 1, p. 109 (1953).

407 We are confident that we can penetrate any enemy defenses with our missiles. We know that we are more than the equal of any nation in the world.

ROBERT S. MCNAMARA, secretary of defense, conversation with newsmen after testifying before a joint session of the Senate Armed Services Committee and Defense Appropriations subcommittee, January 24, 1967, as reported by *The New York Times,* January 25, 1967, p. 17. McNamara denied there was an antimissile gap.

408 Fifth Column.

EMILIO MOLA. A term used by General Mola during the seige of Madrid in 1936, referring to the contingent of supporters within the city who would aid the army's four columns attacking from outside.

A fully documented account of the term, its spread, its popularity, and its change of meaning may be found in Dwight L. Bolinger, "Fifth Column Marches On," *American Speech,* February 1944, pp. 47–49. The first use in English, in a report from Spain, appears in *The New York Times,* October 17, 1936, p. 9, col. 4.

409 That is not to say that we can relax our readiness to defend ourselves. Our armament must be adequate to the needs, but our faith is not primarily in these machines of defense but in ourselves.

Admiral CHESTER W. NIMITZ, speech at the University of California, Berkeley, March 22, 1950.—The *San Francisco Chronicle,* March 23, 1950, p. 7, reported only the second sentence, but both can be found on a typed line of quotations by Admiral Nimitz received from the Navy Department Library.

410 If we desire to avoid insult, we must be able to repel it; if we desire to secure peace, one of the most powerful instruments of our rising prosperity, it must be known, that we are at all times ready for War.

President GEORGE WASHINGTON, fifth annual address to Congress, December 13, 1793.—*The Writings of George Washington,* ed. John C. Fitzpatrick, vol. 33, p. 166 (1940).

411 To be prepared for War is one of the most effectual means of preserving peace.

President GEORGE WASHINGTON, first annual address to Congress, January 8, 1790.—*The Writings of George Washington,* ed. John C. Fitzpatrick, vol. 30, p. 491 (1939).

412 A government without the power of defence! it is a solecism.

JAMES WILSON, speech, Pennsylvania Convention on the adoption of the Federal Constitution, Philadelphia, Pennsylvania, December 11, 1787.—*The Debates in the Several State Conventions on the Adoption of the Federal Constitution,* ed. Jonathan Elliot, vol. 2, p. 520 (1836).

Wilson, the leader of the Federalist forces at the convention, was the only member of the Pennsylvania Convention who had been part of the Federal Convention writing the Constitution.

Democracy

413 Remember, democracy never lasts long. It soon wastes, exhausts, and murders itself. There never was a democracy yet that did not commit suicide.

JOHN ADAMS, letter to John Taylor, April 15, 1814.—*The Works of John Adams*, ed. Charles Francis Adams, vol. 6, p. 484 (1851).

414 When I examined my political faith I found that my strongest belief was in democracy according to my own definition. Democracy—the essential thing as distinguished from this or that democratic government—was primarily an attitude of mind, a spiritual testament, and not an economic structure or a political machine. The testament involved certain basic beliefs—that the personality was sacrosanct, which was the meaning of liberty; that policy should be settled by free discussion; that normally a minority should be ready to yield to a majority, which in turn should respect a minority's sacred things. It seemed to me that democracy had been in the past too narrowly defined and had been identified illogically with some particular economic or political system such as *laissez-faire* or British parliamentarism. I could imagine a democracy which economically was largely socialist and which had not our constitutional pattern.

JOHN BUCHAN, LORD TWEEDSMUIR, *Pilgrim's Way*, p. 222 (1940, reprinted 1979).

415 Democracy will prevail when men believe the vote of Judas as good as that of Jesus Christ.

Attributed to THOMAS CARLYLE, by Wendell Phillips, in "The Scholar in a Republic," address at the centennial anniversary of the Phi Beta Kappa of Harvard College, Cambridge, Massachusetts, June 30, 1881.—Carlos Martyn, *Wendell Phillips, the Agitator*, p. 581 (1890). Unverified.

416 You can never have a revolution in order to establish a democracy. You must have a democracy in order to have a revolution.

G. K. CHESTERTON, *Tremendous Trifles*, chapter 12, p. 63 (1955).

417 Many forms of Government have been tried, and will be tried in this world of sin and woe. No one pretends that democracy is perfect or all-wise. Indeed, it has been said that democracy is the worst form of Government except all those other forms that have been tried from time to time.

WINSTON CHURCHILL, speech, House of Commons, November 11, 1947.—*Winston S. Churchill: His Complete Speeches, 1897–1963*, ed. Robert Rhodes James, vol. 7, p. 7566 (1974).

418 A democracy unsatisfied [by support of the people] cannot long survive. . . . We live in probably the most turbulent and tormented times in the history of this nation. Criticize . . . disagree, yes, but also we have as leaders an obligation to be fair and keep in perspective what we are and what we hope to be.

JOHN B. CONNALLY, JR., secretary of the treasury, off-the-cuff remarks at American Society of Newspaper Editors luncheon, Washington, D.C., April 19, 1972, as reported by *The Washington Post*, April 20, 1972, p. C3.

419 Here is Democracy's opportunity. Here is the opportunity to be of service to the people. Here is the chance for this party to have been of service to the people of the United States. Here is our chance to have been of help to the poor man. Here is our chance to have relieved him of the burdens and to have given him the benefits of a government that could have promoted the enterprises and furnished the conveniences and the facilities needed by every man, woman, and child in this country.

Senator HUEY LONG, remarks in the Senate, May 17, 1932, *Congressional Record*, vol. 75, p. 10394.

420 I have long been convinced that institutions purely democratic must, sooner or later, destroy liberty, or civilisation, or both.

THOMAS BABINGTON MACAULAY, letter to Henry Stephens Randall, May 23, 1857.—*The Letters of Thomas Babington Macaulay*, ed. Thomas Pinney, vol. 6, p. 94 (1981).

See note at No. 334 about this letter.

421 I have not the smallest doubt that, if we had a purely democratic government here, the effect would be the same. Either the poor would plunder the rich, and civilisation would perish; or order and property would be saved by a strong military government, and liberty would perish.

THOMAS BABINGTON MACAULAY, letter to Henry Stephens Randall, May 23, 1857.—*The Letters of Thomas Babington Macaulay*, ed. Thomas Pinney, vol. 6, pp. 94–95 (1981).

See note at No. 334 about this letter.

422 The cure for the evils of democracy is more democracy!

H. L. MENCKEN, *Notes on Democracy*, pp. 4, 73 (1926).

423 Democracy is the theory that the common people know what they want, and deserve to get it good and hard.

H. L. MENCKEN, *A Little Book in C Major*, p. 19 (1916).

424 A democracy cannot exist as a permanent form of government. It can only exist until the voters discover that they can vote themselves largesse from the public treasury. From that moment on, the majority always votes for the candidates promising the most benefits from the public treasury with the result that a democracy always collapses over loose fiscal policy, always followed by a dictatorship. The average age of the world's greatest civilizations has been 200 years.

Attributed to ALEXANDER FRASER TYTLER, LORD WOODHOUSELEE. Unverified.

425 It is not, perhaps, unreasonable to conclude, that a pure and perfect democracy is a thing not attainable by man, constituted as he is of contending elements of vice and virtue, and ever mainly influenced by the predominant principle of self-interest. It may, indeed, be confidently asserted, that there never was that government called a republic, which was not ultimately ruled by a single will, and, therefore, (however bold may seem the paradox,) virtually and substantially a monarchy.

ALEXANDER FRASER TYTLER, LORD WOODHOUSELEE, *University History*, vol. 1, book 2, chapter 6, p. 216 (1838).

426 Democracy is cumbersome, slow and inefficient, but in due time, the voice of the people will be heard and their latent wisdom will prevail.

Author unknown. Attributed to Thomas Jefferson, but unverified.

Democratic party

427 No, sir, th' dimmycratic party ain't on speakin' terms with itsilf. Whin ye see two men with white neckties go into a sthreet car an' set in opposite corners while wan mutthers "Thraiter" an' th' other hisses "Miscreent" ye can bet they're two dimmycratic leaders thryin' to reunite th' gran' ol' party.

FINLEY PETER DUNNE, *Mr. Dooley's Opinions*, p. 93 (1901).

428 The southern Democrats are in the saddle and the northern Democrats must tag along as best they may, no matter what ill may betide.

Representative JOHN JACOB ROGERS, remarks in the House, May 2, 1913, *Congressional Record*, vol. 50, p. 42.

429 I am not a member of any organized party—I am a Democrat.

WILL ROGERS.—P. J. O'Brien, *Will Rogers, Ambassador of Good Will, Prince of Wit and Wisdom*, chapter 9, p. 162 (1935).

"Rogers was a lifelong Democrat but he studiously avoided partisanship. He contributed to the Democratic campaign funds, but at the same time he frequently appeared on benefit programs to raise money for the Republican treasury. Republican leaders sought his counsel in their campaigns as often as did the Democrats" (p. 162).

430 We can make this thing into a Party, instead of a Memory.

WILL ROGERS, letter to Al Smith regarding the Democratic party, January 19, 1929.—*The Autobiography of Will Rogers*, ed. Donald Day, p. 197 (1949).

431 You've got to be [an] optimist to be a Democrat, and you've got to be a humorist to stay one.

WILL ROGERS, Good Gulf radio show, June 24, 1934.—*Radio Broadcasts of Will Rogers*, ed. Steven K. Gragert, p. 92 (1983).

Destiny

432 [Ivan:] "Imagine that you are creating a fabric of human destiny with the object of making men happy in the end, giving them peace and rest at last, but that it was essential and inevitable to torture to death only one tiny creature—that baby beating its breast with its fist, for instance—and to found that edifice on its unavenged tears, would you consent to be the architect on those conditions? Tell me, and tell the truth."

"No, I wouldn't consent," said Alyosha softly.

FYODOR DOSTOYEVSKY, *The Brothers Karamazov*, part 2, book 5, chapter 4, p. 291 (1945).

Destiny

433 Nature—pitiless in a pitiless universe—is certainly not concerned with the survival of Americans or, for that matter, of any of the two billion people now inhabiting this earth. Hence, our destiny, with the aid of God, remains in our own hands.

Senator J. WILLIAM FULBRIGHT, remarks in the Senate, February 2, 1954, *Congressional Record,* vol. 100, p. 1106.

Devil

434 *Roper*: So now you'd give the Devil benefit of law!
[*Sir Thomas*] *More*: Yes. What would you do? Cut a great road through the law to get after the Devil? . . . . Yes, I'd give the Devil benefit of law, for my own safety's sake.

ROBERT BOLT, *A Man for All Seasons,* act I, p. 39 (1967).

435 When there is question of saving souls, or preventing greater harm to souls, We feel the courage to treat with the devil in person.

POPE PIUS XI, speech to the students of the Mondragone college, May 14, 1929. Unverified but recounted in Robert A. Graham, *Vatican Diplomacy,* p. 351 (1959).

Differences

436 So, let us not be blind to our differences—but let us also direct attention to our common interests and to the means by which those differences can be resolved. And if we cannot end now our differences, at least we can help make the world safe for diversity.

President JOHN F. KENNEDY, commencement address at The American University, Washington, D.C., June 10, 1963.—*Public Papers of the Presidents of the United States: John F. Kennedy, 1963,* p. 462.

Diplomacy

437 DIPLOMACY, n. The patriotic art of lying for one's country.

AMBROSE BIERCE, *The Devil's Dictionary,* p. 72 (1948). Originally published in 1906 as *The Cynic's Word Book.*

438 A Foreign Secretary—and this applies also to a prospective Foreign Secretary—is always faced with this cruel dilemma. Nothing he can say can do very much good, and almost anything he may say may do a great deal of harm. Anything he says that is not obvious is dangerous; whatever is not trite is risky. He is forever poised between the cliché and the indiscretion.

HAROLD MACMILLAN, secretary of state for foreign affairs, remarks in the House of Commons, July 27, 1955.—*Parliamentary Debates (Hansard), House of Commons Official Report,* vol. 544, col. 1301.

439 These, then, are the qualities of my ideal diplomatist. Truth, accuracy, calm, patience, good temper, modesty and loyalty. They are also the qualities of an ideal diplomacy. "But," the reader may object, "you have forgotten intelligence, knowledge, discernment, prudence, hospitality, charm, industry, courage and even tact." I have not forgotten them. I have taken them for granted.

HAROLD NICOLSON, *Diplomacy,* chapter 3, p. 126 (1939).

440 Once upon a time all the animals in the zoo decided that they would disarm, and they arranged to have a conference to arrange the matter. So the Rhinoceros said when he opened the proceedings that the use of teeth was barbarous and horrible and ought to be strictly prohibited by general consent. Horns, which were mainly defensive weapons, would, of course, have to be allowed. The Buffalo, the Stag, the Porcupine, and even the little Hedgehog all said they would vote with the Rhino, but the Lion and the Tiger took a different view. They defended teeth and even claws, which they described as honourable weapons of immemorial antiquity. The Panther, the Leopard, the Puma, and the whole tribe of small cats all supported the Lion and the Tiger. Then the Bear spoke. He proposed that both teeth and horns should be banned and never used again for fighting by any animal. It would be quite enough if animals were allowed to give each other a good hug when they quarreled. No one could object to that. It was so fraternal, and that would be a great step towards peace. However, all the other animals were very offended with the Bear, and the Turkey fell into a perfect panic.

The discussion got so hot and angry, and all those animals began thinking so much about horns and teeth and hugging when they argued about the peaceful intentions that had brought them together that they began to look at one another in a very nasty way. Luckily the keepers were able to calm them down and persuade them to go back quietly to their cages, and they began to feel quite friendly with one another again.

WINSTON CHURCHILL, chancellor of the exchequer, speech, Aldersbrook, England, October 24, 1928.—*Winston S. Churchill: His Complete Speeches, 1897–1963,* ed. Robert Rhodes James, vol. 5, p. 4521 (1974). This is "a disarmament fable."

Dissent

441 Freedom of speech is useless without freedom of thought. And I fear that the politics of protest is shutting out the process of thought, so necessary to rational discussion. We are faced with the Ten Commandments of Protest:

Thou Shalt Not Allow Thy Opponent to Speak.
Thou Shalt Not Set Forth a Program of Thine Own.
Thou Shalt Not Trust Anybody Over Thirty.
Thou Shalt Not Honor Thy Father or Thy Mother.
Thou Shalt Not Heed the Lessons of History.
Thou Shalt Not Write Anything Longer than a Slogan.
Thou Shalt Not Present a Negotiable Demand.
Thou Shalt Not Accept Any Establishment Idea.
Thou Shalt Not Revere Any but Totalitarian Heroes.
Thou Shalt Not Ask Forgiveness for Thy Transgressions, Rather Thou Shalt Demand Amnesty for Them.

Vice President SPIRO T. AGNEW, speech to governors and their families, Washington, D.C., December 3, 1969.—*Collected Speeches of Spiro Agnew,* pp. 98–99 (1971).

442 There are only two choices: A police state in which all dissent is suppressed or rigidly controlled; or a society where law is responsive to human needs. If society is to be responsive to human needs, a vast restructuring of our laws is essential.

Realization of this need means adults must awaken to the urgency of the young people's unrest—in other words there must be created an adult unrest against the inequities and injustices in the present system. If the government is in jeopardy, it is not because we are unable to cope with revolutionary situations. Jeopardy means that either the leaders or the people do not realize they have all the tools required to make the revolution come true. The tools and the opportunity exist. Only the moral imagination is missing.

Justice WILLIAM O. DOUGLAS, *Points of Rebellion*, pp. 92–93 (1970).

443 If there is no struggle there is no progress. Those who profess to favor freedom and yet deprecate agitation, are men who want crops without plowing up the ground, they want rain without thunder and lightning. They want the ocean without the awful roar of its many waters. This struggle may be a moral one, or it may be a physical one, and it may be both moral and physical, but it must be a struggle. Power concedes nothing without a demand. It never did and it never will.

FREDERICK DOUGLASS, "West India Emancipation," speech delivered at Canandaigua, New York, August 4, 1857.—*The Life and Writings of Frederick Douglass*, ed. Philip S. Foner, vol. 2, p. 437 (1950).

444 We see political leaders replacing moral imperatives with a Southern strategy. We have seen all too clearly that there are men—now in power in this country—who do not respect dissent, who cannot cope with turmoil, and who believe that the people of America are ready to support repression as long as it is done with a quiet voice and a business suit. And it is up to us to prove that they are wrong.

JOHN V. LINDSAY, mayor of New York City, speech at University of California, Berkeley, April 2, 1970, as reported by *The Washington Post*, April 3, 1970, p. 3.

445 There are a lot of bleeding hearts around who just don't like to see people with helmets and guns. All I can say is go and bleed . . . It is more important to keep law and order in society than to be worried about weak-kneed people . . . Society must take every means at its disposal to defend itself against the emergence of a parallel power which defies the elected power.

PIERRE ELLIOTT TRUDEAU, prime minister of Canada, impromptu exchange with reporters, criticizing those who questioned his decision to use soldiers to protect federal officials and diplomats in Ottawa, October 13, 1970.—*Time*, October 26, 1970, p. 33.

On October 16 Trudeau invoked the 1914 War Measures Act, for the first time in peacetime, to deal with Separatist terrorists who had kidnapped two high-ranking officials.

Dog

446 Gentlemen of the jury, the best friend a man has in this world may turn against him and become his enemy. His son or daughter whom he has reared with loving care may prove ungrateful. Those who are nearest and dearest to us—those whom we trust with our happiness and our good name—may become traitors to their faith. The money that a man has he may lose. It flies away from him, perhaps when he needs it most. A man's reputation may be sacrificed in a moment of ill-considered action. The people who are prone to fall on their knees to do us honor when success is with us may be the first to throw the stone of malice when failure settles its cloud upon our heads. The one absolute, unselfish friend that man can have in this selfish world—the one that never deserts him, the one that never proves ungrateful or treacherous—is his dog.

Gentlemen of the jury, a man's dog stands by him in prosperity and in poverty, in health and in sickness. He will sleep on the cold ground, where the wintry winds blow and the snow drives fiercely, if only he can be near his master's side. He will kiss the hand that had no food to offer, he will lick the wounds and sores that come in encounter with the roughness of the world. He guards the sleep of his pauper master as if he were a prince. When all other friends desert, he remains. When riches take wings and reputation falls to pieces he is as constant in his love as the sun in its journey through the heavens. If fortune drives the master forth an outcast in the world, friendless and homeless, the faithful dog asks no higher privilege than that of accompanying him to guard against danger, to fight against his enemies. And when the last scene of all comes, and death takes the master in its embrace, and his body is laid away in the cold ground, no matter if all other friends pursue their way, there by his graveside will the noble dog be found, his head between his paws, his eyes sad but open in alert watchfulness, faithful and true even to death.

GEORGE GRAHAM VEST, "Eulogy on the Dog," speech during lawsuit, 1870.—*Congressional Record,* October 16, 1914, vol. 51, Appendix, pp. 1235–36.

A foxhound named Drum "was known far and near as one of the fastest and least uncertain of hunting dogs." He was shot and his owner sued for damages, $150 being the maximum allowed. The case started before a Justice of the Peace, was appealed to another court and transferred to another. It was in the final trial, in the State Circuit Court at Warrensburg, Missouri, that Vest made his speech, the peroration of which is above.

According to the recollection of Thomas T. Crittenden, counsel for the defendant and later governor of Missouri, Vest made no reference to the evidence but confined himself to a tribute to canine affection and fidelity. "He seemed to recall from history all the instances where dogs had displayed intelligence and fidelity to man. He quoted more lines of history and poetry about them than I had supposed had been written . . . It was as perfect a piece of oratory as ever was heard from pulpit or bar. Court, jury, lawyers, and audience were entranced. I looked at the jury and saw all were in tears."—Gustav Kobbe, *A Tribute to the Dog,* pp. 9–18 (1911).

According to John F. Phillips, former law partner of Vest and a member of the House of Representatives, whose comments appear in the *Congressional Record* with the eulogy on the dog, the jury returned a verdict for the plaintiff for $500, far more than the sum sued for. The excess was remitted. Vest was elected to the Senate eight years later and served 1879–1904.

Doing

447 Ye been oure lord, dooth with youre owene thyng
Right as yow list.

GEOFFREY CHAUCER, "Clerk's Tale," lines 652–53, *The Canterbury Tales,* p. 108 (1957).

An early version of "Do your own thing."

448 It is better to light one candle than curse the darkness.

Christopher Society, motto, the sentiment of which is an old Chinese proverb.—Bergen Evans, *Dictionary of Quotations,* p. 87, no. 7 (1968).

"I have lost more than a beloved friend. I have lost an inspiration. She would rather light a candle than curse the darkness, and her glow has warmed the world."—Adlai E. Stevenson, U.S. ambassador to the United Nations, tribute to Eleanor Roosevelt after her death on November 7, 1962, as reported by *The New York Times,* November 8, 1962, p. 34.

449 It is some time since so few have been asked to do so much for so many on so little.

ELFAN B. REES, "The Refugee and the United Nations," *International Conciliation,* June 1953, p. 281.

Dr. Rees, secretary of the United Nations Commission of the Churches on International Affairs, was speaking of the U.N. budget designated to assist World War II refugees.

Doing good

450 But ye, brethren, be not weary in well doing. And if any man obey not our word by this epistle, note that man, and have no company with him, that he may be ashamed.

The Bible, II Thessalonians 3:13–14.

451 [Only by] the good influence of our conduct may we bring salvation in human affairs; or like a fatal comet we may bring destruction in our train.

Attributed to DESIDERIUS ERASMUS by Senator J. William Fulbright, "In Need of a Consensus," Penrose Memorial Lecture, delivered to the American Philosophical Society, Philadelphia, Pennsylvania, April 20, 1961.—*Proceedings* of the Society, August 1961, p. 352. Unverified.

452 Do all the good you can,
By all the means you can,
In all the ways you can,
In all the places you can,
At all the times you can,
To all the people you can,
As long as ever you can.

JOHN WESLEY, "Rule of Conduct," *Letters of John Wesley*, ed. George Eayrs, p. 423, footnote (1915).

453 Through this toilsome world, alas!
Once and only once I pass;
If a kindness I may show,
If a good deed I may do
To a suffering fellow man,
Let me do it while I can.
No delay, for it is plain
I shall not pass this way again.

Author unknown, "I Shall Not Pass This Way Again."—*The Best Loved Poems of the American People*, ed. Hazel Felleman, p. 77 (1936).

Doomsday

454 Turning and turning in the widening gyre
The falcon cannot hear the falconer;
Things fall apart; the centre cannot hold;
Mere anarchy is loosed upon the world,
The blood-dimmed tide is loosed, and everywhere
The ceremony of innocence is drowned;
The best lack all conviction, while the worst
Are full of passionate intensity.

WILLIAM BUTLER YEATS, "The Second Coming," lines 1–8, *The Variorum Edition of the Poems of W. B. Yeats*, ed. Peter Allt and Russell K. Alspach, pp. 401–2 (1957).

455 Due to the lack of experienced trumpeters, the end of the world has been postponed for three weeks.

Author unknown. Handmade cardboard sign hung in the United States Capitol, House Rules Committee chambers, c. 1970. Photocopies of this sentence have appeared on the walls of other work areas in the Capitol.

456 The world must be coming to an end. Children no longer obey their parents and every man wants to write a book.

Attributed to the writing on a tablet, unearthed not far from Babylon and dated back to 2800 B.C.—Leewin B. Williams, *Encyclopedia of Wit, Humor and Wisdom*, p. 299 (1949).

An expanded version of this appears as, "Our earth is degenerate in these latter days; there are signs that the world is speedily coming to an end; bribery and corruption are common; children no longer obey their parents; every man wants to write a book and the end of the world is evidently approaching," attributed to an Assyrian stone tablet of about 2800 B.C.—William L. Patty and Louise S. Johnson, *Personality and Adjustment*, p. 277 (1953).

Both of the above quotations would seem to be spurious. Perhaps "every man wants to write a book" may be related to "of making many books there is no end," Ecclesiastes 12:12.

Dreams

457 The dreamer dies, but never dies the dream,
Though Death shall call the whirlwind to his aid,
Enlist men's passions, trick their hearts with hate,
Still shall the Vision live! Say nevermore
That dreams are fragile things. What else endures
Of all this broken world save only dreams!

DANA BURNET, "Who Dreams Shall Live," lines 11–16, *Poems*, p. 209 (1915).

458 Perhaps you have heard the story of Christopher Wren, one of the greatest of English architects, who walked one day unrecognized among the men who were at work upon the building of St. Paul's cathedral in London which he had designed. "What are you doing?" he inquired of one of the workmen, and the man replied, "I am cutting a piece of stone." As he went on he put the same question to another man, and the man replied, "I am earning five shillings twopence a day." And to a third man he addressed the same inquiry and the man answered, "I am helping Sir Christopher Wren build a beautiful cathedral." That man had vision. He could see beyond the cutting of the stone, beyond the earning of his daily wage, to the creation of a work of art—the building of a great cathedral. And in your life it is important for you to strive to attain a vision of the larger whole.

Attributed to LOUISE BUSH-BROWN, director of the Pennsylvania School of Horticulture for Women. Unverified.

459 To dream the impossible dream,
To fight the unbeatable foe,
To bear with unbearable sorrow,
To run where the brave dare not go.

To right the unrightable wrong,
To love pure and chaste from afar,
To try when your arms are too weary,
To reach the unreachable star!

JOE DARION (lyrics) and MITCH LEIGH (music), "The Impossible Dream (The Quest)," stanzas 1 and 2, *Man of La Mancha* (1965), © Helena Music Corp./Andrew Scott, Inc.

460 They are not long, the days of wine and roses:
Out of a misty dream
Our path emerges for a while, then closes
Within a dream.

ERNEST DOWSON, "They are not long, the weeping and the laughter," stanza 2, *The Poems and Prose of Ernest Dowson*, p. 22 (1919).

461 *What happens to a dream deferred?*
Does it dry up
like a raisin in the sun?
Or fester like a sore—
And then run?
Does it stink like rotten meat?
Or crust and sugar over—
like a syrupy sweet?

Maybe it just sags
like a heavy lead.

Or does it explode?

LANGSTON HUGHES, "Harlem," *Selected Poems of Langston Hughes*, p. 268 (1959).

462 I have a dream that one day this nation will rise up and live out the true meaning of its creed: "We hold these truths to be self-evident that all men are created equal.". . . I have a dream that my four little children will one day live in a nation where they will not be judged by the color of their skin but by the content of their character. I have a dream today.

MARTIN LUTHER KING, JR., "I Have a Dream," speech at the Lincoln Memorial, Washington, D.C., August 28, 1963.—*Congressional Record*, April 18, 1968, vol. 114, p. 9165.

This speech culminated a march on Washington for jobs and freedom.

463 There are those, I know, who will reply that the liberation of humanity, the freedom of man and mind, is nothing but a dream. They are right. It is. It is the American Dream.

ARCHIBALD MACLEISH, "We Have Purpose . . . We All Know It," *Life*, May 30, 1960, p. 93.

This was one of a series of essays in *Life* magazine and *The New York Times* on "The National Purpose."

464 The republic is a dream
Nothing happens unless first a dream.

CARL SANDBURG, "Washington Monument by Night," stanza 4, *The Complete Poems of Carl Sandburg*, rev. and expanded ed., p. 282 (1970).

President Ronald Reagan quoted this before a joint session of Congress, April 28, 1981, and added: "As Carl Sandburg said, all we need to begin with is a dream that we can do better than before. All we need to have is faith, and that dream will come true. All we need to do is act, and the time for action is now."—*Public Papers of the Presidents of the United States: Ronald Reagan, 1981*, p. 394.

465 You see things; and you say "Why?" But I dream things that never were; and I say "Why not?"

GEORGE BERNARD SHAW, *Back to Methuselah*, act I, *Selected Plays with Prefaces*, vol. 2, p. 7 (1949). The serpent says these words to Eve.

President John F. Kennedy quoted these words in his address to the Irish Parliament, Dublin, June 28, 1963.—*Public Papers of the Presidents of the United States: John F. Kennedy, 1963*, p. 537.

Senator Robert F. Kennedy used a similar quotation as a theme of his 1968 campaign for the presidential nomination: "Some men see things as they are and say, why; I dream things that never were and say, why not." Senator Edward M. Kennedy quoted these words of Robert Kennedy's in his eulogy for his brother in 1968.—*The New York Times*, June 9, 1968, p. 56.

466 If you have built castles in the air, your work need not be lost; that is where they should be. Now put the foundations under them.

HENRY DAVID THOREAU, *Walden*, chapter 18, p. 427 (1966). Originally published in 1854.

Duty

467 *Let no guilty man escape if it can be avoided.* Be specially vigilant—or instruct those engaged in the prosecution of fraud to be—against all who insinuate that they have high influence to protect—or to protect them. No personal consideration should stand in the way of performing a public duty.

President ULYSSES S. GRANT, endorsement added to letter received July 29, 1875.

The exposure of the Whisky Ring, a secret association of distillers and federal officials defrauding the government, was a major scandal in 1875. W. D. W. Barnard, a St. Louis banker, wrote to Grant that officials in St. Louis claimed Grant would sustain them to protect Orville Babcock, his private secretary. Grant added the above endorsement and referred the letter to Benjamin H. Bristow, secretary of the treasury, who led the efforts to expose the ring.—Louis A. Coolidge, *Ulysses S. Grant*, p. 479 (1922). Also see John A. Carpenter, *Ulysses S. Grant*, p. 150 and p. 196, note 5 (1970).

468 When occasions present themselves, in which the interests of the people are at variance with their inclinations, it is the duty of the persons whom they have appointed to be the guardians of those interests, to withstand the temporary delusion, in order to give them time and opportunity for more cool and sedate reflection.

ALEXANDER HAMILTON, *The Federalist*, ed. Benjamin F. Wright, no. 71, p. 459 (1961).

469 Duty, then is the sublimest word in our language. Do your duty in all things . . . You cannot do more, you should never wish to do less.

Attributed to ROBERT E. LEE, in a letter to his son, G. W. Custis Lee, dated April 5, 1852, and published in the New York *Sun*, November 26, 1864, p. 2.

Although accepted as authentic by many nineteenth century writers, and used for the inscription under Lee's bust in New York University's Hall of Fame in 1901, repudiation of its authenticity began shortly after its publication, beginning with articles in two Richmond, Virginia, newspapers. The most complete summary of evidence indicating the letter was spurious may be found in Charles Alfred Graves, *The Forged Letter of General Robert E. Lee* (1914) and its *Supplementary Paper* (1915).

Duty

470 The lark is up to meet the sun,
The bee is on the wing;
The ant its la-bor has be-gun,
The woods with music ring.
Shall birds, and bees, and ants, be wise,
While I my mo-ments waste?
O let me with the morn-ing rise,
And to my du-ty haste.

WILLIAM HOLMES MCGUFFEY, "The lark is up to meet the sun," *McGuffey's Eclectic Primer,* newly rev., lesson 81, p. 54 (1849).

471 We all know our duty better than we discharge it.

JOHN RANDOLPH of Roanoke.—William Cabell Bruce, *John Randolph of Roanoke, 1773–1833,* vol. 2, chapter 7, p. 205 (1922, reprinted 1970).

Randolph was a member of Congress 1799–1813, 1815–1817, and 1819–1829.

472 Majesty: when a stupid man is doing something he is ashamed of, he always declares that it is his duty.

GEORGE BERNARD SHAW, *Caesar and Cleopatra,* act III, in *Selected Plays with Prefaces,* vol. 3, p. 418 (1948). Apollodorus is speaking to Cleopatra.

473 There is no duty we so much underrate as the duty of being happy.

ROBERT LOUIS STEVENSON, "An Apology for Idlers," *Virginibus Puerisque and Later Essays,* p. 88 (1969). Written between 1874–1879.

474 We live in an age disturbed, confused, bewildered, afraid of its own forces, in search not merely of its road but even of its direction. There are many voices of counsel, but few voices of vision; there is much excitement and feverish activity, but little concert of thoughtful purpose. We are distressed by our own ungoverned, undirected energies and do many things, but nothing long. It is our duty to find ourselves.

WOODROW WILSON, president of Princeton, baccalaureate address, Princeton University, Princeton, New Jersey, June 9, 1907.—*The Papers of Woodrow Wilson,* ed. Arthur S. Link, vol. 17, p. 194.

Earth

475 The land was ours before we were the land's.
She was our land more than a hundred years
Before we were her people. She was ours
In Massachusetts, in Virginia,
But we were England's, still colonials,
Possessing what we still were unpossessed by,
Possessed by what we now no more possessed.
Something we were withholding made us weak
Until we found out that it was ourselves
We were withholding from our land of living,
And forthwith found salvation in surrender.
Such as we were we gave ourselves outright
(The deed of gift was many deeds of war)

To the land vaguely realizing westward,
But still unstoried, artless, unenhanced,
Such as she was, such as she would become.

ROBERT FROST, "The Gift Outright," *The Poetry of Robert Frost*, ed. Edward C. Lathem, p. 348 (1967).

Frost read this poem at President John F. Kennedy's inauguration, January 20, 1961.

476 I have very large ideas of the mineral wealth of our Nation. I believe it practically inexhaustible. It abounds all over the western country, from the Rocky Mountains to the Pacific, and its development has scarcely commenced. . . . Immigration, which even the war has not stopped, will land upon our shores hundred of thousands more per year from overcrowded Europe. I intend to point them to the gold and silver that waits for them in the West. Tell the miners from me, that I shall promote their interests to the utmost of my ability; because their prosperity is the prosperity of the Nation, and we shall prove in a very few years that we are indeed the *treasury of the world.*

President ABRAHAM LINCOLN, message for the miners of the West, delivered verbally to Speaker of the House Schuyler Colfax, who was about to depart on a trip to the West, in the afternoon of April 14, 1865, before Lincoln left for Ford's Theatre. Colfax delivered the message to a large crowd of citizens in Denver, Colorado, May 27, 1865.—Edward Winslow Martin, *The Life and Public Services of Schuyler Colfax*, pp. 187–88 (1868).

477 We travel together, passengers on a little space ship, dependent on its vulnerable reserves of air and soil; all committed for our safety to its security and peace; preserved from annihilation only by the care, the work, and, I will say, the love we give our fragile craft. We cannot maintain it half fortunate, half miserable, half confident, half despairing, half slave—to the ancient enemies of man—half free in a liberation of resources undreamed of until this day. No craft, no crew can travel safely with such vast contradictions. On their resolution depends the survival of us all.

ADLAI E. STEVENSON, U.S. ambassador to the United Nations, last major speech, to the Economic and Social Council of the United Nations, Geneva, Switzerland, July 9, 1965.—*Adlai Stevenson of the United Nations*, ed. Albert Roland, Richard Wilson, and Michael Rahill, p. 224 (1965).

478 The materials of wealth are in the earth, in the seas, and in their natural and unaided productions.

DANIEL WEBSTER, remarks in the Senate, March 12, 1838.—*The Writings and Speeches of Daniel Webster*, vol. 8, p. 177 (1903).

Economy

479 The first theory is that if we make the rich richer, somehow they will let a part of their prosperity trickle down to the rest of us. The second theory . . . was the theory that if we make the average of mankind comfortable and secure, their prosperity will rise upward . . . through the ranks.

FRANKLIN D. ROOSEVELT, governor of New York, campaign address, Detroit, Michigan, October 2, 1932.—*The Public Papers and Addresses of Franklin D. Roosevelt, 1928–1932*, p. 772 (1938).

Economy

480 Too often in recent history liberal governments have been wrecked on rocks of loose fiscal policy.

President FRANKLIN D. ROOSEVELT, request to Congress to effect drastic economies in the government, March 10, 1933.—*The Public Papers and Addresses of Franklin D. Roosevelt, 1933*, p. 50 (1938).

Education

481 The Science of Government it is my Duty to study, more than all other Sciences: the Art of Legislation and Administration and Negotiation, ought to take Place, indeed to exclude in a manner all other Arts.—I must study Politicks and War that my sons may have liberty to study Mathematicks and Philosophy. My sons ought to study Mathematicks and Philosophy, Geography, natural History, Naval Architecture, navigation, Commerce and Agriculture, in order to give their Children a right to study Painting, Poetry, Musick, Architecture, Statuary, Tapestry and Porcelaine.

JOHN ADAMS, letter to Abigail Adams, after May 12, 1780.—*Adams Family Correspondence*, ed. L. H. Butterfield, vol. 3, p. 342 (1973).

This letter has not been dated precisely, but appears to have been written after Adams's letter to his wife on May 12, and before one written to her on May 15.

482 [The educated differ from the uneducated] as much as the living from the dead.

Attributed to ARISTOTLE.—Diogenes Laertius, *Lives of Eminent Philosophers*, trans. R. D. Hicks, vol. 1, book 5, section 19, p. 463 (1942).

He also credits Aristotle with saying: "Teachers who educated children deserved more honour than parents who merely gave them birth; for bare life is furnished by the one, the other ensures a good life" (p. 463).

Diogenes Laertius, a third century A.D. Greek writer, was a literary compiler rather than a philosopher. Considered the most significant secondary source of information covering the history of philosophy, his book is the only work of its kind that has come down to us substantially intact. A special feature of it is the citation of original excerpts.—Michael Grant, *Greek and Latin Authors*, pp. 131–32 (1980).

483 Education is the cheap defence of nations.

Attributed to EDMUND BURKE.—Charles Noël Douglas, comp., *Forty Thousand Quotations*, p. 573 (1921). Unverified.

484 Give a man a fish and you feed him for a day. Teach a man to fish and you feed him for a lifetime.

Chinese proverb.—*The International Thesaurus of Quotations*, ed. Rhoda Thomas Tripp, p. 76, no. 3 (1970).

485 Upon the education of the people of this country the fate of this country depends.

BENJAMIN DISRAELI, speech, House of Commons, June 15, 1874.—*Parliamentary Debates (Commons)*, 3d series, vol. 219, col. 1618 (1874).

486 An education isn't how much you have committed to memory, or even how much you know. It's being able to differentiate between what you do know and what you don't. It's knowing where to go to find out what you need to know; and it's knowing how to use the information you get.

Attributed to WILLIAM FEATHER.—August Kerber, *Quotable Quotes on Education*, p. 17 (1968). Unverified.

487 The whole art of teaching is only the art of awakening the natural curiosity of young minds for the purpose of satisfying it afterwards; and curiosity itself can be vivid and wholesome only in proportion as the mind is contented and happy.

ANATOLE FRANCE, *The Crime of Sylvestre Bonnard* (vol. 1 of *The Works of Anatole France*), trans. Lafcadio Hearn, part 2, chapter 4, June 6, 1860, p. 198 (1924).

488 By educating the young generation along the right lines, the People's State will have to see to it that a generation of mankind is formed which will be adequate to this supreme combat that will decide the destinies of the world.

ADOLF HITLER, *Mein Kampf*, trans. James Murphy, p. 357 (1939).

489 The benefits of education and of useful knowledge, generally diffused through a community, are essential to the preservation of a free government.

Attributed to SAM HOUSTON by the University of Texas. This quotation appears on the verso of the title-page of all University of Texas publications. Unverified.

490 Enlighten the people generally, and tyranny and oppressions of body and mind will vanish like evil spirits at the dawn of day.

THOMAS JEFFERSON, letter to P. S. du Pont de Nemours, April 24, 1816.—*The Writings of Thomas Jefferson*, ed. Paul L. Ford, vol. 10, p. 25 (1899).

This sentence is one of many quotations inscribed on Cox Corridor II, a first floor House corridor, U.S. Capitol.

491 I know no safe depository of the ultimate powers of the society but the people themselves; and if we think them not enlightened enough to exercise their control with a wholesome discretion, the remedy is not to take it from them, but to inform their discretion by education. This is the true corrective of abuses of constitutional power.

THOMAS JEFFERSON, letter to William Charles Jarvis, September 28, 1820.—*The Writings of Thomas Jefferson*, ed. Paul L. Ford, vol. 10, p. 161 (1899).

492 If a nation expects to be ignorant and free, in a state of civilization, it expects what never was and never will be. The functionaries of every government have propensities to command at will the liberty and property of their constituents. There is no safe deposit for these but with the people themselves; nor can they be safe with them without information. Where the press is free, and every man able to read, all is safe.

THOMAS JEFFERSON, letter to Colonel Charles Yancey, January 6, 1816.—*The Writings of Thomas Jefferson*, ed. Paul L. Ford, vol. 10, p. 4 (1899).

493 Every child must be encouraged to get as much education as he has the ability to take. We want this not only for his sake—but for the nation's sake. Nothing matters more to the future of our country: not military preparedness—for armed might is worthless if we lack the brain power to build a world of peace; not our productive economy—for we cannot sustain growth without trained manpower; not our democratic system of government—for freedom is fragile if citizens are ignorant.

President LYNDON B. JOHNSON, special message to the Congress, "Toward Full Educational Opportunity," January 12, 1965.—*Public Papers of the Presidents of the United States: Lyndon B. Johnson, 1965,* book 1, p. 26.

494 I ask that you offer to the political arena, and to the critical problems of our society which are decided therein, the benefit of the talents which society has helped to develop in you. I ask you to decide, as Goethe put it, whether you will be an anvil—or a hammer. The question is whether you are to be a hammer—whether you are to give to the world in which you were reared and educated the broadest possible benefits of that education.

Senator JOHN F. KENNEDY, commencement address, Smith College, Northampton, Massachusetts, June 8, 1958.—Transcript, p. 2.

The Home Book of Quotations, ed. Burton Stevenson, 9th ed., p. 84, no. 8 (1964) gives the quotation from Goethe as follows: "Thou must (in commanding and winning, or serving and losing, suffering or triumphing) be either anvil or hammer," citing his play, *Der Gross-Cophta,* act II, though it has not been found there.

495 If you plan for a year, plant a seed. If for ten years, plant a tree. If for a hundred years, teach the people. When you sow a seed once, you will reap a single harvest. When you teach the people, you will reap a hundred harvests.

KUAN CHUNG, *Kuan-tzu (Book of Master Kuan).—Kuan tzu chi p'ing,* ed. Ling Juheng, vol. 1, p. 12 (1970). Title romanized.

496 Learned Institutions ought to be favorite objects with every free people. They throw that light over the public mind which is the best security against crafty & dangerous encroachments on the public liberty.

JAMES MADISON, letter to W. T. Barry, August 4, 1822.—*The Writings of James Madison,* ed. Gaillard Hunt, vol. 9, p. 105 (1910).

These words are inscribed in the Madison Memorial Hall, Library of Congress James Madison Memorial Building.

497 What spectacle can be more edifying or more seasonable, than that of Liberty & Learning, each leaning on the other for their mutual & surest support?

JAMES MADISON, letter to W. T. Barry, August 4, 1822.—*The Writings of James Madison,* ed. Gaillard Hunt, vol. 9, p. 108 (1910).

These words are inscribed to the right of the main entrance of the Library of Congress James Madison Memorial Building.

498 Education, then, beyond all other devices of human origin, is the great equalizer of the conditions of men,—the balance-wheel of the social machinery.

HORACE MANN, twelfth annual report to the Massachusetts State Board of Education, 1848.—*Life and Works of Horace Mann,* ed. Mrs. Mary Mann, vol. 3, p. 669 (1868).

Mann served in Congress 1848–1853.

499 I also desire to encourage and foster an appreciation of the advantages which I implicitly believe will result from the union of the English-speaking peoples throughout the world and to encourage in the students from the United States of North America[,] who will benefit from the American Scholarships to be established for the reason above given at the University of Oxford under this my Will[,] an attachment to the country from which they have sprung but without I hope withdrawing them or their sympathies from the land of their adoption or birth.

CECIL J. RHODES, *The Last Will and Testament of Cecil John Rhodes*, ed. W. T. Stead, pp. 24–29 (1902). The will was dated July 1, 1899.

500 To educate a man in mind and not in morals is to educate a menace to society.

Attributed to THEODORE ROOSEVELT.—August Kerber, *Quotable Quotes of Education*, p. 138 (1968). Unverified.

501 Education has for its object the formation of character. To curb restive propensities, to awaken dormant sentiments, to strengthen the perceptions, and cultivate the tastes, to encourage this feeling and repress that, so as finally to develop the child into a man of well proportioned and harmonious nature—this is alike the aim of parent and teacher.

HERBERT SPENCER, *Social Statics*, part 2, chapter 17, p. 180 (1851).

502 These ceremonies and the National Statuary Hall will teach the youth of the land in succeeding generations as they come and go that the chief end of human effort in a sublunary view should be usefulness to mankind, and that all true fame which should be perpetuated by public pictures, statues, and monuments, is to be acquired only by noble deeds and high achievements and the establishment of a character founded upon the principles of truth, uprightness, and inflexible integrity.

Representative ALEXANDER H. STEPHENS, remarks in the House, February 15, 1881, upon Vermont's presentation of a statue of Jacob Collamer to Statuary Hall.—*Congressional Record*, vol. 11, p. 1611.

503 "Via ovicipitum dura est," or, for the benefit of the engineers among you: "The way of the egghead is hard."

ADLAI E. STEVENSON, lecture at Harvard University, Cambridge, Massachusetts, March 17, 1954.—Stevenson, *Call to Greatness*, p. xi (1954).

504 In point of substantial merit the law school belongs in the modern university no more than a school of fencing or dancing.

THORSTEIN VEBLEN, *The Higher Learning in America*, p. 211 (1918).

505 In the conditions of modern life the rule is absolute, the race which does not value trained intelligence is doomed. Not all your heroism, not all your social charm, not all your wit, not all your victories on land or at sea, can move back the finger of fate. To-day we maintain ourselves. To-morrow science will have moved forward yet one more step, and there will be no appeal from the judgment which will then be pronounced on the uneducated.

ALFRED NORTH WHITEHEAD, "The Aims of Education—a Plea for Reform," *The Organisation of Thought*, chapter 1, p. 28 (1917, reprinted 1974).

Elections

506 How shall we avert the dire calamities with which we are threatened? The answer comes from the graves of our fathers: By the frequent election of new men. Other help or hope for the salvation of free government there is none under heaven. If history does not teach this, we have read it all wrong.

JEREMIAH S. BLACK, "The Third Term: Reasons Against It," *Essays and Speeches of Jeremiah S. Black*, ed. Chauncey F. Black, p. 383 (1886). First published in *The North American Review*, March 1880.

507 What is it we all seek for in an election? To answer its real purposes, you must first possess the means of knowing the fitness of your man; and then you must retain some hold upon him by personal obligation or dependence.

EDMUND BURKE, "Reflections on the Revolution in France," 1790, *The Works of the Right Honorable Edmund Burke*, vol. 3, p. 483 (1899).

508 I have serious doubts about the value of debates in a presidential election. They tend to be a test of reaction time rather than a genuine exposition of the participants' philosophies and programs. Further, in debate, candidates tend to overstate their views. In the 1960 situation I had a very practical objection: Nixon was widely known; Kennedy was not; dramatic debates would therefore help Kennedy.

DWIGHT D. EISENHOWER, *The White House Years*, vol. 2, p. 599, footnote (1965).

509 An election is coming. Universal peace is declared, and the foxes have a sincere interest in prolonging the lives of the poultry.

GEORGE ELIOT (Mary Ann Evans), *Felix Holt, the Radical*, chapter 5, p. 63 (1980). First published 1866.

510 When the shadow of the Presidential and Congressional election is lifted we shall, I hope be in a better temper to legislate.

Representative JAMES A. GARFIELD, letter to General Hazen, August 1, 1867, concerning his difficulty in getting legislation passed to reduce the size of the military.—*The Life and Letters of James Abram Garfield*, vol. 1, p. 421 (1925).

511 I am superstitious. I have scarcely known a party, preceding an election, to call in help from the neighboring states, but they lost the state.

ABRAHAM LINCOLN, letter to James W. Grimes, governor of Iowa, July 12, 1856.—*The Collected Works of Abraham Lincoln*, ed. Roy P. Basler, vol. 2, p. 348 (1953).

512 And as it [the federal district] is to be appropriated to this use with the consent of the State ceding it; as the State will no doubt provide in the compact for the rights, and the consent of the citizens inhabiting it; as the inhabitants will find sufficient inducements of interest to become willing parties to the cession; as they will have had their voice in the election of the Government which is to exercise authority over them; as a municipal Legislature for local purposes, derived from their own suffrages, will of course be allowed them; and as the authority of the Legislature of the State, and of the inhabitants of the ceded part of it, to concur in the cession, will be derived from the whole people of the State, in their adoption of the Constitution, every imaginable objection seems to be obviated.

JAMES MADISON, *The Federalist*, ed. Benjamin F. Wright, no. 43, p. 310 (1961).

513 Looking back, I am content. Win or lose, I have told you the truth as I see it. I have said what I meant and meant what I said. I have not done as well as I should like to have done, but I have done my best, frankly and forthrightly; no man can do more, and you are entitled to no less.

ADLAI E. STEVENSON, governor of Illinois, remarks on a radio and television broadcast summing up his presidential campaign on election eve, Chicago, Illinois, November 3, 1952.—*Major Campaign Speeches of Adlai E. Stevenson, 1952*, p. 315 (1953).

514 I know nothing grander, better exercise, better digestion, more positive proof of the past, the triumphant result of faith in human kind, than a well-contested American national election.

WALT WHITMAN, "Democratic Vistas," *Collect*, in *The Complete Poetry and Prose of Walt Whitman*, vol. 2, p. 228 (1948).

Enemies

515 Have you forgotten the story of "Lorna Doone"—how the Doones, men of high family, who had fallen under the displeasure of the Government, had betaken themselves to the Doone Valley, surrounded on all sides by precipitous mountains, and from this strongly fortified position levied their blackmail upon the surrounding country, killing and robbing and outraging the people of the land until the citizens were aroused and determined to extirpate them? Do you recall how the men of the eastern county gathered together on the eastern mountain, and the men from the western county gathered on the western mountain, with their arms and cannon ready to fall upon the Doones and destroy them, when by some untoward accident a cannon from the western ranks was trained across the valley and shot into the ranks of the men of the east, and how, inflamed by this accident, the men on the east trained their guns across the valley into the ranks of the men of the west, and while these foolish people were slaughtering one another, the Doones sallied forth and put both counties to flight and continued to rob and kill and outrage for years to come.

Let us heed the lesson, my countrymen! Let me say to Governor Kitchin and Senator Simmons and Chief Justice Clark: The Doones are in the valley. I pray you, gentlemen, train your guns a little lower.

CHARLES B. AYCOCK, governor of North Carolina, address prepared for delivery in Raleigh, North Carolina, April 12, 1912.—R. D. W. Connor and Clarence Poe, *The Life and Speeches of Charles Brantley Aycock*, p. 361–62 (1912).

Aycock did not give the address because he died while making a speech on April 4. The story is from *Lorna Doone* by R. D. Blackmore.

516 Now the trumpet summons us again—not as a call to bear arms, though arms we need—not as a call to battle, though embattled we are—but a call to bear the burden of a long twilight struggle, year in and year out, "rejoicing in hope, patient in tribulation"—a struggle against the common enemies of man: tyranny, poverty, disease and war itself.

President JOHN F. KENNEDY, inaugural address, January 20, 1961.—*The Public Papers of the Presidents of the United States: John F. Kennedy, 1961*, p. 2. The words in quotation marks are from the Bible, Romans 12:12.

This is one of seven inscriptions carved on the walls at the gravesite of John F. Kennedy, Arlington National Cemetery.

517 He who forgiveth, and is reconciled unto his enemy, shall receive his reward from God; for he loveth not the unjust doers.

Koran, sura 42.—*The Koran*, trans. George Sale, chapter 42, p. 361 (1887).

Enemies

518 We have met the enemy and they are ours—two ships, two brigs, one schooner and a sloop.

OLIVER HAZARD PERRY, message to General William Henry Harrison, September 10, 1813.

The earliest printed source for this is found in Robert B. McAfee, *History of the Late War in the Western Country,* chapter 8, p. 354 (1816), and the message in its entirety as given here is reprinted in *Messages and Letters of William Henry Harrison,* ed. Logan Esarey, vol. 2, p. 539 (1922, reprinted 1975).

Benson J. Lossing, *The Pictorial Field-Book of the War of 1812,* p. 530 (1868), has a facsimile of the Perry message, with the introduction, "When Perry's eye perceived at a glance that victory was secure, he wrote, in pencil, on the back of an old letter, resting it upon his navy cap, that remarkable dispatch to General Harrison whose first clause has been so often quoted." No source for the original message is given. The circumstances under which the message was written have been told in many biographies of both Perry and Harrison.

519 I have political enemies, of course—men who, influenced by party feeling, are not above attacking methods and possibly my official reputation; but personal ones—wretches willing to stab me in my homelife and affections, that I can not believe. My life has been as an open book. I have harmed no man knowingly and, as far as I know, no man has ever cherished a wish to injure me.

ANNA KATHERINE ROHLFS, *The Mayor's Wife,* p. 25 (1907).

520 To mortify and even to injure an opponent, reproach him with the very defect or vice . . . you feel . . . in yourself.

IVAN TURGENEV, "The Rule of Life," *Poems in Prose,* in his *A Reckless Character and Other Stories,* trans. Isabel F. Hapgood, p. 317 (1904).

This appeared in *Time,* March 5, 1951, p. 31, in a different translation: "If you desire to put your enemy in the wrong or even to damage his reputation, blame him for the very vice which you feel in yourself."

Enemies from within

521 We have met the enemy and he is us.

WALT KELLY, the words of Pogo in an Earth Day, 1971, cartoon strip, *The Best of Pogo,* ed. Mrs. Walt Kelly and Bill Crouch, Jr., p. 163 (1982).

This succinct expression was derived from a sentence in the Foreword of an earlier publication, *The Pogo Papers* (1953): "Resolve then, that on this very ground, with small flags waving and tinny blasts on tiny trumpets, we shall meet the enemy, and not only may he be ours, he may be us."

See also No. 518.

522 At what point then is the approach of danger to be expected? I answer, if it ever reach us, it must spring up amongst us. It cannot come from abroad. If destruction be our lot, we must ourselves be its author and finisher. As a nation of freemen, we must live through all time, or die by suicide.

President ABRAHAM LINCOLN, address before the Young Men's Lyceum, Springfield, Illinois, January 27, 1838.—*The Collected Works of Abraham Lincoln,* ed. Roy P. Basler, vol. 1, p. 109 (1953).

See also No. 334.

523 Since the general civilization of mankind, I believe there are more instances of the abridgment of the freedom of the people, by gradual and silent encroachments of those in power, than by violent and sudden usurpations.

JAMES MADISON, speech in the Virginia Convention, Richmond, Virginia, June 6, 1788.—*The Papers of James Madison*, ed. Robert A. Rutland and Charles F. Hobson, vol. 11, p. 79 (1977).

This general defense of the Constitution was presented by Madison in response to Patrick Henry's lengthy attack on the Constitution the preceding day.

524 Again people are looking for scapegoats. But this time the attack comes not from the outside but from within, from extremist splinter groups of the New Left made up of students and—I am sorry to acknowledge—also of some faculty who would like to see our colleges and universities denigrated, maligned and even shut down. They insinuate, distort, accuse, their aim being not to identify and correct real abuses, but always rather by crying alarm intentionally to arouse and inflame passions in order to build support for "non-negotiable demands." Clearly the old McCarthy technique is at work again. . . . It is more difficult to maintain a realistic sense of human limitation, to refuse to become frustrated and angry; to analyze, to assess, to seek to understand and explain; to determine to be adult and fair; and thus to work patiently to improve while refusing to succumb to either cynicism or hopelessness. It is the long way around, but it is the civilized way, and the only way for those [who] have come truly to understand the role of humane learning.

NATHAN M. PUSEY, president of Harvard, speech at baccalaureate service, Cambridge, Massachusetts, June 9, 1970.—*The New York Times*, June 10, 1970, pp. 1, 30.

525 I have beheld no day since the commencement of hostilities that I have thought her liberties in such eminent danger as at present. Friends and foes seem now to combine to pull down the goodly fabric as we have hitherto been raising at the expence of so much time, blood, and treasure; and unless the bodies politick will exert themselves to bring things back to first principles, correct abuses, and punish our internal foes, inevitable ruin must follow.

General GEORGE WASHINGTON, letter to George Mason, March 27, 1779.—*The Writings of George Washington*, ed. John C. Fitzpatrick, vol. 14, p. 300 (1936).

Energy

526 Our decision about energy will test the character of the American people and the ability of the President and the Congress to govern this Nation. This difficult effort will be the "moral equivalent of war," except that we will be uniting our efforts to build and not to destroy.

President JIMMY CARTER, address to the nation on the energy problem, April 18, 1977.—*Public Papers of the Presidents of the United States: Jimmy Carter, 1977*, book 1, p. 656.

Carter was quoting William James, who used the phrase in his essay, "The Moral Equivalent of War": "So long as anti-militarists propose no substitute for war's disciplinary function, no *moral equivalent* of war, analogous, as one might say, to the mechanical equivalent of heat, so long they fail to realize the full inwardness of the situation. . . . We must make new energies and hardihoods continue the manliness to which the military mind so faithfully clings. Martial virtues must be the enduring cement; intrepidity, contempt of softness, surrender of private interest, obedience to command, must still remain the rock upon which states are built."—*International Conciliation,* February 1910, pp. 13, 15. The entire issue consisted of James's essay.

527 We must proceed with our own energy development. Exploitation of domestic petroleum and natural gas potentialities, along with nuclear, solar, geothermal, and nonfossil fuels is vital. We will never again permit any foreign nation to have Uncle Sam over a barrel of oil.

Vice President GERALD R. FORD, speech to the Anti-Defamation League of B'nai B'rith, West Palm Beach, Florida, January 26, 1974.—*Congressional Record,* February 4, 1974, vol. 120, p. 2044.

England

528 I have not become the King's First Minister in order to preside over the liquidation of the British Empire.

Prime Minister WINSTON CHURCHILL, speech, Lord Mayor's luncheon, London, November 10, 1942.—*Winston S. Churchill: His Complete Speeches, 1897–1963,* ed. Robert Rhodes James, vol. 6, p. 6695 (1974).

529 The late M. Venizelos observed that in all her wars England—he should have said Britain, of course—always wins one battle—the last.

Prime Minister WINSTON CHURCHILL, speech at Lord Mayor's luncheon, London, November 10, 1942.—*Winston S. Churchill: His Complete Speeches, 1897–1963,* ed. Robert Rhodes James, vol. 6, p. 6693 (1974).

Eleuthérios Venizélos was a Greek statesman who lived from 1864–1936. During World War I, he championed the cause of the Allies.

530 Go into the length and breadth of the world, ransack the literature of all countries, find, if you can, a single voice, a single book—find, I would almost say, as much as a single newspaper article, unless the product of the day, in which the conduct of England towards Ireland is anywhere treated except with profound and bitter condemnation.

WILLIAM E. GLADSTONE, speech on home rule, June 7, 1886.—*The Speeches of the Right Hon. W. E. Gladstone,* ed. A. W. Hutton and H. J. Cohen, vol. 9, p. 127 (1902).

531 We do not intend to part from the Americans and we do not intend to be satellites. I am sure they do not want us to be so. The stronger we are, the better partners we shall be; and I feel certain that as the months pass we shall draw continually closer together with mutual confidence and respect.

Prime Minister HAROLD MACMILLAN, broadcast to the nation, London, January 17, 1957.—*Vital Speeches of the Day,* February 1, 1957, p. 247.

This was his first broadcast as prime minister.

532 [Britons] would rather take the risk of civilizing communism than being kicked around by the unlettered pot-bellied money magnates of the United States.

TOM O'BRIEN, M.P., as quoted by *The New York Times,* August 23, 1949, p. 4.

533 I hold that the real policy of England—apart from questions which involve her own particular interests—is to be the champion of justice and right; pursuing that course with moderation and prudence, not becoming the Quixote of the world, but giving the weight of her moral sanction and support wherever she thinks that justice is, and wherever she thinks that wrong has been done.

LORD PALMERSTON, remarks in the House of Commons defending his foreign policy, March 1, 1848.—*Hansard's Parliamentary Debates,* 3d series, vol. 97, col. 122.

534 I return you many thanks for the honour you have done me; but Europe is not to be saved by any single man. England has saved herself by her exertions, and will, as I trust, save Europe by her example.

WILLIAM PITT, the younger, response to the Lord Mayor's toast to Pitt's health as the "Saviour of Europe," Lord Mayor's banquet, London, November 9, 1805.—Philip Henry Stanhope, *Life of the Right Honourable William Pitt,* vol. 4, p. 346 (1867, reprinted 1970).

This was Pitt's last public utterance.

535 There is nothing so bad or so good that you will not find an Englishman doing it; but you will never find an Englishman in the wrong. He does everything on principle. He fights you on patriotic principles; he robs you on business principles; he enslaves you on imperial principles.

GEORGE BERNARD SHAW, *Man of Destiny,* one act play, in his *Complete Plays with Prefaces,* vol. 1, p. 743 (1962). Napoleon is speaking.

536 They [the British] are like their own beer: froth on top, dregs at bottom, the middle excellent.

Attributed to VOLTAIRE (François Marie Arouet).—*The Home Book of Quotations,* ed. Burton Stevenson, 9th ed., p. 560, no. 1 (1964).

English language

537 The gift of a common tongue is a priceless inheritance and it may well some day become the foundation of a common citizenship.

Prime Minister WINSTON CHURCHILL, speech at Harvard University, Cambridge, Massachusetts, September 6, 1943.—*Winston S. Churchill: His Complete Speeches, 1897–1963,* ed. Robert Rhodes James, vol. 7, p. 6825 (1974).

538 This is the sort of pedantry up with which I will not put.

WINSTON CHURCHILL, marginal note after receiving a civil servant's objection to the ending of a sentence with a preposition and the use of a dangling participle in official documents.—Kay Halle, *Irrepressible Churchill,* p. 166 (1966).

In other versions of this anecdote, the word "English" is often used instead of "pedantry."

539 England and America are two countries separated by the same language.

Attributed to GEORGE BERNARD SHAW.—"Picturesque Speech and Patter," *Reader's Digest,* November 1942, p. 100.

This has not been verified in his published writings, but a number of quotation books published after 1942 have included this quotation, without naming the original published source.

540 The difference between the almost right word and the right word is really a large matter—'tis the difference between the lightning-bug and the lightning.

MARK TWAIN (Samuel L. Clemens).—George Bainton, *The Art of Authorship*, pp. 87–88 (1890).

Bainton asked leading authors for "literary reminiscences, methods of work, and advice to young beginners," and compiled their answers to produce his book.

Environment

541 I've often thought that if our zoning boards could be put in charge of botanists, of zoologists and geologists, and people who know about the earth, we would have much more wisdom in such planning than we have when we leave it to the engineers.

Justice WILLIAM O. DOUGLAS, remarks at conference sponsored by the American Histadrut Cultural Exchange Institute, Harriman, New York, February 17–19, 1967.—*Government and the Democratic Process; A Symposium by American and Israeli Experts*, ed. Judd L. Teller, p. 16 (1969).

542 You could cover the whole world with asphalt, but sooner or later green grass would break through.

Attributed to ILYA EHRENBURG.—*The New York Times Book Review*, October 22, 1967, p. 1. Unverified.

Patricia Blake, author of the book review, obtained this quotation from the late Max Hayward, who may have gotten it directly from Ehrenburg.

543 We have come tardily to the tremendous task of cleaning up our environment. We should have moved with similar zeal at least a decade ago. But no purpose is served by post-mortems. With visionary zeal but the greatest realism, we must now address ourselves to the vast problems that confront us.

Representative GERALD R. FORD, Earth Day address, Grand Rapids, Michigan, April 22, 1970.—*Gerald R. Ford, Selected Speeches*, ed. Michael V. Doyle, p. 84 (1973).

544 In the last few decades entire new categories of waste have come to plague and menace the American scene. . . . Pollution is growing at a rapid rate. . . . Pollution destroys beauty and menaces health. It cuts down on efficiency, reduces property values and raises taxes. . . . Almost all these wastes and pollutions are the result of activities carried on for the benefit of man. A prime national goal must be an environment that is pleasing to the senses and healthy to live in. Our Government is already doing much in this field. We have made significant progress. But more must be done.

President LYNDON B. JOHNSON, special message to the Congress on conservation and restoration of natural beauty, February 8, 1965.—*Public Papers of the Presidents of the United States: Lyndon B. Johnson, 1965*, book 1, pp. 161–62.

545 Never before has man had such capacity to control his own environment, to end thirst and hunger, to conquer poverty and disease, to banish illiteracy and massive human misery. We have the power to make this the best generation of mankind in the history of the world—or to make it the last.

President JOHN F. KENNEDY, address before the General Assembly of the United Nations, New York City, September 20, 1963.—*Public Papers of the Presidents of the United States: John F. Kennedy, 1963,* p. 696.

Epitaphs

546 Here was buried
Thomas Jefferson
author
of the Declaration of
American Independence
of
the Statute of Virginia
for Religious Freedom, and
Father of the University
of Virginia

THOMAS JEFFERSON, epitaph he wrote for himself and wanted on his tombstone.—*The Writings of Thomas Jefferson,* ed. Paul L. Ford, vol. 10, p. 396 (1899).

It is on his gravestone at Monticello.

547 Free at last, free at last
Thank God almighty
We are free at last

MARTIN LUTHER KING, JR., epitaph, South View Cemetery, Atlanta, Georgia.

King was buried on a site adjoining Ebenezer Baptist Church. He had quoted these words from a Negro spiritual to end his "I Have a Dream" speech given during the march on Washington, August 28, 1963, Washington, D.C.—Coretta Scott King, *The Words of Martin Luther King, Jr.,* p. 98 (1984).

See No. 462 for a quotation from the "I Have a Dream" speech.

548 If I take the wings of the morning, and dwell in the uttermost parts of the sea.

Inscription on the tombstone of Charles A. Lindbergh, on the island of Maui, Hawaii.—The Bible, Psalms 139:9.

549 Future times will hardly know how great a life
This simple stone commemorates—
The tradition of his Eloquence, his
Wisdom and his Wit may fade:
But he lived for ends more durable than fame,
His Eloquence was the protection of the poor and wronged;
His Learning illuminated the principles of Law—
In the admiration of his Peers,
In the respect of his People,
In the affection of his Family,
His was the highest place;
The just meed
Of his kindness and forbearance
His dignity and simplicity

Epitaphs

His brilliant genius and his unwearied industry
Unawed by Opinion,
Unseduced by Flattery,
Undismayed by Disaster,
He confronted Life with antique Courage
And Death with Christian Hope.

Excerpt from inscription on the monument over the grave of James Louis Petigru, St. Michael's churchyard, Charleston, South Carolina.—James Petrigru Carson, *Life, Letters and Speeches of James Louis Petigru, the Union Man of South Carolina*, p. 487 (1920).

Equality

550 Legislation to apply the principle of equal pay for equal work without discrimination because of sex is a matter of simple justice.

President DWIGHT D. EISENHOWER, annual message to the Congress on the State of the Union, January 5, 1956.—*Public Papers of the Presidents of the United States: Dwight D. Eisenhower, 1956*, p. 23.

Read before a joint session of Congress by a clerk of the House of Representatives.

551 It is a wise man who said that there is no greater inequality than the equal treatment of unequals.

Justice FELIX FRANKFURTER, dissenting, *Dennis* v. *United States*, 339 U.S. 184 (1949).

552 Equal laws protecting equal rights . . . the best guarantee of loyalty & love of country.

JAMES MADISON, letter to Jacob De La Motta, August 1820.—*The Writings of James Madison*, ed. Gaillard Hunt, vol. 9, p. 30 (1910).

These words are inscribed in the Madison Memorial Hall, Library of Congress James Madison Memorial Building.

553 All animals are equal
But some animals are more equal than others

GEORGE ORWELL, *Animal Farm*, chapter 10, p. 112 (1946).

554 In regard to this principle, that all men are born free and equal, if there is an animal on earth to which it does not apply—that is not born free, it is man—he is born in a state of the most abject want, and in a state of perfect helplessness and ignorance, which is the foundation of the connubial tie. . . . Who should say that all the soil in the world is equally rich, the first rate land in Kentucky and the Highlands of Scotland because the superficial content of the acre is the same, would be just as right as he who should maintain the absolute equality of man in virtue of his birth. The ricketty and scrofulous little wretch who first sees the light in a work-house, or in a brothel, and who feels the effects of alcohol before the effects of vital air, is not equal in any respect to the ruddy offspring of the honest yeoman; nay, I will go further, and say that a prince, provided he is no better born than royal blood will make him, is not equal to the healthy son of a peasant.

Senator JOHN RANDOLPH of Roanoke, remarks in the Senate, *Register of Debates*, vol. 2, March 2, 1826, col. 126.

Error

555 No mans error becomes his own Law; nor obliges him to persist in it.

THOMAS HOBBES, *Leviathan*, part 2, p. 237 (1950).

Europe

556 My conclusion will be simple. It will consist of saying, in the very midst of the sound and the fury of our history: "Let us rejoice." Let us rejoice, indeed, at having witnessed the death of a lying and comfort-loving Europe and at being faced with cruel truths.

ALBERT CAMUS, "Create Dangerously," lecture given at the University of Uppsala, Sweden, December 1957.—Camus, *Resistance, Rebellion and Death*, trans. Justin O'Brien, p. 270 (1961).

557 Europe extends to the Alleghenies; America lies beyond.

Attributed to RALPH WALDO EMERSON. Unverified.

558 Europe has been at peace since 1945. But it is a restless peace that's shadowed by the threat of violence.

Europe is partitioned. An unnatural line runs through the heart of a very great and a very proud nation [Germany]. History warns us that until this harsh division has been resolved, peace in Europe will never be secure.

We must turn to one of the great unfinished tasks of our generation—and that unfinished task is making Europe whole again.

President LYNDON B. JOHNSON, remarks before the National Conference of Editorial Writers, New York City, October 7, 1966.—*Public Papers of the Presidents of the United States: Lyndon B. Johnson, 1966*, book 2, p. 1126.

559 When France has a cold, all Europe sneezes.

KLEMENS VON METTERNICH.—This quotation could not be verified in the English translations of his *Mémoires*. It is attributed to him in George P. Gooch, *The Second Empire*, p. 18 (1960) and, in variant form, in Alan W. Palmer, *Quotations in History*, p. 154 (1976).

An American variation on this is: "There are those in South Carolina, and Mr. Pickens among the number who do not 'sneese when Mr. Calhoun takes snuff.' We are always amused when we hear the oft repeated slang—that South Carolina never speaks until Mr. Calhoun is heard."—*The Charleston Mercury*, June 20, 1846, p. 2, referring to former Representative Francis W. Pickens and to Senator John C. Calhoun.

Evil

560 The only thing necessary for the triumph of evil is for good men to do nothing.

Attributed to EDMUND BURKE, but never found in his works. It may be a paraphrase of Burke's view that "When bad men combine, the good must associate; else they will fall one by one, an unpitied sacrifice in a contemptible struggle" (*Thoughts on the Cause of the Present Discontents*, April 23, 1770).—*Bartlett's Familiar Quotations*, 15th ed., p. ix (1980).

See also No. 565.

561 The true rule, in determining to embrace, or reject any thing, is not whether it have *any* evil in it; but whether it have more of evil, than of good. There are few things *wholly* evil, or *wholly* good. Almost every thing, especially of governmental policy, is an inseparable compound of the two; so that our best judgment of the preponderance between them is continually demanded.

Representative ABRAHAM LINCOLN, remarks in the House, June 20, 1848.—*The Collected Works of Abraham Lincoln,* ed. Roy P. Basler, vol. 1, p. 484 (1953).

562 EVIL. That which one believes of others. It is a sin to believe evil of others, but it is seldom a mistake.

H. L. MENCKEN, *A Book of Burlesques,* p. 203 (1924).

563 He that has light within his own cleer brest
May sit i'th center, and enjoy bright day,
But he that hides a dark soul, and foul thoughts
Benighted walks under the mid-day Sun;
Himself is his own dungeon.

JOHN MILTON, "A Mask Presented at Ludlow Castle, 1634," lines 380–84, *The Works of John Milton,* vol. 1, part 1, p. 99 (1931). The title was changed to "Comus" for the stage version in 1737.

564 A good End cannot *sanctifie* evil Means; nor must we ever do *Evil,* that Good may come of it.

WILLIAM PENN, *Some Fruits of Solitude in Reflections & Maxims,* no. 537, p. 102 (1903, reprinted 1976).

565 The penalty good men pay for indifference to public affairs is to be ruled by evil men.

Attributed to PLATO on the letterhead of the Constitution Party. Unverified.

The Constitution Party was founded in 1952 and ceased in 1968, according to Edward L. and Frederick H. Schapsmeier, *Political Parties and Civil Action Groups,* pp. 122–23 (1981).

See also No. 560.

566 There are a thousand hacking at the branches of evil to one who is striking at the root, and it may be that he who bestows the largest amount of time and money on the needy is doing the most by his mode of life to produce that misery which he strives in vain to relieve.

HENRY DAVID THOREAU, *Walden,* chapter 1, p. 98 (1966). Originally published in 1854.

Excellence

567 The Good of man is the active exercise of his soul's faculties in conformity with excellence or virtue, or if there be several human excellences or virtues, in conformity with the best and most perfect among them.

ARISTOTLE, *Nicomachean Ethics,* trans. H. Rackham, book 1, chapter 7, section 15, p. 33 (1934).

President John F. Kennedy often paraphrased this idea. On May 8, 1963, he said to a group of foreign students: "The ancient Greek definition of happiness was the full use of your powers along lines of excellence."—*Public Papers of the Presidents of the United States: John F. Kennedy, 1963*, p. 380.

568 As I said in another connection: "An excellent plumber is infinitely more admirable than an incompetent philosopher. The society which scorns excellence in plumbing because plumbing is a humble activity and tolerates shoddiness in philosophy because it is an exalted activity will have neither good plumbing nor good philosophy. Neither its pipes nor its theories will hold water."

JOHN W. GARDNER, *Excellence, Can We Be Equal and Excellent Too?*, p. 86 (1961).
Gardner was secretary of health, education, and welfare 1965–1968.

569 Difficult, say you? Difficult to be a man of virtue, truly good, shaped and fashioned without flaw in the perfect figure of four-squared excellence, in body and mind, in act and thought?

SIMONIDES of Ceos.—*The Oedipus Tyrannus of Sophocles*, trans. J. T. Sheppard, Introduction, p. xxxi (1920).

Experience

570 Rulers, Statesmen, Nations, are wont to be emphatically commended to the teaching which experience offers in history. But what experience and history teach is this—that peoples and governments never have learned anything from history, or acted on principles deduced from it. Each period is involved in such peculiar circumstances, exhibits a condition of things so strictly idiosyncratic, that its conduct must be regulated by considerations connected with itself, and itself alone.

GEORG WILHELM FRIEDRICH HEGEL, *The Philosophy of History*, trans. J. Sibree, vol. 10, Introduction, p. 6 (1899).
See also Nos. 574 and 1292.

571 I have but one lamp by which my feet are guided; and that is the lamp of experience. I know of no way of judging the future but by the past.

PATRICK HENRY, speech to the Virginia Convention, Richmond, Virginia, March 23, 1775.—William Wirt, *Sketches of the Life and Character of Patrick Henry*, 9th ed., pp. 138–39 (1836, reprinted 1970). Language altered to first person.
For information on the authenticity of the text of this speech, see the notes at No. 1061.

572 Like anybody, I would like to live a long life. Longevity has its place. But I'm not concerned about that now. I just want to do God's will. And He's allowed me to go up to the mountain. And I've looked over, and I've seen the promised land. I may not get there with you, but I want you to know tonight that we as a people will get to the promised land.

MARTIN LUTHER KING, JR., address to sanitation workers, Memphis, Tennessee, April 3, 1968.—*The New York Times*, April 5, 1968, p. 24.
Dr. King made this statement the day before his assassination in Memphis.

573 We know nothing of what will happen in future, but by the analogy of experience.

ABRAHAM LINCOLN, speech on the sub-Treasury, in the hall of the House of Representatives, Springfield, Illinois, December 26, 1839.—*The Collected Works of Abraham Lincoln,* ed. Roy P. Basler, vol. 1, p. 166 (1953).

574 If history repeats itself, and the unexpected always happens, how incapable must Man be of learning from experience!

GEORGE BERNARD SHAW, appendix 2 to *Man and Superman,* "Maxims for Revolutionists," in his *Selected Plays with Prefaces,* vol. 3, p. 742 (1948).

See also Nos. 570 and 1292.

575 If little profits that an idle king,
By this still hearth, among these barren crags,
Match'd with an aged wife, I mete and dole
Unequal laws unto a savage race,
That hoard, and sleep, and feed, and know not me.
I cannot rest from travel; I will drink
Life to the lees. All times I have enjoy'd
Greatly, have suffer'd greatly, both with those
That loved me, and alone; on shore, and when
Thro' scudding drifts the rainy Hyades
Vext the dim sea. I am become a name;
For always roaming with a hungry heart
Much have I seen and known,—cities of men
And manners, climates, councils, governments,
Myself not least, but honor'd of them all,—
And drunk delight of battle with my peers,
Far on the ringing plains of windy Troy.
I am a part of all that I have met;
Yet all experience is an arch wherethro'
Gleams that untravell'd world whose margin fades
For ever and for ever when I move.
How dull it is to pause, to make an end,
To rust unburnish'd, not to shine in use!
As tho' to breathe were life! Life piled on life
Were all too little, and of one to me
Little remains; but every hour is saved
From that eternal silence, something more,
A bringer of new things; and vile it were
For some three suns to store and hoard myself,
And this gray spirit yearning in desire
To follow knowledge like a sinking star,
Beyond the utmost bound of human thought.
. . . .
It may be we shall touch the Happy Isles,
And see the great Achilles, whom we knew.
Tho' much is taken, much abides; and tho'
We are not now that strength which in old days
Moved earth and heaven, that which we are, we are,—
One equal temper of heroic hearts,
Made weak by time and fate, but strong in will
To strive, to seek, to find, and not to yield.

ALFRED, LORD TENNYSON, "Ulysses," lines 1–32 and 63–70, *The Poetic and Dramatic Works of Alfred Lord Tennyson*, pp. 117–18 (1899).

See also Nos. 11 and 1118.

576 We should be careful to get out of an experience only the wisdom that is in it—and stop there; lest we be like the cat that sits down on a hot stove-lid. She will never sit down on a hot stove-lid again—and that is well; but also she will never sit down on a cold one anymore.

MARK TWAIN (Samuel L. Clemens), *Following the Equator*, vol. 1 (vol. 5 of *The Writings of Mark Twain*), chapter 11, epigraph, p. 125 (1897, reprinted 1968).

577 I've seen the elephant, and I've heard the owl, and I've been to the other side of the mountain.

Author unknown. " 'Seeing the elephant,' though it has pre- and post-gold rush currency, was an immensely popular expression among the overlanders [those journeying in covered wagons to Oregon and California] . . . connoting, in the main, experiencing hardship and difficulty and somehow surviving. Emigrant diaries and letters are filled with humorous references to that ubiquitous animal."—John D. Unruh, Jr., *The Plains Across: The Overland Emigrants and the Trans-Mississippi West, 1840–60*, chapter 4, p. 443, note 22 (1979).

Experts

578 All my life I've known better than to depend on the experts. How could I have been so stupid, to let them go ahead?

President JOHN F. KENNEDY, conversation with Theodore C. Sorensen concerning the Bay of Pigs.—Sorensen, *Kennedy*, p. 309 (1965).

Exploration

579 We shall not cease from exploration
And the end of all our exploring
Will be to arrive where we started
And know the place for the first time.

T. S. ELIOT, "Little Gidding," last stanza, *Collected Poems, 1909–1962*, p. 208 (1963).

Secretary of Defense Robert S. McNamara was asked what major changes he would have made in United States policies in Vietnam during the previous week. He responded it was not yet an appropriate time to be talking with hindsight and then quoted the lines above to answer the question.—"Meet the Press" television program, February 4, 1968, transcript, p. 15.

Extremism

580 It seems to me that it is these extremists who are advocating a soft approach. Their oversimplifications and their baseless generalizations reflect the softness of those who cannot bear to face the burdens of a continuing struggle against a powerful and resourceful enemy. A truly tough approach, in my judgment, is one which accepts the challenge of communism with the courage and determination to meet it with every instrumentality of foreign policy—political and economic as well as military, and with the willingness to see the struggle through as far into the future as may be necessary. Those who seek to meet the challenge—or, in reality, to evade it—by bold adventures abroad and witch hunts at home are the real devotees of softness—the softness of seeking escape from painful realities by resort to illusory panaceas.

Senator J. WILLIAM FULBRIGHT, "Public Policy and Military Responsibility," speech at the opening session of the National War College and the Industrial College of the Armed Forces, Washington, D.C., August 21, 1961, *Congressional Record*, vol. 107, p. 16444. He was referring to radicals of the right.

581 Extremism in the defense of liberty is no vice. Moderation in the pursuit of justice is no virtue.

Senator BARRY GOLDWATER, speech accepting nomination for president, Republican national convention, San Francisco, California, July 16, 1964.—*Congressional Record*, July 21, 1964, vol. 110, p. 16388.

Senator Goldwater comments that the remark was not original with him: "In fact, I believe Cicero used it in some form at one time, and I have been able to trace it rather faintly back to some of the early Greeks so, while I was very proud of the fact that I made the speech, it's certainly not original."

Facts

582 The power of administrative bodies to make finding of fact which may be treated as conclusive, if there is evidence both ways, is a power of enormous consequence. An unscrupulous administrator might be tempted to say "Let me find the facts for the people of my country, and I care little who lays down the general principles."

Chief Justice CHARLES EVANS HUGHES, "Important Work of Uncle Sam's Lawyers," *American Bar Association Journal*, April 1931, p. 238.

This reprinted an address to the Federal Bar Association, Washington, D.C., February 11, 1931, where the chief justice spoke of the "extraordinary development of administrative agencies of the government and of the lawyer's part in making them work satisfactorily and also in protecting the public against bureaucratic excesses," according to the article's subtitle.

583 Sit down before fact as a little child, be prepared to give up every preconceived notion, follow humbly wherever and to whatever abysses nature leads, or you shall learn nothing.

THOMAS HENRY HUXLEY, letter to Charles Kingsley, September 23, 1860.—Leonard Huxley, *Life and Letters of Thomas Henry Huxley*, vol. 1, p. 235 (1900, reprinted 1979).

See also No. 263.

584 Facts have a cruel way of substituting themselves for fancies. There is nothing more remorseless, just as there is nothing more helpful, than truth.

WILLIAM C. REDFIELD, secretary of commerce, address at Case School, Cleveland, Ohio, May 27, 1915.—Ashley H. Thorndike, *Modern Eloquence*, vol. 7, p. 392 (1936).

585 I often wish . . . that I could rid the world of the tyranny of facts. What are facts but compromises? A fact merely marks the point where we have agreed to let investigation cease.

Author unknown, "On Having Known a Poet," *The Atlantic Monthly*, May 1906, p. 712.—*The Home Book of American Quotations*, ed. Bruce Bohle, p. 90 (1967), attributes this article to Bliss Carman, a frequent contributor.

Failure

586 A man's life is interesting primarily when he has failed—I well know. For it's a sign that he tried to surpass himself.

GEORGES CLEMENCEAU, conversation with Jean Martet, June 1, 1928—*Clemenceau, The Events of His Life as Told by Himself to His Former Secretary, Jean Martet*, trans. Milton Waldman, chapter 30, p. 220 (1930).

587 Not failure, but low aim, is crime.

JAMES RUSSELL LOWELL, "For an Autograph," stanza 5, *The Writings of James Russell Lowell*, vol. 9, p. 175 (1890).

588 I have no use for men who fail. The cause of their failure is no business of mine, but I want successful men as my associates.

JOHN D. ROCKEFELLER.—Silas Hubbard, *John D. Rockefeller and His Career*, p. 72 (1904).

Hubbard states that this was a favorite saying of Rockefeller's.

589 It is hard to fail, but it is worse never to have tried to succeed.

THEODORE ROOSEVELT, governor of New York, speech before the Hamilton Club, Chicago, Illinois, April 10, 1899.—*The Strenuous Life* (vol. 13 of *The Works of Theodore Roosevelt*, national ed.), chapter 1, p. 320 (1926).

590 Ambition is the last refuge of the failure.

OSCAR WILDE, "Phrases and Philosophies for the Use of the Young," *The Complete Works of Oscar Wilde*, vol. 10, p. 213 (1923).

See also No. 1306.

Faith

591 Cast thy bread upon the waters: for thou shalt find it after many days.

The Bible, Ecclesiastes 11:1.

592 And Jesus said unto them, Because of your unbelief: for verily I say unto you, If ye have faith as a grain of mustard seed, ye shall say unto this mountain, Remove hence to yonder place; and it shall remove; and nothing shall be impossible unto you.

The Bible, Matthew 17:20.

Fame

593 There is a proud undying thought in man,
That bids his soul still upward look
To fame's proud cliff!

SAM HOUSTON, "There is a proud undying thought in man," lines 1–3, *The Autobiography of Sam Houston*, ed. Donald Day and Harry H. Ullom, p. 56 (1954).

594 Scarce any Tale was sooner heard than told;
And all who told it, added something new,
And all who heard it, made Enlargements too,
In ev'ry Ear it spread, on ev'ry Tongue it grew.

ALEXANDER POPE, "Temple of Fame," lines 469–72, *Poems of Alexander Pope*, ed. Geoffrey Tillotson, vol. 2, p. 269 (1940, revised 1954).

Fear

595 Early and provident fear is the mother of safety.

EDMUND BURKE, speech on the petition of the Unitarians, House of Commons, May 11, 1792.—*The Works of the Right Honorable Edmund Burke*, vol. 7, p. 50 (1899).

596 There is a courageous wisdom; there is also a false, reptile prudence, the result not of caution but of fear.

Attributed to EDMUND BURKE. Unverified.

597 O friend, never strike sail to a fear! Come into port greatly, or sail with God the seas.

RALPH WALDO EMERSON, "Heroism," *Essays: First Series* (vol. 2 of *The Complete Works of Ralph Waldo Emerson*), pp. 259–60 (1903).

598 Let us never negotiate out of fear. But let us never fear to negotiate.

President JOHN F. KENNEDY, inaugural address, January 20, 1961.—*Public Papers of the Presidents of the United States: John F. Kennedy, 1961*, p. 2.

599 Let me assert my firm belief that the only thing we have to fear is fear itself—nameless, unreasoning, unjustified terror which paralyzes needed efforts to convert retreat into advance.

President FRANKLIN D. ROOSEVELT, inaugural address, March 4, 1933.—*The Public Papers and Addresses of Franklin D. Roosevelt, 1933*, p. 11 (1938).

600 Nothing is so much to be feared as fear.

HENRY DAVID THOREAU, journal entry for September 7, 1851.—Thoreau, *Journal*, ed. Bradford Torrey, vol. 2 (vol. 8 of *The Writings of Henry David Thoreau*), p. 468 (1906, reprinted 1968).

Flag

601 Rally round the flag, boys—
Give it to the breeze!
That's the banner that we bore
On the land and seas.
Brave hearts are under it,
Let the traitors brag,

Gallant lads, fire away!
And fight for the flag.
Their flag is but a rag—
Ours is the true one;
Up with the Stars and Stripes!
Down with the new one!
Let our colors fly, boys—
Guard them day and night;
For victory is liberty,
And God will bless the right.

JAMES T. FIELDS, "The Stars and Stripes."—Florence Adams and Elizabeth McCarrick, *Highdays & Holidays*, pp. 182–83 (1927).

602 Your flag and my flag,
And how it flies to-day
In your land and my land
And half a world away!
Rose-red and blood-red
The stripes for ever gleam;
Snow-white and soul-white—
The good forefathers' dream;
Sky-blue and true-blue, with stars to gleam aright—
The gloried guidon of the day; a shelter through the night.

WILBUR D. NESBIT, "A Song for Flag Day," stanza 1, *The Trail to Boyland*, p. 96 (1904).

Flying

603 Oh! I have slipped the surly bonds of Earth
And danced the skies on laughter-silvered wings;
Sunward I've climbed, and joined the tumbling mirth
of sun-split clouds,—and done a hundred things
You have not dreamed of—wheeled and soared and swung
High in the sunlit silence. Hov'ring there,
I've chased the shouting wind along, and flung
My eager craft through footless halls of air. . . .

Up, up the long, delirious, burning blue
I've topped the wind-swept heights with easy grace
Where never lark nor ever eagle flew—
And, while with silent lifting mind I've trod
The high untrespassed sanctity of space,
Put out my hand, and touched the face of God.

JOHN G. MAGEE, JR., "High Flight," September 3, 1941.

Magee was born in Shanghai, China, of missionary parents—an American father and an English mother—and spoke Chinese before English. He was educated at Rugby school in England and at Avon Old Farms School in Connecticut. He won a scholarship to Yale, but instead joined the Royal Canadian Air Force in late 1940, trained in Canada, and was sent to Britain. He flew in a Spitfire squadron and was killed on a routine training mission on December 11, 1941. The sonnet above was sent to his parents written on the back of a letter which said, "I am enclosing a verse I wrote the other day. It started at

30,000 feet, and was finished soon after I landed." He also wrote of his course ending soon and of his then going on operations, and added, "I think we are very lucky as we shall just be in time for the autumn blitzes (which are certain to come)."

Magee's parents lived in Washington, D.C., at the time of his death, and the sonnet came to the attention of Librarian of Congress Archibald MacLeish. He acclaimed Magee the first poet of the War, and included the poem in an exhibition of poems of "faith and freedom" at the Library of Congress in February 1942. The poem was then widely reprinted, and the R.C.A.F. distributed plaques with the words of the poem to all airfields and training stations.

The reprintings vary in punctuation, capitalization, and indentation from the original manuscript, which is in the Manuscript Division of the Library of Congress. Some portions are faded and difficult to read, but the version above follows Magee's as exactly as can be made out, following his pencilled note on another poem, "If anyone should want this please see that it is accurately copied, capitalized, and punctuated." Nearly all versions use ". . . even eagle," but to the editor's careful scrutiny, it was "ever," formed exactly like the preceding "never."

President Ronald Reagan quoted from the first and last lines in a televised address to the nation after the space shuttle *Challenger* exploded, January 28, 1986.—*Weekly Compilation of Presidential Documents*, February 3, 1986, p. 105.

604 According to the theory of aerodynamics, as may be readily demonstrated through wind tunnel experiments, the bumblebee is unable to fly. This is because the size, weight and shape of his body in relation to the total wingspread make flying impossible. *But the bumblebee, being ignorant of these scientific truths, goes ahead and flies anyway—and makes a little honey every day.*

Sign in a General Motors Corporation plant.—Ralph L. Woods, *The Businessman's Book of Quotations*, pp. 249–50 (1951).

"Antoine Magnan, a French zoologist, in 1934 made some very careful studies of bumblebee flight and came to the conclusion that bumblebees cannot fly at all! Fortunately, the bumblebees never heard this bit of news and so went on flying as usual."—Ross E. Hutchins, *Insects*, p. 68 (1968). Magnan's 1934 work was *Le Vol des Insectes* (vol. 1 of *La Locomotion Chez les Animaux*).

Fools

605 But I say unto you, That whosoever is angry with his brother without a cause shall be in danger of the judgment: and whosoever shall say to his brother, Raca, shall be in danger of the council: but whosoever shall say, Thou fool, shall be in danger of hell fire.

The Bible, Matthew 5:22.

606 Twenty-seven millions, mostly fools.

THOMAS CARLYLE, *Latter-Day Pamphlets*, no. 6, p. 15 (1850).

Carlyle used this phrase several times in the pamphlet to refer to the citizens of Great Britain.

Champ Clark, referring to this remark added, "While the percentage of fools in this country is not so large, there are still enough to fatten the swindlers. . . . The percentage of fools in this country is not so great as Carlyle states it, but nevertheless it is quite large."—Champ Clark, *My Quarter Century of American Politics*, p. 213 (1920). Clark was Speaker of the House from 1911–1919.

607 Young men think old men are fools, but old men know young men are fools.

GEORGE CHAPMAN, *All Fools*, act V, scene ii, lines 205–6, p. 87 (1968).

This was a common proverb which appeared not only in Chapman's play, first published in 1605, but in other works as well. See *The Oxford Dictionary of English Proverbs*, pp. 927–28 (1970).

608 We assemble parliaments and councils, to have the benefit of their collected wisdom; but we necessarily have, at the same time, the inconvenience of their collected passions, prejudices, and private interests. By the help of these, artful men overpower their wisdom, and dupe its possessors; and if we may judge by the acts, *arrêts*, and edicts, all the world over, for regulating commerce, an assembly of great men is the greatest fool upon earth.

BENJAMIN FRANKLIN, letter to Benjamin Vaughan, July 26, 1784.—*The Writings of Benjamin Franklin*, ed. Albert H. Smyth, vol. 9, p. 241 (1906).

609 You may fool all the people some of the time; you can even fool some of the people all the time; but you can't fool all of the people all the time.

Attributed to ABRAHAM LINCOLN.—Alexander K. McClure, *"Abe" Lincoln's Yarns and Stories*, p. 184 (1904).

Many quotation books have also attributed this to Lincoln, and the sources given have varied. According to Roy P. Basler, ed., *The Collected Works of Abraham Lincoln*, vol. 3, p. 81 (1953), "Tradition has come to attribute to the Clinton [Illinois] speeches [September 2, 1858] one of Lincoln's most famous utterances—'You can fool all the people some of the time and some of the people all the time, but you cannot fool all the people all the time.' " But he goes on to say that the epigram and any references to it have not been located in surviving Lincoln documents.

This remark has also been attributed to P. T. Barnum.

610 The best way in which to silence any friend of yours whom you know to be a fool is to induce him to hire a hall. Nothing chills pretense like exposure.

President WOODROW WILSON, remarks to the Motion Picture Board of Trade, New York City, January 27, 1916.—*The Papers of Woodrow Wilson*, ed. Arthur S. Link, vol. 36, p. 17 (1981).

See also No. 681.

Foreign aid

611 Is this Nation stating it cannot afford to spend an additional $600 million to help the developing nations of the world become strong and free and independent—an amount less than this country's annual outlay for lipstick, face cream, and chewing gum?

President JOHN F. KENNEDY, remarks at the dinner of the Protestant Council of the City of New York, November 8, 1963.—*Public Papers of the Presidents of the United States: John F. Kennedy, 1963*, p. 842.

612 We have tried to make it clear that the United States is not just an old cow that gives more milk the more it is kicked in the flanks.

Foreign aid

DEAN RUSK, secretary of state, testimony, May 4, 1967.—*Foreign Assistance Act of 1967*, hearings before the Committee on Foreign Affairs, House of Representatives, 90th Congress, 1st session, part 4, p. 844 (1967).

Foreign policy

613 Wherever the standard of freedom and independence has been or shall be unfurled, there will her [America's] heart, her benedictions and her prayers be. But she goes not abroad in search of monsters to destroy. She is the well-wisher to the freedom and independence of all. She is the champion and vindicator only of her own. She will recommend the general cause, by the countenance of her voice, and the benignant sympathy of her example. She well knows that by once enlisting under other banners than her own, were they even the banners of foreign independence, she would involve herself, beyond the power of extrication, in all the wars of interest and intrigue, of individual avarice, envy, and ambition, which assume the colors and usurp the standard of freedom. The fundamental maxims of her policy would insensibly change from liberty to force. . . . She might become the dictatress of the world: she would be no longer the ruler of her own spirit.

JOHN QUINCY ADAMS, *An Address . . . Celebrating the Anniversary of Independence, at the City of Washington on the Fourth of July 1821 . . .* , p. 32 (1821).

This appears with minor variations in punctuation and with italics in the phrase "change from *liberty* to *force*," in *John Quincy Adams and American Continental Empire*, ed. Walter LaFeber, p. 45 (1965).

614 Yes, sir, from Constantinople, or from the Brazils; from Turk or christian; from black or white; from the dey of Algiers or the bey of Tunis; from the devil himself, if he wore a crown, we should receive a minister.

Representative HENRY CLAY, "Emancipation of South America," speech in the House of Representatives, March 28, 1818.—*The Life and Speeches of the Honorable Henry Clay*, ed. Daniel Mallory, vol. 1, p. 359 (1844).

Clay was Speaker of the House 1811–1814, 1815–1820, and 1823–1825.

615 The history of human conduct does not warrant that exalted opinion of human virtue which would make it wise in a nation to commit interests of so delicate and momentous a kind as those which concern its intercourse with the rest of the world to the sole disposal of a magistrate, created and circumstanced, as would be a President of the United States.

ALEXANDER HAMILTON, *The Federalist*, ed. Benjamin F. Wright, no. 75, p. 477 (1961).

616 The desire to preserve our country from the calamities and ravages of war, by cultivating a disposition, and pursuing a conduct, conciliatory and friendly to all nations, has been sincerely entertained and faithfully followed. It was dictated by the principles of humanity, the precepts of the gospel, and the general wish of our country, and it was not to be doubted that the Society of Friends, with whom it is a *religious* principle, would sanction it by their support.

President THOMAS JEFFERSON, letter to Messrs. Thomas, Ellicot, and others, November 13, 1807.—*The Writings of Thomas Jefferson*, ed. H. A. Washington, vol. 8, p. 118 (1871).

617 I have come to a resolution myself as I hope every good citizen will, never again to purchase any article of foreign manufacture which can be had of American make be the difference of price what it may.

THOMAS JEFFERSON, letter to B. S. Barton, February 26, 1815.—*The Writings of Thomas Jefferson,* ed. Andrew A. Lipscomb, vol. 19, p. 223 (1904).

618 It is, therefore, with the sincerest pleasure I have observed on the part of the British government various manifestations of a just and friendly disposition towards us; we wish to cultivate peace and friendship with all nations, believing that course most conducive to the welfare of our own; it is natural that these friendships should bear some proportion to the common interests of the parties.

THOMAS JEFFERSON, letter to Sir John Sinclair, July 31, 1816.—*The Writings of Thomas Jefferson,* ed. Andrew A. Lipscomb, vol. 15, p. 54 (1904).

619 Peace, commerce, and honest friendship, with all nations—entangling alliances with none.

President THOMAS JEFFERSON, inaugural address, March 4, 1801.—*The Writings of Thomas Jefferson,* ed. Andrew A. Lipscomb, vol. 3, p. 321 (1904).

This thought had been similarly expressed earlier in his letter to Edward Carrington, December 21, 1787: "I know too that it is a maxim with us, and I think it a wise one, not to entangle ourselves with the affairs of Europe."—*The Papers of Thomas Jefferson,* ed. Julian P. Boyd, vol. 12, p. 447 (1955).

George Washington did not use any form of "entangle," but shared a like political view in his letters to Patrick Henry, October 9, 1795: "My ardent desire is . . . to keep the U States free from *political* connexions with *every* other Country. To see that they *may be* independent of *all*, and under the influence of *none*," and to Gouverneur Morris, December 22, 1795: "My policy has been . . . to be upon friendly terms with, but independent of, all the nations of the earth. To share in the broils of none."—*Writings of George Washington,* ed. John C. Fitzpatrick, vol. 34, pp. 335, 401 (1940).

620 By this I mean that a political society does not live to conduct foreign policy; it would be more correct to say that it conducts foreign policy in order to live.

GEORGE F. KENNAN, "The Two Planes of International Reality," *Realities of American Foreign Policy,* p. 4 (1954).

This was originally delivered as the first of the Stafford Little Lectures, Princeton University, Princeton, New Jersey, March 1954.

621 Now this problem of the adjustment of man to his natural resources, and the problem of how such things as industrialization and urbanization can be accepted without destroying the traditional values of a civilization and corrupting the inner vitality of its life—these things are not only the problems of America; they are the problems of men everywhere. To the extent that we Americans become able to show that we are aware of these problems, and that we are approaching them with coherent and effective ideas of our own which we have the courage to put into effect in our own lives, to that extent a new dimension will come into our relations with the peoples beyond our borders, to that extent, in fact, the dreams of these earlier generations of Americans who saw us as leaders and helpers to the peoples of the world at large will begin to take on flesh and reality.

GEORGE F. KENNAN, "The Unifying Factor," *Realities of American Foreign Policy,* p. 116 (1954).

This was originally delivered as the fourth of the Stafford Little Lectures, Princeton University, Princeton, New Jersey, March 1954.

622 The purpose of foreign policy is not to provide an outlet for our own sentiments of hope or indignation; it is to shape real events in a real world.

President JOHN F. KENNEDY, address at the Mormon Tabernacle, Salt Lake City, Utah, September 26, 1963.—*Public Papers of the Presidents of the United States: John F. Kennedy, 1963*, p. 736.

623 To those peoples in the huts and villages of half the globe struggling to break the bonds of mass misery, we pledge our best efforts to help them help themselves, for whatever period is required—not because the communists may be doing it, not because we seek their votes, but because it is right. If a free society cannot help the many who are poor, it cannot save the few who are rich.

President JOHN F. KENNEDY, inaugural address, January 20, 1961.—*Public Papers of the Presidents of the United States: John F. Kennedy, 1961*, p. 1.

624 The challenges before us are monumental. But it is not every generation that is given the opportunity to shape a new international order. If the opportunity is missed, we shall live in a world of chaos and danger. If it is realized we will have entered an era of peace and progress and justice. But we can realize our hopes only as a united people. Our challenge—and its solution—lies in ourselves. Our greatest foreign policy problem is our divisions at home. Our greatest foreign policy need is national cohesion and a return to the awareness that in foreign policy we are all engaged in a common national endeavor.

HENRY A. KISSINGER, secretary of state, speech to Boston World Affairs Council, Boston, Massachusetts, March 11, 1976.—Excerpts of official text, *The New York Times*, March 12, 1976, p. 4.

625 But much of what Mr. Wallace calls his global thinking is, no matter how you slice it, still "globaloney." Mr. Wallace's warp of sense and his woof of nonsense is very tricky cloth out of which to cut the pattern of a post-war world.

Representative CLARE BOOTHE LUCE, remarks in the House, February 9, 1943, *Congressional Record*, vol. 89, p. 761.

It was in her maiden speech in the House that Mrs. Luce coined the term *globaloney* to describe then Vice President Henry Wallace's post-war theories.

626 Our idea is to create a situation in which those lands to which we have obligations or in which we have interests, if they are ready to fight a fire, should be able to count on us to furnish the hose and water.

President RICHARD M. NIXON, on-the-record interview with C. L. Sulzberger, March 8, 1971.—*The New York Times*, March 10, 1971, p. 14.

627 The fundamental question for the United States is how it can cooperate to help meet the basic needs of the people of the hemisphere despite the philosophical disagreements it may have with the nature of particular regimes. It must seek pragmatic ways to help people without necessarily embracing their governments. It should recognize that diplomatic relations are merely practical conveniences and not measures of moral judgment.

NELSON A. ROCKEFELLER, governor of New York, "Quality of Life in the Americas," text of the Rockefeller Mission report, *The Department of State Bulletin*, December 8, 1969, p. 515.

Rockefeller was appointed by President Nixon to head a Latin American mission.

628 A man must first care for his own household before he can be of use to the state. But no matter how well he cares for his household, he is not a good citizen unless he also takes thought of the state. In the same way, a great nation must think of its own internal affairs; and yet it cannot substantiate its claim to be a great nation unless it also thinks of its position in the world at large.

THEODORE ROOSEVELT, "Nationalism and International Relations," *Social Justice and Popular Rule* (vol. 17 of *The Works of Theodore Roosevelt*, national ed.), chapter 12, p. 108 (1926).

629 There is a homely old adage which runs: "Speak softly and carry a big stick; you will go far." If the American Nation will speak softly, and yet build, and keep at a pitch of the highest training, a thoroughly efficient navy, the Monroe Doctrine will go far.

President THEODORE ROOSEVELT, speech, Chicago, Illinois, April 2, 1903.—*Presidential Addresses and State Papers*, part 1 (vol. 13 of *The Works of Theodore Roosevelt*, executive ed.), p. 266 (n.d.).

In *America and the World War*, chapter 2, p. 24, he referred to "the homely proverb: 'Speak softly and carry a big stick.' "—*The Works of Theodore Roosevelt*, national ed., vol. 18 (1926). In the last chapter of *Theodore Roosevelt, An Autobiography*, p. 524 (vol. 20 of *Works*, national ed.), he says: "The only safe rule is to promise little, and faithfully to keep every promise; to 'speak softly and carry a big stick.' "

630 The Government of the United States is not entitled to affirm as a universal proposition, with reference to a number of independent States for whose conduct it assumes no responsibility, that its interests are necessarily concerned in whatever may befall those States simply because they are situated in the Western Hemisphere.

LORD SALISBURY, letter to Sir Julian Pauncefote, November 26, 1895.—U.S. Department of State, *Papers Relating to the Foreign Relations of the United States . . . 1895*, part 1, p. 566 (1896).

Lord Salisbury was objecting to U.S. Secretary of State Richard Olney's interpretation of the Monroe Doctrine in Venezuela's boundary dispute with Great Britain. This interpretation, which maintained U.S. right to intervene in international disputes in the Western Hemisphere, is known as the Olney Corollary to the Monroe Doctrine.

631 Every day, for example, politicians, of which there are plenty, swear eternal devotion to the ends of peace and security. They always remind me of the elder Holmes' apostrophe to a katydid: "Thou say'st an undisputed thing in such a solemn way." And every day statesmen, of which there are few, must struggle with limited means to achieve these unlimited ends, both in fact and in understanding. For the nation's purposes always exceed its means, and it is finding a balance between means and ends that is the heart of foreign policy and that makes it such a speculative, uncertain business.

ADLAI E. STEVENSON, *Call to Greatness*, p. 2 (1954).

The quotation from Holmes is from "To an Insect," lines 7–8, *The Complete Poetical Works of Oliver Wendell Holmes*, p. 3 (1900).

Foreign policy

632 We have noted that the federal Constitution put the permanent control of the nation's foreign interests in the hands of the President and the Senate, which to some extent frees the Union's general policy from direct and daily popular control. One should not therefore assert without qualification that American democracy controls the state's external affairs.

ALEXIS DE TOCQUEVILLE, *Democracy in America*, ed. J. P. Mayer, trans. George Lawrence, vol. 1, part 2, chapter 5, p. 226 (1969). Originally published in 1835–1840.

633 If the establishment of an "unlimited" treaty power is to be the ultimate conclusion on this great question, it must be admitted that the incorporation of the treaty-making power into the Constitution of the United States was the introduction into our governmental citadel of a Trojan horse, whose armored soldiery, for years concealed within it, now step forth armed *cap-à-pie*, shameless in their act of deception, eager and ready to capture the citadel upon which they pretended to bestow their gift. If such construction be possible it would be of interest to know for what purpose the Tenth Amendment was ever demanded and incorporated into the Constitution.

HENRY ST. GEORGE TUCKER, *Limitations on the Treaty-Making Power*, p. 339, section 296 (1915).

634 To me "bipartisan foreign policy" means a mutual effort, under our indispensable two-Party system, to unite our official voice at the water's edge so that America speaks with maximum authority against those who would divide and conquer us and the free world. It does not involve the remotest surrender of free debate in determining our position. On the contrary, frank cooperation and free debate are indispensable to ultimate unity. In a word, it simply seeks national security ahead of partisan advantage. Every foreign policy must be *totally* debated (and I think the record proves it has been) and the "loyal opposition" is under special obligation to see that this occurs.

Senator ARTHUR H. VANDENBERG, *The Private Papers of Senator Vandenberg*, ed. Arthur H. Vandenberg, Jr., pp. 552–53 (1952).

The phrase "his majesty's opposition" was coined by John Cam Hobhouse, later Lord Broughton, in the House of Commons, April 10, 1826.—*Parliamentary Debates (Hansard)*, vol. 15, col. 135. It is usually heard now as "loyal opposition." Bergen Evans, *Dictionary of Quotations*, p. 499, no. 9 (1968), notes that Hobhouse said he was praised by Canning, but at the time Canning merely repeated the phrase. The praise came from the Rt. Hon. George Tierney: "[Hobhouse] could not have invented a better phrase to designate us . . . for we are certainly to all intents and purposes, a branch of his majesty's government."—Op. cit., col. 145.

Forgiveness

635 And he said, A certain man had two sons:

And the younger of them said to his father, Father, give me the portion of goods that falleth to me. And he divided unto them his living.

And not many days after the younger son gathered all together, and took his journey into a far country, and there wasted his substance with riotous living.

And when he had spent all, there arose a mighty famine in that land; and he began to be in want.

And he went and joined himself to a citizen of that country; and he sent him into his fields to feed swine.

And he would fain have filled his belly with the husks that the swine did eat: and no man gave unto him.

And when he came to himself, he said, How many hired servants of my father's have bread enough and to spare, and I perish with hunger!

I will arise and go to my father, and will say unto him, Father, I have sinned against heaven, and before thee,

And am no more worthy to be called thy son: make me as one of thy hired servants.

And he arose, and came to his father. But when he was yet a great way off, his father saw him, and had compassion, and ran, and fell on his neck, and kissed him.

And the son said unto him, Father, I have sinned against heaven, and in thy sight, and am no more worthy to be called thy son.

But the father said to his servants, Bring forth the best robe, and put it on him; and put a ring on his hand, and shoes on his feet:

And bring hither the fatted calf, and kill it; and let us eat, and be merry:

For this my son was dead, and is alive again; he was lost, and is found. And they began to be merry.

Now his elder son was in the field: and as he came and drew nigh to the house, he heard musick and dancing.

And he called one of the servants, and asked what these things meant.

And he said unto him, Thy brother is come; and thy father hath killed the fatted calf, because he hath received him safe and sound.

And he was angry, and would not go in: therefore came his father out, and intreated him.

And he answering said to his father, Lo, these many years do I serve thee, neither transgressed I at any time thy commandment: and yet thou never gavest me a kid, that I might make merry with my friends:

But as soon as this thy son was come, which hath devoured thy living with harlots, thou hast killed for him the fatted calf.

And he said unto him, Son, thou art ever with me, and all that I have is thine.

It was meet that we should make merry, and be glad: for this thy brother was dead, and is alive again; and was lost, and is found.

The Bible, Luke 15:11–32. Parable of the prodigal son.

Fortune

636 Fortune, that with malicious joy
Does man her slave oppress,
Proud of her office to destroy,
Is seldom pleas'd to bless.

JOHN DRYDEN, "Horace, the Twenty-Ninth Ode of the Third Book," stanza 9, *The Poetical Works of Dryden*, new ed. rev. and enl., ed. George R. Noyes, p. 200 (1950).

637 Men's fortunes are on a wheel, which in its turning suffers not the same man to prosper for ever.

HERODOTUS, *Herodotus*, trans. A. D. Godley, vol. 1, book 1, section 207, p. 261 (1931).

638 I have a wife, I have sons; all these hostages have I given to fortune.
(Coniunx est mihi, sunt nati; dedimus tot pignora fatis.)

LUCAN, *Pharsalia*, book 7, line 662, *Lucan*, trans. J. D. Duff, pp. 418–19 (1928).

639 Modern life means democracy, democracy means freeing intelligence for independent effectiveness—the emancipation of mind as an individual organ to do its own work. We naturally associate democracy, to be sure, with freedom of action, but freedom of action without freed capacity of thought behind it is only chaos.

JOHN DEWEY, "Democracy in Education," *John Dewey, The Middle Works, 1899–1924*, ed. Jo Ann Boydston, vol. 3, p. 229 (1977). First published in *The Elementary School Teacher*, December 1903.

640 But we know that freedom cannot be served by the devices of the tyrant. As it is an ancient truth that freedom cannot be legislated into existence, so it is no less obvious that freedom cannot be censored into existence. And any who act as if freedom's defenses are to be found in suppression and suspicion and fear confess a doctrine that is alien to America.

President DWIGHT D. EISENHOWER, letter on intellectual freedom to Dr. Robert B. Downs, president of the American Library Association, June 24, 1953.—*Public Papers of the Presidents of the United States: Dwight D. Eisenhower, 1953*, p. 456.

641 For what avail the plough or sail,
Or land or life, if freedom fail?

RALPH WALDO EMERSON, "Boston," stanza 15, *The Complete Writings of Ralph Waldo Emerson*, vol. 2, p. 897 (1929).

These words were also inscribed on a plaque in the stairwell of the pedestal of the Statue of Liberty.

642 You can muffle the drum, and you can loosen the strings of the lyre, but who shall command the skylark not to sing?

KAHLIL GIBRAN, "On Laws," final sentence, *The Prophet*, p. 46 (1968).

643 What the people wanted was a government which would provide a comfortable life for them, and with this as the foremost object ideas of freedom and self-reliance and service to the community were obscured to the point of disappearing. Athens was more and more looked on as a co-operative business possessed of great wealth in which all citizens had a right to share. . . . Athens had reached the point of rejecting independence, and the freedom she now wanted was freedom from responsibility. There could be only one result. . . . If men insisted on being free from the burden of a life that was self-dependent and also responsible for the common good, they would cease to be free at all. Responsibility was the price every man must pay for freedom. It was to be had on no other terms.

EDITH HAMILTON, *The Echo of Greece*, chapter 2, p. 47 (1957).

644 The greatest Glory of a free-born People,
Is to transmit that Freedom to their Children.

WILLIAM HAVARD, "Regulus, a Tragedy," act IV, scene iv.—Francis Longe, *Collection of Plays*, vol. 35, no. 2, p. 59 (1744). Regulus is speaking.

645 When we lose the right to be different, we lose the privilege to be free.

CHARLES EVANS HUGHES, address at Faneuil Hall, Boston, Massachusetts, on the 150th anniversary of the Battle of Bunker Hill, June 17, 1925.—Hughes Papers, Library of Congress.

646 A man's worst difficulties begin when he is able to do as he likes.

THOMAS HENRY HUXLEY, address on university education, delivered at the formal opening of The Johns Hopkins University, Baltimore, Maryland, September 12, 1876.—*Science and Education* (vol. 3 of *Collected Essays*), p. 236 (1898, reprinted 1968).

647 If there is any fixed star in our constitutional constellation, it is that no official, high or petty, can prescribe what shall be orthodox in politics, nationalism, religion, or other matters of opinion or force citizens to confess by word or act their faith therein.

Justice ROBERT H. JACKSON, *West Virginia State Board of Education* v. *Barnette*, 319 U.S. 642 (1943).

648 This is a world of compensation; and he who would be no slave must consent to have no slave. Those who deny freedom to others deserve it not for themselves, and, under a just God, cannot long retain it.

ABRAHAM LINCOLN, letter to H. L. Pierce and others, April 6, 1859.—*The Collected Works of Abraham Lincoln,* ed. Roy P. Basler, vol. 3, p. 375 (1953).

649 The maxims are, first, that the individual is not accountable to society for his actions, in so far as these concern the interests of no person but himself. Advice, instruction, persuasion, and avoidance by other people if thought necessary by them for their own good, are the only measures by which society can justifiably express its dislike or disapprobation of his conduct. Secondly, that for such actions as are prejudicial to the interests of others, the individual is accountable, and may be subjected either to social or to legal punishment, if society is of opinion that the one or the other is requisite for its protection.

JOHN STUART MILL, *On Liberty,* ed. David Spitz, chapter 5, p. 87 (1975). Originally published in 1859.

650 The only freedom which deserves the name, is that of pursuing our own good in our own way, so long as we do not attempt to deprive others of theirs, or impede their efforts to obtain it.

JOHN STUART MILL, *On Liberty,* ed. David Spitz, chapter 1, p. 14 (1975). Originally published in 1859.

651 The only part of the conduct of any one, for which he is amenable to society, is that which concerns others. In the part which merely concerns himself, his independence, is, of right, absolute. Over himself, over his own body and mind, the individual is sovereign.

JOHN STUART MILL, *On Liberty,* ed. David Spitz, chapter 1, p. 11 (1975). Originally published in 1859.

652 There is a limit to the legitimate interference of collective opinion with individual independence: and to find that limit, and maintain it against encroachment, is as indispensable to a good condition of human affairs, as protection against political despotism.

JOHN STUART MILL, *On Liberty,* ed. David Spitz, chapter 1, p. 6 (1975). Originally published in 1859.

653 Yet we can maintain a free society only if we recognize that in a free society no one can win all the time. No one can have his own way all the time, and no one is right all the time.

President RICHARD M. NIXON, Alfred M. Landon lecture, Kansas State University, Manhattan, Kansas, September 16, 1970.—*Public Papers of the Presidents of the United States: Richard Nixon, 1970,* p. 758.

654 If the fires of freedom and civil liberties burn low in other lands, they must be made brighter in our own. If in other lands the press and books and literature of all kinds are censored, we must redouble our efforts here to keep them free. If in other lands the eternal truths of the past are threatened by intolerance we must provide a safe place for their perpetuation.

President FRANKLIN D. ROOSEVELT, address to the National Education Association, New York City, June 30, 1938.—*The Public Papers and Addresses of Franklin D. Roosevelt, 1938,* p. 418 (1941).

655 In the future days, which we seek to make secure, we look forward to a world founded upon four essential human freedoms. The first is freedom of speech and expression—everywhere in the world. The second is freedom of every person to worship God in his own way—everywhere in the world. The third is freedom from want—which, translated into world terms, means economic understandings which will secure to every nation a healthy peacetime life for its inhabitants—everywhere in the world. The fourth is freedom from fear—which, translated into world terms, means a world-wide reduction of armaments to such a point and in such a thorough fashion that no nation will be in a position to commit an act of physical aggression against any neighbor—anywhere in the world.

President FRANKLIN D. ROOSEVELT, State of the Union message to the Congress, January 6, 1941.—*The Public Papers and Addresses of Franklin D. Roosevelt, 1940,* p. 672 (1941).

A plaque in the stairwell of the pedestal of the Statue of Liberty is inscribed: "Liberty is the air America breathes. . . . In the future days, which we seek to make secure, we look forward to a world founded upon four essential freedoms . . . freedom of speech and expression . . . freedom of worship . . . freedom from want . . . freedom from fear."

656 What would you have me do?
Search out some powerful patronage, and be
Like crawling ivy clinging to a tree?
No thank you. Dedicate, like all the others,
Verses to plutocrats, while caution smothers
Whatever might offend my lord and master?
No thank you. Kneel until my knee-caps fester,
Bend my back until I crack my spine,
And scratch another's back if he'll scratch mine?
No thank you. Dining out to curry favour,
Meeting the influential till I slaver,
Suiting my style to what the critics want
With slavish copy of the latest cant?
No thanks! Ready to jump through any hoop
To be the great man of a little group?
Be blown off course, with madrigals for sails,
By the old women sighing through their veils?
Labouring to write a line of such good breeding
Its only fault is—that it's not worth reading?
To ingratiate myself, abject with fear,

And fawn and flatter to avoid a sneer?
No thanks, no thanks, no thanks! But . . . just to sing,
Dream, laugh, and take my tilt of wing,
To cock a snook whenever I shall choose,
To fight for "yes" and "no", come win or lose,
To travel without thought of fame or fortune
Wherever I care to go to under the moon!
Never to write a line that hasn't come
Directly from my heart: and so, with some
Modesty, to tell myself: "My boy,
Be satisfied with a flower, a fruit, the joy
Of a single leaf, so long as it was grown
In your own garden. Then, if success is won
By any chance, you have nothing to render to
A hollow Caesar: the merit belongs to you."
In short, I won't be a parasite; I'll be
My own intention, stand alone and free,
And suit my voice to what my own eyes see!

EDMOND ROSTAND, *Cyrano de Bergerac*, act II, trans. Christopher Fry, pp. 56–57 (1975). Originally published in 1897.

This is Cyrano's declaration of independence.

657 Eastward I go only by force; but westward I go free.

HENRY DAVID THOREAU, "Walking," *Excursions*, p. 266 (1894).

The essay on walking was first published after Thoreau's death, in *Atlantic Monthly*, June 1862.

658 I must walk toward Oregon, and not toward Europe. And that way the nation is moving, and I may say that mankind progress from east to west. . . . We go eastward to realize history and study the works of art and literature, retracing the steps of the race; we go westward as into the future, with a spirit of enterprise and adventure.

HENRY DAVID THOREAU, "Walking," *Excursions*, p. 267 (1894).

See note at No. 657.

659 To be what no one ever was,
To be what everyone has been:
Freedom is the mean of those
Extremes that fence all effort in.

MARK VAN DOREN, "Freedom," *Morning Worship and Other Poems*, p. 124 (1960).

Freedom—defense of

660 A nation which makes the final sacrifice for life and freedom does not get beaten.

KEMAL ATATÜRK.—M. M. Mousharrafa, *Ataturk*, p. 130 (1944).

He was the first president of the Republic of Turkey.

661 In the long history of the world, only a few generations have been granted the role of defending freedom in its hour of maximum danger. I do not shrink from this responsibility—I welcome it.

President JOHN F. KENNEDY, inaugural address, January 20, 1961.—*The Public Papers of the Presidents of the United States: John F. Kennedy, 1961*, pp. 2–3.

This is one of seven inscriptions carved on the walls at the gravesite of John F. Kennedy, Arlington National Cemetery.

662 We in this country, in this generation, are—by destiny rather than choice—the watchmen on the walls of world freedom. We ask, therefore, that we may be worthy of our power and responsibility, that we may exercise our strength with wisdom and restraint, and that we may achieve in our time and for all time the ancient vision of "peace on earth, good will toward men." That must always be our goal, and the righteousness of our cause must always underlie our strength. For as was written long ago: "except the Lord keep the city, the watchman waketh but in vain."

President JOHN F. KENNEDY, remarks prepared for delivery at the Trade Mart in Dallas, Texas, November 22, 1963.—*Public Papers of the Presidents of the United States: John F. Kennedy, 1963*, p. 894.

This speech was never delivered. President Kennedy was on his way to the Trade Mart when he was assassinated. The quotations are from the Bible, Luke 2:14 and Psalms 127:1, respectively.

663 No man is entitled to the blessings of freedom unless he be vigilant in its preservation.

DOUGLAS MACARTHUR, title of speech to the people of Japan, May 3, 1948, upon the first anniversary of the Japanese constitution.—MacArthur, *A Soldier Speaks*, p. 194 (1965).

Francis T. Miller, *General Douglas MacArthur, Fighter for Freedom*, p. 1 (1942), wrote, "[MacArthur] has said many times to friends: '*The man who will not defend his freedom does not deserve to be free!*' "

See also No. 1191.

664 Those who expect to reap the blessings of freedom, must, like men, undergo the fatigues of supporting it.

THOMAS PAINE, "The Crisis," no. 4, September 11, 1777.—*The Writings of Thomas Paine*, ed. Moncure D. Conway, vol. 1, p. 229 (1894).

665 We fight not to enslave, but to set a country free, and to make room upon the earth for honest men to live in.

THOMAS PAINE, "The Crisis," no. 4, September 11, 1777, final paragraph.—*The Writings of Thomas Paine*, ed. Moncure D. Conway, vol. 1, p. 232 (1902, reprinted 1969).

666 The great German poet, Goethe, who also lived through a crisis of freedom, said to his generation: "What you have inherited from your fathers, earn over again for yourselves or it will not be yours." We inherited freedom. We seem unaware that freedom has to be remade and re-earned in each generation of man.

ADLAI E. STEVENSON, "Politics and Morality," *Saturday Review*, February 7, 1959, p. 12.

He quoted Goethe's *Faust*, act I, scene i, "Was du ererbt von deinen Vätern hast, / Erwirb es, um es zu besitzen." In Randall Jarrell's translation, "That which you inherit from your fathers / You must earn in order to possess."—*Goethe's Faust*, p. 35 (1976).

667 Almighty God hath created the mind free. All attempts to influence it by temporal punishments or burthens . . . are a departure from the plan of the holy author of our religion . . . No man shall be compelled to frequent or support any religious worship or ministry or shall otherwise suffer on account of his religious opinions or belief, but all men shall be free to profess and by argument to maintain, their opinions in matters of religion.[a] I know but one code of morality for men whether acting singly or collectively.[b]

THOMAS JEFFERSON. Inscription on the northwest quadrant of the Jefferson Memorial, Washington, D.C., selected by the Thomas Jefferson Memorial Commission.
[a]"A Bill for Establishing Religious Freedom," *The Papers of Thomas Jefferson*, ed. Julian P. Boyd, vol. 2, pp. 545–6 (1950). The inscription contains the ellipses above, but it omits other words without ellipses.
[b]Letter to James Madison, August 28, 1789, *The Papers of Thomas Jefferson*, ed. Julian P. Boyd, vol. 15, p. 367 (1958).

668 That to compel a man to furnish contributions of money for the propagation of opinions which he disbelieves and abhors, is sinful and tyrannical.

THOMAS JEFFERSON, "A Bill for Establishing Religious Freedom," *The Papers of Thomas Jefferson*, ed. Julian P. Boyd, vol. 2, p. 545 (1950).

669 I believe in an America where the separation of church and state is absolute—where no Catholic prelate would tell the President (should he be Catholic) how to act, and no Protestant minister would tell his parishioners for whom to vote—where no church or church school is granted any public funds or political preference—and where no man is denied public office merely because his religion differs from the President who might appoint him or the people who might elect him.

I believe in an America that is officially neither Catholic, Protestant nor Jewish—where no public official either requests or accepts instructions on public policy from the Pope, the National Council of Churches or any other ecclesiastical source—where no religious body seeks to impose its will directly or indirectly upon the general populace or the public acts of its officials—and where religious liberty is so indivisible that an act against one church is treated as an act against all.

For while this year it may be a Catholic against whom the finger of suspicion is pointed, in other years it has been, and may someday be again, a Jew—or a Quaker—or a Unitarian—or a Baptist. It was Virginia's harassment of Baptist preachers, for example, that helped lead to Jefferson's statute of religious freedom. Today I may be the victim—but tomorrow it may be you—until the whole fabric of our harmonious society is ripped at a time of great national peril.

Finally, I believe in an America where religious intolerance will someday end—where all men and all churches are treated as equal—where every man has the same right to attend or not attend the church of his choice—where there is no Catholic vote, no anti-Catholic vote, no bloc voting of any kind—and where Catholics, Protestants and Jews, at both the lay and pastoral level, will refrain from those attitudes of disdain and division which have so often marred their works in the past, and promote instead the American ideal of brotherhood.

That is the kind of America in which I believe. And it represents the kind of Presidency in which I believe—a great office that must neither be humbled by making it the instrument of any one religious group nor tarnished by arbitrarily withholding its occupancy from the members of any one religious group. I believe in a President whose religious views are his own private affair, neither imposed by him upon the Nation or imposed by the Nation upon him as a condition to holding that office.

Freedom of religion

Senator JOHN F. KENNEDY, speech to the Greater Houston Ministerial Association, Houston, Texas, September 12, 1960.—*Freedom of Communications*, final report of the Committee on Commerce, United States Senate, part 1, pp. 208–9 (1961). Senate Rept. 87-994.

670 For happily the government of the United States, which gives to bigotry no sanction, to persecution no assistance, requires only that they who live under its protection should demean themselves as good citizens, in giving it on all occasions their effectual support. . . . May the children of the Stock of Abraham, who dwell in this land, continue to merit and enjoy the good will of the other inhabitants, while every one shall sit in safety under his own vine and fig-tree, and there shall be none to make him afraid.

President GEORGE WASHINGTON, letter to the Hebrew congregation of Newport, Rhode Island, August 17, 1790.—*The Writings of George Washington*, ed. John C. Fitzpatrick, vol. 31, p. 93, footnote (1939).

Freedom of speech

671 Without an unfettered press, without liberty of speech, all the outward forms and structures of free institutions are a sham, a pretense—the sheerest mockery. If the press is not free; if speech is not independent and untrammelled; if the mind is shackled or made impotent through fear, it makes no difference under what form of government you live you are a subject and not a citizen. Republics are not in and of themselves better than other forms of government except in so far as they carry with them and guarantee to the citizen that liberty of thought and action for which they were established.

Senator WILLIAM E. BORAH, remarks in the Senate, April 19, 1917, *Congressional Record*, vol. 55, p. 837.

672 Without free speech no search for truth is possible, without free speech no discovery of truth is useful, without free speech progress is checked and the nations no longer march forward toward the nobler life which the future holds for man. Better a thousandfold abuse of speech than a denial of free speech. The abuse dies in a day, but the denial slays the life of the people, and entombs the hope of the race.

Attributed to CHARLES BRADLAUGH.—Edmund Fuller, *Thesaurus of Quotations*, p. 398 (1941). Unverified.

673 I realize that, in speaking to you this afternoon, there are certain limitations placed upon the right of free speech. I must be exceedingly careful, prudent, as to what I say, and even more careful and prudent as to how I say it. I may not be able to say all I think; but I am not going to say anything that I do not think.

EUGENE V. DEBS, speech to the Socialist party of Ohio state convention, Canton, Ohio, June 16, 1918.—*Eugene V. Debs Speaks*, ed. Jean Y. Tussey, p. 244 (1970).

This was Debs's most famous speech. It was a socialist antiwar speech while the United States was at war, and it was used against him at his trial. He was convicted under the Espionage Law and sentenced to 10 years in prison. President Harding commuted the sentence in 1921.

674 Without Freedom of Thought, there can be no such Thing as Wisdom; and no such Thing as publick Liberty, without Freedom of Speech.

BENJAMIN FRANKLIN, letter from "Silence Dogood," no. 8, printed in *The New-England Courant*, Boston, Massachusetts, July 9, 1722. Franklin, writing under the pseudonym Silence Dogood, was quoting the *London Journal*, no. 80, February 4, 1720/1.—*The Papers of Benjamin Franklin*, ed. Leonard W. Labaree, vol. 1, p. 27 (1959).

This sentence is one of many quotations inscribed on Cox Corridor II, a first floor House corridor, U.S. Capitol.

675 But the character of every act depends upon the circumstances in which it is done. . . . The most stringent protection of free speech would not protect a man in falsely shouting fire in a theatre and causing a panic. It does not even protect a man from an injunction against uttering words that may have all the effect of force. . . . The question in every case is whether the words used are used in such circumstances and are of such a nature as to create a clear and present danger that they will bring about the substantive evils that Congress has a right to prevent. It is a question of proximity and degree.

Justice OLIVER WENDELL HOLMES, *Schenck* v. *United States, Baer* v. *United States*, 249 U.S. 52 (1919).

676 To preserve the freedom of the human mind . . . and freedom of the press, every spirit should be ready to devote itself to martyrdom; for as long as we may think as we will, and speak as we think the condition of man will proceed in improvement. The generation which is going off the stage has deserved well of mankind for the struggles it has made, and for having arrested the course of despotism which had overwhelmed the world for thousands and thousands of years. If there seems to be danger that the ground they have gained will be lost again, that danger comes from the generation your contemporary. But that the enthusiasm which characterizes youth should lift its parricide hands against freedom and science would be such a monstrous phenomenon as I cannot place among possible things in this age and country.

THOMAS JEFFERSON, letter to William Green Mumford, June 18, 1799.—Merrill D. Peterson, *Thomas Jefferson and the New Nation*, p. 616 (1970).

In Peterson's book, the letter is identified merely as "a ringing affirmation of the larger faith to a college student," omitting the recipient's name and date. The ellipses stand for a single word that is indecipherable.

677 For in the absence of debate unrestricted utterance leads to the degradation of opinion. By a kind of Gresham's law the more rational is overcome by the less rational, and the opinions that will prevail will be those which are held most ardently by those with the most passionate will. For that reason the freedom to speak can never be maintained merely by objecting to interference with the liberty of the press, of printing, of broadcasting, of the screen. It can be maintained only by promoting debate.

WALTER LIPPMANN, *Essays in the Public Philosophy*, chapter 9, section 3, pp. 129–30 (1955).

See also No. 1275.

678 I yield to no man—if I may borrow that majestic parliamentary phrase—I yield to no man in my belief in the principle of free debate, inside or outside the halls of Congress. The sound of tireless voices is the price we pay for the right to hear the music of our own opinions. But there is also, it seems to me, a moment at which democracy must prove its capacity to act. Every man has a right to be heard; but no man has the right to strangle democracy with a single set of vocal cords.

ADLAI E. STEVENSON, speech to the state committee of the Liberal party, New York City, August 28, 1952.—*The Papers of Adlai E. Stevenson*, vol. 4, p. 63 (1974).

Freedom of speech

679 For if Men are to be precluded from offering their Sentiments on a matter, which may involve the most serious and alarming consequences, that can invite the consideration of Mankind, reason is of no use to us; the freedom of Speech may be taken away, and, dumb and silent we may be led, like sheep, to the Slaughter.

General GEORGE WASHINGTON, address to the officers of the army, Newburgh, New York, March 15, 1783.—*The Writings of George Washington*, ed. John C. Fitzpatrick, vol. 26, p. 225 (1938).

680 So, dear friend, put fear out of your heart. This nation will survive, this state will prosper, the orderly business of life will go forward if only men can speak in whatever way given them to utter what their hearts hold—by voice, by posted card, by letter or by press. Reason never has failed men. Only force and repression have made the wrecks in the world.

WILLIAM ALLEN WHITE, "To an Anxious Friend," editorial, *The Emporia* (Kansas) *Gazette*, July 27, 1922.—White, *Forty Years on Main Street*, comp. Russell H. Fitzgibbon, p. 285 (1937).

681 I have always been among those who believed that the greatest freedom of speech was the greatest safety, because if a man is a fool, the best thing to do is to encourage him to advertise the fact by speaking. It cannot be so easily discovered if you allow him to remain silent and look wise, but if you let him speak, the secret is out and the world knows that he is a fool. So it is by the exposure of folly that it is defeated; not by the seclusion of folly, and in this free air of free speech men get into that sort of communication with one another which constitutes the basis of all common achievement.

WOODROW WILSON, "That Quick Comradeship of Letters," address at the Institute of France, Paris, May 10, 1919.—*The Public Papers of Woodrow Wilson*, ed. Ray Stannard Baker and William E. Dodd, vol. 5, p. 484 (1927).

See also No. 610.

Friendship

682 For no one, in our long decline,
So dusty, spiteful and divided,
Had quite such pleasant friends as mine,
Or loved them half as much as I did. [stanza 3]

The library was most inviting:
The books upon the crowded shelves
Were mainly of our private writing:
We kept a school and taught ourselves. [stanza 15]

From quiet homes and first beginning,
Out to the undiscovered ends,
There's nothing worth the wear of winning,
But laughter and the love of friends. [stanza 22]

You do retain the song we set,
And how it rises, trips and scans?
You keep the sacred memory yet,
Republicans? Republicans? [stanza 36]

HILAIRE BELLOC, "Dedicatory Ode," *Sonnets and Verse*, pp. 70, 73, 74, 76 (1923). Republicans was the name of the friends' club

683 Give me one friend, just one, who meets
The needs of all my varying moods.

ESTHER M. CLARK, "A Plea," lines 1 and 2, *Verses by a Commonplace Person* (1906).

684 The happiest business in all the world is that of making friends,
And no investment on the street pays larger dividends,
For life is more than stocks and bonds, and love than rate percent,
And he who gives in friendship's name shall reap what he has spent.

ANNE S. EATON, "The Business of Friendship," lines 1-4.—Seth Parker, *Fireside Poems*, p. 34 (1933).

685 "He was a friend to man, and lived in a house by the side of the road."—HOMER

There are hermit souls that live withdrawn
In the peace of their self-content;
There are souls, like stars, that dwell apart,
In a fellowless firmament;
There are pioneer souls that blaze their paths
Where highways never ran;
But let me live by the side of the road
And be a friend to man.

Let me live in a house by the side of the road,
Where the race of men go by—
The men who are good and the men who are bad,
As good and as bad as I.
I would not sit in the scorner's seat,
Or hurl the cynic's ban;—
Let me live in a house by the side of the road
And be a friend to man.

I see from my house by the side of the road,
By the side of the highway of life,
The men who press with the ardor of hope,
The men who are faint with the strife.
But I turn not away from their smiles nor their tears—
Both parts of an infinite plan;—
Let me live in my house by the side of the road
And be a friend to man.

I know there are brook-gladdened meadows ahead
And mountains of wearisome height;
That the road passes on through the long afternoon
And stretches away to the night.
But still I rejoice when the travellers rejoice,
And weep with the strangers that moan.
Nor live in my house by the side of the road
Like a man who dwells alone.

Let me live in my house by the side of the road
Where the race of men go by—
They are good, they are bad, they are weak, they are strong,
Wise, foolish—so am I.
Then why should I sit in the scorner's seat
Or hurl the cynic's ban?—
Let me live in my house by the side of the road
And be a friend to man.

SAM WALTER FOSS, "The House by the Side of the Road," *Dreams in Homespun*, pp. 11–12 (1898).

686 Never Explain—your Friends do not need it and your Enemies will not believe you anyway

ELBERT HUBBARD, *The Note Book of Elbert Hubbard*, opposite p. 176 (1927).

See also No. 1113.

687 But friendship is precious, not only in the shade, but in the sunshine of life; and thanks to a benevolent arrangement of things, the greater part of life is sunshine.

President THOMAS JEFFERSON, letter to Maria Cosway, October 12, 1786.—*The Papers of Thomas Jefferson*, ed. Julian P. Boyd, vol. 10, pp. 449–50 (1954).

688 Our cause, then, must be intrusted to, and conducted by, its own undoubted friends—those whose hands are free, whose hearts are in the work—who *do care* for the result. Two years ago the Republicans of the nation mustered over thirteen hundred thousand strong. We did this under the single impulse of resistance to a common danger, with every external circumstance against us. Of *strange, discordant,* and even, *hostile* elements, we gathered from the four winds, and *formed* and fought the battle through, under the constant hot fire of a disciplined, proud, and pampered enemy. Did we brave all *then* to *falter* now?—*now* when that same enemy is *wavering,* dissevered, and belligerent? The result is not doubtful. We shall not fail—if we stand firm, we shall not fail. *Wise councils* may *accelerate* or *mistakes delay* it, but, sooner or later, the victory is *sure to come.*

ABRAHAM LINCOLN, speech delivered at the close of the Republican state convention, which named him the candidate for the United States Senate, Springfield, Illinois, June 16, 1858.—*The Collected Works of Abraham Lincoln*, ed. Roy P. Basler, vol. 2, pp. 468–69 (1953).

See note about this speech at No. 1851.

689 When someone asked Abraham Lincoln, after he was elected president, what he was going to do about his enemies, he replied, "I am going to destroy them. I am going to make them my friends."

Attributed to ABRAHAM LINCOLN. Unverified.

690 Think where man's glory most begins and ends,
And say my glory was I had such friends.

WILLIAM BUTLER YEATS, "The Municipal Gallery Revisited," lines 54–55, *The Variorum Edition of the Poems of W. B. Yeats*, ed. Peter Allt and Russell K. Alspach, p. 604 (1957).

Senator George McGovern quoted these words of Yeats's in his concession speech following the 1972 presidential election.

691 The challenge of the next half century is whether we have the wisdom to use that wealth to enrich and elevate our national life, and to advance the quality of our American civilization. . . .

The Great Society rests on abundance and liberty for all. It demands an end to poverty and racial injustice, to which we are totally committed in our time. But that is just the beginning.

The Great Society is a place where every child can find knowledge to enrich his mind and to enlarge his talents. It is a place where leisure is a welcome chance to build and reflect, not a feared cause of boredom and restlessness. It is a place where the city of man serves not only the needs of the body and the demands of commerce but the desire for beauty and the hunger for community.

It is a place where man can renew contact with nature. It is a place which honors creation for its own sake and for what it adds to the understanding of the race. It is a place where men are more concerned with the quality of their goals than the quantity of their goods.

But most of all, the Great Society is not a safe harbor, a resting place, a final objective, a finished work. It is a challenge constantly renewed, beckoning us toward a destiny where the meaning of our lives matches the marvelous products of our labor.

President LYNDON B. JOHNSON, remarks at the University of Michigan, Ann Arbor, May 22, 1964.—*Public Papers of the Presidents of the United States: Lyndon B. Johnson, 1963–64*, book 1, p. 704.

692 For if Freedom and Communism were to compete for man's allegiance in a world at peace, I would look to the future with ever increasing confidence.

President JOHN F. KENNEDY, State of the Union address, January 30, 1961.—*Public Papers of the Presidents of the United States: John F. Kennedy, 1961*, p. 23.

693 But this *long run* is a misleading guide to current affairs. *In the long run* we are all dead.

JOHN MAYNARD KEYNES, *A Tract on Monetary Reform*, chapter 3, p. 80 (1923).

694 Yet this corporate being, though so insubstantial to our senses, binds, in Burke's words, a man to his country with "ties which though light as air, are as strong as links of iron." That is why young men die in battle for their country's sake and why old men plant trees they will never sit under.

WALTER LIPPMANN, *Essays in the Public Philosophy*, chapter 3, part 2, p. 36 (1955).

The quotation is from Edmund Burke's speech on "Conciliation with America" (1775).

695 The only limit to our realization of tomorrow will be our doubts of today. Let us move forward with strong and active faith.

President FRANKLIN D. ROOSEVELT.—"This is the latest draft of the President's proposed speech [for Jefferson Day, April 13, 1945]. The last sentence [quoted above] was written into the typed draft in his own hand. The draft was not the final one; the preparation of the final draft was prevented by death."—*The Public Papers and Addresses of Franklin D. Roosevelt, 1944–45*, p. 616 (1950).

FDR died April 12, 1945.

Future

696 "So you've been over into Russia?" said Bernard Baruch, and I answered very literally, "I have been over into the future and it works."

LINCOLN STEFFENS, *The Autobiography of Lincoln Steffens*, vol. 2, chapter 18, p. 799 (1931, reprinted 1958).

Steffens had made his second trip to Russia in 1919, as part of a mission sent by President Woodrow Wilson.

697 The nation is burdened with the heavy curse on those who come afterwards. The generation before us was inspired by an activism and a naive enthusiasm, which we cannot rekindle, because we confront tasks of a different kind from those which our fathers faced.

MAX WEBER, address to convention of the Verein für Socialpolitik, Germany, 1893.—Reinhard Bendix, *Max Weber*, p. 53 (1960).

698 My clients are the children; my clients are the next generation. They do not know what promises and bonds I undertook when I ordered the armies of the United States to the soil of France, but I know, and I intend to redeem my pledges to the children; they shall not be sent upon a similar errand.

President WOODROW WILSON, address in Pueblo, Colorado, September 25, 1919.—*The Messages and Papers of Woodrow Wilson*, ed. Albert Shaw, vol. 2, p. 1127 (1924).

God

699 For I would rather be a servant in the House of the Lord than to sit in the seats of the mighty.

Senator ALBEN W. BARKLEY, address to a mock Democratic convention, Washington and Lee University, Lexington, Virginia, April 30, 1956.—*Memorial Services Held in the Senate and House of Representatives of the United States, Together with Remarks Presented in Eulogy of Alben William Barkley, Late a Senator from Kentucky*, p. 106 (1956).

After speaking these words, Senator Barkley collapsed and died. In her book, *I Married the Veep* (1958), Jane R. Barkley says (p. 312), "I am not sure, even now, how these words came into being, where they came from. I believe they were original with him but were based on the Old Testament, 84th Psalm: 10, 'I had rather be a doorkeeper in the house of my God, than to dwell in the tents of wickedness.' "

700 I say, the acknowledgment of God in Christ
Accepted by thy reason, solves for thee
All questions in the earth and out of it,
And has so far advanced thee to be wise.

ROBERT BROWNING, "A Death in the Desert," stanza 21, *The Complete Poetic and Dramatic Works of Robert Browning*, p. 390 (1895).

701 "Let us hope," I prayed, "that a kind Providence will put a speedy end to the acts of God under which we have been laboring."

PETER DE VRIES, *The Mackerel Plaza*, p. 28 (1958).

702 It is the final proof of God's omnipotence that he need not exist in order to save us.

PETER DE VRIES, *The Mackerel Plaza*, p. 8 (1958).

703 I have lived, Sir, a long time, and the longer I live, the more convincing proofs I see of this truth—*that God governs in the affairs of men.* And if a sparrow cannot fall to the ground without his notice, is it probable that an empire can rise without his aid?

BENJAMIN FRANKLIN, debates in the Constitutional Convention, Philadelphia, Pennsylvania, June 28, 1787.—James Madison, *Journal of the Federal Convention,* ed. E. H. Scott, pp. 259–60 (1893).

Franklin suggests that the Convention begin its sessions with prayers "imploring the assistance of Heaven, and its blessings on our deliberations."

704 I know that the LORD is *always* on the side of the *right.* But it is my constant anxiety and prayer that *I* and *this nation* should be on the LORD's *side.*

President ABRAHAM LINCOLN.—Francis B. Carpenter, *Six Months at the White House with Abraham Lincoln,* p. 282 (1867).

Reply to a clergyman who said to Lincoln that he hoped "the Lord was on our side." See note at No. 731.

705 Had I but serv'd my God with half the zeal
I serv'd my king, He would not in mine age
Have left me naked to mine enemies.

WILLIAM SHAKESPEARE, *Henry VIII,* act II, scene ii, lines 455–57. Cardinal Wolsey is speaking to his servant, Cromwell.

During the Watergate hearings, on June 12, 1973, Senator Sam Ervin quoted these words to Herbert Porter.

Government

706 And thus Bureaucracy, the giant power wielded by pigmies, came into the world.

HONORÉ DE BALZAC, *Bureaucracy* (vol. 12 in *The Works of Honoré de Balzac*), p. 13 (1901, reprinted 1971).

707 If the Government becomes a lawbreaker, it breeds contempt for law; it invites every man to become a law unto himself; it invites anarchy. To declare that in the administration of the criminal law the end justifies the means—to declare that the Government may commit crimes in order to secure the conviction of a private criminal—would bring terrible retribution.

Justice LOUIS D. BRANDEIS, dissenting, *Olmstead et al.* v. *United States,* 277 U.S. 485 (1928).

708 We cannot meet it [the threat of dictatorship] if we turn this country into a wishy-washy imitation of totalitarianism, where every man's hand is out for pabulum and virile creativeness has given place to the patronizing favor of swollen bureaucracy.

VANNEVAR BUSH, speech at Massachusetts Institute of Technology, Cambridge, Massachusetts, December 5, 1949, as reported by *The New York Times,* December 6, 1949, p. 12.

Bush was president of the Carnegie Institution, Washington, D.C.

709 The nearest approach to immortality on earth is a government bureau.

JAMES F. BYRNES, *Speaking Frankly,* p. 7 (1947).

Byrnes served in Congress 1911–1925 and 1930–1941.

710 In the long-run every Government is the exact symbol of its People, with their wisdom and unwisdom; we have to say, Like People like Government.

THOMAS CARLYLE, *Past and Present*, ed. Richard D. Altick, book 4, chapter 4, p. 267 (1965). First published in 1843.

711 Only perhaps in the United States, which alone of countries can do *without* governing,—every man being at least able to live, and move off into the wilderness, let Congress jargon as it will,—can such a form of so-called "Government" continue for any length of time to torment men with the semblance, when the indispensable substance is not there.

THOMAS CARLYLE, *Latter-Day Pamphlets*, no. 6, pp. 16–17 (1850).

712 The administration of government, like a guardianship ought to be directed to the good of those who confer, not of those who receive the trust.

Attributed to MARCUS TULLIUS CICERO.—Tryon Edwards, *Dictionary of Thoughts*, p. 204 (1891). Unverified.

713 For nearly five years the present Ministers have harassed every trade, worried every profession, and assailed or menaced every class, institution, and species of property in the country. Occasionally they have varied this state of civil warfare by perpetrating some job which outraged public opinion, or by stumbling into mistakes which have been always discreditable, and sometimes ruinous. All this they call a policy, and seem quite proud of it; but the country has, I think, made up its mind to close this career of plundering and blundering.

BENJAMIN DISRAELI, letter to Lord Grey de Wilton, October 3, 1873.—W. F. Monypenny and George Earl Buckle, *The Life of Benjamin Disraeli*, vol. 5, chapter 7, p. 262 (1920).

Lord Grey was standing for Parliament, and was a personal friend of Disraeli's, who "wrote for publication . . . a full-blooded letter, conceived in the hustings spirit, but it only restated, in pointed fashion, charges which Disraeli had often brought against Ministers in public speeches and . . . [in] the House of Commons. A vehement outcry was, however, raised against its tone and language; and even many of his own party attributed to this indiscretion Grey de Wilton's failure by a small majority" to win the seat. Disraeli "was quite impenitent" (p. 262).

A footnote indicates that the "plundering and blundering" phrase had been used before by Disraeli, in *Coningsby*, book 2, chapter 4.

714 The American wage earner and the American housewife are a lot better economists than most economists care to admit. They know that a government big enough to give you everything you want is a government big enough to take from you everything you have.

President GERALD R. FORD, remarks to a joint session of Congress, August 12, 1974.—*The Public Papers of the Presidents of the United States: Gerald R. Ford, 1974*, p. 6.

Representative Ford was quoted as having expressed the same idea nearly fifteen years earlier: "If the government is big enough to give you everything you want, it is big enough to take away everything you have."—John F. Parker, "*If Elected, I Promise . . . ,*" *Stories and Gems of Wisdom by and About Politicians*, p. 193 (1960). No source is given.

715 In a political sense, there is one problem that currently underlies all of the others. That problem is making Government sufficiently responsive to the people. If we don't make government responsive to the people, we don't make it believable. And we must make government believable if we are to have a functioning democracy.

Representative GERALD R. FORD, address at Robert A. Taft government seminar banquet, Jacksonville University, Jacksonville, Florida, December 16, 1971.—*Gerald R. Ford, Selected Speeches*, ed. Michael V. Doyle, p. 170 (1973).

716 The small progress we have made after four or five weeks close attendance and continual reasonings with each other . . . is, methinks, a melancholy proof of the imperfection of the human understanding. We indeed seem to feel our own want of political wisdom, since we have been running about in search of it. We have gone back to ancient history for models of government, and examined the different forms of those republics which, having been formed with seeds of their own dissolution, now no longer exist.

BENJAMIN FRANKLIN, debates in the Constitutional Convention, Philadelphia, Pennsylvania, June 28, 1787.—James Madison, *Journal of the Federal Convention*, ed. E. H. Scott, p. 259 (1893).

717 Our form of government may remain notwithstanding legislation or decision, but, as long ago observed, it is with governments, as with religion, the form may survive the substance of the faith.

Chief Justice MELVILLE W. FULLER, dissenting, the Lottery Case, 188 U.S. 375 (1903).

718 Fellow-citizens! Clouds and darkness are round about Him! His pavilion is dark waters and thick clouds of the skies! Justice and judgment are the habitation of his throne! Mercy and truth shall go before his face! Fellow-citizens! God reigns and the government at Washington still lives.

Representative JAMES A. GARFIELD, address to calm a crowd in New York City, April 17, 1865, two days after the death of President Lincoln.—Theodore Clarke Smith, *The Life and Letters of James Abram Garfield*, vol. 1, p. 383 (1925).

Smith notes that while the tradition of this speech was so well established during Garfield's own lifetime as to become "a familiar commonplace," no clipping of it exists among Garfield's papers, nor did Garfield himself, so far as known, refer to it in later times.

719 Which is the best government? That which teaches us to govern ourselves.
(Welche Regierung die beste sei? Diejenige, die uns lehrt, uns selbst zu regieren.)

JOHANN WOLFGANG VON GOETHE, *The Maxims and Reflections of Goethe*, trans. Bailey Saunders, maxim 225, p. 107 (1893).

720 A wise government knows how to enforce with temper, or to conciliate with dignity, but a weak one is odious in the former, and contemptible in the latter.

GEORGE GRENVILLE, speech against the motion for expelling John Wilkes, House of Commons, February 3, 1769.—*The Parliamentary History of England*, printed by T. C. Hansard, vol. 16, col. 570 (1813).

"Though Grenville had taken a prominent part in the early measures against Wilkes, he opposed his expulsion from the House of Commons on 3 Feb. 1769, in probably the ablest speech that he ever made."—*The Dictionary of National Biography*, vol. 8, p. 559.

721 The system . . . is the best that the present views and circumstances of the country will permit.

ALEXANDER HAMILTON, *The Federalist*, ed. Benjamin F. Wright, no. 85, p. 544 (1961).

Hamilton acknowledged the imperfect nature of the government that would result from adopting the Constitution, but he felt it imprudent "to prolong the precarious state of our national affairs . . . in the chimerical pursuit of the perfect plan."

722 But, sir, I have said I do not dread these corporations as instruments of power to destroy this country, because there are a thousand agencies which can regulate, restrain, and control them; but there is a corporation we may all well dread. That corporation is the Federal Government.

Senator BENJAMIN H. HILL, remarks in the Senate on the Pacific Railroad funding bill, March 27, 1878, *Congressional Record*, vol. 7, p. 2067.

723 Far more important to me is, that I should be loyal to what I regard as the law of my political life, which is this: a belief that that country is best governed, which is least governed . . .

GEORGE HOADLY, remarks in Ohio constitutional convention, June 19, 1873.—*Official Report of the Proceedings and Debates of the Third Constitutional Convention of Ohio* . . . , p. 436 (1873).

724 It was once said that the moral test of government is how that government treats those who are in the dawn of life, the children; those who are in the twilight of life, the elderly; and those who are in the shadows of life—the sick, the needy and the handicapped.

Senator HUBERT H. HUMPHREY, remarks at the dedication of the Hubert H. Humphrey Building, November 1, 1977.—*Congressional Record*, November 4, 1977, vol. 123, p. 37287.

725 I confess I have the same fears for our South American brethren; the qualifications for self-government in society are not innate. They are the result of habit and long training, and for these they will require time and probably much suffering.

THOMAS JEFFERSON, letter to Edward Everett, March 27, 1824.—*The Writings of Thomas Jefferson*, ed. Andrew A. Lipscomb, vol. 16, p. 22 (1904).

726 I think our governments will remain virtuous for many centuries; as long as they are chiefly agricultural; and this will be as long as there shall be vacant lands in any part of America. When they get piled upon one another in large cities, as in Europe, they will become corrupt as in Europe.

THOMAS JEFFERSON, letter to James Madison, December 20, 1787.—*The Papers of Thomas Jefferson*, ed. Julian P. Boyd, vol. 12, p. 442 (1955).

727 If we can prevent the government from wasting the labors of the people, under the pretence of taking care of them, they must become happy.

President THOMAS JEFFERSON, letter to Thomas Cooper, November 29, 1802.—*The Writings of Thomas Jefferson*, ed. Paul L. Ford, vol. 8, p. 178 (1897).

728 Were we directed from Washington when to sow, & when to reap, we should soon want bread.

THOMAS JEFFERSON, "Autobiography," *The Writings of Thomas Jefferson*, ed. Paul L. Ford, vol. 1, p. 113 (1892).

729 I believe that the essence of government lies with unceasing concern for the welfare and dignity and decency and innate integrity of life for every individual. I don't like to say this and wish I didn't have to add these words to make it clear but I will—regardless of color, creed, ancestry, sex or age.

LYNDON B. JOHNSON, remarks at a civil rights symposium, LBJ Library, Austin, Texas, December 12, 1972.—Text, p. 1.

730 Before my term has ended, we shall have to test anew whether a nation organized and governed such as ours can endure. The outcome is by no means certain.

President JOHN F. KENNEDY, annual message to Congress on the State of the Union, January 30, 1961.—*Public Papers of the Presidents of the United States: John F. Kennedy, 1961*, p. 19.

731 Gentlemen, suppose all the property you were worth was in gold, and you had put it in the hands of Blondin to carry across the Niagara River on a rope, would you shake the cable, or keep shouting out to him—"Blondin, stand up a little straighter—Blondin, stoop a little more—go a little faster—lean a little more to the north—lean a little more to the south?" No, you would hold your breath as well as your tongue, and keep your hands off until he was safe over. The Government are carrying an immense weight. Untold treasures are in their hands. They are doing the very best they can. Don't badger them. Keep silence, and we'll get you safe across.

President ABRAHAM LINCOLN, reply to critics of his administration, 1864.—Francis B. Carpenter, "Anecdotes and Reminiscences of President Lincoln" in Henry Jarvis Raymond, *The Life and Public Services of Abraham Lincoln . . .*, p. 752 (1865).

Carpenter, a portrait artist, lived in the White House for six months beginning February 1864, to paint the president and the entire Cabinet. His relations with the president became of an "intimate character," and he was permitted "the freedom of his private office at almost all hours, . . . privileged to see and know more of his daily life" than most people. He states that he "endeavored to embrace only those [anecdotes] which bear the marks of authenticity. Many . . . I myself heard the President relate; others were communicated to me by persons who either heard or took part in them" (p. 725).

Blondin (real name Jean François Gravelet) was a French tightrope walker who crossed Niagara Falls on a tightrope in 1855, 1859, and 1860.

732 I am struggling to maintain the government, not to overthrow it. I am struggling especially to prevent others from overthrowing it.

President ABRAHAM LINCOLN, response to a serenade, October 19, 1864.—*The Collected Works of Abraham Lincoln*, ed. Roy P. Basler, vol. 8, p. 52 (1953).

733 Must a government, of necessity, be too *strong* for the liberties of its own people, or too *weak* to maintain its own existence?

President ABRAHAM LINCOLN, message to Congress in special session, July 4, 1861.—*The Collected Works of Abraham Lincoln*, ed. Roy P. Basler, vol. 4, p. 426 (1953).

734 There is an important sense in which government is distinctive from administration. One is perpetual, the other is temporary and changeable. A man may be loyal to his government and yet oppose the particular principles and methods of administration.

Attributed to Representative ABRAHAM LINCOLN.—W. T. Roche, address at Washington, Kansas, April 9, 1942: "These words were spoken by Lincoln, then a Congressman, in defense of his condemnation of President Polk for provoking the Mexican War."—*Congressional Record,* April 15, 1942, vol. 88, Appendix, p. A1493. Not found in *The Collected Works of Abraham Lincoln,* ed. Roy P. Basler (1953).

735 While the people retain their virtue, and vigilance, no administration, by any extreme of wickedness or folly, can very seriously injure the government, in the short space of four years.

President ABRAHAM LINCOLN, first inaugural address (final text), March 4, 1861.—*The Collected Works of Abraham Lincoln,* ed. Roy P. Basler, vol. 4, p. 270 (1953).

736 We must judge of a form of government by its general tendency, not by happy accidents.

THOMAS BABINGTON MACAULAY, speech on parliamentary reform, March 2, 1831.—*The Complete Writings of Lord Macaulay,* vol. 17, p. 13 (1900).

737 Yes, Gentlemen; if I am asked why we are free with servitude all around us, why our Habeas Corpus Act has not been suspended, why our press is still subject to no censor, why we still have the liberty of association, why our representative institutions still abide in all their strength, I answer, It is because in the year of revolutions we stood firmly by our government in its peril; and, if I am asked why we stood by our government in its peril, when men all around us were engaged in pulling governments down, I answer, It was because we knew that though our government was not a perfect government, it was a good government, that its faults admitted of peaceable and legal remedies, that it had never inflexibly opposed just demands, that we had obtained concessions of inestimable value, not by beating the drum, not by ringing the tocsin, not by tearing up the pavement, not by running to the gunsmiths' shops to search for arms, but by the mere force of reason and public opinion.

THOMAS BABINGTON MACAULAY, speech on his re-election to Parliament, November 2, 1852.—Macaulay, *Miscellanies,* vol. 2 (vol. 18 of *The Complete Writings of Lord Macaulay*), pp. 170–71 (1900).

738 The free system of government we have established is so congenial with reason, with common sense, and with a universal feeling, that it must produce approbation and a desire of imitation, as avenues may be found for truth to the knowledge of nations.

JAMES MADISON, letter to Pierre E. Duponceau, January 23, 1826.—James Madison papers, Library of Congress.

These words are inscribed in the Madison Memorial Hall, Library of Congress James Madison Memorial Building.

739 If men were angels, no government would be necessary. If angels were to govern men, neither external nor internal controls on government would be necessary.

JAMES MADISON, *The Federalist,* ed. Benjamin F. Wright, no. 51, p. 356 (1961).

740 Every country has the government it deserves.
(Toute nation a le gouvernement qu'elle mérite.)

JOSEPH MARIE DE MAISTRE, letter to M. le chevalier de . . . , August 15, 1811.—*Lettres et Opuscules Inédits du Comte J. De Maistre,* 5th ed., book 1, p. 264 (1869).

741 Thus, a people may prefer a free government, but if, from indolence, or carelessness, or cowardice, or want of public spirit, they are unequal to the exertions necessary for preserving it; if they will not fight for it when it is directly attacked; if they can be deluded by the artifices used to cheat them out of it; if by momentary discouragement, or temporary panic, or a fit of enthusiasm for an individual, they can be induced to lay their liberties at the feet even of a great man, or trust him with powers which enable him to subvert their institutions; in all these cases they are more or less unfit for liberty: and though it may be for their good to have had it even for a short time, they are unlikely long to enjoy it.

JOHN STUART MILL, *Considerations on Representative Government*, p. 6 (1861).

742 When the people are too much attached to savage independence, to be tolerant of the amount of power to which it is for their good that they should be subject, the state of society (as already observed) is not yet ripe for representative government.

JOHN STUART MILL, *Considerations on Representative Government*, chapter 6, p. 108 (1861).

743 You have the God-given right to kick the government around—don't hesitate to do so.

Senator EDMUND S. MUSKIE, speech in South Bend, Indiana, September 11, 1968, as reported by the Louisville, Kentucky, *Courier-Journal*, September 12, 1968, p. A3.

744 The great art of governing consists in not letting men grow old in their jobs.
(Ne pas laisser vieillir les hommes doit être le grand art du gouvernement.)

NAPOLEON, letter to Lazare Nicolas Marguerite Carnot, August 9, 1796.—*Correspondance de Napoléon Ier*, vol. 1, p. 532 (1858).

745 Governments, like clocks, go from the motion men give them, and as governments are made and moved by men, so by them they are ruined too. Wherefore governments rather depend upon men, than men upon governments. Let men be good, and the government cannot be bad; if it be ill, they will cure it. But if men be bad, let the government be never so good, they will endeavour to warp and spoil it to their turn.

WILLIAM PENN, in his Preface to the First Frame of Government [constitution] for Pennsylvania, which was formally adopted in England, April 25, 1682.—The William Penn Tercentenary Committee, *Remember William Penn*, 2d ed., p. 81 (1945).

The committee noted that the preface was perhaps "Penn's best expression of his ideas of government" (p. 80).

746 Men must be governed by God or they will be ruled by tyrants.

Attributed to WILLIAM PENN.—Virginia Ely, *I Quote*, p. 189 (1947). Unverified. Numerous sources cite this remark but it has not been found in Penn's writings.

747 To be governed is to be watched over, inspected, spied on, directed, legislated at, regulated, docketed, indoctrinated, preached at, controlled, assessed, weighed, censored, ordered about, by men who have neither the right nor the knowledge nor the virtue.

PIERRE-JOSEPH PROUDHON.—From an English translation of his *Idée Générale de la Révolution au XIXe Siècle* (1851) quoted in James Joll, *The Anarchists*, chapter 3, p. 78 (1964).

748 There is no credit to being a comedian, when you have the whole Government working for you. All you have to do is report the facts. I don't even have to exaggerate.

WILL ROGERS.—P.J. O'Brien, *Will Rogers, Ambassador of Good Will, Prince of Wit and Wisdom,* chapter 9, p. 157 (1935).

749 Governments can err, Presidents do make mistakes, but the immortal Dante tells us that divine justice weighs the sins of the cold-blooded and the sins of the warm-hearted in different scales. Better the occasional faults of a Government that lives in a spirit of charity than the consistent omissions of a Government frozen in the ice of its own indifference.

President FRANKLIN D. ROOSEVELT, speech accepting renomination for the presidency, June 27, 1936.—*The Public Papers and Addresses of Franklin D. Roosevelt, 1936,* p. 235 (1938).

Senator John F. Kennedy quoted these words of Roosevelt's in a campaign speech in Houston, Texas, September 12, 1960.—*Freedom of Communications,* final report of the Committee on Commerce, United States Senate, part 1, p. 203 (1961). Senate Rept. 87-994.

750 History proves that dictatorships do not grow out of strong and successful governments, but out of weak and helpless ones. If by democratic methods people get a government strong enough to protect them from fear and starvation, their democracy succeeds; but if they do not, they grow impatient. Therefore, the only sure bulwark of continuing liberty is a government strong enough to protect the interests of the people, and a people strong enough and well enough informed to maintain its sovereign control over its government.

President FRANKLIN D. ROOSEVELT, fireside chat on economic conditions, April 14, 1938.—*The Public Papers and Addresses of Franklin D. Roosevelt, 1938,* pp. 242–43 (1941).

751 The true art of government consists in *not governing too much.*

JONATHAN SHIPLEY, bishop of St. Asaph, sermon, at parish church of St. Mary-Le-Bow, London, February 19, 1773.—*A Sermon Preached Before the Incorporated Society for the Propagation of the Gospel in Foreign Parts,* p. 11 (1773). Reprinted in *English Defenders of American Freedoms, 1774–1778,* ed. Paul H. Smith, pp. 22–23 (1972).

752 Public confidence in the integrity of the Government is indispensable to faith in democracy; and when we lose faith in the system, we have lost faith in everything we fight and spend for.

ADLAI E. STEVENSON, governor of Illinois, speech before the Los Angeles Town Club, Los Angeles, California, September 11, 1952.—*Speeches of Adlai Stevenson,* p. 31 (1952).

753 I heartily accept the motto,—"That government is best which governs least;" and I should like to see it acted up to more rapidly and systematically. Carried out, it finally amounts to this, which I also believe,—"That government is best which governs not at all;" and when men are prepared for it, that will be the kind of government which they will have. Government is at best but an expedient; but most governments are usually, and all governments are sometimes, inexpedient.

HENRY DAVID THOREAU, *Civil Disobedience,* first paragraph, *Walden and Civil Disobedience,* ed. Owen Thomas, p. 224 (1966). This essay was first published in 1849.

The motto Thoreau referred to was almost certainly that of *The United States Magazine and Democratic Review,* a literary-political monthly: "The best government is that which governs least."

Ralph Waldo Emerson expressed a similar sentiment in his essay "Politics": "Hence the less government we have the better—the fewer laws and the less confided power."—*Essays: Second Series*, in *The Complete Writings of Ralph Waldo Emerson*, vol. 1, p. 302 (1929).

754 Government is not reason, it is not eloquence, it is force; like fire, a troublesome servant and a fearful master. Never for a moment should it be left to irresponsible action.

Attributed to GEORGE WASHINGTON.—Frank J. Wilstach, *A Dictionary of Similes*, 2d ed., p. 526 (1924). This can be found with minor variations in wording and in punctuation, and with "fearful" for "troublesome," in George Seldes, *The Great Quotations*, p. 727 (1966). Unverified.

In his most recent book of quotations, *The Great Thoughts* (1985), Seldes says, p. 441, col. 2, footnote, this paragraph "although credited to the 'Farewell' [address] cannot be found in it. Lawson Hamblin, who owns a facsimile, and Horace Peck, America's foremost authority on quotations, informed me this paragraph is apocryphal."

755 Other misfortunes may be borne, or their effects overcome. If disastrous war should sweep our commerce from the ocean, another generation may renew it; if it exhaust our treasury, future industry may replenish it; . . . It were but a trifle even if the walls of yonder Capitol were to crumble, if its lofty pillars should fall, and its gorgeous decorations be all covered by the dust of the valley. All these might be rebuilt. But who shall reconstruct the fabric of demolished government? Who shall rear again the well-proportioned columns of constitutional liberty? . . . No, if these columns fall, they will be raised not again. . . . they will be the remnants of a more glorious edifice than Greece or Rome ever saw, the edifice of constitutional American liberty.

Senator DANIEL WEBSTER, "The Character of Washington," speech delivered in Washington, D.C., at a public dinner in honor of the centennial birthday of George Washington, February 22, 1832.—*The Works of Daniel Webster*, 10th ed., vol. 1, p. 231 (1857).

756 Whatever government is not a government of laws, is a despotism, let it be called what it may.

Senator DANIEL WEBSTER, at a reception in Bangor, Maine, August 25, 1835.—*The Writings and Speeches of Daniel Webster*, vol. 2, p. 165 (1903).

757 Trust nothing to the enthusiasm of the people. Give them a strong and a just, and, if possible, a good, government; but, above all, a strong one.

ARTHUR WELLESLEY, DUKE OF WELLINGTON, letter to Lieutenant-General Lord William Bentinck, December 24, 1811.—John Gurwood, *Selections from the Dispatches and General Orders of Field Marshal, the Duke of Wellington*, p. 545 (1851).

758 My reading of history convinces me that most bad government has grown out of too much government.

Senator JOHN SHARP WILLIAMS, *Thomas Jefferson: His Permanent Influence on American Institutions*, p. 49 (1913). Lecture delivered at Columbia University, New York City, 1912.

759 Too much law was too much government; and too much government was too little individual privilege,—as too much individual privilege in its turn was selfish license.

WOODROW WILSON, "The Author and Signers of the Declaration of Independence," address at Jamestown exposition, Norfolk, Virginia, July 4, 1907.—*The Papers of Woodrow Wilson*, ed. Arthur S. Link, vol. 17, p. 254 (1974).

Government—by the people

760 Our present political position has been achieved in a manner unprecedented in the history of nations. It illustrates the American idea that governments rest on the consent of the governed, and that it is the right of the people to alter or abolish them at will whenever they become destructive of the ends for which they were established.

JEFFERSON DAVIS, inaugural address as president of the Confederate States of America, Montgomery, Alabama, February 18, 1861.—*Jefferson Davis, Constitutionalist, His Letters, Papers and Speeches*, ed. Dunbar Rowland, vol. 5, p. 50 (1923).

Davis served in Congress 1845–1846 and 1847–1851.

761 My fellow Americans, our long national nightmare is over. Our Constitution works; our great Republic is a government of laws and not of men. Here the people rule. But there is a higher Power, by whatever name we honor Him, who ordains not only righteousness but love, not only justice but mercy.

President GERALD R. FORD, remarks on taking the oath of office, August 9, 1974.—*Public Papers of the Presidents of the United States: Gerald R. Ford, 1974*, p. 2.

762 Here, sir, the people govern; here they act by their immediate representatives.

ALEXANDER HAMILTON, remarks at the New York convention on the adoption of the federal Constitution, Poughkeepsie, New York, June 27, 1788.—Jonathan Elliot, *The Debates in the Several State Conventions on the Adoption of the Federal Constitution* . . . , vol. 2, p. 348 (1836, reprinted 1937).

Hamilton was referring to the House of Representatives.

763 The only legitimate right to govern is an express grant of power from the governed.

President WILLIAM HENRY HARRISON, inaugural address, March 4, 1841.—*Inaugural Addresses of the Presidents of the United States from George Washington, 1789, to John F. Kennedy, 1961*, p. 72 (1961). House Doc. 87-218.

This sentence is one of many quotations inscribed on Cox Corridor II, a first floor House corridor, U.S. Capitol.

764 The people who own the country ought to govern it.

Attributed to JOHN JAY.—Frank Monaghan, *John Jay*, chapter 15, p. 323 (1935). According to Monaghan, this "was one of his favorite maxims." Unverified in the writings of Jay, although the essence of this is expressed in several passages.

765 The genius of Republican liberty, seems to demand on one side, not only that all power should be derived from the people; but, that those entrusted with it should be kept in dependence on the people, by a short duration of their appointments; and, that, even during this short period, the trust should be placed not in a few, but in a number of hands. Stability, on the contrary, requires, that the hands, in which power is lodged, should continue for a length of time, the same. A frequent change of men will result from a frequent return of electors, and a frequent change of measures, from a frequent change of men; whilst energy in Government requires not only a certain duration of power, but the execution of it by a single hand.

JAMES MADISON, *The Federalist*, ed. Benjamin F. Wright, no. 37, p. 268 (1961).

Government—citizen participation

766 Are you a politician asking *what your country can do for you* or a zealous one *asking what you can do for your country?* If you are the first, then you are a parasite; if the second, then you are an oasis in the desert.

KAHLIL GIBRAN.—*A Third Treasury of Kahlil Gibran*, ed. Andrew Dib Sherfan, p. 53 (1975).

"This statement appeared in an article written by Gibran in Arabic, over fifty years ago. The heading of that article can be translated either *The New Deal* or *The New Frontier*" (p. 52).

The following translation was made before John F. Kennedy's 1961 inaugural address:

Are you a politician who says to himself: "I will use my country for my own benefit"? If so, you are naught but a parasite living on the flesh of others. Or are you a devoted patriot, who whispers into the ear of his inner self: "I love to serve my country as a faithful servant." If so, you are an oasis in the desert, ready to quench the thirst of the wayfarer.—Kahlil Gibran, *The Voice of the Master*, trans. Anthony R. Ferris, p. 34 (1958).

767 I like people in the cities, in the States and in the Nation to ask themselves now and then: "What can I do for my city?" not "How much can I get out of my city?" I like people to speak now and then in the same devotion to State and Nation, because, after all, my countrymen, whenever a man contributes to the betterment of his community, whenever he contributes to the enlarged influence of his State, whenever he contributes to the greater glory of the Republic and makes it a better place in which to live and in which to invite men to participate and aspire, he contributes to himself as he contributes to the welfare of his fellow men.

President WARREN G. HARDING, address at the laying of the cornerstone of the City Club Building, St. Louis, Missouri, June 21, 1923.—*Speeches and Addresses of Warren G. Harding, President of the United States, . . . 1923*, p. 31 (1923).

768 It is now the moment when by common consent we pause to become conscious of our national life and to rejoice in it, to recall what our country has done for each of us, and to ask ourselves what we can do for our country in return.

OLIVER WENDELL HOLMES, justice of the supreme court of Massachusetts, Memorial Day speech, May 30, 1884, Keene, New Hampshire.—Holmes, *Speeches*, pp. 2–3 (1934).

769 And so, my fellow Americans: ask not what your country can do for you—ask what you can do for your country. My fellow citizens of the world: ask not what America will do for you, but what together we can do for the freedom of man.

President JOHN F. KENNEDY, inaugural address, January 20, 1961.—*The Public Papers of the Presidents of the United States: John F. Kennedy, 1961*, p. 3.

This is one of seven inscriptions carved on the walls at the gravesite of John F. Kennedy, Arlington National Cemetery.

He foreshadowed this remark earlier: "But the New Frontier of which I speak is not a set of promises—it is a set of challenges. It sums up not what I intend to offer the

American people, but what I intend to ask of them."—Acceptance speech, Democratic national convention, Los Angeles, California, July 15, 1960, *Vital Speeches of the Day,* August 1, 1960, p. 611.

770 The energy, the faith, the devotion which we bring to this endeavor will light our country and all who serve it—and the glow from that fire can truly light the world.

President JOHN F. KENNEDY, inaugural address, January 20, 1961.—*The Public Papers of the Presidents of the United States: John F. Kennedy, 1961,* p. 3.

This is one of seven inscriptions carved on the walls at the gravesite of John F. Kennedy, Arlington National Cemetery.

771 In our own lives, let each of us ask—not just what government will do for me, but what can I do for myself?

President RICHARD M. NIXON, second inaugural address, January 20, 1973.—*Public Papers of the Presidents of the United States: Richard Nixon, 1973,* p. 14.

772 The value of government to the people it serves is in direct relationship to the interest citizens themselves display in the affairs of state.

Attributed to WILLIAM SCRANTON, governor of Pennsylvania. Unverified.

Government—definition of

773 Government is a contrivance of human wisdom to provide for human *wants.* Men have a right that these wants should be provided for by this wisdom.

EDMUND BURKE, "Reflections on the Revolution in France," 1790, *The Works of the Right Honorable Edmund Burke,* vol. 3, p. 310 (1899).

774 If any ask me what a free government is, I answer, that, for any practical purpose, it is what the people think so,—and that they, and not I, are the natural, lawful, and competent judges of this matter.

EDMUND BURKE, letter to the sheriffs of Bristol, April 3, 1777.—*The Works of the Right Honorable Edmund Burke,* vol. 2, p. 227 (1899).

775 Government is like a big baby—an alimentary canal with a big appetite at one end and no sense of responsibility at the other.

RONALD REAGAN, governor of California, joke during 1965 campaign for governor.—*The Reagan Wit,* ed. Bill Adler, p. 30 (1981). Quoted lacking "sense of" in *The New York Times Magazine,* November 14, 1965, p. 174, as a typical wisecrack.

Government—purpose of

776 The chief duty of governments, in so far as they are coercive, is to restrain those who would interfere with the inalienable rights of the individual, among which are the right to life, the right to liberty, the right to the pursuit of happiness and the right to worship God according to the dictates of one's conscience.

WILLIAM JENNINGS BRYAN, secretary of state, speech before the City Club, Baltimore, Maryland, April 24, 1915.—"Bryan's Ten Rules for the New Voter," rule 3, *The Sun,* Baltimore, Maryland, April 25, 1915, p. 16.

Bryan prepared the ten rules as a synopsis of his speech so the newspapers might get the exact sense of it.

777 The lessons of paternalism ought to be unlearned and the better lesson taught that while the people should patriotically and cheerfully support their Government its functions do not include the support of the people.

President GROVER CLEVELAND, second inaugural address, March 4, 1893.—*A Compilation of the Messages and Papers of the Presidents, 1789–1897*, comp. James D. Richardson, vol. 9, p. 390 (1898).

778 If, in my retirement to the humble station of a private citizen, I am accompanied with the esteem and approbation of my fellow citizens, trophies obtained by the blood-stained steel, or the tattered flags of the tented field, will never be envied. The care of human life and happiness, and not their destruction, is the first and only legitimate object of good government.

THOMAS JEFFERSON, letter to the Republican Citizens of Washington County, Maryland, March 31, 1809.—*The Writings of Thomas Jefferson*, ed. H.A. Washington, vol. 8, p. 165 (1871).

779 The main objects of all science, the freedom and happiness of man. . . . [are] the sole objects of all legitimate government.

THOMAS JEFFERSON, letter to General Thaddeus Kosciusko, February 26, 1810.—*The Writings of Thomas Jefferson*, ed. Andrew A. Lipscomb, vol. 12, pp. 369–70 (1904).

In the stairwell of the pedestal of the Statue of Liberty is a plaque inscribed with this quotation, lacking the first clause above.

780 The legitimate object of government, is to do for a community of people, whatever they need to have done, but can not do, *at all*, or can not, *so well do*, for themselves—in their separate, and individual capacities.

In all that the people can individually do as well for themselves, government ought not to interfere.

The desirable things which the individuals of a people can not do, or can not well do, for themselves, fall into two classes: those which have relation to *wrongs*, and those which have not. Each of these branch off into an infinite variety of subdivisions.

The first—that in relation to wrongs—embraces all crimes, misdemeanors, and nonperformance of contracts. The other embraces all which, in its nature, and without wrong, requires combined action, as public roads and highways, public schools, charities, pauperism, orphanage, estates of the deceased, and the machinery of government itself.

From this it appears that if all men were just, there still would be *some*, though not *so much*, need for government.

ABRAHAM LINCOLN, fragment on government (July 1, 1854?)—*The Collected Works of Abraham Lincoln*, ed. Roy P. Basler, vol. 2, pp. 220–21 (1953).

781 The business of government is not directly to make the people rich, but to protect them in making themselves rich; and a government which attempts more than this is precisely the government which is likely to perform less. Governments do not and cannot support the people.

THOMAS BABINGTON MACAULAY, speech on parliamentary reform, March 2, 1831.—*The Complete Writings of Lord Macaulay*, vol. 17, p. 39 (1900).

782 The safety and happiness of society are the objects at which all political institutions aim, and to which all such institutions must be sacrificed.

JAMES MADISON, *The Federalist*, ed. Benjamin F. Wright, no. 43, p. 316 (1961).

These words are inscribed in the Madison Memorial Hall, Library of Congress James Madison Memorial Building.

783 We all know of course that we cannot abolish all the evils in this world by statute or by the enforcement of statutes, nor can we prevent the inexorable law of nature which decrees that suffering shall follow vice, and all the evil passions and folly of mankind. Law cannot give to depravity the rewards of virtue, to indolence the rewards of industry, to indifference the rewards of ambition, or to ignorance the rewards of learning. The utmost that government can do is measurably to protect men, not against the wrong they do themselves but against wrong done by others and to promote the long, slow process of educating mind and character to a better knowledge and nobler standards of life and conduct. We know all this, but when we see how much misery there is in the world and instinctively cry out against it, and when we see some things that government may do to mitigate it, we are apt to forget how little after all it is possible for any government to do, and to hold the particular government of the time and place to a standard of responsibility which no government can possibly meet.

ELIHU ROOT, *Experiments in Government and the Essentials of the Constitution*, pp. 13–14 (1913). The Stafford Little Lectures given at Princeton University, Princeton, New Jersey, 1913.

784 It is customary in democratic countries to deplore expenditure on armaments as conflicting with the requirements of the social services. There is a tendency to forget that the most important social service that a government can do for its people is to keep them alive and free.

SIR JOHN COTESWORTH SLESSOR, marshal of the Royal Air Force, *Strategy for the West*, chapter 4, p. 75 (1954).

785 The ultimate aim of government is not to rule, or restrain, by fear, nor to exact obedience, but contrariwise, to free every man from fear, that he may live in all possible security; in other words, to strengthen his natural right to exist and work without injury to himself or others.

No, the object of government is not to change men from rational beings into beasts or puppets, but to enable them to develop their minds and bodies in security, and to employ their reason unshackled; neither showing hatred, anger, or deceit, nor watched with the eyes of jealousy and injustice. In fact, the true aim of government is liberty.

BENEDICTUS DE SPINOZA, "Tractatus Theologico-Politicus," *Writings on Political Philosophy*, ed. A. G. A. Balz, trans. R. H. M. Elwes, p. 65 (1937). Other translations vary.

786 It is only the novice in political economy who thinks it is the duty of government to *make* its citizens happy.—Government has no such office. To protect the weak and the minority from the impositions of the strong and the majority—to prevent any one from positively working to render the people unhappy, (if we may so express it,) to do the labor not of an officious inter-meddler in the affairs of men, but of a prudent watchman who prevents outrage—these are rather the proper duties of a government. Under the specious pretext of effecting "the happiness of the whole community," nearly all the wrongs and intrusions of government have been carried through. The legislature may, and should, when such things fall in its way, lend its potential weight to the cause of virtue and happiness—

but to legislate in direct behalf of those objects is never available, and rarely effects any even temporary benefit.

WALT WHITMAN, "Duties of Government," editorial, Brooklyn *Eagle*, April 4, 1846.—Whitman, *The Gathering of the Forces*, ed. Cleveland Rodgers and John Black, vol. 1, pp. 56–57 (1920).

787 Government should not be made an end in itself; it is a means only,—a means to be freely adapted to advance the best interests of the social organism. The State exists for the sake of Society, not Society for the sake of the State.

WOODROW WILSON, *The State; Elements of Historical and Practical Politics*, rev. ed., chapter 16, section 1528, p. 636 (1911).

Government—separation of powers

788 In all tyrannical governments the supreme magistracy, or the right both of *making* and of *enforcing* the laws, is vested in one and the same man, or one and the same body of men; and wherever these two powers are united together, there can be no public liberty.

SIR WILLIAM BLACKSTONE, *Commentaries on the Laws of England*, 9th ed., book 1, chapter 2, p. 146 (1783, reprinted 1978).

789 The doctrine of the separation of powers was adopted by the Convention of 1787, not to promote efficiency but to preclude the exercise of arbitrary power. The purpose was, not to avoid friction, but, by means of the inevitable friction incident to the distribution of the governmental powers among three departments, to save the people from autocracy.

Justice LOUIS D. BRANDEIS, dissenting, *Myers* v. *United States*, 272 U.S. 293 (1926).

790 The accumulation of all powers, legislative, executive, and judiciary, in the same hands, whether of one, a few, or many, and whether hereditary, self-appointed, or elective, may justly be pronounced the very definition of tyranny.

JAMES MADISON, *The Federalist*, ed. Benjamin F. Wright, no. 47, p. 336 (1961).

791 It is important, likewise, that the habits of thinking in a free Country should inspire caution in those entrusted with its administration, to confine themselves within their respective Constitutional Spheres; avoiding in the exercise of the Powers of one department to encroach upon another.

President GEORGE WASHINGTON, farewell address, September 19, 1796.—*The Writings of George Washington*, ed. John C. Fitzpatrick, vol. 35, p. 228 (1940).

See note at No. 339 about the farewell address.

792 To admit then a right in the House of Representatives to demand, and to have as a matter of course, all the Papers respecting a negotiation with a foreign power, would be to establish a dangerous precedent. It does not occur that the inspection of the papers asked for, can be relative to any purpose under the cognizance of the House of Representatives, except that of an impeachment, which the resolution has not expressed. I repeat, that I have no disposition to withhold any information which the duty of my station will permit, or the public good shall require to be disclosed: and in fact, all the Papers affecting the negotiation with Great Britain were laid before the Senate, when the Treaty itself was communicated for their consideration and advice. The course which the debate has taken, on the resolution of the House, leads to some observations on the mode of making treaties under the Constitution of the United States.

President GEORGE WASHINGTON, address to the House of Representatives, March 30, 1796.—*The Writings of George Washington*, ed. John C. Fitzpatrick, vol. 35, p. 3 (1940).

Washington refused to provide papers relating to the Jay Treaty, since the assent of the House was unnecessary.

Government officials

793 Decency, security and liberty alike demand that government officials shall be subjected to the same rules of conduct that are commands to the citizen. In a government of laws, existence of the government will be imperilled if it fails to observe the law scrupulously.

Justice LOUIS D. BRANDEIS, dissenting, *Olmstead et al.* v. *United States*, 277 U.S. 485 (1928).

794 It is undoubtedly the business of ministers very much to consult the inclinations of the people, but they ought to take great care that they do not receive that inclination from the few persons who may happen to approach them.

EDMUND BURKE, "Letters on a Regicide Peace," letter 3, 1796–1797, *The Works of the Right Honorable Edmund Burke*, vol. 5, p. 431 (1899).

Government spending

795 The budget should be balanced, the treasury should be refilled, public debt should be reduced, the arrogance of officialdom should be tempered and controlled, assistance to foreign lands should be curtailed lest Rome become bankrupt, the mobs should be forced to work and not depend on government for subsistence.

Attributed to Marcus Tullius Cicero, *Congressional Record*, April 25, 1968, vol. 114, p. 10635.

This passage was reprinted in *U.S. News & World Report*, July 29, 1968, p. 15. Still later, a contributor reported this to *The Review of the News*, June 30, 1971, p. 19, and he also attributed this to Cicero. No evidence has been found to confirm that Cicero said these words, and it is almost certainly spurious.

796 It is the duty of those serving the people in public place closely to limit public expenditures to the actual needs of the government economically administered, because this bounds the right of the government to extract tribute from the earnings of labor or the property of the citizen, and because public extravagance begets extravagance among the people. We should never be ashamed of the simplicity and prudential economies which are best suited to the operation of a republican form of government and most compatible with the mission of the American people. Those who are selected for a limited time to manage public affairs are still of the people, and may do much by their example to encourage, consistently with the diginity of their official functions, that plain way of life which among their fellow-citizens aids integrity and promotes thrift and prosperity.

President GROVER CLEVELAND, first inaugural address, March 4, 1885.—*The Writings and Speeches of Grover Cleveland*, ed. George F. Parker, p. 35 (1892).

797 The appropriation of public money always is perfectly lovely until some one is asked to pay the bill. If we are to have a billion dollars of navy, half a billion of farm relief, [etc.] . . . the people will have to furnish more revenue by paying more taxes. It is for them, through their Congress, to decide how far they wish to go.

CALVIN COOLIDGE, syndicated column, *New York Herald Tribune*, August 5, 1930, p. 1.

798 I favor the policy of economy, not because I wish to save money, but because I wish to save people. The men and women of this country who toil are the ones who bear the cost of the Government. Every dollar that we carelessly waste means that their life will be so much the more meager. Every dollar that we prudently save means that their life will be so much the more abundant. Economy is idealism in its most practical form.

President CALVIN COOLIDGE, inaugural address, March 4, 1925.—Coolidge, *Foundations of the Republic*, p. 201 (1926).

799 Nothing is easier than spending the public money. It does not appear to belong to anybody. The temptation is overwhelming to bestow it on somebody.

Attributed to CALVIN COOLIDGE.—*Readers Digest*, June 1960, p. 178. Unverified.

800 A billion here, a billion there, and pretty soon you're talking about real money.

Attributed to Senator EVERETT M. DIRKSEN by John Kriegsman, confidant of Dirksen's and one-time Republican official in Illinois. Kriegsman reportedly heard this and similar statements as off-the-cuff remarks during campaigns and meetings in Illinois. This remark does not appear in any formal address or in Dirksen's papers.

801 So that here we have, really, the compound, the overall philosophy of Lincoln: in all those things which deal with people, be liberal, be human. In all those things which deal with the people's money or their economy, or their form of government, be conservative—and don't be afraid to use the word.

And so today, Republicans come forward with programs in which there are such words as "balanced budgets," and "cutting expenditures," and all the kind of thing that means this economy must be conservative, it must be solvent.

But they also come forward and say we are concerned with every American's health, with a decent house for him, we are concerned that he will have a chance for health, and his children for education. We are going to see that he has power available to him. We are going to see that everything takes place that will enrich his life and let him as an individual, hard-working American citizen, have full opportunity to do for his children and his family what any decent American should want to do.

President DWIGHT D. EISENHOWER, remarks at Lincoln Day box supper, Washington, D.C., February 5, 1954.—*Public Papers of the Presidents of the United States: Dwight D. Eisenhower, 1954*, p. 242.

802 The same prudence which in private life would forbid our paying our own money for unexplained projects, forbids it in the dispensation of the public moneys.

President THOMAS JEFFERSON, letter to Shelton Gilliam, June 19, 1808.—*The Writings of Thomas Jefferson*, ed. Andrew A. Lipscomb, vol. 12, p. 73 (1903).

803 We are endeavoring, too, to reduce the government to the practice of a rigorous economy, to avoid burdening the people, and arming the magistrate with a patronage of money, which might be used to corrupt and undermine the principles of our government.

President THOMAS JEFFERSON, letter to Mr. Pictet, February 5, 1803.—*The Writings of Thomas Jefferson,* ed. Andrew A. Lipscomb, vol. 10, pp. 356–57 (1903).

804 No; no; not a sixpence.

CHARLES COTESWORTH PINCKNEY, American minister to France, letter to Timothy Pickering, October 27, 1797, relating the American response to a French request for a tribute or bribe.—*State Papers and Publick Documents of the United States,* 3d ed., vol. 3, p. 492 (1819). The French had seized several American ships.

The wording of this quotation usually reads: ". . . not a penny." For further discussion of the wording used by Pinckney and of the quotation frequently but mistakenly attributed to Pinckney—"Millions for defense, but not one cent for tribute," actually said by Robert Goodloe Harper—see *The Home Book of Quotations,* ed. Burton Stevenson, 10th ed., p. 63 (1967) and "Notes and Queries," *South Carolina Historical and Genealogical Magazine,* vol. 1, pp. 100–103, 178–79 (1901).

805 That most delicious of all privileges—spending other people's money.

JOHN RANDOLPH of Roanoke.—William Cabell Bruce, *John Randolph of Roanoke, 1773–1833,* vol. 2, chapter 7, p. 204 (1922, reprinted 1970).

Randolph was a member of Congress 1799–1813, 1815–1817, and 1819–1829.

806 There is no doubt that many expensive national projects may add to our prestige or serve science. But none of them must take precedence over human needs. As long as Congress does not revise its priorities, our crisis is not just material, it is a crisis of the spirit.

NELSON A. ROCKEFELLER, governor of New York, letter to Mayor John V. Lindsay, April 24, 1971.—*The New York Times,* April 25, 1971, p. 69.

This letter concerned New York City's financial problems.

807 Lord, the money we do spend on Government and it's not one bit better than the government we got for one-third the money twenty years ago.

WILL ROGERS.—Paula McSpadden Love, *The Will Rogers Book,* p. 20 (1972).

Paula McSpadden Love was a niece of Will Rogers's and curator of the Will Rogers Memorial in Claremore, Oklahoma.

808 Any Government, like any family, can for a year spend a little more than it earns. But you and I know that a continuation of that habit means the poorhouse.

FRANKLIN D. ROOSEVELT, governor of New York, radio speech discussing the national Democratic platform, July 30, 1932.—*The Public Papers and Addresses of Franklin D. Roosevelt, 1928–1932,* p. 663 (1938).

809 If the Nation is living within its income, its credit is good. If, in some crises, it lives beyond its income for a year or two, it can usually borrow temporarily at reasonable rates. But if, like a spendthrift, it throws discretion to the winds, and is willing to make no sacrifice at all in spending; if it extends its taxing to the limit of the people's power to pay and continues to pile up deficits, then it is on the road to bankruptcy.

FRANKLIN D. ROOSEVELT, governor of New York, campaign address on the federal budget, Pittsburgh, Pennsylvania, October 19, 1932.—*The Public Papers and Addresses of Franklin D. Roosevelt, 1928–1932,* p. 797 (1938).

810 None of us really understands what's going on with all these numbers.

DAVID STOCKMAN, director, Office of Management and Budget.—William Greider, "The Education of David Stockman," *The Atlantic Monthly,* December 1981, p. 38.

He served in Congress 1977-1981.

811 There are four categories of voting on the floor of the Senate. The first are those who have been described as ones who can hear the farthest drum before the cry of a single hungry child. Then there is the group who can hear every child, whether he is hungry or not, before they can hear a single drum. Then you have a third group, who say, "Nothing can happen to the almighty dollar, so we will vote for all the children and all the drums." The time has come when we must have some priorities with respect to the way we are allocating our steadily decreasing resources, else it should be clear to everybody—that the economy of the United States could well be destroyed.

Senator STUART SYMINGTON, remarks in the Senate, November 23, 1971.—*Congressional Record,* vol. 117, p. 2896.

The theme of this was used earlier by Herbert Block, *Herblock Gallery,* p. 9 (1968): "This is particularly true of those bellicose Republican 'conservatives' and Dixiecrats who are more ready to lay down lives than prejudices and who can hear the most distant drum more clearly than the cry of a hungry child in the street."

812 Countries, therefore, when lawmaking falls exclusively to the lot of the poor cannot hope for much economy in public expenditure; expenses will always be considerable, either because taxes cannot touch those who vote for them or because they are assessed in a way to prevent that.

ALEXIS DE TOCQUEVILLE, *Democracy in America,* ed. J. P. Mayer, trans. George Lawrence, vol. 1, part 2, chapter 5, p. 210 (1969). Originally published in 1835–1840.

813 He smote the rock of the national resources, and abundant streams of revenue gushed forth. He touched the dead corpse of the Public Credit, and it sprung upon its feet. The fabled birth of Minerva, from the brain of Jove, was hardly more sudden or more perfect than the financial system of the United States, as it burst forth from the conceptions of Alexander Hamilton.

Senator DANIEL WEBSTER, speech at a dinner in New York City, March 10, 1831.—*The Writings and Speeches of Daniel Webster,* vol. 2, p. 50 (1903).

Greatness

814 There are some men who lift the age they inhabit, till all men walk on higher ground in that lifetime.

MAXWELL ANDERSON, *Valley Forge,* act II, scene ii, p. 92 (1937). Mary Philipse is referring to George Washington.

815 There be three things which make a nation great and prosperous: a fertile soil, busy workshops, easy conveyance for men and goods from place to place.

SIR FRANCIS BACON. This sentence was inscribed on one side of the Golden Door of the Transportation Building at the World's Columbian Exposition held in Chicago in 1893.

816 Great men are the guideposts and landmarks in the state.

EDMUND BURKE, speech on American taxation, House of Commons, April 19, 1774.—*The Works of the Right Honorable Edmund Burke*, vol. 2, p. 65 (1899).

817 Let every man or woman here, if you never hear me again, remember this, that if you wish to be great at all, you must begin where you are and what you are, in Philadelphia, now. He that can give to his city any blessing, he who can be a good citizen while he lives here, he that can make better homes, he that can be a blessing whether he works in the shop or sits behind the counter or keeps house, whatever be his life, he who would be great anywhere must first be great in his own Philadelphia.

RUSSELL H. CONWELL, *Acres of Diamonds*, p. 59 (1915).

Conwell gave this public address more than 6,000 times from 1877 until his death in 1925. He tailored his speech to individual cities by changing Philadelphia, his home town, to the name of the city where he was speaking.

818 Not he is great who can alter matter, but he who can alter my state of mind.

RALPH WALDO EMERSON, "The American Scholar," oration delivered before the Phi Beta Kappa Society, Cambridge, Massachusetts, August 31, 1837.—*Nature, Addresses and Lectures* (vol. 3 of *The Works of Ralph Waldo Emerson*), p. 100 (1906).

819 There aren't any great men. There are just great challenges that ordinary men like you and me are forced by circumstances to meet.

Attributed to Admiral WILLIAM F. HALSEY. Unverified. Though these words have not been found as spoken by Halsey, they were said by James Cagney, portraying Halsey, in the United Artists film version of Halsey's life, *The Gallant Hours* (dialogue continuity, p. 38), © 1960 Cagney-Montgomery Productions, Inc.

820 He was a foe without hate; a friend without treachery; a soldier without cruelty; a victor without oppression, and a victim without murmuring. He was a public officer without vices; a private citizen without wrong; a neighbor without reproach; a Christian without hypocrisy, and a man without guile. He was a Caesar, without his ambition; Frederick, without his tyranny; Napoleon, without his selfishness, and Washington, without his reward.

BENJAMIN HARVEY HILL, SR., address before the Southern Historical Society, Atlanta, Georgia, February 18, 1874.—Benjamin H. Hill, Jr., *Senator Benjamin H. Hill of Georgia; His Life, Speeches and Writings*, p. 406 (1893). These words were spoken about Robert E. Lee.

Hill served in Congress 1875–1882.

821 I am convinced that nothing will happen to me, for I know the greatness of the task for which Providence has chosen me.

ADOLF HITLER, remark when running for the presidency of the Reich against Hindenburg in 1932.—*The Speeches of Adolf Hitler, April 1922–August 1939*, trans. Norman H. Baynes, vol. 1, p. 193 (1969).

822 I am against bigness and greatness in all their forms, and with the invisible molecular moral forces that work from individual to individual, stealing in through the crannies of the world like so many soft rootlets, or like the capillary oozing of water, and yet rending the hardest monuments of man's pride, if you give them time. The bigger the unit you deal with, the hollower, the more brutal, the more mendacious is the life displayed. So I am against all big organizations as such, national ones first and foremost; against all big successes and big results; and in favor of the eternal forces of truth which always work in the individual and immediately unsuccessful way, under-dogs always, till history comes, after they are long dead, and puts them on top.—You need take no notice of these ebullitions of spleen, which are probably quite unintelligible to anyone but myself.

WILLIAM JAMES, letter to Mrs. Henry Whitman, June 7, 1899.—*The Letters of William James*, ed. Henry James, vol. 2, p. 90 (1926).

823 I think this is the most extraordinary collection of talent, of human knowledge, that has ever been gathered together at the White House, with the possible exception of when Thomas Jefferson dined alone.

President JOHN F. KENNEDY, remarks at a dinner honoring Nobel prize winners of the Western Hemisphere, April 29, 1962.—*Public Papers of the Presidents of the United States: John F. Kennedy, 1962*, p. 347.

824 Four things greater than all things are,—
Women and Horses and Power and War.

RUDYARD KIPLING, "The Ballad of the King's Jest," stanza 5, *The Collected Works of Rudyard Kipling: Departmental Ditties and Barrack-Room Ballads*, vol. 25, p. 234 (1941, reprinted 1970).

825 No one should be astonished if in the following discussion of completely new princedoms and of the prince and of government, I bring up the noblest examples. Because, since men almost always walk in the paths beaten by others and carry on their affairs by imitating—even though it is not possible to keep wholly in the paths of others or to attain the ability of those you imitate—a prudent man will always choose to take paths beaten by great men and to imitate those who have been especially admirable, in order that if his ability does not reach theirs, at least it may offer some suggestion of it; and he will act like prudent archers, who, seeing that the mark they plan to hit is too far away and knowing what space can be covered by the power of their bows, take an aim much higher than their mark, not in order to reach with their arrows so great a height, but to be able, with the aid of so high an aim, to attain their purpose.

NICCOLÒ MACHIAVELLI, *The Prince*, chapter 6.—*Machiavelli, the Chief Works and Others*, trans. Allan Gilbert, vol. 1, pp. 24–25 (1965).

826 I do not admire a virtue like valour when it is pushed to excess, if I do not see at the same time the excess of the opposite virtue, as one does in Epaminondas, who displayed extreme valour and extreme benevolence. For otherwise it is not an ascent, but a fall. We do not display our greatness by placing ourselves at one extremity, but rather by being at both at the same time, and filling up the whole of the space between them.

BLAISE PASCAL, *Pascal's Pensées*, trans. Martin Turnell, part 1, section 6, p. 164 (1962).

Greatness

827 If we are to be a really great people, we must strive in good faith to play a great part in the world. We cannot avoid meeting great issues. All that we can determine for ourselves is whether we shall meet them well or ill.

THEODORE ROOSEVELT, governor of New York, speech before the Hamilton Club, Chicago, Illinois, April 10, 1899.—*The Strenuous Life* (vol. 13 of *The Works of Theodore Roosevelt*, national ed.), chapter 1, p. 322 (1926).

828 In my stars I am above thee, but be not afraid of greatness. Some are born great, some achieve greatness, and some have greatness thrust upon 'em.

WILLIAM SHAKESPEARE, *Twelfth Night*, act II, scene v, lines 155–59. Malvolio is speaking.

829 I sought for the greatness and genius of America in her commodious harbors and her ample rivers—and it was not there . . . in her fertile fields and boundless forests—and it was not there . . . in her rich mines and her vast world commerce—and it was not there . . . in her democratic Congress and her matchless Constitution—and it was not there. Not until I went into the churches of America and heard her pulpits flame with righteousness did I understand the secret of her genius and power. America is great because she is good, and if America ever ceases to be good, America will cease to be great.

Attributed to ALEXIS DE TOCQUEVILLE by Dwight D. Eisenhower in his final campaign address in Boston, Massachusetts, November 3, 1952. Unverified.

The last two sentences are attributed to de Tocqueville's *Democracy in America* by Sherwood Eddy, *The Kingdom of God and the American Dream*, chapter 1, p. 6 (1941). This appears with minor variations in *A Third Treasury of the Familiar*, ed. Ralph L. Woods, p. 347 (1970), as "attributed to de Tocqueville but not found in his works."

830 This is the bare chronology of as great an American as ever lived. Ten thousand pages would be required to fill in the full story of his talents, his genius and his impact upon the foundation of America. He was ever the subject of white-heat controversy—in death even as in life. But for myself, summing it all up, I say that five words might be his epitaph: THE REPUBLIC IS HIS MONUMENT.

Senator ARTHUR H. VANDENBERG, "Story of Alexander Hamilton as Told by Senator Arthur H. Vandenberg," *The Sons of the American Revolution Magazine*, February 1950, p. 9. Also *Congressional Record*, February 24, 1950, vol. 96, Appendix, p. A1378.

831 There was never a nation great until it came to the knowledge that it had nowhere in the world to go for help.

CHARLES DUDLEY WARNER, "Comments on Canada," section 3, *Studies in the South and West with Comments on Canada*, p. 483 (1889).

Greed

832 We find greedy men, blind with the lust for money, trafficking in human misery.

Attorney General THOMAS C. CLARK, address before the Boston Chamber of Commerce, Boston, Massachusetts, October 8, 1947.—*Boston Business*, November 1947, p. 16.

833 what man calls civilization
always results in deserts

man is never on the square
he uses up the fat and greenery of the earth
each generation wastes a little more
of the future with greed and lust for riches

DON MARQUIS, "What the Ants Are Saying," stanza 5, *Archy Does His Part*, in *The Lives and Times of Archy & Mehitabel*, p. 475 (1950).

Guilt

834 Friends and comrades! On that side [south] are toil, hunger, nakedness, the drenching storm, desertion, and death; on this side ease and pleasure. There lies Peru with its riches; here, Panama and its poverty. Choose, each man, what best becomes a brave Castilian. For my part, I go to the south.

FRANCISCO PIZARRO.—This English translation of a 1527 manuscript is in William H. Prescott, *History of the Conquest of Peru*, vol. 1, p. 263 (1848).

835 He who flies proves himself guilty.

Danish proverb.—Robert Christy, *Proverbs, Maxims and Phrases of All Ages*, vol. 1, p. 471 (1888).

The Bible says, "The wicked flee when no man pursueth."—Proverbs 28:1.

836 That deed which in our guilt we today call weakness, will appear tomorrow as an essential link in the complete chain of Man.

KAHLIL GIBRAN, *The Voice of the Master*, trans. Anthony R. Ferris, p. 32 (1958).

837 He declares himself guilty who justifies himself before accusation.

Proverb.—Robert Christy, *Proverbs, Maxims and Phrases of All Ages*, p. 470, no. 12 (1888).

The Oxford Dictionary of English Proverbs, 3d ed., rev. F. P. Wilson, p. 234 (1970), has "He who excuses himself, accuses himself." Shakespeare expressed it as, "And oftentimes excusing of a fault / Doth make the fault the worse by the excuse."—*King John*, act IV, scene ii, lines 30–31.

Haiti

838 Those of you who have been there [Haiti] know it is one of the most beautiful countries in the world. It has everything. It has everything above the ground, and everything under the ground. . . . It is an amazing place. I strongly recommend that whenever you get a chance, if you haven't been there, that you go to Haiti. I think it was a certain Queen of England who said that after her death "Calais" would be found written on her heart. When I die, I think that "Haiti" is going to be written on my heart.

President FRANKLIN D. ROOSEVELT, toast to the President of Haiti, White House dinner, October 14, 1943.—*The Public Papers and Addresses of Franklin D. Roosevelt, 1943*, p. 430 (1950).

It was Queen Mary I of England who said, "When I am dead and opened, you shall find Calais laying in my heart."—John Foxe, *The Acts and Monuments of John Foxe*, ed. Stephen Reed Cattley, vol. 8, book 12, p. 625 (1839). During her reign, England had lost Calais to the French.

839 The great end of all human industry, is the attainment of happiness. For this were arts invented, sciences cultivated, laws ordained, and societies modelled, by the most profound wisdom of patriots and legislators. Even the lonely savage, who lies exposed to the inclemency of the elements and the fury of wild beasts, forgets not, for a moment, this grand object, of his being.

DAVID HUME, "The Stoic," *Essays, Moral, Political and Literary*, part 1, essay 16, in *The Philosophical Works of David Hume*, vol. 3, p. 167 (1826).

840 Believing that the happiness of mankind is best promoted by the useful pursuits of peace, that on these alone a stable prosperity can be founded, that the evils of war are great in their endurance, and have a long reckoning for ages to come, I have used my best endeavors to keep our country uncommitted in the troubles which afflict Europe, and which assail us on every side.

President THOMAS JEFFERSON, letter to the Young Republicans of Pittsburg, December 2, 1808.—*The Writings of Thomas Jefferson*, ed. H. A. Washington, vol. 8, p. 142 (1871).

841 Perfect happiness I believe was never intended by the deity to be the lot of any one of his creatures in this world; but that he has very much put in our power the nearness of our approaches to it, is what I as stedfastly believe.

THOMAS JEFFERSON, letter to John Page, July 15, 1763.—*The Papers of Thomas Jefferson*, ed. Julian P. Boyd, vol. 1, p. 10 (1950). Jefferson used the spelling "beleive."

This letter was written in hopes that John Page would talk to Belinda, a young woman with whom Jefferson, then 20, was infatuated. Jefferson was normally cool and level-headed, but Belinda had a devastating effect on his poise, leaving him tongue-tied and stammering.—Saul K. Padover, *Jefferson*, chapter 2, p. 20 (1942).

842 The happiest moments of my life have been the few which I have past at home in the bosom of my family. . . . public emploiment contributes neither to advantage nor happiness. It is but honorable exile from one's family and affairs.

THOMAS JEFFERSON, secretary of state, letter to Francis Willis, Jr., April 18, 1790.—*The Papers of Thomas Jefferson*, ed. Julian P. Boyd, vol. 16, p. 353 (1961).

Willis served in Congress 1791–1793.

843 We meet this evening, not in sorrow, but in gladness of heart.

President ABRAHAM LINCOLN, last public address, April 11, 1865.—*The Collected Works of Abraham Lincoln*, ed. Roy P. Basler, vol. 8, p. 399 (1953).

On April 9 Lee had surrendered.

844 Three ounces are necessary, first of *Patience*, Then, of *Repose & Peace;* of *Conscience*
A pound entire is needful;
of *Pastimes* of all sorts, too,
Should be gathered as much as the hand can hold;
Of *Pleasant Memory &* of *Hope* three good drachms
There must be at least. But they should moistened be
With a liquor made from *True Pleasures* which rejoice the heart. Then of *Love's Magic Drops*, a few—
But use them sparingly, for they may bring a flame
Which naught but tears can drown,

Grind the whole and mix therewith of *Merriment,* an ounce
To even. Yet all this may not bring happiness
Except in your *Orisons* you lift your voice
To Him who holds the gift of health.

MARGARET of Navarre, *Recipe for a Happy Life, Written by Margaret of Navarre in the Year Fifteen Hundred,* ed. Marie West King, p. 1 (1911).

A modern "happy home recipe," author unknown, includes: "4 cups of love, 2 cups of loyalty, 3 cups of forgiveness, 1 cup of friendship, 5 spoons of hope, 2 spoons of tenderness, 4 quarts of faith, 1 barrel of laughter. Take love and loyalty, mix thoroughly with faith. Blend it with tenderness, kindness and understanding. Add friendship and hope, sprinkle abundantly with laughter. Bake it with sunshine. Serve daily with generous helpings."

845 There are only two roads that lead to something like human happiness. They are marked by the words: love and achievement. . . . In order to be happy oneself it is necessary to make at least one other person happy. . . . The secret of human happiness is not in self-seeking but in self-forgetting.

THEODORE REIK, *A Psychologist Looks at Love,* chapter 3, final page, in *Of Love and Lust,* p. 194 (1957).

846 All the things I really like to do are either immoral, illegal, or fattening.

Attributed to ALEXANDER WOOLLCOTT in various sources. Unverified. Sometimes heard, "immoral, illegal, fattening, or too expensive."

Harm

847 As to diseases, make a habit of two things—to help, or at least to do no harm. The art has three factors, the disease, the patient, the physician. The physician is the servant of the art. The patient must co-operate with the physician in combating the disease.

HIPPOCRATES, *Epidemics,* book 1, section 11.—*Hippocrates,* trans. W. H. S. Jones, vol. 1, p. 165 (1923).

"To do no harm" is echoed in two places in the Hippocratic Oath, as given in this translation: "I will use treatment to help the sick according to my ability and judgment, but never with a view to injury and wrong-doing" and "In whatsoever houses I enter, I will enter to help the sick, and I will abstain from all intentional wrong-doing and harm" (pp. 299, 301).

848 I wish to have no connection with any ship that does not sail *fast;* for I intend *to go in harm's way.*

JOHN PAUL JONES, letter to M. Le Ray de Chaumont, November 16, 1778.—Lincoln Lorenz, *John Paul Jones, Fighter for Freedom and Glory,* p. xiii (1943).

Hate

849 I make it a practice to avoid hating anyone. If someone's been guilty of despicable actions, especially toward me, I try to forget him. I used to follow a practice—somewhat contrived, I admit—to write the man's name on a piece of scrap paper, drop it into the lowest drawer of my desk, and say to myself: "That finishes the incident, and so far as I'm concerned, that fellow." The drawer became over the years a sort of private wastebasket for crumbled-up spite and discarded personalities.

DWIGHT D. EISENHOWER, *At Ease: Stories I Tell to Friends,* p. 52 (1967).

Hate

850 I could never hate anyone I knew.

Attributed to CHARLES LAMB.—Alfred Ainger, *Charles Lamb,* chapter 6, p. 124 (1882). Other biographers have also attributed this sentence to him, although the circumstances under which he said it are given variously.

Health

851 With your talents and industry, with science, and that stedfast honesty which eternally pursues right, regardless of consequences, you may promise yourself every thing—but health, without which there is no happiness. An attention to health then should take place of every other object. The time necessary to secure this by active exercises, should be devoted to it in preference to every other pursuit.

THOMAS JEFFERSON, letter to Thomas Mann Randolph, Jr., July 6, 1787.—*The Papers of Thomas Jefferson,* ed. Julian P. Boyd, vol. 11, p. 558 (1955).

Heroin

852 King Heroin is my shepherd, I shall always want. He maketh me to lie down in the gutters. He leadeth me beside the troubled waters. He destroyeth my soul. He leadeth me in the paths of wickedness for the effort's sake. Yea, I shall walk through the valley of poverty and will fear all evil for thou, Heroin, art with me. Thy Needle and capsule try to comfort me. Thou strippest the table of groceries in the presence of my family. Thou robbest my head of reason. My cup of sorrow runneth over. Surely heroin addiction shall stalk me all the days of my life and I will dwell in the House of the Damned forever.

Author unknown, "The Psalm of the Addict."—*Congressional Record,* July 31, 1971, vol. 117, p. 28511.

A newspaper clipping of this was found with the body of a young woman suicide in Rockingham County, North Carolina, and it was subsequently reprinted in an editorial in the Morganton, North Carolina, *News-Herald,* May 12, 1971.

History

853 History gives us a kind of chart, and we dare not surrender even a small rushlight in the darkness. The hasty reformer who does not remember the past will find himself condemned to repeat it.

JOHN BUCHAN, general introduction to *The Nations of Today,* a series of popular histories published in 1923–1924 under Buchan's editorship. Each work contained Buchan's introduction.—*Great Britain,* vol. 1, p. 12 (1923).

See No. 1292 for Santayana's similar remark.

854 Want of foresight, unwillingness to act when action would be simple and effective, lack of clear thinking, confusion of counsel until the emergency comes, until self-preservation strikes its jarring gong—these are the features which constitute the endless repetition of history.

WINSTON CHURCHILL, speech, House of Commons, May 2, 1935.—*Winston S. Churchill: His Complete Speeches, 1897–1963,* ed. Robert Rhodes James, vol. 6, p. 5592 (1974).

Quoted by Senator John Tower, address delivered before the American Defense Preparedness Association, April 14, 1983.—*Congressional Record,* April 20, 1983, vol. 129, p. S4989 (daily edition).

855 What has once happened, will invariably happen again, when the same circumstances which combined to produce it, shall again combine in the same way.

ABRAHAM LINCOLN, speech on the sub-Treasury, in the hall of the House of Representatives, Springfield, Illinois, December 26, 1839.—*The Collected Works of Abraham Lincoln,* ed. Roy P. Basler, vol. 1, p. 165 (1953).

856 Hegel remarks somewhere that all great world-historic facts and personages appear, so to speak, twice. He forgot to add: the first time as tragedy, the second time as farce.

KARL MARX, "The Eighteenth Brumaire of Louis Napoleon," part 1, in *On Revolution* (vol. 1 of *The Karl Marx Library*), ed. and trans. Saul K. Padover, p. 245 (1971).

857 "A land without ruins is a land without memories—a land without memories is a land without history."

ABRAM JOSEPH RYAN, "A Land Without Ruins," Preface quoting an unnamed source.—Edd Winfield Parks, *Southern Poets,* p. 165 (1936).

Father Ryan was a chaplain in the Civil War.

858 Human history becomes more and more a race between education and catastrophe.

H. G. WELLS, *The Outline of History,* vol. 2, chapter 41, p. 594 (1921).

Home

859 For a man's house is his castle, *& domus sua cuique est tutissimum refugium;* for where shall a man be safe, if it be not in his house?

EDWARD COKE, *The Third Part of the Institutes of the Laws of England,* chapter 73, p. 162 (1644).

860 Home is the place where, when you have to go there,
They have to take you in.

ROBERT FROST, "The Death of the Hired Man," lines 118–19, *The Poetry of Robert Frost,* ed. Edward C. Lathem, p. 38 (1967).

861 The poorest man may in his cottage bid defiance to all the forces of the Crown. It may be frail—its roof may shake—the wind may blow through it—the storm may enter—the rain may enter—but the King of England cannot enter!—all his force dares not cross the threshold of the ruined tenement!

WILLIAM PITT, the elder, Earl of Chatham, speech in the House of Lords.—Henry Peter Brougham, *Historical Sketches of Statesmen Who Flourished in the Time of George III,* vol. 1, p. 52 (1839).

Lord Brougham notes, "There are other celebrated passages of his speeches in all men's mouths. . . . Perhaps the finest of them all is his allusion to the maxim of English law, that every man's home is his castle," given above.

According to Francis Thackeray, *A History of the Right Honorable William Pitt,* vol. 2, p. 29 (1827), the speech was delivered in 1763 in opposition to an excise tax on perry and cider.

Honesty

862 A man is sorry to be honest for nothing.

OVID.—Henry T. Riley, *A Dictionary of Latin and Greek Quotations, Proverbs, Maxims and Mottos,* p. 138 (1876).

This is a translation of Ovid's "gratis paenitet esse probum" from his *Ex Ponto,* book 2, chapter 3. The translation in *Bartlett's Familiar Quotations,* 15th ed., p. 114 (1980) reads: "It is annoying to be honest to no purpose."

Hope

863 So, cutting the lashing of the waterproof match keg, after many failures Starbuck contrived to ignite the lamp in the lantern; then stretching it on a waif pole, handed it to Queequeg as the standard-bearer of this forlorn hope. There, then, he sat, holding up that imbecile candle in the heart of that almighty forlornness. There, then, he sat, the sign and symbol of a man without faith, hopelessly holding up hope in the midst of despair.

HERMAN MELVILLE, *Moby-Dick,* chapter 48, p. 251 (1851).

Human rights

864 On September 17, 1914, Erzberger, the well-known German statesman, an eminent member of the Catholic Party, wrote to the Minister of War, General von Falkenhayn, "*We must not worry about committing an offence against the rights of nations nor about violating the laws of humanity. Such feelings today are of secondary importance*"? A month later, on October 21, 1914, he wrote in *Der Tag,* "*If a way was found of entirely wiping out the whole of London it would be more humane to employ it* than to allow the blood of A SINGLE GERMAN SOLDIER to be shed on the battlefield!"

GEORGES CLEMENCEAU, quoting Matthias Erzberger, *Grandeur and Misery of Victory,* trans. F. M. Atkinson, p. 279 (1930).

865 The sacred rights of mankind are not to be rummaged for among old parchments or musty records. They are written, as with a sunbeam, in the whole volume of human nature, by the hand of the divinity itself; and can never be erased or obscured by mortal power.

ALEXANDER HAMILTON, "The Farmer Refuted," *The Works of Alexander Hamilton,* ed. John C. Hamilton, vol. 2, p. 80 (1850).

866 Where, after all, do universal human rights begin? In small places, close to home—so close and so small that they cannot be seen on any map of the world. Yet they *are* the world of the individual person: the neighborhood he lives in; the school or college he attends; the factory, farm or office where he works. Such are the places where every man, woman and child seeks equal justice, equal opportunity, equal dignity without discrimination. Unless these rights have meaning there, they have little meaning anywhere. Without concerted citizen action to uphold them close to home, we shall look in vain for progress in the larger world.

ELEANOR ROOSEVELT, remarks at presentation of booklet on human rights, *In Your Hands,* to the United Nations Commission on Human Rights, United Nations, New York, March 27, 1958.—United Nations typescript of statements at presentation (microfilm).

This quotation, lacking the final sentence, was used by Adlai E. Stevenson in 1963 on his Christmas card.

Human rights

867 My position as regards the monied interests can be put in a few words. In every civilized society property rights must be carefully safeguarded; ordinarily and in the great majority of cases, human rights and property rights are fundamentally and in the long run, identical; but when it clearly appears that there is a real conflict between them, human rights must have the upper hand; for property belongs to man and not man to property.

THEODORE ROOSEVELT, address at the Sorbonne, Paris, France, April 23, 1910.—"Citizenship in a Republic," *The Strenuous Life* (vol. 13 of *The Works of Theodore Roosevelt,* national ed.), chapter 21, pp. 515–16 (1926).

Idealists

868 An idealist believes the short run doesn't count. A cynic believes the long run doesn't matter. A realist believes that what is done or left undone in the short run determines the long run.

SIDNEY J. HARRIS, in his column "Thoughts at Large," for the *Chicago Sun-Times.* Reprinted in Ann Landers's column, *The Washington Post,* November 12, 1979, p. B7.

869 Man is born a predestined idealist, for he is born to act. To act is to affirm the worth of an end, and to persist in affirming the worth of an end is to make an ideal.

Justice OLIVER WENDELL HOLMES, "The Class of '61," speech delivered at the 50th anniversary of graduation, Harvard University, Cambridge, Massachusetts, June 28, 1911.—*Speeches by Oliver Wendell Holmes,* pp. 96–97 (1934).

870 An idealist is one who, on noticing that a rose smells better than a cabbage, concludes that it is also more nourishing.

H. L. MENCKEN, *A Little Book in C Major,* p. 19 (1916).

He later altered this to read ". . . concludes that it will also make better soup."—*A Book of Burlesques,* p. 205 (1924) and *A Mencken Chrestomathy,* p. 617 (1949).

871 Sometimes people call me an idealist. Well, that is the way I know I am an American. America, my fellow citizens—I do not say it in disparagement of any other great people—America is the only idealistic nation in the world.

President WOODROW WILSON, address supporting the League of Nations, Sioux Falls, South Dakota, September 8, 1919.—*The Messages and Papers of Woodrow Wilson,* ed. Albert Shaw, vol. 2, p. 822 (1924).

Ideas

872 Mr Kremlin himself was distinguished for ignorance, for he had only one idea,—and that was wrong.

BENJAMIN DISRAELI, *Sybil,* book 4, chapter 5, p. 273 (1980). First published in 1845.

873 The key to every man is his thought. . . . He can only be reformed by showing him a new idea which commands his own.

RALPH WALDO EMERSON, "Circles," *Essays: First Series,* p. 303 (1903).

874 The real Antichrist is he who turns the wine of an original idea into the water of mediocrity.

ERIC HOFFER, "Thoughts of Eric Hoffer, Including: 'Absolute Faith Corrupts Absolutely,' " *The New York Times Magazine*, April 25, 1971, p. 60.

875 The composition of this book has been for the author a long struggle of escape, and so must the reading of it be for most readers if the author's assault upon them is to be successful,—a struggle of escape from habitual modes of thought and expression. The ideas which are here expressed so laboriously are extremely simple and should be obvious. The difficulty lies, not in the new ideas, but in escaping from the old ones, which ramify, for those brought up as most of us have been, into every corner of our minds.

JOHN MAYNARD KEYNES, *The General Theory of Employment, Interest and Money*, Preface, p. viii (1936).

Idleness

876 La molesse est douce, et sa suite est cruelle.
(Idleness is sweet, and its consequences are cruel.)

Attributed to **JOHN QUINCY ADAMS**, in his diary. Unverified.

Ignorance

877 Nothing is worse than active ignorance.
(Es ist nichts schrecklicher als eine tätige Unwissenheit.)

JOHANN WOLFGANG VON GOETHE, *Goethe's World View Presented in His Reflections and Maxims*, ed. Frederick Ungar, pp. 58–59 (1963).

878 Everybody is ignorant only on different subjects.

WILL ROGERS.—Paula McSpadden Love, *The Will Rogers Book*, p. 119 (1972).
The author was a niece of Will Rogers's and curator of the Will Rogers Memorial in Claremore, Oklahoma.

879 So oft in theologic wars,
The disputants, I ween,
Rail on in utter ignorance
Of what each other mean,
And prate about an Elephant
Not one of them has seen!

JOHN GODFREY SAXE, "The Blind Men and the Elephant," moral.—*The Poetical Works of John Godfrey Saxe*, p. 112 (1887).
While Saxe said this was a Hindu fable, the story may be found in *The Udāna, or The Solemn Utterances of the Buddha*, chapter 6, section 4, trans. Dawsonne M. Strong, pp. 93–96 (1902).

880 Ignorant men
Don't know what good they hold in their hands until
They've flung it away.

SOPHOCLES, "Ajax," trans. John Moore, *The Complete Greek Tragedies*, ed. David Grene and Richmond Lattimore, vol. 2, p. 250 (1959).

Since there have been numerous translations of this play by Sophocles, these words—spoken by Tecmessa—vary. The translation by George Young, *The Dramas of Sophocles*, p. 102 (1888) reads, "Men of perverse opinion do not know / The excellence of what is in their hands, / Till some one dash it from them."

Immigrants

881 It almost seems that nobody can hate America as much as native Americans. America needs new immigrants to love and cherish it.

ERIC HOFFER, "Thoughts of Eric Hoffer, Including: 'Absolute Faith Corrupts Absolutely,' " *The New York Times Magazine*, April 25, 1971, p. 25.

882 Remember, remember always that all of us, and you and I especially, are descended from immigrants and revolutionists.

President FRANKLIN D. ROOSEVELT, remarks before the Daughters of the American Revolution, Washington, D.C., April 21, 1938.—*The Public Papers and Addresses of Franklin D. Roosevelt, 1938*, p. 259 (1941).

FDR is often quoted as having addressed the DAR as "my fellow immigrants." The above words are believed to be the source.

883 Every man has a right to one country. He has a right to love and serve that country and to feel that it is absolutely his country and that he has in it every right possessed by anyone else. It is our duty to require the man of German blood who is an American citizen to give up all allegiance to Germany wholeheartedly and without on his part any mental reservation whatever. If he does this it becomes no less our duty to give him the full rights of an American, including our loyal respect and friendship without on our part any mental reservation whatever. The duties are reciprocal, and from the standpoint of American patriotism one is as important as the other.

THEODORE ROOSEVELT, "Every Man Has a Right to One Country," *The Kansas City* (Missouri) *Star*, July 15, 1918, p. 2.

884 The bosom of America is open to receive not only the Opulent and respectable Stranger, but the oppressed and persecuted of all Nations And Religions; whom we shall wellcome to a participation of all our rights and previleges, if by decency and propriety of conduct they appear to merit the enjoyment.

General GEORGE WASHINGTON, letter to the members of the Volunteer Association and other Inhabitants of the Kingdom of Ireland who have lately arrived in the City of New York, December 2, 1783.—*The Writings of George Washington*, ed. John C. Fitzpatrick, vol. 27, p. 254 (1938).

Immortality

885 Nothing is lasting but change; nothing perpetual but death.

Attributed to LUDWIG BÖRNE, in his *Denkrede auf Jean Paul*. Unverified.

886 The fame of the brave outlives him; his portion is immortality. What more flattering homage could we pay to the manes of Paul Jones, than to swear on his tomb to live or to die free? It is the vow, it is the watch-word of every Frenchman.

PAUL HENRI MARRON, officiating Protestant clergyman, discourse at the funeral of John Paul Jones, Paris, France, July 20, 1792.—*Life and Correspondence of John Paul Jones . . .* , p. 68 (1830).

887 What we have done for ourselves alone dies with us; what we have done for others and the world remains and is immortal.

Attributed to ALBERT PIKE. Unverified.

Impeachment

888 May I now pass on to this Congress advice which I received recently from a fellow Vermonter—Either impeach him or get off his back.

Senator GEORGE AIKEN, remarks in the Senate, November 7, 1973, *Congressional Record,* vol. 119, p. 36086.
He was referring to President Richard M. Nixon.

889 The only honest answer is that an impeachable offense is whatever a majority of the House of Representatives considers [it] to be at a given moment in history; conviction results from whatever offense or offenses two-thirds of the other body considers to be sufficiently serious to require removal of the accused from office.

Representative GERALD R. FORD, remarks in the House, April 15, 1970, *Congressional Record,* vol. 116, p. 11913.

890 Dr. FRANKLIN mentioned the case of the Prince of Orange [William V], during the late war. An arrangement was made between France and Holland, by which their two fleets were to unite at a certain time and place. The Dutch fleet did not appear. Every body began to wonder at it. At length it was suspected that the stadtholder was at the bottom of the matter. This suspicion prevailed more and more. Yet, as he could not be impeached, and no regular examination took place, he remained in his office; and strengthening his own party, as the party opposed to him became formidable, he gave birth to the most violent animosities and contentions. Had he been impeachable, a regular and peaceful inquiry would have taken place, and he would, if guilty, have been duly punished,—if innocent, restored to the confidence of the public.

BENJAMIN FRANKLIN, debates in the Constitutional Convention, Philadelphia, Pennsylvania, July 20, 1787.—James Madison, *Debates on the Adoption of the Federal Constitution,* ed. Jonathan Elliot, vol. 5, p. 342 (1845).

891 Dr. Franklin was for retaining the clause [on impeachment], as favorable to the executive. History furnishes one example only of a first magistrate being formally brought to public justice. Every body cried out against this as unconstitutional. What was the practice before this, in cases where the chief magistrate rendered himself obnoxious? Why, recourse was had to assassination, in which he was not only deprived of his life, but of the opportunity of vindicating his character. It would be the best way, therefore, to provide in the Constitution for the regular punishment of the executive, where his misconduct should deserve it, and for his honorable acquittal, where he should be unjustly accused.

BENJAMIN FRANKLIN, debates in the Constitutional Convention, Philadelphia, Pennsylvania, July 20, 1787.—James Madison, *Debates on the Adoption of the Federal Constitution,* ed. Jonathan Elliot, vol. 5, pp. 340–41 (1845).

Impeachment

892 In the case of impeachments, which are the groans of the people, . . . and carry with them a greater supposition of guilt than any other accusation, there all the Lords must judge.

JOHN HATSELL, *Precedents of Proceedings in the House of Commons,* vol. 4, appendix 3, p. 343 (1769).

This quotation is used in a footnote by Raoul Berger, *Impeachment: The Constitutional Problems,* p. 51 (1973).

893 The power of impeachment is, of course, solely entrusted by the Constitution to the House of Representatives. However, the Executive Branch is clearly obligated, both by precedent and by the necessity of the House of Representatives having all of the facts before reaching its decision, to supply relevant information to the Legislative Branch, as it does in aid of other inquiries being conducted by committees of the Congress, to the extent compatible with the public interest.

President RICHARD M. NIXON, letter to the Hon. Emanuel Cellar, chairman of the House Committee on the Judiciary, May 19, 1970.—*Public Papers of the Presidents of the United States: Richard Nixon, 1970,* p. 441.

This letter concerned H. Res. 920, a resolution of impeachment of Justice William O. Douglas.

894 Conditions may, and are not unlikely to arise, some day, when the exercise of the power to impeach and remove the President may be quite as essential to the preservation of our political system as it threatened to become in this instance destructive of that system. Should that day ever come, it is to be hoped that the remedy of impeachment, as established by the Constitution, may be as patriotically, as fearlessly, and as unselfishly applied as it was on this occasion rejected.

Senator EDMUND G. ROSS, *History of the Impeachment of Andrew Johnson . . . 1868,* p. 173 (1896, reprinted 1965).

Ross voted against conviction of Johnson for lack of evidence, though he knew it was political suicide.—*Dictionary of American Biography,* vol. 8, pp. 175–76.

Impropriety

895 Does it *really* matter what these affectionate people do—so long as they don't do it in the streets *and frighten the horses!*

Attributed to MRS. PATRICK CAMPBELL, rebuke to a young actress reporting that an old actor in the company was too fond of the young and handsome leading-man.—Alan Dent, *Mrs. Patrick Campbell,* p. 78 (1961).

Various versions of the first clause occur in different sources. *The Oxford Dictionary of Quotations,* 3d ed., p. 128 (1970), has "I don't mind where people make love . . ." and *Bartlett's Familiar Quotations,* 15th ed., p. 706, no. 16 (1982), "My dear, I don't care what they do . . ."

Independence Day

896 The Second Day of July 1776, will be the most memorable Epocha, in the History of America.—I am apt to believe that it will be celebrated, by succeeding Generations, as the great anniversary Festival. It ought to be commemorated, as the Day of Deliverance by solemn Acts of Devotion to God Almighty. It ought to be solemnized with Pomp and Parade, with Shews, Games, Sports, Guns, Bells, Bonfires and Illuminations from one End of this Continent to the other from this Time forward forever more.

JOHN ADAMS, letter to Abigail Adams, July 3, 1776.—*Adams Family Correspondence*, ed. L. H. Butterfield, vol. 2, p. 30 (1963).

897 Americans can celebrate the Fourth of July and bring its spirit anywhere in the world. . . . But it is celebrated with more sentiment and fervor by Americans away from home in France than in any country, for Lafayette and Rochambeau equally with Washington made the Fourth of July possible. French aid, French armies and French gallantry joining with the American army saved liberty for the United States and the world. So Americans can say of the French on the Fourth of July what my old friend, Colonel Somers of South Carolina, said in closing a hot discussion on the merits of religious sects. The Colonel said, "I admit that Catholics can go to Heaven, so can Baptists, Presbyterians, Unitarians and others, but if you wish to go to Heaven as a gentleman with gentlemen, you must be an Episcopalian."

CHAUNCEY M. DEPEW, speech at the Fourth of July banquet of the American Chamber of Commerce, Paris, France, July 4, 1914.—Depew, *Addresses and Literary Contributions on the Threshold of Eighty-Two*, p. 103–4 (1916).

He served in Congress 1899–1911.

Individual

898 Could Hamlet have been written by a committee, or the Mona Lisa painted by a club? Could the New Testament have been composed as a conference report? Creative ideas do not spring from groups. They spring from individuals. The divine spark leaps from the finger of God to the finger of Adam, whether it takes ultimate shape in a law of physics or a law of the land, a poem or a policy, a sonata or a mechanical computer.

A. WHITNEY GRISWOLD, president of Yale, baccalaureate address, Yale University, New Haven, Connecticut, June 9, 1957.—*Congressional Record*, June 11, 1957, vol. 103, Appendix, p. A4545.

899 I am only one,
But still I am one.
I cannot do everything,
But still I can do something;
And because I cannot do everything
I will not refuse to do the something that I can do.

EDWARD EVERETT HALE, "Lend a Hand."—*Masterpieces of Religious Verse*, ed. James Dalton Morrison, p. 416 (1948).

See note at No. 1434.

900 One man with courage makes a majority.

Attributed to ANDREW JACKSON by Robert F. Kennedy in his Foreward to the Young Readers Memorial Edition of John F. Kennedy's *Profiles in Courage*, p. xiii (1964). Unverified.

Kennedy continued, "That is the effect President Kennedy had on others." A variation of the phrase above, "One man can make a difference and every man should try," was written by Jacqueline Kennedy on a card to accompany an exhibit that travelled around the country when the John F. Kennedy Library in Boston was first opened.

901 At the heart of that western freedom and democracy is the belief that the individual man, the child of God, is the touchstone of value, and all society, groups, the state, exist for his benefit. Therefore the enlargement of liberty for individual human beings must be the supreme goal and the abiding practice of any western society.

Senator ROBERT F. KENNEDY, "Day of Affirmation," address delivered at the University of Capetown, South Africa, June 6, 1966.—*Congressional Record*, June 6, 1966, vol. 112, p. 12429.

902 First, is the dangers of futility; the belief there is nothing one man or one woman can do against the enormous array of the world's ills—against misery and ignorance, injustice and violence. Yet many of the world's great movements, of thought and action, have flowed from the work of a single man.

Senator ROBERT F. KENNEDY, "Day of Affirmation," address delivered at the University of Capetown, South Africa, June 6, 1966.—*Congressional Record*, June 6, 1966, vol. 112, p. 12430.

903 But society has now fairly got the better of individuality; and the danger which threatens human nature is not the excess, but the deficiency, of personal impulses and preferences.

JOHN STUART MILL, *On Liberty*, ed. David Spitz, chapter 3, pp. 57–58 (1975). Originally published in 1859.

904 If it were felt that the free development of individuality is one of the leading essentials of well-being; that it is not only a coordinate element with all that is designated by the terms civilisation, instruction, education, culture, but is itself a necessary part and condition of all those things; there would be no danger that liberty should be undervalued.

JOHN STUART MILL, *On Liberty*, ed. David Spitz, chapter 3, p. 54 (1975). Originally published in 1859.

905 If a man does not keep pace with his companions, perhaps it is because he hears a different drummer. Let him step to the music which he hears, however measured or far away.

HENRY DAVID THOREAU, *Walden*, chapter 18, p. 430 (1966). Originally published in 1854.

Ingratitude

906 People who bite the hand that feeds them usually lick the boot that kicks them.

ERIC HOFFER, "Thoughts of Eric Hoffer, Including: 'Absolute Faith Corrupts Absolutely,' " *The New York Times Magazine*, April 25, 1971, p. 52.

Injustice

907 I know there is a God, and that He hates injustice and slavery. I see the storm coming, and I know that His hand is in it. If he has a place and work for me—and I think He has—I believe I am ready.

Attributed to ABRAHAM LINCOLN.—Joseph Gilbert Holland, *The Life of Abraham Lincoln*, p. 237 (1886). Unverified.

This comment was made in a private conversation with Newton Bateman, superintendent of public instruction for the state of Illinois, a few days before the election of 1860.

During the election of 1960, Senator John F. Kennedy used the same words in a speech to the United Steelworkers of America convention, Atlantic City, New Jersey, September 19, 1960.—*Freedom of Communications*, final report of the Committee on Commerce, United States Senate, part 1, p. 286 (1961). Senate Rept. 87-994.

As president, he used a variation of these words at the 10th annual presidential prayer breakfast, March 1, 1962.—*Public Papers of the Presidents of the United States: John F. Kennedy, 1962*, p. 176.

908 If you give me six lines written by the hand of the most honest of men, I will find something in them which will hang him.

(Qu'on me donne six lignes écrites de la main du plus honnête homme, j'y trouverai de quoi le faire pendre.)

Cardinal RICHELIEU, *Mirame.—The Home Book of Quotations*, ed. Burton Stevenson, 9th ed., p. 2259 (1964).

However, the other source Stevenson cites, Édouard Fournier's *L'Esprit dans l'Histoire*, 3d ed., chapter 51, p. 260 (1867), does not accept the traditional attribution and suggests one or another of Richelieu's agents as possible authors.

Adlai Stevenson was reminded "with a shudder" of Richelieu's words, "Give me six sentences written by the most innocent of men and I will hang him with them," in his *Call to Greatness*, p. 51 (1954).

909 Men's indignation, it seems, is more excited by legal wrong than by violent wrong; the first looks like being cheated by an equal, the second like being compelled by a superior.

THUCYDIDES, *The History of the Peloponnesian War*, trans. Richard Crawley, book 1, p. 50 (1876).

Isolationism

910 Perfectionism, no less than isolationism or imperialism or power politics, may obstruct the paths to international peace. Let us not forget that the retreat to isolationism a quarter of a century ago was started not by a direct attack against international cooperation but against the alleged imperfections of the peace.

President FRANKLIN D. ROOSEVELT, annual message to Congress on the State of the Union, January 6, 1945.—*The Public Papers and Addresses of Franklin D. Roosevelt, 1944–45*, p. 498 (1950).

911 I have no confidence in the system of *isolement* [isolation]. It does not answer in social life for individuals, nor in politics for nations. Man is a social animal.

ARTHUR WELLESLEY, DUKE OF WELLINGTON, letter to Thomas Raikes, March 1, 1841.—*Private Correspondence of Thomas Raikes*, ed. Harriet Raikes, pp. 262–63 (1861).

Israel

912 This life as a simple citizen and laborer has its benefits not only for the person himself but perhaps also for his country. After all, there is room for only one Prime Minister, but for those who make the desert bloom there is room for hundreds, thousands and even millions. And the destiny of the state is in the hands of the many rather than of a single individual. There are times when an individual feels he should do those things which only can and should be done by the many.

DAVID BEN-GURION, "Why I Retired to the Desert," *The New York Times Magazine*, March 28, 1954, p. 47.

913 Should a nation which attacks and occupies foreign territory in the face of United Nations disapproval be allowed to impose conditions on its own withdrawal?

President DWIGHT D. EISENHOWER, radio and television broadcast on the situation in the Middle East, Washington, D.C., February 20, 1957.—*Public Papers of the Presidents of the United States: Dwight D. Eisenhower, 1957*, p. 151.

Israel had invaded Egypt on October 29, 1956, precipitating the Suez Crisis.

914 On May 14 I was informed that the Provisional Government of Israel was planning to proclaim a Jewish state at midnight that day, Palestine time, which was when the British mandate came to an end. . . . I decided to move at once and give American recognition to the new nation. I instructed a member of my staff to communicate my decision to the State Department and prepare it for transmission to Ambassador Austin at the United Nations in New York. About thirty minutes later, exactly eleven minutes after Israel had been proclaimed a state, Charlie Ross, my press secretary, handed the press the announcement of the *de facto* recognition by the United States of the provisional government of Israel.

HARRY S. TRUMAN, *Memoirs by Harry S. Truman*, vol. 2, p. 164 (1956).

Italy

915 We who have seen Italia in the throes,
Half risen but to be hurled to ground, and now,
Like a ripe field of wheat where once drove plough,
All bounteous as she is fair, we think of those
Who blew the breath of life into her frame:
Cavour, Mazzini, Garibaldi: Three:
Her Brain, her Soul, her Sword; and set her free
From ruinous discords, with one lustrous aim.

GEORGE MEREDITH, "For the Centenary of Garibaldi," stanza 1, *The Times* (London), July 1, 1907, p. 9. This poem is also in *Poems of George Meredith*, ed. Phyllis B. Bartlett, p. 790 (1978).

Jesus Christ

916 Here is a man who was born in an obscure village, the child of a peasant woman. He grew up in another obscure village, where He worked in a carpenter shop until He was thirty, and then for three years He was an itinerant preacher. He never wrote a book. He never held an office. He never owned a home. He never had a family. He never went to college. He never put his foot inside a big city. He never traveled two hundred miles from the place where He was born. He never did one of the things that usually accompany greatness. He had no credentials but Himself. He had nothing to do with this world except the naked power of His divine manhood. While still a young man, the tide of public opinion turned against Him. His friends ran away. One of them denied Him. He was turned over to His enemies. He went through the mockery of a trial. He was nailed to a cross between two thieves. His executioners gambled for the only piece of property He had on earth while He was dying—and that was his coat. When he was dead He was taken down and laid in a borrowed grave through the pity of a friend. Nineteen wide centuries have come and gone and today He is the centerpiece of the human race and the leader of the column of progress. I am far within the mark when I say that all the armies that ever marched, and all the navies that ever were built, and all the parliaments that ever sat, all the kings that ever reigned, put together have not affected the life of man upon this earth as powerfully as has that One Solitary Life.

JAMES ALLAN FRANCIS, *One Solitary Life*, pp. 1–7 (1963).

This miniature book, made up entirely of the text above, was hand set and printed by Doris V. Welsh, a former staff member of the Newberry Library, in an edition of 150 copies. No information in the book is given for the first published source of this essay by James Allan Francis, D.D. (1864–1928), nor could it be found in the essays and sermons by Francis in the collections of his writings in the Library of Congress. Nor was the Newberry Library able to identify the original published source.

As an anonymous work and with some variations in the text, "One Solitary Life" was published in *The Irish Echo*, December 27, 1969, p. 10; in the *Congressional Record*, December 23, 1969, vol. 115, p. 13105; and on a variety of Christmas greeting cards in the 1970s and 1980s.

917 Listen, Christ,
You did alright in your day, I reckon—
But that day's gone now.
They ghosted you up a swell story, too,
Called it Bible—
But it's dead now.
The popes and the preachers've
Made too much money from it.
They've sold you too many

Kings, generals, robbers, and killers—
Even to the Czar and the Cossacks,
Even to Rockefeller's church,
Even to THE SATURDAY EVENING POST.
You ain't no good no more.
They've pawned you
Till you've done wore out.

Goodbye,
Christ Jesus Lord God Jehova,
Beat it on away from here now.
Make way for a new guy with no religion at all—
A real guy named
Marx Communist Lenin Peasant Stalin Worker ME—
I said, ME!

Go Ahead on now,
You're getting in the way of things, Lord.
And please take Saint Ghandi [sic] with you when you go,
And Saint Pope Pius,
And Saint Aimee McPherson,
And big black Saint Becton
Of the Consecrated Dime.
And step on the gas, Christ!

Move!
Don't be so slow about movin'!
The world is mine from now on—
And nobody's gonna sell ME
To a king, or a general,
Or a millionaire.

LANGSTON HUGHES, "Goodbye Christ," *The Negro Worker*, November/December 1932, p. 32.

918 At the time of the Crucifixion the dogwood had been the size of the oak and other forest trees. So firm and strong was the tree that it was chosen as the timber for the cross. To be used thus for such a cruel purpose greatly distressed the tree, and Jesus, nailed upon it, sensed this, and, in His gentle pity for all sorrow and suffering, said to it: "Because of your regret and pity for My suffering, never again shall the dogwood tree grow large enough to be used as a cross.

"Henceforth it shall be slender and bent and twisted and its blossoms shall be in the form of a cross—two long and two short petals. And in the center of each petal there will be nail prints, brown with rust and stained with red, and in the center of the flower will be a crown of thorns, and all who see it will remember."

Legend of the Dogwood.—Maxwell Droke, *The Speaker's Special Occasion Book*, pp. 159–60 (1954).

919 For man he seems
In all his lineaments, though in his face
The glimpses of his Fathers glory shine.

JOHN MILTON, *Paradise Regain'd*, lines 91–93, *The Works of John Milton*, vol. 2, part 2, p. 408 (1931). Originally published in 1671. Satan is speaking of Christ.

920 Yes, if the life and death of Socrates are those of a wise man, the life and death of Jesus are those of a god.

JEAN JACQUES ROUSSEAU, *Émile*, trans. Allan Bloom, book 4, p. 308 (1979). Originally published in 1762.

921 Whosoever on the night of the nativity of the young Lord Jesus, in the great snows, shall fare forth bearing a succulent bone for the lost and lamenting hounds, a wisp of hay for the shivering horse, a cloak of warm raiment for the stranded wayfarer, a bundle of fagots for the twittering crone, a flagon of red wine for him whose marrow withers, a garland of bright red berries for one who has worn chains, a dish of crumbs with a song of love for all huddled birds who thought that song was dead, and divers lush sweetmeats for such babes' faces as peer from lonely windows, to him shall be proffered and returned gifts of such an astonishment as will rival the hues of the peacock and the harmonies of heaven, so that though he live to the great age when man goes stooping and querulous because of the nothing that is left of him, yet shall he walk upright and remembering, as one whose heart shines like a great star in his breast.

Author unknown.

Joy

922 Occasionally in life there are those moments of unutterable fulfillment which cannot be completely explained by those symbols called words. Their meanings can only be articulated by the inaudible language of the heart.

MARTIN LUTHER KING, JR., Nobel lecture, Oslo, Norway, December 11, 1964.—*Nobel Lecture by The Reverend Dr. Martin Luther King, Jr.*, p. 1 (1964).

He was the 1964 recipient of the Nobel Peace Prize.

923 Joy is not the same as pleasure or happiness. A wicked and evil man may have pleasure, while any ordinary mortal is capable of being happy. Pleasure generally comes from things, and always through the senses; happiness comes from humans through fellowship. Joy comes from loving God and neighbor. Pleasure is quick and violent, like a flash of lightning. Joy is steady and abiding, like a fixed star. Pleasure depends on external circumstances, such as money, food, travel, etc. Joy is independent of them, for it comes from a good conscience and love of God.

Bishop FULTON J. SHEEN, *Fulton J. Sheen's Guide to Contentment*, p. 120 (1967).

Judges

924 Biggest damfool mistake I ever made.

DWIGHT D. EISENHOWER, referring to his appointment of Earl Warren as chief justice of the Supreme Court.—Fred Rodell, "The Complexities of Mr. Justice Fortas," *The New York Times Magazine*, July 28, 1968, p. 12.

William B. Ewald, Jr., research assistant for Eisenhower's memoirs, says in *Eisenhower the President*, p. 95 (1981), "I myself once, and once only, heard him say in Gettysburg in 1961, 'The two worst appointments I ever made came out of recommendations from the Justice Department: that fellow who headed the Antitrust Division, Bicks, and Earl Warren.' "

925 When twenty years ago a vague terror went over the earth and the word socialism began to be heard, I thought and still think that fear was translated into doctrines that had no proper place in the Constitution or the common law. Judges are apt to be naif, simple-minded men, and they need something of Mephistopheles. We too need education in the obvious—to learn to transcend our own convictions and to leave room for much that we hold dear to be done away with short of revolution by the orderly change of law.

Justice OLIVER WENDELL HOLMES, speech at Harvard Law School Association of New York, New York City, February 15, 1913.—*Speeches by Oliver Wendell Holmes*, p. 101 (1934).

926 As, for the safety of society, we commit honest maniacs to Bedlam, so judges should be withdrawn from their bench, whose erroneous biases are leading us to dissolution. It may indeed injure them in fame or in fortune; but it saves the republic, which is the first and supreme law.

THOMAS JEFFERSON, "Autobiography," *The Writings of Thomas Jefferson*, ed. Paul L. Ford, vol. 1, p. 114 (1892).

927 Jefferson was against any needless official apparel, but if the gown was to carry, he said: "For Heaven's sake discard the monstrous wig which makes the English judges look like rats peeping through bunches of oakum."

THOMAS JEFFERSON, commenting on judges' apparel.—Benjamin Harrison, *The Constitution and Administration of the United States of America*, p. 320 (1897).

928 In the public interest, therefore, it is better that we lose the services of the exceptions who are good Judges after they are seventy and avoid the presence on the Bench of men who are not able to keep up with the work, or to perform it satisfactorily.

WILLIAM HOWARD TAFT, *Popular Government: Its Essence, Its Permanence and Its Perils*, chapter 7, p. 159 (1913).

929 Judges, like people, may be divided roughly into four classes: judges with neither head nor heart—they are to be avoided at all costs; judges with head but no heart—they are almost as bad; then judges with heart but no head—risky but better than the first two; and finally, those rare judges who possess both head and a heart—thanks to blind luck, that's our judge.

ROBERT TRAVER, *Anatomy of a Murder*, chapter 17, pp. 313–14 (1958).

930 When the spotless ermine of the judicial robe fell on John Jay, it touched nothing less spotless than itself.

Senator DANIEL WEBSTER, at a public dinner, New York City, March 10, 1831.—*The Writings and Speeches of Daniel Webster*, vol. 2, p. 51 (1903).

The dinner, given in Webster's honor by the citizens of New York, was to thank him for his defense of the Constitution in the previous session of Congress. John Jay was the first chief justice of the Supreme Court of the United States.

Judgment

931 But let judgment run down as waters, and righteousness as a mighty stream.

The Bible, Amos 5:24.

932 In the last analysis sound judgment will prevail.

Representative JOSEPH G. CANNON, maxim quoted in a tribute to Cannon on his retirement, *The Sun*, Baltimore, Maryland, March 4, 1923.—*Congressional Record*, March 4, 1923, vol. 64, p. 5714.

"Uncle Joe" Cannon, who was Speaker of the House 1903-1911, served in the House for 46 years.

933 The lack of objectivity, as far as foreign nations are concerned, is notorious. From one day to another, another nation is made out to be utterly depraved and fiendish, while one's own nation stands for everything that is good and noble. Every action of the enemy is judged by one standard—every action of oneself by another. Even good deeds by the enemy are considered a sign of particular devilishness, meant to deceive us and the world, while our bad deeds are necessary and justified by our noble goals which they serve.

ERICH FROMM, *The Art of Loving*, pp. 100–101 (1956).

934 Nature has but one judgment on wrong conduct—if you can call that a judgment which seemingly has no reference to conduct as such—the judgment of death.

OLIVER WENDELL HOLMES, justice of the supreme court of Massachusetts, address at the dedication of the Northwestern University Law School Building, Chicago, Illinois, October 20, 1902.—Holmes, *Collected Legal Papers*, p. 272 (1937).

935 The firmness with which the people have withstood the late abuses of the press, the discernment they have manifested between truth and falsehood, show that they may safely be trusted to hear everything true and false, and to form a correct judgment between them.

President THOMAS JEFFERSON, letter to Judge John Tyler, June 28, 1804.—*The Writings of Thomas Jefferson*, ed. Andrew A. Lipscomb, vol. 11, p. 33 (1904).

936 If we could first know *where* we are, and *whither* we are tending, we could then better judge *what* to do, and *how* to do it.

ABRAHAM LINCOLN, speech delivered at the close of the Republican state convention, which named him the candidate for the United States Senate, Springfield, Illinois, June 16, 1858.—*The Collected Works of Abraham Lincoln*, ed. Roy P. Basler, vol. 2, p. 461 (1953).

This is the opening sentence of the "house divided" speech. See note about this speech at No. 1851.

937 One cool judgment is worth a thousand hasty counsels. The thing to be supplied is light, not heat.

President WOODROW WILSON, address on preparedness, Pittsburgh, Pennsylvania, January 29, 1916.—*The Papers of Woodrow Wilson*, ed. Arthur S. Link, vol. 36, p. 33 (1981).

Judiciary

938 I do not think the United States would come to an end if we lost our power to declare an Act of Congress void. I do think the Union would be imperiled if we could not make that declaration as to the laws of the several States.

Justice OLIVER WENDELL HOLMES, address to the Harvard Law School Association of New York, New York City, February 15, 1913.—*Speeches by Oliver Wendell Holmes*, p. 102 (1934).

939 John Marshall has made his decision: *now let him enforce it!*

President ANDREW JACKSON.—Horace Greeley, *The American Conflict, A History of the Great Rebellion* . . . , vol. 1, p. 106 (1864), noting that "I am indebted for this fact to the late Governor George N. Briggs, of Massachusetts, who was in Washington as a member of Congress when the decision was rendered" (footnote 27, p. 106).

Chief Justice Marshall had read the Supreme Court's opinion in a dispute between the state of Georgia and two missionaries, who had been convicted of and imprisoned for living among the Cherokee Indians. The Supreme Court's decision was in favor of the missionaries. "The attorneys for the missionaries sought to have this judgment enforced, but could not. General Jackson was President, and would do nothing of the sort. . . . So the missionaries languished years in prison" (p. 106).

940 At the establishment of our constitutions, the judiciary bodies were supposed to be the most helpless and harmless members of the government. Experience, however, soon showed in what way they were to become the most dangerous; that the insufficiency of the means provided for their removal gave them a freehold and irresponsibility in office; that their decisions, seeming to concern individual suitors only, pass silent and unheeded by the public at large; that these decisions, nevertheless, become law by precedent, sapping, by little and little, the foundations of the constitution, and working its change by construction, before any one has perceived that that invisible and helpless worm has been busily employed in consuming its substance. In truth, man is not made to be trusted for life, if secured against all liability to account.

THOMAS JEFFERSON, letter to Monsieur A. Coray, October 31, 1823.—*The Writings of Thomas Jefferson*, ed. Andrew A. Lipscomb, vol. 15, pp. 486–87 (1904).

941 The germ of dissolution of our federal government is in the constitution of the federal judiciary; an irresponsible body, (for impeachment is scarcely a scare-crow,) working like gravity by night and by day, gaining a little to-day and a little to-morrow, and advancing its noiseless step like a thief, over the field of jurisdiction, until all shall be usurped from the States, and the government of all be consolidated into one.

THOMAS JEFFERSON, letter to Charles Hammond, August 18, 1821.—*The Writings of Thomas Jefferson*, ed. Andrew A. Lipscomb, vol. 15, pp. 331–32 (1903).

942 The great object of my fear is the federal judiciary. That body, like gravity, ever acting, with noiseless foot, and unalarming advance, gaining ground step by step, and holding what it gains, is ingulfing insidiously the special governments into the jaws of that which feeds them.

THOMAS JEFFERSON, letter to Judge Spencer Roane, March 9, 1821.—*The Writings of Thomas Jefferson*, ed. Andrew A. Lipscomb, vol. 15, p. 326 (1903).

943 The judiciary of the United States is the subtle corps of sappers and miners constantly working under ground to undermine the foundations of our confederated fabric. . . . A judiciary independent of a king or executive alone, is a good thing; but independence of the will of the nation is a solecism, at least in a republican government.

THOMAS JEFFERSON, letter to Thomas Ritchie, December 25, 1820.—*The Writings of Thomas Jefferson*, ed. Paul L. Ford, vol. 10, pp. 170–71 (1899).

A similar statement is made in Jefferson's "Autobiography," *Writings*, vol. 1, pp. 112–13 (1892).

944 If the policy of the government, upon vital questions affecting the whole people, is to be irrevocably fixed by decisions of the Supreme Court, . . . the people will have ceased, to be their own rulers, having, to that extent, practically resigned their government into the hands of that eminent tribunal. Nor is there, in this view, any assault upon the court, or the judges. It is a duty, from which they may not shrink, to decide cases properly brought before them; and it is no fault of theirs, if others seek to turn their decisions to political purposes.

President ABRAHAM LINCOLN, first inaugural address (final text), March 4, 1861.—*The Collected Works of Abraham Lincoln*, ed. Roy P. Basler, vol. 4, p. 268 (1953).

Justice

945 Justice, voiceless, unseen, seeth thee when thou sleepest and when thou goest forth and when thou liest down. Continually doth she attend thee, now aslant thy course, now at a later time.

AESCHYLUS (?), "Fragments," fragment 253.—*Aeschylus*, trans. Herbert W. Smyth, vol. 2, p. 513 (1926). These lines are from a section of doubtful or spurious fragments.

946 Consequently, if the republic is the weal of the people, and there is no people if it be not associated by a common acknowledgment of right, and if there is no right where there is no justice, then most certainly it follows that there is no republic where there is no justice.

ST. AUGUSTINE, *The City of God*, book 19, chapter 21.—*The Works of Aurelius Augustine*, trans. Marcus Dods, vol. 2, p. 331 (1871). *De Civitate Dei* was written 413–426.

947 What doth the Lord require of thee, but to do justly, and to love mercy, and to walk humbly with thy God?

The Bible, Micah 6:8.

948 Justice is itself the great standing policy of civil society; and any eminent departure from it, under any circumstances, lies under the suspicion of being no policy at all.

EDMUND BURKE, "Reflections on the Revolution in France," 1790, *The Works of the Right Honorable Edmund Burke*, vol. 3, pp. 438–39 (1899).

949 "No, no!" said the Queen. "Sentence first—verdict afterwards."

LEWIS CARROLL (Charles L. Dodgson), *Alice in Wonderland*, chapter 12.—*Logical Nonsense: The Works of Lewis Carroll*, ed. Philip C. Blackburn and Lionel White, p. 177 (1934). First published in 1865.

950 "There's the King's Messenger. He's in prison now, being punished: and the trial doesn't begin until next Wednesday: and of course the crime comes last of all."

"Suppose he never commits the crime?" said Alice.

"That would be all the better, wouldn't it?" the Queen said.

LEWIS CARROLL (Charles L. Dodgson), *Through the Looking-Glass*, chapter 5.—*Logical Nonsense: The Works of Lewis Carroll*, ed. Philip C. Blackburn and Lionel White, p. 195 (1934). First published in 1872.

951 If there has been any crime, it must be prosecuted. If there has been any property of the United States illegally transferred or leased, it must be recovered. . . . I propose to employ special counsel of high rank drawn from both political parties to bring such actions for the enforcement of the law. Counsel will be instructed to prosecute these cases in the courts so that if there is any guilt it will be punished; if there is any civil liability it will be enforced; if there is any fraud it will be revealed; and if there are any contracts which are illegal they will be canceled. Every law will be enforced. And every right of the people and the Government will be protected.

President CALVIN COOLIDGE, statement on the Teapot Dome scandal.—*The New York Times*, January 27, 1924, p. 1.

Quoted by Senator Edward Martin, address to the Mifflin County Republican Committee, Lewistown, Pennsylvania, January 25, 1952.—*Congressional Record*, January 28, 1952, vol. 98, Appendix, p. A400.

952 Sir, I say that justice is truth in action.

BENJAMIN DISRAELI, "Agricultural Distress," speech in the House of Commons, February 11, 1851.—*Selected Speeches of the Late Right Honourable Earl of Beaconsfield*, ed. T. E. Kebbel, vol. 1, p. 321 (1882).

953 That it is better 100 guilty Persons should escape than that one innocent Person should suffer, is a Maxim that has been long and generally approved.

BENJAMIN FRANKLIN, letter to Benjamin Vaughan, March 14, 1785.—*The Writings of Benjamin Franklin*, ed. Albert H. Smyth, vol. 9, p. 293 (1906).

He was echoing Voltaire, "that generous Maxim, *that 'tis much more Prudence to acquit two Persons, tho' actually guilty, than to pass Sentence of Condemnation on one that is virtuous and innocent.*"—*Zadig*, chapter 6, p. 53 (1749, reprinted 1974).

Sir William Blackstone, in his *Commentaries on the Laws of England*, 9th ed., book 4, chapter 27, p. 358 (1783, reprinted 1978), says, "For the law holds, that it is better that ten guilty persons escape, than that one innocent suffer."

954 Justice delayed is justice denied.

Attributed to WILLIAM E. GLADSTONE.—Laurence J. Peter, *Peter's Quotations*, p. 276 (1977). Unverified.

955 Oh Justice, when expelled from other habitations, make this thy dwelling place.

WILLIAM JEWELL, inscription over the door of the Boone County, Missouri, Court House.—North Todd Gentry, *The Bench and Bar of Boone County, Missouri*, pp. 81–82 (1916).

Lawyers trying cases in the court house were known to make "eloquent and effective" references to the motto.—Walter Ridgway, "Boone County's Justice Motto," *Missouri Historical Review*, October 1926, pp. 114–16.

956 Dear son, if you come to reign do that which befits a king, that is, be so just as to deviate in nothing from justice, whatever may befall you. If a poor man goes to law with one who is rich, support the poor rather than the rich man until you know the truth, and when the truth is known, do that which is just.

LOUIS IX, king of France.—Louis Gazagne, *The Saint on Horseback: A Story of St. Louis IX, King of France*, p. 73 (1953).

Another translation: "To keep right and justice be thou righteous and steady with thy people, without turning to the right hand or to the left, but straight forward, and uphold the poor man's suit until the truth be made manifest."—Jean de Joinville, *The History of St. Louis*, ed. Natalis de Wailly, trans. Joan Evans, book 2, chapter 145, p. 225 (1938). In some translations, this is paragraph 747.

957 Let me make one more remark suggested by this trial and by others. There is no accepted test of civilization. It is not wealth, or the degree of comfort, or the average duration of life, or the increase of knowledge. All such tests would be disputed. In default of any other measure, may it not be suggested that as good a measure as any is the degree to which justice is carried out, the degree to which men are sensitive as to wrong-doing and desirous to right it? If that be the test, a trial such as that of Servetus is a trial of the people among whom it takes place, and his condemnation is theirs also.

SIR JOHN MACDONELL, *Historical Trials*, chapter 7, p. 148 (1927).

Miguel Serveto, known as Michael Servetus, was imprisoned in Geneva at John Calvin's request and burned at the stake as a heretic in 1553.

958 We said that a single injustice, a single crime, a single illegality, particularly if it is officially recorded, confirmed, a single wrong to humanity, a single wrong to justice and to right, particularly if it is universally, legally, nationally, commodiously accepted, that a single crime shatters and is sufficient to shatter the whole social pact, the whole social contract, that a single legal crime, a single dishonorable act will bring about the loss of one's honor, the dishonor of a whole people. It is a touch of gangrene that corrupts the entire body.

CHARLES-PIERRE PÉGUY, in reference to the Dreyfus trial, *Men and Saints*, trans. Anne and Julian Green, p. 11 (1944).

959 They have a Right to censure, that have a *Heart* to help: The rest is Cruelty, not Justice.

WILLIAM PENN, *Some Fruits of Solitude in Reflections & Maxims*, no. 46, p. 15 (1903, reprinted 1976).

960 Salvation for a race, nation, or class must come from within. Freedom is never granted; it is won. Justice is never given; it is exacted. Freedom and justice must be struggled for by the oppressed of all lands and races, and the struggle must be continuous, for freedom is never a final fact, but a continuing evolving process to higher and higher levels of human, social, economic, political and religious relationships.

A. PHILIP RANDOLPH.—Jervis Anderson, *A. Philip Randolph, a Biographical Portrait*, epigraph, p. vii (1972).

961 Of all the officers of the Government, those of the Department of Justice should be kept most free from any suspicion of improper action on partisan or factional grounds, so that there shall be gradually a growth, even though a slow growth, in the knowledge that the Federal courts and the representatives of the Federal Department of Justice insist on meting out even-handed justice to all.

President THEODORE ROOSEVELT, letter to Attorney General William H. Moody, August 9, 1904.—Homer S. Cummings, *Federal Justice*, p. 500 (1937).

962 But Justice, though her dome [doom] she doe prolong,
Yet at the last she will her owne cause right.

EDMUND SPENSER, *The Faerie Queene*, book 5, canto 11, stanza 1, p. 434 (1903).

963 Justice in the life and conduct of the State is possible only as first it resides in the hearts and souls of the citizens.

Author unknown. Inscription over the 10th Street entrance of the U.S. Department of Justice Building, Washington, D.C. This has been attributed to Plato, but is unverified.

Kentucky

964 The song birds are the sweetest
In Kentucky;
The thoroughbreds are fleetest
In Kentucky;
Mountains tower proudest,
Thunder peals the loudest,

Kentucky

The landscape is the grandest—
And politics—the damnedest
In Kentucky.

JAMES H. MULLIGAN, "In Kentucky," stanza 7.—John W. Townsend, *"In Kentucky" and its Author, "Jim" Mulligan*, pp. 8–9 (1935).

Kings

965 His hands would plait the priest's guts, if he had no rope, to strangle kings.
(Et ses mains ourdiraient les entrailles du prêtre,
Au défaut d'un cordon pour étrangler les rois.)

DENIS DIDEROT, "Les Éleuthéromanes," *Poésies Diverses*, p. 16 (1875).

Another version frequently cited is: "Let us strangle the last king with the guts of the last priest." (Et des boyaux du dernier prêtre / Serrons le cou du dernier roi.)—Attributed to Diderot by Jean-François de La Harpe, *Cours de Littérature Ancienne et Moderne*, vol. 3, book 4, chapter 3, p. 415 (1840).

Knowledge

966 The trouble with people is not that they don't know but that they know so much that ain't so.

Attributed to JOSH BILLINGS (Henry Wheeler Shaw) by *The Oxford Dictionary of Quotations*, 3d ed., p. 491 (1979). Not verified in his writings, although some similar ideas are found in *Everybody's Friend, or Josh Billing's Encyclopedia and Proverbial Philosophy of Wit and Humor* (1874). Original spelling is corrected:

"What little I do know I hope I am certain of" (p. 502).

"Wisdom don't consist in knowing more that is new, but in knowing less that is false" (p. 430).

"I honestly believe it is better to know nothing than to know what ain't so" (p. 286).

Walter Mondale echoed the words above in his first debate with President Ronald Reagan, October 7, 1984, in Louisville, Kentucky: "I'm reminded a little bit of what Will Rogers once said of Hoover. He said it's not what he doesn't know that bothers me, it's what he knows for sure just ain't so."—Transcript, *The New York Times*, October 8, 1984, p. B4. This has not been found in Rogers's work.

967 If a man empties his purse into his head no one can take it away from him. An investment in knowledge always pays the best interest.

Attributed to BENJAMIN FRANKLIN, *Poor Richard*, in *The Home Book of Quotations*, ed. Burton Stevenson, 10th ed., p. 1054 (1967), and in *The Home Book of American Quotations*, ed. Bruce Bohle, p. 220 (1967). Unverified.

968 Perplexity is the beginning of knowledge.

KAHLIL GIBRAN, *The Voice of the Master*, trans. Anthony R. Ferris, p. 87 (1958).

969 A popular Government, without popular information, or the means of acquiring it, is but a Prologue to a Farce or a Tragedy; or, perhaps both. Knowledge will forever govern ignorance: And a people who mean to be their own Governors, must arm themselves with the power which knowledge gives.

JAMES MADISON, letter to W. T. Barry, August 4, 1822.—*The Writings of James Madison*, ed. Gaillard Hunt, vol. 9, p. 103 (1910).

These words, using the older spelling "Governours," are inscribed to the left of the main entrance, Library of Congress James Madison Memorial Building.

970 They never open their mouths without subtracting from the sum of human knowledge.

Representative THOMAS B. REED, referring to two of his colleagues in the House of Representatives.—Samuel W. McCall, *The Life of Thomas Brackett Reed*, chapter 21, p. 248 (1914).

971 Give light and the people will find their own way.

SCRIPPS-HOWARD newspapers, motto. It is still in current use and may be found on the masthead of the papers they publish, e.g., *The Rocky Mountain News*.

972 Every man is a valuable member of society who, by his observations, researches, and experiments, procures knowledge for men . . . it is in his knowledge that man has found his greatness and his happiness, the high superiority which he holds over the other animals who inhabit the earth with him, and consequently no ignorance is probably without loss to him, no error without evil . . . the particle and the planet are subject to the same laws, and what is learned of one will be known of the other . . . I bequeath the whole of my property . . . to the United States of America to found at Washington, under the name of the Smithsonian Institution, an establishment for the increase and diffusion of knowledge among men.

JAMES SMITHSON, various writings, including his will. Inscription, National Museum of American History, Washington, D.C.

973 Knowledge comes, but wisdom lingers, . . .

ALFRED, LORD TENNYSON, "Locksley Hall," line 141, *The Poetic and Dramatic Works of Alfred Lord Tennyson*, p. 124 (1899).

974 We have not the reverent feeling for the rainbow that a savage has, because we know how it is made. We have lost as much as we gained by prying into that matter.

MARK TWAIN (Samuel L. Clemens), *A Tramp Abroad*, vol. 2 (vol. 4 of *The Writings of Mark Twain*), chapter 14, p. 189 (1879, reprinted 1968).

Labor

975 I've had the best possible chance of learning that what the working-classes really need is to be allowed some part in the direction of public affairs, Doctor—to develop their abilities, their understanding and their self-respect.

HENRIK IBSEN, *An Enemy of the People*, English adaptation by Max Faber, act II, p. 28 (1970). Mr. Hovstad is speaking.

976 I agree with you, Mr. Chairman, that the working men are the basis of all governments, for the plain reason that they are the more numerous, and as you added that those were the sentiments of the gentlemen present, representing not only the working class, but citizens of other callings than those of the mechanic, I am happy to concur with you in these sentiments, not only of the native born citizens, but also of the Germans and foreigners from other countries.

ABRAHAM LINCOLN, speech to Germans at Cincinnati, Ohio, February 12, 1861 [*Commercial* version].—*The Collected Works of Abraham Lincoln,* ed. Roy P. Basler, vol. 4, p. 202 (1953).

977 In the early days of the world, the Almighty said to the first of our race "In the sweat of thy face shalt thou eat bread"; and since then, if we except the *light* and the *air* of heaven, no good thing has been, or can be enjoyed by us, without having first cost labour. And inasmuch [as] most good things are produced by labour, it follows that [all] such things of right belong to those whose labour has produced them. But it has so happened in all ages of the world, that *some* have labored, and *others* have, without labour, enjoyed a large proportion of the fruits. This is wrong, and should not continue. To [secure] to each labourer the whole product of his labour, or as nearly as possible, is a most worthy object of any good government.

ABRAHAM LINCOLN, fragments of a tariff discussion, December 1, 1847 ?, *The Collected Works of Abraham Lincoln,* ed. Roy P. Basler, vol. 1, pp. 407–8 (1953).

978 It is better, then, to save the work while it is begun. You have done the labor; maintain it—keep it. If men choose to serve you, go with them; but as you have made up your organization upon principle, stand by it; for, as surely as God reigns over you, and has inspired your mind, and given you a sense of propriety, and continues to give you hope, so surely will you still cling to these ideas, and you will at last come back after your wanderings, merely to do your work over again.

ABRAHAM LINCOLN, speech at Chicago, Illinois, July 10, 1858.—*The Collected Works of Abraham Lincoln,* ed. Roy P. Basler, vol. 2, p. 498 (1953).

979 Labor is prior to, and independent of, capital. Capital is only the fruit of labor, and could never have existed if labor had not first existed. Labor is the superior of capital, and deserves much the higher consideration.

President ABRAHAM LINCOLN, annual message to Congress, December 3, 1861.—*The Collected Works of Abraham Lincoln,* ed. Roy P. Basler, vol. 5, p. 52 (1953).

980 The most notable feature of a disturbance in your city last summer, was the hanging of some working people by other working people. It should never be so. The strongest bond of human sympathy, outside of the family relation, should be one uniting all working people, of all nations, and tongues, and kindreds.

President ABRAHAM LINCOLN, reply to New York Workingmen's Democratic Republican Association, March 21, 1864.—*The Collected Works of Abraham Lincoln,* ed. Roy P. Basler, vol. 7, p. 259 (1953).

981 They are usually denominated labor-*saving* machines, but it would be more just to call them labor-*doing* machines.

Senator DANIEL WEBSTER, remarks in the Senate, March 12, 1838.—*The Writings and Speeches of Daniel Webster,* vol. 8, p. 177 (1903).

982 There may be here and there a worker who for certain reasons unexplainable to us does not join a union of labor. That is his right. It is his legal right, no matter how morally wrong he may be. It is his legal right, and no one can or dare question his exercise of that legal right.

SAMUEL GOMPERS, address delivered to the Council of Foreign Relations, New York City, December 10, 1918.—*American Federationist,* February 1919, p. 160.

983 We will stand by our friends and administer a stinging rebuke to men or parties who are either indifferent, negligent, or hostile, and, wherever opportunity affords, to secure the election of intelligent, honest, earnest trade unionists, with clear, unblemished, paid-up union cards in their possession.

SAMUEL GOMPERS, "Men of Labor! Be Up and Doing," editorial, *American Federationist,* May 1906, p. 319.

984 Don't waste any time mourning—organize!

JOE HILL, letter to William D. Haywood, November 18, 1915.—Philip S. Foner, *The Letters of Joe Hill,* p. 84 (1965).

Joe Hill was a member of the Industrial Workers of the World (IWW), and was "the Wobblies' most famous and most prolific writer of working class songs." Hill had been convicted "on the flimsiest of evidence—all circumstantial" of slaying a Salt Lake City grocer, and sentenced to death. "It appears obvious that a real effort had been made to 'fix' the case against him." Despite an international movement to reverse the conviction or grant a new trial, Hill was shot and killed by a firing squad on November 19, 1915 (pp. 7, 9, 10).

985 It ill behooves one who has supped at labor's table and who has been sheltered in labor's house to curse with equal fervor and fine impartiality both labor and its adversaries when they become locked in deadly embrace.

JOHN L. LEWIS, president of the Congress of Industrial Organizations (CIO), radio broadcast, September 3, 1937.—*Vital Speeches of the Day*, September 15, 1937, p. 733.

The New York Times account said, "The fact that Mr. Lewis did not mention the President by name did not dull the point in the eyes of those who had followed labor developments through the violent days of last Winter and Spring. These observers unanimously accepted this part of his speech as a direct reference to Mr. [Franklin D.] Roosevelt's invocation of 'a plague on both your houses' when the labor unions and steel mill operators were 'locked in deadly embrace' only a few months ago."—September 4, 1937, p. 1.

"A plague on both your houses" is from Shakespeare's *Romeo and Juliet,* act III, scene i, line 112.

986 The United Mine Workers and the CIO have paid cash on the barrel for every piece of legislation that we have gotten. We have the Wagner Act. The Wagner Act cost us many dollars in contributions which the United Mine Workers have made to the Roosevelt administration with the explicit understanding of a quid pro quo for labor. These contributions far exceed the notions held by the general public or the press.

JOHN L. LEWIS, president of the Congress of Industrial Organizations (CIO).—Saul David Alinsky, *John L. Lewis: An Unauthorized Biography,* p. 177 (1949).

987 To remember the loneliness, the fear and the insecurity of men who once had to walk alone in huge factories, beside huge machines—to realize that labor unions have meant new dignity and pride to millions of our countrymen—human companionship on the job, and music in the home—to be able to see what larger pay checks mean, not to a man as an employee, but as a husband and as a father—to know these things is to understand what American labor means.

ADLAI E. STEVENSON, governor of Illinois, speech to the American Federation of Labor, New York City, September 22, 1952.—*Speeches of Adlai Stevenson*, p. 62 (1952).

Last Words

988 To die will be an awfully big adventure.

SIR JAMES M. BARRIE, *Peter Pan*, act III, final sentence, p. 94 (1930, reprinted 1975).

This line was quoted by Barrie's friend, American impresario Charles Frohman, as he plunged to his death on the *Lusitania*.—*The Dictionary of National Biography, 1931–1940*, p. 49.

989 "What is the answer?" she asked, and when no answer came she laughed and said: "Then, what is the question?"

GERTRUDE STEIN, last words, according to Elizabeth Sprigge, *Gertrude Stein, Her Life and Work*, p. 265 (1957).

"What is the answer? . . . In that case . . . what is the question?" is the version in *What Is Remembered* (1963) by Alice B. Toklas, p. 173, though these are not specifically labeled Stein's last words.

990 Don't give up the ship.

Although this quotation has been attributed to several historical figures, the only documented source is the blue battle-flag inscribed with these words ordered and used by Oliver Hazard Perry as a signal during the battle of Lake Erie, September 10, 1813.

Although popularly attributed to Captain James Lawrence as his dying words during a battle with a British frigate off the coast of Boston on June 1, 1813, there remains the possibility these words were not his, but those of someone reporting the battle.

For other attributed sources and theories, see: *Macmillan Book of Proverbs, Maxims, and Famous Phrases*, ed. Burton Stevenson, p. 2091 (1965); Charles C. Bombaugh, *Facts and Fancies for the Curious*, pp. 388–89 (1905); William S. Walsh, *Hand-Book of Literary Curiosities*, pp. 1004–5 (1929); *Dictionary of American History*, rev. ed., vol. 2, p. 364 (1976); and *Motor Boating*, October 1965, p. 72.

Law

991 A government of laws and not of men.

JOHN ADAMS, "Novanglus Papers," no. 7.—*The Works of John Adams*, ed. Charles Francis Adams, vol. 4, p. 106 (1851).

Adams published articles in 1774 in the Boston, Massachusetts, *Gazette* using the pseudonym "Novanglus." In this paper he credited James Harrington with expressing the idea this way. Harrington described government as "the empire of laws and not of men" in his 1656 work, *The Commonwealth of Oceana*, p. 35 (1771). The phrase gained wider currency when Adams used it in the Massachusetts Constitution, Bill of Rights, article 30 (1780).—*Works*, vol. 4, p. 230.

992 Law is a Bottomless-Pit, it is a Cormorant, a Harpy, that devours every thing.

JOHN ARBUTHNOT, *The History of John Bull*, ed. Alan W. Bower and Robert A. Erickson, chapter 6, p. 10 (1976). First published in 1712.

993 You would oppose law to socialism. But it is the law which socialism invokes. It aspires to legal, not extra-legal plunder. . . . You wish to prevent it from taking any part in the making of laws. You would keep it outside the Legislative Palace. In this you will not succeed, I venture to prophesy, so long as legal plunder is the basis of the legislation within.

It is absolutely necessary that this question of legal plunder should be determined, and there are only three solutions of it:—

1. When the few plunder the many.
2. When everybody plunders everybody else.
3. When nobody plunders anybody.

Partial plunder, universal plunder, absence of plunder, amongst these we have to make our choice. The law can only produce one of these results.

Partial plunder.—This is the system which prevailed so long as the elective privilege was *partial*; a system which is resorted to, to avoid the invasion of socialism.

Universal plunder.—We have been threatened by this system when the elective privilege has become universal; the masses having conceived the idea of making law, on the principle of legislators who had preceded them.

Absence of plunder.—This is the principle of justice, peace, order, stability, conciliation, and of good sense.

FRÉDÉRIC BASTIAT, *Essays on Political Economy*, part 4, "The Law," p. 20 (185–?).

994 Any law that takes hold of a man's daily life cannot prevail in a community, unless the vast majority of the community are actively in favor of it. The laws that are the most operative are the laws which protect life.

HENRY WARD BEECHER, "Civil Law and the Sabbath," sermon delivered December 3, 1882.—*Plymouth Pulpit*, vol. 5 (new series), p. 416 (1883).

995 He that keepeth the law of the Lord getteth the understanding thereof: and the perfection of the fear of the Lord is wisdom.

The Bible (Apocrypha), Ecclesiasticus 21:11.

996 If you like laws and sausages, you should never watch either one being made.

Widely attributed to OTTO VON BISMARCK. Unverified.

997 So great moreover is the regard of the law for private property, that it will not authorize the least violation of it; no, not even for the general good of the whole community.

SIR WILLIAM BLACKSTONE, *Commentaries on the Laws of England*, 9th ed., book 1, chapter 1, section 3, p. 139 (1783, reprinted 1978).

998 The law is not a "light" for you or any man to see by; the law is not an instrument of any kind. The law is a causeway upon which so long as he keeps to it a citizen may walk safely.

ROBERT BOLT, *A Man for All Seasons*, act II, p. 92 (1967). Sir Thomas More is speaking.

999 Law never *is*, but is always about to be.

BENJAMIN CARDOZO, justice, Court of Appeals of New York State, lecture to Yale Law School, 1921.—*The Nature of the Judicial Process*, lecture 3, p. 126 (1921).

1000 True law is right reason in agreement with nature; it is of universal application, unchanging and everlasting; it summons to duty by its commands, and averts from wrong-doing by its prohibitions. And it does not lay its commands or prohibitions upon good men in vain, though neither have any effect on the wicked. It is a sin to try to to [sic] alter this law, nor is it allowable to attempt to repeal any part of it, and it is impossible to abolish it entirely. We cannot be freed from its obligations by senate or people, and we need not look outside ourselves for an expounder or interpreter of it. And there will not be different laws at Rome and at Athens, or different laws now and in the future, but one eternal and unchangeable law will be valid for all nations and all times, and there will be one master and ruler, that is, God, over us all, for he is the author of this law, its promulgator, and its enforcing judge. Whoever is disobedient is fleeing from himself and denying his human nature, and by reason of this very fact he will suffer the worst penalties, even if he escapes what is commonly considered punishment.

MARCUS TULLIUS CICERO, *De Re Publica (The Republic)*, book 3, paragraph 22.—*De Re Publica, De Legibus*, trans. Clinton W. Keyes, p. 211 (1943).

1001 There is no jewel in the world comparable to learning; no learning so excellent both for Prince and subject, as knowledge of laws; and no knowledge of any laws (I speak of human) so necessary for all estates and for all causes, concerning goods, lands or life, as the common laws of England.

SIR EDWARD COKE, *Le Second Part Des Reportes Del Edward Coke*, p. vi (1600–1659). Spelling modernized.

1002 "If the law supposes that," said Mr. Bumble, . . . "the law is a ass—a idiot. If that's the eye of the law, the law is a bachelor; and the worst I wish the law is that his eye may be opened by experience—by experience."

CHARLES DICKENS, *Oliver Twist*, chapter 51, p. 489 (1970). First published serially 1837–1839.

1003 Good men must not obey the laws too well.

RALPH WALDO EMERSON, "Politics," *Essays: Second Series*, in *Complete Writings of Ralph Waldo Emerson*, vol. 1, p. 300 (1929).

1004 Republics abound in young civilians who believe that the laws make the city, that grave modifications of the policy and modes of living and employments of the population, that commerce, education and religion may be voted in or out; and that any measure, though it were absurd, may be imposed on a people if only you can get sufficient voices to make it a law. But the wise know that foolish legislation is a rope of sand which perishes in the twisting; that the State must follow and not lead the character and progress of the citizen; that the form of government which prevails is the expression of what cultivation exists in the population which permits it. The law is only a memorandum.

RALPH WALDO EMERSON, "Politics," *Essays: Second Series* (vol. 3 of *The Complete Works of Ralph Waldo Emerson*), pp. 199–200 (1903).

1005 If one man can be allowed to determine for himself what is law, every man can. That means first chaos, then tyranny. Legal process is an essential part of the democratic process.

Justice FELIX FRANKFURTER, concurring, *United States* v. *Mine Workers*, 330 U.S. 312 (1946).

1006 It cannot be helped, it is as it should be, that the law is behind the times.

Justice OLIVER WENDELL HOLMES, speech at Harvard Law School Association of New York, New York City, February 15, 1913.—*Speeches by Oliver Wendell Holmes*, p. 101 (1934).

1007 It is revolting to have no better reason for a rule of law than that so it was laid down in the time of Henry IV.

OLIVER WENDELL HOLMES, associate justice, supreme court of Massachusetts, address delivered at the dedication of the new hall of Boston University School of Law, Boston, Massachusetts, January 8, 1897.—Holmes, *Address Delivered at the Dedication . . .*, p. 18 (1897).

1008 The laws of God, the laws of man,
He may keep that will and can;
Not I: let God and man decree
Laws for themselves and not for me;
And if my ways are not as theirs
Let them mind their own affairs.

A. E. HOUSMAN, "The laws of God, the laws of man," line 1–6, *Last Poems*, in *The Collected Poems*, p. 79 (1967).

1009 A strict observance of the written laws is doubtless *one* of the high duties of a good citizen, but it is not *the highest*. The laws of necessity, of self-preservation, of saving our country when in danger, are of higher obligation. To lose our country by a scrupulous adherence to written law, would be to lose the law itself, with life, liberty, property and all those who are enjoying them with us; thus absurdly sacrificing the end to the means.

THOMAS JEFFERSON, letter to John B. Colvin, September 20, 1810.—*The Writings of Thomas Jefferson*, ed. Paul L. Ford, vol. 9, p. 279 (1898).

1010 There is, therefore, only one categorical imperative. It is: Act only according to that maxim by which you can at the same time will that it should become a universal law.

IMMANUEL KANT, *Foundations of the Metaphysics of Morals*, trans. Lewis W. Beck, ed. Robert P. Wolff, section 2, p. 44 (1969).

1011 Because just as good morals, if they are to be maintained, have need of the laws, so the laws, if they are to be observed, have need of good morals.

NICCOLÒ MACHIAVELLI, *Discourses on the First Decade of Titus Livius*, trans. Allan Gilbert, book 1, chapter 18, p. 241 (1965).

1012 It will be of little avail to the people, that the laws are made by men of their own choice, if the laws be so voluminous that they cannot be read, or so incoherent that they cannot be understood; if they be repealed or revised before they are promulgated, or undergo such incessant changes that no man, who knows what the law is to-day, can guess what it will be to-morrow.

JAMES MADISON (?), *The Federalist*, ed. Benjamin F. Wright, no. 62, pp. 411–12 (1961).

1013 It is important, of course, that controversies be settled right, but there are many civil questions which arise between individuals in which it is not so important the controversy be settled one way or another as that it be settled. Of course a settlement of a controversy on a fundamentally wrong principle of law is greatly to be deplored, but there must of necessity be many rules governing the relations between members of the same society that are more important in that their establishment creates a known rule of action than that they proceed on one principle or another. Delay works always for the man with the longest purse.

Chief Justice WILLIAM HOWARD TAFT, informal address to the judicial section of the American Bar Association, Cincinnati, Ohio, August 30, 1921.—"Adequate Machinery for Judicial Business," *American Bar Association Journal*, September 1921, p. 453.

Lawyers

1014 America is the paradise of lawyers.

Attributed to Justice DAVID J. BREWER.—Champ Clark, *My Quarter Century of American Politics*, vol. 2, p. 130 (1920).
Clark was Speaker of the House from 1911–1919.

1015 The purpose of the University of Washington cannot be to produce black lawyers for blacks, Polish lawyers for Poles, Jewish lawyers for Jews, Irish lawyers for Irish. It should be to produce good lawyers for Americans and not to place First Amendment barriers against anyone.

Justice WILLIAM O. DOUGLAS, dissenting, *DeFunis* v. *Odegaard*, 416 U.S. 342 (1974).

1016 That makes me think, my friend, as I have often done before, how natural it is that those who have spent a long time in the study of philosophy appear ridiculous when they enter the courts of law as speakers. . . . Those who have knocked about in courts and the like from their youth up seem to me, when compared with those who have been brought up in philosophy and similar pursuits, to be as slaves in breeding compared with freemen.

PLATO, *Theaetetus*, trans. H. N. Fowler, p. 115 (1921).

1017 The first thing we do, let's kill all the lawyers.

William Shakespeare, *Henry VI, part II*, act IV, scene ii, lines 83–84. Dick the butcher is speaking.

Leadership

1018 As we look over the list of the early leaders of the republic, Washington, John Adams, Hamilton, and others, we discern that they were all men who insisted upon being themselves and who refused to truckle to the people. With each succeeding generation, the growing demand of the people that its elective officials shall not lead but merely register the popular will has steadily undermined the independence of those who derive their power from popular election. The persistent refusal of the Adamses to sacrifice the integrity of their own intellectual and moral standards and values for the sake of winning public office or popular favor is another of the measuring rods by which we may measure the divergence of American life from its starting point.

JAMES TRUSLOW ADAMS, *The Adams Family*, p. 95 (1930).

1019 Ye call me chief, and ye do well to call him chief who, for twelve long years, has met upon the arena every shape of man or beast that the broad Empire of Rome could furnish, and has never yet lowered his arm. And if there be one among you who can say that, ever, in public fight or private brawl, my actions did belie my tongue, let him step forth and say it. If there be three in all your throng dare face me on the bloody sand, let them come on! Yet I was not always thus, a hired butcher, a savage chief of still more savage men.

ELIJAH KELLOGG, "Spartacus to the Gladiators."—Wilmot B. Mitchell, *Elijah Kellogg: The Man and His Work*, p. 206 (1903).

This declamation was written by Kellogg when he was a student at Andover Theological Seminary in 1840–1843, and has been published elsewhere in books on public speaking and oratory.

1020 Of the best rulers
The people (only) know that they exist;
The next best they love and praise;
The next they fear;
And the next they revile.

When they do not command the people's faith,
Some will lose faith in them,
And then they resort to oaths!
But (of the best) when their task is accomplished, their work done,
The people all remark, "We have done it ourselves."

LAO-TZU, *The Wisdom of Laotse*, trans. and ed. Lin Yutang, chapter 17, p. 114 (1948).

1021 There go the people. I must follow them, for I am their leader.

Attributed to ALEXANDRE LEDRU-ROLLIN, one of the leaders of the February Revolution of 1848 in France.

James Michael Curley uses this quotation as an epigraph at the beginning of chapter 4 of his autobiography, *I'd Do It Again*, p. 44 (1957), and attributes it to a French Revolutionist.

Attribution to Gandhi of "I must follow the people for I am their leader" is made by Leon Howell, "The Delta Ministry," *Christianity and Crisis*, August 8, 1966, p. 192.

Alvin R. Calman, *Ledru-Rollin and the Second French Republic* (*Studies in History, Economics and Public Law*, vol. 103, no. 2), p. 374 (1922), says Ledru-Rollin's use of "I am their chief; I must follow them" is probably apocryphal.

1022 He made the city [Athens], great as it was when he took it, the greatest and richest of all cities, and grew to be superior in power to kings and tyrants. Some of these actually appointed him guardian of their sons, but he did not make his estate a single drachma greater than it was when his father left it to him.

PLUTARCH, *Plutarch's Lives*, trans. Bernadotte Perrin, life of Pericles, vol. 3, p. 51 (1915).

1023 You cannot be a leader, and ask other people to follow you, unless you know how to follow, too.

Speaker of the House SAM RAYBURN.—*The Leadership of Speaker Sam Rayburn, Collected Tributes of His Congressional Colleagues*, p. 34 (1961). House Doc. 87-247.

"A compilation of tributes paid him in the Hall of the House of Representatives, June 12, 1961, and other pertinent material, to celebrate the occasion of his having served as Speaker twice as long as any of his predecessors in the history of the United States: *Sixteen years and 273 days*" (title page).

1024 A great nation is not led by a man who simply repeats the talk of the street-corners or the opinions of the newspapers. A nation is led by a man who hears more than those things; or who, rather, hearing those things, understands them better, unites them, puts them into a common meaning; speaks, not the rumors of the street, but a new principle for a new age; a man in whose ears the voices of the nation do not sound like the accidental and discordant notes that come from the voice of a mob, but concurrent and concordant like the united voices of a chorus, whose many meanings, spoken by melodious tongues, unite in his understanding in a single meaning and reveal to him a single vision, so that he can speak what no man else knows, the common meaning of the common voice. Such is the man who leads a great, free, democratic nation.

WOODROW WILSON, president of Princeton, address, "Abraham Lincoln: A Man of the People," Chicago, Illinois, February 12, 1909.—*The Papers of Woodrow Wilson*, ed. Arthur S. Link, vol. 19, p. 42 (1975).

1025 Some citizens are so good that nothing a leader can do will make them better. Others are so incorrigible that nothing can be done to improve them. But the great bulk of the people go with the moral tide of the moment. The leader must help create that tide.

Author unknown. Attributed to a nineteenth century Japanese philosopher by John W. Gardner, as quoted by Edward P. Morgan in his syndicated column.—*The Washington Post*, September 29, 1970, p. A18.

League of Nations

1026 I have loved but one flag and I can not share that devotion and give affection to the mongrel banner invented for a league.

Senator HENRY CABOT LODGE, remarks in the Senate, August 12, 1919, *Congressional Record*, vol. 58, p. 3784.

1027 The program of the world's peace, therefore, is our program; and that program, the only possible program, as we see it, is this:

1. Open covenants of peace, openly arrived at, after which there shall be no private international understandings of any kind but diplomacy shall proceed always frankly and in the public view.

President WOODROW WILSON, first of the "Fourteen Points," address to a joint session of Congress, January 8, 1918.—*The Messages and Papers of Woodrow Wilson*, ed. Albert Shaw, vol. 1, p. 468 (1924).

This speech on war aims and peace terms laid the groundwork for the proposal of a League of Nations.

Legislators

1028 I did not obey your instructions. No. I conformed to the instructions of truth and Nature, and maintained your interest, against your opinions, with a constancy that became me. A representative worthy of you ought to be a person of stability. I am to look, indeed, to your opinions,—but to such opinions as you and I *must* have five years hence. I was not to look to the flash of the day. I knew that you chose me, in my place, along with others, to be a pillar of the state, and not a weathercock on the top of the edifice, exalted for my levity and versatility, and of no use but to indicate the shiftings of every fashionable gale.

EDMUND BURKE, speech at Bristol, previous to the election, September 6, 1780.—*The Works of the Right Honorable Edmund Burke,* vol. 2, p. 382 (1899).

1029 In all forms of government the people is the true legislator.

EDMUND BURKE, "Tract on the Popery Laws," chapter 3, part 1, *The Works of the Right Honorable Edmund Burke,* vol. 6, p. 320 (1899).

1030 The legislator is an indispensable guardian of our freedom. It is true that great executives have played a powerful role in the development of civilization, but such leaders appear sporadically, by chance. They do not always appear when they are most needed. The great executives have given inspiration and push to the advancement of human society, but it is the legislator who has given stability and continuity to that slow and painful progress.

Senator J. WILLIAM FULBRIGHT, "The Legislator," lecture delivered at the University of Chicago in 1946.—*The Works of the Mind,* ed. for the University's Committee on Social Thought by Robert B. Heywood, p. 119 (1947).

1031 Two deputies, one of whom is a radical, have more in common than two radicals, one of whom is a deputy.

(Il y a moins de différence entre deux députés dont l'un est révolutionnaire et l'autre ne l'est pas, qu'entre deux révolutionnaires, dont l'un est député et l'autre ne l'est pas.)

ROBERT DE JOUVENEL, *La République des Camarades,* part 1, chapter 1, p. 17 (1914).

1032 Legislators represent people, not trees or acres. Legislators are elected by voters, not farms or cities or economic interests.

Chief Justice EARL WARREN, *Reynolds* v. *Sims,* 377 U.S. 562 (1964).

Legislature

1033 Parliament will train you to talk; and above all things to hear, with patience, unlimited quantities of foolish talk.

THOMAS CARLYLE, *Latter-Day Pamphlets,* no. 5, p. 33 (1850).

1034 That a Parliament, especially a Parliament with Newspaper Reporters firmly established in it, is an entity which by its very nature cannot do work, but can do talk only.

THOMAS CARLYLE, *Latter-Day Pamphlets,* no. 6, pp. 14–15 (1850).

1035 He [Oliver Cromwell] in a furious manner, bid the Speaker leave his chair; told the house "That they had sat long enough, unless they had done more good; . . . and that it was not fit they should sit as a parliament any longer, and desired them to go away."

OLIVER CROMWELL, dissolving Parliament, April 20, 1653, as reported by Bulstrode Whitlocke.—*Cobbett's Parliamentary History of England, from the Norman Conquest, in 1066, to the Year 1803,* vol. 3, col. 1383 (1808).

There is no official version of this speech because the journal entry was expunged by order of Parliament, January 7, 1659. The version most often quoted is that of Thomas Carlyle, who combined three original sources, including Whitlocke, to obtain an "authentic, moderately conceivable account": "You have sat too long here for any good you have been doing lately. . . . Depart, I say; and let us have done with you. In the name of God,—go!"—Thomas Carlyle, *Oliver Cromwell's Letters and Speeches,* vol. 3, part 7, pp. 34–35 (1897).

On May 7, 1940, Leopold Amery quoted the Carlyle version (omitting "lately") in the House of Commons, urging Prime Minister Neville Chamberlain to resign.—Winston Churchill, *The Gathering Storm* (vol. 1 of *The Second World War*), p. 659 (1948).

Senator George J. Mitchell quoted the Carlyle version on December 23, 1982.—*Congressional Record,* vol. 128, no. 17, p. S16068 (daily ed.).

1036 A plural Legislature is as necessary to good Government as a single Executive. It is not enough that your Legislature should be numerous; it should also be divided. Numbers alone are not a sufficient Barrier against the Impulses of Passion, the Combinations of Interest, the Intrigues of Faction, the Haste of Folly, or the Spirit of Encroachment. One Division should watch over and controul the other, supply its Wants, correct its Blunders, and cross its Designs, should they be criminal or erroneous. Wisdom is the specific Quality of the Legislature, grows out of the Number of the Body, and is made up of the Portions of Sense and Knowledge which each Member brings to it.

BENJAMIN FRANKLIN, "Queries and Remarks Respecting Alterations in the Constitution of Pennsylvania," *The Writings of Benjamin Franklin,* ed. Albert H. Smith, vol. 10, pp. 55–56 (1907, reprinted 1970).

This section of his "Queries and Remarks" is a rearrangement and slight rewording of a portion of an anonymous article, "Hints for the Members of the Convention," *Federal Gazette,* November 3, 1789, p. 2, which had been reprinted from the *Carlisle Gazette,* October 21, 1789.

1037 Great constitutional provisions must be administered with caution. Some play must be allowed for the joints of the machine, and it must be remembered that legislatures are ultimate guardians of the liberties and welfare of the people in quite as great a degree as the courts.

Justice OLIVER WENDELL HOLMES, *Missouri, Kansas and Texas Railway Company* v. *May,* 194 U.S. 270 (1904).

1038 The commons, faithful to their system, remained in a wise and masterly inactivity.

SIR JAMES MACKINTOSH, *Vindiciae Gallicae,* section 1, p. 14 (1838). Originally published in 1791.

The phrase "a wise and masterly inactivity" was used in America by Representative John Randolph of Roanoke: "We ought to observe that practice which is the hardest of all—especially for young physicians—we ought to throw in no medicine at all—to abstain—to observe a wise and masterly inactivity."—*Register of Debates in Congress,* January 25, 1828, vol. 4, col. 1170.

The phrase was mostly associated, however, with John C. Calhoun, who used it during the nullification crisis and later during the Oregon controversy in 1843. While vice president, Calhoun spoke to the people of South Carolina by addressing the legislature at the close of the session of 1831: "If the Government should be taught thereby, that the highest wisdom of a State is, 'a wise and masterly inactivity,'—an invaluable blessing will be conferred."—*The Works of John C. Calhoun*, vol. 6, p. 143 (1859). See Hans Sperber and Travis Trittschuh, *American Political Terms*, pp. 263–64 (1962).

1039 The legislature, like the executive, has ceased to be even the creature of the people: it is the creature of pressure groups, and most of them, it must be manifest, are of dubious wisdom and even more dubious honesty. Laws are no longer made by a rational process of public discussion; they are made by a process of blackmail and intimidation, and they are executed in the same manner. The typical lawmaker of today is a man wholly devoid of principle—a mere counter in a grotesque and knavish game. . . . If the right pressure could be applied to him he would be cheerfully in favor of chiropractic, astrology or cannibalism.

H. L. MENCKEN, "The Library," *The American Mercury*, May 1930, p. 123.

This view of Mencken's comes from his book review of *The Dissenting Opinions of Mr. Justice Holmes* (1930).

1040 Lawyers are apt to speak as though the legislature were omnipotent, as they do not require to go beyond its decisions. It is, of course, omnipotent in the sense that it can make whatever laws it pleases, inasmuch as a law means any rule which has been made by the legislature. But from the scientific point of view, the power of the legislature is of course strictly limited. It is limited, so to speak, both from within and from without; from within, because the legislature is the product of a certain social condition, and determined by whatever determines the society; and from without, because the power of imposing laws is dependent upon the instinct of subordination, which is itself limited. If a legislature decided that all blue-eyed babies should be murdered, the preservation of blue-eyed babies would be illegal; but legislators must go mad before they could pass such a law, and subjects be idiotic before they could submit to it.

LESLIE STEPHEN, *The Science of Ethics*, p. 145 (1882).

1041 No man's life, liberty or property are safe while the Legislature is in session.

Saying quoted by Gideon J. Tucker, Surrogate, in 1866 report of the final accounting in the estate of A. B.—*New York Surrogate Reports*, 1 Tucker (N.Y. Surr.) 249 (1866).

Liberals

1042 Ultraliberalism today translates into a whimpering isolationism in foreign policy, a mulish obstructionism in domestic policy, and a pusillanimous pussyfooting on the critical issue of law and order.

Vice President SPIRO T. AGNEW, speech before Illinois Republican meeting, Springfield, Illinois, September 10, 1970.—*Collected Speeches of Spiro Agnew*, p. 193 (1971).

1043 A liberal is a person whose interests aren't at stake at the moment.

WILLIS PLAYER, quoted by *The Washington Post, Potomac* magazine, November 15, 1972, p. 12. Unverified.

1044 What bothers me about today's "liberals" is this: through the ages, those called liberal fought to take the power away from the kings and the emperors and to give it to the parliaments; now it is the "liberals" who are anxious to give more and more power to the executive, at the expense of the legislative branch.

BURTON K. WHEELER, *Yankee from the West,* chapter 19, p. 428 (1962).
Wheeler served in Congress 1923–1947.

Liberty

1045 This liberty will look easy by and by when nobody dies to get it.

MAXWELL ANDERSON, *Valley Forge,* act III, final sentence, p. 110 (1937). George Washington is speaking.

1046 Proclaim liberty throughout all the land unto all the inhabitants thereof.

The Bible, Leviticus 25:10.

"In a letter written by a committee of the Pennsylvania Provincial Assembly, 1 Nov., 1751, ordering a bell for the tower of the new State House, it was directed that this quotation from the Bible should be inscribed around it 'well-shaped in large letters.' "—*The Home Book of Quotations,* 10th ed., ed. Burton Stevenson, pp. 1104–5 (1967).

The bell was ordered to celebrate fifty years of William Penn's Charter of Privileges. Penn left England in 1699 to return to America, where he drew up a document known as the Charter of Privileges, which was confirmed by the Assembly on October 28, 1701, and "remained substantially the fundamental law of Pennsylvania until 1776."—[Federal] Writer's Program, Pennsylvania, *Pennsylvania: A Guide to the Keystone State,* p. 30 (1940). The verse above is more fitting for a fiftieth anniversary than it appears, for it begins: "And ye shall hallow the fiftieth year . . ."

This bell, known as the Liberty Bell since about 1839, was rung July 8, 1776, with other church bells, announcing the adoption of the Declaration of Independence. The bell may be seen in Liberty Bell Pavilion, just north of Independence Hall in Philadelphia.

These words are also inscribed on a plaque in the stairwell of the pedestal of the Statue of Liberty.

1047 The United States appear to be destined by Providence to plague America with misery in the name of liberty.

Attributed to SIMÓN BOLÍVAR. Unverified.

1048 The defendants' objections to the evidence obtained by wire-tapping must, in my opinion, be sustained. It is, of course, immaterial where the physical connection with the telephone wires leading into the defendants' premises was made. And it is also immaterial that the intrusion was in aid of law enforcement. Experience should teach us to be most on our guard to protect liberty when the Government's purposes are beneficent. Men born to freedom are naturally alert to repel invasion of their liberty by evil-minded rulers. The greatest dangers to liberty lurk in insidious encroachment by men of zeal, well-meaning but without understanding.

Justice LOUIS D. BRANDEIS, dissenting, *Olmstead* v. *United States,* 277 U.S. 479 (1928).

The last sentence is one of many quotations inscribed on Cox Corridor II, a first floor House corridor, U.S. Capitol.

1049 Those who won our independence believed that the final end of the State was to make men free to develop their faculties; and that in its government the deliberative forces should prevail over the arbitrary. They valued liberty both as an end and as a means. They believed liberty to be the secret of happiness and courage to be the secret of liberty.

Justice LOUIS D. BRANDEIS, concurring, *Whitney* v. *California*, 274 U.S. 375 (1927).

1050 The distinguishing part of our Constitution is its liberty. To preserve that liberty inviolate seems the particular duty and proper trust of a member of the House of Commons. But the liberty, the only liberty, I mean is a liberty connected with order: that not only exists along with order and virtue, but which cannot exist at all without them. It inheres in good and steady government, as in its substance and vital principle.

EDMUND BURKE, speech at his arrival at Bristol, October 13, 1774.—*The Works of the Right Honorable Edmund Burke*, vol. 2, p. 87 (1899).

1051 Men are qualified for civil liberty in exact proportion to their disposition to put moral chains upon their own appetites,—in proportion as their love to justice is above their rapacity,—in proportion as their soundness and sobriety of understanding is above their vanity and presumption,—in proportion as they are more disposed to listen to the counsels of the wise and good, in preference to the flattery of knaves. Society cannot exist, unless a controlling power upon will and appetite be placed somewhere; and the less of it there is within, the more there must be without. It is ordained in the eternal constitution of things, that men of intemperate minds cannot be free. Their passions forge their fetters.

EDMUND BURKE, "Letter to a Member of the National Assembly," 1791.—*The Works of the Right Honorable Edmund Burke*, vol. 4, pp. 51–52 (1899).

1052 That the greatest security of the people, against the encroachments and usurpations of their superiors, is to keep the Spirit of Liberty constantly awake, is an undeniable truth.

EDMUND BURKE, "A Free Briton's Advice to the Free Citizens of Dublin," no. 2, 1748.—*The Early Life, Correspondence and Writings of the Rt. Hon. Edmund Burke*, p. 338 (1923).

1053 The true danger is when liberty is nibbled away, for expedients, and by parts.

EDMUND BURKE, letter to the Sheriffs of Bristol, April 3, 1777.—*The Works of the Right Honorable Edmund Burke*, vol. 2, p. 199 (1899).

1054 It is the common fate of the indolent to see their rights become a prey to the active. The condition upon which God hath given liberty to man is eternal vigilance; which condition if he break, servitude is at once the consequence of his crime and the punishment of his guilt.

JOHN PHILPOT CURRAN, "Election of Lord Mayor of Dublin," speech before the Privy Council, July 10, 1790.—*The Speeches of the Right Honorable John Philpot Curran*, ed. Thomas Davis, pp. 94–95 (1847).

An early use of the words "eternal vigilance." *Bartlett's Familiar Quotations*, at least, lists this as the source of "eternal vigilance is the price of liberty" (15th ed., p. 397, footnote 8, 1980). But see also No. 1073.

1055 True liberty consists only in the power of doing what we ought to will, and in not being constrained to do what we ought not to will.

Attributed to JONATHAN EDWARDS.—George Seldes, *The Great Quotations*, p. 220 (1966). Unverified.

In the editor's introduction to Edwards's *Freedom of the Will*, ed. Paul Ramsey, p. 12 (1957), is a succinct summary of a portion of Edwards's definition of terms, part 1, section 5 (p. 164): "In other words, a man is free to do what he wills, but not to do what he does not will."

1056 Those who would give up essential Liberty, to purchase a little temporary Safety, deserve neither Liberty nor Safety.

BENJAMIN FRANKLIN, Pennsylvania Assembly: Reply to the Governor, November 11, 1755.—*The Papers of Benjamin Franklin*, ed. Leonard W. Labaree, vol. 6, p. 242 (1963).

This quotation, slightly altered, is inscribed on a plaque in the stairwell of the pedestal of the Statue of Liberty: "They that can give up essential liberty to obtain a little safety deserve neither liberty nor safety."

1057 Where liberty is, there is my country.

Attributed to BENJAMIN FRANKLIN.

H. L. Mencken, *A New Dictionary of Quotations*, p. 682 (1942) gives "Where liberty dwells, there is my country," with a note that this was in a Franklin letter to Benjamin Vaughan, March 14, 1783, but the on-going project, *Papers of Benjamin Franklin*, has been unable to identify this letter.

Alfred Owen Aldridge, *Man of Reason*, p. 169 (1959) says, "According to a tradition repeated by many biographers of Paine, Franklin at one time remarked in his hearing: 'Where liberty is, there is my country. . . .' " Aldridge adds, "the story must be written off as apocryphal."

Bartlett's Familiar Quotations, 15th ed., p. 367 (1982), attributes this to James Otis, as his motto (Ubi libertas, ibi patria), but this has not been verified in either his speeches or biographical sources. It has also been attributed to Algernon Sidney, but has not been verified in any source.

See also No. 347.

1058 The fundamental source of all your errors, sophisms, and false reasonings, is a total ignorance of the natural rights of mankind. Were you once to become acquainted with these, you could never entertain a thought, that all men are not, by nature, entitled to a parity of privileges. You would be convinced, that natural liberty is a gift of the beneficent Creator, to the whole human race; and that civil liberty is founded in that; and cannot be wrested from any people, without the most manifest violation of justice. *Civil liberty is only natural liberty, modified and secured by the sanctions of civil society*. It is not a thing, in its own nature, precarious and dependent on human will and caprice; but it is conformable to the constitution of man, as well as necessary to the *well-being* of society.

ALEXANDER HAMILTON, "The Farmer Refuted," *The Works of Alexander Hamilton*, ed. John C. Hamilton, vol. 2, p. 61 (1850).

1059 Liberty lies in the hearts of men and women; when it dies there, no constitution, no law, no court can save it; no constitution, no law, no court can even do much to help it. . . . The spirit of liberty is the spirit which is not too sure that it is right; the spirit of liberty is the spirit which seeks to understand the minds of other men and women; the spirit of liberty is the spirit which weighs their interests alongside its own without bias; the spirit of liberty remembers that not even a sparrow falls to earth unheeded; the spirit of liberty is the spirit of Him who, near two thousand years ago, taught mankind that lesson it has never learned, but has never quite forgotten; that there may be a kingdom where the least shall be heard and considered side by side with the greatest.

LEARNED HAND, "The Spirit of Liberty," speech at an "I Am an American Day" ceremony, Central Park, New York City, May 21, 1944.—Hand, *The Spirit of Liberty*, 3d ed., enl., ed. Irving Dilliard, p. 190 (1960).

1060 Is the relinquishment of the trial by jury and the liberty of the press necessary for your liberty? Will the abandonment of your most sacred rights tend to the security of your liberty? Liberty, the greatest of all earthly blessings—give us that precious jewel, and you may take every thing else! . . . Guard with jealous attention the public liberty. Suspect every one who approaches that jewel.

PATRICK HENRY, speech to the Virginia Convention, Richmond, Virginia, June 5, 1788.—*The Debates in the Several State Conventions on the Adoption of the Federal Constitution*, ed. Jonathan Elliot, vol. 3, p. 45 (1836, reprinted 1937).

1061 There is a just God who presides over the destinies of nations, and who will raise up friends to fight our battles for us. The battle, sir, is not to the strong alone; it is to the vigilant, the active, the brave. . . . It is vain, sir, to extenuate the matter. Gentlemen may cry, peace, peace—but there is no peace. The war is actually begun! The next gale that sweeps from the north will bring to our ears the clash of resounding arms! Our brethren are already in the field! Why stand we here idle? What is it that gentlemen wish? What would they have? Is life so dear, or peace so sweet, as to be purchased at the price of chains and slavery? Forbid it, Almighty God!—I know not what course others may take; but as for me, give me liberty, or give me death!

PATRICK HENRY, speech to the Virginia Convention, Richmond, Virginia, March 23, 1775.—William Wirt, *Sketches of the Life and Character of Patrick Henry*, 9th ed., pp. 141–42 (1836, reprinted 1970). The Biblical allusion is from Jeremiah 6:14.

"While there is no doubt as to the general effect of Henry's speech, questions as to its actual wording are not so easily disposed of. Not only is there no manuscript copy of the oration, there is no stenographic report. . . . It was not until some forty years later that William Wirt first reprinted a reconstruction of Henry's oration. In the absence of contemporary written information" there was much criticism of Wirt's text. Wirt collected much of the information for his biography of Patrick Henry "when many of Henry's auditors at St. John's [church] were still in their clear-minded fifties or sixties." Wirt collected information from "intelligent and reliable" auditors, including John Tyler, Judge St. George Tucker, and Edmund Randolph. "Wirt's text was based on a few very helpful sources plus many bits of information. He had ample proof for certain burning phrases . . . a remarkable resemblance to Henry's other speeches during that period," the fact that the speech conforms to others in "oratorical style and technique, even in the use of Biblical quotations or analogies. Of course, Wirt may have used fragments" from earlier speeches for the reconstruction. "Yet the information on the text as a whole is more precise than for many other great speeches in history."—Robert Douthat Meade, *Patrick Henry, Practical Revolutionary*, vol. 2, pp. 38–40 (1969).

"I can find no evidence that Patrick Henry's 'Give me liberty, or give me death' went ringing round the country in 1775, when he thus burst forth to the Virginia delegates, or in fact that it was quoted at all until after William Wirt's official life in 1817."—Carroll A. Wilson, "Familiar 'Small College' Quotations, II: Mark Hopkins and the Log," *The Colophon*, spring 1938, p. 204.

1062 God who gave us life gave us liberty.[a] Can the liberties of a nation be secure when we have removed a conviction that these liberties are the gift of God? Indeed I tremble for my country when I reflect that God is just, that his justice cannot sleep forever.[b] Commerce between master and slave is despotism.[c] Nothing is more certainly written in the book of fate than that these people are to be free.[d] Establish the law for educating the common people.[e] This it is the business of the State to effect and on a general plan.[f]

THOMAS JEFFERSON. Inscription on the northeast quadrant of the Jefferson Memorial, Washington, D.C., selected by the Thomas Jefferson Memorial Commission, from several writings of Jefferson's. The inscription omits words without ellipses.

[a] "Draft of Instructions to the Virginia Delegates in the Continental Congress," *The Papers of Thomas Jefferson*, ed. Julian P. Boyd, vol. 1, p. 135 (1950).

[b] *"Notes on the State of Virginia,"* query 18, *The Writings of Thomas Jefferson*, ed. Paul L. Ford, vol. 3, p. 267 (1894).

[c] Ibid., p. 266.

[d] "Autobiography," in *The Writings of Thomas Jefferson*, ed. Andrew A. Lipscomb, vol. 1, p. 72 (1903).

[e] Letter to George Wythe, August 13, 1786.—*The Papers of Thomas Jefferson*, ed. Julian P. Boyd, vol. 10, p. 245 (1954).

[f] Letter to George Washington, January 4, 1785 (i.e., 1786).—*The Papers of Thomas Jefferson*, ed. Julian P. Boyd, vol. 9, p. 151 (1954).

1063 I would rather be exposed to the inconveniencies attending too much liberty than those attending too small a degree of it.

THOMAS JEFFERSON, letter to Archibald Stuart, December 23, 1791.—*The Writings of Thomas Jefferson*, ed. Paul L. Ford, vol. 5, p. 409 (1895).

1064 It behoves every man who values liberty of conscience for himself, to resist invasions of it in the case of others; or their case may, by change of circumstances, become his own.

President THOMAS JEFFERSON, letter to Benjamin Rush, April 21, 1803.—*The Writings of Thomas Jefferson*, ed. Paul L. Ford, vol. 8, p. 224, footnote 1 (1897).

1065 The tree of liberty must be refreshed from time to time with the blood of patriots and tyrants. It is it's natural manure.

THOMAS JEFFERSON, letter to William Stephens Smith, November 13, 1787.—*The Papers of Thomas Jefferson*, ed. Julian P. Boyd, vol. 12, p. 356 (1955).

A related idea was later expressed by Bertrand Barère de Vieuzac in a speech to the French national assembly, January 16, 1793: "L'arbre de la liberté . . . croît lorsqu'il est arrosé du sang de toute espèce de tyrans (The tree of liberty grows only when watered by the blood of tyrants)," *Archives Parliamentaires de 1787 à 1860*, vol. 57, p. 368 (1900).

And much earlier Tertullian had said: "Plures efficimur quotiens metimur a vobis; semen est sanguis Christianorum (We multiply whenever we are mown down by you; the blood of Christians is seed)," *Apology*, trans. T. R. Glover, pp. 226–27 (1931).

1066 Let every nation know, whether it wishes us well or ill, that we shall pay any price, bear any burden, meet any hardship, support any friend, oppose any foe to assure the survival and the success of liberty.

President JOHN F. KENNEDY, inaugural address, January 20, 1961.—*The Public Papers of the Presidents of the United States: John F. Kennedy, 1961*, p. 1.

This is one of seven inscriptions carved on the walls at the gravesite of John F. Kennedy, Arlington National Cemetery.

1067 To one however who adores liberty, and the noble virtues of which it is the parent, there is some consolation in seeing, while we lament the fall of British liberty, the rise of that of America. Yes, my friend, like a young phoenix she will rise full plumed and glorious from her mother's ashes.

ARTHUR LEE, letter to Samuel Adams, December 24, 1772.—Richard Henry Lee, *Life of Arthur Lee,* vol. 1, p. 225 (1829, reprinted 1969).

Adams repeated the striking phrase in a letter to Lee, April 9, 1773: "But America 'shall rise full plumed and glorious from her Mothers Ashes.' "—*The Writings of Samuel Adams,* ed. Harry A. Cushing, vol. 3, p. 21 (1907, reprinted 1968).

1068 The Democracy of to-day hold the *liberty* of one man to be absolutely nothing, when in conflict with another man's right of *property.* Republicans, on the contrary, are for both the *man* and the *dollar;* but in cases of conflict, the man *before* the dollar.

ABRAHAM LINCOLN, letter to Henry L. Pierce and others, April 6, 1859.—*The Collected Works of Abraham Lincoln,* ed. Roy P. Basler, vol. 3, p. 375 (1953).

1069 What constitutes the bulwark of our own liberty and independence? It is not our frowning battlements, our bristling sea coasts, the guns of our war steamers, or the strength of our gallant and disciplined army. These are not our reliance against a resumption of tyranny in our fair land. All of them may be turned against our liberties, without making us stronger or weaker for the struggle. Our reliance is in the *love of liberty* which God has planted in our bosoms. Our defense is in the preservation of the spirit which prizes liberty as the heritage of all men, in all lands, every where. Destroy this spirit, and you have planted the seeds of despotism around your own doors.

ABRAHAM LINCOLN, speech at Edwardsville, Illinois, September 11, 1858.—*The Collected Works of Abraham Lincoln,* ed. Roy P. Basler, vol. 3, p. 95 (1953).

The last two sentences appear in slightly varying form inscribed on a plaque in the stairwell of the pedestal of the Statue of Liberty: "Our defense is in the spirit which prized liberty as the heritage of all men, in all lands everywhere. Destroy this spirit and you have planted the seeds of despotism at your own doors."

1070 The world has never had a good definition of the word liberty, and the American people, just now, are much in want of one. We all declare for liberty; but in using the same *word* we do not all mean the same *thing.* With some the word liberty may mean for each man to do as he pleases with himself, and the product of his labor; while with others the same word may mean for some men to do as they please with other men, and the product of other men's labor. Here are two, not only different, but incompatable things, called by the same name—liberty. And it follows that each of the things is, by the respective parties, called by two different and incompatable names—liberty and tyranny.

President ABRAHAM LINCOLN, address at sanitary fair, Baltimore, Maryland, April 18, 1864.—*The Collected Works of Abraham Lincoln,* ed. Roy P. Basler, vol. 7, pp. 301–2 (1953).

1071 The struggle between Liberty and Authority is the most conspicuous feature in the portions of history with which we are earliest familiar, particularly in that of Greece, Rome, and England.

JOHN STUART MILL, *On Liberty,* ed. David Spitz, chapter 1, p. 3 (1975). Originally published in 1859.

1072 He that would make his own liberty secure, must guard even his enemy from oppression; for if he violates this duty, he establishes a precedent that will reach to himself.

THOMAS PAINE, "Dissertation on First Principles of Government," *The Writings of Thomas Paine,* ed. Moncure D. Conway, vol. 3, p. 277 (1895). Originally published in 1795.

1073 Eternal vigilance is the price of liberty—power is ever stealing from the many to the few. . . . The hand entrusted with power becomes . . . the necessary enemy of the people. Only by continual oversight can the democrat in office be prevented from hardening into a despot: only by unintermitted Agitation can a people be kept sufficiently awake to principle not to let liberty be smothered in material prosperity.

WENDELL PHILLIPS, speech in Boston, Massachusetts, January 28, 1852.—*Speeches Before the Massachusetts Anti-Slavery Society,* p. 13 (1853).

The memorable and oft-quoted phrase, "eternal vigilance is the price of liberty," was not in quotation marks in the printed edition of this speech. *The Home Book of Quotations,* ed. Burton Stevenson, 9th ed., p. 1106 (1964), notes that "It has been said that Mr. Phillips was quoting Thomas Jefferson, but in a letter dated 14 April, 1879, Mr. Phillips wrote: ' "Eternal vigilance is the price of liberty" has been attributed to Jefferson, but no one has yet found it in his works or elsewhere.' It has also been attributed to Patrick Henry."

See also No. 1054.

1074 Liberty means responsibility. That is why most men dread it.

GEORGE BERNARD SHAW, "Maxims for Revolutionists," appendix 2 to *Man and Superman,* in *The Collected Works of Bernard Shaw,* vol. 10, p. 218 (1930).

1075 Liberty—precious boon of Heaven—is meek and reasonable. She admits, that she belongs to all—to the high and the low; the rich and the poor; the black and the white—and, that she belongs to them all equally. . . . But true liberty acknowledges and defends the equal rights of all men, and all nations.

Representative GERRIT SMITH, remarks in the House, June 27, 1854, *Congressional Globe,* vol. 23, Appendix, p. 1016.

1076 The men of the future will yet fight their way to many a liberty that we do not even miss.

MAX STIRNER ([Johann] Kaspar Schmidt), *The Ego and His Own,* trans. Steven T. Byington, ed. James J. Martin, part 1, chapter 2, p. 127 (1973). Originally published in 1845.

1077 For the saddest epitaph which can be carved in memory of a vanished liberty is that it was lost because its possessors failed to stretch forth a saving hand while yet there was time.

Justice GEORGE SUTHERLAND, dissenting, *Associated Press* v. *National Labor Relations Board,* 301 U.S. 141 (1938).

1078 The contest, for ages, has been to rescue Liberty from the grasp of executive power.

Senator DANIEL WEBSTER, speech in the Senate, May 27, 1834, on President Andrew Jackson's protest.—*The Works of Daniel Webster,* 10th ed., vol. 4, p. 133 (1857).

Liberty

1079 God grants liberty only to those who love it, and are always ready to guard and defend it.

Senator DANIEL WEBSTER, remarks in the Senate, June 3, 1834.—*The Writings and Speeches of Daniel Webster,* vol. 7, p. 47 (1903).

1080 The history of liberty is a history of resistance. The history of liberty is a history of the limitation of governmental power, not the increase of it.

WOODROW WILSON, governor of New Jersey, address to the New York Press Club, New York City, September 9, 1912.—*The Papers of Woodrow Wilson,* ed. Arthur S. Link, vol. 25, p. 124 (1978).

1081 I would rather belong to a poor nation that was free than to a rich nation that had ceased to be in love with liberty. But we shall not be poor if we love liberty, because the nation that loves liberty truly sets every man free to do his best and be his best, and that means the release of all the splendid energies of a great people who think for themselves. A nation of employees cannot be free any more than a nation of employers can be.

President WOODROW WILSON, address on Latin American policy to the fifth annual convention of the Southern Commercial Congress, Mobile, Alabama, October 27, 1913.—*The Papers of Woodrow Wilson,* ed. Arthur S. Link, vol. 28, p. 451 (1978).

The first sentence is inscribed on a plaque in the stairwell of the pedestal of the Statue of Liberty.

Lies

1082 Fraud and prevarication are servile vices. They sometimes grow out of the necessities, always out of the habits, of slavish and degenerate spirits. . . . It is an erect countenance, it is a firm adherence to principle, it is a power of resisting false shame and frivolous fear, that assert our good faith and honor, and assure to us the confidence of mankind.

EDMUND BURKE, "Letters on a Regicide Peace," letter 3, 1796–1797, *The Works of the Right Honorable Edmund Burke,* vol. 5, p. 414 (1899).

1083 I think the inherent right of the Government to lie to save itself when faced with nuclear disaster is basic.

ARTHUR SYLVESTER, assistant secretary of defense, speech at a meeting of the New York chapter of Sigma Delta Chi, New York City, December 6, 1962, as reported by *The Washington Post,* December 7, 1962, p. A-2.

Life

1084 You can't make a silk purse out of a sow's ear, and you can't change human nature from intelligent self-interest into pure idealism—not in this life; and if you could, what would be left for paradise?

Representative JOSEPH G. CANNON, maxim quoted in a tribute to Cannon on his retirement, *The Sun,* Baltimore, Maryland, March 4, 1923.—*Congressional Record,* March 4, 1923, vol. 64, p. 5714.

"Uncle Joe" Cannon, who was Speaker of the House 1903–1911, served in the House for 46 years.

1085 Well, as you know, there are many things in life that are not fair, that wealthy people can afford and poor people can't. But I don't believe that the Federal Government should take action to try to make these opportunities exactly equal, particularly when there is a moral factor involved.

President JIMMY CARTER, answer to a question asking whether it is fair that women who can afford abortions can get them while women who cannot afford them are precluded, news conference, Washington, D.C., July 12, 1977.—*Public Papers of the Presidents of the United States: Jimmy Carter, 1977*, book 2, p. 1237.

1086 What is life but the angle of vision? A man is measured by the angle at which he looks at objects. What is life but what a man is thinking of all day? This is his fate and his employer. Knowing is the measure of the man. By how much we know, so much we are.

RALPH WALDO EMERSON, "Natural History of Intellect," part 1, *Natural History of Intellect and Other Papers* (vol. 12 of *The Complete Works of Ralph Waldo Emerson*), p. 10 (1921).

1087 He was, first and last, the born fighter, to whom the consciousness of being matched against a great adversary suffices and who can dispense with success. Life for him was an adventure, perilous indeed, but men are not made for safe havens. The fullness of life is in the hazards of life. And, at the worst, there is that in us which can turn defeat into victory.

EDITH HAMILTON, *The Great Age of Greek Literature*, p. 243 (1942). She was referring to Aeschylus.

1088 I think that, as life is action and passion, it is required of a man that he should share the passion and action of his time at peril of being judged not to have lived.

OLIVER WENDELL HOLMES, justice of the supreme court of Massachusetts, Memorial Day speech, May 30, 1884, Keene, New Hampshire.—Holmes, *Speeches*, p. 3 (1934).

1089 Life is a romantic business. It is painting a picture, not doing a sum—but you have to make the romance, and it will come to the question how much fire you have in your belly.

Justice OLIVER WENDELL HOLMES, letter to Oswald Ryan, March 8, 1911.—Francis Biddle, *Mr. Justice Holmes*, pp. 138–39 (1942).

1090 O Damsel Dorothy! Dorothy Q.!
Strange is the gift that I owe to you;
Such a gift as never a king
Save to daughter or son might bring,—
All my tenure of heart and hand,
All my title to house and land;
Mother and sister and child and wife
And joy and sorrow and death and life!

OLIVER WENDELL HOLMES, "Dorothy Q.," stanza 5, *The Poetical Works of Oliver Wendell Holmes*, p. 187 (1975).

Dorothy Quincy was Holmes's great-grandmother, and, as he explained in a head-note to the poem, pp. 186–87, "the daughter of Judge Edmund Quincy, and the aunt of Josiah Quincy, junior, the young patriot and orator who died just before the American Revolution, of which he was one of the most eloquent and effective promoters."

1091 . . . the giver of life, who gave it for happiness and not for wretchedness.

THOMAS JEFFERSON, letter to James Monroe, May 20, 1782.—*The Papers of Thomas Jefferson,* ed. Julian P. Boyd, vol. 6, p. 186 (1952).

1092 There is always inequity in life. Some men are killed in a war and some men are wounded, and some men never leave the country, and some men are stationed in the Antarctic and some are stationed in San Francisco. It's very hard in military or in personal life to assure complete equality. Life is unfair.

President JOHN F. KENNEDY, news conference, March 21, 1962.—*Public Papers of the Presidents of the United States: John F. Kennedy, 1962,* p. 259.

1093 Life involves suffering and transitoriness. No person can choose his age or the condition of his time. The past may rob the present of much joy and much mystery. The generation of Buchenwald and the Siberian labor camps cannot talk with the same optimism as its fathers. The bliss of Dante has been lost in our civilization.

HENRY A. KISSINGER, "The Meaning of History: Reflections on Spengler, Toynbee and Kant," senior thesis at Harvard College, as quoted in *The New York Times,* April 5, 1976, p. 20.

1094 Yes! Life is a banquet, and most poor sons-of-bitches are *starving* to death! Live!

JEROME LAWRENCE and ROBERT E. LEE, *Auntie Mame,* act II, scene vi (1957). Auntie Mame is speaking. Based on the novel of the same title by Patrick Dennis.

1095 There are three things which are real: God, human folly, and laughter. Since the first two pass our comprehension, we must do what we can with the third.

AUBREY MENEN, *Rama Retold,* p. 231 (1954).

This is a modern retelling of part of the Ramayana. President John F. Kennedy presented his friend, White House appointment secretary David Powers, with a silver beer mug for his birthday, April 26, 1963. The inscription on the mug was a slight variation on the lines above:

There are three things which are real:
God, human folly and laughter.
The first two are beyond our comprehension
So we must do what we can with the third.

—*The New York Times,* April 29, 1963, p. 14.

1096 Unrest of spirit is a mark of life; one problem after another presents itself and in the solving of them we can find our greatest pleasure.

KARL MENNINGER, "Take Your Choice," *This Week Magazine,* October 16, 1949, p. 2.

1097 This is a world in which each of us, knowing his limitations, knowing the evils of superficiality and the terrors of fatigue, will have to cling to what is close to him, to what he knows, to what he can do, to his friends and his tradition and his love, lest he be dissolved in a universal confusion and know nothing and love nothing.

J. ROBERT OPPENHEIMER, *The Open Mind,* p. 144 (1955).

1098 Life is not so important as the duties of life.

JOHN RANDOLPH of Roanoke. "Randolph's best epigram."—William Cabell Bruce, *John Randolph of Roanoke, 1773–1833,* vol. 2, chapter 7, p. 205 (1922, reprinted 1970).

Randolph was a member of Congress 1799–1813, 1815–1817, and 1819–1829.

1099 I bargained with Life for a penny,
And Life would pay no more,
However I begged at evening
When I counted my scanty store;
For Life is a just employer,
He gives you what you ask,
But once you have set the wages,
Why, you must bear the task.
I worked for a menial's hire,
Only to learn, dismayed,
That any wage I had asked of Life,
Life would have paid.

JESSIE B. RITTENHOUSE, "My Wage," *The Door of Dreams*, p. 25 (1918).

1100 A baby is God's opinion that life should go on.

CARL SANDBURG, *Remembrance Rock*, chapter 2, p. 7 (1948).

1101 The great fault of all ethics hitherto has been that they believed themselves to have to deal only with the relations of man to man. In reality, however, the question is what is his attitude to the world and all life that comes within his reach. A man is ethical only when life, as such, is sacred to him, and that of plants and animals as that of his fellow men, and when he devotes himself helpfully to all life that is in need of help. Only the universal ethic of the feeling of responsibility in an ever-widening sphere for all that lives—only that ethic can be founded in thought. . . . The ethic of Reverence for Life, therefore, comprehends within itself everything that can be described as love, devotion, and sympathy whether in suffering, joy, or effort.

ALBERT SCHWEITZER, *Out of My Life and Thought, An Autobiography*, trans. C. T. Campion, chapter 13, p. 188 (1933).

1102 Just as the wave cannot exist for itself, but is ever a part of the heaving surface of the ocean, so must I never live my life for itself, but always in the experience which is going on around me. It is an uncomfortable doctrine which the true ethics whisper into my ear. You are happy, they say; therefore you are called upon to give much.

ALBERT SCHWEITZER, *Civilization and Ethics*, chapter 26.—*The Philosophy of Civilization*, trans. C. T. Campion, part 2, p. 321 (1949, reissued 1981).

1103 So farewell to the little good you bear me.
Farewell! a long farewell, to all my greatness!
This is the state of man: to-day he puts forth
The tender leaves of hopes; to-morrow blossoms,
And bears his blushing honours thick upon him;
The third day comes a frost, a killing frost,
And, when he thinks, good easy man, full surely
His greatness is a-ripening, nips his root,
And then he falls, as I do. I have ventur'd,
Like little wanton boys that swim on bladders,
This many summers in a sea of glory,
But far beyond my depth. My high-blown pride
At length broke under me, and now has left me,
Weary and old with service, to the mercy
Of a rude stream that must for ever hide me.

Vain pomp and glory of this world, I hate ye!
I feel my heart new open'd. O, how wretched
Is that poor man that hangs on princes' favours!
There is, betwixt that smile we would aspire to,
That sweet aspect of princes, and their ruin,
More pangs and fears than wars or women have;
And when he falls, he falls like Lucifer,
Never to hope again.

WILLIAM SHAKESPEARE, *Henry VIII*, act III, scene ii, lines 350–72. Cardinal Wolsey is speaking about his friendship with Henry VIII.

1104 Anyone can carry his burden, however hard, until nightfall. Anyone can do his work, however hard, for one day. Anyone can live sweetly, patiently, lovingly, purely, till the sun goes down. And this is all that life really means.

Attributed to ROBERT LOUIS STEVENSON by Senator Sam Ervin in his last newsletter, *Senator Sam Ervin Says*, January 2, 1975, p. 2. Unverified.

1105 If a man is alive, there is always *danger* that he may die, though the danger must be allowed to be less in proportion as he is dead-and-alive to begin with. A man sits as many risks as he runs.

HENRY DAVID THOREAU, *Walden*, chapter 6, conclusion (vol. 2 of *The Writings of Henry David Thoreau*), p. 170 (1906, reprinted 1968). Originally published in 1854.

1106 Listen to the Exhortation of the Dawn!
Look to this Day!
For it is Life, the very Life of Life.
In its brief course lie all the
Verities and Realities of your Existence;
The Bliss of Growth,
The Glory of Action,
The Splendor of Beauty;
For Yesterday is but a Dream,
And To-morrow is only a Vision:
But To-day well lived makes
Every Yesterday a Dream of Happiness,
And every To-morrow a Vision of Hope.
Look well therefore to this Day!
Such is the Salutation of the Dawn!

Author unknown. From the Sanskrit, "The Salutation of the Dawn."—*Masterpieces of Religious Verse*, ed. James Dalton Morrison, p. 301 (1948). Attributed in some sources to Kālidāsa, Hindu dramatist and lyric poet of the fifth century, A.D.

Lincoln, Abraham (1809–1865)

1107

In this temple
As in the hearts of the people
For whom he saved the Union
The memory of Abraham
Lincoln
Is enshrined forever

ROYAL CORTISSOZ, inscription above the statue of Lincoln at the Lincoln Memorial, Washington, D.C.—*The Washington Star*, April 20, 1976, pp. D1-D2.

Cortissoz was art critic of the *New York Herald Tribune*.

1108 And when he fell in whirlwind, he went down
As when a lordly cedar, green with boughs,
Goes down with a great shout upon the hills,
And leaves a lonesome place against the sky.

EDWIN MARKHAM, "Lincoln, the Man of the People," stanza 4, lines 8–11, *Lincoln & Other Poems*, p. 3 (1901).

1109 Not often in the story of mankind does a man arrive on earth who is both steel and velvet, who is as hard as rock and soft as drifting fog, who holds in his heart and mind the paradox of terrible storm and peace unspeakable and perfect.

CARL SANDBURG, opening sentence in an address to a joint session of Congress marking the 150th anniversary of Abraham Lincoln's birth, February 12, 1959, *Congressional Record*, vol. 105, p. 2265.

1110 No man made great by death offers more hope to lowly pride than does Abraham Lincoln; for while living he was himself so simple as often to be dubbed a fool. Foolish he was, they said, in losing his youthful heart to a grave and living his life on married patience; foolish in pitting his homely ignorance against Douglas, brilliant, courtly, and urbane; foolish in setting himself to do the right in a world where the day goes mostly to the strong; foolish in dreaming of freedom for a long-suffering folk whom the North is as anxious to keep out as the South was to keep down; foolish in choosing the silent Grant to lead to victory the hesitant armies of the North; foolish, finally, in presuming that government for the people must be government of the people and by the people.

Foolish many said; foolish many, many believed.

This Lincoln, whom so many living friends and foes alike deemed foolish, hid his bitterness in laughter; fed his sympathy on solitude; and met recurring disaster with whimsicality to muffle the murmur of a bleeding heart. Out of the tragic sense of life he pitied where others blamed; bowed his own shoulders with the woes of the weak; endured humanely his little day of chance power; and won through death what life disdains to bestow upon such simple souls—lasting peace and everlasting glory.

How prudently—to echo Wendell Phillips—we proud men compete for nameless graves, while now and then some starveling of Fate forgets himself into immortality.

THOMAS VERNOR SMITH, memorial address, the Illinois State Senate, February 12, 1935, the 126th anniversary of Lincoln's birth.—Smith, *Lincoln, Living Legend*, pp. 3–5 (1940).

Smith later served in Congress 1939–1941. The striking final paragraph is unverified in the works of Wendell Phillips.

Living

1111 It is not well for a man to pray, cream; and live skim milk.

HENRY WARD BEECHER, *Life Thoughts*, ed. Edna Dean Proctor, p. 64 (1858).

1112 Man doth not live by bread only, but by every word that proceedeth out of the mouth of the Lord doth man live.

The Bible, Deuteronomy 8:3.

1113 Never complain and never explain.

BENJAMIN DISRAELI.—John Morley, *The Life of William Ewart Gladstone*, vol. 1, p. 123 (1903, reprinted 1968).

See No. 686 for a later variation.

1114 Go placidly amid the noise and the haste, and remember what peace there may be in silence. As far as possible, without surrender, be on good terms with all persons. Speak your truth quietly and clearly; and listen to others, even to the dull and the ignorant; they too have their story. Avoid loud and aggressive persons; they are vexatious to the spirit. If you compare yourself with others, you may become vain or bitter, for always there will be greater and lesser persons than yourself. Enjoy your achievements as well as your plans. Keep interested in your own career, however humble; it is a real possession in the changing fortunes of time. Exercise caution in your business affairs, for the world is full of trickery. But let this not blind you to what virtue there is; many persons strive for high ideals, and everywhere life is full of heroism. Be yourself. Especially do not feign affection. Neither be cynical about love; for in the face of all aridity and disenchantment, it is as perennial as the grass. Take kindly the counsel of the years, gracefully surrendering the things of youth. Nurture strength of spirit to shield you in sudden misfortune. But do not distress yourself with dark imaginings. Many fears are born of fatigue and loneliness. Beyond a wholesome discipline, be gentle with yourself. You are a child of the universe no less than the trees and the stars; you have a right to be here. And whether or not it is clear to you, no doubt the universe is unfolding as it should. Therefore be at peace with God, whatever you conceive Him to be. And whatever your labors and aspirations, in the noisy confusion of life, keep peace in your soul. With all its sham, drudgery and broken dreams, it is still a beautiful world. Be cheerful. Strive to be happy.

MAX EHRMANN, "Desiderata," *The Poems of Max Ehrmann*, p. 165 (1948).

There has been confusion about the authorship of this poem. In 1956, the rector of St. Paul's Church in Baltimore, Maryland, used the poem in a collection of mimeographed inspirational material for his congregation. Someone printing it later said it was found in Old St. Paul's Church, Baltimore, dated 1692. The year 1692 is the founding date of the church and has nothing to do with the poem, which was written in 1927. It was widely distributed with the 1692 date. A copy of it was found on the bedside table of Adlai Stevenson's New York apartment after his death in 1965. He had been planning to use it on his Christmas cards identifying it as an ancient poem. The Stevenson connection helped bring the poem to the attention of the public.—Fred D. Cavinder, "Desiderata," *TWA Ambassador*, August 1973, pp. 14–15.

1115 The riders in a race do not stop short when they reach the goal. There is a little finishing canter before coming to a standstill. There is time to hear the kind voice of friends and to say to one's self: "The work is done." But just as one says that, the answer comes: "The race is over, but the work never is done while the power to work remains." The canter that brings you to a standstill need not be only coming to rest. It cannot be while you still live. For to live is to function. That is all there is in living.

Justice OLIVER WENDELL HOLMES, radio address, March 8, 1931.—*Justice Oliver Wendell Holmes, His Book Notices and Uncollected Letters and Papers*, ed. Harry C. Shriver, p. 142 (1936).

"Justice Holmes' first and only radio address, delivered upon his ninetieth birthday, in response to felicitations from Chief Justice Hughes and the American Bar" (footnote 14, p. 142).

Twenty or thirty years earlier, Holmes had said, "Life is action, the use of one's powers. As to use them to their height is our joy and duty, so it is the one end that justifies itself . . ." "Life is a roar of bargain and battle; but in the very heart of it there rises a mystic spiritual tone that gives meaning to the whole, and transmutes the dull details into romance . . ." "Man is born a predestined idealist, for he is born to act. . . . To act is to affirm the worth of an end and to persist in affirming the worth of an end is to make an ideal."—Holmes, *Speeches*, pp. 85, 96, 97 (1913), as cited by Shriver, footnote 15, p. 142.

1116 *A Decalogue of Canons for observation in practical life.*

1. Never put off till to-morrow what you can do to-day.
2. Never trouble another for what you can do yourself.
3. Never spend your money before you have it.
4. Never buy what you do not want, because it is cheap; it will be dear to you.
5. Pride costs us more than hunger, thirst and cold.
6. We never repent of having eaten too little.
7. Nothing is troublesome that we do willingly.
8. How much pain have cost us the evils which have never happened.
9. Take things always by their smooth handle.
10. When angry, count ten, before you speak; if very angry, an hundred.

THOMAS JEFFERSON, letter to Thomas Jefferson Smith, February 21, 1825.—*Writings of Thomas Jefferson*, ed. Paul L. Ford, vol. 10, p. 341 (1899).

1117

1. You cannot bring about prosperity by discouraging thrift.
2. You cannot strengthen the weak by weakening the strong.
3. You cannot help small men up by tearing big men down.
4. You cannot help the poor by destroying the rich.
5. You cannot lift the wage-earner up by pulling the wage-payer down.
6. You cannot keep out of trouble by spending more than your income.
7. You cannot further the brotherhood of man by inciting class hatred.
8. You cannot establish sound social security on borrowed money.
9. You cannot build character and courage by taking away a man's initiative and independence.
10. You cannot help men permanently by doing for them what they could and should do for themselves.

Erroneously attributed to ABRAHAM LINCOLN. Since the 1940s these "Ten Points" attributed to Lincoln have been widely reprinted. They have appeared in such places as magazines, Christmas cards, and the *Congressional Record*. The Library of Congress and Lincoln scholars believe that any connection made between Lincoln and the "Ten Points" is spurious.

1118 I would rather be ashes than dust! I would rather that my spark should burn out in a brilliant blaze than it should be stifled by dry-rot. I would rather be a superb meteor, every atom of me in magnificent glow, than a sleepy and permanent planet. The proper function of man is to live, not to exist. I shall not waste my days in trying to prolong them. I shall use my time.

JACK LONDON, *Jack London's Tales of Adventure*, ed. Irving Shepard, Introduction, p. vii (1956).

This is generally known as London's Credo. He is known to have said these words, just two months before his death, to a group of friends with whom he was discussing life and living.—*The Bulletin*, San Francisco, California, December 2, 1916, part 2, p. 1.

See also Nos. 11 and 575.

1119 More will sometimes be demanded of you than is reasonable. Bear it meekly, and exhaust your time and strength in performing your duties, rather than in vindicating your rights. Be silent, even when you are misrepresented. Turn aside when opposed, rather than confront opposition with resistance. Bear and forbear, not defending yourselves, so much as trusting to your works to defend you. Yet, in counselling you thus, I would not be understood to be a total non-resistant;—a perfectly passive, non-elastic sand-bag, in society; but I would not have you resist until the blow be aimed, not so much at you, as, through you, at the sacred cause of human improvement, in which you are engaged,—a point at which forbearance would be allied to crime.

HORACE MANN, remarks at the dedication of the Bridgewater State Normal Schoolhouse, Bridgewater, Massachusetts, August 19, 1846.—*Horace Mann on the Crisis in Education*, ed. Louis Filler, p. 167 (1965).

Mann served in Congress 1848–1853.

1120 Man is born to live, not to prepare for life.

BORIS PASTERNAK, *Doctor Zhivago*, p. 297 (1958).

1121 Only those are fit to live who do not fear to die; and none are fit to die who have shrunk from the joy of life and the duty of life. Both life and death are parts of the same Great Adventure.

THEODORE ROOSEVELT, *The Great Adventure* (vol. 19 of *The Works of Theodore Roosevelt*, national ed.), chapter 1, opening sentences, p. 243 (1926).

Douglas MacArthur, speech, July 14, 1935, at the annual reunion of veterans of the Rainbow (42d) Infantry Division, World War I, said, "Only those are fit to live who are not afraid to die."—*A Soldier Speaks: Public Papers and Speeches of General of the Army Douglas MacArthur*, p. 70 (1965).

1122 If you had to define stress, it would not be far off if you said it was the process of living. The process of living is the process of having stress imposed on you and reacting to it.

STANLEY J. SARNOFF.—*Man Under Stress*, conference no. 7, University of California, San Francisco Medical Center, November 15–17, 1963, p. 100.

1123 Every one lives by selling something, whatever be his right to it.

ROBERT LOUIS STEVENSON, *"Beggars," Across the Plains with Other Memories and Essays*, p. 263 (1903).

1124 The mass of men lead lives of quiet desperation. What is called resignation is confirmed desperation. From the desperate city you go into the desperate country, and have to console yourself with the bravery of minks and muskrats. A stereotyped but unconscious despair is concealed even under what are called the games and amusements of mankind. There is no play in them, for this comes after work. But it is a characteristic of wisdom not to do desperate things.

HENRY DAVID THOREAU, *Walden*, chapter 1, p. 8 (1966). Originally published in 1854.

1125 Let us endeavor so to live that when we come to die even the undertaker will be sorry.

MARK TWAIN (Samuel L. Clemens), *Pudd'nhead Wilson* (vol. 14 of *The Writings of Mark Twain*), chapter 6, epigraph, p. 56 (1894, reprinted 1968).

1126 Four things a man must learn to do
If he would make his record true:
To think without confusion clearly;
To love his fellow-men sincerely;
To act from honest motives purely;
To trust in God and Heaven securely.

HENRY VAN DYKE, "Four Things," *Poems*, vol. 1 (vol. 9 of *The Works of Henry Van Dyke*), p. 277 (1920).

1127 It costs so much to be a full human being that there are very few who have the enlightenment, or the courage, to pay the price. . . . One has to abandon altogether the search for security, and reach out to the risk of living with both arms. One has to embrace the world like a lover, and yet demand no easy return of love. One has to accept pain as a condition of existence. One has to court doubt and darkness as the cost of knowing. One needs a will stubborn in conflict, but apt always to the total acceptance of every consequence of living and dying.

MORRIS L. WEST, *The Shoes of the Fisherman*, p. 254 (1963).

Lobbyists

1128 Lobbyists are in many cases expert technicians and capable of explaining complex and difficult subjects in a clear, understandable fashion. They engage in personal discussions with Members of Congress in which they can explain in detail the reasons for positions they advocate. . . . Because our congressional representation is based on geographical boundaries, the lobbyists who speak for the various economic, commercial, and other functional interests of this country serve a very useful purpose and have assumed an important role in the legislative process.

Senator JOHN F. KENNEDY, "To Keep the Lobbyist Within Bounds," *The New York Times Magazine*, February 19, 1956.—*Congressional Record*, March 2, 1956, vol. 102, pp. 3802–3.

Loneliness

1129 It is loneliness that makes the loudest noise. This is as true of men as of dogs.

ERIC HOFFER, "Thoughts of Eric Hoffer, Including: 'Absolute Faith Corrupts Absolutely,' " *The New York Times Magazine*, April 25, 1971, p. 55.

Love

1130 For, you see, each day I love you more,
Today more than yesterday and less than tomorrow.
(Car, vois-tu, chaque jour je t'aime davantage,
Aujourd'hui plus qu'hier et bien moins que demain.)

ROSEMONDE GÉRARD, "L'éternelle chanson," IX, *Les Pipeaux*.—P. Dupré, *Encyclopédie des Citations*, p. 176 (1959).

1131 Love has power that dispels Death; charm that conquers the enemy.

KAHLIL GIBRAN, "Peace," *Tears and Laughter,* trans. Anthony R. Ferris, p. 30 (1949).

1132 Love is the magician, the enchanter, that changes worthless things to joy, and makes right royal kings and queens of common clay. It is the perfume of that wondrous flower, the heart, and without that sacred passion, that divine swoon, we are less than beasts; but with it, earth is heaven, and we are gods.

ROBERT G. INGERSOLL, "Orthodoxy," lecture, *The Works of Robert G. Ingersoll,* vol. 2, p. 420 (1929, reprinted 1978).

1133 First love is only a little foolishness and a lot of curiosity: no really self-respecting woman would take advantage of it.

GEORGE BERNARD SHAW, *John Bull's Other Island,* act IV, *Selected Plays with Prefaces,* vol. 2, p. 596 (1949). These words are spoken by Broadbent.

1134 But as a philosopher said, one day after mastering the winds, the waves, the tides and gravity, after all the scientific and technological achievements, we shall harness for God the energies of love. And then, for the second time in the history of the world, man will have discovered fire.

R. SARGENT SHRIVER, JR., speech before the Democratic National Committee, accepting nomination as the Democratic candidate for vice president, Washington, D.C., August 8, 1972.—Transcript, *The New York Times,* August 9, 1972, p. 18.

He was slightly paraphrasing Pierre Teilhard de Chardin, "The Evolution of Chastity," *Toward the Future,* trans. René Hague, pp. 86–87 (1975): "The day will come when, after harnessing the ether, the winds, the tides, gravitation, we shall harness for God the energies of love. And, on that day, for the second time in the history of the world, man will have discovered fire." This was written in Peking in 1934.

1135 I hold it true, whate'er befall;
I feel it, when I sorrow most;
'Tis better to have loved and lost
Than never to have loved at all.

ALFRED, LORD TENNYSON, "In Memoriam A. H. H." [Arthur Henry Hallam], stanza 27, *The Poetic and Dramatic Works of Alfred Lord Tennyson,* p. 226 (1899).

1136 There is a land of the living and a land of the dead and the bridge is love, the only survival, the only meaning.

THORNTON WILDER, *The Bridge of San Luis Rey,* final sentence, p. 148 (1967).

Majority

1137 A majority can do anything.

Representative JOSEPH G. CANNON, maxim quoted in a tribute to Cannon on his retirement, *The Sun,* Baltimore, Maryland, March 4, 1923.—*Congressional Record,* March 4, 1923, vol. 64, p. 5714.

"Uncle Joe" Cannon, who was Speaker of the House 1903–1911, served in the House for 46 years.

Majority

1138 One with the law is a majority.

CALVIN COOLIDGE, governor of Massachusetts, speech accepting nomination as Republican candidate for vice president, Northampton, Massachusetts, July 27, 1920, as reported by *The New York Times,* July 28, 1920, p. 6.

1139 It is quite plain that your government will never be able to restrain a distressed and discontented majority. For with you the majority is the government, and has the rich, who are always a minority, absolutely at its mercy.

THOMAS BABINGTON MACAULAY, letter to Henry Stephens Randall, May 23, 1857.—*The Letters of Thomas Babington Macaulay,* ed. Thomas Pinney, vol. 6, p. 95 (1981).

See note at No. 334 about this letter.

1140 Let historians not record that when America was the most powerful nation in the world we passed on the other side of the road and allowed the last hopes for peace and freedom of millions of people to be suffocated by the forces of totalitarianism. And so tonight—to you, the great silent majority of my fellow Americans—I ask for your support.

President RICHARD M. NIXON, address to the Nation on the Vietnam war, November 3, 1969.—*Public Papers of the Presidents of the United States: Richard Nixon, 1969,* p. 909.

William Safire claims that this televised speech had a great effect on public opinion and bought time for the Vietnamization program, effectively countering mounting dissent to the war. Safire discusses Nixon's earlier uses of the "silent center."—*Safire's Political Dictionary,* p. 649–50 (1978).

1141 How a minority,
Reaching majority,
Siezing authority,
Hates a minority!

Attributed to LEONARD HARMAN ROBBINS, *Minorities.*—Bergen Evans, *Dictionary of Quotations,* p. 123 (1968). Unverified.

Man

1142 Make no more giants, God!
But elevate the race at once!

ROBERT BROWNING, "Paracelsus," part 1, *Poems,* vol. 1, p. 29 (1850).

1143 Manhood begins when we have in any way made truce with Necessity; begins even when we have surrendered to Necessity, as the most part only do; but begins joyfully and hopefully only when we have reconciled ourselves to Necessity; and thus, in reality, triumphed over it, and felt that in Necessity we are free.

THOMAS CARLYLE, "Burns," *Critical and Miscellaneous Essays,* vol. 1 (vol. 29 of *The Works of Thomas Carlyle,* ed. H. D. Traill), p. 295 (1899, reprinted 1969). Book review in the *Edinburgh Review,* no. 96, 1828.

1144 Man is about to be an automaton; he is identifiable only in the computer. As a person of worth and creativity, as a being with an infinite potential, he retreats and battles the forces that make him inhuman.

The dissent we witness is a reaffirmation of faith in man; it is protest against living under rules and prejudices and attitudes that produce the extremes of wealth and poverty and that make us dedicated to the destruction of people through arms, bombs, and gases, and that prepare us to think alike and be submissive objects for the regime of the computer.

Justice WILLIAM O. DOUGLAS, *Points of Rebellion*, pp. 32–33 (1970).

1145 I decline to accept the end of man. It is easy enough to say that man is immortal simply because he will endure: that when the last ding-dong of doom has clanged and faded from the last worthless rock hanging tideless in the last red and dying evening, that even then there will still be one more sound: that of his puny inexhaustible voice, still talking. I refuse to accept this. I believe that man will not merely endure: he will prevail. He is immortal, not because he alone among creatures has an inexhaustible voice, but because he has a soul, a spirit capable of compassion and sacrifice and endurance. The poet's, the writer's, duty is to write about these things. It is his privilege to help man endure by lifting his heart, by reminding him of the courage and honor and hope and pride and compassion and pity and sacrifice which have been the glory of his past. The poet's voice need not merely be the record of man, it can be one of the props, the pillars to help him endure and prevail.

WILLIAM FAULKNER, address upon receiving the Nobel Prize for literature, Stockholm, Sweden, December 10, 1950.—Faulkner, *Essays, Speeches & Public Letters*, p. 120 (1951).

This text is from Faulkner's original typescript; it was slightly revised from that which he delivered in Stockholm, and which was published in American newspapers at the time (p. 121).

1146 Who is wise? *He that learns from every One.* Who is powerful? *He that governs his Passions.* Who is rich? *He that is content.* Who is that? *Nobody.*

BENJAMIN FRANKLIN, "Poor Richard's Almanack," July 1755, *The Complete Poor Richard Almanacks*, facsimile ed., vol. 2, p. 270 (1970).

1147 What tho' the spicy breezes
Blow soft o'er Ceylon's isle;
Though every prospect pleases,
And only man is vile?

REGINALD HEBER, "From Greenland's Icy Mountains" (hymn), *From Greenland's Icy Mountains*, p. 23 (1884).

1148 There is a great deal of human nature in man.

CHARLES KINGSLEY, *At Last*, chapter 2 (*The Works of Charles Kingsley*, vol. 14), p. 49 (1880–1885, reprinted 1969). Kingsley quotes this as said by "the wise Yankee."

In 1862, Artemus Ward (Charles Farrar Browne) had published *Artemus Ward: His Book* (reprinted 1964), and in "Thrilling Scenes from Dixie," p. 202, says, "There's considerable human nater in a man."

1149 We all are blind until we see
That in the human plan
Nothing is worth the making if
It does not make the man.

Why build these cities glorious
If man unbuilded goes?
In vain we build the world, unless
The builder also grows.

EDWIN MARKHAM, "Man-Making," *Poems of Edwin Markham*, p. 6 (1950).

1150 Men are men before they are lawyers, or physicians, or merchants, or manufacturers; and if you make them capable and sensible men, they will make themselves capable and sensible lawyers or physicians.

JOHN STUART MILL, inaugural address to the University of St. Andrews, St. Andrews, Scotland, February 1, 1867.—*Dissertations and Discussions*, vol. 4, p. 335 (1868).

1151 No particular man is necessary to the state. We may depend on it that, if we provide the country with popular institutions, those institutions will provide it with great men.

THOMAS BABINGTON MACAULAY, speech on parliamentary reform, March 2, 1831.—*The Complete Writings of Lord Macaulay*, vol. 17, p. 14 (1900).

See also No. 1153.

1152 Man, created to God's image and likeness (Gen. 1:26–27), is not just flesh and blood. The sexual instinct is not all that he has. Man is also, and pre-eminently, intelligent and free; and thanks to these powers he is, and must remain, superior to the rest of creation; they give him mastery over his physical, psychological and affective appetites.

Pope PAUL VI, encyclical on priestly celibacy (*Sacerdotalis Caelibatus*), paragraph 53, June 24, 1967.—*Catholic Mind*, October 1967, pp. 56–57.

1153 A great man left a watchword that we can well repeat: "There is no indispensable man."

FRANKLIN D. ROOSEVELT, governor of New York, campaign address before the Republican-for-Roosevelt League, New York City, November 3, 1932.—*The Public Papers and Addresses of Franklin D. Roosevelt, 1928–1932*, p. 860 (1938).

The man whom Roosevelt quotes is probably Macaulay. See No. 1151.

1154 It is said that Napoleon lost the battle of Waterloo because he forgot his infantry—he staked too much upon the more spectacular but less substantial calvary. The present administration in Washington provides a close parallel. It has either forgotten or it does not want to remember the infantry of our economic army. These unhappy times call for the building of plans that rest upon the forgotten, the unorganized but the indispensable units of economic power, for plans like those of 1917 that build from the bottom up and not from the top down, that put their faith once more in the forgotten man at the bottom of the economic pyramid.

FRANKLIN D. ROOSEVELT, governor of New York, radio address, Albany, New York, April 7, 1932.—*The Public Papers and Addresses of Franklin D. Roosevelt, 1928–1932*, pp. 624–25 (1938).

1155 When I die, my epitaph or whatever you call those signs on gravestones is going to read: "I joked about every prominent man of my time, but I never met a man I dident like." I am so proud of that I can hardly wait to die so it can be carved. And when you come to my grave you will find me sitting there, proudly reading it.

WILL ROGERS.—Paula McSpadden Love, *The Will Rogers Book*, pp. 166–67 (1972).

"One of his most famous and most quoted remarks. First printed in the *Boston Globe*, June 16, 1930, after he had attended Tremont Temple Baptist Church, where Dr. James W. Brougher was minister. He asked Will to say a few words after the sermon. The papers were quick to pick up the remark, and it stayed with him the rest of his life. He also said it on various other occasions" (p. 167).

The author was a niece of Will Rogers's and curator of the Will Rogers Memorial in Claremore, Oklahoma.

1156 Every actual animal is somewhat dull and somewhat mad. He will at times miss his signals and stare vacantly when he might well act, while at other times he will run off into convulsions and raise a dust in his own brain to no purpose. These imperfections are so human that we should hardly recognise ourselves if we could shake them off altogether. Not to retain any dulness would mean to possess untiring attention and universal interests, thus realising the boast about deeming nothing human alien to us; while to be absolutely without folly would involve perfect self-knowledge and self-control. The intelligent man known to history flourishes within a dullard and holds a lunatic in leash. He is encased in a protective shell of ignorance and insensibility which keeps him from being exhausted and confused by this too complicated world; but that integument blinds him at the same time to many of his nearest and highest interests. He is amused by the antics of the brute dreaming within his breast; he gloats on his passionate reveries, an amusement which sometimes costs him very dear. Thus the best human intelligence is still decidely barbarous; it fights in heavy armour and keeps a fool at court.

GEORGE SANTAYANA, *The Life of Reason*, vol. 1, chapter 2, pp. 50–51 (1905).

1157 The awareness that we are all human beings together has become lost in war and through politics.

ALBERT SCHWEITZER, radio appeal for peace, Oslo, Norway, April 30, 1958.—Schweitzer, *Peace or Atomic War?*, p. 44 (1972).

This was the third of three appeals broadcast April 28, 29, and 30, 1958.

1158 All the world's a stage,
And all the men and women merely players.
They have their exits and their entrances,
And one man in his time plays many parts,
His acts being seven ages. At first the infant,
Mewling and puking in the nurse's arms.
Then the whining school-boy, with his satchel
And shining morning face, creeping like snail
Unwillingly to school. And then the lover,
Sighing like furnace, with a woeful ballad
Made to his mistress' eyebrow. Then a soldier,
Full of strange oaths, and bearded like the pard,
Jealous in honour, sudden, and quick in quarrel,
Seeking the bubble reputation
Even in the cannon's mouth. And then the justice,
In fair round belly with good capon lin'd,
With eyes severe and beard of formal cut,
Full of wise saws and modern instances;
And so he plays his part. The sixth age shifts
Into the lean and slipper'd pantaloon [dotard],

With spectacles on nose and pouch on side,
His youthful hose, well sav'd, a world too wide
For his shrunk shank; and his big manly voice,
Turning again toward childish treble, pipes
And whistles in his sound. Last scene of all,
That ends this strange eventful history,
Is second childishness and mere oblivion,
Sans teeth, sans eyes, sans taste, sans every thing.

WILLIAM SHAKESPEARE, *As You Like It,* act II, scene vii, lines 139–66. Jaques is speaking.

1159 . . . man, proud man,
Dress'd in a little brief authority, . . .

WILLIAM SHAKESPEARE, *Measure for Measure,* act III, scene ii, lines 117–18. Isabella is speaking.

1160 This was the noblest Roman of them all.
All the conspirators, save only he,
Did that they did in envy of Caesar;
He only, in a general honest thought
And common good to all, made one of them.
His life was gentle, and the elements
So mix'd in him that Nature might stand up
And say to all the world, "This was a man!"

WILLIAM SHAKESPEARE, *Julius Caesar,* act V, scene v, lines 68–75. Antony is speaking.

1161 Every man will be a poet if he can; otherwise a philosopher or man of science. This proves the superiority of the poet.

HENRY DAVID THOREAU, journal entry, April 11, 1852.—*The Heart of Thoreau's Journals,* ed. Odell Shepard, p. 126 (1927).

1162 Mankind which began in a cave and behind a windbreak will end in the disease-soaked ruins of a slum.

H. G. WELLS, *The Fate of Man,* chapter 26, p. 247 (1939, reprinted 1970).

Marriage

1163 He that hath wife and children hath given hostages to fortune, for they are impediments to great enterprises, either of virtue or mischief. Certainly the best works and of greatest merit for the public have proceeded from the unmarried or childless men, which both in affection and means have married and endowed the public. . . . He was reputed one of the wise men that made answer to the question, when a man should marry—"A young man not yet, an elder man not at all."

FRANCIS BACON, "Of Marriage and Single Life," *The Essays or Counsels Civil and Moral of Francis Bacon,* ed. Fred A. Howe, chapter 8, pp. 20, 22 (1908). Based on the 1625 edition but with modernized spelling.

Marriage

1164 I have always thought that every woman should marry, and no man.

BENJAMIN DISRAELI, *Lothair*, chapter 30, p. 109 (1870).

1165 But the main purpose of marriage will compel us to revise the institution so that we shall not waste any useful woman, expecially if she is a woman of notable ability. It is a significant fact that there are no 'unwanted women' in polygamous countries. These derelicts are to be found only in countries which are monogamous; and they represent, less today, perhaps, than formerly, sheer waste of mother-power. Even as things are, the 'unwanted woman' is still doomed to lead a solitary life, unless she has an illicit lover, and can contemplate old age and retirement only with dismay.

ST. JOHN ERVINE, *Bernard Shaw, His Life, Work and Friends*, p. 424 (1956).

In this comment on Shaw's play, "Getting Married," Ervine summarizes one of the arguments in Shaw's lengthy Preface to the play.

1166 The critical period in matrimony is breakfast-time.

A. P. HERBERT, *Uncommon Law*, p. 98 (1935).

1167 A gentleman who had been very unhappy in marriage, married immediately after his wife died: Johnson said, it was the triumph of hope over experience.

SAMUEL JOHNSON.—James Boswell, *Boswell's Life of Johnson*, ed. George B. Hill, rev. and enl. ed., ed. L. F. Powell, entry for 1770, vol. 2, p. 128 (1934).

1168 I don't see why we can't get along just as well with a polygamist who doesn't polyg as we do with a lot of monogamists who don't monog!

Attributed to Senator BOIES PENROSE.—Francis T. Plimpton, speech, quoted in *Reader's Digest*, June 1958, p. 142.

These words were supposedly said in the Senate where a protest had arisen against seating Reed Smoot, the first Mormon senator, in 1903. Not verified in newspapers or accounts of that time.

Also attributed, with variation in the wording, to President Theodore Roosevelt, while he was campaigning in 1902.—Bennett Cerf, *The Laugh's on Me*, p. 350 (1959).

1169 Men marry because they are tired; women because they are curious. Both are disappointed.

OSCAR WILDE, *A Woman of No Importance*, act III, in *The Complete Works of Oscar Wilde*, vol. 7, p. 263 (1923). Lord Illingworth is speaking.

McCarthyism

1170 When public men indulge themselves in abuse, when they deny others a fair trial, when they resort to innuendo and insinuation, to libel, scandal, and suspicion, then our democratic society is outraged, and democracy is baffled. It has no apparatus to deal with the boor, the liar, the lout, and the antidemocrat in general.

Senator J. WILLIAM FULBRIGHT, remarks in the Senate, February 2, 1954, *Congressional Record*, vol. 100, p. 1105.

McCarthyism

1171 Until this moment, Senator, I think I never really gaged [sic] your cruelty or your recklessness. . . . Let us not assassinate this lad further, Senator. You have done enough. Have you no sense of decency, sir, at long last? Have you left no sense of decency?

JOSEPH N. WELCH, remark to Senator Joseph McCarthy, June 9, 1954, during the Army-McCarthy hearings.—*Special Senate Investigation on Charges and Countercharges Involving: Secretary of the Army Robert T. Stevens [et al.]*, hearing before the Special Subcommittee on Investigations of the Committee on Government Operations, United States Senate, 83d Congress, 2d session, part 59, p. 2429.

Welch, counsel for the Army, was responding to Senator McCarthy's charge that a member of Welch's law firm had once belonged to a Communist front group. Many believed that Senator McCarthy's downfall began with this exchange.

Mediocrity

1172 Never were abilities so much below mediocrity so well rewarded; no, not when Caligula's horse was made Consul.

Representative JOHN RANDOLPH of Roanoke, referring to Richard Rush, upon Rush's appointment as secretary of the treasury by President John Quincy Adams. Published as an appendix to a new edition of his speech in the House, February 1, 1828, on retrenchment and reform.—William Cabell Bruce, *John Randolph of Roanoke, 1773–1833*, vol. 2, chapter 7, p. 200 (1922, reprinted 1970).

Caligula, Roman emperor from A.D. 37–41, was a "cruel, prodigal, and insane tyrant," according to *The Oxford Companion to Classical Literature*, ed. Sir Paul Harvey, p. 373 (1937). There is some disagreement whether he actually made his horse, Incitatus, consul to humiliate the Senate, or merely proposed it.

Memory

1173 It is therefore necessary that memorable things should be committed to writing, (the witness of times, the light and the life of truth,) and not wholly betaken [i.e., committed] to slippery memory which seldom yields a certain reckoning.

SIR EDWARD COKE, *Les Reports de Edward Coke*, vol. 1, p. 3 (1660). Spelling modernized.

1174 We can remember minutely and precisely only the things which never really happened to us.

ERIC HOFFER, "Thoughts of Eric Hoffer, Including: 'Absolute Faith Corrupts Absolutely,' " *The New York Times Magazine*, April 25, 1971, pp. 55, 57.

1175 The Right Honourable Gentleman is indebted to his memory for his jests, and to his imagination for his facts.

RICHARD BRINSLEY SHERIDAN, reply in the House of Commons.—Thomas Moore, *Memoirs of the Life of the Right Honourable Richard Brinsley Sheridan*, 3d ed., vol. 2, chapter 21, p. 471 (1825).

"A curious instance of the care with which he treasured up the felicities of his wit appears in the use he made of one of those epigrammatic passages . . . which, in its first form, ran thus:—'He certainly has a great deal of fancy, and a very good memory; but, with a perverse ingenuity, he employs these qualities as no other person does—for he employs his fancy in his narratives, and keeps his recollection for his wit:—when he makes jokes, you applaud the accuracy of his memory, and 'tis only when he states his facts that you admire the flights of his imagination.'

"After many efforts to express this thought more concisely, and to reduce the language of it to that condensed and elastic state, in which alone it gives force to the projectiles of wit, he kept the passage by him patiently some years,—till he at length found an opportunity of turning it to account, in a reply, I believe, to Mr. Dundas, in the House of Commons, when, with the most extemporaneous air, he brought it forth, in the . . . compact and pointed form [above] (p. 471).

Military affairs

1176 Nay, number itself in armies importeth not much, where the people is of weak courage; for, as Virgil saith, "It never troubles the wolf how many the sheep be."

FRANCIS BACON, "Of the True Greatness of Kingdoms and Estates," *The Essays or Counsels Civil & Moral of Francis Bacon*, p. 129 (1905).

Bacon quoted the words of Thyrsis in Virgil's *Eclogue VII.*

1177 In the councils of government, we must guard against the acquisition of unwarranted influence, whether sought or unsought, by the military-industrial complex. The potential for the disastrous rise of misplaced power exists and will persist. We must never let the weight of this combination endanger our liberties or democratic processes. We should take nothing for granted. Only an alert and knowledgeable citzenry can compel the proper meshing of the huge industrial and military machinery of defense with our peaceful methods and goals, so that security and liberty may prosper together.

President DWIGHT D. EISENHOWER, farewell radio and television address to the American people, Washington, D.C., January 17, 1961.—*Public Papers of the Presidents of the United States: Dwight D. Eisenhower, 1960–61*, p. 1038.

1178 Some day there is going to be a man sitting in my present chair who has not been raised in the military services and who will have little understanding of where slashes in their estimates can be made with little or no damage. If that should happen while we still have the state of tension that now exists in the world, I shudder to think of what could happen in this country . . .

President DWIGHT D. EISENHOWER, letter to Everett E. ("Swede") Hazlett, August 20, 1956.—William Bragg Ewald, Jr., *Eisenhower the President*, p. 248 (1981). Date of the letter provided by the Eisenhower Library, Abilene, Kansas.

1179 There was only one catch and that was Catch-22, which specified that a concern for one's own safety in the face of dangers that were real and immediate was the process of a rational mind. Orr was crazy and could be grounded. All he had to do was ask; and as soon as he did, he would no longer be crazy and would have to fly more missions. Orr would be crazy to fly more missions and sane if he didn't, but if he was sane he had to fly them. If he flew them he was crazy and didn't have to; but if he didn't want to he was sane and had to. Yossarian was moved very deeply by the absolute simplicity of this clause of Catch-22 and let out a respectful whistle.

JOSEPH HELLER, *Catch-22*, chapter 5, p. 46 (1961).

A more succinct definition of Catch-22 comes from Jacob Brackman's review of the film, *Catch-22*: "If you're crazy, they have to take you out of combat, but the catch is you have to *ask* them, and if you're trying to get out of combat then you can't be crazy."—*A*

"Catch-22" Casebook, ed. Frederick Kiley and Walter McDonald, p. 363 (1973). The review originally appeared in *Esquire*, September 1970.

1180 I could as easily bail out the Potomac River with a teaspoon as attend to all the details of the army.

Attributed to President ABRAHAM LINCOLN by General James B. Fry.—Allen Thorndike Rice, *Reminiscences of Abraham Lincoln*, chapter 22, p. 393 (1886).

This supposedly had been part of Lincoln's response to a young volunteer soldier who had come to Lincoln's office asking his help with a grievance. The story has been repeated in numerous books on Lincoln: Alexander K. McClure, *"Abe" Lincoln's Yarns and Stories*, p. 162 (1904); Ida M. Tarbell, *The Life of Abraham Lincoln*, vol. 2, p. 153 (1917); and Caroline T. Harnsberger, *The Lincoln Treasury*, p. 14 (1950).

1181 Enjoin this upon the Officers, and let them inculcate, and press home to the Soldiery, the Necessity of Order and Harmony among them, who are embark'd in one common Cause, and mutually contending for all that Freeman [sic] hold dear. I am persuaded, if the Officers will but exert themselves, these Animosities, this Disorder, will in a great Measure subside, and nothing being more essential to the Service than that it should, I am hopeful nothing on their Parts will be wanting to effect it.

General GEORGE WASHINGTON, letter to Major General Philip Schuyler, July 17, 1776.—*The Writings of George Washington*, ed. John C. Fitzpatrick, vol. 5, pp. 290–91 (1932).

1182 Nothing can be more hurtful to the service, than the neglect of discipline; for that discipline, more than numbers, gives one army the superiority over another.

General GEORGE WASHINGTON, general orders, July 6, 1777.—*The Writings of George Washington*, ed. John C. Fitzpatrick, vol. 8, p. 359 (1933).

1183 With willing hearts and skillful hands, the difficult we do at once; the impossible takes a bit longer.

Author unknown. Inscription on the memorial to the Seabees (U.S. Naval Construction Batallions), between Memorial Bridge and Arlington Cemetery.

"The difficult we do immediately. The impossible takes a little longer."—Motto of the U.S. Army Corps of Engineers during World War II, according to *The Home Book of American Quotations*, ed. Bruce Bohle, p. 35 (1967), which says that other branches of the service also used this slogan. *Newsweek*, March 8, 1943, p. 34, attributes this "cocky slogan" to the Army Air Forces.

A higher comparative, "The impossible we do at once; the miraculous takes a little longer," was said to be the motto of the Army Service Forces.—*The New York Times*, November 4, 1945, pp. 2E, 6E. This echoes a remark attributed to Charles-Alexandre de Calonne, Louis XVI's minister of finance. Marie Antoinette asked him something in a tone that brooked no refusal, adding that perhaps it would be difficult. He replied, "If it is only difficult, it is done; if it is impossible, we shall see."—J. F. Michaud, *Biographie Universelle*, vol. 6, p. 427.

1184 Really when I reflect upon the characters and attainments of some of the General Officers of this army, and consider that these are the persons on whom I am to rely to lead columns against the French Generals, and who are to carry my instructions into execution, I tremble; and, as Lord Chesterfield said of the Generals of his day, "I only hope that when the enemy reads the list of their names he trembles as I do."

ARTHUR WELLESLEY, DUKE OF WELLINGTON, letter to Lieutenant-Colonel Henry Torrens, August 29, 1810.—Antony Brett-James, *Wellington at War, 1794–1815,* p. 199 (1961). Lord Chesterfield's comment is unverified.

1185 To know when to retreat; and to dare to do it.

ARTHUR WELLESLEY, DUKE OF WELLINGTON, when asked the best test of a great general.—Sir William Fraser, *Words on Wellington,* p. 37 (1889).

Military service

1186 Any recruiter will tell you that the incentive for enlistment is that it [being drafted] is inevitable if you don't.

Lieutenant General LEWIS B. HERSHEY, director of the Selective Service System, address at The American University, Washington, D.C., December 11, 1966, as reported by *The New York Times,* December 12, 1966, p. 53.

1187 We must train and classify the whole of our male citizens, and make military instruction a regular part of collegiate education.

THOMAS JEFFERSON, letter to James Monroe, June 18, 1813.—*The Writings of Thomas Jefferson,* ed. Andrew A. Lipscomb, vol. 13, p. 261 (1903).

1188 War will exist until that distant day when the conscientious objector enjoys the same reputation and prestige that the warrior does today.

JOHN F. KENNEDY.—Arthur M. Schlesinger, Jr., *A Thousand Days: John F. Kennedy in the White House,* p. 76 (1979).

1189 A young man who does not have what it takes to perform military service is not likely to have what it takes to make a living. Today's military rejects include tomorrow's hard core unemployed.

President JOHN F. KENNEDY, statement on the need for training or rehabilitation of Selective Service rejectees, September 30, 1963.—*Public Papers of the Presidents of the United States: John F. Kennedy, 1963,* p. 753.

1190 Women should be permitted to volunteer for non-combat service, . . . they should not be accepted, voluntarily or through the draft, as combat soldiers. . . . We know of no comparable ways of training women and girls, and we have no real way of knowing whether the kinds of training that teach men both courage and restraint would be adaptable to women or effective in a crisis. But the evidence of history and comparative studies of other species suggest that women as a fighting body might be far less amenable to the rules that prevent warfare from becoming a massacre and, with the use of modern weapons, that protect the survival of all humanity. This is what I meant by saying that women in combat might be too fierce.

MARGARET MEAD, response to question asking her views on the draft, June 1968.—*Margaret Mead, Some Personal Views,* ed. Rhoda Metraux, pp. 35, 36 (1979).

1191 No man who is not willing to bear arms and to fight for his rights can give a good reason why he should be entitled to the privilege of living in a free community.

THEODORE ROOSEVELT, *Thomas Hart Benton,* chapter 2, p. 37 (1897, reprinted 1968). See also No. 663.

1192 It may be laid down as a primary position, and the basis of our system, that every Citizen who enjoys the protection of a free Government, owes not only a proportion of his property, but even his personal services to the defence of it, and consequently that the Citizens of America (with a few legal and official exceptions) from 18 to 50 Years of Age should be borne on the Militia Rolls, provided with uniform Arms, and so far accustomed to the use of them, that the Total strength of the Country might be called forth at a Short Notice on any very interesting Emergency, . . .

GEORGE WASHINGTON, "Sentiments on a Peace Establishment," enclosed in a letter to Alexander Hamilton, chairman of the Committee of Congress on the Peace Establishment, May 2, 1783.—*The Writings of George Washington*, ed. John C. Fitzpatrick, vol. 26, p. 389 (1938).

1193 Where is it written in the Constitution, in what article or section is it contained, that you may take children from their parents, and parents from their children, and compel them to fight the battles of any war in which the folly or the wickedness of government may engage it?

Representative DANIEL WEBSTER, remarks in the House, December 9, 1814.—*The Writings and Speeches of Daniel Webster*, vol. 14, p. 61 (1903).

Mind

1194 A foolish consistency is the hobgoblin of little minds, adored by little statesmen and philosophers and divines.

RALPH WALDO EMERSON, "Self-Reliance," *Essays: First Series* (vol. 2 of *The Complete Works of Ralph Waldo Emerson*), p. 57 (1903).

1195 The mind is never satisfied with the objects immediately before it, but is always breaking away from the present moment, and losing itself in schemes of future felicity. . . . The natural flights of the human mind are not from pleasure to pleasure, but from hope to hope.

SAMUEL JOHNSON, *The Rambler*, no. 2, March 24, 1750.—*The Rambler; A Periodical Paper, Published in 1750, 1751, 1752*, p. 3 (1825).

1196 Cultivated mind is the guardian genius of Democracy, and while guided and controlled by virtue, the noblest attribute of man. It is the only dictator that freemen acknowledge, and the only security which freemen desire.

MIRABEAU BUONAPARTE LAMAR, president of the Republic of Texas, first message to both houses of Congress of the Republic of Texas, Houston, Texas, December 21, 1838.—*The Papers of Mirabeau Buonaparte Lamar*, ed. Charles A. Gulick, Jr., vol. 2, p. 348 (1922).

"When a public school was a novelty and the Republic's treasury and credit were at their lowest, only a daring mind and a champion of enlightened liberty could have conceived the idea for insuring the education of the future Texas generations."—Philip Graham, *The Life and Poems of Mirabeau B. Lamar*, p. 53 (1938).

1197 If there is anything in the world that can really be called a man's property, it is surely that which is the result of his mental activity.

Attributed to ARTHUR SCHOPENHAUER. Unverified.

Mind

1198 If we work upon marble, it will perish; if we work on brass, time will efface it. If we rear temples, they will crumble to dust. But if we work on men's immortal minds, if we impress on them high principles, the just fear of God, and love for their fellow-men, we engrave on those tablets something which no time can efface, and which will brighten and brighten to all eternity.

DANIEL WEBSTER, secretary of state, speech to the City Council, Boston, Massachusetts, May 22, 1852.—*The Writings and Speeches of Daniel Webster*, vol. 13, pp. 518–19 (1903).

Webster served in Congress as a representative from New Hampshire, 1813–1817, and from Massachusetts, 1823–1827, and as a senator from Massachusetts, 1827–1841 and 1845–1850.

Moderation

1199 Those words, "temperate and moderate," are words either of political cowardice, or of cunning, or seduction.—A thing, moderately good is not so good as it ought to be. Moderation in temper, is always a virtue; but moderation in principle, is a species of vice.

THOMAS PAINE, letter to the addressers on the late proclamation against seditious writings.—*The Writings of Thomas Paine*, ed. Moncure D. Conway, vol. 3, pp. 94–95 (1895).

Money

1200 All the perplexities, confusions, and distresses in America arise, not from defects in their constitution or confederation, not from a want of honor or virtue, so much as from downright ignorance of the nature of coin, credit, and circulation.

JOHN ADAMS, letter to Thomas Jefferson, August 25, 1787.—*The Works of John Adams*, ed. Charles Francis Adams, vol. 8, p. 447 (1853).

1201 Money is power, and you ought to be reasonably ambitious to have it.

RUSSELL H. CONWELL, *Acres of Diamonds*, p. 20 (1915).

Conwell, founder and first president of Temple University, delivered this address more than 6,000 times from 1877 until his death in 1925.

1202 As this body has no authority to make anything whatever a tender in payment of private debts, it necessarily follows that nothing but gold and silver coin can be made a legal tender for that purpose, and that Congress cannot authorize the payment in any species of paper currency of any other debts but those due to the United States, or such debts of the United States as may, by special contract, be made payable in such paper.

ALBERT GALLATIN, *Considerations on the Currency and Banking System of the United States*, 1831, in *The Writings of Albert Gallatin*, ed. Henry Adams, vol. 3, p. 235 (1879).

1203 For the folk-community does not exist on the fictitious value of money but on the results of productive labour, which is what gives money its value.

ADOLF HITLER, speech to the German Reichstag, January 30, 1937.—*The Speeches of Adolf Hitler, April 1922–August 1939*, trans. and ed. Norman H. Baynes, vol. 1, p. 937 (1969).

1204 If the American people ever allow private banks to control the issuance of their currency, first by inflation and then by deflation, the banks and corporations that will grow up around them will deprive the people of all their property until their children will wake up homeless on the continent their fathers conquered.

Attributed to THOMAS JEFFERSON. Although Jefferson was opposed to paper money, this quotation is obviously spurious. *Inflation* was listed in Webster's dictionary of 1864, according to the *Oxford English Dictionary*, but the OED gives 1920 as the earliest use of *deflation*.

1205 In truth, the gold standard is already a barbarous relic.

JOHN MAYNARD KEYNES, *Monetary Reform*, p. 187 (1924).

1206 The best way to destroy the capitalist system is to debauch the currency.

Attributed to VLADIMIR ILICH (ULYANOV) LENIN by John Maynard Keynes, *The Economic Consequences of the Peace*, p. 235 (1920, reprinted 1971). Keynes says, "Lenin is said to have declared . . ." Despite careful searching by the European Division of the Library of Congress, this has not been found in Lenin's writings and remains unverified.

1207 God gave me my money. I believe the power to make money is a gift from God . . . to be developed and used to the best of our ability for the good of mankind. Having been endowed with the gift I possess, I believe it is my duty to make money and still more money and to use the money I make for the good of my fellow man according to the dictates of my conscience.

JOHN D. ROCKEFELLER, interview in 1905.—Peter Collier and David Horowitz, *The Rockefellers, an American Dynasty*, chapter 3, p. 48 (1976).

Rockefeller assumed giving to charity was a Christian duty, and did so throughout his life. Later in life he began to "have the semimystical feeling that he had been especially selected as the frail vessel for the great fortune" (p. 48).

1208 "Not worth a Continental dam" had its origin about this time [1780]. It is not a profane expression. A "dam" is an Indian coin of less value than one cent and a Continental one cent was next to worthless when it took six pounds, or about thirty dollars to buy a "warm dinner."

OLIVER TAYLOR, *Historic Sullivan*, p. 97, footnote (1909).

Other versions of this phrase include "Not worth a Continental" and "Not worth a Continental Damn." While other writers do not include the Indian connection, they agree the phrase arose when Continental money became worthless toward the end of the Revolution. See Mitford M. Mathews, *A Dictionary of Americanisms*, p. 383 (1951).

1209 He who tampers with the currency robs labor of its bread.

Senator DANIEL WEBSTER, speech delivered at Niblo's Saloon, New York City, March 15, 1837.—*The Works of Daniel Webster*, 10th ed., vol. 1, p. 377 (1857).

Morality

1210 For what end shall we be connected with men, of whom this is the character and conduct? . . . . Is it, that we may see our wives and daughters the victims of legal prostitution; soberly dishonoured; speciously polluted; the outcasts of delicacy and virtue, and the lothing of God and man?

TIMOTHY DWIGHT, *The Duty of Americans, at the Present Crisis*, pp. 20–21 (1798).

Dwight, president of Yale, preached this sermon on July 4, 1798, at New Haven, Connecticut. In 1798, much of the anti-French feeling was directed at the Jeffersonians, who were the champions in America of the French Revolution. In the congressional elections that year, the Jeffersonians lost heavily as the Federalists won control of both the House and the Senate. In this sermon, Dwight warned that a victory for the Jeffersonians meant lustful moral depravity.—Saul K. Padover, *Jefferson*, pp. 251–52 (1942).

1211 Dante once said that the hottest places in hell are reserved for those who in a period of moral crisis maintain their neutrality.

President JOHN F. KENNEDY, remarks in Bonn, West Germany, at the signing of a charter establishing the German Peace Corps, June 24, 1963.—*Public Papers of the Presidents of the United States: John F. Kennedy, 1963*, p. 503.

This remark may have been inspired by the passage from Dante Alighieri's *La Comedia Divina*, trans. Geoffrey L. Bickersteth, "Inferno," canto 3, lines 35–42 (1972):

by those disbodied wretches who were loth
when living, to be either blamed or praised.

. . . .

Fear to lose beauty caused the heavens to expel
these caitiffs; nor, lest to the damned they then
gave cause to boast, receives them the deep hell.

A more modern-sounding translation: "They are mixed with that repulsive choir of angels . . . undecided in neutrality. Heaven, to keep its beauty, cast them out, but even Hell itself would not receive them for fear the wicked there might glory over them."—*Dante's Inferno*, trans. Mark Musa, p. 21 (1971).

1212 I believe that in this generation those with the courage to enter the moral conflict will find themselves with companions in every corner of the world.

Senator ROBERT F. KENNEDY, "Day of Affirmation," address delivered at the University of Capetown, South Africa, June 6, 1966.—*Congressional Record*, June 6, 1966, vol. 112, p. 12430.

1213 Even in war moral power is to physical as three parts out of four.

Attributed to NAPOLEON.—Maturin M. Ballou, *Treasury of Thought*, p. 407 (1899). Unverified.

A handwritten note in Congressional Research Service files says that the War Department Library had searched many times without success for a different version: "Morale is to material as is the ratio of three to one."

1214 Ethics, too, are nothing but reverence for life. That is what gives me the fundamental principle of morality, namely, that good consists in maintaining, promoting, and enhancing life, and that destroying, injuring, and limiting life are evil.

ALBERT SCHWEITZER, *Civilization and Ethics*, Preface.—*The Philosophy of Civilization*, trans. C. T. Campion, part 2, p. 79 (1949, reissued 1981).

1215 I wrote my name upon the sand,
And trusted it would stand for aye;
But, soon, alas! the refluent sea
Had washed my feeble lines away.

HORATIO ALGER, JR., "Carving a Name," lines 1–4, *Alger Street: The Poetry of Horatio Alger, Jr.*, ed. Gilbert K. Westgard II, p. 53 (1964).

1216 The paths of glory lead but to the grave.

THOMAS GRAY, "Elegy Written in a Country Church Yard," line 36, *The Complete Poems of Thomas Gray*, ed. H. W. Starr and J. R. Hendrickson, p. 38 (1966). Originally published in 1751.

"Nobody knew that [Major General James] Wolfe, reciting Gray's *Elegy* in 1759 as he rowed up the St. Lawrence [to Quebec] the night before his death, said that 'he would prefer being the author of that poem to the glory of beating the French tomorrow,' until in 1815, in Vol. VII of the Transactions of the Royal Society of Edinburgh, appeared a biography of its secretary, John Robison, LL.D., professor of natural philosophy in the University of Edinburgh, who as a young man had been a midshipman in Wolfe's flotilla."—Carroll A. Wilson, "Familiar 'Small College' Quotations, II: Mark Hopkins and the Log," *The Colophon*, spring 1938, p. 204.

1217 Don't strew me with roses after I'm dead.
When Death claims the light of my brow,
No flowers of life will cheer me: instead
You may give me my roses now!

THOMAS F. HEALEY, "Give Me My Roses Now."—*The Home Book of Quotations*, ed. Burton Stevenson, 10th ed., p. 1578 (1967). Unverified.

1218 Closed eyes can't see the white roses,
Cold hands can't hold them, you know,
Breath that is stilled cannot gather
The odors that sweet from them blow,
Death, with a peace beyond dreaming,
Its children of earth doth endow;
Life is the time we can help them,
So give them the flowers now!

Here are the struggles and striving,
Here are the cares and the tears;
Now is the time to be smoothing
The frowns and the furrows and fears.
What to closed eyes are kind sayings?
What to hushed heart is deep vow?
Naught can avail after parting,
So give them the flowers now!

Just a kind word or a greeting;
Just a warm grasp or a smile—
These are the flowers that will lighten
The burdens for many a mile.
After the journey is over

What is the use of them; how
Can they carry them who must be carried?
Oh, give them the flowers now!

Blooms from the happy heart's garden
Plucked in the spirit of love;
Blooms that are earthly reflections
Of flowers that blossom above.
Words cannot tell what a measure
Of blessings such gifts will allow
To dwell in the lives of many,
So give them the flowers now!

Attributed to LEIGH MITCHELL HODGES. Unverified. The authorship of the poem, "Give Them the Flowers Now," is anonymous in *The World's Famous Short Poems and Prose Selections,* comp. James G. Lawson, p. 177 (1927). This poem is credited to Hodges in *Heart Throbs in Prose and Verse,* comp. Joe Mitchell Chapple, p. 35 (1947), a work based on readers' contributions.

1219 Faded the flower and all its budded charms,
Faded the sight of beauty from my eyes,
Faded the shape of beauty from my arms,
Faded the voice, warmth, whiteness, paradise!
Vanish'd unseasonably . . .

JOHN KEATS, "Sonnet to Fanny Brawne," lines 5–9, *The Complete Poetical Works of John Keats,* p. 379 (1900).

1220 So fleet the works of men, back to their earth again;
Ancient and holy things fade like a dream.

CHARLES KINGSLEY, "Old and New," lines 3–4, *Poems,* p. 243 (1902).

1221 It is said an Eastern monarch once charged his wise men to invent him a sentence, to be ever in view, and which should be true and appropriate in all times and situations. They presented him the words: *"And this, too, shall pass away."* How much it expresses! How chastening in the hour of pride!—how consoling in the depth of affliction!

ABRAHAM LINCOLN, address before the Wisconsin State Agricultural Society, Milwaukee, Wisconsin, September 30, 1859.—*The Collected Works of Abraham Lincoln,* ed. Roy P. Basler, vol. 3, pp. 481–82 (1953).

Many versions of this story exist. Another one is: "The Sultan asked for a Signet motto, that should hold good for Adversity or Prosperity. Solomon gave him, 'This also shall pass away.' "—Edward Fitzgerald, *Polonius: A Collection of Wise Saws and Modern Instances,* item 112, p. 80 (1901).

The words *In neez bogzarad,* which can be translated, "This also shall pass," appear in the *Diven* of the twelfth century Persian poet and philosopher, Sana'ī of Ghaznī, ed. Maẓāhir Muṣaffa, p. 92 (1957).

1222 Above all, Hubert was a man with a good heart. And on this sad day it would be good for us to recall Shakespeare's words:

A good leg will fall. A straight back will stoop. A black beard will turn white. A curled pate will grow bald. A fair face will wither. A full eye will wax hollow. But a good heart is the sun and the moon. Or rather the sun and not the moon, for it shines bright and never changes, but keeps its course truly.

He taught us all how to hope and how to live, how to win and how to lose, he taught us how to live, and finally, he taught us how to die.

Vice President WALTER F. MONDALE, eulogy for former Vice President Hubert H. Humphrey, January 15, 1978, in the rotunda of the Capitol.—*The Washington Post*, January 16, 1978, p. 1.

The Shakespeare quotation is a slight variation from *Henry V*, act V, scene ii.

1223 At thirty, man suspects himself a fool;
Knows it at forty, and reforms his plan;
At fifty, chides his infamous delay,
Pushes his prudent purpose to resolve;
In all the magnanimity of thought
Resolves, and re-resolves; then dies the same.
And why? Because he thinks himself immortal.
All men think all men mortal but themselves.

EDWARD YOUNG, *Night Thoughts*, 1, lines 417–24, *The Complete Works, Poetry and Prose*, ed. James Nichols, p. 13 (1854, reprinted 1968).

1224 Philip, remember that thou art mortal.

Author unknown. Supposedly, words Philip of Macedon had a servant repeat in the audience-room.—Samuel A. Bent, *Short Sayings of Great Men*, p. 437 (1882).

Similarly, "Remember thou, too, art a man."—Words a slave would be bidden to whisper now and again to the triumphal conqueror returning in state to Rome.—John L. Stoddard, *Lectures*, vol. 8, pp. 263–64 (1911).

Mothers

1225 All that I am, or hope to be, I owe to my angel mother.

Attributed to ABRAHAM LINCOLN.—Josiah G. Holland, *The Life of Abraham Lincoln*, p. 23 (1866), and George Alfred Townsend, *The Real Life of Abraham Lincoln*, p. 6 (1867). According to the latter, Lincoln made this remark to his law partner, William Herndon.

Lincoln's natural mother, Nancy Hanks Lincoln, died when he was nine years old and his father remarried the following year. His stepmother, Sarah Bush (Johnston) Lincoln, was loved and respected by Lincoln throughout her life, as evidenced in the many biographical studies of Lincoln. Benjamin P. Thomas says in *Abraham Lincoln*, p. 12 (1952): "The boy Abraham adored her. Recollection of his own mother dimmed. And in later years he called this woman, who filled her place so well, 'my angel mother.' "

The Macmillan Book of Proverbs, Maxims, and Famous Phrases, ed. Burton Stevenson, p. 1627 (1965), comments that the remark referred to Lincoln's stepmother. But the biographers of Lincoln's natural mother claim the remark referred to her: Caroline Hanks Hitchcock, *Nancy Hanks*, p. 105 (1899) and Charles Ludwig, *Nancy Hanks: Mother of Lincoln*, p. 84 (1965).

1226 "M" is for the million things she gave me,
"O" means only that she's growing old,
"T" is for the tears were shed to save me,
"H" is for her heart of purest gold;
"E" is for her eyes, with love-light shining,

"R" means right, and right she'll always be,
Put them all together, they spell "MOTHER,"
A word that means the world to me.

M-O-T-H-E-R (A Word That Means the World to Me), words by Howard Johnson, music by Theodore Morse, pp. 2–5, © 1915, renewed 1943 Leo Feist, Inc. Rights assigned to CBS Catalogue Partnership. All rights controlled and administered by CBS Feist Catalog Inc. All rights reserved. International copyright secured. Used by permission.

Motives

1227 Dreadful will be the day when the world becomes contented, when one great universal satisfaction spreads itself over the world. Sad will be the day for every man when he becomes absolutely contented with the life that he is living, with the thoughts that he is thinking, with the deeds that he is doing, when there is not forever beating at the doors of his soul some great desire to do something larger which he knows that he was meant and made to do because he is a child of God.

PHILLIPS BROOKS, *Daily Thoughts from Phillips Brooks,* p. 85 (1893).

1228 We must not inquire too curiously into motives. . . . they are apt to become feeble in the utterance: the aroma is mixed with the grosser air. We must keep the germinating grain away from the light.

GEORGE ELIOT (Mary Ann Evans), *Middlemarch,* chapter 2, p. 13 (1977). Originally published in 1871–1872.

1229 There is a desire deep within the soul which drives man from the seen to the unseen, to philosophy and to the divine.

KAHLIL GIBRAN, "Al Ghazali," *Mirrors of the Soul,* trans. Joseph Sheban, p. 49 (1965).

1230 The value the world sets upon motives is often grossly unjust and inaccurate.

H. L. MENCKEN, *A Mencken Chrestomathy,* p. 12 (1949). This is the opening sentence of his essay, "The Scientist," first published in *The Smart Set,* August 1919.

1231 The plea of good intentions is not one that can be allowed to have much weight in passing historical judgment upon a man whose wrong-headedness and distorted way of looking at things produced, or helped to produce, such incalculable evil; there is a wide political applicability in the remark attributed to a famous Texan, to the effect that he might, in the end, pardon a man who shot him on purpose, but that he would surely never forgive one who did so accidentally.

THEODORE ROOSEVELT, writing of John C. Calhoun, *Thomas Hart Benton,* chapter 5, p. 111 (1897, reprinted 1968).

Murphy's Law

1232 If there is a wrong way to do something, then someone will do it.

EDWARD A. MURPHY, JR., "Murphy's Law."—Robert L. Forward, "Murphy Lives!" *Science 83,* January–February 1983, p. 78. Commonly quoted as, "If anything can go wrong, it will."—*The Concise Oxford Dictionary of Proverbs,* ed. J. A. Simpson, p. 4 (1982), provides interesting historical notes on its origin and use.

A longer version appeared in a story about Murphy and his law in *People,* January 31, 1983, p. 82: "If there's more than one way to do a job and one of those ways will end in disaster, then somebody will do it that way."

Nation

1233 Happy are all free peoples, too strong to be dispossessed.
But blessed are those among nations who dare to be strong for the rest!

ELIZABETH BARRETT BROWNING, "A Court Lady," stanza 20, *The Poetical Works of Elizabeth Barrett Browning,* p. 418 (1974).

1234 Not gold but only men can make
A people great and strong;
Men who for truth and honor's sake
Stand fast and suffer long.

Brave men who work while others sleep,
Who dare while others fly—
They build a nation's pillars deep
And lift them to the sky.

RALPH WALDO EMERSON (?), "A Nation's Strength," stanzas 5 and 6.—*Masterpieces of Religious Verse,* ed. James Dalton Morrison, p. 459 (1948).

Granger's Index to Poetry, 6th ed., p. 898 (1973) says the author is unknown and that this is wrongly attributed to Emerson; the poem is not found in Emerson's *Complete Works* (1903).

1235 Cleanse the body of this nation
Through the glory of the Lord.

HENRY SCOTT HOLLAND, "Judge Eternal, Throned in Splendor."—*Service Book and Hymnal of the Lutheran Church in America,* music ed., no. 343 (1958).

1236 Great nations write their autobiographies in three manuscripts, the book of their deeds, the book of their words and the book of their art. Not one of these books can be understood unless we read the two others, but of the three the only trustworthy one is the last.

JOHN RUSKIN, *St. Mark's Rest: The History of Venice,* Preface, p. 1 (1885).

1237 A nation that can not preserve itself ought to die, and it will die—die in the grasp of the evils it is too feeble to overthrow.

Senator MORRIS SHEPPARD, remarks in the Senate, December 18, 1914, *Congressional Record,* vol. 52, p. 338.

1238 Great nations rise and fall. The people go from bondage to spiritual truth, to great courage, from courage to liberty, from liberty to abundance, from abundance to selfishness, from selfishness to complacency, from complacency to apathy, from apathy to dependence, from dependence back again to bondage.

Author unknown. Attributed to Benjamin Disraeli. Unverified.

Nation

1239 I know three things must always be
To keep a nation strong and free.
One is a hearthstone bright and dear,
With busy, happy loved ones near.
One is a ready heart and hand
To love, and serve, and keep the land.
One is a worn and beaten way
To where the people go to pray.
So long as these are kept alive,
Nation and people will survive.
God keep them always, everywhere—
The home, the heart, the place of prayer.

Author unknown, "Three Things."—*Sourcebook of Poetry,* comp. Al Bryant, p. 514 (1968). A variation of this poem appeared in the *Congressional Record,* January 14, 1959, vol. 105, Appendix, p. A144.

Needs

1240 *For want of a Nail the Shoe was lost; for want of a Shoe the Horse was lost; and for want of a Horse the Rider was lost;* being overtaken and slain by the Enemy, all for want of Care about a Horse-shoe Nail.

BENJAMIN FRANKLIN, "Poor Richard's Almanack," June 1758, *The Complete Poor Richard Almanacks,* facsimile ed., vol. 2, pp. 375, 377 (1970).

New England

1241 The one great poem of New England is her Sunday.

HENRY WARD BEECHER, *Proverbs from Plymouth Pulpit,* comp. William Drysdale, p. 229 (1887).

News

1242 There is good news tonight.

GABRIEL HEATTER, *There's Good News Tonight,* p. 122 (1960).
Heatter began his evening radio newscasts with these words, trying to give hope when the news was grim during World War II.

1243 I well believe it, to unwilling ears;
None love the messenger who brings bad news.

SOPHOCLES, *Antigone,* lines 276–77.—*The Dramas of Sophocles,* trans. Sir George Young, p. 16 (1888). A sentinel is speaking to Creon.

Newspapers

1244 Covers Dixie Like the Dew.

The Atlanta (Georgia) *Journal,* slogan. Still in use.

1245 The basis of our governments being the opinion of the people, the very first object should be to keep that right; and were it left to me to decide whether we should have a government without newspapers, or newspapers without a government, I should not hesitate a moment to prefer the latter. But I should mean that every man should receive those papers and be capable of reading them.

THOMAS JEFFERSON, letter to Edward Carrington, January 16, 1787.—*The Papers of Thomas Jefferson,* ed. Julian P. Boyd, vol. 11, p. 49 (1955).

1246 But let me beseech you, Sir, not to let this letter get into a newspaper. Tranquillity, at my age, is the supreme good of life. I think it a duty, and it is my earnest wish, to take no further part in public affairs. . . . The abuse of confidence by publishing my letters has cost me more than all other pains.

THOMAS JEFFERSON, letter to Charles Hammond, August 18, 1821.—*The Writings of Thomas Jefferson,* ed. Andrew A. Lipscomb, vol. 15, p. 331 (1903).

1247 For the newspaper is in all literalness the bible of democracy, the book out of which a people determines its conduct. It is the only serious book most people read. It is the only book they read every day.

WALTER LIPPMANN, *Liberty and the News,* p. 47 (1920).

1248 I generalized rashly: That is what kills political writing, this absurd pretence that you are delivering a great utterance. You never do. You are just a puzzled man making notes about what you think. You are not building the Pantheon, then why act like a graven image? You are drawing sketches in the sand which the sea will wash away.

WALTER LIPPMANN, "Books and Things," *The New Republic,* August 7, 1915, p. 24.
Lippmann's comments after reading a book on politics that displeased him.

1249 I know that my retirement will make no difference in its cardinal principles, that it will always fight for progress and reform, never tolerate injustice or corruption, always fight demagogues of all parties, never belong to any party, always oppose privileged classes and public plunderers, never lack sympathy with the poor, always remain devoted to the public welfare, never be satisfied with merely printing news, always be drastically independent, never be afraid to attack wrong, whether by predatory plutocracy or predatory poverty.

JOSEPH PULITZER, retirement speech, April 10, 1907.—*St. Louis* (Missouri) *Post-Dispatch,* April 11, 1907.

Since November 1911 this has been in continuous use on the editorial page of that newspaper under the heading, "The Post-Dispatch Platform."

1250 So I became a newspaperman. I hated to do it but I couldn't find honest employment.

Attributed to MARK TWAIN (Samuel L. Clemens). Unverified. Never found by Twain authorities or the Twain Papers staff.

Nobility

1251 As one lamp lights another, nor grows less,
So nobleness enkindleth nobleness.

Nobility

JAMES RUSSELL LOWELL, "Yussouf," lines 17-18, *The Complete Poetical Works of James Russell Lowell,* p. 376 (1900).

Inscription above the statue of Art, Main Reading Room, Library of Congress. The inscription was selected by Charles W. Eliot, president of Harvard.

1252 Be NOBLE! and the nobleness that lies
In other men, sleeping, but never dead,
Will rise in majesty to meet thine own.

JAMES RUSSELL LOWELL, "Sonnet IV," *The Complete Poetical Works of James Russell Lowell,* p. 20 (1900).

Be noble, and the nobleness that
Lies in other men—sleeping but
Never dead—will rise in majesty
To meet thine own

—Inscription on south facade of Union Station, Washington, D.C.

North Carolina

1253 North Carolina is a valley of humility between two mountains of conceit.

Author unknown.—For a discussion of its origin and correct wording ("humility," not "humiliation" as given by Mencken in his *New Dictionary of Quotations . . .*), see the editorial comments by Henry Wiseman Kendall in the *Greensboro* (North Carolina) *Daily News,* August 26, 1962, p. B4.

Nuclear energy

1254 I happen to be one who believes that we will not get very far in working out a peace program, or in lowering the suspicious fingers which are now being pointed toward America by other nations of the world, until we recognize that, after all, the secret of atomic energy does not belong to America, but that, instead, it belongs to all mankind.

Senator WAYNE MORSE, remarks in the Senate, October 22, 1945, *Congressional Record,* vol. 91, p. 9893.

1255 We are not bent on conquest or on threatening others. But we do have a nuclear umbrella that can protect others, above all the states to which we are allied or in which we have a great national interest.

President RICHARD M. NIXON, on-the-record interview with C. L. Sulzberger, March 8, 1971.—*The New York Times,* March 10, 1971, p. 14.

1256 Our children will enjoy in their homes electrical energy too cheap to meter.

LEWIS L. STRAUSS, chairman of the Atomic Energy Commission, speech at the 20th anniversary of the National Association of Science Writers, New York City, September 16, 1954, as reported by *The New York Times,* September 17, 1954, p. 5. The *Times* said he "predicted . . . that industry would have electrical power from atomic furnaces in five to fifteen years."

For controversy over whether this implied nuclear power or fusion power, Atomic Industrial Forum, Inc., issued a four-page *Special Report,* May 1980.

1257 The living will envy the dead.

Attributed to NIKITA S. KHRUSHCHEV, speaking of nuclear war.

Ed Zuckerman, "Hiding from the Bomb—Again," *Harper's*, August 1979, p. 36, attributes "the survivors would envy the dead" to Khrushchev. This issue of *Harper's* was stamped in the Library of Congress on July 12, 1979. Senator Frank Church, chairman of the Senate Committee on Foreign Relations, also attributed this same quotation to Khrushchev in hearings held July 11, 1979, and repeated the quotation in later hearings held July 16, 1979.—*The Salt II Treaty*, hearings before the Committee on Foreign Relations, United States Senate, 96th Congress, 1st session, part 1, p. 333, and part 2, p. 27 (1979).

An Associated Press news release, dated August 4, 1979, summarized these meetings: "In a month of hearings on the SALT II treaty, many senators have . . . quoted and requoted the late Soviet Premier Nikita Khrushchev, who once said that after a nuclear exchange, 'the living would envy the dead.' " The quotation has been widely used in the press since then, including *The Washington Post*, March 20, 1981, p. A23. No form of this quotation has been verified in the speeches or writings of Khrushchev.

1258 But this very triumph of scientific annihilation—this very success of invention—has destroyed the possibility of war's being a medium for the practical settlement of international differences. The enormous destruction to both sides of closely matched opponents makes it impossible for even the winner to translate it into anything but his own disaster. . . . Global war has become a Frankenstein to destroy both sides. No longer is it a weapon of adventure—the shortcut to international power. If you lose, you are annihilated. If you win, you stand only to lose. No longer does it possess even the chance of the winner of a duel. It contains now only the germs of double suicide.

General DOUGLAS MACARTHUR, speech to a joint session of the Congress of the Republic of the Philippines, July 5, 1961.—*Representative Speeches of General of the Army Douglas MacArthur*, p. 98 (1964). Senate Doc. 88–95.

1259 If we have to start over again with another Adam and Eve, then I want them to be Americans and not Russians, and I want them on this continent and not in Europe.

Senator RICHARD RUSSELL, remarks in the Senate during debate on the antiballistic missile, October 2, 1968, *Congressional Record*, vol. 114, p. 29175.

Oath of office

1260 I, AB, do solemnly swear (or affirm) that I will support and defend the Constitution of the United States against all enemies, foreign and domestic; that I will bear true faith and allegiance to the same; that I take this obligation freely, without any mental reservation or purpose of evasion; and that I will well and faithfully discharge the duties of the office on which I am about to enter. So help me God.

Oath of Office.—*United States Code*, 1982 ed., vol. 1, title 5, section 3331, p. 538 (1983).

This oath is taken by any individual, except the president, "elected or appointed to an office of honor or profit in the civil service or uniformed services."

Obscenity

1261 But implicit in the history of the First Amendment is the rejection of obscenity as utterly without redeeming social importance.

Obscenity

Justice WILLIAM J. BRENNAN, JR., *Roth* v. *United States*, 354 U.S. 484 (1957).

This is often quoted as "utterly without redeeming social value." The decision also cited the test used in American courts in judging obscenity: "whether to the average person, applying contemporary community standards, the dominant theme of the material taken as a whole appeals to prurient interest" (p. 489).

"This [decision] was the first definition of obscenity offered by the court. It was modified in several subsequent decisions and finally replaced with another standard in the 1973 case of *Miller* v. *California*."—Congressional Quarterly Inc., *The Supreme Court and Its Work*, p. 215 (1981).

Opinions

1262 Every man has a right to his opinion, but no man has a right to be wrong in his facts.

Attributed to BERNARD M. BARUCH.—*Distilled Wisdom*, ed. Alfred A. Montapert, p. 145 (1964). Unverified.

Baruch placed such great importance on getting the facts, "free from tips, inside dope or wishful thinking," that President Wilson took to calling him "Dr. Facts."—*Baruch*, vol. 1 (*My Own Story*), p. 131 (1957).

1263 The matter does not appear to me now as it appears to have appeared to me then.

Baron GEORGE W. W. BRAMWELL, justice on the Court of the Exchequer, *Andrews* v. *Styrap*, 26 L.T. 706 (1872).—Eugene C. Gerhart, *Quote It!*, p. 558 (1969). Unverified.

1264 Predominant opinions are generally the opinions of the generation that is vanishing.

Attributed to BENJAMIN DISRAELI.—Maturin M. Ballou, *Treasury of Thought*, p. 370 (1899). Unverified.

1265 There is probably an element of malice in the readiness to overestimate people; we are laying up for ourselves the pleasure of later cutting them down to size.

ERIC HOFFER, "Thoughts of Eric Hoffer, Including 'Absolute Faith Corrupts Absolutely,' " *The New York Times Magazine*, April 25, 1971, pp. 60, 62.

1266 A great many people think they are thinking when they are merely rearranging their prejudices.

Attributed to WILLIAM JAMES.—Clifton Fadiman, *American Treasury, 1455–1955*, p. 719 (1955). Unverified.

A similar thought was expressed by Josh Billings (Henry Wheeler Shaw): "Education is a good thing generally, but most folks educate their prejudices."—*Everybody's Friend, or Josh Billing's* [sic] *Encyclopedia and Proverbial Philosophy of Wit and Humor*, p. 592 (1874). Spelling corrected.

1267 If there be any among us who would wish to dissolve this Union or to change its republican form, let them stand undisturbed as monuments of the safety with which error of opinion may be tolerated where reason is left free to combat it.

President THOMAS JEFFERSON, inaugural address, March 4, 1801.—*The Writings of Thomas Jefferson*, ed. Andrew A. Lipscomb, vol. 3, p. 319 (1904).

1268 For the great enemy of the truth is very often not the lie—deliberate, contrived, and dishonest—but the myth—persistent, persuasive, and unrealistic. Too often we hold fast to the cliches of our forebears. We subject all facts to a prefabricated set of interpretations. We enjoy the comfort of opinions without the discomfort of thought.

President JOHN F. KENNEDY, commencement address at Yale University, New Haven, Connecticut, June 11, 1962.—*Public Papers of the Presidents of the United States: John F. Kennedy, 1962*, p. 234.

1269 I have got you together to hear what I have written down. I do not wish your advice about the main matter—for that I have determined for myself.

Attributed to President ABRAHAM LINCOLN.—Salmon P. Chase, diary entry for September 22, 1862, *Diary and Correspondence of Salmon P. Chase*, p. 88 (1903, reprinted 1971).

According to the Chase account, Lincoln spoke these words at a cabinet meeting he had called to inform the members of his decision to issue the Emancipation Proclamation. This quotation is also used in Carl Sandburg, *Abraham Lincoln: The War Years*, p. 584 (1939).

Although these words are not used, the same thought is conveyed in the diary of another member of Lincoln's cabinet, Gideon Welles. See his diary entry for the same date in *Diary of Gideon Welles*, vol. 1, pp. 142–43 (1911).

1270 We cannot ask a man what he will do, and if we should, and he should answer us, we should despise him for it. Therefore we must take a man whose opinions are known.

President ABRAHAM LINCOLN, in conversation with George Sewall Boutwell concerning the nomination of Salmon P. Chase to the U.S. Supreme Court, reported by Boutwell in his *Reminiscences of Sixty Years in Public Affairs*, vol. 2, p. 29 (1902).

1271 This imputation of inconsistency is one to which every sound politician and every honest thinker must sooner or later subject himself. The foolish and the dead alone never change their opinion.

JAMES RUSSELL LOWELL, *My Study Windows*, chapter on Abraham Lincoln, p. 166 (1899).

1272 There is the grand truth about Nathaniel Hawthorne. He says NO! in thunder; but the Devil himself cannot make him say *yes*. For all men who say *yes*, lie; and all men who say *no*,—why, they are in the happy condition of judicious, unincumbered travellers in Europe; they cross the frontiers into Eternity with nothing but a carpet-bag,—that is to say, the Ego. Whereas those *yes*-gentry, they travel with heaps of baggage, and, damn them! they will never get through the Custom House.

HERMAN MELVILLE, letter to Nathaniel Hawthorne, April 16, 1851.—Melville, *Moby-Dick: An Authoritative Text, Reviews and Letters . . .*, ed. Harrison Hayford and Hershel Parker, p. 555 (1967).

1273 There are as many opinions as there are experts.

President FRANKLIN D. ROOSEVELT, radio appeal on the scrap rubber campaign, June 12, 1942.—*The Public Papers and Addresses of Franklin D. Roosevelt, 1942*, p. 272 (1950). The speech was reprinted in the *Congressional Record*, June 15, 1942, vol. 88, Appendix, p. A2228.

Opinions

1274 After the war, and until the day of his death, his position on almost every public question was either mischievous or ridiculous, and usually both.

THEODORE ROOSEVELT, *Thomas Hart Benton* (vol. 7 of *The Works of Theodore Roosevelt,* national ed.), chapter 8, p. 104 (1926).

He was referring to Wendell Phillips, well-known nineteenth century Abolitionist.

1275 The opinions that are held with passion are always those for which no good ground exists; indeed the passion is the measure of the holder's lack of rational conviction. Opinions in politics and religion are almost always held passionately.

BERTRAND RUSSELL, *Sceptical Essays,* Introduction, p. 10 (1961).

See also No. 677.

Oratory

1276 I was very glad that Mr. Attlee described my speeches in the war as expressing the will not only of Parliament but of the whole nation. Their will was resolute and remorseless and, as it proved, unconquerable. It fell to me to express it, and if I found the right words you must remember that I have always earned my living by my pen and by my tongue. It was a nation and race dwelling all round the globe that had the lion heart. I had the luck to be called upon to give the roar.

WINSTON CHURCHILL, address marking his 80th birthday, Westminster Hall, London, November 30, 1954.—*Winston S. Churchill: His Complete Speeches, 1897–1963,* ed. Robert Rhodes James, vol. 8, pp. 8608–9 (1974).

1277 One woman who managed to corner him, the story runs, said in a treacly gushing voice:

"Doesn't it thrill you, Mr. Churchill, to know that every time you make a speech the hall is packed to overflowing?"

"It is quite flattering," Mr. Churchill replied, "but whenever I feel this way I always remember that if instead of making a political speech I was being hanged, the crowd would be twice as big."

WINSTON CHURCHILL, remark on a transatlantic tour.—Norman McGowan, *My Years with Churchill,* p. 138 (1958).

1278 When I see a bird that walks like a duck and swims like a duck and quacks like a duck, I call that bird a duck.

Attributed to RICHARD CARDINAL CUSHING.—Everett Dirksen and Herbert V. Prochnow, *Quotation Finder,* p. 55 (1971). Unverified.

1279 Then there was a maiden speech, so inaudible, that it was doubted whether, after all, the young orator really did lose his virginity.

BENJAMIN DISRAELI, *The Young Duke,* chapter 6, p. 19 (1859). First published in 1831.

1280 It is reputed that Mr. Disraeli when he was once asked by a new member whether he advised him to take part often in debate replied:—

> No, I do not think you ought to do so, because it is much better that the House should wonder why you do not speak than why you do.

My advice in this matter is very much the same as that given by Mr. Disraeli; it is much better when a member resumes his seat after he has made a speech for the House to have the feeling that they wish he had gone on longer instead of wondering why he did not stop sooner.

EDWARD ALGERNON FITZROY, remarks in the House of Commons, May 25, 1939, as reported by *The Times* (London), May 26, 1939, p. 7.—FitzRoy, Speaker of the House of Commons, was quoting the nineteenth century Prime Minister Benjamin Disraeli, Lord Beaconsfield. Quoted in slightly different form in the *Congressional Record,* June 2, 1939, vol. 84, pp. 6538–39.

1281 It is amazing how soon one becomes accustomed to the sound of one's voice, when forced to repeat a speech five or six times a day. As election day approaches, the size of the crowds grows; they are more responsive and more interested; and one derives a certain exhilaration from that which, only a few weeks before, was intensely painful. This is one possible explanation of unlimited debate in the Senate.

Senator J. WILLIAM FULBRIGHT, "The Legislator," lecture delivered at the University of Chicago, Chicago, Illinois, in 1946.—*The Works of the Mind,* ed. for the University's Committee on Social Thought by Robert B. Heywood, p. 123 (1947).

1282 Every living sentence which shows a mind at work for itself is to be welcomed. It is not the first use but the tiresome repetition of inadequate catch words which I am observing—phrases which originally were contributions, but which, by their very felicity, delay further analysis for fifty years. That comes from the same source as dislike of novelty—intellectual indolence or weakness—a slackening in the eternal pursuit of the more exact.

OLIVER WENDELL HOLMES, "Law in Science and Science in Law," address before the New York State Bar Association, January 17, 1899.—*Collected Legal Papers by Oliver Wendell Holmes,* pp. 230–31 (1937).

Holmes was an associate justice of the supreme court of Massachusetts.

1283 The art of reasoning becomes of first importance. In this line antiquity has left us the finest models for imitation; . . . I should consider the speeches of Livy, Sallust, and Tacitus, as pre-eminent specimens of logic, taste, and that sententious brevity which, using not a word to spare, leaves not a moment for inattention to the hearer. Amplification is the vice of modern oratory.

THOMAS JEFFERSON, letter to David Harding, April 20, 1824.—*The Writings of Thomas Jefferson,* ed. Andrew A. Lipscomb, vol. 16, p. 30 (1904).

1284 Also the two-edged tongue of mighty Zeno, who, Say what one would, could argue it untrue.

PLUTARCH, *Plutarch's Lives,* trans. John Dryden, rev. A. H. Clough, life of Pericles, vol. 1, p. 323 (1859).

1285 Middle-aged clubwoman, with a flutter in her voice: "Oh, Mr. Stevenson, your speech was superfluous."

"Thank you, madam. I've been thinking of having it published posthumously."

"Oh, won't that be nice. The sooner the better."

ADLAI E. STEVENSON, U.S. ambassador to the United Nations, favorite anecdote on public occasions.—Richard J. Walton, *The Remnants of Power: The Tragic Last Years of Adlai Stevenson,* p. 24 (1968).

Oratory

1286 When the mariner has been tossed for many days in thick weather, and on an unknown sea, he naturally avails himself of the first pause in the storm, the earliest glance of the sun, to take his latitude, and ascertain how far the elements have driven him from his true course. Let us imitate this prudence, and, before we float farther on the waves of this debate, refer to the point from which we departed, that we may at least be able to conjecture where we now are.

Senator DANIEL WEBSTER, second speech on Foote's resolution, delivered in the Senate, January 26, 1830.—*The Works of Daniel Webster,* 10th ed., vol. 3, p. 270 (1857).

His opening remarks on the sixth day of debate.

1287 It was a bit of campaign oratory.

WENDELL WILLKIE, testimony, February 11, 1941.—*To Promote the Defense of the United States,* hearings before the Committee on Foreign Relations, United States Senate, 77th Congress, 1st session, part 3, p. 905 (1941).

In 1940 Willkie had been the Republican party candidate for president.

1288 A member of the Cabinet congratulated Wilson on introducing the vogue of short speeches and asked him about the time it took him to prepare his speeches. He said: "It depends. If I am to speak ten minutes, I need a week for preparation; if fifteen minutes, three days; if half an hour, two days; if an hour, I am ready now."

President WOODROW WILSON.—Josephus Daniels, *The Wilson Era; Years of War and After, 1917–1923,* p. 624 (1946).

See also No. 2078.

Order

1289 Oh, order! Material order, intellectual order, moral order! What a comfort and strength, and what an economy! To know where we are going and what we want; that is order. To keep one's word, to do the right thing, and at the right time: more order. To have everything under one's hand, to put one's whole army through its manoeuvres, to work with all one's resources: still order. To discipline one's habits and efforts and wishes, to organize one's life and distribute one's time, to measure one's duties and assert one's rights, to put one's capital and resources, one's talents and opportunities to profit: again and always order. Order is light, peace, inner freedom, self-determination: it is power. To conceive order, to return to order, to realize order in oneself, around oneself, by means of oneself, this is aesthetic and moral beauty, it is well-being, it is what ought to be.

HENRI FRÉDÉRIC AMIEL, journal entry, January 27, 1860.—*The Private Journal of Henri Frédéric Amiel,* trans. Van Wyck Brooks and Charles Van Wyck Brooks, enl. and rev. ed., pp. 131–32 (1935).

1290 If you delay till to-morrow what ought to be done to-day, you overcharge the morrow with a burden which belongs not to it. You load the wheels of time, and prevent it from carrying you along smoothly. He who every morning plans the transactions of the day, and follows out the plan, carries on a thread which will guide him through the labyrinth of the most busy life. The orderly arrangement of his time is like a ray of light which darts itself through all his affairs. But where no plan is laid, where the disposal of time is surrendered merely to the chance of incidents, all things lie huddled together in one chaos, which admits neither of distribution nor review.

Order

HUGH BLAIR, "On the Importance of Order in Conduct," *Sermons*, vol. 1, no. 16, p. 195 (1822).

Early time management advice.

Past

1291 One thing alone not even God can do,
To make undone whatever hath been done.

ARISTOTLE, *The Nicomachean Ethics of Aristotle*, trans. Robert Williams, book 6, chapter 2, p. 154 (1879). Aristotle attributed these words to Agathon, an Athenian tragic poet who lived in the latter half of the fifth century B.C.

In his column, "Today and Tomorrow," Walter Lippmann attributed the same idea to George Santayana: "He might meditate on Santayana's saying that not even God can change the past."—*New York Herald Tribune*, June 11, 1951, p. 17. Unverified.

1292 Progress, far from consisting in change, depends on retentiveness. . . . when experience is not retained, as among savages, infancy is perpetual. Those who cannot remember the past are condemned to repeat it. . . . This is the condition of children and barbarians, in whom instinct has learned nothing from experience.

GEORGE SANTAYANA, *The Life of Reason*, vol. 1, chapter 12, p. 284 (1905).

See also Nos. 570, 574, and 853.

1293 How can we live without our lives? How will we know it's us without our past?

JOHN STEINBECK, *The Grapes of Wrath*, p. 120 (1939).

Past and future

1294 There must be what Mr. Gladstone many years ago called "a blessed act of oblivion." We must all turn our backs upon the horrors of the past. We must look to the future. We cannot afford to drag forward across the years that are to come the hatreds and revenges which have sprung from the injuries of the past.

WINSTON CHURCHILL, speech at Zurich University, Zurich, Switzerland, September 19, 1946.—*The Sinews of Peace: Post-War Speeches by Winston S. Churchill*, p. 200 (1949).

1295 Our duty is to preserve what the past has had to say for itself, and to say for ourselves what shall be true for the future.

Attributed to JOHN RUSKIN. Unverified.

1296 Whereof what's past is prologue, what to come
In yours and my discharge.

WILLIAM SHAKESPEARE, *The Tempest*, act II, scene i, lines 253–54. Antonio is speaking.

"What's past is prologue" is carved on the National Archives Building, Washington, D.C.

1297 More and more Emerson recedes grandly into history, as the future he predicted becomes a past.

Past and future

ROBERT PENN WARREN, speech upon receipt of the 1970 National Medal for Literature, New York City, December 2, 1970.—Transcript, p. 2.

Past and present

1298 The question Whether one generation of men has a right to bind another, seems never to have been started either on this or our side of the water. . . . I set out on this ground, which I suppose to be self evident, *"that the earth belongs in usufruct to the living*:" that the dead have neither powers nor rights over it.

THOMAS JEFFERSON, letter to James Madison, September 6, 1789.—*The Papers of Thomas Jefferson,* ed. Julian P. Boyd, vol. 15, p. 392 (1958).

In an editorial note, Boyd states that "This concept of political relativism was the one great addition to Jefferson's thought that emerged from his years of residence at the center of European intellectual ferment" (p. 384).

1299 Like my three brothers before me, I pick up a fallen standard. Sustained by their memory of our priceless years together I shall try to carry forward that special commitment to justice, to excellence, to courage that distinguished their lives.

Senator EDWARD M. KENNEDY, speech, Holy Cross College, Worcester, Massachusetts, August 21, 1968, as reported by *The New York Times,* August 22, 1968, p. 22.

1300 The dogmas of the quiet past, are inadequate to the stormy present. The occasion is piled high with difficulty, and we must rise with the occasion. As our case is new, so we must think anew and act anew. We must disenthrall ourselves, and then we shall save our country.

President ABRAHAM LINCOLN, annual message to Congress, December 1, 1862.—*The Collected Works of Abraham Lincoln,* ed. Roy P. Basler, vol. 5, p. 537 (1953).

This passage was quoted in the preamble to the 1968 Republican party platform.

1301 There is nothing new under the sun.

Various authors. Some sources give as a first source the Bible, Ecclesiastes 1:9, "The thing that hath been, it is that which shall be; and that which is done is that which shall be done: and there is no new thing under the sun."

However, Marcus Aurelius said in his *Meditations,* "Consider for example, and thou wilt find that almost all of the transactions in the time of Vespasian differed little from those of the present day. Thou there findest marrying and giving in marriage, educating children, sickness, death, war, joyous holidays, traffic, agriculture, flatterers, insolent pride, suspicions, laying of plots, longing for the death of others, newsmongers, lovers, misers, men canvassing for the consulship and for the kingdom;—yet all these passed away, and are nowhere."—Craufurd Tait Ramage, *Familiar Quotations from Greek Authors,* p. 47 (1895, reprinted 1968).

For a range of variations of the above quotation, see *The Concise Oxford Dictionary of Proverbs,* pp. 164–65 (1982).

Patriotism

1302 America now is stumbling through the darkness of hatred and divisiveness. Our values, our principles, and our determination to succeed as a free and democratic people will give us a torch to light the way. And we will survive and become the stronger—not only because of a patriotism that stands for love of country, but a patriotism that stands for love of people.

Representative GERALD R. FORD, address to the state conference of the Order of DeMolay, Grand Rapids, Michigan, September 7, 1968.—*Gerald R. Ford, Selected Speeches,* ed. Michael V. Doyle, p. 77 (1973).

1303 We would rather starve than sell our national honor.

INDIRA GANDHI, prime minister of India, remark at election meeting in Nagpur, India, as reported by *The New York Times,* January 23, 1967, p. 1.

India had accepted trade restrictions with North Vietnam and Cuba to get grain from the United States. Prime Minister Gandhi said this did not compromise the country's honor because India had not been trading with North Vietnam, and her trade with Cuba was limited to the selling of jute products, which was not objected to by the United States.

1304 I only regret that I have but one life to lose for my country.

NATHAN HALE, last words before being hanged by the British as a spy, September 22, 1776. Possibly inspired by Joseph Addison's celebrated tragedy, *Cato* (act IV, scene iv), in which Cato says, when the body of his son is brought before him: "How beautiful is death when earned by virtue. Who would not be that youth? What pity is it that we can die but once to serve our country!"—George Dudley Seymour, *Captain Nathan Hale, Major John Palsgrave Wyllys, A Digressive History,* p. 39 (1933).

See note at No. 1561.

1305 With earnest prayers to all my friends to cherish mutual good will, to promote harmony and conciliation, and above all things to let the love of our country soar above all minor passions, I tender you the assurance of my affectionate esteem and respect.

THOMAS JEFFERSON, letter to John Hollins, May 5, 1811.—*The Writings of Thomas Jefferson,* ed. Andrew A. Lipscomb, vol. 13, pp. 58-59 (1903).

1306 Patriotism is the last refuge of a scoundrel.

SAMUEL JOHNSON.—James Boswell, *Life of Johnson,* entry for Friday, April 7, 1775, p. 615 (1970).

"In Dr. Johnson's famous dictionary patriotism is defined as the last resort of a scoundrel. With all due respect to an enlightened but inferior lexicographer, I beg to submit that it is the first."—Ambrose Bierce, *The Devil's Dictionary,* at entry for patriotism, *The Collected Writings of Ambrose Bierce,* p. 323 (1946, reprinted 1973).

H. L. Mencken added this to Johnson's dictum: "But there is something even worse: it is the first, last, and middle range of fools."—*The World,* New York City, November 7, 1926, p. 3E.

1307 True patriotism sometimes requires of men to act exactly contrary, at one period, to that which it does at another, and the motive which impels them—the desire to do right—is precisely the same.

ROBERT E. LEE, letter to General P. G. T. Beauregard, October 3, 1865.—John William Jones, *Life and Letters of Robert Edward Lee, Soldier and Man,* p. 390 (1906).

1308 Intellectually I know America is no better than any other country; emotionally I know she is better than every other country.

SINCLAIR LEWIS, radio interview in Berlin, Germany, December 29, 1930, as reported by *The New York Times*, December 30, 1930, p. 5.

1309 Whenever you hear a man speak of his love for his country it is a sign that he expects to be paid for it.

H. L. MENCKEN, *A Mencken Chrestomathy*, chapter 30, p. 616 (1949).

1310 Breathes there the man, with soul so dead,
Who never to himself hath said,
This is my own, my native land!
Whose heart hath ne'er within him burn'd,
As home his footsteps he hath turn'd,
From wandering on a foreign strand!

SIR WALTER SCOTT, *The Lay of the Last Minstrel*, ed. Margaret A. Allen, canto sixth, 1, lines 1–6, p. 123 (1915).

1311 I venture to suggest that what we mean is a sense of national responsibility which will enable America to remain master of her power—to walk with it in serenity and wisdom, with self-respect and the respect of all mankind; a patriotism that puts country ahead of self; a patriotism which is not short, frenzied outbursts of emotion, but the tranquil and steady dedication of a lifetime. These are words that are easy to utter, but this is a mighty assignment. For it is often easier to fight for principles than to live up to them.

ADLAI E. STEVENSON, governor of Illinois, speech to the American Legion convention, New York City, August 27, 1952.—*Speeches of Adlai Stevenson*, p. 81 (1952).

1312 Citizens by birth or choice, of a common country, that country has a right to concentrate your affections. The name of AMERICAN, which belongs to you, in your national capacity, must always exalt the just pride of Patriotism, more than any appellation derived from local discriminations.

President GEORGE WASHINGTON, farewell address, September 19, 1796.—*The Writings of George Washington*, ed. John C. Fitzpatrick, vol. 35, pp. 219–20 (1940).

See note at No. 339 about the farewell address.

Patronage

1313 Senator [Stephen] Douglas is of world-wide renown. All the anxious politicians of his party, or who have been of his party for years past, have been looking upon him as certainly, at no distant day, to be the President of the United States. They have seen in his round, jolly, fruitful face, postoffices, landoffices, marshalships, and cabinet appointments, chargeships and foreign missions, bursting and sprouting out in wonderful exuberance ready to be laid hold of by their greedy hands.

ABRAHAM LINCOLN, speech at Springfield, Illinois, July 17, 1858.—*The Collected Works of Abraham Lincoln*, ed. Roy P. Basler, vol. 2, p. 506 (1953).

1314 It may be, sir, that the politicians of the United States are not so fastidious as some gentlemen are, as to disclosing the principles on which they act. They boldly preach what they practise. When they are contending for victory, they avow their intention of enjoying the fruits of it. If they are defeated, they expect to retire from office. If they are successful, they claim, as a matter of right, the advantages of success. They see nothing wrong in the rule, that to the victor belong the spoils of the enemy.

Senator WILLIAM LEARNED MARCY, remarks in the Senate, January 25, 1832, *Register of Debates in Congress*, vol. 8, col. 1325.

Marcy was defending Martin Van Buren, nominated as minister to England, against the attacks of Senator Henry Clay.

Peace

1315 Glory to God in the highest, and on earth peace, good will toward men.

The Bible, Luke 2:14.

1316 They have healed also the hurt of the daughter of my people slightly, saying, Peace, peace; when there is no peace.

The Bible, Jeremiah 6:14.
See also No. 1061.

1317 When things are investigated, then true knowledge is achieved; when true knowledge is achieved, then the will becomes sincere; when the will is sincere, then the heart is set right (or then the mind sees right); when the heart is set right, then the personal life is cultivated; when the personal life is cultivated, then the family life is regulated; when the family life is regulated, then the national life is orderly; and when the national life is orderly, then there is peace in this world.

CONFUCIUS, *Liki (Record of Rites)*, chapter 42.—*The Wisdom of Confucius*, ed. and trans. Lin Yutang, chapter 4, pp. 139–40 (1938).

1318 Yes, God and the politicians willing, the United States can declare peace upon the world, and win it.

ELY CULBERTSON, *Must We Fight Russia*, chapter 5, p. 19 (1946).

1319 At present the peace of the world has been preserved, not by statesmen, but by capitalists.

BENJAMIN DISRAELI, letter to Mrs. Sarah Brydges Willyams, October 17, 1863.—W. F. Monypenny and George E. Buckle, *The Life of Benjamin Disraeli*, vol. 4, p. 339 (1916).

He foresaw the possibility of a European war, "on the pretext of restoring Poland." The Rothschilds had made large loans to Italy and Russia, and "are naturally very nervous."—Disraeli, letter to Mrs. Brydges Willyams of July 21, 1863. Following the words above, he wrote, "For the last three months it has been a struggle between the secret societies and the European millionaires. Rothschild hitherto has won" (p. 339).

1320 Peace is an unstable equilibrium, which can be preserved only by acknowledged supremacy or equal power.

WILL DURANT and ARIEL DURANT, *The Lessons of History*, chapter 11, p. 81 (1968).

1321 I like to believe that people, in the long run, are going to do more to promote peace than our governments. Indeed, I think that people want peace so much that one of these days governments had better get out of the way and let them have it.

President DWIGHT D. EISENHOWER, radio and television broadcast with Prime Minister Harold Macmillan, London, August 31, 1959.—*Public Papers of the Presidents of the United States: Dwight D. Eisenhower, 1959*, p. 625.

1322 Peace with all nations, and the right which that gives us with respect to all nations, are our object.

THOMAS JEFFERSON, letter to Mr. Dumas, March 24, 1793.—*The Writings of Thomas Jefferson*, ed. H. A. Washington, vol. 3, p. 535.

1323 That peace, safety, and concord may be the portion of our native land, and be long enjoyed by our fellow-citizens, is the most ardent wish of my heart, and if I can be instrumental in procuring or preserving them, I shall think I have not lived in vain.

President THOMAS JEFFERSON, letter to Benjamin Waring and others, March 23, 1801.—*The Writings of Thomas Jefferson*, ed. Andrew A. Lipscomb, vol. 10, p. 235 (1903).

1324 So let us here resolve that Dag Hammarskjöld did not live, or die, in vain. Let us call a truce to terror. Let us invoke the blessings of peace. And, as we build an international capacity to keep peace, let us join in dismantling the national capacity to wage war.

President JOHN F. KENNEDY, address before the General Assembly of the United Nations, New York City, September 25, 1961.—*Public Papers of the Presidents of the United States: John F. Kennedy, 1961*, p. 619.

1325 With malice toward none; with charity for all; with firmness in the right, as God gives us to see the right, let us strive on to finish the work we are in; to bind up the nation's wounds; to care for him who shall have borne the battle, and for his widow, and his orphan—to do all which may achieve and cherish a just, and a lasting peace, among ourselves, and with all nations.

President ABRAHAM LINCOLN, second inaugural address, conclusion, March 4, 1865.—*The Collected Works of Abraham Lincoln*, ed. Roy P. Basler, vol. 8, p. 333 (1953).

"Both the Gettysburg address and the Second Inaugural Address mark the height of Lincoln's eloquence. The *London Times* called the latter the most sublime state paper of the century. Exactly two months later it was read over its author's grave."—*Complete Works of Abraham Lincoln*, new and enl. ed., ed. John G. Nicolay and John Hay, vol. 9, p. 44, footnote (1905).

An excerpt appears on a plaque on the Veterans Administration building in Washington, D.C.: "To care for him who shall have borne the battle and for his widow, and his orphan."

1326 The plain truth is the day is coming when no single nation, however powerful, can undertake by itself to keep the peace outside its own borders. Regional and international organizations for peace-keeping purposes are as yet rudimentary; but they must grow in experience and be strengthened by deliberate and practical cooperative action.

ROBERT S. MCNAMARA, secretary of defense, address before the American Society of Newspaper Editors, Montreal, Canada, May 19, 1966.—*Congressional Record*, May 19, 1966, vol. 112, p. 11114.

1327 It is not enough just to *be* for peace. The point is, what can we do about it?

President RICHARD M. NIXON, on-the-record interview with C. L. Sulzberger, March 8, 1971.—*The New York Times*, March 10, 1971, p. 14.

Peace

1328 For peace is not mere absence of war, but is a virtue that springs from force of character.

BENEDICTUS DE SPINOZA, "Tractatus Politicus," *Writings on Political Philosophy,* ed. A. G. A. Balz, trans. R. H. M. Elwes, p. 110 (1937). Other translations vary.

1329 Only a peace between equals can last. Only a peace the very principle of which is equality and a common participation in a common benefit.

President WOODROW WILSON, address to the United States Senate on essential terms of peace in Europe, January 22, 1917.—*The Messages and Papers of Woodrow Wilson,* ed. Albert Shaw, vol. 1, p. 352 (1924).

People

1330 There are people in our society who should be separated and discarded. I think it's one of the tendencies of the liberal community to feel that every person in a nation of over 200 million people can be made into a productive citizen.

I'm realist enough to believe this can't be. We're always going to have our prisons, we're always going to have our places of preventive detention for psychopaths, and we're always going to have a certain number of people in our community who have no desire to achieve or who have no desire to even fit in an amicable way with the rest of society.

And these people should be separated from the community, not in a callous way but they should be separated as far as any idea that their opinions shall have any effect on the course we follow.

Vice President SPIRO T. AGNEW, comments during interview for European audiences which was recorded in Washington, D.C., then broadcast over British Independent Television on June 30, 1970, as reported by *The Washington Post,* July 2, 1970, p. A3.

1331 Where there is no vision, the people perish.

The Bible, Proverbs 29:18.

1332 I can not wish you success in your effort to reject the treaty because while it may win the fight it may destroy our cause. My plan cannot fail if the people are with us and we ought not to succeed unless we do have the people with us.

WILLIAM JENNINGS BRYAN, letter to Andrew Carnegie, January 13, 1899.—Bryan papers, Library of Congress.

Andrew Carnegie, working to defeat the treaty of peace with Spain, unsuccessfully sought Bryan's help.

See also No. 1557.

1333 I am a child of the House of Commons. I was brought up in my father's house to believe in democracy. "Trust the people"—that was his message.

Prime Minister WINSTON CHURCHILL, speech to a joint session of Congress, Washington, D.C., December 26, 1941.—*Winston S. Churchill: His Complete Speeches, 1897–1963,* ed. Robert Rhodes James, vol. 6, p. 6536 (1974).

1334 Your *people,* sir, is nothing but a great beast!

Attributed to ALEXANDER HAMILTON, in a political argument with Thomas Jefferson.—David S. Muzzey, *An American History,* p. 192 (1911).

For similar expressions of this idea going back to Horace, see *Bartlett's Familiar Quotations*, 15th ed., p. 108, no. 19 and footnotes (1982), and *The Home Book of Quotations*, ed. Burton Stevenson, 9th ed., p. 1483–84, section 7 (1964).

1335 Would yee *both eat your cake, and have your cake?*

JOHN HEYWOOD, *The Proverbs of John Heywood*, part 2, chapter 9, p. 162 (1598, reprinted 1874, 1978).

The idea that if you spend a thing you cannot have it goes back much further than Heywood's original 1546 work. Plautus wrote c. 194 B.C. in *Trinummus* (act II, scene iv, line 414), "Non tibi illud apparere si sumas potest" (if you spend a thing you cannot have it), translated as "You cannot eat your cake and have it too" by one Englishman.—*Comedies of Plautus*, trans. Bonnell Thornton, 2d ed., rev., vol. 2, p. 29 (1769).

1336 People don't eat in the long run—they eat every day.

Attributed to HARRY L. HOPKINS, who headed the Federal Emergency Relief Administration in 1933.—Robert E. Sherwood, *Roosevelt and Hopkins: An Intimate History*, p. 52 (1948).

1337 The mobs of great cities add just so much to the support of pure government, as sores do to the strength of the human body. It is the manners and spirit of a people which preserve a republic in vigor. A degeneracy in these is a canker which soon eats to the heart of its laws and constitution.

THOMAS JEFFERSON, *Notes on Virginia*, query 19, reprinted in *The Writings of Thomas Jefferson*, ed. Andrew A. Lipscomb, vol. 2, p. 230 (1903).

1338 A sense of this necessity, and a submission to it, is to me a new and consolatory proof that wherever the people are well informed they can be trusted with their own government; that whenever things get so far wrong as to attract their notice, they may be relied on to set them to rights.

THOMAS JEFFERSON, letter to Richard Price, January 8, 1789.—*The Papers of Thomas Jefferson*, ed. Julian P. Boyd, vol. 14, p. 420 (1958).

1339 The President to-night has a dream:—He was in a party of plain people, and, as it became known who he was, they began to comment on his appearance. One of them said:—"He is a very common-looking man." The President replied:—"The Lord prefers common-looking people. That is the reason he makes so many of them."

Attributed to President ABRAHAM LINCOLN, December 23, 1863.—John Hay, *Letters of John Hay and Extracts from Diary*, vol. 1, pp. 142–43 (1908, reprinted 1969).

1340 No democracy has ever long survived the failure of its adherents to be ready to die for it. . . . My own conviction is this, the people must either go on or go under.

Prime Minister DAVID LLOYD GEORGE, address, conference of trade union delegates, London, January 18, 1918, as reported by *The Times* (London), January 19, 1918, p. 8.

1341 I do not want the voice of the people shut out.

Senator HUEY LONG, remarks in the Senate, May 16, 1932, *Congressional Record*, vol. 75, p. 10297.

1342 Your country is calling you. Our people are calling us. The people of America are calling us to relieve them from the distress that has infested this entire Nation as the result of following the Cabinet officers of the present administration. Your people are asking you to deliver them from this condition that now exists. They are asking relief.

Senator HUEY LONG, remarks in the Senate, May 16, 1932, *Congressional Record*, vol. 75, p. 10307.

1343 If I were to attempt to put my political philosophy tonight into a single phrase, it would be this: Trust the people. Trust their good sense, their decency, their fortitude, their faith. Trust them with the facts. Trust them with the great decisions. And fix as our guiding star the passion to create a society where people can fulfill their own best selves—where no American is held down by race or color, by worldly condition or social status, from gaining what his character earns him as an American citizen, as a human being and as a child of God.

ADLAI E. STEVENSON, speech at Harrisburg, Pennsylvania, September 13, 1956.—Stevenson, *The New America*, ed. Seymour E. Harris, Jr., pp. 13–14 (1971).

1344 No People can be bound to acknowledge and adore the invisible hand, which conducts the Affairs of men more than the People of the United States. Every step, by which they have advanced to the character of an independent nation, seems to have been distinguished by some token of providential agency.

President GEORGE WASHINGTON, first inaugural address, April 30, 1789.—*The Writings of George Washington*, ed. John C. Fitzpatrick, vol. 30, p. 293 (1939).

1345 People are not an interruption of our business. People are our business.

WALTER E. WASHINGTON, mayor of Washington, D.C., c. 1971.

1346 In the last analysis, my fellow countrymen, as we in America would be the first to claim, a people are responsible for the acts of their government.

President WOODROW WILSON, address, Columbus, Ohio, September 4, 1919.—*The Messages and Papers of Woodrow Wilson*, ed. Albert Shaw, vol. 2, p. 728 (1924).

1347 Let them eat cake.

Author unknown. Commonly attributed to Marie Antoinette. There is a good deal of conflicting evidence, however.

"At length I recollected the thoughtless saying of a great princess, who, on being informed that the country people had no bread, replied, 'Then let them eat cake.' "—Jean Jacques Rousseau, *Confessions*, book 6, as cited by *The Home Book of Quotations*, ed. Burton Stevenson, 9th ed., p. 1571, which adds this note: "Usually attributed to Marie Antoinette, after her arrival in France in 1770, but the sixth book of the *Confessions* was written two or three years before that date. It is difficult to translate 'brioche,' which is not exactly cake, but a bun or fancy bread something like Scotch scones."

Rousseau wrote the first six books of his *Confessions* in 1766–1767, though the work was not published until 1782–1789. Marie Antoinette lived 1755–1793.

In the London *Sunday Telegraph* of January 23, 1983, p. 6, an unidentified columnist responded to a reader's inquiry about this remark: "[You] may be surprised to learn that it was not attributed to her until more than half a century after her death. However, 15 years before Marie Antoinette's birth, Rousseau, in his 'Confessions,' pinned the yarn on an Italian noblewoman. King Louis XVIII of France in the 1820's wrote that the culprit was the wife of his predecessor, Louis XIV, who had reigned a couple of centuries before him: the only slight difference is that she is supposed to have said pastry instead of cake. And in 1959 one of those numerous know-alls who write to the *Times* said that John Peckham, a thirteenth century Archbishop of Canterbury, tells the same story in a letter written in Latin."

A similar remark was attributed to Joseph François Foullon, appointed minister of the king's household in 1789, who "was reported, probably quite without foundation to have said, 'If the people cannot get bread, let them eat hay.' "—*Encyclopaedia Britannica*, 11th ed., vol. 10, p. 738 (1910).

Perfection

1348 I never expect to see a perfect work from imperfect man.

ALEXANDER HAMILTON, *The Federalist*, ed. Benjamin F. Wright, no. 85, p. 544 (1961).

1349 We are morally and intellectually superior to all men. We are peerless. So, too, are our organizations and our institutions. [Germany was] the most perfect political creation known to history, [the Kaiser] deliciae humani generis, [and the Imperial Chancellor, Herr von Bethmann-Hollweg] the most eminent of living men.

ADOLF LASSON.—*The Times* (London), *History of the War*, vol. 5, p. 170 (1915).

This noted Hegelian philosopher and German nationalist is also quoted by Georges Clemenceau, *Grandeur and Misery of Victory*, p. 278 (1930).

1350 No one can be perfectly free till all are free; no one can be perfectly moral till all are moral; no one can be perfectly happy till all are happy.

HERBERT SPENCER, *Social Statics*, part 4, chapter 30, last sentence, p. 456 (1851).

1351 We are all imperfect. We can not expect perfect government.

President WILLIAM HOWARD TAFT, address at a banquet given in his honor by the Board of Trade and Chamber of Commerce of Washington, D.C., May 8, 1909.—*Presidential Addresses and State Papers of William Howard Taft*, vol. 1, chapter 7, p. 82 (1910).

1352 By his father he is English, by his mother he is American—to my mind the blend which makes the perfect man.

MARK TWAIN (Samuel L. Clemens), introducing Winston Churchill, New York City, December 12, 1900.—*Mark Twain Speaking*, ed. Paul Fatout, p. 368 (1976).

Perseverance

1353 Never give in, never give in, *never, never, never, never*—in nothing, great or small, large or petty—never give in except to convictions of honour and good sense.

Prime Minister WINSTON CHURCHILL, speech at Harrow School, Harrow, England, October 29, 1941.—*Winston S. Churchill: His Complete Speeches, 1897-1963*, ed. Robert Rhodes James, vol. 6, p. 6499 (1974).

1354 We shall fight on the beaches, we shall fight on the landing grounds, we shall fight in the fields and in the streets, we shall fight in the hills; we shall never surrender, and even if, which I do not for a moment believe, this island or a large part of it were subjugated and starving, then our Empire beyond the seas, armed and guarded by the British Fleet, would carry on the struggle, until, in God's good time, the New World, with all its power and might, steps forth to the rescue and the liberation of the old.

Prime Minister WINSTON CHURCHILL, speech in the House of Commons after successful evacuation of Allied troops at Dunkirk, France, June 4, 1940.—*Winston S. Churchill: His Complete Speeches, 1897–1963*, ed. Robert Rhodes James, vol. 6, p. 6231 (1974).

1355 Nothing in the World can take the place of persistence. Talent will not; nothing is more common than unsuccessful men with talent. Genius will not; unrewarded genius is almost a proverb. Education will not; the world is full of educated derelicts. Persistence and determination are omnipotent. The slogan "press on" has solved and always will solve the problems of the human race.

Attributed to CALVIN COOLIDGE. Unverified, though this appeared on the cover of the program of a memorial service for him in 1933. The Forbes Library, Northampton, Massachusetts, has searched its Coolidge collection many times for this.

1356 Diamonds are only chunks of coal,
That stuck to their jobs, you see.

MINNIE RICHARD SMITH, "Stick to Your Job," lines 1–2.—Christian F. Kleinknecht, *Poor Richard's Anthology of Thoughts on Success*, p. 44 (1947).

1357 We should never despair, our Situation before has been unpromising and has changed for the better, so I trust, it will again. If new difficulties arise, we must only put forth New Exertions and proportion our Efforts to the exigency of the times.

General GEORGE WASHINGTON, letter to Major General Philip Schuyler, July 15, 1777.—*The Writings of George Washington*, ed. John C. Fitzpatrick, vol. 8, p. 408 (1933).

This letter concerns the loss of Fort Ticonderoga.

1358 When things go wrong, as they sometimes will,
When the road you're trudging seems all up hill,
. . . When care is pressing you down a bit,
Rest, if you must—but don't you quit.
. . . Often the goal is nearer than
It seems to a faint and faltering man,
Often the struggler has given up
When he might have captured the victor's cup.

Author unknown, "Don't Quit."—Hazel Felleman, *The Best Loved Poems of the American People*, pp. 113–14 (1936, reprinted 1957).

Perverseness

1359 Yet I am not more sure that my soul lives, than I am that perverseness is one of the primitive impulses of the human heart—one of the indivisible primary faculties, or sentiments, which give direction to the character of Man.

EDGAR ALLAN POE, "The Black Cat," *Edgar Allan Poe*, ed. Philip Van Doren Stern, p. 299 (1945). Originally published in 1843.

1360 Make no little plans; they have no magic to stir men's blood and probably themselves will not be realized. Make big plans; aim high in hope and work, remembering that a noble, logical diagram once recorded will never die, but long after we are gone will be a living thing, asserting itself with ever-growing insistency. Remember that our sons and grandsons are going to do things that would stagger us. Let your watchword be order and your beacon beauty.

Attributed to DANIEL H. BURNHAM. While Burnham expressed these thoughts in a paper he read before the Town Planning Conference, London, 1910, the exact words were reconstructed by Willis Polk, Burnham's San Francisco partner. Polk used the paragraph on Christmas cards in 1912 after Burnham's death in June of that year.—Henry H. Saylor, "Make No Little Plans," *Journal of the American Institute of Architects*, March 1957, pp. 95–99.

1361 The hardest strokes of heaven fall in history upon those who imagine that they can control things in a sovereign manner, as though they were kings of the earth, playing Providence not only for themselves but for the far future—reaching out into the future with the wrong kind of far-sightedness, and gambling on a lot of risky calculations in which there must never be a single mistake. And it is a defect in such enthusiasts that they seem unwilling to leave anything to Providence, unwilling even to leave the future flexible, as one must do; and they forget that in any case, for all we know, our successors may decide to switch ideals and look for a different utopia before any of our long shots have reached their objective, or any of our long-range projects have had fulfillment. It is agreeable to all the processes of history, therefore, that each of us should rather do the good that is straight under our noses. Those people work more wisely who seek to achieve good in their own small corner of the world and then leave the leaven to leaven the whole lump, than those who are for ever thinking that life is vain unless one can act through the central government, carry legislation, achieve political power and do big things.

HERBERT BUTTERFIELD, *Christianity and History*, p. 104 (1949).

1362 In the space of two days I had evolved two plans, wholly distinct, both of which were equally feasible. The point I am trying to bring out is that one does not plan and then try to make circumstances fit those plans. One tries to make plans fit the circumstances.

General GEORGE S. PATTON, JR., *War as I Knew It*, p. 116 (1947).

Pledge of allegiance

1363 I pledge allegiance to the Flag of the United States of America, and to the Republic for which it stands, one Nation under God, indivisible, with liberty and justice for all.

Pledge of allegiance to the flag.—36 *United States Code* 172 (1982 ed.).

This pledge was first used at the dedication of the World's Fair Grounds in Chicago, Illinois, on October 21, 1892, the four hundredth anniversary of the discovery of America and the first celebration of Columbus Day, which had been proclaimed by the president and made a national holiday by Congress. It was published in *The Youth's Companion*, September 8, 1892, p. 446, with this wording: "I pledge allegiance to my Flag and the Republic for which it stands: one Nation indivisible, with Liberty and Justice for all."

No single author was named; the program bore the names of the executive committee, including the chairman, Francis Bellamy. A story in *The Youth's Companion*, December 20, 1917, p. 722, credits the authorship of the pledge to James B. Upham with the assistance of the 1892 committee, but in 1939 a scholarly committee of the United States Flag Association studied the question of authorship and "decided that to Francis Bellamy unquestionably belongs the honor and distinction of being the author of the original Pledge to the Flag."—Margarette S. Miller, *I Pledge Allegiance*, pp. 162–69 (1946). Also *Pledge of Allegiance to the Flag*, p. 4 (1955). House Doc. 84-225.

The wording of the 1892 pledge was originally the twenty-two words above, but the word "to" preceding "the Republic" was added immediately after the first celebration. The First National Flag Conference, 1923, altered the wording from "my Flag" to "the Flag of the United States," and the following year the Second National Flag Conference added "of America" to that phrase.—Miller, op. cit., pp. 156–58.

Public Law 79-287, December 28, 1945, made this officially the Pledge of Allegiance to the Flag. Public Law 83-396, signed on Flag Day, June 14, 1954, added the phrase "under God."

1364 If I may I would like to recite the Pledge of Allegiance and give you a definition for each word.

I—me, an individual, a committee of one.

Pledge—dedicate all of my worldly goods to give without self-pity.

Allegiance—my love and my devotion.

To the Flag—our standard, Old Glory, a symbol of freedom. Wherever she waves, there is respect because your loyalty has given her a dignity that shouts freedom is everybody's job.

Of the United—that means that we have all come together.

States—individual communities that have united into 48 great states, 48 individual communities with pride and dignity and purpose, all divided with imaginary boundaries, yet united to a common purpose, and that's love for country.

Of America.

And to the Republic—a state in which sovereign power is invested in representatives chosen by the people to govern. And government is the people and it's from the people to the leaders, not from the leaders to the people.

For which it stands.

One nation—meaning, so blessed by God.

Indivisible—incapable of being divided.

With liberty—which is freedom and the right of power to live one's own life without threats or fear or some sort of retaliation.

And justice—The principle or quality of dealing fairly with others.

For all—which means "it's as much your country as it is mine."

RED SKELTON, remarks in the House, Flag Day, June 14, 1972, *Congressional Record*, vol. 118, p. 20859.

Point of view

1365 But there are some people, nevertheless—and I am one of them—who think that the most practical and important thing about a man is still his view of the universe. We think that for a landlady considering a lodger, it is important to know his income, but still more important to know his philosophy. We think that for a general about to fight an enemy, it is important to know the enemy's numbers, but still more important to know the enemy's philosophy.

G. K. CHESTERTON, *Heretics*, introductory remarks, pp. 15–16 (1905).

1366 You have your Lebanon and its dilemma. I have my Lebanon and its beauty. Your Lebanon is an arena for men from the West and men from the East. My Lebanon is a flock of birds fluttering in the early morning as shepherds lead their sheep into the meadow and

Point of view

rising in the evening as farmers return from their fields and vineyards. *You have your Lebanon and its people. I have my Lebanon and its people.*

KAHLIL GIBRAN, "You Have Your Lebanon and I Have My Lebanon," *Mirrors of the Soul*, trans. Joseph Sheban, pp. 30–31 (1965).

Policy

1367 In a scheme of policy which is devised for a nation, we should not limit our views to its operation during a single year, or even for a short term of years. We should look at its operation for a considerable time, and in war as well as in peace.

HENRY CLAY.—*The Clay Code, or Text-Book of Eloquence, a Collection of Axioms, Apothegms, Sentiments . . . Gathered from the Public Speeches of Henry Clay*, ed. G. Vandenhoff, p. 95 (1844).

Clay served in the House of Representatives 1811–1814, 1815–1821, and 1823–1825; he was Speaker every year except 1821. He was a senator 1806–1807, 1810–1811, 1831–1842, and 1849–1852.

1368 You have despoiled churches. You have threatened every corporation and endowment in the country. You have examined into everybody's affairs. You have criticised every profession and vexed every trade. No one is certain of his property, and nobody knows what duties he may have to perform to-morrow. This is the policy of confiscation as compared with that of concurrent endowment.

BENJAMIN DISRAELI, speech on the University Education Bill (Ireland), House of Commons, March 11, 1873.—*Selected Speeches of the Late Right Honourable the Earl of Beaconsfield*, ed. T. E. Kebbel, vol. 2, p. 390 (1882).

1369 [Policy] is like a play in many acts, which unfolds inevitably once the curtain is raised. To declare then that the performance will not take place is an absurdity. The play will go on, either by means of the actors . . . or by means of the spectators who mount the stage. . . . Intelligent people never consider this the essence of the problem, however. For them it lies in the decision whether the curtain is to be raised at all, whether the spectators are to be assembled and in the intrinsic quality of the play.

KLEMENS VON METTERNICH, *Aus Metternich's Nachgelassenen Papieren* , vol. 8, p. 190 (1880), as quoted by Henry Kissinger, *A World Restored*, chapter 4, p. 41 (1957).

1370 There is no such thing as a fixed policy, because policy like all organic entities is always in the making.

Attributed to LORD SALISBURY.—M. R. D. Foot, *British Foreign Policy Since 1898*, p. 9 (1956). Not verified in Salisbury's writings.

1371 There is an eternal dispute between those who imagine the world to suit their policy, and those who correct their policy to suit the realities of the world.

Attributed to ALBERT SOREL. Unverified.

1372 In the tragic days of Mussolini, the trains in Italy ran on time as never before and I am told in their way, their horrible way, that the Nazi concentration-camp system in

Germany was a model of horrible efficiency. The really basic thing in government is policy. Bad administration, to be sure, can destroy good policy, but good administration can never save bad policy.

ADLAI E. STEVENSON, governor of Illinois, speech before the Los Angeles Town Club, Los Angeles, California, September 11, 1952.—*Speeches of Adlai Stevenson*, p. 36 (1952).

Political parties

1373 It's a damned good thing to remember in politics to stick to your party and never attempt to buy the favor of your enemies at the expense of your friends.

Representative JOSEPH G. CANNON.—L. White Busby, *Uncle Joe Cannon*, p. 269 (1927).

"Uncle Joe" Cannon, who was Speaker of the House from 1903–1911, served in the House for 46 years.

1374 Anyone can rat, but it takes a certain amount of ingenuity to re-rat.

WINSTON CHURCHILL, remark in 1923 after rejoining the Conservatives, having left them earlier to join the Liberals.—Kay Halle, *Irrepressible Churchill*, pp. 52–53 (1966). Other sources say this remark was made in 1924.

1375 It is necessary to have party organization if we are to have effective and efficient government. The only difference between a mob and a trained army is organization, and the only difference between a disorganized country and one that has the advantage of a wise and sound government is fundamentally a question of organization.

CALVIN COOLIDGE, address to women.—Eward Elwell Whiting, *Calvin Coolidge*, p. 154 (1924).

1376 The two great political parties of the nation have existed for the purpose, each in accordance with its own principles, of undertaking to serve the interests of the whole nation. Their members of the Congress are chosen with that great end in view.

Vice President CALVIN COOLIDGE, Memorial Day address, Northampton, Massachusetts, May 30, 1923.—Coolidge, *The Price of Freedom*, p. 348 (1925).

1377 You cannot choose between party government and Parliamentary government. I say you can have no Parliamentary government if you have no party government; and therefore when gentlemen denounce party government, they strike at the scheme of government which, in my opinion, has made this country great, and which, I hope, will keep it great.

BENJAMIN DISRAELI, speech in the House of Commons, August 30, 1848.—*Selected Speeches of the Late Right Honourable the Earl of Beaconsfield*, ed. T. E. Kebbel, vol. 2, p. 455 (1882).

The editor notes, p. 415, "this particular speech enjoys a special and superlative distinction above all its fellows: as I am authorised to state that, in Mr. Disraeli's own opinion, it made him leader of the Conservative Party in the House of Commons."

1378 There can be but two great political parties in this country.

Senator STEPHEN A. DOUGLAS, speech delivered at Bloomington, Illinois, July 16, 1858.—*Complete Works of Abraham Lincoln*, new and enl. ed., ed. John G. Nicolay and John Hay, vol. 3, p. 66 (1905).

1379 The two parties which divide the state, the party of Conservatism and that of Innovation, are very old, and have disputed the possession of the world ever since it was made.

RALPH WALDO EMERSON, "The Conservative," lecture delivered at the Masonic Temple, Boston, Massachusetts, December 9, 1841.—*Nature, Addresses and Lectures* (vol. 3 of *The Works of Ralph Waldo Emerson*), p. 273 (1906).

1380 The President of the United States of necessity owes his election to office to the suffrage and zealous labors of a political party, the members of which cherish with ardor and regard as of essential importance the principles of their party organization; but he should strive to be always mindful of the fact that he serves his party best who serves the country best.

President RUTHERFORD B. HAYES, inaugural address, March 5, 1877.—*Inaugural Addresses of the Presidents of the United States from George Washington, 1789, to Richard Milhous Nixon, 1973*, p. 138 (1974). House Doc. 93-208.

1381 Of course, both major parties today seek to serve the national interest. They would do so in order to obtain the broadest base of support, if for no nobler reason. But when party and officeholder differ as to how the national interest is to be served, we must place first the responsibility we owe not to our party or even to our constituents but to our individual consciences.

Senator JOHN F. KENNEDY, *Profiles in Courage*, p. 15 (1956).

1382 Sometimes party loyalty asks too much.

Senator JOHN F. KENNEDY.—Arthur M. Schlesinger, Jr., *A Thousand Days: John F. Kennedy in the White House*, p. 26 (1979).

1383 There is no Democratic or Republican way of cleaning the streets.

Attributed to FIORELLO LA GUARDIA, mayor of New York City, by Murray W. Stand.—Charles Garrett, *The La Guardia Years, Machine and Reform Politics in New York City*, p. 274 (1961).

1384 We're the party that wants to see an America in which people can still get rich.

President RONALD REAGAN, remarks at a Republican congressional dinner saluting him, Washington, D.C., May 4, 1982.—*Public Papers of the Presidents of the United States: Ronald Reagan, 1982*, p. 558.

1385 I have no Politics. I am for the Party that is out of Power, no matter which one it is. But I will give you my word that, in case of my appointment, I will not be a Republican; I will do my best to pull with you, and not embarrass you. In fact, my views on European affairs are so in accord with You, Mr. President, that I might almost be suspected of being a Democrat.

WILL ROGERS, letter to President Warren Harding offering to replace the American ambassador to the Court of St. James's in England.—Rogers, *The Illiterate Digest*, p. 172 (1924).

1386 I don't care to be involved in the crash-landing unless I can be in on the take-off.

HAROLD STASSEN, comment on bipartisanship, attributed to him by Senator Arthur H. Vandenberg.

"Once again, it was the procedure of a hurried call to senators and a last-minute meeting to inform them of an impending development or of the execution of a policy, and not to consult on the formation of policy. Vandenberg then and thereafter insisted that real bipartisanship meant consultation in advance and not a perfunctory reading to legislators of an impending press announcement or policy statement. . . . Stassen's comment, the Senator used to say, was such a good statement of the Republican case that he wished it were his."—*The Private Papers of Senator Vandenberg*, ed. Arthur H. Vandenberg, Jr., p. 230 (1952).

1387 I have been thinking that I would make a proposition to my Republican friends. . . . That if they will stop telling lies about the Democrats, we will stop telling the truth about them.

ADLAI E. STEVENSON, governor of Illinois, campaign remark, Fresno, California, September 10, 1952.—John Bartlow Martin, *Adlai Stevenson of Illinois*, pp. 673–74 (1976).

Martin called this remark a favorite of Stevenson's, but it is not original with him. It was attributed to Senator Chauncey Depew, but in reverse, in John F. Parker's *"If Elected, I Promise . . . ," Stories and Gems of Wisdom by and About Politicians*, p. 41 (1969): "If you will refrain from telling any lies about the Republican party, I'll promise not to tell the truth about the Democrats." Depew was a senator 1899–1911.

1388 Now is the time for all good men to come to the aid of the party.

Author unknown. Sentence devised to test the speed of the first typewriter, Milwaukee, Wisconsin, fall of 1867, during "an exciting political campaign."—Charles E. Weller, *The Early History of the Typewriter*, p. 21 (1918).

Other sources credit Weller as author of the famous sentence, but he does not claim the credit in his book. The sentence is still in use, though it is often written as "their" party.

Politicians

1389 Some of the politicians in this country, in their feverish search for group acceptance, are ready to endorse tumultuous confrontation as a substitute for debate, and the most illogical and unfitting extensions of the Bill of Rights as protections for psychotic and criminal elements in our society. . . . We have seen all too clearly that there are men—now in power in this country—who do not represent authority, who cannot cope with tradition, and who believe that the people of America are ready to support revolution as long as it is done with a cultured voice and a handsome profile.

Vice President SPIRO T. AGNEW, address to the American Retail Federation, Washington, D.C., May 4, 1970.—John R. Coyne, Jr., *The Impudent Snobs*, p. 324 (1972).

1390 Man is by nature a political animal.

ARISTOTLE, *Politics*, book 1, chapter 2.—*Aristotle's Politics and Poetics*, trans. Benjamin Jowett and Thomas Twining, p. 5 (1957). Jowett translated *Politics*. This statement appears again in book 3, chapter 6, p. 68.

1391 [Recipe for political success:] If a politician during a campaign finds it necessary to resort to flattery, he should spread it on, not in thin layers, but with a trowel, or better yet, a shovel. Politicians should not forget that voters never grow weary of illusory promises.

Politicians should ever remember that the electorate suspects and distrusts men of superb intellect, calmness, and serenity. And, finally, the politician must always tell people what they want to hear.

Attributed to Senator HENRY FOUNTAIN ASHURST.—John Rustgard, *The Problem of Poverty*, 2d ed., pp. 211–12 (1936).

1392 I would he were better, I would he were worse.

Attributed to Senator JOSEPH WELDON BAILEY. Unverified. Said to have been applied to President Theodore Roosevelt during debate on the Railroad Rate Bill of 1906.

1393 POLITICIAN, n. An eel in the fundamental mud upon which the superstructure of organized society is reared. When he wriggles he mistakes the agitation of his tail for the trembling of the edifice. As compared with the statesman, he suffers the disadvantage of being alive.

AMBROSE BIERCE, *The Devil's Dictionary*, p. 259 (1948). Originally published in 1906 as *The Cynic's Word Book*.

1394 [Trying to obtain information from Mr. Mitchell was] Like trying to nail a drop of water to the wall.

Representative GEORGE E. DANIELSON, remark referring to former Attorney General John N. Mitchell's testimony during the Watergate hearings held by the House Judiciary Committee, Washington, D.C., July 10, 1974.—*The New York Times*, July 11, 1974, p. 14.

1395 A garden, you know, is a very usual refuge of a disappointed politician. Accordingly, I have purchased a few acres about nine miles from town, have built a house, and am cultivating a garden.

ALEXANDER HAMILTON, letter to Charles Cotesworth Pinckney, December 29, 1802.—*The Works of Alexander Hamilton*, ed. John C. Hamilton, vol. 6, p. 551 (1851).

1396 I don't believe in labels. I want to do the best I can, all the time. I want to be progressive without getting both feet off the ground at the same time. I want to be prudent without having my mind closed to anything that is new or different. I have often said that I was proud that I was a free man first and an American second, and a public servant third and a Democrat fourth, in that order, and I guess as a Democrat, if I had to take—place a label on myself, I would want to be a progressive who is prudent.

President LYNDON B. JOHNSON, television and radio interview, March 15, 1964.—*Public Papers of the Presidents of the United States: Lyndon B. Johnson, 1963–64*, book 1, p. 368.

1397 "Don't teach my boy poetry," an English mother recently wrote the Provost of Harrow. "Don't teach my boy poetry; he is going to stand for Parliament." Well, perhaps she was right—but if more politicians knew poetry, and more poets knew politics, I am convinced the world would be a little better place to live on this Commencement Day of 1956.

Senator JOHN F. KENNEDY, address to the annual meeting of the Harvard Alumni Association, Cambridge, Massachusetts, June 14, 1956.—Text, pp. 11–12.

1398 [Politicians] are the same all over. They promise to build a bridge even where there is no river.

NIKITA S. KHRUSHCHEV, impromptu remark made during a visit to Belgrade, Yugoslavia, August 21, 1963, as reported by the *New York Herald Tribune,* August 22, 1963, p. 16.

1399 I once said cynically of a politician, "He'll double-cross that bridge when he comes to it."

OSCAR LEVANT, *The Memoirs of an Amnesiac,* p. 13 (1965).

1400 You have to pursue the ideals of a Joan of Arc with the political prowess of an Adam Clayton Powell. Whatever you say about Joan, her purpose was noble. And whatever you say about Adam, his politics is effective; it gets things done he wants done.

BILL D. MOYERS, remarks, conference on the returned Peace Corps volunteer, Washington, D.C., March 5–7, 1965.—*Citizen in a Time of Change: The Returned Peace Corps Volunteer, Report of the Conference,* p. 69 (1965).

1401 In my youth, I, too, entertained some illusions; but I soon recovered from them. The great orators who rule the assemblies by the brilliancy of their eloquence are in general men of the most mediocre political talents: they should not be opposed in their own way; for they have always more noisy words at command than you. Their eloquence should be opposed by a serious and logical argument; their strength lies in vagueness; they should be brought back to the reality of facts; practical arguments destroy them. In the council, there were men possessed of much more eloquence than I was: I always defeated them by this simple argument—*two and two make four.*

NAPOLEON, dictated to Count Montholon to be passed on to Napoleon's son.—Charles-Tristan de Montholon, *History of the Captivity of Napoleon at St. Helena,* vol. 3, p. 187 (1847).

1402 There is no such thing as a nonpolitical speech by a politician.

Vice President RICHARD M. NIXON, address to Radio-Television Executives Society, New York City, September 14, 1955, as reported by *The Christian Science Monitor,* September 15, 1955, p. 6.

This is not in the press release of the speech.

1403 He has been called a mediocre man; but this is unwarranted flattery. He was a politician of monumental littleness.

THEODORE ROOSEVELT, writing of John Tyler, *Thomas Hart Benton,* chapter 11, p. 239 (1897, reprinted 1968).

1404 I was really too honest a man to be a politician and live.

Attributed to SOCRATES, but unverified in his writings or in interpretive writings about him. Possibly this is an interpretation of a passage from Plato, *The Trial and Death of Socrates (The Apology),* trans. F. J. Church, p. 61 (1880, reprinted 1972): "I do not venture to come forward in the assembly, and take part in public councils. . . . For, Athenians, it is quite certain that if I had attempted to take part in politics, I should have perished at once and long ago, without doing any good either to you or to myself. And do not be vexed with me for telling the truth."

Politicians

1405 I'm proud that I'm a politician. A politician is a man who understands government, and it takes a politician to run a government. A statesman is a politician who's been dead 10 or 15 years.

HARRY S. TRUMAN, impromptu remarks before the Reciprocity Club, Washington, D.C., April 11, 1958, as reported by the *New York World-Telegram and Sun*, April 12, 1958, p. 4.

1406 I think politicians and movie actors and movie executives are similar in more ways than they're different. There is an egocentric quality about both; there is a very sensitive awareness of the public attitude, because you live or die on public favor or disfavor. There is the desire for publicity and for acclaim, because, again, that's part of your life. . . . And in a strange and bizarre way, when movie actors come to Washington, they're absolutely fascinated by the politicians. And when the politicians go to Hollywood, they're absolutely fascinated by the movie stars. It's a kind of reciprocity of affection by people who both recognize in a sense they're in the same racket.

JACK VALENTI, special assistant to President Lyndon Johnson, interview on National Public Radio, December 13, 1974. This excerpt was printed in *The Washingtonian*, March 1975, p. 162.

1407 I'm not a politician and my other habits are good. I've no enemys to reward, nor friends to sponge. But I'm a Union man.

ARTEMUS WARD (Charles Farrar Browne), Fourth of July oration delivered at Weathersfield, Connecticut, July 4, 1859.—*The Complete Works of Artemus Ward*, pp. 175–76 (1898).

Bartlett's Familiar Quotations, 15th ed., p. 616, footnote 2 (1980), says the first sentence was a favorite quotation of John F. Kennedy's.

1408 I'd rather keep my promises to other politicians than to God. God, at least, has a degree of forgiveness.

Author unknown.—*The Washington Post*, June 9, 1978, p. C1, quoting a "veteran Virginia Democrat."

Politics

1409 Practical politics consists in ignoring facts.

HENRY ADAMS, *The Education of Henry Adams*, ed. Ernest Samuels, chapter 24, p. 373 (1973). Originally published in 1906.

He was the son of Charles Francis Adams, the grandson of John Quincy Adams, and the great-grandson of John Adams.

1410 People who think the mighty in Washington can be persuaded, or corrupted, if you will, by anything less than votes just don't understand what it's all about and never will. They don't know what Washington juice is made of.

GEORGE E. ALLEN, *Presidents Who Have Known Me*, chapter 16, p. 219 (1950).

Allen was a longtime personal aide to President Harry Truman and was director of the Reconstruction Finance Corporation 1946–1947.

1411 The only way you can do that [decrease taxes, balance the budget, and increase military spending] is with mirrors, and that's what it would take.

Representative JOHN B. ANDERSON, remarks at GOP Presidential Forum, Des Moines, Iowa, January 5, 1980, as reported by the *Des Moines Sunday Register*, January 6, 1980, p. 4A.

1412 PUSH, n. One of the two things mainly conducive to success, especially in politics. The other is Pull.

AMBROSE BIERCE, *The Devil's Dictionary*, p. 270 (1948). Originally published in 1906 as *The Cynic's Word Book*.

1413 Politics is not an exact science.
(Die Politik ist keine exakte Wissenschaft.)

OTTO VON BISMARCK, Prussian Chamber, December 18, 1863.—*The Oxford Dictionary of Quotations*, 3d ed., p. 84 (1979).

1414 Politics is the art of the possible.
(Die Politik ist die Lehre von Moglichen.)

OTTO VON BISMARCK, conversation with Meyer von Waldeck, August 11, 1867.—*The Oxford Dictionary of Quotations*, 3d ed., p. 84 (1979).

1415 All political power is primarily an illusion. . . . Illusion. Mirrors and blue smoke, beautiful blue smoke rolling over the surface of highly polished mirrors, first a thin veil of blue smoke, then a thick cloud that suddenly dissolves into wisps of blue smoke, the mirrors catching it all, bouncing it back and forth.

JIMMY BRESLIN, *How the Good Guys Finally Won, Notes from an Impeachment Summer*, pp. 33–34 (1975).

The phrase is usually quoted as "blue smoke and mirrors."

1416 A political career brings out the basest qualities in human nature.

LORD BRYCE.—Owen Wister, *Roosevelt: The Story of a Friendship*, p. 66 (1930).

This remark was made during a conversation with Wister in London in 1921.

1417 Politics and the pulpit are terms that have little agreement. No sound ought to be heard in the church but the healing voice of Christian charity. The cause of civil liberty and civil government gains as little as that of religion by this confusion of duties. Those who quit their proper character to assume what does not belong to them are, for the greater part, ignorant both of the character they leave and of the character they assume.

EDMUND BURKE, "Reflections on the Revolution in France," 1790, *The Works of the Right Honorable Edmund Burke*, vol. 3, p. 246 (1899).

1418 The pendulum will swing back.

Representative JOSEPH G. CANNON, maxim indicating that in life and politics the things detested today may be praised tomorrow. Quoted in a tribute to Cannon on his retirement, *The Sun*, Baltimore, Maryland, March 4, 1923.—*Congressional Record*, March 4, 1923, vol. 64, p. 5714.

"Uncle Joe" Cannon, who was Speaker of the House 1903–1911, served in the House for 46 years.

1419 Thus, then, on the night of the tenth of May, at the outset of this mighty battle, I acquired the chief power in the State, which henceforth I wielded in ever-growing measure for five years and three months of world war, at the end of which time, all our enemies having surrendered unconditionally or being about to do so, I was immediately dismissed by the British electorate from all further conduct of their affairs.

WINSTON CHURCHILL, *The Gathering Storm* (vol. 1 of *The Second World War*), pp. 666–67 (1948).

However, he was prime minister again, 1951–1955.

1420 Politics ought to be the part-time profession of every citizen who would protect the rights and privileges of free people and who would preserve what is good and fruitful in our national heritage.

President DWIGHT D. EISENHOWER, address recorded for the Republican Lincoln Day dinners, January 28, 1954.—*Public Papers of the Presidents of the United States: Dwight D. Eisenhower, 1954*, p. 219.

1421 The whole aim of practical politics is to keep the populace alarmed (and hence clamorous to be led to safety) by menacing it with an endless series of hobgoblins, all of them imaginary.

H. L. MENCKEN, "Women as Outlaws," *A Mencken Chrestomathy*, p. 29 (1949). This essay was first published in *The Smart Set*, December 1921.

1422 The whole art of politics consists in directing rationally the irrationalities of men.

REINHOLD NIEBUHR.—This statement is attributed to him in his obituary in *The New York Times*, June 2, 1971, p. 45. Unverified.

1423 They are wrong who think that politics is like an ocean voyage or a military campaign, something to be done with some particular end in view, something which leaves off as soon as that end is reached. It is not a public chore, to be got over with. It is a way of life. It is the life of a domesticated political and social creature who is born with a love for public life, with a desire for honor, with a feeling for his fellows; and it lasts as long as need be.

Attributed to PLUTARCH.—*The Great Quotations*, ed. George Seldes, p. 570 (1966). Unverified.

1424 The most practical kind of politics is the politics of decency.

Vice President THEODORE ROOSEVELT, remarks to Harvard and Yale undergraduates invited to Sagamore Hill, Oyster Bay, Long Island, June 1901.—Hermann Hagedorn, *The Roosevelt Family of Sagamore Hill*, p. 112 (1954).

1425 Politics is the practical exercise of the art of self-government, and somebody must attend to it if we are to have self-government; somebody must study it, and learn the art, and exercise patience and sympathy and skill to bring the multitude of opinions and wishes of self-governing people into such order that some prevailing opinion may be expressed and peaceably accepted. Otherwise, confusion will result either in dictatorship or anarchy. The principal ground of reproach against any American citizen should be that he is not a politician. Everyone ought to be, as Lincoln was.

ELIHU ROOT, "Lincoln as a Leader of Men," *Men and Policies, Addresses by Elihu Root*, ed. Robert Bacon and James B. Scott, p. 75 (1924).

1426 Who put up that cage?
Who hung it up with bars, doors?
Why do those on the inside want to get out?
Why do those outside want to get in?
What is this crying inside and out all the time?
What is this endless, useless beating of baffled wings at these bars, doors, this cage?

CARL SANDBURG, "Money, Politics, Love and Glory," *The Complete Poems of Carl Sandburg*, rev. and expanded ed., p. 394 (1970).

1427 Politics is perhaps the only profession for which no preparation is thought necessary.

ROBERT LOUIS STEVENSON, "Yoshida-Torajiro," *Familiar Studies of Men and Books*, p. 175 (1902).

1428 The political activity prevailing in the United States is something one could never understand unless one had seen it. No sooner do you set foot on American soil than you find yourself in a sort of tumult; a confused clamor rises on every side, and a thousand voices are heard at once, each expressing some social requirements. All around you everything is on the move: here the people of a district are assembled to discuss the possibility of building a church; there they are busy choosing a representative; further on, the delegates of a district are hurrying to town to consult about some local improvements; elsewhere it's the village farmers who have left their furrows to discuss the plan for a road or a school.

ALEXIS DE TOCQUEVILLE, *Democracy in America*, ed. J. P. Mayer, trans. George Lawrence, vol. 1, part 2, chapter 6, p. 242 (1969). Originally published in 1835–1840.

1429 There is hardly a political question in the United States which does not sooner or later turn into a judicial one.

ALEXIS DE TOCQUEVILLE, *Democracy in America*, ed. J. P. Mayer, trans. George Lawrence, vol. 1, part 2, chapter 8, p. 270 (1969). Originally published in 1835–1840.

1430 Politics is a fascinating game, because politics is government. It is the art of government.

HARRY S. TRUMAN.—William Hillman, *Mr. President: The First Publication from the Personal Diaries, Private Letters, Papers and Revealing Interviews of Harry S. Truman*, p. 198 (1952).

1431 Politics makes strange bed-fellows.

CHARLES DUDLEY WARNER, *My Summer in a Garden*, 15th week, p. 131 (1871).

1432 Until you've been in politics
you've never really been alive
it's rough and sometimes it's
dirty and it's always hard
work and tedious details
But, it's the only sport for grownups—all other
games are for kids.

— Heinlein

Author unknown. Framed saying on the mantel of Senator John C. Culver's private office, 1978.—Elizabeth Drew, "A Reporter at Large (Senator John C. Culver—part I)," *The New Yorker,* September 11, 1978, p. 60. Disclaimed by Robert A. Heinlein, noted science-fiction author.

Positive thinking

1433 For myself I am an optimist—it does not seem to be much use being anything else.

Prime Minister WINSTON CHURCHILL, speech, Lord Mayor's banquet, London, November 9, 1954.—*Winston S. Churchill: His Complete Speeches, 1897–1963,* ed. Robert Rhodes James, vol. 8, pp. 8603–4 (1974).

1434 Look up and not down;
Look forward and not back;
Look out and not in;
Lend a Hand.

EDWARD EVERETT HALE, motto of the Lend a Hand Society.

The first Lend a Hand Club was founded in 1871, followed by the incorporation of a league of clubs, the Lend a Hand Society, in 1891. Edward E. Hale, who founded the first club in Boston, Massachusetts, later became chaplain to the United States Senate.

See also No. 899.

1435 Keep your face to the sunshine and you cannot see the shadow.

Attributed to HELEN KELLER, inscription in autograph album of Lafayette E. Cornwell, Yonkers, New York.—Walter Fogg, *One Thousand Sayings of History,* p. 17 (1929).

While this sentence has been attributed to Keller several times, Keller experts at the American Federation for the Blind in New York City have never been able to find it.

1436 If you think you are beaten, you are;
If you think you dare not, you don't.
If you'd like to win, but think you can't,
It's almost a cinch you won't.
If you think you'll lose, you're lost,
For out in the world we find
Success begins with a fellow's will;
It's all in the state of mind.

If you think you're outclassed, you are;
You've got to think high to rise.
You've got to be sure of yourself before
You can ever win a prize.
Life's battles don't always go
To the stronger or faster man;
But soon or late the man who wins
Is the one who thinks he can.

WALTER D. WINTLE, "The Man Who Thinks He Can."—*Poems That Live Forever,* comp. Hazel Felleman, p. 310 (1965).

1437 The Post Office Department is like a great root spreading many feet under ground and nourishing the mighty oak. It is the tap root of civilization.

Representative JOSEPH G. CANNON.—L. White Busby, *Uncle Joe Cannon*, p. 294 (1927).

"Uncle Joe" Cannon, who was Speaker of the House from 1903–1911, served in the House for 46 years.

1438 Carrier of news and knowledge
Instrument of trade and industry
Promoter of mutual acquaintance
Of peace and of goodwill
Among men and nations

Messenger of sympathy and love
Servant of parted friends
Consoler of the lonely
Bond of the scattered family
Enlarger of the common life

CHARLES W. ELIOT, revised by Woodrow Wilson, inscriptions on the main Post Office, Washington, D.C.—*Inscriptions Written by Charles William Eliot*, p. 40 (1934).

In 1877 Charles W. Eliot, president of Harvard University 1869-1909, was asked to provide an inscription for a Civil War monument. "The brevity, cogency, and lyric quality of what he wrote . . . won wide acclaim and . . . he was constantly asked to provide inscriptions" until his death in 1926. He achieved considerable "success in this difficult form of composition. . . . it meant not only the happy exercise of his gift for concise and descriptive phrasing, but also appealed to his experience as a mathematician" because the words had to fit particular, sometimes restrictive spaces.

"In 1911, at the close of a long day's work at Northeast Harbor, Maine, Mr. Eliot went out on his boat in company with two or three friends. Presently he produced a scrap of paper and an infinitesimal pencil and began to write. When he had finished, he read aloud the original draft of the two inscriptions for the Post Office at Washington. Possibly he had meditated these inscriptions for some time, but it appeared to those present like an inspiration of the moment. In time they came, unsigned, to the notice of President Wilson who made a few alterations and consigned the inscriptions to the stonecutters. Only later did he learn the name of the author."—Ibid., Foreword by Grace Eliot Dudley, pp. 7, 9.

1439 It is said that as many days as there are in the whole journey, so many are the men and horses that stand along the road, each horse and man at the interval of a day's journey; and these are stayed neither by snow nor rain nor heat nor darkness from accomplishing their appointed course with all speed.

HERODOTUS, *Herodotus*, trans. A. D. Godley, vol. 4, book 8, verse 98, pp. 96–97 (1924).

A paraphrase of this motto—"Neither snow, nor rain, nor heat, nor gloom of night stays these couriers from the swift completion of their appointed rounds"—is carved over the entrance to the central post office building in New York City. The method of carrying messages Herodotus describes was a Persian invention and enabled the messengers to travel swiftly. In this fashion King Xerxes sent a message home to Persia that the Greeks had destroyed his fleet off Salamis in 480 B.C.—George Stimpson, *A Book About a Thousand Things*, pp. 69–70 (1946).

Poverty

1440 This administration today, here and now, declares unconditional war on poverty in America. I urge this Congress and all Americans to join with me in that effort.

President LYNDON B. JOHNSON, State of the Union address, delivered to a joint session of Congress, January 8, 1964.—*Public Papers of the Presidents of the United States: Lyndon B. Johnson, 1963–64*, book 1, p. 114.

1441 It is easy enough to tell the poor to accept their poverty as God's will when you yourself have warm clothes and plenty of food and medical care and a roof over your head and no worry about the rent. But if you want them to believe you—try to share some of their poverty and see if you can accept it as God's will yourself!

THOMAS MERTON, *Seeds of Contemplation*, chapter 14, p. 107 (1949).

1442 The poor in Resurrection City have come to Washington to show that the poor in America are sick, dirty, disorganized, and powerless—and they are criticized daily for being sick, dirty, disorganized, and powerless.

CALVIN TRILLIN, "U.S. Journal: Resurrection City," *The New Yorker*, June 15, 1968, p. 71.

Power

1443 Power tends to corrupt and absolute power corrupts absolutely. Great men are almost always bad men, even when they exercise influence and not authority: still more when you superadd the tendency or the certainty of corruption by authority.

LORD ACTON, letter to Mandell Creighton, April 5, 1887.—Acton, *Essays on Freedom and Power*, ed. Gertrude Himmelfarb, pp. 335–36 (1972).

1444 There is no worse heresy than that the office sanctifies the holder of it.

LORD ACTON, letter to Mandell Creighton, April 5, 1887.—Acton, *Essays on Freedom and Power*, ed. Gertrude Himmelfarb, p. 336 (1972).

1445 We have, in truth, resorted to power [in Cuba, the Dominican Republic, Vietnam] because our politics has failed. Since no politician can afford to admit this, we must pretend that we are resorting to power in order to make our politics succeed.

THEODORE DRAPER, *Abuse of Power*, p. 164 (1967).

1446 In the main it will be found that a power over a man's support [salary] is a power over his will.

ALEXANDER HAMILTON, *The Federalist*, ed. Benjamin F. Wright, no. 73, p. 468 (1961).

1447 More power than any good man should want, and more power than any other kind of man ought to have.

Senator DANIEL O. HASTINGS, remark in the Senate on the power to be given President Franklin D. Roosevelt by the proposed work-relief program, March 23, 1935. Hastings said the bill as passed by the House was remarkable in two ways. "First, the huge amount involved, it being probably the largest appropriation ever made by any legislative body. Second, the amount was not only shocking to the average American citizen, but what was more alarming was the fact that its expenditure was left entirely in the discretion of the Executive."—*Congressional Record*, vol. 79, p. 4353.

Hastings's remark repeats the sound of words made famous in an exchange in the Senate between Senators Lucius Q. C. Lamar of Mississippi and Roscoe Conkling of New York. Conkling, whose arrogance made him unpopular, was humiliated by Lamar, who was considered one of the coolest, most courteous members of the Senate. Lamar's reputation for self-control gave his words an added sting. Conkling said that if Lamar charged him with falsehood outside the Senate, he would denounce him as a blackguard, a coward, and a liar.

Lamar responded: "Mr. President, I have only to say that the Senator from New York understood me correctly. I did mean to say just precisely the words, and all that they imported. I beg pardon of the Senate for the unparliamentary language. It was very harsh; it was very severe; it was such as no good man would deserve, and no brave man would wear." Though Conkling had served notice that he would attend to the insult at some other time, he never did, and his prestige was lost. He resigned from the Senate two years later.—*Congressional Record*, June 18, 1879, vol. 9, p. 2144. Also see Wirt Armistead Cate, *Lucius Q. C. Lamar*, pp. 348–58 (1932, reprinted 1969).

1448 There are similarities between absolute power and absolute faith: a demand for absolute obedience, a readiness to attempt the impossible, a bias for simple solutions—to cut the knot rather than unravel it, the viewing of compromise as surrender. Both absolute power and absolute faith are instruments of dehumanization. Hence, absolute faith corrupts as absolutely as absolute power.

ERIC HOFFER, "Thoughts of Eric Hoffer, Including: 'Absolute Faith Corrupts Absolutely,' " *The New York Times Magazine*, April 25, 1971, p. 24.

1449 From this we learn that a wise prince sees to it that never, in order to attack someone, does he become the ally of a prince more powerful than himself, except when necessity forces him, as I said above. If you win, you are the powerful king's prisoner, and wise princes avoid as much as they can being in other men's power.

NICCOLÒ MACHIAVELLI, *The Prince*, chapter 21, in *Machiavelli: The Chief Works and Others*, trans. Allan Gilbert, vol. 1, pp. 83–84 (1965).

1450 The essence of Government is power; and power, lodged as it must be in human hands, will ever be liable to abuse.

JAMES MADISON, speech in the Virginia constitutional convention, Richmond, Virginia, December 2, 1829.—*The Writings of James Madison*, ed. Gaillard Hunt, vol. 9, p. 361 (1910).

These words are inscribed in the Madison Memorial Hall, Library of Congress James Madison Memorial Building.

1451 Every Communist must grasp the truth: "Political power grows out of the barrel of a gun."

MAO TSE-TUNG, concluding speech at the sixth plenary session of the Central Committee, Communist party, China, November 6, 1938.—Mao, *Selected Works*, vol. 2, p. 272 (1954).

1452 Beware of the man who rises to power
From one suspender.

EDGAR LEE MASTERS, "John Hancock Otis," *Spoon River Anthology*, p. 123 (1915, reprinted 1916).

In this poem, the rich John Hancock Otis describes a man "born in a shanty and beginning life as a water carrier . . . then section hand . . . afterwards foreman . . . who rose to the superintendency of the railroad" as "a veritable slave driver, grinding the faces of labor, and a bitter enemy of democracy."

1453 The power of Kings and Magistrates is nothing else, but what is only derivative, transferr'd and committed to them in trust from the People, to the Common good of them all, in whom the power yet remaines fundamentally, and cannot be tak'n from them, without a violation of thir natural birthright.

JOHN MILTON, "The Tenure of Kings," *The Works of John Milton*, vol. 5, p. 10 (1932).

1454 For we put the power in the people.

WILLIAM PENN.—Robert Proud, *The History of Pennsylvania in North America*, vol. 1, p. 139 (1797).

1455 They realize that in thirty-four months we have built up new instruments of public power. In the hands of a people's Government this power is wholesome and proper. But in the hands of political puppets of an economic autocracy such power would provide shackles for the liberties of the people.

President FRANKLIN D. ROOSEVELT, annual message to the Congress, January 3, 1936.—*The Public Papers and Addresses of Franklin D. Roosevelt, 1936*, p. 16 (1938).

1456 Every institution which grapples with the problem of molding recalcitrant material into a fairer shape—and nothing is more recalcitrant than the passions and interests of men—runs the risk of being defeated by its material. And since the institution which proposes the ideal is itself served by fallible human beings, the danger is not only that the experiment may fail but that the artists themselves, wrestling with such insidious substances as power, responsibility, and material goods, may themselves be caught by these powerful instincts, may appropriate to themselves the power they sought to tame or the riches they had hoped to divert to a nobler cause.

BARBARA WARD, *Faith and Freedom*, chapter 7, p. 94 (1954).

1457 My cool judgement is, that if all the other doctrines of devils which have been committed to writing since letters were in the world were collected together in one volume, it would fall short of this; and that, should a Prince form himself by this book, so calmly recommending hypocrisy, treachery, lying, robbery, oppression, adultery, whoredom, and murder of all kinds, Domitian or Nero would be an angel of light compared to that man.

JOHN WESLEY, comment after reading *The Works of Nicholas Machiavel*, journal entry for January 26, 1737.—*The Journal of the Rev. John Wesley, A.M.*, ed. Nehemiah Curnock, vol. 1, p. 313 (1909).

1458 When I resist, therefore, when I as a Democrat resist the concentration of power, I am resisting the processes of death, because the concentration of power is what always precedes the destruction of human initiative, and, therefore of human energy.

WOODROW WILSON, governor of New Jersey, speech, New York City, September 4, 1912.—*The Papers of Woodrow Wilson*, ed. Arthur S. Link, vol. 25, p. 100 (1978).

This speech was delivered to the Woodrow Wilson Workingmen's League "dollar dinner," at the Yorkville Casino.

1459 It is not for minds like ours to give or to receive flattery; yet the praises of sincerity have ever been permitted to the voice of friendship.

GEORGE GORDON, LORD BYRON, "Childe Harold's Pilgrimage," canto 4, dedication, *The Complete Poetical Works of Lord Byron,* ed. Paul E. More, p. 54 (1905).

1460 I am about courting a girl I have had but little acquaintance with. How shall I come to a knowledge of her faults, and whether she has the virtues I imagine she has? *Answer.* Commend her among her female acquaintance.

BENJAMIN FRANKLIN, "Miscellaneous Observations," *The Works of Benjamin Franklin,* ed. Jared Sparks, vol. 2, p. 550 (1836).

1461 He who praises every body, praises nobody.

Attributed to SAMUEL JOHNSON, "Johnsoniana," *The European Magazine and London Review,* January 1785, p. 55.

The anecdote which quotes this line was reprinted in *The Works of Samuel Johnson,* vol. 11 *(Apophthegms, Sentiments, Opinions and Occasional Reflections),* p. 216 (1787). According to George Birkbeck Hill, *Johnsonian Miscellanies,* vol. 2, pp. 1, 312 (1897, reprinted 1966), the author of this anecdote was George Steevens.

Prayers

1462 I Pray Heaven to Bestow The Best of Blessing on THIS HOUSE, and on All that shall hereafter Inhabit it. May none but Honest and Wise Men ever rule under This Roof!

President JOHN ADAMS, letter to his wife Abigail, November 2, 1800, the day after he moved into the White House.—*Letters of John Adams Addressed to His Wife,* ed. Charles Francis Adams, p. 267 (1841).

President Franklin D. Roosevelt had this lettered in gold in the marble over the fireplace in the State Dining Room of the White House. The quotation above follows the capitalization used in the inscription.

1463 Grant us a common faith that man shall know bread and peace—that he shall know justice and righteousness, freedom and security, an equal opportunity and an equal chance to do his best not only in our own lands, but throughout the world. And in that faith let us march toward the clean world our hands can make.

STEPHEN VINCENT BENÉT, *Prayer,* concluding sentences (1942).

Archibald MacLeish, poet and Librarian of Congress, asked Benét to write "The United Nations Prayer" to be used in the celebration of Flag Day, 1942. President Franklin D. Roosevelt used it to close his radio address on Flag Day, June 14, 1942. Adlai E. Stevenson used this final section of the prayer on his Christmas cards in 1964.

1464 For Mercy has a human heart
Pity, a human face:
And Love, the human form divine,
And Peace, the human dress.

Then every man of every clime,
That prays in his distress,
Prays to the human form divine
Love Mercy Pity Peace.

WILLIAM BLAKE, "The Divine Image," stanzas 3 and 4, lines 9–16, *The Complete Poetry and Prose of William Blake*, ed. David V. Erdman, pp. 12–13 (1982). First published in 1789.

1465 "God bless us every one!" said Tiny Tim, the last of all.

CHARLES DICKENS, *A Christmas Carol*, stave 3, p. 74 (1963). First published in 1843.

1466 Lord, make me a channel of your peace.
Where there is hatred, let me bring love.
Where there is offense, forgiveness.
Where there is discord, reconciliation.
Where there is doubt, faith.
Where there is despair, hope.
Where there is sadness, joy.
Where there is darkness, your light.
If we give, we are made rich.
If we forget ourselves, we find peace.
If we forgive, we receive forgiveness.
If we die, we receive eternal resurrection.
Give us peace, Lord.

Attributed to ST. FRANCIS of Assisi.—Auspicius van Corstanje, *Francis: Bible of the Poor*, p. 203 (1977).

"This prayer cannot be found in any of the early texts written by Francis. In its present form, it is probably not even a hundred years old. All the same, it clearly reflects the spirit of Francis. He *could* have written it, and that is why it is generally attributed to him" (p. 203). A slightly different version ("Lord, make me an instrument of thy peace") can be found in *Masterpieces of Religious Verse*, ed. James Dalton Morrison, p. 130 (1948).

1467 There is nothing I can give you which you have not got; but there is much, very much, that, while I cannot give it, you can take. No Heaven can come to us unless our hearts find rest in it to-day. Take Heaven! No peace lies in the future which is not hidden in this present little instant. Take peace!

The gloom of the world is but a shadow. Behind it, yet within our reach, is joy. There is radiance and glory in the darkness, could we but see; and to see, we have only to look. Contessina I beseech you to look.

Life is so generous a giver, but we, judging its gifts by their covering, cast them away as ugly or heavy or hard. Remove the covering, and you will find beneath it a living splendour, woven of love, by wisdom, with power. Welcome it, grasp it, and you touch the Angel's hand that brings it to you. Everything we call a trial, a sorrow, or a duty: believe me, that angel's hand is there; the gift is there, and the wonder of an overshadowing Presence. Our joys, too: be not content with them as joys, they too conceal diviner gifts.

Life is so full of meaning and of purpose, so full of beauty—beneath its covering—that you will find that earth but cloaks your heaven. Courage, then to claim it: that is all! But courage you have; and the knowledge that we are pilgrims together, wending through unknown country, home.

And so, at this Christmas time, I greet you; not quite as the world sends greetings, but with profound esteem, and with the prayer that for you, now and forever, the day breaks and the shadows flee away.

FRA GIOVANNI, *A Letter to the Most Illustrious the Contessina Allagia Dela Aldobrandeschi, Written Christmas Eve Anno Domini 1513* (193?)

The British Museum stated in 1970 that it had "proved impossible" to identify Fra Giovanni, the purported author of this letter. This was published, probably in the 1930s, "with Christmas Greetings" from Greville MacDonald, son of novelist George MacDonald, and Mary MacDonald.

1468 Almighty God, who hast given us this good land for our heritage; We humbly beseech Thee that we may always prove ourselves a people mindful of Thy favor and glad to do Thy will. Bless our land with honourable industry, sound learning, and pure manners. Save us from violence, discord, and confusion; from pride and arrogancy, and from every evil way. Defend our liberties, and fashion into one united people the multitudes brought hither out of many kindreds and tongues. Endure with the spirit of wisdom those to whom in Thy Name we entrust the authority of government, that there may be justice and peace at home, and that, through obedience to Thy law, we may show forth Thy praise among the nations of the earth. In the time of prosperity, fill our hearts with thankfulness, and in the day of trouble, suffer not our trust in Thee to fail; Amen.

GEORGE L. LOCKE, prayer, c. 1880.

President Franklin D. Roosevelt included it as "an old prayer" without attribution, in his final radio speech of the 1940 presidential campaign, November 4, 1940.—*The Public Papers and Addresses of Franklin D. Roosevelt, 1940*, pp. 557–58 (1941). *Life* magazine reproduced the prayer in its issue of November 18, 1940, and in a letter to the editor in the December 9 issue, p. 4, the Rev. Mr. Locke's daughter wrote about his authorship and the circumstances of his composing the prayer.

1469 Build me a son, O Lord, who will be strong enough to know when he is weak, and brave enough to face himself when he is afraid; one who will be proud and unbending in honest defeat, and humble and gentle in victory. Build me a son whose wishes will not take the place of deeds; a son who will know Thee—and that to know himself is the foundation stone of knowledge. Lead him, I pray, not in the path of ease and comfort, but under the stress and spur of difficulties and challenge. Here let him learn to stand up in the storm; here let him learn compassion for those who fail. Build me a son whose heart will be clear, whose goal will be high; a son who will master himself before he seeks to master other men; one who will reach into the future, yet never forget the past. And after all these things are his, add, I pray, enough of a sense of humor, so that he may always be serious, yet never take himself too seriously. Give him humility, so that he may always remember the simplicity of true greatness, the open mind of true wisdom, and the meekness of true strength. Then, I, his father, will dare to whisper, "I have not lived in vain."

General DOUGLAS MACARTHUR, "A Father's Prayer."—Courtney Whitney, *MacArthur, His Rendevous with History*, p. 547 (1956).

Written "during the early days of the desperate campaigns in the Far East in World War II."

1470 Our earnest prayer is that God will graciously vouchsafe prosperity, happiness, and peace to all our neighbors, and like blessings to all the peoples and powers of earth.

President WILLIAM MCKINLEY, speech delivered at the Pan-American Exposition, Buffalo, New York, September 5, 1901.—*Modern Eloquence*, ed. Ashley H. Thorndike, rev. Adam Ward, vol. 11, p. 401 (1936).

This was McKinley's last speech, as he was mortally wounded the next day at the Exposition. He served in Congress 1877–1884 and 1885–1891.

1471 The things, good Lord, that I pray for, give me thy grace to labour for. Amen.

SIR THOMAS MORE, *English Prayers and Treatise on the Holy Eucharist*, ed. Philip E. Hallett, p. 20 (1938). His English works were published in 1557.

1472 God give me the serenity to accept things which cannot be changed;
Give me courage to change things which must be changed;
And the wisdom to distinguish one from the other.

Attributed to REINHOLD NIEBUHR.—*The A.A. Grapevine*, January 1950, pp. 6–7; also June Bingham, *Courage to Change*, p. iii (1961), where the version differs somewhat: "O God, give us serenity to accept what cannot be changed, courage to change what should be changed, and wisdom to distinguish the one from the other."

Alcoholics Anonymous has used this prayer, with minor changes in wording, since about 1940. According to the first source, Dr. Niebuhr said, "It may have been spooking around for years, even centuries, but I don't think so. I honestly do believe that I wrote it myself."

The Anglican publishing house, Mobray of London, for more than a century has identified it as a General or Common Prayer of fourteenth-century England, according to a reader of *American Notes and Queries*, June 1970, p. 154. He added that "Reinhold Niebuhr has acknowledged, more than once, both in seminar and publicly that he was *not* the original author of the Serenity Prayer."

In *Ausblick von der Weibertreu* by Christoph Duncker, p. 1 (1973), the following lines are attributed to a Johann Christoph Oetinger, deacon in Weinsberg from 1762 to 1769: "Gib mir Gelassenheit, Dinge hinzunehmen, die ich nicht ändern kann, Den Mut, Dinge zu ändern, die ich ändern kann, und die Weisheit, das eine vom andern zu untersheiden," which can be translated as above. Another reader of *American Notes and Queries*, October 1969, p. 25, gives a nearly identical quotation and states that it can be traced to Friedrich Christoph Oetinger (1702–1782), German theologian and theosophist, without giving a source.

Whatever the original source or wording, Niebuhr and A.A. have made the prayer well-known in the United States.

1473 Almighty and most merciful Father, we humbly beseech Thee, of Thy great goodness, to restrain these immoderate rains with which we have had to contend. Grant us fair weather for Battle. Graciously hearken to us as soldiers who call upon Thee that, armed with Thy power, we may advance from victory to victory, and crush the oppression and wickedness of our enemies, and establish Thy justice among men and nations. Amen.

Colonel JAMES H. O'NEILL, prayer for good weather, December 1944.—Ladislas Farago, *Patton, Ordeal and Triumph*, chapter 36, p. 690 (1964).

General George S. Patton, Jr., ordered Colonel O'Neill, chaplain of the Third Army, to produce this prayer.

1474 Stars above our cornfields,
Morning-colored wind,
Snow, and wood-fires burning
On hearths we leave behind.
(Shine for us, dear beacons.)

God of the hidden purpose,
Let our embarking be
The prayer of proud men asking
Not to be safe, but free.

HENRY MORTON ROBINSON, "Litany for D-Day: 1944," stanzas 4 and 5, *The Enchanted Grindstone and Other Poems*, p. 93 (1952).

1475 Give us courage and gaiety and the quiet mind. Spare to us our friends, soften to us our enemies. Bless us, if it may be, in all our innocent endeavors. If it may not, give us the strength to encounter that which is to come, that we be brave in peril, constant in tribulation, temperate in wrath, and in all changes of fortune and down to the gates of death, loyal and loving one to another.

ROBERT LOUIS STEVENSON, prayer "For Success," *Vailima Papers and a Footnote to History*, p. 7 (1925).

This was used by Adlai E. Stevenson on his Christmas card in 1962.

1476 I now make it my earnest prayer, that God would have you, and the State over which you preside, in his holy protection, that he would incline the hearts of the Citizens to cultivate a spirit of subordination and obedience to Government, to entertain a brotherly affection and love for one another, for their fellow Citizens of the United States at large, and particularly for their brethren who have served in the Field, and finally, that he would most graciously be pleased to dispose us all, to do Justice, to love mercy, and to demean [i.e., comport] ourselves with that Charity, humility and pacific temper of mind, which were the Characteristicks of the Divine Author of our blessed Religion, and without an humble imitation of whose example in these things, we can never hope to be a happy Nation.

General GEORGE WASHINGTON, circular to the states, Newburgh, New York, June 8, 1783.—*The Writings of George Washington*, ed. John C. Fitzpatrick, vol. 26, p. 496 (1938).

1477 I asked God for strength, that I might achieve
I was made weak, that I might learn humbly to obey . . .
I asked for health, that I might do greater things
I was given infirmity, that I might do better things . . .
I asked for riches, that I might be happy
I was given poverty, that I might be wise . . .
I asked for power, that I might have the praise of men
I was given weakness, that I might feel the need of God . . .
I asked for all things, that I might enjoy life
I was given life that I might enjoy all things . . .
I got nothing that I asked for—but everything I had hoped for
Almost despite myself, my unspoken prayers were answered.
I am, among all men, most richly blessed.

Author unknown.

As "A Creed for Those Who Have Suffered," this has been used by rehabilitation centers. Adlai E. Stevenson used these lines on his Christmas card, 1955.

1478 May the road rise to meet you.
May the wind be ever at your back
May the Good Lord keep you in the hollow of His hand.
May your heart be as warm as your hearthstone.
And when you come to die
may the wail of the poor
be the only sorrow
you'll leave behind.
May God bless you always.

Author unknown, "An Irish Wish."—Ralph L. Woods, *A Third Treasury of the Familiar,* p. 644 (1970).

Another version of this popular Irish blessing:

May the road rise to meet you,
May the wind be always at your back,
May the sun shine warm upon your face,
May the rain fall soft upon your fields,
And, until we meet again,
May God hold you in the palm of His hand.

1479 O God, thy sea is so great, and my boat is so small.

Author unknown. Prayer of Breton fishermen.

President John F. Kennedy had on his desk a plaque with these words, given to him by Admiral Hyman Rickover, who gave one like it to the commanding officer of each new Polaris submarine.—Tazewell Taylor Shepard, Jr., *John F. Kennedy, Man of the Sea,* p. 23 (1965).

1480 Slow me down, Lord! Ease the pounding of my heart by the quieting of my mind. Steady my hurried pace with a vision of the eternal reach of time. Give me, amidst the confusion of my day, the calmness of the everlasting hills. Break the tensions of my nerves and muscles with the soothing music of singing streams that live in my memory. Teach me the art of taking minute vacations . . . of slowing down to look at a flower, to chat with a friend, to pat a dog, to read a few lines from a good book. Remind me each day of the fable of the hare and the tortoise, that I may know that the race is not always to the swift; that there is more to life than measuring its speed. Let me look upward into the branches of the towering oak and know that it grew great and strong because it grew slowly and well. Slow me down, Lord, and inspire me to send my roots deep into the soil of life's enduring values that I may grow toward the stars of my greater destiny.

Author unknown.

Prejudice

1481 We are all citizens of one world, we are all of one blood. To hate a man because he was born in another country, because he speaks a different language, or because he takes a different view on this subject or that, is a great folly. Desist, I implore you, for we are all equally human. . . . Let us have but one end in view, the welfare of humanity.

Attributed to JOHANN AMOS COMENIUS.—Laurence J. Peter, *Peter's Quotations,* p. 76 (1977).

This passage was used by Adlai E. Stevenson on his Christmas card in 1961.

1482 We are a nation of many nationalities, many races, many religions—bound together by a single unity, the unity of freedom and equality. Whoever seeks to set one nationality against another, seeks to degrade all nationalities. Whoever seeks to set one race against another seeks to enslave all races. Whoever seeks to set one religion against another, seeks to destroy all religion.

President FRANKLIN D. ROOSEVELT, campaign address, Brooklyn, New York, November 1, 1940.—*The Public Papers and Addresses of Franklin D. Roosevelt, 1940,* p. 537 (1941).

1483 Sex prejudice is so ingrained in our society that many who practice it are simply unaware that they are hurting women. *It is the last socially acceptable prejudice.*

BERNICE SANDLER, testimony, June 19, 1970.—*Discrimination Against Women,* hearings before the special subcommittee on education of the Committee on Education and Labor, House of Representatives, 91st Congress, 2d session, part 1, p. 302 (1970).

She was chairman of the Action Committee for Federal Contract Compliance in Education of the Women's Equity Action League.

1484 Consider: if you incorporate those tropical countries with the Republic of the United States, you will have to incorporate their people too.

Senator CARL SCHURZ, remarks in the Senate on the annexation of San Domingo, January 11, 1871, *The Congressional Globe,* vol. 43, p. 26.

Presidency

1485 PRESIDENT, n. The leading figure in a small group of men of whom—and of whom only—it is positively known that immense numbers of their countrymen did not want any of them for President.

AMBROSE BIERCE, *The Devil's Dictionary,* p. 266 (1948). Originally published in 1906 as *The Cynic's Word Book.*

1486 I thought a lot about our Nation and what I should do as President. And Sunday night before last, I made a speech about two problems of our country—energy and malaise.

President JIMMY CARTER, remarks at a town meeting, Bardstown, Kentucky, July 31, 1979.—*Public Papers of the Presidents of the United States: Jimmy Carter, 1979,* book 2, p. 1340.

Carter was referring to the speech on energy and national goals broadcast from the White House on July 15. He did not use the term "malaise" in that earlier speech.

1487 The cheek of every American must tingle with shame as he reads the silly, flat, and dish-watery utterances of the man who has to be pointed out to intelligent foreigners as President of the United States.

Attributed to *The Chicago Times,* following President Abraham Lincoln's address at Gettysburg on November 19, 1863.—Carl Sandburg, *Abraham Lincoln: The War Years,* vol. 2, p. 472 (1939); no date of issue for the *Times* is given.

This quotation also appears in Robert S. Harper, *Lincoln and the Press,* chapter 33, p. 287 (1951), but he also gives no specific date for the *Times,* citing only Sandburg. This same quotation and attribution is used in Gore Vidal, *Lincoln,* part 3, chapter 2, p. 494 (1984, reprinted 1985). This quotation could not be found in *The Chicago Times,* November 20–25, 1863.

1488 And still the question, "What shall be done with our ex-Presidents?" is not laid at rest; and I sometimes think Watterson's solution of it, "Take them out and shoot them," is worthy of attention.

GROVER CLEVELAND, letter to William F. Vilas, April 19, 1889.—*Letters of Grover Cleveland, 1850–1908,* ed. Allan Nevins, p. 204 (1933).

Henry Watterson, editor of the Louisville, Kentucky, *Courier-Journal* for fifty years, feared that a president's ambitions would lead him to seek a third term and then life tenancy. Because any other position after the presidency would seem anticlimactic, Watterson believed the country was not safe from any president while he was alive. He especially worried about Theodore Roosevelt, a young president who greatly enjoyed the presidency, and he frequently editorialized on this theme during Roosevelt's second term, though the remark was facetious.—Joseph Henry Wall, *Henry Watterson*, pp. 254–55 (1956).

1489 But I believe this: by and large, the United States ought to be able to choose for its President anybody that it wants, regardless of the number of terms he has served. That is what I believe. Now, some people have said "You let him get enough power and this will lead toward a one-party government." That, I don't believe. I have got the utmost faith in the long-term common sense of the American people. Therefore, I don't think there should be any inhibitions other than those that were in the 35-year age limit and so on. I think that was enough, myself.

President DWIGHT D. EISENHOWER, answer to question seeking his views on limiting U.S. presidents to two terms, news conference, Washington, D.C., October 5, 1956.—*Public Papers of the Presidents of the United States: Dwight D. Eisenhower, 1956*, p. 862.

1490 I do believe that the buck stops here, that I cannot rely upon public opinion polls to tell me what is right. I do believe that right makes might and that if I am wrong, 10 angels swearing I was right would make no difference. I do believe, with all my heart and mind and spirit, that I, not as President but as a humble servant of God, will receive justice without mercy if I fail to show mercy.

President GERALD R. FORD, announcing his decision to pardon Richard Nixon, September 8, 1974.—*Public Papers of the Presidents of the United States: Gerald R. Ford, 1974*, p. 103.

See also No. 1610.

1491 I once told you that I am not a saint, and I hope never to see the day that I cannot admit having made a mistake. So I will close with another confession. Frequently, along the tortuous road of recent months from this chamber to the President's House, I protested that I was my own man. Now I realize that I was wrong. I am your man, for it was your carefully weighed confirmation that changed my occupation. The truth is I am the people's man, for you acted in their name, and I accepted and began my new and solemn trust with a promise to serve all the people and do the best that I can for America.

President GERALD R. FORD, address to a joint session of Congress, August 12, 1974.—*Public Papers of the Presidents of the United States: Gerald R. Ford, 1974.*, p. 13.

1492 If you have not chosen me by secret ballot, neither have I gained office by any secret promises. I have not campaigned either for the Presidency or the Vice Presidency. I have not subscribed to any partisan platform. I am indebted to no man, and only to one woman—my dear wife—as I begin this very difficult job.

President GERALD R. FORD, remarks on taking the oath of office, August 9, 1974.—*Public Papers of the Presidents of the United States: Gerald R. Ford, 1974*, p. 1.

1493 The second office of this government is honorable & easy, the first is but a splendid misery.

Vice President THOMAS JEFFERSON, letter to Elbridge Gerry, May 13, 1797.—*The Writings of Thomas Jefferson*, ed. Paul L. Ford, vol. 7, p. 120 (1896).

1494 And so it is that I carry with me from this State to that high and lonely office to which I now succeed more than fond memories and fast friendships. The enduring qualities of Massachusetts—the common threads woven by the Pilgrim and the Puritan, the fisherman and the farmer, the Yankee and the immigrant—will not be and could not be forgotten in the Nation's Executive Mansion. They are an indelible part of my life, my convictions, my view of the past, my hopes for the future.

President-elect JOHN F. KENNEDY, address to the Massachusetts legislature, January 9, 1961.—*Congressional Record,* January 10, 1961, vol. 107, Appendix, p. A169.

For another portion of this address, see No. 1611.

1495 Allow the President to invade a neighboring nation, whenever *he* shall deem it necessary to repel an invasion, and you allow him to do so, *whenever he may choose to say* he deems it necessary for such purpose—and you allow him to make war at pleasure. Study to see if you can fix *any limit* to his power in this respect, after you have given him so much as you propose. If, to-day, he should choose to say he thinks it necessary to invade Canada, to prevent the British from invading us, how could you stop him? You may say to him, "I see no probability of the British invading us" but he will say to you "be silent; I see it, if you dont."

The provision of the Constitution giving the war-making power to Congress, was dictated, as I understand it, by the following reasons. Kings had always been involving and impoverishing their people in wars, pretending generally, if not always, that the good of the people was the object. This, our Convention understood to be the most oppressive of all Kingly oppressions; and they resolved to so frame the Constitution that *no one man* should hold the power of bringing this oppression upon us. But your view destroys the whole matter, and places our President where kings have always stood.

Representative ABRAHAM LINCOLN, letter to William H. Herndon, February 15, 1848.—*The Collected Works of Abraham Lincoln,* ed. Roy P. Basler, vol. 1, pp. 451–52 (1953).

1496 In a certain sense, and to a certain extent, he [the president] is the representative of the people. He is elected by them, as well as congress is. But can he, in the nature [of] things, know the wants of the people, as well as three hundred other men, coming from all the various localities of the nation? If so, where is the propriety of having a congress?

Representative ABRAHAM LINCOLN, remarks in the House, July 27, 1848.—*The Collected Works of Abraham Lincoln,* ed. Roy P. Basler, vol. 1, p. 504 (1953).

1497 My friends— . . . I now leave, not knowing when, or whether ever, I may return, with a task before me greater than that which rested upon Washington. Without the assistance of that Divine Being, who ever attended him, I cannot succeed. With that assistance, I cannot fail.

President-elect ABRAHAM LINCOLN, farewell address at Springfield, Illinois, February 11, 1861.—*The Collected Works of Abraham Lincoln,* ed. Roy P. Basler, vol. 4, p. 190 (1953).

"W. H. Lamon, who witnessed this scene of farewell, says: 'having reached the train he [Lincoln] ascended the rear platform, and, facing the throng which had closed around him, drew himself up to his full height, removed his hat, and stood for several seconds in profound silence. . . . There was an unusual quiver on his lip, and a still more unusual tear on his furrowed cheek. . . . At length he began in a husky tone of voice, and slowly and impressively delivered his farewell to his neighbors. Imitating his example, every man in the crowd stood with his head uncovered in the fast-falling rain.' "—*Complete Works of Abraham Lincoln,* new and enl. ed., ed. John G. Nicolay and John Hay, vol. 6, p. 110 (1905).

1498 You have heard the story, haven't you, about the man who was tarred and feathered and carried out of town on a rail? A man in the crowd asked him how he liked it. His reply was that if it was not for the honor of the thing, he would much rather walk.

President ABRAHAM LINCOLN, response to a friend from Springfield asking how he liked being president, c. 1861.—Emanuel Hertz, *Lincoln Talks: A Biography in Anecdote*, pp. 258–59 (1939).

1499 Franklin D. Roosevelt is no crusader. He is no tribune of the people. He is no enemy of entrenched privilege. He is a pleasant man who, without any important qualifications for the office, would very much like to be President.

WALTER LIPPMANN, *Interpretations, 1931–1932*, ed. Allan Nevins, p. 262 (1932).

1500 I think it absolutely necessary that the President should have the power of removing [his subordinates] from office; it will make him, in a peculiar manner, responsible for their conduct, and subject him to impeachment himself, if he suffers them to perpetrate with impunity high crimes or misdemeanors against the United States, or neglects to superintend their conduct, so as to check their excesses.

Representative JAMES MADISON, remarks in the House, May 19, 1789, *Annals of Congress*, vol. 1, col. 387.

1501 "Why would *anyone* want to be President today?" The answer is not one of glory, or fame; today the burdens of the office outweigh its privileges. It's not because the Presidency offers a chance to *be* somebody, but because it offers a chance to *do* something.

RICHARD M. NIXON, television address on NBC and CBS, September 19, 1968.—*Nixon Speaks Out, Major Speeches and Statements . . . in the Presidential Campaign of 1968*, p. 1 (1968).

1502 When I am the candidate, I run the campaign.

President RICHARD M. NIXON, remarks during an interview with representatives of the television networks, January 4, 1971.—*Public Papers of the Presidents of the United States: Richard Nixon, 1971*, p. 21.

1503 Representative William McK. Springer, remarks in the House, quoting Henry Clay: "As for me, I would rather be right than be President."

Reed: "Well, the gentleman will never be either."

Representative THOMAS B. REED.—Samuel W. McCall, *The Life of Thomas Brackett Reed*, chapter 21, p. 246 (1914).

1504 The Presidency is not merely an administrative office. That's the least of it. It is more than an engineering job, efficient or inefficient. It is pre-eminently a place of moral leadership. All our great Presidents were leaders of thought at times when certain historic ideas in the life of the nation had to be clarified.

FRANKLIN D. ROOSEVELT, governor of New York, as reported by *The New York Times Magazine*, September 11, 1932, p. 2.

1505 My view was that every executive officer, and above all every executive officer in high position, was a steward of the people bound actively and affirmatively to do all he could for the people, and not to content himself with the negative merit of keeping his talents undamaged in a napkin. I declined to adopt the view that what was imperatively necessary for the Nation could not be done by the President unless he could find some specific authorization to do it. My belief was that it was not only his right but his duty to do anything that the needs of the Nation demanded unless such action was forbidden by the Constitution or by the laws. Under this interpretation of executive power I did and caused to be done many things not previously done by the President and the heads of the departments. I did not usurp power, but I did greatly broaden the use of executive power. In other words, I acted for the public welfare, I acted for the common well-being of all our people, whenever and in whatever manner was necessary, unless prevented by direct constitutional or legislative prohibition.

THEODORE ROOSEVELT, *Theodore Roosevelt, An Autobiography* (vol. 20 of *The Works of Theodore Roosevelt,* national ed.), chapter 10, pp. 347–48 (1926).

1506 Our loyalty is due entirely to the United States. It is due to the President only and exactly to the degree in which he efficiently serves the United States. It is our duty to support him when he serves the United States well. It is our duty to oppose him when he serves it badly. This is true about Mr. Wilson now and it has been true about all our Presidents in the past. It is our duty at all times to tell the truth about the President and about every one else, save in the cases where to tell the truth at the moment would benefit the public enemy.

THEODORE ROOSEVELT, "Lincoln and Free Speech," *The Great Adventure* (vol. 19 of *The Works of Theodore Roosevelt,* national ed.), chapter 7, p. 297 (1926).

1507 The President is merely the most important among a large number of public servants. He should be supported or opposed exactly to the degree which is warranted by his good conduct or bad conduct, his efficiency or inefficiency in rendering loyal, able, and disinterested service to the nation as a whole. Therefore it is absolutely necessary that there should be full liberty to tell the truth about his acts, and this means that it is exactly as necessary to blame him when he does wrong as to praise him when he does right. Any other attitude in an American citizen is both base and servile. To announce that there must be no criticism of the President, or that we are to stand by the President, right or wrong, is not only unpatriotic and servile, but is morally treasonable to the American public. Nothing but the truth should be spoken about him or any one else. But it is even more important to tell the truth, pleasant or unpleasant, about him than about any one else.

THEODORE ROOSEVELT, "Lincoln and Free Speech," *The Great Adventure* (vol. 19 of *The Works of Theodore Roosevelt,* national ed.), chapter 7, p. 289 (1926).

1508 Yes, Haven, most of us enjoy preaching, and I've got such a bully pulpit!

President THEODORE ROOSEVELT, reply to George Haven Putnam, who had accused him of a tendency to preaching, sometime during his first presidential term.—George Haven Putnam, introductory essay, *The Works of Theodore Roosevelt,* national ed., vol. 9, p. x (1926).

1509 The President must be greater than anyone else, but not better than anyone else. We subject him and his family to close and constant scrutiny and denounce them for things that we ourselves do every day. A Presidential slip of the tongue, a slight error in judgment—social, political, or ethical—can raise a storm of protest. We give the President more work than a man can do, more responsibility than a man should take, more pressure than a man can bear. We abuse him often and rarely praise him. We wear him out, use him up, eat him up. And with all this, Americans have a love for the President that goes beyond loyalty or party nationality; he is ours, and we exercise the right to destroy him.

JOHN STEINBECK, *America and Americans*, p. 46 (1966).

1510 Ike has picked a cabinet of eight millionaires and one plumber.

T. R. B. (RICHARD STROUT), "Washington Wire," *New Republic*, December 15, 1952, p. 3.

The plumber was secretary of labor Martin Durkin of Chicago, head of the Journeyman Plumbers and Steamfitters Union. See William Safire, *Safire's Political Dictionary*, pp. 195–96 (1968).

1511 The President can exercise no power which cannot be fairly and reasonably traced to some specific grant of power . . . in the Federal Constitution or in an act of Congress passed in pursuance thereof. There is no undefined residuum of power which he can exercise because it seems to him to be in the public interest.

WILLIAM HOWARD TAFT, *Our Chief Magistrate and His Powers*, chapter 6, pp. 139–40 (1916).

1512 But the PRESIDENT is the Chief Executive of the nation as well as a party leader, and it has been objected that for him to take an active and overt part in influencing the choice of party candidates derogates from the dignity of his high position and is almost a constitutional impropriety.

The Times, London, editorial about President Franklin D. Roosevelt's campaign in the South to influence voting in the forthcoming primary elections, August 16, 1938, p. 13.

1513 There has been a lot of talk lately about the burdens of the Presidency. Decisions that the President has to make often affect the lives of tens of millions of people around the world, but that does not mean that they should take longer to make. Some men can make decisions and some cannot. Some men fret and delay under criticism. I used to have a saying that applies here, and I note that some people have picked it up, "If you can't stand the heat, get out of the kitchen."

HARRY S. TRUMAN, *Mr. Citizen*, p. 229 (1960).

1514 When contemplating General Eisenhower winning the Presidential election, Truman said, "He'll sit here, and he'll say, 'Do this! Do that!' *And nothing will happen.* Poor Ike—it won't be a bit like the Army. He'll find it very frustrating."

HARRY S. TRUMAN.—Richard E. Neustadt, *Presidential Power, the Politics of Leadership*, p. 9 (1960).

1515 You know, the greatest epitaph in the country is here in Arizona. It's in Tombstone, Ariz., and this epitaph says, "Here lies Jack Williams. He done his damndest." I think that is the greatest epitaph a man could have. Whenever a man does the best he can, then that is all he can do; and that is what your President has been trying to do for the last 3 years for this country.

President HARRY S. TRUMAN, remarks in Winslow, Arizona, June 15, 1948.—*Public Papers of the Presidents of the United States: Harry S. Truman, 1948*, p. 356.

1516 The legislative job of the President is especially important to the people who have no special representatives to plead their cause before Congress—and that includes the great majority. I sometimes express it by saying the President is the only lobbyist that one hundred and fifty million Americans have. The other twenty million are able to employ people to represent them—and that's all right, it's the exercise of the right of petition—but someone has to look after the interests of the one hundred and fifty million that are left.

HARRY S. TRUMAN, speech to the Press and Union League Club, San Francisco, California, October 25, 1956.—Transcript, pp. 19–20.

1517 I sleep each night a little better, a little more confidently because Lyndon Johnson is my President. For I know he lives and thinks and works to make sure that for all America and indeed, the growing body of the free world, the morning shall always come.

JACK VALENTI, special assistant to the president, address before the Advertising Federation of America convention, Boston, Massachusetts, June 28, 1965.—*Congressional Record*, July 7, 1965, vol. 111, Appendix, p. A3583.

1518 Following the trail of some of these [President Lyndon Johnson's financial] transactions resembles the action in a Western movie, where the cowboys ride off in a cloud of dust to the south, the herd stampedes northeastward, the Indians start to westward but, once out of sight, circle toward the north, the rustlers drift eastward and the cavalry, coming to the rescue, gets lost entirely—all over stony ground leaving little trace.

KEITH WHEELER and MICHAEL LAMBERT, "The Man Who Is President," part 2, *Life*, August 21, 1964, p. 69.

1519 [Hoover was the greatest engineer in the world since] he had drained, ditched, and damned the United States in three years.

Attributed to a Kansas farmer.—Roy Victor Peel, *The 1932 Campaign*, p. 56 (1935, reprinted 1973).

Press

1520 Well, I am reading more and enjoying it less—*[laughter]*—and so on, but I have not complained nor do I plan to make any general complaints. I read and talk to myself about it, but I don't plan to issue any general statement on the press. I think that they are doing their task, as a critical branch, the fourth estate. And I am attempting to do mine. And we are going to live together for a period, and then go our separate ways. *[Laughter]*.

President JOHN F. KENNEDY, when asked to comment on the press in general, news conference, May 9, 1962.—*Public Papers of the Presidents of the United States: John F. Kennedy, 1962*, p. 376 (1963).

1521 To the press alone, chequered as it is with abuses, the world is indebted for all the triumphs which have been gained by reason and humanity over error and oppression.

JAMES MADISON, "Report on the Resolutions," *The Writings of James Madison*, ed. Gaillard Hunt, vol. 6, p. 389 (1906).

This report of the resolutions of the Virginia House of Delegates in 1799 was submitted by a committee headed by Madison and is widely known as the Virginia Report of 1799.

Press

1522 Government has an obligation not to inhibit the collection and dissemination of news. . . . I'm convinced that if reporters should ever lose the right to protect the confidentiality of their sources then serious investigative reporting will simply dry up. The kind of resourceful, probing journalism that first exposed most of the serious scandals, corruption and injustice in our nation's history would simply disappear. . . . And let me tell you, reading about one's failings in the daily papers is one of the privileges of high office in this free country of ours.

NELSON A. ROCKEFELLER, governor of New York, speech to the Anti-Defamation League, Syracuse, New York, November 29, 1972, as reported by *The New York Times*, November 30, 1972, pp. 1, 86.

1523 Whenever the press quits abusing me I know I'm in the wrong pew. I don't mind it because when they throw bricks at me—I'm a pretty good shot myself and I usually throw 'em back at 'em.

HARRY S. TRUMAN, speech at a dinner in his honor, Washington, D.C., February 22, 1958.—Text as recorded by *The New York Times*, February 23, 1958, p. 46.

1524 In America the President reigns for four years, and Journalism governs for ever and ever.

OSCAR WILDE, "The Soul of Man Under Socialism," *The Works of Oscar Wilde*, ed. G. F. Maine, p. 1033 (1954).

Prisons

1525 Nothing can be more abhorrent to democracy than to imprison a person or keep him in prison because he is unpopular. This is really the test of civilisation.

Prime Minister WINSTON CHURCHILL, letter to Home Secretary Herbert Morrison, November 21, 1943.—Churchill, *Closing the Ring* (vol. 5 of *The Second World War*), p. 679 (1951).

1526 A prison taint was on everything there. The imprisoned air, the imprisoned light, the imprisoned damps, the imprisoned men, were all deteriorated by confinement. As the captive men were faded and haggard, so the iron was rusty, the stone was slimy, the wood was rotten, the air was faint, the light was dim. Like a well, like a vault, like a tomb, the prison had no knowledge of the brightness outside; and would have kept its polluted atmosphere intact, in one of the spice islands of the Indian Ocean.

CHARLES DICKENS, *Little Dorrit*, ed. Harvey P. Sucksmith, book 1, chapter 1, pp. 2, 5 (1979). First published 1855–1857.

1527 The degree of civilization in a society can be judged by entering its prisons.

Attributed to FYODOR DOSTOEVSKY. Unverified.

1528 Mr. Emerson visited Thoreau at the jail, and the meeting between the two philosophers must have been interesting and somewhat dramatic. The account of the meeting was told me by Miss Maria Thoreau [Henry Thoreau's aunt]—"Henry, why are you here?" "Waldo, why are you *not* here?"

Attributed to RALPH WALDO EMERSON and HENRY DAVID THOREAU.—Arthur Samuel Jones, *Thoreau's Incarceration [As Told by His Jailer]*, p. 15 (1962).

This exchange was supposed to have taken place on July 23 or 24, 1846, in the Concord, Massachusetts, jail where Thoreau was placed for nonpayment of poll taxes. There are many versions of this story, but Thoreau's account does not mention a visit by Emerson, in his *Reform Papers*, ed. Wendell Glick, pp. 79–84 (1973), so it is probably apocryphal.

Privacy

1529 We are rapidly entering the age of no privacy, where everyone is open to surveillance at all times; where there are no secrets from government.

Justice WILLIAM O. DOUGLAS, dissenting, *Osborn* v. *United States*, 385 U.S. 341 (1966).

1530 Every man should know that his conversations, his correspondence, and his personal life are private. I have urged Congress—except when the Nation's security is at stake—to take action to that end.

President LYNDON B. JOHNSON, remarks at the swearing-in of Ramsey Clark as attorney general, March 10, 1967.—*Public Papers of the Presidents of the United States: Lyndon B. Johnson, 1967*, book 1, p. 313.

1531 Gentlemen do not read each other's mail.

HENRY L. STIMSON. As secretary of state under Herbert Hoover, Stimson closed the Department of State's code-breaking office, the so-called Black Chamber, in 1929. He later justified his action with this remark.—Stimson and McGeorge Bundy, *On Active Service in Peace and War*, p. 188 (1948). Also see David Kahn, *The Codebreakers*, p. 360 (1967).

Progress

1532 The advancement of the arts from year to year taxes our credulity, and seems to presage the arrival of that period when human improvement must end.

HENRY L. ELLSWORTH, U.S. commissioner of patents, *Annual Report*, p. 5 (1843).

1533 According to the ancient Chinese proverb, "A journey of a thousand miles must begin with a single step."

President JOHN F. KENNEDY, radio and television address to the American people on the nuclear test ban treaty, July 26, 1963.—*Public Papers of the Presidents of the United States: John F. Kennedy, 1963*, p. 606.

1534 I walk slowly, but I never walk backward.

Attributed to ABRAHAM LINCOLN.—Representative Everett M. Dirksen, remarks in the House, September 18, 1941, *Congressional Record*, vol. 87, p. 7479. Unverified in *The Collected Works of Abraham Lincoln*, ed. Roy P. Basler (1953).

He may have been paraphrasing this: "I hope to 'stand firm' enough to not go backward, and yet not go forward fast enough to wreck the country's cause."—President Lincoln, letter to Zachariah Chandler, November 20, 1863.—*Collected Works*, vol. 7, p. 24.

1535 Next came the Patent laws. These began in England in 1624; and, in this country, with the adoption of our constitution. Before then [these?], any man might instantly use what another had invented; so that the inventor had no special advantage from his own invention. The patent system changed this; secured to the inventor, for a limited time, the exclusive use of his invention; and thereby added the fuel of *interest* to the *fire* of genius, in the discovery and production of new and useful things.

ABRAHAM LINCOLN, second lecture on discoveries and inventions, delivered to the Phi Alpha Society of Illinois College at Jacksonville, Illinois, February 11, 1859.—*The Collected Works of Abraham Lincoln,* ed. Roy P. Basler, vol. 3, p. 357 (1953).

1536 The chief cause which made the fusion of the different elements of society so imperfect was the extreme difficulty which our ancestors found in passing from place to place. Of all inventions, the alphabet and the printing press alone excepted, those inventions which abridge distance have done most for the civilisation of our species. Every improvement of the means of locomotion benefits mankind morally and intellectually as well as materially, and not only facilitates the interchange of the various productions of nature and art, but tends to remove national and provincial antipathies, and to bind together all the branches of the great human family.

THOMAS BABINGTON MACAULAY, *The History of England,* 5th ed., vol. 1, chapter 3, p. 370 (1849).

"Of all inventions, the alphabet and the printing press alone excepted, those inventions which abridge distance have done most for civilization" was inscribed on one side of the Golden Door of the Transportation Building at the World's Columbian Exposition, held in Chicago in 1893.

1537 Expositions are the timekeepers of progress.

President WILLIAM MCKINLEY, speech delivered at the Pan-American Exposition, Buffalo, New York, September 5, 1901.—*Modern Eloquence,* ed. Ashley H. Thorndike, rev. Adam Ward, vol. 11, p. 401 (1936).

This was McKinley's last speech, as he was mortally wounded the next day at the Exposition. He served in Congress 1877–1884 and 1885–1891.

1538 Two conditions render difficult this historic situation of mankind: It is full of tremendously deadly armament, and it has not progressed morally as much as it has scientifically and technically.

POPE PAUL VI, sermon at the Shrine of Fatima, Portugal, May 13, 1967, as reported by *The New York Times,* May 14, 1967, p. 47.

1539 I was to learn later in life that we tend to meet any new situation by reorganizing; and a wonderful method it can be for creating the illusion of progress while producing confusion, inefficiency, and demoralization.

Attributed to PETRONIUS ARBITER.—Robert Townsend, *Up the Organization,* p. 162 (1970). Unverified.

1540 Our inventions are wont to be pretty toys, which distract our attention from serious things. They are but improved means to an unimproved end, . . . We are in great haste to construct a magnetic telegraph from Maine to Texas; but Maine and Texas, it may be, have nothing important to communicate.

HENRY DAVID THOREAU, *Walden,* chapter 1, p.67 (1966). Originally published in 1854.

Progress

1541 The day of large profits is probably past. There may be room for further intensive, but not extensive, development of industry in the present area of civilization.

D. CARROLL WRIGHT, U.S. commissioner of labor.—*Industrial Depressions*, first annual report of the U.S. Bureau of Labor, 1885, chapter 3, p. 257. House Executive Doc. 49–1, part 5.

Promise

1542 But not the first Illusion, the new earth,
The march upon the solitary fire,
The casting of the dice of death and birth
Against a giant, for a blind desire,
The stream uncrossed, the promise still untried,
The metal sleeping in the mountainside.

STEPHEN VINCENT BENÉT, *Western Star*, prelude, section 3, stanza 6, pp. 7–8 (1943).

The last two lines were quoted by Senator George McGovern in his remarks nominating R. Sargent Shriver as his vice presidential running mate on the Democratic ticket, in a television address from the Capitol, August 5, 1972.

Promises

1543 All men have a feeling, that they would rather you told them a civil lie than give them a point blank refusal. . . . If you make a promise, the thing is still uncertain, depends on a future day, and concerns but few people; but if you refuse you alienate people to a certainty and at once, and many people too.

QUINTUS TULLIUS CICERO, "On Standing for the Consulship," section 12.—*The Treatises of M. T. Cicero*, trans. C. D. Yonge, pp. 499, 500 (1872).

This work, also known as the "Handbook of Electioneering," was addressed to Marcus Tullius Cicero, the author's brother. Another translation of the passage is: "Human nature being what it is, all men prefer a false promise to a flat refusal. At the worst the man to whom you have lied may be angry. That risk, if you make a promise, is uncertain and deferred, and it affects only a few. But if you refuse you are sure to offend many, and that at once."—H. J. Haskell, *The New Deal in Old Rome*, p. 169 (1939).

1544 We must not promise what we ought not, lest we be called on to perform what we cannot.

Attributed to ABRAHAM LINCOLN, speech delivered before the first Republican state convention of Illinois, Bloomington, Illinois, May 29, 1856.—*The Writings of Abraham Lincoln*, ed. Arthur B. Lapsley, vol. 2, p. 249 (1905).

This version of the speech has been questioned because it was reconstructed by Henry C. Whitney, who made notes at the time but did not write it out until 1896. He did not claim that it was literally correct, only that he had followed the argument and that in many cases the sentences were as Lincoln spoke them. The only contemporary account of the so-called "Lost Speech" was a brief report in the Alton, Illinois, *Weekly Courier*, June 5, 1856, which does not contain this sentence.

Some historians believe the Whitney reconstruction "is not . . . worthy of serious consideration."—*The Collected Works of Abraham Lincoln*, ed. Roy P. Basler, vol. 2, p. 341 (1953).

Promises

1545 The Great Spirit placed me and my people on this land poor and naked. When the white men came we gave them lands, and did not wish to hurt them. But the white man drove us back and took our lands. Then the Great Father [president] made us many promises, but they are not kept. He promised to give us large presents, and when they came to us they were small; they seemed to be lost on the way.

Sioux Indian Chief RED CLOUD, speech at the Council of Peace, New York City, June 15, 1870, as reported by *The New York Times*, June 16, 1870, p. 2.

1546 Promises and Pye-Crusts, . . . are made to be broken.

JONATHAN SWIFT, "Polite Conversation," *The Prose Works of Jonathan Swift*, ed. Herbert Davis, vol. 4, p. 146 (1957).

Property

1547 Property is the fruit of labor—property is desirable——is a positive good in the world. That some should be rich, shows that others may become rich, and hence is just encouragement to industry and enterprize. Let not him who is houseless pull down the house of another; but let him labor diligently and build one for himself, thus by example assuring that his own shall be safe from violence when built.

President ABRAHAM LINCOLN, reply to New York Workingmen's Democratic Republican Association, March 21, 1864.—*The Collected Works of Abraham Lincoln*, ed. Roy P. Basler, vol. 7, p. 259–60 (1953).

1548 As a man is said to have a right to his property, he may be equally said to have a property in his rights.

JAMES MADISON, "Property," *National Gazette*, March 29, 1792.—*The Writings of James Madison*, ed. Gaillard Hunt, vol. 6, p. 101 (1906).

These words are inscribed in the Madison Memorial Hall, Library of Congress James Madison Memorial Building.

1549 The freest government, if it could exist, would not be long acceptable, if the tendency of the laws were to create a rapid accumulation of property in few hands, and to render the great mass of the population dependent and penniless. In such a case, the popular power would be likely to break in upon the rights of property, or else the influence of property to limit and control the exercise of popular power. Universal suffrage, for example, could not long exist in a community where there was great inequality of property. . . . In the nature of things, those who have not property, and see their neighbors possess much more than they think them to need, cannot be favorable to laws made for the protection of property. When this class becomes numerous, it grows clamorous. It looks on property as its prey and plunder, and is naturally ready, at all times, for violence and revolution.

DANIEL WEBSTER, "First Settlement of New England," speech delivered at Plymouth, Massachusetts, December 22, 1820, to commemorate the 200th anniversary of the landing of the Pilgrims at Plymouth.—*The Writings and Speeches of Daniel Webster*, vol. 1, p. 214 (1903).

Webster served in Congress as a representative from New Hampshire, 1813–1817, and from Massachusetts, 1823–1827, and as a senator from Massachusetts, 1827–1841 and 1845–1850.

Property

1550 Give a man the secure possession of a bleak rock, and he will turn it into a garden; give him a nine years lease of a garden, and he will convert it into a desert. . . . The magic of PROPERTY turns sand to gold.

ARTHUR YOUNG, journal entries for July 30 and November 7, 1787, *Travels* . . . , 2d ed., vol. 1, pp. 51, 88 (1794, reprinted 1970).

Public affairs

1551 My rule, in which I have always found satisfaction, is, never to turn aside in public affairs through views of private interest; but to go straight forward in doing what appears to me right at the time, leaving the consequences with Providence.

BENJAMIN FRANKLIN, letter to Mrs. Jane Mecom, December 30, 1770.—*The Works of Benjamin Franklin*, ed. Jared Sparks, vol. 7, p. 497 (1838).

1552 An Athenian citizen does not neglect the state because he takes care of his own household; and even those of us who are engaged in business have a very fair idea of politics. We alone regard a man who takes no interest in public affairs, not as a harmless, but as a useless character, and if few of us are originators, we are all sound judges of a policy.

THUCYDIDES, "Funeral Speech of Pericles," book 2, section 40.—*Thucydides Translated into English*, 2d ed., trans. Benjamin Jowett, vol. 1, pp. 129–30 (1900).

Public opinion

1553 In the United States today, we have more than our share of the nattering nabobs of negativism. They have formed their own 4-H Club—the "hopeless, hysterical hyponchondriacs of history."

Vice President SPIRO T. AGNEW, address to the California Republican state convention, San Diego, California, September 11, 1970.—*Congressional Record*, September 16, 1970, vol. 116, p. 32017.

William Safire, then a speechwriter for President Nixon, was the author of "nattering nabobs of negativism," according to *The Washingtonian*, March 1985, p. 11, and *The Washington Post*, August 27, 1987, p. C4.

1554 Nothing is more dangerous in wartime than to live in the temperamental atmosphere of a Gallup Poll, always feeling one's pulse and taking one's temperature. I see that a speaker at the week-end said that this was a time when leaders should keep their ears to the ground. All I can say is that the British nation will find it very hard to look up to leaders who are detected in that somewhat ungainly posture.

Prime Minister WINSTON CHURCHILL, speech, House of Commons, September 30, 1941.—*Winston S. Churchill: His Complete Speeches, 1897-1963*, ed. Robert Rhodes James, vol. 6, p. 6495 (1974).

1555 I had grown tired of standing in the lean and lonely front line facing the greatest enemy that ever confronted man—public opinion.

CLARENCE DARROW, *The Story of My Life*, p. 232 (1932).

Public opinion

1556 Heroes are created by popular demand, sometimes out of the scantiest materials, or none at all.

GERALD W. JOHNSON, *American Heroes and Hero-Worship,* p. 11 (1943).

1557 In this and like communities, public sentiment is everything. With public sentiment, nothing can fail; without it nothing can succeed.

ABRAHAM LINCOLN, reply in the first debate with Senator Stephen A. Douglas, Ottawa, Illinois, August 21, 1858.—*The Collected Works of Abraham Lincoln,* ed. Roy P. Basler, vol. 3, p. 27 (1953).

See also No. 1332.

1558 Private opinion creates public opinion. Public opinion overflows eventually into national behaviour and national behaviour, as things are arranged at present, can make or mar the world. That is why private opinion, and private behaviour, and private conversation are so terrifyingly important.

JAN STRUTHER (Joyce Anstruther), "The Weather of the World," *A Pocketful of Pebbles,* p. 341 (1946).

1559 What news? *Ma foi!*
The tiger has broken out of his den.
The monster was three days at sea.
The wretch has landed at Fréjus.
The Brigand has arrived at Antibes.
The Invader has reached Grenoble.
The General has entered Lyons.
Napoleon slept last night at Fontainebleau.
The Emperor proceeds to the Tuileries to-day.
His Imperial Majesty will address his loyal subjects to-morrow.

Author unknown.—Louis Cohen, *Napoleonic Anecdotes,* p. 229 (1925).

Taken from a skit of 1815, this purports to show how Napoleon's return from Elba was progressively regarded in Paris.

Public service

1560 We must not in the course of public life expect immediate approbation and immediate grateful acknowledgment of our services. But let us persevere through abuse and even injury. The internal satisfaction of a good conscience is always present, and time will do us justice in the minds of the people, even those at present the most prejudiced against us.

BENJAMIN FRANKLIN, letter to Joseph Galloway, December 2, 1772.—*The Works of Benjamin Franklin,* ed. Jared Sparks, vol. 8, p. 23 (1839).

1561 I am not influenced by the expectation of promotion or pecuniary reward. I wish to be useful, and every kind of service necessary for the public good, becomes honorable by being necessary.

Captain NATHAN HALE, remark to his friend, Captain William Hull, who attempted to dissuade him from volunteering for spy duty, early September 1776.—Isaac William Stuart, *Life of Captain Nathan Hale,* p. 94 (1856).

While General Washington desperately needed someone to provide information on the strength and location of the enemy, he could not command someone to be a spy. He needed a paid spy or a volunteer. Hale was the sole volunteer. At the end of his mission, Hale was captured by the British and hanged on September 22, 1776. He was twenty-one years old.

See also No. 1304.

1562 When a man assumes a public trust, he should consider himself as public property.

Attributed to THOMAS JEFFERSON.—B. L. Rayner, *Life of Thomas Jefferson*, p. 356 (1834).

Rayner says the remark was made during a conversation in the president's office with Baron Alexander von Humboldt, the celebrated naturalist and traveler.

1563 In government offices which are sensitive to the vehemence and passion of mass sentiment public men have no sure tenure. They are in effect perpetual office seekers, always on trial for their political lives, always required to court their restless constituents. They are deprived of their independence. Democratic politicians rarely feel they can afford the luxury of telling the whole truth to the people. And since not telling it, though prudent, is uncomfortable, they find it easier if they themselves do not have to hear too often too much of the sour truth. The men under them who report and collect the news come to realize in their turn that it is safer to be wrong before it has become fashionable to be right.

WALTER LIPPMANN, *Essays in the Public Philosophy*, p. 26 (1935).

1564 I made my mistakes, but in all of my years in public life, I have never profited, never profited from public service—I have earned every cent. And in all of my years of public life, I have never obstructed justice. And I think, too, that I could say that in my years of public life, that I welcome this kind of examination, because people have got to know whether or not their President is a crook. Well, I am not a crook. I have earned everything I have got.

President RICHARD M. NIXON, televised question and answer session at the annual convention of the Associated Press Managing Editors Association, Orlando, Florida, November 17, 1973.—*Public Papers of the Presidents of the United States: Richard Nixon, 1973*, p. 956.

1565 A private Life is to be preferr'd; the Honour and Gain of publick Posts, bearing no proportion with the Comfort of it.

WILLIAM PENN, *Some Fruits of Solitude in Reflections & Maxims*, no. 370, p. 73 (1903, reprinted 1976).

1566 The weakling and the coward are out of place in a strong and free community. In a republic like ours the governing class is composed of the strong men who take the trouble to do the work of government; and if you are too timid or too fastidious or too careless to do your part in this work, then you forfeit your right to be considered one of the governing and you become one of the governed instead—one of the driven cattle of the political arena.

President THEODORE ROOSEVELT, address at the Harvard Union, Cambridge, Massachusetts, February 23, 1907.—"Athletics, Scholarship and Public Service," *The Strenuous Life* (vol. 13 of *The Works of Theodore Roosevelt*, national ed.), chapter 27, p. 563 (1926).

1567 We believe above all else that those who hold in their hands the power of government must themselves be independent—and this kind of independence means the wisdom, the experience, the courage to identify the special interests and the pressures that are always at work, to see the public interest steadily, to resist its subordination no matter what the political hazards.

ADLAI E. STEVENSON, governor of Illinois, speech before the Colorado Volunteers-for-Stevenson dinner, Denver, Colorado, September 5, 1952.—*Speeches of Adlai Stevenson,* p. 23 (1952).

1568 Our form of government does not enter into rivalry with the institutions of others. We do not copy our neighbours, but are an example to them. It is true that we are called a democracy, for the administration is in the hands of the many and not of the few. But while the law secures equal justice to all alike in their private disputes, the claim of excellence is also recognised; and when a citizen is in any way distinguished, he is preferred to the public service, not as a matter of privilege, but as the reward of merit. Neither is poverty a bar, but a man may benefit his country whatever be the obscurity of his condition.

THUCYDIDES, "Funeral Speech of Pericles," *Thucydides,* trans. Benjamin Jowett, 2d ed., rev., vol. 1, book 2, section 37, pp. 127–28 (1900).

1569 Shortly after I was elected, in Nineteen Hundred and Forty-eight, I made up my mind that I would not seek another term. I have seen a great many men in public life, and one of their besetting sins is to stay in office too long. Nowadays, in such organizations as the Army and the civil service and industry, there is compulsory retirement, but no such regulations prevail in politics. I decided that I would not be guilty of this common failing, and that I should make way for younger men—and the Constitutional Amendment Number twenty-two, the two-term amendment, does not apply to me. The people responsible for the 22nd amendment thought I was not worth considering and that I'd be beaten in 1948—so I was exempted.

HARRY S. TRUMAN, speech to the Press and Union League Club, San Francisco, California, October 25, 1956.—Transcript, p. 30. The last sentence was added in longhand to the typewritten speech.

Truman had made similar remarks at a political rally in John Hancock Hall, Boston, Massachusetts, September 29, 1956, as reported by *The Boston Sunday Globe,* September 30, 1956, p. 38: "There is an old girl called Anno Domini that catches up with us and she has been trying to catch up with me. It just seems to me to make sense to move on and make way for younger men. It seems to me to make sense to move out of the White House voluntarily without waiting to be carried out."

1570 There is no cause half so sacred as the cause of a people. There is no idea so uplifting as the idea of the service of humanity.

WOODROW WILSON, governor of New Jersey, presidential campaign address, Madison Square Garden, New York City, October 31, 1912.—*The Papers of Woodrow Wilson,* ed. Arthur S. Link, vol. 25, p. 493 (1978).

Wilson spoke to an audience estimated at between 12,000 and 16,000 persons. For two hours before he arrived, the crowd listened to various other speakers. Upon his arrival there was a "tumultuous ovation which lasted for more than an hour. Wilson was so moved that he forgot his prepared speech" (p. 493, footnote).

1571 The office should seek the man, not man the office.

Attributed to SILAS WRIGHT.—Edward Parsons Day, *Day's Collacon,* p. 684 (1884). Unverified.

According to biographies, this is in character. Wright was a nineteenth century representative and senator from New York, and served as governor of New York. In 1844, he declined a Supreme Court appointment, refused to be considered for the presidential nomination and declined, when nominated, to be a candidate for the vice presidency.—*Dictionary of American Biography*, vol. 10, part 2, p. 556.

Publicity

1572 Publicity is justly commended as a remedy for social and industrial diseases. Sunlight is said to be the best of disinfectants; electric light the most efficient policeman.

LOUIS D. BRANDEIS, "What Publicity Can Do," *Other People's Money*, chapter 5, p. 92 (1932). First published in *Harper's Weekly*, December 20, 1913.

1573 The government being the people's business, it necessarily follows that its operations should be at all times open to the public view. Publicity is therefore as essential to honest administration as freedom of speech is to representative government. "Equal rights to all and special privileges to none" is the maxim which should control in all departments of government.

WILLIAM JENNINGS BRYAN, secretary of state, speech before the City Club, Baltimore, Maryland, April 24, 1915.—"Bryan's Ten Rules for the New Voter," rule 8, *The Sun*, Baltimore, Maryland, April 25, 1915, p. 16.

Bryan prepared the ten rules as a synopsis of his speech so the newspapers might get the exact sense of it.

Puritans

1574 The fact is, there were all kinds of Puritans. There were dismal precisians, like William Prynne, illiberal and vulgar fanatics, the Tribulation Wholesomes, Hope-on-high Bombys, and Zeal-of-the-land Busys, whose absurdities were the stock in trade of contemporary satirists from Johnson to Butler. But there were also gentlemen and scholars, like Fairfax, Marvell, Colonel Hutchinson, Vane, whose Puritanism was consistent with all elegant tastes and accomplishments. Was Milton's Puritanism hurtful to his art? No and yes. It was in many ways an inspiration; it gave him *zeal*, a Puritan word much ridiculed by the Royalists; it gave refinement, distinction, selectness, elevation to his picture of the world. But it would be uncritical to deny that it also gave a certain narrowness and rigidity to his view of human life.

HENRY A. BEERS, "Milton's Tercentenary," *The Connecticut Wits and Other Essays*, p. 230 (1920).

Race

1575 For it is not light that is needed, but fire; it is not the gentle shower, but thunder. We need the storm, the whirlwind, and the earthquake. The feeling of the nation must be quickened; the conscience of the nation must be roused; the propriety of the nation must be startled; the hypocrisy of the nation must be exposed; and its crimes against God and man must be proclaimed and denounced.

FREDERICK DOUGLASS, "What to the Slave Is the Fourth of July?," address delivered in Rochester, New York, July 5, 1852.—*The Frederick Douglass Papers*, ed. John W. Blassingame, series 1, vol. 2, p. 371 (1982).

Race

1576 Nothing is more certainly written in the book of fate, than that these people are to be free; nor is it less certain that the two races, equally free, cannot live in the same government. Nature, habit, opinion have drawn indelible lines of distinction between them.

THOMAS JEFFERSON, "Autobiography," *The Writings of Thomas Jefferson*, ed. Andrew A. Lipscomb, vol. 1, pp. 72–73 (1903).

1577 And if we are to open employment opportunities in this country for members of all races and creeds, then the Federal Government must set an example. . . . The President himself must set the key example. I am not going to promise a Cabinet post or any other post to any race or ethnic group. That is racism in reverse at its worst. So I do not promise to consider race or religion in my appointments if I am successful. I promise only that I will not consider them.

Senator JOHN F. KENNEDY, campaign speech, Wittenberg College, Springfield, Ohio, October 17, 1960.—*Freedom of Communications*, final report of the Committee on Commerce, United States Senate, part 1, p. 635 (1961). Senate Rept. 87-994.

1578 I will say then that I am not, nor ever have been in favor of bringing about in any way the social and political equality of the white and black races,—that I am not nor ever have been in favor of making voters or jurors of negroes, nor of qualifying them to hold office, nor to intermarry with white people; and I will say in addition to this that there is a physical difference between the white and black races which I believe will forever forbid the two races living together on terms of social and political equality. And inasmuch as they cannot so live, while they do remain together there must be the position of superior and inferior, and I as much as any other man am in favor of having the superior position assigned to the white race.

ABRAHAM LINCOLN, fourth debate with Senator Stephen A. Douglas, Charleston, Illinois, September 18, 1858.—*The Collected Works of Abraham Lincoln*, ed. Roy P. Basler, vol. 3, p. 145–46 (1953).

1579 The time may have come when the issue of race could benefit from a period of "benign neglect." The subject has been too much talked about. The forum has been too much taken over to hysterics, paranoids, and boodlers on all sides. We may need a period in which Negro progress continues and racial rhetoric fades. The administration can help bring this about by paying close attention to such progress—as we are doing—while seeking to avoid situations in which extremists of either race are given opportunities for martyrdom, heroics, histrionics or whatever.

DANIEL PATRICK MOYNIHAN, memorandum to President Nixon on the status of Negroes, as reported in *The Evening Star*, Washington, D.C., March 2, 1970, p. A-5.

Moynihan has served in Congress since 1977.

1580 I have one great fear in my heart, that one day when they are turned to loving, they will find we are turned to hating.

ALAN PATON, *Cry, the Beloved Country*, p. 40 (1960).

Reading

1581 I read my eyes out and can't read half enough. . . . The more one reads the more one sees we have to read.

Reading

Vice President JOHN ADAMS, letter to Abigail Adams, December 28, 1794.—Adams papers, Massachusetts Historical Society, Boston, Massachusetts.

Reasons

1582 A man always has two reasons for what he does—a good one, and the real one.

Attributed to J. PIERPONT MORGAN.—Owen Wister, *Roosevelt: The Story of a Friendship*, p. 280 (1930).

Reform

1583 A rayformer thinks he was ilicted because he was a rayformer, whin th' thruth iv th' matther is he was ilicted because no wan knew him.

FINLEY PETER DUNNE, *Observations by Mr. Dooley*, p. 167 (1906, reprinted 1968).

1584 The voice of great events is proclaiming to us, Reform, that you may preserve.

THOMAS BABINGTON MACAULAY, speech on parliamentary reform, March 2, 1831.—*The Complete Writings of Lord Macaulay*, vol. 17, p. 18 (1900).

President Franklin D. Roosevelt paraphrased slightly "The words of the great essayist," not named: "The voice of great events is proclaiming to us. Reform if you would preserve," in his address at the Democratic state convention, Syracuse, New York, September 29, 1936.—*The Public Papers and Addresses of Franklin D. Roosevelt, 1936,* p. 390 (1938).

1585 The best reformers the world has ever seen are those who commence on themselves.

Attributed to GEORGE BERNARD SHAW.—Evan Esar, *The Dictionary of Humorous Quotations*, p. 178 (1949). Unverified in Shaw's published writings.

Regulation

1586 The general rule, at least, is that while property may be regulated to a certain extent, if regulation goes too far it will be recognized as a taking.

Justice OLIVER WENDELL HOLMES, *Pennsylvania Coal Company* v. *H. J. Mahon*, 260 U.S. 415 (1922).

1587 It is hardly lack of due process for the Government to regulate that which it subsidizes.

Justice ROBERT H. JACKSON, *Wickard* v. *Filburn*, 317 U.S. 131 (1943).

1588 Will one of you gentlemen tell me in what civilized country of the earth there are important government boards of control on which private interests are represented? Which of you gentlemen thinks the railroads should select members of the Interstate Commerce Commission?

Attributed to WOODROW WILSON, at a meeting of bankers and the president shortly before he asked Congress to enact legislation creating a Federal Reserve System.—Carter Glass, *An Adventure in Constructive Finance*, chapter 7, p. 116 (1927, reprinted 1975).

Regulation

This appears to be the origin of what is frequently quoted as "You don't put robbers to work in a bank."

Relevance

1589 If, in the middle of World War II, a general could be writing a poem, then maybe I was not so irrelevant after all. Maybe the general was doing more for victory by writing a poem than he would be by commanding an army. At least, he might be doing less harm. By applying the same logic to my own condition [consultant in poetry at the Library of Congress], I decided that I might be relevant in what I called a negative way. I have clung to this concept ever since—negative relevance. In moments of vain-glory I even entertain the possibility that if my concept were more widely accepted, the world might be a better place to live in. There are a lot of people who would make better citizens if they were content to be just negatively relevant.

ROBERT PENN WARREN, speech upon receipt of the 1970 National Medal for Literature, New York City, December 2, 1970.—Transcript, p. 1.

Representation

1590 One half of our brethren who fight and pay taxes, are excluded, like Helots, from the rights of representation, as if society were instituted for the soil, and not for the men inhabiting it; or one half of these could dispose of the rights and the will of the other half, without their consent.

THOMAS JEFFERSON, letter to John Taylor, May 28, 1816.—*The Writings of Thomas Jefferson,* ed. Paul L. Ford, vol. 10, p. 30 (1899).

1591 Were our State a pure democracy, in which all its inhabitants should meet together to transact all their business, there would yet be excluded from their deliberations, 1. infants, until arrived at years of discretion. 2. Women, who, to prevent depravation of morals and ambiguity of issue, could not mix promiscuously in the public meetings of men. 3. Slaves, from whom the unfortunate state of things with us takes away the right of will and of property. Those then who have no will could be permitted to exercise none in the popular assembly; and of course, could delegate none to an agent in a representative assembly. The business, in the first case, would be done by qualified citizens only.

THOMAS JEFFERSON, letter to Samuel Kercheval, September 5, 1816.—*The Writings of Thomas Jefferson,* ed. Paul L. Ford, vol. 10, pp. 45–46, footnote 1 (1899).

1592 [Many agricultural counties] are far more important in the life of the State than their population bears to the entire population of the State. It is for this reason that I have never been in favor of restricting their representation in our State Senate to a strictly population basis. It is the same reason that the founding fathers of our country gave balanced representation to the States of the Union, equal representation in one House and proportionate representation based upon population in the other.

EARL WARREN, governor of California, speech at Merced, California, October 29, 1948, as reported by the *San Francisco Chronicle,* October 30, 1948, p. 3.

Warren was asking for a "no" vote on a proposition which would reconstitute the state senate on the basis of population.

1593 "Well, Doctor, what have we got—a Republic or a Monarchy?"
"A Republic, if you can keep it."

The response is attributed to BENJAMIN FRANKLIN—at the close of the Constitutional Convention of 1787, when queried as he left Independence Hall on the final day of deliberation—in the notes of Dr. James McHenry, one of Maryland's delegates to the Convention.

McHenry's notes were first published in *The American Historical Review,* vol. 11, 1906, and the anecdote on p. 618 reads: "A lady asked Dr. Franklin Well Doctor what have we got a republic or a monarchy. A republic replied the Doctor if you can keep it." When McHenry's notes were included in *The Records of the Federal Convention of 1787,* ed. Max Farrand, vol. 3, appendix A, p. 85 (1911, reprinted 1934), a footnote stated that the date this anecdote was written is uncertain.

1594 The Republic needed to be passed through chastening, purifying fires of adversity and suffering: so these came and did their work and the verdure of a new national life springs greenly, luxuriantly, from their ashes.

HORACE GREELEY, *Greeley on Lincoln,* ed. Joel Benton, pp. 78–79 (1893). He is referring to the Civil War.

1595 You and your descendants have to ascertain whether this great mass will hold together under the forms of a republic, and the despotic reality of universal suffrage; whether state rights will hold out against centralisation, without separation, whether centralisation will get the better, without actual or disguised monarchy; whether shifting corruption is better than a permanent bureaucracy; and as population thickens in your great cities, and the pressure of what is felt, the gaunt spectre of pauperism will stalk among you, and communism and socialism will claim to be heard.

THOMAS HENRY HUXLEY, *Science and Education,* p. 138 (1904).

1596 But every difference of opinion is not a difference of principle. We have called by different names brethren of the same principle. We are all republicans we are federalists.

President THOMAS JEFFERSON, inaugural address, March 4, 1801.—*The Writings of Thomas Jefferson,* ed. Andrew A. Lipscomb, vol. 3, p. 319 (1904).

1597 In truth, the abuses of monarchy had so much filled all the space of political contemplation, that we imagined everything republican which was not monarchy. We had not yet penetrated to the mother principle, that "governments are republican only in proportion as they embody the will of their people, and execute it." Hence, our first constitutions had really no leading principles in them. But experience and reflection have but more and more confirmed me in the particular importance of the equal representation then proposed.

THOMAS JEFFERSON, letter to Samuel Kercheval, July 12, 1816.—*The Writings of Thomas Jefferson,* ed. Paul L. Ford, vol. 10, p. 37 (1899).

1598 When a monarchy gradually transforms itself into a republic, the executive power there preserves titles, honors, respect, and even money long after it has lost the reality of power. The English, having cut off the head of one of their kings and chased another off the throne, still go on their knees to address the successors of those princes. On the other hand, when a republic falls under one man's yoke, the ruler's demeanor remains simple, unaffected, and modest, as if he had not already been raised above everybody.

ALEXIS DE TOCQUEVILLE, *Democracy in America,* ed. J. P. Mayer, trans. George Lawrence, vol. 1, part 1, chapter 8, p. 123 (1969). Originally published in 1835–1840.

Republican Party

1599 I am a Republican, a black, dyed in the wool Republican, and I never intend to belong to any other party than the party of freedom and progress.

Attributed to FREDERICK DOUGLASS. Unverified.

1600 I knew that however bad the Republican party was, the Democratic party was much worse. The elements of which the Republican party was composed gave better ground for the ultimate hope of the success of the colored man's cause than those of the Democratic party.

FREDERICK DOUGLASS, *Life and Times of Frederick Douglass,* chapter 47, p. 579 (1941).

1601 I recognize the Republican party as the sheet anchor of the colored man's political hopes and the ark of his safety.

FREDERICK DOUGLASS, letter to men from Petersburg, Virginia, August 15, 1888.—Douglass papers, Library of Congress.

The Petersburg men had written Douglass seeking advice about supporting John M. Langston as their Republican candidate for Congress. He would be their first black representative, but earlier he had worked against the Republican party. Douglass called him a trickster and said not to support anyone "whose mad ambition would imperil the success of the Republican party."

1602 Indeed there are some Republicans I would trust with anything—anything, that is, except public office.

ADLAI E. STEVENSON, governor of Illinois, campaign speech, Illinois state fair, Springfield, Illinois, August 14, 1952.—*Major Campaign Speeches of Adlai E. Stevenson, 1952,* p. 14 (1953).

Responsibility

1603 A hundred times every day I remind myself that my inner and outer life are based on the labors of other men, living and dead, and that I must exert myself in order to give in the same measure as I have received and am still receiving.

ALBERT EINSTEIN, "The World as I See It," *Ideas and Opinions,* trans. Sonja Bargmann, p. 8 (1954).

1604 For of those to whom much is given, much is required. And when at some future date the high court of history sits in judgment on each of us—recording whether in our brief span of service we fulfilled our responsibilities to the state—our success or failure, in whatever office we hold, will be measured by the answers to four questions:

First, were we truly men of courage—with the courage to stand up to one's enemies—and the courage to stand up, when necessary, to one's associates—the courage to resist public pressure, as well as private greed?

Secondly, were we truly men of judgment—with perceptive judgment of the future as well as the past—of our mistakes as well as the mistakes of others—with enough wisdom to know what we did not know and enough candor to admit it.

Third, were we truly men of integrity—men who never ran out on either the principles in which we believed or the men who believed in us—men whom neither financial gain nor political ambition could ever divert from the fulfillment of our sacred trust?

Finally, were we truly men of dedication—with an honor mortgaged to no single individual or group, and comprised of no private obligation or aim, but devoted solely to serving the public good and the national interest?

Courage—judgment—integrity—dedication—these are the historic qualities . . . which, with God's help . . . will characterize our Government's conduct in the 4 stormy years that lie ahead.

President-elect JOHN F. KENNEDY, address to the Massachusetts legislature, January 9, 1961.—*Congressional Record,* January 10, 1961, vol. 107, Appendix, p. A169.

1605 Upon the standard to which the wise and honest will now repair it is written: "You have lived the easy way; henceforth, you will live the hard way. . . . You came into a great heritage made by the insight and the sweat and the blood of inspired and devoted and courageous men; thoughtlessly and in utmost self-indulgence you have all but squandered this inheritance. Now only by the heroic virtues which made this inheritance can you restore it again. . . . You took the good things for granted. Now you must earn them again. . . . For every right that you cherish, you have a duty which you must fulfill. For every hope that you entertain, you have a task that you must perform. For every good that you wish to preserve, you will have to sacrifice your comfort and your ease. There is nothing for nothing any longer."

WALTER LIPPMANN, speech to the Harvard Class of 1910 at their thirtieth reunion, June 18, 1940.—Walter Lippmann papers, Yale University Library.

President Jimmy Carter quoted from the latter part of this passage, with slight variations, in his State of the Union address to Congress, January 23, 1980.—*Public Papers of the Presidents of the United States: Jimmy Carter, 1980–81,* book 1, p. 200.

1606 If I knew something useful to me and harmful to my family, I should put it out of my mind. If I knew something useful to my family and not to my country, I should try to forget it. If I knew something useful to my country and harmful to Europe, or useful to Europe and harmful to the human race, I should consider it a crime.

MONTESQUIEU.—Robert John Loy, *Montesquieu,* chapter 3, p. 122 (1968).

Before giving this translation, Loy says, "Montesquieu was so fond of the passage that he composed it in several forms; it stands as his philosophical emblem." For the original French, see Montesquieu, *Oeuvres Completes,* p. 981 (1949).

1607 There is a mysterious cycle in human events. To some generations much is given. Of other generations much is expected. This generation of Americans has a rendezvous with destiny.

President FRANKLIN D. ROOSEVELT, speech accepting renomination for the presidency, Philadelphia, Pennsylvania, June 27, 1936.—*The Public Papers and Addresses of Franklin D. Roosevelt, 1936,* p. 235 (1938).

1608 God has lent us the earth for our life; it is a great entail. It belongs as much to those who are to come after us, and whose names are already written in the book of creation, as to us; and we have no right, by anything that we do or neglect, to involve them in unnecessary penalties, or deprive them of benefits which it was in our power to bequeath.

JOHN RUSKIN, "The Lamp of Memory," *The Seven Lamps of Architecture,* chapter 6, section 9, p. 248 (1907).

Responsibility

1609 Physical misery is great everywhere out here [Africa]. Are we justified in shutting our eyes and ignoring it because our European newspapers tell us nothing about it? We civilised people have been spoilt. If any one of us is ill the doctor comes at once. Is an operation necessary, the door of some hospital or other opens to us immediately. But let every one reflect on the meaning of the fact that out here millions and millions live without help or hope of it. Every day thousands and thousands endure the most terrible sufferings, though medical science could avert them. Every day there prevails in many and many a far-off hut a despair which we could banish. Will each of my readers think what the last ten years of his family history would have been if they had been passed without medical or surgical help of any sort? It is time that we should wake from slumber and face our responsibilities!

ALBERT SCHWEITZER, *On the Edge of the Primeval Forest*, trans. C. T. Campion, p. 115 (1948, reprinted 1976).

1610 The Buck Stops Here

President HARRY S. TRUMAN, motto on his White House desk.—Alfred Steinberg, *Harry S. Truman*, p. 185 (1963).

See also No. 1490.

1611 For we must consider that we shall be as a City upon a hill. The eyes of all people are upon us. Soe that if we shall deal falsely with our God in this work we have undertaken, and so cause him to withdraw his present help from us, we shall be made a story and a byword throughout the world.

JOHN WINTHROP, governor of Massachusetts Bay Colony, "A Modell of Christian Charity," discourse written aboard the *Arbella* during the voyage to Massachusetts, 1630.—Robert C. Winthrop, *Life and Letters of John Winthrop*, p. 19 (1867).

Robert C. Winthrop was a representative from Massachusetts, 1840–1850, and was Speaker of the House 1847–1849; he was a senator from Massachusetts 1850–1851.

Walter F. Mondale referred to the "city on a hill" in a presidential campaign speech in Cleveland, Ohio, October 25, 1984; *The Washington Post* account notes that this quotation from Winthrop is a favorite of President Reagan's.—October 26, 1984, p. 1.

President-elect John F. Kennedy said, in an address to the Massachusetts Legislature on January 9, 1961, "During the last 60 days I have been engaged in the task of constructing an administration. . . . I have been guided by the standard John Winthrop set before his shipmates on the flagship *Arabella* [sic] 331 years ago, as they, too, faced the task of building a government on a new and perilous frontier. 'We must always consider,' he said, 'that we shall be as a city upon a hill—the eyes of all people are upon us.' Today the eyes of all people are truly upon us—and our governments, in every branch, at every level, national, State, and local, must be as a city upon a hill—constructed and inhabited by men aware of their grave trust and their great responsibilities."—*Congressional Record*, January 10, 1961, vol. 107, Appendix, p. A169. For another portion of this speech, see No. 1494.

Retribution

1612 Retribution often means that we eventually do to ourselves what we have done unto others.

ERIC HOFFER, "Thoughts of Eric Hoffer, Including: 'Absolute Faith Corrupts Absolutely,' " *The New York Times Magazine*, April 25, 1971, p. 57.

1613 This means we must subject the machine—technology—to control and cease despoiling the earth and filling people with goodies merely to make money. The search of the young today is more specific than the ancient search for the Holy Grail. The search of the youth today is for ways and means to make the machine—and the vast bureaucracy of the corporation state and of government that runs that machine—the servant of man.

That is the revolution that is coming.

That revolution—now that the people hold the residual powers of government—need not be a repetition of 1776. It could be a revolution in the nature of an explosive political regeneration. It depends on how wise the Establishment is. If, with its stockpile of arms, it resolves to suppress the dissenters, America will face, I fear, an awful ordeal.

Justice WILLIAM O. DOUGLAS, *Points of Rebellion*, pp. 96–97 (1970).

1614 We must realize that today's Establishment is the new George III. Whether it will continue to adhere to his tactics, we do not know. If it does, the redress, honored in tradition, is also revolution.

Justice WILLIAM O. DOUGLAS, *Points of Rebellion*, p. 95 (1970).

1615 As it was 189 years ago, so today the cause of America is a revolutionary cause. And I am proud this morning to salute you as fellow revolutionaries. Neither you nor I are willing to accept the tyranny of poverty, nor the dictatorship of ignorance, nor the despotism of ill health, nor the oppression of bias and prejudice and bigotry. We want change. We want progress. We want it both abroad and at home—and we aim to get it.

President LYNDON B. JOHNSON, remarks to college students employed by the government during the summer, August 4, 1965.—*Public Papers of the Presidents of the United States: Lyndon B. Johnson, 1965*, book 2, p. 830.

1616 Those who make peaceful revolution impossible will make violent revolution inevitable.

President JOHN F. KENNEDY, address to the diplomatic corps of the Latin American republics on the first anniversary of the Alliance for Progress, March 13, 1962.—*Public Papers of the Presidents of the United States: John F. Kennedy, 1962*, p. 223.

1617 But above all, what this Congress can be remembered for is opening the way to a new American revolution—a peaceful revolution in which power was turned back to the people—in which government at all levels was refreshed and renewed and made truly responsive. This can be a revolution as profound, as far-reaching, as exciting as that first revolution almost 200 years ago—and it can mean that just 5 years from now America will enter its third century as a young nation new in spirit, with all the vigor and the freshness with which it began its first century.

President RICHARD M. NIXON, State of the Union address to a joint session of Congress, January 22, 1971.—*Public Papers of the Presidents of the United States: Richard Nixon, 1971*, p. 58.

1618 Many of the world's troubles are not due just to Russia or communism. They would be with us in any event because we live in an era of revolution—the revolution of rising expectations. In Asia, the masses now count for something. Tomorrow, they will count for more. And, for better or for worse, the future belongs to those who understand the hopes and fears of masses in ferment. The new nations want independence, including the inalienable right to make their own mistakes. The people want respect—and something to eat every day. And they want something better for their children.

ADLAI E. STEVENSON, *The Papers of Adlai E. Stevenson,* vol. 5, p. 411 (1974).

First published in *Look,* September 22, 1953, p. 46, in the concluding article in a series about his five-month trip around the world.

Revolutionary War (1775–1783)

1619 As to the history of the revolution, my ideas may be peculiar, perhaps singular. What do we mean by the revolution? The war? That was no part of the revolution; it was only an effect and consequence of it. The revolution was in the minds of the people, and this was effected from 1760 to 1775, in the course of fifteen years, before a drop of blood was shed at Lexington.

JOHN ADAMS, letter to Thomas Jefferson, August 24, 1815.—*The Works of John Adams,* ed. Charles Francis Adams, vol. 10, p. 172 (1856).

1620 You say that at the time of the Congress, in 1765, "The great mass of the people were zealous in the cause of America." "The great mass of the people" is an expression that deserves analysis. New York and Pennsylvania were so nearly divided, if their propensity was not against us, that if New England on one side and Virginia on the other had not kept them in awe, they would have joined the British. Marshall, in his life of Washington, tells us, that the southern States were nearly equally divided. Look into the Journals of Congress, and you will see how seditious, how near rebellion were several counties of New York, and how much trouble we had to compose them. The last contest, in the town of Boston, in 1775, between whig and tory, was decided by five against two. Upon the whole, if we allow two thirds of the people to have been with us in the revolution, is not the allowance ample? Are not two thirds of the nation now with the administration? Divided we ever have been, and ever must be. Two thirds always had and will have more difficulty to struggle with the one third than with all our foreign enemies.

JOHN ADAMS, letter to Thomas McKean, August 31, 1813.—*The Works of John Adams,* ed. Charles Francis Adams, vol. 10, p. 63 (1856).

He referred to a Congress "held at New York, A.D. 1765, on the subject of the American stamp act" (p. 62).

1621 The country shall be independent, and we will be satisfied with nothing short of it.

SAMUEL ADAMS, remark in "small confidential companies."—William Gordon, *The History of the Rise, Progress, and Establishment, of the Independence of the United States of America,* vol. 1, entry for March 9, 1774, p. 347 (1788, reprinted 1969).

1622 Americans developed the resourcefulness and wisdom to solve the problem of organizing a nation in the midst of war and crisis, one of the greatest achievements of modern political history. The Americans of the Revolutionary generation proved themselves the most creative statesmen in modern history, perhaps in all history. They established institutions that have had a more lasting influence than any established anywhere else.

HENRY STEELE COMMAGER, interview with John A. Garraty.—Garraty, *Interpreting American History, Conversations with Historians,* part 1, p. I-100 (1970).

1623 Yet where does this anarchy exist? Where did it ever exist, except in the single instance of Massachusets? And can history produce an instance of a rebellion so honourably conducted? . . . God forbid we should ever be 20. years without such a rebellion. The people can not be all, and always, well informed. The part which is wrong will be discontented in proportion to the importance of the facts they misconceive. If they remain quiet under such misconceptions it is a lethargy, the forerunner of death to the public liberty.

THOMAS JEFFERSON, letter to William Stephens Smith, November 13, 1787.—*The Papers of Thomas Jefferson,* ed. Julian P. Boyd, vol. 12, p. 356 (1955).

1624 An honorable Peace is and always was my first wish! I can take no delight in the effusion of human Blood; but, if this War should continue, I wish to have the most active part in it.

JOHN PAUL JONES, letter to Gouverneur Morris, September 2, 1782.—Robert Morris Letter Book, Rosenbach Collection No. 33, Manuscript Collection, U.S. Naval Academy Museum, Annapolis, Maryland. This sentence is reprinted in Lincoln Lorenz, *John Paul Jones, Fighter for Freedom and Glory,* p. xiv (1943).

1625 I have not yet begun to fight.

JOHN PAUL JONES, captain of the *Bonhomme Richard,* reply to the British ship *Serapis,* September 23, 1779.

The exact wording of his reply is uncertain, and several accounts exist. The standard version above is from an account of the engagement by one of Jones's officers, First Lieutenant Richard Dale.—John Henry Sherburne, *The Life and Character of John Paul Jones,* 2d ed., p. 121 (1851).

Sherburne includes Jones's letter of October 3, 1779, to Benjamin Franklin, where he says, p. 116, "The English commodore asked me if I demanded quarters, and I having answered him in the most determined negative, they renewed the battle with double fury."

Benjamin Rush writes, "I heard a minute account of his engagement with the Seraphis in a small circle of gentlemen at a dinner. It was delivered with great apparent modesty and commanded the most respectful attention. Towards the close of the battle, while his deck was swimming in blood, the captain of the Seraphis called him to strike. 'No, Sir,' said he, 'I will not, we have had but a small fight as yet.' "—*The Autobiography of Benjamin Rush,* ed. George W. Corner, p. 157 (1948).

1626 Every proceeding respecting myself has been so thoroughly mortifying, that nothing but the integrity of my heart, and the fervency of my Zeal Supports me under it. . . . Change then your opinion of one foreigner, who from his intrance into your Service, has never the cause to be pleased; who, in Europe, is by Rank superior to all that are in your Service; who certainly is not inferior in Zeal and Capacity and who perhaps, may have been considered as one who came to beg your favour. Be more just, Gentlemen, and Know that as I could not Submit to Stoop before the Sovereigns of Europe, So I came to hazard all the freedom of America, and desirous of passing the rest of my life in a Country truly free and before settling as a Citizen, to fight for Liberty.

CASIMIR PULASKI, farewell address to Congress, Charleston, South Carolina, August 19, 1779.—R. D. Jamro, *Pulaski: A Portrait of Freedom,* appendix Y, pp. 199, 200 (1981).

1627 The time is now near at hand which must probably determine, whether Americans are to be, Freemen, or Slaves; whether they are to have any property they can call their own; whether their Houses, and Farms, are to be pillaged and destroyed, and they consigned to a State of Wretchedness from which no human efforts will probably deliver them. The fate of unborn Millions will now depend, under God, on the Courage and Conduct of this army—Our cruel and unrelenting Enemy leaves us no choice but a brave resistance, or the most abject submission; that is all we can expect—We have therefore to resolve to conquer or die.

General GEORGE WASHINGTON, general orders, July 2, 1776.—*The Writings of George Washington,* ed. John C. Fitzpatrick, vol. 5, p. 211 (1932).

1628 To morrow being the day set apart by the Honorable Congress for public Thanksgiving and Praise; and duty calling us devoutely to express our grateful acknowledgements to God for the manifold blessings he has granted us. The General directs that the army remain in it's present quarters, and that the Chaplains perform divine service with their several Corps and brigades. And earnestly exhorts, all officers and soldiers, whose absence is not indispensibly necessary, to attend with reverence the solemnities of the day.

General GEORGE WASHINGTON, general orders, December 17, 1777.—*The Writings of George Washington,* ed. John C. Fitzpatrick, vol. 10, p. 168 (1933).

1629 You will therefore send me none but Natives, and Men of some property, if you have them.

General GEORGE WASHINGTON, letter to his regimental commanders, April 30, 1777.—*The Writings of George Washington,* ed. John C. Fitzpatrick, vol. 7, p. 495 (1932).

Washington wanted a contingent of guards he could trust. This order is often quoted as "Put none but Americans on guard tonight."

1630

HERE were held the
town-meetings that
ushered in the Revolution
HERE Samuel Adams, James Otis
and Joseph Warren exhorted
HERE the men of Boston proved
themselves independent
courageous freemen
worthy to raise issues
which were to concern the
liberty and happiness
of millions yet unborn

Author unknown. Sign at the main entrance of the Old South Meeting House, Boston, Massachusetts.

Rich

1631 "I was told," continued Egremont, "that an impassable gulf divided the Rich from the Poor; I was told that the Privileged and the People formed Two Nations, governed by different laws, influenced by different manners, with no thoughts or sympathies in common; with an innate inability of mutual comprehension."

BENJAMIN DISRAELI, *Sybil, or, The Two Nations,* ed. Thom Braun, book 4, chapter 8, p. 299 (1980). First published in 1845.

1632 This country cannot afford to be materially rich and spiritually poor.

President JOHN F. KENNEDY, State of the Union address, January 14, 1963.—*Public Papers of the Presidents of the United States: John F. Kennedy, 1963,* p. 13.

Inscription on the John F. Kennedy Center for the Performing Arts, Washington, D.C.

See also No. 230.

1633 I take it that it is best for all to leave each man free to acquire property as fast as he can. Some will get wealthy. I don't believe in a law to prevent a man from getting rich; it would do more harm than good.

ABRAHAM LINCOLN, speech at New Haven, Connecticut, March 6, 1860.—*The Collected Works of Abraham Lincoln*, ed. Roy P. Basler, vol. 4, p. 24 (1953).

Right

1634 Still, if you will not fight for the right when you can easily win without bloodshed; if you will not fight when your victory will be sure and not too costly; you may come to the moment when you will have to fight with all the odds against you and only a precarious chance of survival. There may even be a worse case. You may have to fight when there is no hope of victory, because it is better to perish than live as slaves.

WINSTON CHURCHILL, *The Gathering Storm* (vol. 1 of *The Second World War*), p. 348 (1948).

On March 31, 1939, Prime Minister Neville Chamberlain had informed the House of Commons that Britain would support Poland against any action threatening its independence. This marked the end of submission to Germany. Churchill thought the decision should have been made sooner when it would have been easier to stop Germany.

1635 To see what is right and not to do it is want of courage.

CONFUCIUS, *Analects*, book 2, chapter 24, *Confucian Analects, the Great Learning, and the Doctrine of the Mean*, trans. James Legge, p. 154 (1893, reprinted 1971).

1636 Let us not be content to wait and see what will happen, but give us the determination to make the right things happen.

PETER MARSHALL, Senate chaplain, prayer offered at the opening of the session, March 10, 1948.—*Prayers Offered by the Chaplain, the Rev. Peter Marshall . . . 1947–1948*, p. 49 (1949). Senate Doc. 80–170.

1637 Aggressive fighting for the right is the noblest sport the world affords.

THEODORE ROOSEVELT, saying.—Gifford Pinchot, "Roosevelt as President" in *State Papers as Governor and President, 1899–1909* (vol. 15 of *The Works of Theodore Roosevelt*, national ed.), p. xxxiii (1926).

Pinchot commented, "There are few sayings of his that hold for me so much of him as this."

Right and wrong

1638 You may burn my body to ashes, and scatter them to the winds of heaven; you may drag my soul down to the regions of darkness and despair to be tormented forever; but you will never get me to support a measure which I believe to be wrong, although by doing so I may accomplish that which I believe to be right.

Attributed to ABRAHAM LINCOLN.—Ida M. Tarbell, *The Life of Abraham Lincoln*, vol. 1, p. 139 (1900).

This book is based on the reminiscences of contemporaries of Lincoln's. General T. H. Henderson of Illinois related this story—told by his father, who had served with Lincoln in the Illinois legislature—which "illustrates his character for integrity and his firmness in maintaining what he regarded as right in his public acts."

This incident is supposed to have occurred during the session of 1836–1837, when efforts were made to move the capital of Illinois to Springfield; a bill to that effect was coupled with another measure that Lincoln did not approve of. "Finally, after midnight . . . Mr. Lincoln rose amid the silence and solemnity which prevailed, and, my father said, made one of the most eloquent and powerful speeches to which he had ever listened. He concluded his remarks" with the words above (pp. 138–39).

1639 Stand with anybody that stands RIGHT. Stand with him while he is right and PART with him when he goes wrong.

ABRAHAM LINCOLN, speech in reply to Senator Stephen Douglas, Peoria, Illinois, October 16, 1854.—*The Collected Works of Abraham Lincoln*, ed. Roy P. Basler, vol. 2, p. 273 (1953).

"This speech, together with one delivered twelve days before at Springfield, made Lincoln a power in national politics. He had had little to do with politics since the expiration of his term in Congress, but the repeal of the Missouri Compromise aroused him to instant action. . . . When closely studied the Peoria speech reveals germs of many of the powerful arguments elaborated by Lincoln later in his career."—*The Complete Works of Abraham Lincoln*, new and enl. ed., ed. John G. Nicolay and John Hay, vol. 2, p. 190, footnote (1905).

1640 Nothing is politically right which is morally wrong.

Attributed to DANIEL O'CONNELL.—Wendell Phillips, speech on the 100th anniversary of O'Connell's birth, August 6, 1875, *Speeches, Lectures, and Letters*, 2d series, p. 398 (1891). Unverified.

1641 The Senator from Wisconsin cannot frighten me by exclaiming, "My country, right or wrong." In one sense I say so too. My country; and my country is the great American Republic. My country, right or wrong; if right, to be kept right; and if wrong, to be set right.

Senator CARL SCHURZ, remarks in the Senate, February 29, 1872, *The Congressional Globe*, vol. 45, p. 1287. *The Globe* merely notes "[Manifestations of applause in the galleries]" but according to Schurz's biographer, "The applause in the gallery was deafening." This is "one of Schurz's most frequently quoted replies."—Hans L. Trefousse, *Carl Schurz: A Biography*, chapter 11, p. 180 (1982).

Schurz expanded on this theme in a speech delivered at the Anti-Imperialistic Conference, Chicago, Illinois, October 17, 1899: "I confidently trust that the American people will prove themselves . . . too wise not to detect the false pride or the dangerous ambitions or the selfish schemes which so often hide themselves under that deceptive cry of mock patriotism: 'Our country, right or wrong!' They will not fail to recognize that our dignity, our free institutions and the peace and welfare of this and coming generations of Americans will be secure only as we cling to the watchword of *true* patriotism: 'Our country—when right to be kept right; when wrong to be put right.' "—Schurz, "The Policy of Imperialism," *Speeches, Correspondence and Political Papers of Carl Schurz*, vol. 6, pp. 119–20 (1913).

1642 The greatest right in the world is the right to be wrong. If the Government or majorities think an individual is right, no one will interfere with him; but when agitators talk against the things considered holy, or when radicals criticise, or satirize the political gods, or question the justice of our laws and institutions, or pacifists talk against war, how the old inquisition awakens, and ostracism, the excommunication of the church, the prison, the wheel, the torture-chamber, the mob, are called to suppress the free expression of thought.

HARRY WEINBERGER, "The First Casualties in War," letter to the editor, *The Evening Post,* New York City, April 10, 1917, p. 11.

Rights

1643 The public good is in nothing more essentially interested, than in the protection of every individual's private rights.

SIR WILLIAM BLACKSTONE, *Commentaries on the Laws of England,* 9th ed., book 1, chapter 1, section 3, p. 139 (1783, reprinted 1978).

1644 [On completely popular government:] Its superiority in reference to present well-being rests upon two principles, of as universal truth and applicability as any general propositions which can be laid down respecting human affairs. The first is, that the rights and interests of every or any person are only secure from being disregarded, when the person interested is himself able, and habitually disposed, to stand up for them. The second is, that the general prosperity attains a greater height, and is more widely diffused, in proportion to the amount and variety of the personal energies enlisted in promoting it.

JOHN STUART MILL, *Considerations on Representative Government,* chapter 3, p. 55 (1861).

River

1645 A river is more than an amenity, it is a treasure.

Justice OLIVER WENDELL HOLMES, *New Jersey* v. *New York, et al.,* 283 U.S. 342 (1931).

Rome

1646 A great civilization is not conquered from without until it has destroyed itself within. The essential causes of Rome's decline lay in her people, her morals, her class struggle, her failing trade, her bureaucratic despotism, her stifling taxes, her consuming wars.

WILL DURANT, *Caesar and Christ,* Epilogue, p. 665 (1944).

1647 It was scarcely possible that the eyes of contemporaries should discover in the public felicity the latent causes of decay and corruption. This long peace, and the uniform government of the Romans, introduced a slow and secret poison into the vitals of the empire. The minds of men were gradually reduced to the same level, the fire of genius was extinguished, and even the military spirit evaporated. The natives of Europe were brave and robust. Spain, Gaul, Britain, and Illyricum, supplied the legions with excellent soldiers, and constituted the real strength of the monarchy. Their personal valour remained, but they no longer possessed that public courage which is nourished by the love of independence, the sense of national honour, the presence of danger, and the habit of command. They received laws and governors from the will of their sovereign, and trusted for their defence to a mercenary army. The posterity of their boldest leaders was contented with the rank of citizens and subjects. The most aspiring spirits resorted to the court or standard of the emperors; and the deserted provinces, deprived of political strength or union, insensibly sunk into the languid indifference of private life.

EDWARD GIBBON, *History of the Decline and Fall of the Roman Empire,* chapter 2, third paragraph from the end, p. 32 (1838).

1648 The teacher reminded us that Rome's liberties were not auctioned off in a day, but were bought slowly, gradually, furtively, little by little; first with a little corn and oil for the exceedingly poor and wretched, later with corn and oil for voters who were not quite so poor, later still with corn and oil for pretty much every man that had a vote to sell—exactly our own history over again.

MARK TWAIN (Samuel L. Clemens), "Purchasing Civic Virtue," *Mark Twain in Eruption,* ed. Bernard DeVoto, pp. 68–69 (1940).

Rules

1649 Rules are mostly made to be broken and are too often for the lazy to hide behind.

DOUGLAS MACARTHUR.—William A. Ganoe, *MacArthur Close-Up,* p. 137 (1962).

Running

1650 Now, *here* you see, it takes all the running *you* can do, to keep in the same place. If you want to get somewhere else, you must run at least twice as fast as that!

LEWIS CARROLL (Charles L. Dodgson), *Through the Looking-Glass,* chapter 2.—*Logical Nonsense: The Works of Lewis Carroll,* ed. Philip C. Blackburn and Lionel White, p. 177 (1934). First published in 1872.

1651 He can run. But he can't hide.

JOE LOUIS, remark to a reporter prior to the Joe Louis—Billy Conn boxing match, June 19, 1946.—Louis, *My Life Story,* p. 176 (1947).

Russia

1652 I cannot forecast to you the action of Russia. It is a riddle wrapped in a mystery inside an enigma; but perhaps there is a key. That key is Russian national interest.

WINSTON CHURCHILL, first lord of the admiralty, radio broadcast, London, October 1, 1939.—*Winston S. Churchill: His Complete Speeches, 1897–1963,* ed. Robert Rhodes James, vol. 6, p. 6161 (1974).

1653 Judged by every standard which history has applied to Governments, the Soviet Government of Russia is one of the worst tyrannies that has ever existed in the world. It accords no political rights. It rules by terror. It punishes political opinions. It suppresses free speech. It tolerates no newspapers but its own. It persecutes Christianity with a zeal and a cunning never equalled since the times of the Roman Emperors. It is engaged at this moment in trampling down the peoples of Georgia and executing their leaders by hundreds.

WINSTON CHURCHILL, chancellor of the exchequer, speech to the Scottish Unionist Association, Edinburgh, Scotland, September 25, 1924.—*Winston S. Churchill: His Complete Speeches, 1897–1963,* ed. Robert Rhodes James, vol. 4, p. 3472 (1974).

1654 It would appear that the natural frontier of Russia runs from Dantzic or perhaps Stettin to Trieste.

FREIDRICH ENGELS, "The Real Issue in Turkey," Karl Marx and Engels, *Collected Works*, vol. 12, p. 16 (1979).

This article was originally published in *The New York Daily Tribune*, April 12, 1853, p. 4, and since that paper's European correspondent was at that time Karl Marx, it has generally been assumed the author was Marx. *Collected Works*, vol. 12, p. 639, note 17, makes it clear that Engels was the author.

The same geographic area figures in No. 234.

1655 In a Russian tragedy, everybody dies. In a Russian comedy, everybody dies, too. But they die happy.

BARRY FARBER, radio talk-show host in New York City, during a program on radio station WMCA.

1656 If I had to choose between life in the Soviet Union and life in the U.S.A., I would certainly choose the Soviet Union.

Attributed to GRAHAM GREENE.—*Parade* magazine, October 29, 1967, p. 2. Unverified.

1657 My letter to Castro concluded an episode of world history in which, bringing the world to the brink of atomic war, we won a Socialist Cuba. It's very consoling for me personally to know that our side acted correctly and that we did a great revolutionary deed by not letting American imperialism intimidate us. The Caribbean crisis was a triumph of Soviet foreign policy and a personal triumph in my own career as a statesman and as a member of the collective leadership. We achieved, I would say, a spectacular success without having to fire a single shot!

NIKITA S. KHRUSHCHEV, *Khrushchev Remembers*, trans. Strobe Talbott, p. 504 (1971).

1658 I got very well acquainted with Joe Stalin, and I like old Joe! He is a decent fellow. But Joe is a prisoner of the Politburo.

President HARRY S. TRUMAN, informal remarks, Eugene, Oregon, June 11, 1948.—*Public Papers of the Presidents of the United States: Harry S. Truman, 1948*, p. 329.

Truman refers to his meeting with Stalin at the Potsdam conference in July 1945.

Sacrifice

1659 Too long a sacrifice
Can make a stone of the heart.
O when may it suffice?

WILLIAM BUTLER YEATS, "Easter 1916," lines 57–59, *The Variorum Edition of the Poems of W. B. Yeats*, ed. Peter Allt and Russell K. Alspach, p. 394 (1957).

Santa Claus

1660 We take pleasure in answering at once and thus prominently the communication below, expressing at the same time our great gratification that its faithful author is numbered among the friends of *The Sun:*

Santa Claus

"Dear Editor: I am 8 years old.
"Some of my little friends say there is no Santa Claus.
"Papa says 'If you see it in *The Sun* it's so.'
"Please tell me the truth; is there a Santa Claus?

"Virginia O'Hanlon.
"115 West Ninety-fifth Street."

Virginia, your little friends are wrong. They have been affected by the skepticism of a skeptical age. They do not believe except they see. They think that nothing can be which is not comprehensible by their little minds. All minds, Virginia, whether they be men's or children's are little. In this great universe of ours man is a mere insect, an ant, in his intellect, as compared with the boundless world about him, as measured by the intelligence capable of grasping the whole of truth and knowledge.

Yes, Virginia, there is a Santa Claus. He exists as certainly as love and generosity and devotion exist, and you know that they abound and give to your life its highest beauty and joy. Alas! how dreary would be the world if there were no Santa Claus. It would be as dreary as if there were no Virginias. There would be no childlike faith then, no poetry, no romance to make tolerable this existence. We should have no enjoyment, except in sense and sight. The eternal light with which childhood fills the world would be extinguished.

Not believe in Santa Claus! You might as well not believe in fairies! You might get your papa to hire men to watch in all the chimneys on Christmas Eve to catch Santa Claus, but even if they did not see Santa Claus coming down, what would that prove? Nobody sees Santa Claus, but that is no sign that there is no Santa Claus. The most real things in the world are those that neither children nor men can see. Did you ever see fairies dancing on the lawn? Of course not, but that's no proof that they are not there. Nobody can conceive or imagine all the wonders there are unseen and unseeable in the world.

You may tear apart the baby's rattle and see what makes the noise inside, but there is a veil covering the unseen world which not the strongest man, nor even the united strength of all the strongest men that ever lived, could tear apart. Only faith, fancy, poetry, love, romance, can push aside that curtain and view and picture the supernal beauty and glory beyond. Is it all real? Ah, Virginia, in all this world there is nothing else real and abiding.

No Santa Claus! Thank God! he lives, and he lives forever. A thousand years from now, Virginia, nay, ten times ten thousand years from now, he will continue to make glad the heart of childhood.

FRANCIS P. CHURCH, "Is There a Santa Claus," editorial, *The Sun*, New York City, September 21, 1897, p. 6.

After Church's death on April 11, 1906, *The Sun* broke its policy of editorial anonymity to announce that he had written this editorial.

Science

1661 It is not enough that you should understand about applied science in order that your work may increase man's blessings. Concern for the man himself and his fate must always form the chief interest of all technical endeavors; concern for the great unsolved problems of the organization of labor and the distribution of goods in order that the creations of our mind shall be a blessing and not a curse to mankind. Never forget this in the midst of your diagrams and equations.

ALBERT EINSTEIN, speech at the California Institute of Technology, Pasadena, California, February 16, 1931, as reported in *The New York Times*, February 17, 1931, p. 6.

1662 Science without religion is lame, religion without science is blind.

ALBERT EINSTEIN, paper prepared for initial meeting of the Conference on Science, Philosophy and Religion in Their Relation to the Democratic Way of Life, New York City, September 9–11, 1940.—Einstein, *Out of My Later Years*, chapter 8, part 1, p. 26 (1950, rev. and reprinted 1970).

1663 Modern civilization depends on science . . . James Smithson was well aware that knowledge should not be viewed as existing in isolated parts, but as a whole, each portion of which throws light on all the other, and that the tendency of all is to improve the human mind, and give it new sources of power and enjoyment . . . narrow minds think nothing of importance but their own favorite pursuit, but liberal views exclude no branch of science or literature, for they all contribute to sweeten, to adorn, and to embellish life . . . science is the pursuit above all which impresses us with the capacity of man for intellectual and moral progress and awakens the human intellect to aspiration for a higher condition of humanity.

JOSEPH HENRY, first secretary of the Smithsonian Institution. Inscription on the National Museum of American History, Washington, D.C.

1664 What is a scientist? . . . We give the name scientist to the type of man who has felt experiment to be a means guiding him to search out the deep truth of life, to lift a veil from its fascinating secrets, and who, in this pursuit, has felt arising within him a love for the mysteries of nature, so passionate as to annihilate the thought of himself.

MARIA MONTESSORI, *The Montessori Method*, trans. Anne E. George, p. 8 (1964).

1665 A new scientific truth does not triumph by convincing its opponents and making them see the light, but rather because its opponents eventually die, and a new generation grows up that is familiar with it.

MAX PLANCK, *Scientific Autobiography and Other Papers*, trans. Frank Gaynor, pp. 33–34 (1950).

Sea

1666 I have seen the sea lashed into fury and tossed into spray, and its grandeur moves the soul of the dullest man; but I remember that it is not the billows, but the calm level of the sea from which all heights and depths are measured.

Representative JAMES A. GARFIELD, speech nominating John Sherman for president.—*Proceedings of the Republican National Convention*, Chicago, Illinois, June 2–8, 1880, p. 184 (1881).

Garfield himself was ultimately nominated at this convention.

1667 As they say on my own Cape Cod, a rising tide lifts all the boats. And a partnership, by definition, serves both partners, without domination or unfair advantage. Together we have been partners in adversity—let us also be partners in prosperity.

President JOHN F. KENNEDY, address in the Assembly Hall at the Paulskirche, Frankfurt, West Germany, June 25, 1963.—*Public Papers of the Presidents of the United States: John F. Kennedy, 1963*, p. 519.

Kennedy used the "rising tide" image a number of times.

Secrecy

1668 Everything secret degenerates, even the administration of justice; nothing is safe that does not show how it can bear discussion and publicity.

Attributed to LORD ACTON. Unverified.

1669 I request that they may be considered in confidence, until the members of Congress are fully possessed of their contents, and shall have had opportunity to deliberate on the consequences of their publication; after which time, I submit them to your wisdom.

President JOHN ADAMS, message to both houses of Congress transmitting dispatches from France, April 3, 1798.—*The Works of John Adams*, ed. Charles Francis Adams, vol. 9, p. 158 (1854).

1670 I believe that the public temper is such that the voters of the land are prepared to support the party which gives the best promise of administering the government in the honest, simple, and plain manner which is consistent with its character and purposes. They have learned that mystery and concealment in the management of their affairs cover tricks and betrayal. The statesmanship they require consists in honesty and frugality, a prompt response to the needs of the people as they arise, and a vigilant protection of all their varied interests.

GROVER CLEVELAND, letter accepting nomination as the Democratic candidate for president, August 8, 1884.—*The Writings and Speeches of Grover Cleveland*, p. 13 (1892).

Security

1671 If all that Americans want is security, they can go to prison. They'll have enough to eat, a bed and a roof over their heads. But if an American wants to preserve his dignity and his equality as a human being, he must not bow his neck to any dictatorial government.

DWIGHT D. EISENHOWER, president of Columbia University, speech to luncheon clubs, Galveston, Texas, December 8, 1949.—*The New York Times*, December 9, 1949, p. 23.

1672 There is no security on this earth; there is only opportunity.

Attributed to DOUGLAS MACARTHUR.—James B. Simpson, *Contemporary Quotations*, p. 316 (1964). Unverified.

Self

1673 If I am not for myself, who will be for me? And if I am only for myself, what am I? And if not now—when?

Aboth 1:14, saying of Hillel. Pirkay Avot, often known in English as the "Chapters of the Fathers," is the best known of the books of the Mishnah, first part of the Talmud. Translations vary; that above is from *Leo Rosten's Treasury of Jewish Quotations*, p. 459 (1972).

1674 How much easier is self-sacrifice than self-realization!

ERIC HOFFER, "Thoughts of Eric Hoffer, Including: 'Absolute Faith Corrupts Absolutely,' " *The New York Times Magazine*, April 25, 1971, p. 60.

1675 This above all: to thine own self be true,
And it must follow, as the night the day,
Thou canst not then be false to any man.

Self

WILLIAM SHAKESPEARE, *Hamlet,* act I, scene iii, lines 78–80. Polonius is speaking to Laertes.

1676 What we do belongs to what we are; and what we are is what becomes of us.

HENRY VAN DYKE, *Ships and Havens,* chapter 2, p. 10 (1898).

Self-deception

1677 Nothing is easier than self-deceit. For what each man wishes, that he also believes to be true.

DEMOSTHENES, *Third Olynthiac,* paragraph 19, *Olynthiacs, Phillippics, Minor Public Speeches . . . ,* trans. J. H. Vince, p. 53 (1954).

Self-examination

1678 How queer everything is to-day! And yesterday things went on just as usual. I wonder if I've been changed in the night? Let me think: *was* I the same when I got up this morning? I almost think I can remember feeling a little different. But if I'm not the same, the next question is, "Who in the world am I?" Ah, *that's* the great puzzle!

LEWIS CARROLL (Charles L. Dodgson), *Alice in Wonderland,* chapter 2.—*Logical Nonsense: The Works of Lewis Carroll,* ed. Philip C. Blackburn and Lionel White, p. 177 (1934). First published in 1865.

1679 I have sometimes asked myself whether my country is the better for my having lived at all? I do not know that it is. I have been the instrument of doing the following things; but they would have been done by others; some of them, perhaps, a little better.

THOMAS JEFFERSON, "Services of Jefferson" (1800?), *The Writings of Thomas Jefferson,* ed. Paul L. Ford, vol. 7, p. 475 (1896).

Self-importance

1680 I now know all the people worth knowing in America, and I find no intellect comparable to my own.

MARGARET FULLER.—*Memoirs of Margaret Fuller Ossoli,* by Ralph Waldo Emerson, William Henry Channing, and James Freeman Clarke, vol. 1, part 4 (written by Emerson), p. 234 (1884, reprinted 1972).

Perry Miller, "I Find No Intellect Comparable to My Own," *American Heritage,* February 1957, p. 22, says she made the remark at Emerson's table and adds, "she was speaking the truth."

1681 The compulsion to take ourselves seriously is in inverse proportion to our creative capacity. When the creative flow dries up, all we have left is our importance.

ERIC HOFFER, "Thoughts of Eric Hoffer, Including: 'Absolute Faith Corrupts Absolutely,' " *The New York Times Magazine,* April 25, 1971, p. 52.

Self-pity

1682 I never complained of the vicissitudes of fortune, nor suffered my face to be overcast at the revolution of the heavens, except once, when my feet were bare, and I had not the means of obtaining shoes. I came to the chief of Kūfah in a state of much dejection, and saw there a man who had no feet. I returned thanks to God and acknowledged his mercies, and endured my want of shoes with patience, and exclaimed,

"Roast fowl to him that's sated will seem less
Upon the board than leaves of garden cress.
While, in the sight of helpless poverty,
Boiled turnip will a roasted pullet be."

SADI, *The Gulistān, or Rose Garden,* trans. Edward B. Eastwick, chapter 3, story 19, p. 129 (1880).

A modern version, often cited as an old Arabian proverb, is: "I thought I was abused because I had no shoes until I met a man who had no feet."—J. M. Braude, *Speaker's Encyclopedia of Stories, Quotations and Anecdotes,* p. 338, no. 2320 (1955).

Self-respect

1683 It is my ambition and desire to so administer the affairs of the government while I remain President that if at the end I have lost every other friend on earth I shall at least have one friend remaining and that one shall be down inside me.

Attributed to President ABRAHAM LINCOLN by Enos Clarke, one of the seventy-member delegation of Radicals from Missouri, who met with Lincoln, September 30, 1863. This attribution was made by Clarke in an interview with Walter B. Stevens, who later published it in his *Lincoln and Missouri,* p. 100 (1916).

All contemporary accounts indicate there were no reporters at this meeting. Lincoln's secretary, John Hay, took notes, but this statement is not in his notebooks. For that day's notes, see John G. Nicolay and John Hay, *Abraham Lincoln, A History,* vol. 8, pp. 215–20 (1890).

Sex

1684 I lose my respect for the man who can make the mystery of sex the subject of a coarse jest, yet when you speak earnestly and seriously on the subject, is silent.

HENRY DAVID THOREAU, journal entry, April 12, 1852.—*The Heart of Thoreau's Journals,* ed. Odell Shepard, p. 126 (1927).

1685 The state has no business in the bedrooms of the nation.

PIERRE ELLIOTT TRUDEAU, Canadian minister of justice, remark to newsmen, Ottawa, Canada, December 21, 1967, as reported by *The Globe and Mail,* Toronto, December 22, 1967, p. 1.

He was commenting on the government's proposal to overhaul Canadian criminal law, giving new recognition to individual rights in several areas, including sexual behavior.

Shakespeare, William (1564–1616)

1686 England's genius filled all measure
Of heart and soul, of strength and pleasure,
Gave to the mind its emperor,
And life was larger than before:
Nor sequent centuries could hit

Orbit and sum of SHAKESPEARE's wit.
The men who lived with him became
Poets, for the air was fame.

RALPH WALDO EMERSON, "Solution," lines 35–42, *Poems*, p. 222 (1918).

These lines are inscribed above the fireplace in the old reading room of the Folger Shakespeare Library, Washington, D.C.

Ships and shipping

1687 It is a national humiliation that we are now compelled to pay from twenty to thirty million dollars annually (exclusive of passage money which we should share with vessels of other nations) to foreigners for doing the work which should be done by American vessels American built, American owned, and American manned. This is a direct drain upon the resources of the country of just so much money; equal to casting it into the sea, so far as this nation is concerned.

President ULYSSES S. GRANT, message to the Senate and House of Representatives, March 23, 1870, *Congressional Globe*, vol. 42, p. 2177.

1688 It is cheering to see that the rats are still around—the ship is not sinking.

ERIC HOFFER, "Thoughts of Eric Hoffer, Including: 'Absolute Faith Corrupts Absolutely,' " *The New York Times Magazine*, April 25, 1971, p. 24.

1689 [A ship is always referred to as "she"] Because it costs so much to keep one in paint and powder.

Rear Admiral CHESTER W. NIMITZ, answer when asked why a ship is always referred to as "she," to Society of Sponsors of the United States Navy, Washington, D.C., February 13, 1940.—Associated Press dispatch, *The New York Times*, February 15, 1940, p. 39.

Silence

1690 In some causes silence is dangerous; so if any know of conspiracies against their country or king, or any that might greatly prejudice their neighbor, they ought to discover it.

Attributed to ST. AMBROSE. Unverified.

1691 Under all speech that is good for anything there lies a silence that is better. Silence is deep as Eternity; speech is shallow as Time.

THOMAS CARLYLE, essay on Sir Walter Scott, *Critical and Miscellaneous Essays*, vol. 4, p. 190 (1881).

Carlyle refers to this theme elsewhere, one example being: "As the Swiss Inscription says: *Sprechen ist silbern, Schweigen ist golden* (Speech is silvern, Silence is golden); or as I might express it: Speech is of Time, Silence is of Eternity."—Carlyle, *Sartor Resartus and Selected Prose*, book 3, chapter 3, p. 205 (1970).

1692 Blessed is the man who, having nothing to say, abstains from giving us wordy evidence of the fact.

GEORGE ELIOT, *Impressions of Theophrastus Such*, chapter 4, p. 51 (1900). First published in 1879.

1693 I am coming to feel that the people of ill will have used time much more effectively than the people of goodwill. We will have to repent in this generation not merely for the vitriolic words and actions of the bad people, but for the appalling silence of the good people. We must come to see that human progress never rolls in on wheels of inevitability. It comes through the tireless efforts and persistent work of men willing to be co-workers with God, and without this hard work time itself becomes an ally of the forces of social stagnation. We must use time creatively, and forever realize that the time is always ripe to do right. Now is the time to make real the promise of democracy, and transform our pending national elegy into a creative psalm of brotherhood. Now is the time to lift our national policy from the quicksand of racial injustice to the solid rock of human dignity.

MARTIN LUTHER KING, JR., letter to several clergymen from the Birmingham City Jail, Birmingham, Alabama, April 16, 1963.—Microfilm of original typescript, p. 6. This has been widely reprinted, with occasional textual variations.

1694 Great souls endure in silence.
(Grosse Seelen dulden still.)

FRIEDRICH SCHILLER, *Don Carlos*, act I, scene iv, *Don Carlos, Mary Stuart*, trans. R. D. Boylan and Joseph Mellish, p. 30 (1902). The Marquis is speaking.

"Great spirits suffer patiently" is the translation in Friedrich Schiller, *Plays*, ed. Walter Hinderer, *Don Carlos* trans. A. Leslie and Jeanne R. Willson, p. 124 (1983).

1695 To sin by silence, when we should protest,
Makes cowards out of men. The human race
Has climbed on protest. Had no voice been raised
Against injustice, ignorance, and lust,
The inquisition yet would serve the law,
And guillotines decide our least disputes.
The few who dare, must speak and speak again
To right the wrongs of many. Speech, thank God,
No vested power in this great day and land
Can gag or throttle. Press and voice may cry
Loud disapproval of existing ills;
May criticise oppression and condemn
The lawlessness of wealth-protecting laws
That let the children and childbearers toil
To purchase ease for idle millionaires.

Therefore I do protest against the boast
Of independence in this mighty land.
Call no chain strong, which holds one rusted link.
Call no land free, that holds one fettered slave.
Until the manacled slim wrists of babes
Are loosed to toss in childish sport and glee,
Until the mother bears no burden, save
The precious one beneath her heart, until
God's soil is rescued from the clutch of greed
And given back to labor, let no man
Call this the land of freedom.

ELLA WHEELER WILCOX, "Protest," *Poems of Problems*, pp. 154–55 (1914).

Sincerity

1696 A little sincerity is a dangerous thing, and a great deal of it is absolutely fatal.

OSCAR WILDE, *The Critic as Artist*, part 2, in *The Complete Works of Oscar Wilde*, vol. 5, p. 209 (1923).

Sins

1697 According to Gandhi, the seven sins are wealth without works, pleasure without conscience, knowledge without character, commerce without morality, science without humanity, worship without sacrifice, and politics without principle. Well, Hubert Humphrey may have sinned in the eyes of God, as we all do, but according to those definitions of Gandhi's, it was Hubert Humphrey without sin.

President JIMMY CARTER, eulogy at funeral services for former Vice President Hubert Humphrey, St. Paul, Minnesota, January 16, 1978.—*Public Papers of the Presidents of the United States: Jimmy Carter, 1978,* book 1, p. 80.

President Carter told of finding "The Seven Sins" engraved on the wall of Gandhi's memorial during a recent trip to India.

Slavery

1698 I did more for the Russian serf in giving him land as well as personal liberty, than America did for the negro slave set free by the proclamation of President Lincoln. I am at a loss to understand how you Americans could have been so blind as to leave the negro slave without tools to work out his salvation. In giving him personal liberty, you have him an obligation to perform to the state which he must be unable to fulfill. Without property of any kind he cannot educate himself and his children. I believe the time must come when many will question the manner of American emancipation of the negro slaves in 1863. The vote, in the hands of an ignorant man, without either property or self respect, will be used to the damage of the people at large; for the rich man, without honor or any kind of patriotism, will purchase it, and with it swamp the rights of a free people.

ALEXANDER II, emperor of Russia, conversation with Wharton Barker, Pavlovski Palace, August 17, 1879.—Barker, "The Secret of Russia's Friendship," *The Independent*, March 24, 1904, p. 647.

1699 But this is slavery, not to speak one's thought.

EURIPIDES, *The Phoenician Women*, line 392.—*The Complete Greek Tragedies*, ed. David Grene and Richmond Lattimore, vol. 4, p. 392 (1958).

1700 But this momentous question, like a fire bell in the night, awakened and filled me with terror.

THOMAS JEFFERSON, letter to John Holmes, April 22, 1820.—*The Writings of Thomas Jefferson*, ed. Paul L. Ford, vol. 10, p. 157 (1899).

Jefferson refers to the Missouri question, whether to admit Missouri as a slave state but prohibit slavery in the rest of the Louisiana Purchase.

Holmes was a representative from Massachusetts from 1817 to March 15, 1820, when he resigned to attend the Maine constitutional convention. He was elected to the Senate from Maine and served from June 13, 1820, to 1827, and 1829–1833.

1701 Fellow-citizens, *we* cannot escape history. We of this Congress and this administration, will be remembered in spite of ourselves. No personal significance, or insignificance, can spare one or another of us. The fiery trial through which we pass, will light us down, in honor or dishonor, to the latest generation. We *say* we are for the Union. The world will not forget that we say this. We know how to save the Union. The world knows we do know how to save it. We—even *we here*—hold the power, and bear the responsibility. In *giving* freedom to the *slave*, we *assure* freedom to the *free*—honorable alike in what we give, and what we preserve. We shall nobly save, or meanly lose, the last best, hope of earth.

President ABRAHAM LINCOLN, annual message to Congress, December 1, 1862.—*The Collected Works of Abraham Lincoln,* ed. Roy P. Basler, vol. 5, p. 537 (1953).

1702 I do not understand that because I do not want a negro woman for a slave I must necessarily want her for a wife. My understanding is that I can just let her alone.

ABRAHAM LINCOLN, fourth debate with Senator Stephen A. Douglas, Charleston, Illinois, September 18, 1858.—*The Collected Works of Abraham Lincoln,* ed. Roy P. Basler, vol. 3, p. 146 (1953).

Lincoln used similar wording in a speech in Springfield, Illinois, June 26, 1857: "Now I protest against that counterfeit logic which concludes that, because I do not want a black woman for a *slave* I must necessarily want her for a *wife.* I need not have her for either. I can just leave her alone."—*Collected Works,* vol. 2, p. 405 (1953).

1703 Those arguments that are made, that the inferior race are to be treated with as much allowance as they are capable of enjoying; that as much is to be done for them as their condition will allow. What are these arguments? They are the arguments that kings have made for enslaving the people in all ages of the world. You will find that all the arguments in favor of kingcraft were of this class; they always bestrode the necks of the people, not that they wanted to do it, but because the people were better off for being ridden. That is their argument, and this argument of the Judge is the same old serpent that says you work and I eat, you toil and I will enjoy the fruits of it. Turn in whatever way you will—whether it comes from the mouth of a King, an excuse for enslaving the people of his country, or from the mouth of men of one race as a reason for enslaving the men of another race, it is all the same old serpent, and I hold if that course of argumentation that is made for the purpose of convincing the public mind that we should not care about this, should be granted, it does not stop with the negro.

ABRAHAM LINCOLN, speech at Chicago, Illinois, July 10, 1858.—*The Collected Works of Abraham Lincoln,* ed. Roy P. Basler, vol. 2, p. 500 (1953).

1704 Whenever [I] hear any one, arguing for slavery I feel a strong impulse to see it tried on him personally.

President ABRAHAM LINCOLN, speech to 140th Indiana regiment, March 17, 1865.—*The Collected Works of Abraham Lincoln,* ed. Roy P. Basler, vol. 8, p. 361 (1953).

1705 All socialism involves slavery. . . . That which fundamentally distinguishes the slave is that he labours under coercion to satisfy another's desires.

HERBERT SPENCER, "The Coming Slavery," *The Contemporary Review,* April 1884, p. 474. This essay was reprinted in chapter 2 of his book, *Man vs. the State* (1884).

1706 Not only do I pray for it, on the score of human dignity, but I can clearly forsee that nothing but the rooting out of slavery can perpetuate the existence of our union, by consolidating it in a common bond of principle.

Slavery

Attributed to GEORGE WASHINGTON.—John Bernard, *Retrospections of America, 1797–1811*, p. 91 (1887). This is from Bernard's account of a conversation he had with Washington in 1798. Unverified.

Sleep

1707 "Laugh and the world laughs with you, snore and you sleep alone."

MRS. PATRICK CAMPBELL, letter to George Bernard Shaw, August 13, 1912.—*Bernard Shaw and Mrs. Patrick Campbell: Their Correspondence*, ed. Alan Dent, p. 32 (1952).

Since this was in quotation marks in the letter, it may have been her own version of the familiar lines, "Laugh, and the world laughs with you; / Weep, and you weep alone." These are the first two lines of Ella Wheeler Wilcox's poem, "Solitude," first published in 1883 in her *Poems of Passion* and widely reprinted in newspapers, often without attribution.—Burton Stevenson, *Famous Single Poems*, pp. 223–242 (1935).

Smile

1708 Comrades, this man has a nice smile, but he's got iron teeth.

Attributed to ANDREI GROMYKO, speech to the Soviet Communist party central committee, Moscow, March 11, 1985, as reported by *The Washington Post*, March 17, 1985, p. A1.

He was referring to Soviet leader Mikhail Gorbachev. This statement is not found in translations of official materials.

1709 When you call me that, *smile!*

OWEN WISTER, *The Virginian*, pp. 29–30 (1902).

Presumably the forerunner of "Smile when you say that, partner," familiar to generations of moviegoers.

Smithsonian Institution

1710 Of all the foundations of establishments for pious or charitable uses, which ever signalized the spirit of the age, or the comprehensive beneficence of the founder, none can be named more deserving of the approbation of mankind than this. Should it be faithfully carried into effect, with an earnestness and sagacity of application, and a steady perseverance of pursuit, proportioned to the means furnished by the will of the founder, and to the greatness and simplicity of his design as by himself declared, "the increase and diffusion of knowledge among men," it is no extravagance of anticipation to declare, that his name will be hereafter enrolled among the eminent benefactors of mankind. . . . Whoever increases his knowledge, multiplies the uses to which he is enabled to turn the gift of his Creator.

Representative JOHN QUINCY ADAMS, House Report 181, pp. 2, 3, January 19, 1836, and William J. Rhees, *The Smithsonian Institution: Documents Relative to Its Origin and History, 1835–1899*, vol. 1, pp. 131–32 (1901).

This passage, in a slightly altered form, is inscribed on the exterior of the National Museum of American History, Washington, D.C.: "Of all the foundations of establishments for pious or charitable uses which ever signalized the spirit of the age or the comprehensive beneficence of the founder none can be named more deserving of the approbation of mankind than the Smithsonian Institution. Should it be faithfully carried into effect with an earnestness and sagacity of application . . . proportioned to the means furnished by the will of the founder and to the greatness and simplicity of his design as by himself declared,

Smithsonian Institution

'The increase and diffusion of knowledge among men,' his name will be hereafter enrolled among the eminent benefactors of mankind . . . whoever increases knowledge multiplies the uses to which he is able to turn the gift of his creator.

John Quincy Adams 1767–1848,
Sixth President of the United States"

Socialism

1711 Socialists propose to supplant the competitive planning of capitalism with a highly centralized planned economy. Our aim is frankly international and not narrowly patriotic (Daughters of the American Revolution please notice), but I cannot here discuss socialism's international policies.

If we gained control of the American Government, we would probably begin with a complete revision of the national governmental system. We would do one of two things. We would write an amendment to the Constitution giving the Federal Government the right to regulate all private business and to enter into any business which it deemed proper, or we would abolish the Constitution altogether and give the National Congress the power to interpret the people's will subject only to certain general principles of free speech and free assemblage.

PAUL BLANSHARD, "Socialist and Capitalist Planning," *The Annals of the American Academy of Political and Social Science*, July 1932, p. 10.

1712 I believe that for the past twenty years there has been a creeping socialism spreading in the United States.

President DWIGHT D. EISENHOWER, off-the-cuff speech to Republican leaders, Custer State Park, South Dakota, June 11, 1953.—Robert J. Donovan, *Eisenhower: The Inside Story*, p. 336 (1956).

At his press conference in Washington, D.C., June 17, 1953, President Eisenhower was asked what he meant by "creeping socialism." Donovan writes, "He replied: continued Federal expansion of the T.V.A. He reiterated for what he said was the thousandth time that he would not destroy the T.V.A., but he said that he thought it was socialistic to continue putting money paid by all the taxpayers into a single region which could then attract industry away from other areas" (p. 336). Also see *Public Papers of the Presidents of the United States: Dwight D. Eisenhower, 1953*, p. 433.

1713 The socialist economy has become so strong, so vigorous that from the summits we have reached we can issue an open challenge of peaceful economic competition to the most powerful capitalist country—the United States of America.

NIKITA S. KHRUSHCHEV, concluding speech to twenty-second congress of the Communist party of the Soviet Union, October 27, 1961.—*Khrushchev Speaks: Selected Speeches, Articles, and Press Conferences, 1949–1961*, ed. Thomas P. Whitney, p. 450 (1963).

Society

1714 Now, the vicissitudes that afflict the individual have their source in society. It is this situation that has given currency to the phrase "social forces." Personal relations have given way to impersonal ones. The Great Society has arrived and the task of our generation is to bring it under control. The study of how it is to be done is the function of politics.

ANEURIN BEVAN, *In Place of Fear;* chapter 3, p. 38 (1952).

Society

1715 [Society] is a partnership in all science, a partnership in all art, a partnership in every virtue and in all perfection. As the ends of such a partnership cannot be obtained in many generations, it becomes a partnership not only between those who are living, but between those who are living, those who are dead, and those who are to be born.

EDMUND BURKE, "Reflections on the Revolution in France," 1790, *The Works of the Right Honorable Edmund Burke,* vol. 3, p. 359 (1899).

1716 We must beware of trying to build a society in which nobody counts for anything except a politician or an official, a society where enterprise gains no reward and thrift no privileges.

WINSTON CHURCHILL, radio broadcast, London, March 21, 1943.—*Winston S. Churchill: His Complete Speeches, 1897–1963,* ed. Robert Rhodes James, vol. 7, p. 6761 (1974).

1717 The truth is that a vast restructuring of our society is needed if remedies are to become available to the average person. Without that restructuring the good will that holds society together will be slowly dissipated. It is that sense of futility which permeates the present series of protests and dissents. Where there is a persistent sense of futility, there is violence; and that is where we are today.

Justice WILLIAM O. DOUGLAS, *Points of Rebellion,* p. 56 (1970).

1718 The nature of a society is largely determined by the direction in which talent and ambition flow—by the tilt of the social landscape.

ERIC HOFFER, *The Temper of Our Time,* p. 104 (1967).

1719 The principles of Jefferson are the definitions and axioms of free society.

ABRAHAM LINCOLN, letter to Henry L. Pierce and others, April 6, 1859.—*The Collected Works of Abraham Lincoln,* ed. Roy P. Basler, vol. 3, p. 375 (1953).

Soldiers

1720 If I should die, think only this of me:
That there's some corner of a foreign field
That is for ever England.

RUPERT BROOKE, "The Soldier," lines 1–3, *Rupert Brooke: The Complete Poems,* 2d ed., p. 150 (1942, reprinted 1977).

1721 Soldiers! When it is announced that a respected and beloved leader has died for our freedom in the course of the battle, do not grieve, do not lose hope! Observe that anyone who dies for his country is a fortunate man, but death takes what it wants, indiscriminately, in peace-time as well as in war. It is better to die with freedom than without it.

Our fathers who have maintained our country in freedom for us have offered us their life in sacrifice; so let them be an example to you!

Soldier, trader, peasant, young and old, man and woman, be united! Defend your country by helping each other! According to ancient custom, the women will stand in defence of their country by giving encouragement to the soldier and by caring for the wounded. Although Italy is doing everything possible to disunite us, whether Christian or Muslim we will unitedly resist.

Our shelter and our shield is God. May our attackers' new weapons not deflect you from your thoughts which are dedicated to your defence of Ethiopia's freedom.

Your King who speaks to you today will at that time be in your midst, prepared to shed his blood for the liberty of Ethiopia.

HAILE SELASSIE I, emperor of Ethiopia, address to the Ethiopian Parliament, July 18, 1935.—*"My Life and Ethiopia's Progress," 1892–1937,* trans. Edward Ullendorff, p. 220 (1976).

1722 The patriot volunteer, fighting for country and his rights, makes the most reliable soldier on earth.

Attributed to THOMAS J. (STONEWALL) JACKSON.—Hunter McGuire, *Stonewall Jackson: An Address*, p. 16 (1897).

1723 Oh, it's Tommy this, an' Tommy that, an' 'Tommy, go away';
But it's 'Thank you, Mister Atkins', when the band begins to play—
The band begins to play, my boys, the band begins to play,
Oh, it's 'Thank you, Mister Atkins,' when the band begins to play.

RUDYARD KIPLING, "Tommy," stanza 1, chorus, *The Collected Works of Rudyard Kipling: Departmental Ditties and Barrack-Room Ballads*, vol. 25, p. 168 (1941, reprinted 1970).

1724 Honor to the Soldier, and Sailor everywhere, who bravely bears his country's cause. Honor also to the citizen who cares for his brother in the field, and serves, as he best can, the same cause—honor to him, only less than to him, who braves, for the common good, the storms of heaven and the storms of battle.

President ABRAHAM LINCOLN, letter to George Opdyke and others, December 2, 1863.—*The Collected Works of Abraham Lincoln*, ed. Roy P. Basler, vol. 7, p. 32 (1953).

1725 This extraordinary war in which we are engaged falls heavily upon all classes of people, but the most heavily upon the soldier. For it has been said, all that a man hath will he give for his life; and while all contribute of their substance the soldier puts his life at stake, and often yields it up in his country's cause. The highest merit, then, is due to the soldier.

President ABRAHAM LINCOLN, remarks at closing of sanitary fair, Washington, D.C., March 18, 1864.—*The Collected Works of Abraham Lincoln*, ed. Roy P. Basler, vol. 7, pp. 253–54 (1953).

1726 I have every confidence in the ultimate success of our joint cause; but success in modern war requires something more than courage and a willingness to die: it requires careful preparation. This means the furnishing of sufficient troops and sufficient material to meet the known strength of a potential enemy. No general can make something out of nothing. My success or failure will depend primarily upon the resources which the respective governments place at my disposal. My faith in them is complete. In any event I shall do my best. I shall keep the soldier's faith.

General DOUGLAS MACARTHUR, first public statement upon arriving in Australia, March 1942.—*A Soldier Speaks, Public Papers and Speeches of General of the Army Douglas MacArthur*, ed. Vorin E. Whan, Jr., p. 115 (1965).

1727 Old soldiers never die; they just fade away.

General DOUGLAS MACARTHUR, address to a joint session of Congress, April 19, 1951, *Congressional Record,* vol. 97, p. 4125.

According to *The Home Book of Quotations,* ed. Burton Stevenson, 9th ed., p. 2298h, col. 2 (1964), this is a line from a soldier's parody of a nineteenth century gospel hymn, "Kind Words Can Never Die." The parody was known at West Point where MacArthur was graduated in 1903. However, since the earliest printed version of the song "Old Soldiers Never Die" is found in the London publication, *Tommy's Tunes,* compiled by Frederick T. Nettleingham, p. 58 (1917), there is also the theory that the origin of the parody was English. That version's line read: "Old soldiers never die, they always fade away." Several other variations have been used by English authors: "They simply fade away," Frank Richards, *Old Soldiers Never Die,* chapter 23, p. 324 (1933); and "they only fade away," James Ronald, *Old Soldiers Never Die,* p. 7 (1942).

1728 The soldier, above all other men, is required to perform the highest act of religious teaching—sacrifice. In battle and in the face of danger and death he discloses those divine attributes which his Maker gave when He created man in his own image. No physical courage and no brute instincts can take the place of the divine annunciation and spiritual uplift which will alone sustain him.

General DOUGLAS MACARTHUR, speech at the annual reunion of veterans of the Rainbow (42d) Infantry Division of World War I, Washington, D.C., July 14, 1935.—MacArthur, *A Soldier Speaks,* p. 69 (1965).

1729 An atheist could not be as great a military leader as one who is not an atheist.

THOMAS H. MOORER, as reported by *The Washington Post,* April 29, 1970, p. C1.

Admiral Moorer, then chairman-designate of the Joint Chiefs of Staff, testified in U.S. District Court supporting the policy of compulsory chapel attendance at the service academies.

1730 It is foolish and wrong to mourn the men who died. Rather we should thank God that such men lived.

Attributed to General GEORGE S. PATTON, JR., speech at the Copley Plaza Hotel, Boston Massachusetts, June 7, 1945.—These words were reported by William Blair in *The New York Times,* June 8, 1945, p. 6, and by Stephen Lynch in the *Boston Herald,* June 8, 1945, pp. 1, 16 (where "the" appears as "these"). Other newspapers of that day have variant wordings.

The speech was extemporaneous and is not included in his published papers. Biographers of Patton have used variant wordings of this quotation, and Mike Wallace as narrator of the 1965 David Wolper television production, *General George Patton,* quoted this as, "Let me not mourn for the men who have died fighting, but rather let me be glad that such heroes have lived."

Patton had expressed himself in similar words at a memorial service at an Allied cemetery near Palermo, Italy, November 11, 1943: "I consider it no sacrifice to die for my country. In my mind we came here to thank God that men like these have lived rather than to regret that they have died."—Harry H. Semmes, *Portrait of Patton,* p. 176 (1955).

1731 Our *God* and *Souldiers* we alike adore,
Ev'n at the Brink of danger; not before:
After deliverance, both alike required;
Our *God's* forgotten, and our *Souldiers* slighted.

Soldiers

FRANCIS QUARLES, "Of Common Devotion," *The Complete Works in Prose and Verse of Francis Quarles*, ed. Alexander B. Grosart, vol. 2, p. 205 (1880).

President John F. Kennedy quoted this in remarks to members of the First Armored Division, Fort Stewart, Georgia, November 26, 1962: "Many years ago, according to the story, there was found in a sentry box in Gibraltar a poem which said:

God and the soldier, all men adore
In time of danger and not before
When the danger is passed and all things righted,
God is forgotten and the soldier slighted.

This country does not forget God or the soldier. Upon both we now depend. Thank you."—*Public Papers of the Presidents of the United States: John F. Kennedy, 1962*, p. 840. The First Armored Division had been deployed during the Cuban crisis.

1732 So, as you go into battle, remember your ancestors and remember your descendants.

TACITUS, *Agricola, an English Version of a Roman Tale*, trans. G. J. Acheson, chapter 4, paragraph 22, final sentence, p. 72 (1938).

1733 These endured all and gave all that justice among nations might prevail and that mankind might enjoy freedom and inherit peace.

Author unknown. Normandy Chapel, inscription on the exterior of the lintel of the chapel.—American Battle Monuments Commission, *Normandy American Cemetery and Memorial*, p. 16 (1975, rev. 1984).

This World War II memorial inscription is very similar to the World War I memorial inscription at Oise-Aisne Cemetery: These endured all and gave that honor and justice might prevail and that the world might enjoy freedom and inherit peace.—American Battle Monuments Commission, *Oise-Aisne American Cemetery and Memorial*, p. 9 (1978).

1734 Here rests in honored glory an American soldier known but to God.

Author unknown. Incription on the Tomb of the Unknown Soldier, Arlington National Cemetery.

Solution

1735 And we must face the fact that the United States is neither omnipotent or omniscient—that we are only 6 percent of the world's population—that we cannot impose our will upon the other 94 percent of mankind—that we cannot right every wrong or reverse every adversity—and that therefore there cannot be an American solution to every world problem.

President JOHN F. KENNEDY, address at the University of Washington's 100th anniversary program, Seattle, Washington, November 16, 1961.—*Public Papers of the Presidents of the United States: John F. Kennedy, 1961*, p. 726.

1736 There is always an easy solution to every human problem—neat, plausible, and wrong.

H. L. MENCKEN, "The Divine Afflatus," *A Mencken Chrestomathy*, chapter 25, p. 443 (1949).

This essay was originally published in the New York *Evening Mail*, November 16, 1917, and reprinted in *Predjudices: Second Series* (1920).

Space exploration

1737 The *Eagle* has landed.

NEIL A. ARMSTRONG, radio message announcing the first landing on the moon, July 20, 1969.—*The Washington Post*, July 21, 1969, p. 1.

1738 That's one small step for a man, one giant leap for mankind.

NEIL A. ARMSTRONG, message on first stepping on the moon, July 20, 1969.—*The Washington Post*, July 21, 1969, p. 1.

In the original transmission, the article "a" was lost, causing the message to be printed erroneously in countless newspapers.—Richard Hanser, "Of Deathless Remarks," *American Heritage*, June 1970, p. 59.

1739 The emergence of this new world poses a vital issue: will outer space be preserved for peaceful use and developed for the benefit of all mankind? Or will it become another focus for the arms race—and thus an area of dangerous and sterile competition? The choice is urgent. And it is ours to make. The nations of the world have recently united in declaring the continent of Antarctica "off limits" to military preparations. We could extend this principle to an even more important sphere. National vested interests have not yet been developed in space or in celestial bodies. Barriers to agreement are now lower than they will ever be again.

President DWIGHT D. EISENHOWER, address before the fifteenth General Assembly of the United Nations, New York City, September 22, 1960.—*Public Papers of the Presidents of the United States: Dwight D. Eisenhower, 1960–61*, p. 714.

1740 First, I believe that this nation should commit itself to achieving the goal, before this decade is out, of landing a man on the moon and returning him safely to the earth. . . . I believe we should go to the moon. But . . . there is no sense in agreeing or desiring that the United States take an affirmative position in outer space, unless we are prepared to do the work and bear the burdens to make it successful.

President JOHN F. KENNEDY, special message to a joint session of Congress on urgent national needs, May 25, 1961.—*Public Papers of the Presidents of the United States: John F. Kennedy, 1961*, pp. 404, 405.

1741 Many years ago the great British explorer George Mallory, who was to die on Mount Everest, was asked why did he want to climb it. He said "Because it is there." Well, space is there, and we're going to climb it, and the moon and the planets are there, and new hopes for knowledge and peace are there.

President JOHN F. KENNEDY, address on the nation's space effort, Rice University, Houston, Texas, September 12, 1962.—*Public Papers of the Presidents of the United States: John F. Kennedy, 1962*, p. 668.

Mallory's remark, "Because it's there," was reported in *The New York Times*, March 18, 1923, p. 11, during his visit to New York.

Space exploration

1742 To see the earth as we now see it, small and blue and beautiful in that eternal silence where it floats, is to see ourselves as riders on the earth together, brothers on that bright loveliness in the unending night—brothers who *see* now they are truly brothers.

ARCHIBALD MACLEISH, "Bubble of Blue Air," *Riders on the Earth; Essays and Recollections by Archibald MacLeish,* epigraph, p. xiv (1978).

This was written by MacLeish for *The New York Times* "after the Appollo mission of 1968 returned from space with a photograph of what earth looked like as seen from beyond the moon: the photograph which gave mankind its first understanding of its actual situation; riders on the earth together, brothers on that bright loveliness in the unending night—brothers who *see* now they are truly brothers" (p. ix).

The article has slightly different wording and reads as follows: "To see the earth as it truly is, small and blue and beautiful in that eternal silence where it floats, is to see ourselves as riders on the earth together, brothers on that bright loveliness in the eternal cold—brothers who know now they are truly brothers."—*The New York Times,* December 25, 1968, p. 1.

1743 Some say God is living there [in space]. I was looking around very attentively, but I did not see anyone there. I did not detect either angels or gods. . . . I don't believe in God. I believe in man—his strength, his possibilities, his reason.

GHERMAN TITOV, Soviet cosmonaut, comments at world's fair, Seattle, Washington, May 6, 1962, as reported by *The Seattle Daily Times,* May 7, 1962, p. 2.

1744 Yet I do seriously and on good grounds affirm it possible to make a flying chariot in which a man may sit and give such a motion unto it as shall convey him through the air. And this perhaps might be made large enough to carry divers men at the same time, together with food for their viaticum and commodities for traffic. It is not the bigness of anything in this kind that can hinder its motion, if the motive faculty be answerable thereunto. We see a great ship swims as well as a small cork, and an eagle flies in the air as well as a little gnat. . . . 'Tis likely enough that there may be means invented of journeying to the moon; and how happy they shall be that are first successful in this attempt.

JOHN WILKINS, *A Discourse Concerning a New World and Another Planet,* book 1, chapter 14, pp. 238–39 (1640). Spelling modernized.

Speaking out

1745 Try to raise a voice that shall be heard from here to Albany and watch what it is that comes forward to shut off the sound. It is not a German sergeant, nor a Russian officer of the precinct. It is a note from a friend of your father's offering you a place in his office. This is your warning from the secret police. Why, if any of you young gentlemen have a mind to get heard a mile off, you must make a bonfire of your reputation, and a close enemy of most men who wish you well.

And what will you get in return? Well, if I must for the benefit of the economists, charge you up with some selfish gain, I will say that you get the satisfaction of having been heard, and that this is the whole possible scope of human ambition.

JOHN JAY CHAPMAN, "The Unity of Human Nature," address delivered before the Hobart Chapter of Phi Beta Kappa, Hobart College, Geneva, New York, on commencement day, June 20, 1900.—Chapman, *Learning and Other Essays,* p. 185 (1910, reprinted 1968).

1746 Laws can embody standards; governments can enforce laws—but the final task is not a task for government. It is a task for each and every one of us. Every time we turn our heads the other way when we see the law flouted—when we tolerate what we know to be wrong—when we close our eyes and ears to the corrupt because we are too busy, or too frightened—when we fail to speak up and speak out—we strike a blow against freedom and decency and justice.

ROBERT F. KENNEDY, attorney general, remarks before the Joint Defense Appeal of the American Jewish Committee and the Anti-Defamation League of the B'nai B'rith, Chicago, Illinois, June 21, 1961.—*A New Day: Robert F. Kennedy,* ed. Bill Adler, p. 26 (1968).

1747 Singular indeed that the people should be writhing under oppression and injury, and yet not one among them to be found, to raise the voice of complaint.

ABRAHAM LINCOLN, remarks in the Illinois legislature, January 11, 1837.—*The Collected Works of Abraham Lincoln,* ed. Roy P. Basler, vol. 1, p. 65 (1953).

A related expression is, "You must be vocal at all times on political matters, pro or con, voicing your opinion so that it may be heard by those who govern," attributed to David L. Lawrence, governor of Pennsylvania 1958–1962. Unverified.

1748 The historian should be fearless and incorruptible; a man of independence, loving frankness and truth; one who, as the poet says, calls a fig a fig and a spade a spade. He should yield to neither hatred nor affection, but should be unsparing and unpitying. He should be neither shy nor deprecating, but an impartial judge, giving each side all it deserves but no more. He should know in his writings no country and no city; he should bow to no authority and acknowledge no king. He should never consider what this or that man will think, but should state the facts as they really occurred.

LUCIAN, *How History Should Be Written (De Historia Conscribenda).—The Great Thoughts,* ed. George Seldes, p. 251 (1985).

1749 When Hitler attacked the Jews . . . I was not a Jew, therefore, I was not concerned. And when Hitler attacked the Catholics, I was not a Catholic, and therefore, I was not concerned. And when Hitler attacked the unions and the industrialists, I was not a member of the unions and I was not concerned. Then, Hitler attacked me and the Protestant church—and there was nobody left to be concerned.

Attributed to MARTIN NIEMÖLLER.—*Congressional Record,* October 14, 1968, vol. 114, p. 31636.

This statement has not been documented in biographies of Niemöller, nor was it contained in the 1945 Stuttgart Statement of Guilt, but the attribution is widely accepted.

Spirit

1750 The sword conquered for a while, but the spirit conquers for ever!

SHOLEM ASCH, *The Apostle,* trans. Maurice Samuel, p. 804 (1943).

1751 Never the spirit was born; the spirit shall cease to be never;
Never was time it was not; End and Beginning are dreams!
Birthless and deathless and changeless remaineth the spirit for ever;
Death hath not touched it at all, dead though the house of it seems!
Who knoweth it exhaustless, self-sustained,
Immortal, indestructible,—shall such
Say, "I have killed a man, or caused to kill?"

Nay, but as when one layeth
His worn-out robes away,
And, taking new ones, sayeth,
"These will I wear to-day!"
So putteth by the spirit
Lightly its garb of flesh,
And passeth to inherit
A residence afresh.

Bhagavad Gita.—*The Song Celestial or Bhagavad-Gita,* trans. Sir Edwin Arnold, pp. 10–11 (1934). This is chapter 2, sections 20–22 in other editions.

1752 If that vital spark that we find in a grain of wheat can pass unchanged through countless deaths and resurrections, will the spirit of man be unable to pass from this body to another?

WILLIAM JENNINGS BRYAN, eulogy, Elks Lodge annual memorial service, Lincoln, Nebraska, December 2, 1906, as reported by the *Nebraska State Journal,* December 3, 1906, p. 3.

In "The Prince of Peace," a lecture delivered at Chautauquas and religious gatherings, starting in 1904, he phrased the idea this way: "If this invisible germ of life in the grain of wheat can thus pass unimpaired through three thousand resurrections, I shall not doubt that my soul has power to clothe itself with a body suited to its new existence when this earthly frame has crumbled into dust."—*Speeches of William Jennings Bryan,* vol. 2, p. 284 (1909).

1753 I am certain that after the dust of centuries has passed over our cities, we, too, will be remembered not for victories or defeats in battle or in politics, but for our contribution to the human spirit.

President JOHN F. KENNEDY, remarks at a closed-circuit television broadcast on behalf of the national cultural center, November 29, 1962.—*Public Papers of the Presidents of the United States: John F. Kennedy, 1962,* pp. 846–47.

Inscription on the John F. Kennedy Center for the Performing Arts, Washington, D.C.

1754 *Glendower:* I can call spirits from the vasty deep.
Hotspur: Why, so can I, or so can any man;
But will they come when you do call for them?

WILLIAM SHAKESPEARE, *Henry IV, Part I,* act III, scene i, lines 53–55.

State

1755 It is one of the happy incidents of the federal system that a single courageous State may, if its citizens choose, serve as a laboratory; and try novel social and economic experiments without risk to the rest of the country.

Justice LOUIS D. BRANDEIS, dissenting, *New State Ice Co.* v. *Liebmann,* 285 U.S. 311 (1932).

1756 We are gong down the road to stateism. Where we will wind up, no one can tell, but if some of the new programs seriously proposed should be adopted, there is danger that the individual—whether farmer, worker, manufacturer, lawyer, or doctor—will soon be an economic slave pulling an oar in the galley of the state.

JAMES F. BYRNES, "Great Decisions Must Be Made," speech delivered at the bicentennial celebration of Washington and Lee University, Lexington, Virginia, June 18, 1949.—*Vital Speeches of the Day*, July 15, 1949, p. 580.

Byrnes served in Congress 1911–1925 and 1930–1941.

1757 The first act by virtue of which the State really constitutes itself the representative of the whole of society—the taking possession of the means of production in the name of society—this is, at the same time, its last independent act as a State. State interference in social relations becomes, in one domain after another, superfluous, and then dies out of itself; the government of persons is replaced by the administration of things, and by the conduct of processes of production. The State is not "abolished." *It dies out.*

FRIEDRICH ENGELS, *Socialism, Utopian and Scientific*, trans. Edward Aveling, p. 49 (1901).

1758 A question like the present should be disposed of without undue delay. But a State cannot be expected to move with the celerity of a private business man; it is enough if it proceeds, in the language of the English Chancery, with all deliberate speed.

Justice OLIVER WENDELL HOLMES, *Virginia* v. *West Virginia*, 222 U.S. 19–20 (1911).

The best known use of the phrase "all deliberate speed" is in Chief Justice Earl Warren's opinion of the court, *Brown et al.* v. *Board of Education of Topeka, et al.*, 349 U.S. 301 (1954).

1759 The church must be reminded that it is not the master or the servant of the state, but rather the conscience of the state.

MARTIN LUTHER KING, JR., *Strength to Love*, p. 47 (1963).

1760 The worth of a State, in the long run, is the worth of the individuals composing it; and a State which postpones the interests of *their* mental expansion and elevation, to a little more of administrative skill, or of that semblance of it which practice gives, in the details of business; a State which dwarfs its men, in order that they may be more docile instruments in its hands even for beneficial purposes—will find that with small men no great thing can really be accomplished; and that the perfection of machinery to which it has sacrificed everything, will in the end avail it nothing, for want of the vital power which, in order that the machine might work more smoothly, it has preferred to banish.

JOHN STUART MILL, *On Liberty*, ed. David Spitz, chapter 5, p. 106 (1975). Originally published in 1859.

States rights

1761 I believe each individual is naturally entitled to do as he pleases with himself and the fruit of his labor, so far as it in no wise interferes with any other man's rights—that each community, as a State, has a right to do exactly as it pleases with all the concerns within that State that interfere with the right of no other State, and that the general government, upon principle, has no right to interfere with anything other than that general class of things that does concern the whole.

ABRAHAM LINCOLN, speech at Chicago, Illinois, July 10, 1858.—*The Collected Works of Abraham Lincoln*, ed. Roy P. Basler, vol. 2, p. 493 (1953).

States rights

1762 No political dreamer was ever wild enough to think of breaking down the lines which separate the States, and of compounding the American people into one common mass.

Chief Justice JOHN MARSHALL, *McCulloch* v. *Maryland*, 17 U.S. 403 (1819).

1763 Is the United States going to decide, are the people of this country going to decide that their Federal Government shall in the future have no right under any implied power or any court-approved power to enter into a solution of a national economic problem, but that that national economic problem must be decided only by the States? . . . We thought we were solving it, and now it has been thrown right straight in our faces. We have been relegated to the horse-and-buggy definition of interstate commerce.

President FRANKLIN D. ROOSEVELT, remarks at press conference, May 31, 1935.—*The Public Papers and Addresses of Franklin D. Roosevelt, 1935*, pp. 215, 221 (1938).

Monday, May 27, 1935, became known as "Black Monday." One of the decisions the Supreme Court handed down that day was the case of *Schechter Poultry Corporation* v. *United States*, to which Roosevelt refers.

Statesman

1764 When statesmen forsake their own private conscience for the sake of their public duties . . . they lead their country by a short route to chaos.

ROBERT BOLT, *A Man for All Seasons*, act I, p. 12 (1968). Sir Thomas More is speaking. Ellipses in original.

1765 But a good patriot, and a true politician, always considers how he shall make the most of the existing materials of his country. A disposition, to preserve, and an ability to improve, taken together, would be my standard of a statesman. Everything else is vulgar in the conception, perilous in the execution.

EDMUND BURKE, "Reflections on the Revolution in France," 1790, *The Works of the Right Honorable Edmund Burke*, vol. 3, p. 440 (1899).

1766 A great statesman is he who knows when to depart from traditions, as well as when to adhere to them.

JOHN STUART MILL, *Considerations on Representative Government*, chapter 5, p. 93 (1861).

1767 Statesmen have to bend to the collective will of their peoples or be broken.

Attributed to WOODROW WILSON. Unverified.

Statistics

1768 The individual source of the statistics may easily be the weakest link. Harold Cox tells a story of his life as a young man in India. He quoted some statistics to a Judge, an Englishman, and a very good fellow. His friend said, "Cox, when you are a bit older, you will not quote Indian statistics with that assurance. The Government are very keen on amassing statistics—they collect them, add them, raise them to the *n*th power, take the cube root and prepare wonderful diagrams. But what you must never forget is that every one of those figures comes in the first instance from the *chowty dar* [chowkidar] (village watchman), who just puts down what he damn pleases."

Josiah Stamp, *Some Economic Factors in Modern Life*, pp. 258–59 (1929).

1769 There are three kinds of lies: lies, damned lies, and statistics.

MARK TWAIN, *Mark Twain's Autobiography*, p. 246 (1924), quotes this as a remark attributed to Disraeli.

Current quotation books, in addition to naming Mark Twain or Disraeli, have suggested Henry Labouchère, Abram S. Hewitt, and Holloway H. Frost; one bravely says "author unidentified."

The quotation, or a variation, seems to be known internationally. When a Russian citizen was interviewed, following the death of Chernenko, he began by saying, "As one of your writers said, 'There are three kinds of lie: a small lie, a big lie and politics.' "—*Time*, March 25, 1985, p. 21.

Statue of Liberty

1770 Not like the brazen giant of Greek fame,
With conquering limbs astride from land to land;
Here at our sea-washed, sunset gates shall stand
A mighty woman with a torch, whose flame
Is the imprisoned lightning, and her name
Mother of Exiles. From her beacon-hand
Glows world-wide welcome; her mild eyes command
The air-bridged harbor that twin cities frame.
"Keep, ancient lands, your storied pomp!" cries she
With silent lips. "Give me your tired, your poor,
Your huddled masses yearning to breathe free,
The wretched refuse of your teeming shore.
Send these, the homeless, tempest-tost to me,
I lift my lamp beside the golden door!"

EMMA LAZARUS, "The New Colossus," *Emma Lazarus, Selection from Her Poetry and Prose*, ed. Morris U. Schappes, pp. 40–41 (1944).

Congress had allocated money to erect Frédéric Bartholdi's Statue of Liberty Enlightening the World, but had provided no money for a pedestal. A citizens committee invited famous authors to write appropriate words and donate their manuscripts for auction. Lazarus wrote this sonnet (1883), which can be found on a plaque in the pedestal of the Statue of Liberty. The last four and a half lines are also engraved on the wall of the reception hall of John F. Kennedy International Airport, New York City.—Dan Vogel, *Emma Lazarus*, pp. 157, 159 (1980).

1771 You have set up in New York Harbor a monstrous idol which you call Liberty. The only thing that remains to complete that monument is to put on its pedestal the inscription written by Dante on the gate of hell: "All hope abandon ye who enter here."

GEORGE BERNARD SHAW, *The Future of Political Science in America*, pp. 7–8 (1933).

This address was given at the Metropolitan Opera House, New York City, April 11, 1933, before a special meeting of the Academy of Political Science held in honor of Shaw's first visit to America.

Strength

1772 Our real problem, then, is not our strength today; it is rather the vital necessity of action today to ensure our strength tomorrow.

President DWIGHT D. EISENHOWER, State of the Union address to a joint session of Congress, January 9, 1958.—*Public Papers of the Presidents of the United States: Dwight D. Eisenhower, 1958,* p. 5.

1773 We all have enough strength to endure the misfortunes of others.

FRANÇOIS DE LA ROCHEFOUCAULD. The saying, "Nous avons tous assez de force pour supporter les maux d'autrui," was first published in his *Réflexions ou Sentences et Maximes Morales,* 1655. There are several English translations, including that above from his *Selected Maxims and Reflections,* trans. Edward M. Stack, p. 26 (1956).

1774 It is from weakness that people reach for dictators and concentrated government power. Only the strong can be free. And only the productive can be strong.

WENDELL WILLKIE, speech accepting nomination as Republican candidate for president, Elwood, Indiana, August 17, 1940.—Willkie, *This Is Wendell Willkie,* pp. 273–74 (1940).

Strike

1775 There is no right to strike against the public safety by anybody, anywhere, any time.

CALVIN COOLIDGE, governor of Massachusetts, telegram to Samuel Gompers, September 14, 1919, regarding the Boston police strike.—Coolidge, *Have Faith in Massachusetts,* p. 223 (1919).

1776 I am glad to know that there is a system of labor where the laborer can strike if he wants to! I would to God that such a system prevailed all over the world.

ABRAHAM LINCOLN, speech at Hartford, Connecticut, March 5, 1860, as reported in the Hartford *Daily Courant,* March 6, 1860.—*The Collected Works of Abraham Lincoln,* ed. Roy P. Basler, vol. 4, p. 7 (1953).

Success

1777 The road to success is filled with women pushing their husbands along.

Attributed to LORD THOMAS R. DEWAR.—*The Home Book of Quotations,* ed. Burton Stevenson, 10th ed., p. 1263 (1967). Unverified.

1778 I have climbed to the top of the greasy pole!

BENJAMIN DISRAELI, remark to a friend after being named prime minister.—Sir William Fraser, *Disraeli and His Day,* 2d ed., p. 52 (1891).

1779 The secret of success is constancy of purpose.

BENJAMIN DISRAELI, speech at banquet of National Union of Conservative and Constitutional Associations, Crystal Palace, London, June 24, 1872.—*Selected Speeches of the Right Honourable the Earl of Beaconsfield,* ed. T. E. Kebbel, vol. 2, p. 535 (1882).

1780 If a man can write a better book, preach a better sermon, or make a better mouse-trap than his neighbor, though he build his house in the woods, the world will make a beaten path to his door.

Attributed to RALPH WALDO EMERSON by Sarah B. Yule, *Borrowings*, p. 138 (1889).

While this sentence has never been found in Emerson's works, he is believed to have used it in a lecture either at San Francisco or Oakland, California, in 1871. *Borrowings* was an anthology compiled by women of the First Unitarian Church of Oakland, and Sarah Yule contributed this sentence, which she had copied from an address years before. There has been some controversy because others, including Elbert Hubbard, have claimed authorship. See *The Home Book of Quotations*, ed. Burton Stevenson, 10th ed., pp. 630, 2275 (1967).

1781 But I like not these great successes of yours; for I know how jealous are the gods.

HERODOTUS, *Herodotus*, trans. A. D. Godley, vol. 2, book 3, paragraph 40, pp. 53, 55 (1928). Excerpt from a letter from Amasis to Polycrates.

1782 Even on the most exalted throne in the world we are only sitting on our own bottom.

MICHEL EYQUEM DE MONTAIGNE, *The Essays of Michel de Montaigne*, trans. Jacob Zeitlin, vol. 3, p. 317 (1936). His essays were first published in 1580.

The translation of "Et au plus eslevé throne du monde, si ne sommes assis que sus nôstre cul" varies in other editions.

1783 There is only one success . . . to be able to spend your life in your own way, and not to give others absurd maddening claims upon it.

CHRISTOPHER MORLEY, *Where the Blue Begins*, p. 85 (1922).

1784 Is the proposed operation likely to succeed? What might be the consequences of failure? Is it in the realm of practicability in terms of matériel and supplies?

Admiral CHESTER W. NIMITZ.—*Life*, July 10, 1944, p. 84, describes these as "three favorite rules of thumb which . . . he has printed on a card he keeps on his desk."

1785 Success is the necessary misfortune of life, but it is only to the very unfortunate that it comes early.

ANTHONY TROLLOPE, *Orley Farm*, chapter 49, pp. 438–39 (1950). First published in 1862.

1786 We must walk consciously only part way toward our goal, and then leap in the dark to our success.

Author unknown. Attributed to Henry David Thoreau, but not found in his works.

Taxation

1787 To please universally was the object of his life; but to tax and to please, no more than to love and to be wise, is not given to men.

EDMUND BURKE, speech on American taxation, House of Commons, April 19, 1774.—*The Writings and Speeches of Edmund Burke*, ed. Paul Langford, vol. 2, p. 454 (1981).

Burke was referring to the chancellor of the exchequer, Charles Townshend.

1788 The art of taxation consists in so plucking the goose as to obtain the largest possible amount of feathers with the smallest possible amount of hissing.

Attributed to JEAN BAPTISTE COLBERT, minister of finance to Louis XIV of France. It has also been attributed to Cardinal Mazarin, under whom Colbert served.—*The Home Book of Quotations,* ed. Burton Stevenson, 10th ed., p. 2300f, no. 5 (1967).

1789 Of all debts men are least willing to pay the taxes. What a satire is this on government! Everywhere they think they get their money's worth, except for these.

RALPH WALDO EMERSON, "Politics," *Essays: Second Series,* in *The Complete Writings of Ralph Waldo Emerson,* vol. 1, p. 302 (1929).

1790 Mr. Gladstone, then Chancellor of the Exchequer, had interrupted him in a description of his work on electricity to put the impatient inquiry: 'But, after all, what use is it?' Like a flash of lightning came the response: 'Why, sir, there is every probability that you will soon be able to tax it!'

MICHAEL FARADAY.—James Kendall, *Michael Faraday, Man of Simplicity,* Introduction, p. 14 (1955).

1791 *In the usual progress of things, the necessities of a nation in every stage of its existence will be found at least equal to its resources.*

ALEXANDER HAMILTON, *The Federalist,* ed. Benjamin F. Wright, no. 30, p. 234 (1961).

1792 The power to tax is not the power to destroy while this Court sits.

Justice OLIVER WENDELL HOLMES, dissenting, *Panhandle Oil Company* v. *Mississippi ex rel. Knox, Attorney General,* 277 U.S. 223 (1928).

1793 We shall tax and tax, and spend and spend, and elect and elect.

Attributed to HARRY L. HOPKINS, administrator of the Works Progress Administration.

Although Frank R. Kent mentioned the subject of "spending, taxes, and election" in reference to Hopkins in his column, "The Great Game of Politics" (Baltimore, Maryland, *Sun,* September 25, 1938, pp. 1, 16) he first attributed "we are going to spend and spend and spend, and tax and tax and tax, and elect and elect and elect" to Hopkins in the *Sun,* October 14, 1938, p. 15.

Joseph Alsop and Robert Kintner in their column, "The Capital Parade" (Washington, D.C., *Evening Star,* November 9, 1938, p. A–11), elaborated Hopkins's "probably apocryphal" words to: "Now, get this through your head. We're going to spend and spend and spend, and tax and tax and tax, and re-elect and re-elect and re-elect, until you're dead or forgotten."

Arthur Krock, in his column, "In the Nation" (*The New York Times,* November 10, 1938, p. 26), reported the wording as "we will spend and spend, and tax and tax, and elect and elect." He also repeated this wording in an article in *The New York Times,* November 13, 1938, sec. 4, p. E–3. A letter by Hopkins denying this attributed quotation and a response by Krock were published in *The New York Times,* November 24, 1938, p. 26.

Over the years the quotation attributed to Hopkins has evolved into the wording above.

1794 Every good citizen . . . should be willing to devote a brief time during some one day in the year, when necessary, to the making up of a listing of his income for taxes . . . to contribute to his Government, not the scriptural tithe, but a small percentage of his net profits.

Representative CORDELL HULL, remarks in the House, April 26, 1913, *Congressional Record,* vol. 50, p. 505.

1795 If the Government cannot reduce the "terrific" tax burden on the country, I will predict that you will have a depression that will curl your hair, because we are just taking too much money out of this economy that we need to make the jobs that you have to have as time goes on.

GEORGE M. HUMPHREY, secretary of the treasury, at a news conference on January 15, 1957, as reported by *The New York Times,* January 17, 1957, p. 20. On January 16, President Eisenhower sent to Congress a record peacetime budget of $71.8 billion.

1796 A government which robs Peter to pay Paul can always depend on the support of Paul.

GEORGE BERNARD SHAW, *Everybody's Political What's What?,* chapter 30, p. 256 (1944).

Shaw wrote this book "to track down some of the mistakes that have landed us in a gross misdistribution of domestic income and two world wars in twentyfive years" (p. 1).

1797 In other words, a democratic government is the only one in which those who vote for a tax can escape the obligation to pay it.

ALEXIS DE TOCQUEVILLE, *Democracy in America,* ed. J. P. Mayer, trans. George Lawrence, vol. 1, part 2, chapter 5, p. 210 (1969). Originally published in 1835–1840.

1798 The power to tax is the power to destroy.

This quotation comes from the words of Daniel Webster and those of John Marshall in the Supreme Court case, *McCulloch* v. *Maryland.*

Webster, in arguing the case, said: "An unlimited power to tax involves, necessarily, a power to destroy," 17 U.S. 327 (1819).

In his decision, Chief Justice Marshall said: "That the power of taxing it [the bank] by the States may be exercised so as to destroy it, is too obvious to be denied" (p. 427), and "That the power to tax involves the power to destroy . . . [is] not to be denied" (p. 431).

Teachers

1799 Who dares to teach must never cease to learn.

JOHN COTTON DANA. In 1912 Dana, a Newark, New Jersey, librarian, was asked to supply a Latin quotation suitable for inscription on a new building at Newark State College (now Kean College of New Jersey), Union, New Jersey. Unable to find an appropriate quotation, Dana composed what became the college motto.—*The New York Times Book Review,* March 5, 1967, p. 55.

1800 He who can, does. He who cannot, teaches.

GEORGE BERNARD SHAW, "Maxims for Revolutionists," appendix 2 to *Man and Superman,* in his *Selected Plays with Prefaces,* vol. 3, p. 733 (1948).

Television

1801 I invite you to sit down in front of your television set when your station goes on the air . . . and keep your eyes glued to that set until the station signs off. I can assure you that you will observe a vast wasteland.

NEWTON N. MINOW, chairman of the Federal Communications Commission, speech before the National Association of Broadcasters, Washington, D.C., May 9, 1961.—Minow, *Equal Time*, p. 52 (1964).

1802 Unless and until there is unmistakable proof to the contrary, the presumption must be that television is and will be a main factor in influencing the values and moral standards of our society. . . . Television does not, and cannot, merely reflect the moral standards of society. It must affect them, either by changing or by reinforcing them.

Pilkington Report. Great Britain, Committee on Broadcasting, 1960, *Report* (Cmnd. 1753), chapter 3, pp. 15, 19 (1962).

1803 Those who say they give the public what it wants begin by underestimating public taste, and end by debauching it.

Pilkington Report, quoting an unknown source. Great Britain, Committee on Broadcasting, 1960, *Report* (Cmnd. 1753), chapter 3, p. 17 (1962).

Ten Commandments

1804 Thou shalt have no other gods before me.

Thou shalt not make unto thee any graven image, or any likeness of any thing that is in heaven above, or that is in the earth beneath, or that is in the water under the earth: Thou shalt not bow down thyself to them, nor serve them: for I the Lord thy God am a jealous God, visiting the iniquity of the fathers upon the children unto the third and fourth generation of them that hate me; And shewing mercy unto thousands of them that love me, and keep my commandments.

Thou shalt not take the name of the Lord thy God in vain; for the Lord will not hold him guiltless that taketh his name in vain.

Remember the sabbath day, to keep it holy. Six days shalt thou labor, and do all thy work: But the seventh day is the sabbath of the Lord thy God: in it thou shalt not do any work, thou, nor thy son, nor thy daughter, thy manservant, nor thy maidservant, nor thy cattle, nor thy stranger that is within thy gates: For in six days the Lord made heaven and earth, the sea, and all that in them is, and rested the seventh day: wherefore the Lord blessed the sabbath day, and hallowed it.

Honor thy father and thy mother: that thy days may be long upon the land which the Lord thy God giveth thee.

Thou shalt not kill.

Thou shalt not commit adultery.

Thou shalt not steal.

Thou shalt not bear false witness against thy neighbor.

Thou shalt not covet thy neighbor's wife, nor his manservant, nor his maidservant, nor his ox, nor his ass, nor anything that is thy neighbor's.

The Bible, Exodus 20:3–17. This appears with minor differences in Deuteronomy 5:7–21.

1805 Thou shalt have one God only; who
Would be at the expense of two?
No graven images may be

Worshipped, except the currency:
Swear not at all; for for thy curse
Thine enemy is none the worse:
At church on Sunday to attend
Will serve to keep the world thy friend:
Honour thy parents; that is, all
From whom advancement may befall:
Thou shalt not kill; but needst not strive
Officiously to keep alive:
Do not adultery commit;
Advantage rarely comes of it:
Thou shalt not steal; an empty feat,
When it's so lucrative to cheat:
Bear not false witness: let the lie
Have time on its own wings to fly:
Thou shalt not covet; but tradition
Approves all forms of competition.

The sum of all is, thou shalt love,
If any body, God above:
At any rate shall never labour
More than thyself to love thy neighbour.

ARTHUR HUGH CLOUGH, "The Latest Decalogue," *The Poems of Arthur Hugh Clough*, ed. A. L. P. Norrington, pp. 60–61 (1968).

Theory

1806 It is a condition which confronts us—not a theory.

President GROVER CLEVELAND, third annual message to Congress, December 6, 1887.—*The Writings and Speeches of Grover Cleveland*, ed. George F. Parker, p. 86 (1892).
He was referring to the tariff.

Thought

1807 No brain is stronger than its weakest think.

THOMAS L. MASSON, *Laughs*, p. 167 (1926).
This quotation appears as "The brain is as strong as its weakest think," in Eleanor Doan, *The Speaker's Sourcebook*, p. 263 (1960) with no source acknowledged, and is repeated in A. K. Adams, *The Home Book of Humorous Quotations*, p. 238 (1969).

1808 To him whose elastic and vigorous thought keeps pace with the sun, the day is a perpetual morning.

HENRY DAVID THOREAU, *Walden*, chapter 2, pp. 116–17 (1966). Originally published in 1854.

Three-mile limit

1809 The character of our coasts, remarkable in considerable parts of it for admitting no vessels of size to pass near the shores, would entitle us, in reason, to as broad a margin of protected navigation, as any nation whatever. Not proposing, however, at this time, and without a respectful and friendly communication with the Powers interested in this navigation, to fix on a distance to which we may ultimately insist on the right of protection, the President gives instructions to the officers, acting under this authority, to consider those heretofore given them as restrained for the present to the distance of one sea-league, or three geographical miles from the sea-shore. This distance can admit of no opposition as it is recognized by treaties between some of the Powers with whom we are connected in commerce and navigation, and is as little or less than is claimed by any of them on their own coasts.

THOMAS JEFFERSON, secretary of state, letter to the French Minister, Edmond Charles Genêt, November 8, 1793.—*The Writings of Thomas Jefferson*, ed. Paul L. Ford, vol. 6, pp. 440–41 (1895).

Time

1810 To every thing there is a season, and time to every purpose under the heaven:
A time to be born, and a time to die; a time to plant, and a time to pluck up that which is planted;
A time to kill, and a time to heal; a time to break down, and a time to build up;
A time to weep, and a time to laugh; a time to mourn, and a time to dance;
A time to cast away stones, and a time to gather stones together; a time to embrace, and a time to refrain from embracing;
A time to get, and a time to lose; a time to keep, and a time to cast away;
A time to rend, and a time to sew; a time to keep silence, and a time to speak;
A time to love, and a time to hate; a time of war, and a time of peace.

The Bible, Ecclesiastes 3:1–8.

1811 "The time has come," the Walrus said,
"To talk of many things:
Of shoes—and ships—and sealing-wax—
Of cabbages—and kings—
And why the sea is boiling hot—
And whether pigs have wings."

LEWIS CARROLL (Charles L. Dodgson), "The Walrus and the Carpenter," stanza 11, *Through the Looking-Glass*, chapter 4.—*Logical Nonsense: The Works of Lewis Carroll*, ed. Philip C. Blackburn and Lionel White, p. 188 (1934). First published in 1871.

1812 What though the tide of years may roll.

EDWARD A. CRAIGHILL, "Goōd Old Song," first line of second stanza, 1895. This song from the University of Virginia is set to the tune of "Auld Lang Syne."—John S. Patton, Sallie J. Doswell, and Lewis D. Crenshaw, *Jefferson's University*, pp. 72–73 (1915).

1813 One always has time enough, if one will apply it well.
(Man hat immer Zeit genug, wenn man sie gut anwenden will.)

JOHANN WOLFGANG VON GOETHE, *The Autobiography of Johann Wolfgang Von Goethe*, trans. John Oxenford, vol. 2, book 10, p. 16 (1974).

1814 There is no time like the old time, when you and I were young,
When the buds of April blossomed, and the birds of spring-time sung!
The garden's brightest glories by summer suns are nursed,
But oh, the sweet, sweet violets, the flowers that opened first!

There is no place like the old place, where you and I were born,
Where we lifted first our eyelids on the splendors of the morn
From the milk-white breast that warmed us, from the clinging arms that bore,
Where the dear eyes glistened o'er us that will look on us no more!

There is no friend like the old friend, who has shared our morning days,
No greeting like his welcome, no homage like his praise:
Fame is the scentless sunflower, with gaudy crown of gold;
But friendship is the breathing rose, with sweets in every fold.

There is no love like the old love, that we courted in our pride;
Though our leaves are falling, falling, and we're fading side by side,
There are blossoms all around us with the colors of our dawn,
And we live in borrowed sunshine when the day-star is withdrawn.

There are no times like the old times,—they shall never be forgot!
There is no place like the old place,—keep green the dear old spot!
There are no friends like our old friends,—may Heaven prolong their lives!
There are no loves like our old loves,—God bless our loving wives!

OLIVER WENDELL HOLMES, "No Time Like the Old Time," *The Poetical Works of Oliver Wendell Holmes*, p. 222 (1895, reprinted 1975).

1815 In its [knowledge's] light, we must think and act not only for the moment but for our time. I am reminded of the great French Marshal Lyautey, who once asked his gardener to plant a tree. The gardener objected that the tree was slow-growing and would not reach maturity for a hundred years. The Marshal replied, "In that case, there is no time to lose, plant it this afternoon."

President JOHN F. KENNEDY, address at the University of California, Berkeley, California, March 23, 1962.—*Public Papers of the Presidents of the United States: John F. Kennedy, 1962*, p. 266.

Kennedy used this story a number of times. The attribution to Marshal Lyautey is unverified.

1816 Time is at once the most valuable and the most perishable of all our possessions.

JOHN RANDOLPH of Roanoke.—William Cabell Bruce, *John Randolph of Roanoke, 1773–1833*, vol. 2, chapter 7, p. 205 (1922, reprinted 1970).

Randolph was a member of Congress 1799–1813, 1815–1817, and 1819–1829.

1817 The opera ain't over till the fat lady sings.

DAN COOK, sports broadcaster and writer for the *San Antonio* (Texas) *Express-News*, on television newscast in April 1978, after the first basketball playoff game between the San Antonio Spurs and the Washington Bullets, to illustrate that while the Spurs had won once, the series was not over yet. Bullets coach Dick Motta borrowed the phrase later during the Bullets' eventually successful championship drive, and it became widely known and was often mistakenly attributed to him.—*The Washington Post*, June 11, 1978, p. D6. Cook may well have said *isn't*, but this remark is generally heard with *ain't*.

Times

1818 It was the best of times, it was the worst of times, it was the age of wisdom, it was the age of foolishness, it was the epoch of belief, it was the epoch of incredulity, it was the season of Light, it was the season of Darkness, it was the spring of hope, it was the winter of despair, we had everything before us, we had nothing before us, we were all going direct to Heaven, we were all going direct the other way—in short, the period was so far like the present period, that some of its noisiest authorities insisted on its being received, for good or for evil, in the superlative degree of comparison only.

CHARLES DICKENS, *A Tale of Two Cities*, chapter 1, opening paragraph, p. 3 (1958). Originally published in 1859.

1819 These times of ours are serious and full of calamity, but all times are essentially alike. As soon as there is life there is danger.

RALPH WALDO EMERSON, "Public and Private Education," lecture before the Parker Fraternity, Boston, Massachusetts, November 27, 1864.—Emerson, *Uncollected Lectures*, ed. Clarence Gohdes, p. 14 (1932).

1820 This time, like all times, is a very good one, if we but know what to do with it.

RALPH WALDO EMERSON, "The American Scholar," oration delivered before the Phi Beta Kappa Society, Cambridge, Massachusetts, August 31, 1837.—*Nature, Addresses and Lectures* (vol. 3 of *The Works of Ralph Waldo Emerson*), p. 105 (1906).

1821 These are the times that try men's souls. The summer soldier and the sunshine patriot will, in this crisis, shrink from the service of their country; but he that stands it *now*, deserves the love and thanks of man and woman.

THOMAS PAINE, "The Crisis," no. 1, *The Writings of Thomas Paine*, ed. Moncure D. Conway, vol. 1, p. 170 (1894).

"The first 'Crisis' is of especial historical interest. It was written during the retreat of Washington across the Delaware, and by order of the Commander was read to groups of his dispirited and suffering soldiers. Its opening sentence [above] was adopted as the watchword of the movement on Trenton, a few days after its publication, and is believed to have inspired much of the courage which won that victory, which, though not imposing in extent, was of great moral effect on Washington's little army" (p. 169).

1822 The man and the hour have met.

WILLIAM YANCEY, introducing Jefferson Davis, president-elect of the Confederacy, in Montgomery, Alabama, February 16, 1861. Attributed to Yancey by the biographers of Davis, including Hudson Strode, *Jefferson Davis*, vol. 1, p. 407 (1955).

Timing

1823 On the Plains of Hesitation bleach the bones of countless millions who, at the Dawn of Victory, sat down to wait, and waiting—died!

GEORGE W. CECIL. Under the pseudonym of William A. Lawrence, Cecil wrote and published an advertisement for the International Correspondence Schools in *The American Magazine*, March 1923, p. 87, in which this sentence is used. For further information and later paraphrase, see *The Home Book of American Quotations*, ed. Bruce Bohle, p. 208 (1967).

1824 There is something peculiar in the temper of the House. A clear strong statement of a case if made too soon or too late fails. If well made at the right time it is effective. It is a nice point to study the right time.

Timing

Representative JAMES A. GARFIELD, journal entry on June 12, 1874.—Theodore C. Smith, *The Life and Letters of James Abram Garfield*, vol. 1, p. 511 (1925).

Today

1825 Today is the first day of the rest of your life.

Attributed to CHARLES DEDERICH by *The Washington Post*, December 10, 1978, p. C5.

He was the founder of Synanon, a self-help community for drug abusers and alcoholics, based in California.

Treason

1826 Treason doth never prosper, what's the reason?
For if it prosper, none dare call it Treason.

SIR JOHN HARINGTON, "Of Treason," *The Letters and Epigrams of Sir John Harington . . .*, ed. Norman E. McClure, book 4, epigram 5, p. 255 (1977). The complete edition of his epigrams was published in 1618.

Trust

1827 Preserve me, O God: for in thee do I put my trust.

The Bible, Psalms 16:1.

The stained glass window of the Prayer Room in the United States Capitol contains this verse.

1828 We have a saying in the movement that we don't trust anybody over 30.

JACK WEINBERG, twenty-four year old leader of the Free Speech Movement at the University of California, Berkeley, California, interview with *San Francisco Chronicle* reporter, c. 1965. Weinberg later said he did not actually believe the statement, but said it as a kind of taunt to a question asking if there were outside adults manipulating the organization.—*The Washington Post*, March 23, 1970, p. A1.

Truth

1829 Truth, crushed to earth, shall rise again;
Th' eternal years of God are hers;
But Error, wounded, writhes in pain,
And dies among his worshippers.

WILLIAM CULLEN BRYANT, "The Battle-Field," stanza 9, *The Poetical Works of William Cullen Bryant*, ed. Parke Godwin, vol. 1, p. 276 (1883, reprinted 1967). Written in 1837.

1830 Hell is truth seen too late—duty neglected in its season.

Attributed to TRYON EDWARDS.—Edwards, *A Dictionary of Thoughts*, p. 225 (1891).

1831 I believe that truth is the glue that holds government together, not only our Government but civilization itself. That bond, though strained, is unbroken at home and abroad.

President GERALD R. FORD, remarks on taking the oath of office, August 9, 1974.—*Public Papers of the Presidents of the United States: Gerald R. Ford, 1974*, p. 2.

See also No. 255.

1832 Another one of the old poets, whose name has escaped my memory at present, called Truth the daughter of Time.

AULUS GELLIUS, *The Attic Nights of Aulus Gellius*, trans. John C. Rolfe, vol. 2, book 12, chapter 11, verse 7, pp. 394–95 (1927).

1833 Persecution cannot harm him who stands by Truth. Did not Socrates fall proudly a victim in body? Was not Paul stoned for the sake of the Truth? It is our inner selves that hurt us when we disobey it, and it kills us when we betray it.

KAHLIL GIBRAN, *The Secrets of the Heart*, trans. Anthony R. Ferris, p. 157 (1947).

1834 It is natural to man to indulge in the illusions of hope. We are apt to shut our eyes against a painful truth—and listen to the song of that syren, till she transforms us into beasts. Is this the part of wise men, engaged in a great and arduous struggle for liberty? Are we disposed to be of the number of those, who having eyes, see not, and having ears, hear not, the things which so nearly concern their temporal salvation? For my part, whatever anguish of spirit it might cost, I am willing to know the whole truth; to know the worst, and to provide for it.

PATRICK HENRY, speech to the Virginia Convention, Richmond, Virginia, March 23, 1775.—William Wirt, *Sketches of the Life and Character of Patrick Henry*, 9th ed., p. 138 (1836, reprinted 1970). Language altered to first person.

For information on the authenticity of the text of this speech, see the notes at No. 1061.

1835 But when men have realized that time has upset many fighting faiths, they may come to believe even more than they believe the very foundations of their own conduct that the ultimate good desired is better reached by free trade in ideas—that the best test of truth is the power of the thought to get itself accepted in the competition of the market, and that truth is the only ground upon which their wishes safely can be carried out.

Justice OLIVER WENDELL HOLMES, dissenting, *Abrams et al.* v. *United States*, 250 U.S. 630 (1919).

1836 We should face reality and our past mistakes in an honest, adult way. Boasting of glory does not make glory, and singing in the dark does not dispel fear.

HUSSEIN, king of Jordan, remarks during a conference of Arab chiefs of state, Khartoum, Sudan, August 30, 1967, as reported by *The New York Times*, August 31, 1967, p. 6.

1837 The most violent revolutions in an individual's beliefs leave most of his old order standing. Time and space, cause and effect, nature and history, and one's own biography remain untouched. New truth is always a go-between, a smoother-over of transitions. It marries old opinion to new fact so as ever to show a minimum of jolt, a maximum of continuity.

WILLIAM JAMES, "What Pragmatism Means," *Pragmatism*, pp. 60–61 (1931). Lectures delivered at the Lowell Institute, Boston, Massachusetts, December 1906, and at Columbia University, New York City, January 1907.

1838 Careless seems the great Avenger; history's pages but record
One death-grapple in the darkness 'twixt old systems and the Word;
Truth forever on the scaffold, Wrong forever on the throne,—
Yet that scaffold sways the future, and, behind the dim unknown,
Standeth God within the shadow, keeping watch above his own.

New occasions teach new duties; Time makes ancient good uncouth;
They must upward still, and onward, who would keep abreast of Truth;
Lo, before us gleam her camp-fires! we ourselves must Pilgrims be,
Launch our Mayflower, and steer boldly through the desperate winter sea,
Nor attempt the Future's portal with the Past's blood-rusted key.

JAMES RUSSELL LOWELL, "The Present Crisis," stanzas 8 and 18, *The Poetical Works of James Russell Lowell*, p. 68 (1978). Originally published in 1844.

1839 You'll never get mixed up if you simply tell the truth. Then you don't have to remember what you have said, and you never forget what you have said.

Representative SAM RAYBURN, private conversation.—W. B. Ragsdale, "An Old Friend Writes of Rayburn," *U.S. News & World Report*, October 23, 1961, p. 72.

Trying

1840 Ah, but a man's reach should exceed his grasp,
Or what's a heaven for?

ROBERT BROWNING, "Andrea Del Sarto," *The Complete Poetic and Dramatic Works of Robert Browning*, p. 346 (1895).

1841 Somebody said that it couldn't be done,
But he with a chuckle replied
That "maybe it couldn't," but he would be one
Who wouldn't say so till he'd tried.
So he buckled right in with the trace of a grin
On his face. If he worried he hid it.
He started to sing as he tackled the thing
That couldn't be done, and he did it.

EDGAR A. GUEST, "It Couldn't Be Done," stanza 1, *Collected Verse of Edgar A. Guest*, p. 285 (1934).

1842 The mode in which the inevitable comes to pass is through effort.

Justice OLIVER WENDELL HOLMES, "Ideals and Doubts," *Collected Legal Papers*, p. 305 (1937).

1843 The country needs and, unless I mistake its temper, the country demands bold, persistent experimentation. It is common sense to take a method and try it; if it fails, admit it frankly and try another. But above all, try something. The millions who are in want will not stand by silently forever while the things to satisfy their needs are within easy reach.

Trying

FRANKLIN D. ROOSEVELT, governor of New York, *Looking Forward,* chapter 2, p. 51 (1933).

Tyranny

1844 I have sworn upon the altar of God, eternal hostility against every form of tyranny over the mind of man.

Vice President THOMAS JEFFERSON, letter to Benjamin Rush, September 23, 1800.—*The Writings of Thomas Jefferson,* ed. Andrew A. Lipscomb, vol. 10, p. 175 (1903).

Carved at the base of the dome, interior of the Jefferson Memorial, Washington, D.C.

1845 Tyranny, like hell, is not easily conquered; yet we have this consolation with us, that the harder the conflict, the more glorious the triumph. What we obtain too cheap, we esteem too lightly: it is dearness only that gives every thing its value.

THOMAS PAINE, "The Crisis," no. 1, *The Writings of Thomas Paine,* ed. Moncure D. Conway, vol. 1, p. 170 (1894).

See note at No. 1821 about "Crisis."

Unemployment

1846 When a great many people are unable to find work, unemployment results.

Attributed to CALVIN COOLIDGE.—Stanley Walker, *City Editor,* p. 131 (1934). Unverified.

1847 But the time will come when New England will be as thickly peopled as old England. Wages will be as low, and will fluctuate as much with you as with us. You will have your Manchesters and Birminghams; and, in those Manchesters and Birminghams, hundreds of thousands of artisans will assuredly be sometimes out of work. Then your institutions will be fairly brought to the test.

THOMAS BABINGTON MACAULAY, letter to Henry Stephens Randall, May 23, 1857.—*The Letters of Thomas Babington Macaulay,* ed. Thomas Pinney, vol. 6, p. 95 (1981).

See note at No. 334 about this letter.

Union

1848 It's a Story they tell in the border country, where Massachusetts joins Vermont and New Hampshire. Yes, Dan'l Webster's dead—or, at least, they buried him.

But every time there's a thunderstorm around Marshfield, they say you can hear his rolling voice in the hollows of the sky. And they say that if you go to his grave and speak loud and clear, "Dan'l Webster—Dan'l Webster!" the ground'll begin to shiver and the trees begin to shake. And after a while you'll hear a deep voice saying, "Neighbor, how stands the Union?" Then you better answer the Union stands as she stood, rock-bottomed and copper-sheathed, one and indivisible, or he's liable to rear right out of the ground. At least, that's what I was told when I was a youngster.

Stephen Vincent Benét, *The Devil and Daniel Webster,* pp. 13–14 (1937).

1849 Our Union: It must be preserved.

President ANDREW JACKSON, toast at a Jefferson Day dinner, April 13, 1830.—Marquis James, *Andrew Jackson: Portrait of a President,* p. 235 (1937).

The account by James emphasizes the shocked reaction of Jackson's vice president, John C. Calhoun, to this toast, since it was clear he had lost Jackson's support of the Southern cause of nullification. When Calhoun's turn came, his toast was: "The Union, next to our liberty, most dear. May we all remember that it can only be preserved by respecting the rights of the States and by distributing equally the benefits and burdens of the Union" (pp. 235–36).

According to Martin Van Buren, *Autobiography,* vol. 2, p. 415 (1920, reprinted 1973), at the urging of General Hayne, Jackson altered his toast to "Our Federal Union" before it was given to the newspapers, and it was reported in this form in many sources including James Parton, *Life of Andrew Jackson,* vol. 3, p. 283 (1860), and Thomas Hart Benton, *Thirty Years View,* vol. 1, p. 148 (1854, reprinted 1883).

1850 Still a Union that can only be maintained by swords and bayonets, and in which strife and civil war are to take the place of brotherly love and kindness, has no charm for me.

ROBERT E. LEE, letter to his son, G. W. Custis Lee, January 23, 1861.—John William Jones, *Personal Reminiscences, Anecdotes, and Letters of Gen. Robert E. Lee,* p. 137 (1876).

1851 "A house divided against itself cannot stand." I believe this government cannot endure, permanently half *slave* and half *free.* I do not expect the Union to be *dissolved*—I do not expect the house to *fall*—but I *do* expect it will cease to be divided. It will become *all* one thing, or *all* the other.

ABRAHAM LINCOLN, speech delivered at the close of the Republican state convention, which named him the candidate for the United States Senate, Springfield, Illinois, June 16, 1858.—*The Collected Works of Abraham Lincoln,* ed. Roy P. Basler, vol. 2, p. 461 (1953). The quotation is a slight paraphrase of the Bible, Mark 3:25.

This "was probably the most carefully prepared address of Lincoln's life. The majority of his friends thought the sentiments nothing short of political suicide. Herndon writes that before delivering the oration Lincoln had declared . . . that 'the time has come when those sentiments should be uttered and if it is decreed that I should go down because of this speech, then let me go down linked with the truth—let me die in the advocacy of what is just and right.' "—*Complete Works of Abraham Lincoln,* new and enl. ed., ed. John G. Nicolay and John Hay, vol. 3, pp. 1–2, footnote 1 (1905).

1852 I am exceedingly anxious that this Union, the Constitution, and the liberties of the people shall be perpetuated in accordance with the original idea for which that struggle was made, and I shall be most happy indeed if I shall be an humble instrument in the hands of the Almighty, and of this, his almost chosen people, for perpetuating the object of that great struggle.

President-elect ABRAHAM LINCOLN, address to the New Jersey Senate, February 21, 1861.—*The Collected Works of Abraham Lincoln,* ed. Roy P. Basler, vol. 4, p. 236 (1953).

1853 Within that door
A man sits or the image of a man
Staring at stillness on a marble floor.
No drum distracts him nor no trumpet can
Although he hears the trumpet and the drum.
He listens for the time to come.

Within this door
A man sits or the image of a man
Remembering the time before.
He hears beneath the river in its choking channel
A deeper river rushing on the stone,
Sits there in his doubt alone,
Discerns the Principle,
The guns begin,
Emancipates—but not the slaves,
The Union—not from servitude but shame:
Emancipates the Union from the monstrous name
Whose infamy dishonored
Even the great Founders in their graves . . .

He saves the Union and the dream goes on.

ARCHIBALD MACLEISH, "At the Lincoln Memorial," stanza 4, lines 1–6, and stanza 5, *New & Collected Poems, 1917–1976*, pp. 433–35 (1976).

This poem was written for ceremonies marking the centennial of the Emancipation Proclamation and was read by MacLeish at the Lincoln Memorial, Washington, D.C., September 22, 1962.

1854 The happy Union of these States is a wonder; their Constitution a miracle; their example the hope of Liberty throughout the world.

JAMES MADISON, "Outline" notes, September 1829.—*The Writings of James Madison*, ed. Gaillard Hunt, vol. 9, p. 357 (1910).

These words are inscribed in the Madison Memorial Hall, Library of Congress James Madison Memorial Building.

1855 While the Union lasts, we have high, exciting, gratifying prospects spread out before us, for us and our children. Beyond that I seek not to penetrate the veil. God grant that in my day, at least, that curtain may not rise! God grant that on my vision never may be opened what lies behind! When my eyes shall be turned to behold for the last time the sun in heaven, may I not see him shining on the broken and dishonored fragments of a once glorious Union; on States dissevered, discordant, belligerent; on a land rent with civil feuds, or drenched, it may be, in fraternal blood! Let their last feeble and lingering glance rather behold the gorgeous ensign of the republic, now known and honored throughout the earth, still full and high advanced, its arms and trophies streaming in their original lustre, not a strip erased or polluted, nor a single star obscured, bearing for its motto, no such miserable interrogatory as "What is all this worth?" nor those other words of delusion and folly, "Liberty first and Union afterwards"; but everywhere, spread all over in characters of living light, blazing on all its ample folds, as they float over the sea and over the land, and in every wind under the whole heavens, that other sentiment, dear to every true American heart,—Liberty *and* Union, now and for ever, one and inseparable!

Senator DANIEL WEBSTER, remarks in the Senate, second speech on Foote's resolution, January 26, 1830.—*The Writings and Speeches of Daniel Webster*, vol. 6, p. 75 (1903).

United Nations

1856 Eagerly, musician,
Sweep your string,
So we may sing,
Elated, optative,

Our several voices
Interblending,
Playfully contending,
Not interfering
But co-inhering,
For all within
The cincture of the sound
Is holy ground,
Where all are Brothers,
None faceless Others.
Let mortals beware
Of words, for
With words we lie,
Can say peace
When we mean war,
Foul thought speak fair
And promise falsely,
But song is true:
Let music for peace
Be the paradigm,
For peace means to change
At the right time,
As the World-Clock,
Goes Tick and Tock.
So may the story
Of our human city
Presently move
Like music, when
Begotten notes
New notes beget,
Making the flowing
Of time a growing,
Till what it could be,
At last it is,
Where even sadness
Is a form of gladness,
Where Fate is Freedom,
Grace and Surprise.

W. H. AUDEN, "Hymn to the United Nations," music by Pablo Casals.—Text in *The New York Times*, October 25, 1971, p. 40.

1857 It is not the Soviet Union or indeed any other big Powers who need the United Nations for their protection. It is all the others. In this sense, the Organization is first of all their Organization and I deeply believe in the wisdom with which they will be able to use it and guide it. I shall remain in my post during the term of my office as a servant of the Organization in the interests of all those other nations, as long as they wish me to do so.

Secretary-General DAG HAMMARSKJÖLD, statement to the General Assembly of the United Nations, October 3, 1960.—*Official Records* of the United Nations, General Assembly, vol. 1, p. 332.

United Nations

1858 Protocol, alcohol, and Geritol.

ADLAI E. STEVENSON, U.S. ambassador to the United Nations, definition of diplomatic life.—Herbert J. Muller, *Adlai Stevenson*, p. 274 (1967).

Unity

1859 In union there is strength.

AESOP, fable, "The Bundle of Sticks," *Aesop's Fables*, with drawings by Fritz Kredel, p. 122 (1947).

"Union gives strength" is the version in *The Fables of Aesop*, ed. Joseph Jacobs, p. 87 (1964).

1860 Behold, how good and how pleasant it is for brethren to dwell together in unity! It is like the precious ointment upon the head, that ran down upon the beard, even Aaron's beard: that went down to the skirts of his garments.

The Bible, Psalms 133:1–2.

1861 Civilisation will not last, freedom will not survive, peace will not be kept, unless a very large majority of mankind unite together to defend them and show themselves possessed of a constabulary power before which barbaric and atavistic forces will stand in awe.

WINSTON CHURCHILL, chancellor's address, University of Bristol, Bristol, England, July 2, 1938.—*Winston S. Churchill: His Complete Speeches, 1897–1963*, ed. Robert Rhodes James, vol. 6, p. 5991 (1974).

1862 All for one, one for all, that is our device, is it not?

ALEXANDRE DUMAS, *The Three Musketeers*, chapter 9, p. 75 (1949). D'Artagnan is speaking.

1863 Even though this is late in an election year, there is no way we can go forward except together and no way anybody can win except by serving the people's urgent needs. We cannot stand still or slip backwards. We must go forward now together.

President GERALD R. FORD, remarks on taking the oath of office, August 9, 1974.—*Public Papers of the Presidents of the United States: Gerald R. Ford, 1974*, p. 2.

1864 What we need in the United States is not division. What we need in the United States is not hatred. What we need in the United States is not violence or lawlessness, but love and wisdom and compassion toward one another, and a feeling of justice toward those who still suffer within our country whether they be white or they be black. Let us dedicate ourselves to what the Greeks wrote so many years ago: To tame the savageness of man and make gentle the life of this world. Let us dedicate ourselves to that and say a prayer for our country and our people.

Senator ROBERT F. KENNEDY. One of the inscriptions at the Robert F. Kennedy gravesite in Arlington National Cemetery.

These words are taken from his extemporaneous eulogy of Martin Luther King, Jr., given at the airport in Indianapolis, Indiana, April 4, 1968.—*Robert F. Kennedy: Promises to Keep*, sel. Arthur Wortman and Richard Rhodes, p. 33 (1969) The printed version lacks the first two sentences above and a few words of the third, and there are other minor variations in wording.

Unity

The quotation from the Greeks has been attributed to Aeschylus but has not been found in his works.

1865 For the strength of the Pack is the Wolf, and the strength of the Wolf is the Pack.

RUDYARD KIPLING, "The Law of the Jungle," *The Second Jungle Book*, p. 29 (1899).

1866 And see the confluence of dreams
That clashed together in our night,
One river born of many streams
Roll in one blaze of blinding light!

GEORGE WILLIAM RUSSELL (AE), "Salutation," last stanza.—Kathleen Hoagland, *1000 Years of Irish Poetry*, p. 617 (1947).

This was written for those who took part in the Irish rebellion against England, 1916.

1867 It manus in gyrum; paullatim singula vires
Deperdunt proprias; color est *E pluribus unus.*

Spins round the stirring hand; lose by degrees
Their separate powers the parts, and comes at last
From many several colors one that rules.

VIRGIL, "Moretum," lines 103–4, *The Works of Virgil*, trans. into English verse by John Augustine Wilstach, vol. 1, p. 123 (1884).

Moretum literally means garden herbs. From Virgil's minor poems, this is a tribute "to common things and plebian associations. The lines are laudatory of early habits and rustic poverty. They close with a description of the ingredients and mode of preparation of a salad composed of garlic, parsley, rue, and onions, seasoned with cheese, salt, coriander, and vinegar, and finally sprinkled with oil.

"The poem is a brief one, of uncertain, but probably early date. But, brief as it is, and insignificant as it seems to be, certain of its words formulate the talisman of our National Government.

"So that we may say, with probable truth, that, in describing an Italian salad, a frugal shepherd of the Roman Republic dictated that motto [E pluribus unum] which has served as the symbol of union for States in a hemisphere then unknown, for a Republic which uses, with enthusiasm, even the language of that illustrious government to which it is indebted, under so many forms, for safe precedents and wise examples" (p. 124).

Values

1868 It is not our affluence, or our plumbing, or our clogged freeways that grip the imagination of others. Rather, it is the values upon which our system is built. These values imply our adherence not only to liberty and individual freedom, but also to international peace, law and order, and constructive social purpose. When we depart from these values, we do so at our peril.

Senator J. WILLIAM FULBRIGHT, remarks in the Senate, June 29, 1961, *Congressional Record*, vol. 107, p. 11703.

Victory

1869 The people who remained victorious were less like conquerors than conquered.

ST. AUGUSTINE, *The City of God,* book 3, chapter 19.—*The Works of Aurelius Augustine,* ed. Marcus Dods, vol. 1, pp. 119–20 (1871). *De Civitate Dei* was written 413–426.

1870 I would say to the House, as I said to those who have joined this Government: "I have nothing to offer but blood, toil, tears and sweat." . . . You ask, what is our aim? I can answer in one word: It is victory, victory at all costs, victory in spite of all terror, victory, however long and hard the road may be; for without victory, there is no survival.

WINSTON CHURCHILL, speech, House of Commons, May 13, 1940.—*Winston S. Churchill: His Complete Speeches, 1897–1963,* ed. Robert Rhodes James, vol. 6, p. 6220 (1974).

1871 No retreat. No retreat. They must conquer or die who've no retreat.

JOHN GAY, "We've Cheated the Parson" (song), *Polly: an Opera,* air 46, act II, scene X, *The Poetical Works of John Gay,* ed. John Underhill, vol. 2, p. 336 (1893).

1872 There's an old saying that victory has 100 fathers and defeat is an orphan.

President JOHN F. KENNEDY, referring to the Bay of Pigs disaster, press conference, April 21, 1961.—*Public Papers of the Presidents of the United States: John F. Kennedy, 1961,* p. 312.

1873 Beware of rashness, but with energy, and sleepless vigilance, go forward and give us victories.

President ABRAHAM LINCOLN, letter to General Joseph Hooker, January 26, 1863.—*The Collected Works of Abraham Lincoln,* ed. Roy P. Basler, vol. 6, p. 79 (1953).

1874 Upon the fields of friendly strife
Are sown the seeds
That, upon other fields, on other days
Will bear the fruits of victory.

General DOUGLAS MACARTHUR, *Reminiscences,* p. 82 (1964).

MacArthur wrote these lines while superintendent of the U.S. Military Academy at West Point, New York, 1919–1922, and had them engraved over the entrance to the gymnasium.

1875 Be ashamed to die until you have won some victory for humanity.

HORACE MANN, baccalaureate address, Antioch College, Yellow Springs, Ohio, 1859.—*Life and Works of Horace Mann,* ed. Mrs. Mary Mann, vol. 1, p. 575 (1868).

"The motivating principle of Mann's life was nowhere better or more clearly expressed than in the oft-quoted words with which he closed his last Commencement address at Antioch College."—*Dictionary of American Biography,* vol. 6, p. 243. Mann died a few weeks later. He had served in Congress 1848–1853.

Vietnam War

1876 A spirit of national masochism prevails, encouraged by an effete corps of impudent snobs who characterize themselves as intellectuals.

Vice President SPIRO T. AGNEW, speech at a Republican fund-raising dinner, New Orleans, Louisiana, October 19, 1969.—*Collected Speeches of Spiro Agnew,* p. 55 (1971).

1877 We cannot remain silent on Viet Nam. We should remember that whatever victory there may be possible, it will have a racial stigma. . . . It will always be the case of a predominantly white power killing an Asian nation. We are interested in peace, not just for Christians but for the whole of humanity.

EUGENE CARSON BLAKE, remarks at a World Council of Churches meeting, Geneva, Switzerland, February 12, 1966, as reported in *The Sunday Star,* Washington, D.C., February 13, 1966, p. A–5.

1878 I am convinced that the French could not win the war because the internal political situation in Vietnam, weak and confused, badly weakened their military position. I have never talked or corresponded with a person knowledgeable in Indochinese affairs who did not agree that had elections been held as of the time of the fighting, possibly 80 per cent of the population would have voted for the Communist Ho Chi Minh as their leader rather than Chief of State Bao Dai. Indeed, the lack of leadership and drive on the part of Bao Dai was a factor in the feeling prevalent among Vietnamese that they had nothing to fight for. As one Frenchman said to me, "What Vietnam needs is another Syngman Rhee, regardless of all the difficulties the presence of such a personality would entail."

DWIGHT D. EISENHOWER, *The White House Years,* vol. 1, p. 372 (1963).

1879 With 450,000 U.S. troops now in Vietnam, it is time that Congress decided whether or not to declare a state of war exists with North Vietnam. Previous congressional resolutions of support provide only limited authority. Although Congress may decide that the previously approved resolution on Vietnam given President Johnson is sufficient, the issue of a declaration of war should at least be put before the Congress for decision.

DWIGHT D. EISENHOWER, remarks to Republican congressmen, Gettysburg, Pennsylvania, July 15, 1967, published in a paraphrased form in *The Washington Post,* July 22, 1967, p. 1.

1880 The Communist leaders in Moscow, Peking and Hanoi must fully understand that the United States considers the freedom of South Viet Nam vital to our interests. And they must know that we are not bluffing in our determination to defend those interests.

Representative GERALD R. FORD, "U.S. Foreign Policy: New Myths and Old Realities," address to the National Press Club, Washington, D.C., July 21, 1965.—*Gerald R. Ford, Selected Speeches,* ed. Michael V. Doyle, p. 199 (1973).

1881 In Asia we face an ambitious and aggressive China, but we have the will and we have the strength to help our Asian friends resist that ambition. Sometimes our folks get a little impatient. Sometimes they rattle their rockets some, and they bluff about their bombs. But we are not about to send American boys 9 or 10,000 miles away from home to do what Asian boys ought to be doing for themselves.

President LYNDON B. JOHNSON, remarks at Akron University, Akron, Ohio, October 21, 1964.—*Public Papers of the Presidents of the United States: Lyndon B. Johnson, 1963–64,* book 2, pp. 1390–91.

1882 I don't think that unless a greater effort is made by the Government to win popular support that the war can be won out there. In the final analysis, it is their war. They are the ones who have to win it or lose it. We can help them, we can give them equipment, we can send our men out there as advisers, but they have to win it, the people of Viet-Nam, against the Communists.

President JOHN F. KENNEDY, televised interview with Walter Cronkite, September 2, 1963.—*Public Papers of the Presidents of the United States: John F. Kennedy, 1963*, p. 652.

1883 The war the soldiers tried to stop.

JOHN F. KERRY, commenting on how Vietnam would be known to future generations, at rally of antiwar demonstrators, west front of the Capitol, April 24, 1971, as reported by *The Evening Star*, Washington, D.C., April 26, 1971, p. A–7.

Kerry, a former Navy lieutenant who was the spokesman for Vietnam Veterans Against the War, was elected to the Senate in 1984.

1884 But also out here in this dreary, difficult war, I think history will record that this may have been one of America's finest hours, because we took a difficult task and we succeeded.

President RICHARD M. NIXON, remarks to American troops of the First Infantry Division, Di An, Vietnam, July 30, 1969.—*Public Papers of the Presidents of the United States: Richard Nixon, 1969*, p. 588.

1885 I would rather be a one-term President and do what I believe is right than to be a two-term President at the cost of seeing America become a second-rate power and to see this Nation accept the first defeat in its proud 190-year history.

President RICHARD M. NIXON, address to the nation on the situation in Southeast Asia, April 30, 1970.—*Public Papers of the Presidents of the United States: Richard Nixon, 1970*, p. 410.

1886 If, when the chips are down, the world's most powerful nation, the United States of America, acts like a pitiful, helpless giant, the forces of totalitarianism and anarchy will threaten free nations and free institutions throughout the world.

President RICHARD M. NIXON, address to the nation on the situation in Southeast Asia, April 30, 1970.—*Public Papers of the Presidents of the United States: Richard Nixon, 1970*, p. 409.

1887 I have been among the officers who have said that a large land war in Asia is the last thing we should undertake. Most of us, when we use that term, are thinking about getting into a land war against Red China. That's the only power in Asia which would require us to use forces in very large numbers. I was slow in joining with those who recommended the introduction of ground forces in South Vietnam. But it became perfectly clear that because of the rate of infiltration from North Vietnam to South Vietnam something had to be done.

General MAXWELL D. TAYLOR, interview, "Top Authority Looks at Vietnam War and Its Future," *U.S. News & World Report*, February 21, 1966, p. 42.

1888 It became necessary to destroy the town to save it.

Author unknown. An unnamed major in the U.S. Army said this about the decision to bomb and shell the town of Bentre, according to an Associated Press dispatch.—*The New York Times*, February 8, 1968, p. 14.

1889 Violence is as American as cherry pie.

H. RAP BROWN, press conference at the Student Nonviolent Co-ordinating Committee headquarters, Washington, D.C., July 27, 1967, as reported by *The Evening Star,* Washington, D.C., July 27, 1967, p. 1.

1890 The use of violence as an instrument of persuasion is therefore inviting and seems to the discontented to be the only effective protest.

Justice WILLIAM O. DOUGLAS, *Points of Rebellion,* p. 78 (1970).

1891 Violence has no constitutional sanction; and every government from the beginning has moved against it. But where grievances pile high and most of the elected spokesmen represent the Establishment, violence may be the only effective response.

Justice WILLIAM O. DOUGLAS, *Points of Rebellion,* pp. 88–89 (1970).

1892 I'd hate to be in those [slum] conditions and I'll tell you if I were in those conditions, you'd have more trouble than you have already because I've got enough spark left in me to lead a mighty good revolt.

Vice President HUBERT H. HUMPHREY, speech to the National Association of Counties in New Orleans, Louisiana, July 18, 1966, as reported by *The Times-Picayune,* New Orleans, July 19, 1966, p. 18.

1893 The ultimate weakness of violence is that it is a descending spiral, begetting the very thing it seeks to destroy. Instead of diminishing evil, it multiplies it. Through violence you may murder the liar, but you cannot murder the lie, nor establish the truth. Through violence you may murder the hater, but you do not murder hate. In fact, violence merely increases hate. So it goes. Returning violence for violence multiplies violence, adding deeper darkness to a night already devoid of stars. Darkness cannot drive out darkness; only light can do that. Hate cannot drive out hate: only love can do that.

MARTIN LUTHER KING, JR., *Where Do We Go from Here: Chaos or Community?,* pp. 62–63 (1967).

1894 I feel that we will continue to have a non-violent movement, and we will continue to find the vast majority of Negroes committed to non-violence, at least as the best tactical approach and from a pragmatic point of view as the best strategy in dealing with the problem of racial injustice. Realism impels me to admit, however, that when there is justice and the pursuit of justice, violence appears, and where there is injustice and frustration, the potentialities for violence are greater, and I would like to strongly stress the point that the more we can achieve victories through non-violence, the more it will be possible to keep the non-violent discipline at the center of the movement. But the more we find individuals facing conditions of frustration, conditions of disappointment and seething despair as a result of the slow pace of things and the failure to change conditions, the more it will be possible for the apostles of violence to interfere.

MARTIN LUTHER KING, JR., televised interview, "Meet the Press," March 28, 1965.—Transcript, p. 9.

1895 Lawlessness is lawlessness. Anarchy is anarchy is anarchy. Neither race nor color nor frustration is an excuse for either lawlessness or anarchy.

Violence

THURGOOD MARSHALL, U.S. solicitor general, speech at the national convention of Alpha Phi Alpha, St. Louis, Missouri, August 15, 1966, as reported by the *St. Louis Globe-Democrat,* August 17, 1966, p. 1.

1896 Our most serious challenges to date have been external—the kind this strong and resourceful country could unite against. While serious external dangers remain, the graver threats today are internal: haphazard urbanization, racial discrimination, disfiguring of the environment, unprecedented interdependence, the dislocation of human identity and motivation created by an affluent society—all resulting in a rising tide of individual and group violence.

To Establish Justice, to Insure Domestic Tranquility, final report of the National Commission on the Causes and Prevention of Violence, p. xxxii (1960).

Dr. Milton S. Eisenhower was chairman of the commission.

Voters and voting

1897 I would relate to the crowds how I called on a certain rural constituent and was shocked to hear him say he was thinking of voting for my opponent. I reminded him of the many things I had done for him as prosecuting attorney, as county judge, as congressman, and senator. I recalled how I had helped get an access road built to his farm, how I had visited him in a military hospital in France when he was wounded in World War I, how I had assisted him in securing his veteran's benefits, how I had arranged his loan from the Farm Credit Administration, how I had got him a disaster loan when the flood destroyed his home, etc., etc.

"How can you think of voting for my opponent?" I exhorted at the end of this long recital. "Surely you remember all these things I have done for you?"

"Yeah," he said, "I remember. But what in hell have you done for me lately?"

ALBEN W. BARKLEY, *That Reminds Me—,* p. 165 (1954).

Barkley first told this story during his 1938 campaign for renomination as Kentucky's Democratic candidate for the United States Senate.

1898 VOTE, n. The instrument and symbol of a freeman's power to make a fool of himself and a wreck of his country.

AMBROSE BIERCE, *The Devil's Dictionary,* p. 359 (1948). Originally published in 1906 as *The Cynic's Word Book.*

1899 We'd all like t'vote fer th'best man, but he's never a candidate.

KIN HUBBARD, *The Best of Kin Hubbard,* part 1, p. 14 (1984).

The sayings of Abe Martin, Hubbard's rural sage, appeared from 1904–1930 in many newspapers.

1900 I am of the opinion that all who can should vote for the most intelligent, honest, and conscientious men eligible to office, irrespective of former party opinions, who will endeavour to make the new constitutions and the laws passed under them as beneficial as possible to the true interests, prosperity, and liberty of all classes and conditions of the people.

ROBERT E. LEE, letter to General James Longstreet, October 29, 1867.—*Recollections and Letters of General Robert E. Lee,* p. 269 (1924).

1901 Our mission is at once the oldest and the most basic of this country: to right wrong, to do justice, to serve man. . . . Because all Americans just must have the right to vote. And we are going to give them that right. All Americans must have the privileges of citizenship regardless of race. And they are going to have those privileges of citizenship regardless of race.

President LYNDON B. JOHNSON, "The American Promise," delivered to a joint session of Congress, March 15, 1965.—*Public Papers of the Presidents of the United States: Lyndon B. Johnson, 1965,* book 1, pp. 281, 286.

He was talking about the civil rights bill he was about to present to Congress.

1902 The margin is narrow, but the responsibility is clear.

President-elect JOHN F. KENNEDY, press conference, November 10, 1963.—Transcript, *The New York Times,* November 11, 1963, p. 20.

In Theodore Sorensen's *Kennedy* (1965), these words are followed by "There may be difficulties with the Congress, but a margin of only one vote would still be a mandate" (p. 219).

1903 To give the victory to the right, not *bloody bullets,* but *peaceful ballots* only, are necessary.

ABRAHAM LINCOLN, speech c. May 18, 1858.—*Collected Works of Abraham Lincoln,* ed. Roy P. Basler, vol. 2, p. 454 (1953).

Other uses of his contrast of ballots and bullets can be found in his message to Congress of July 4, 1861, "That ballots are the rightful, and peaceful, successors of bullets; and that when ballots have fairly, and constitutionally, decided, there can be no successful appeal, back to bullets" (vol. 4, p. 439); and in a letter to James C. Conkling, August 26, 1863, "There can be no successful appeal from the ballot to the bullet" (vol. 6, p. 410).

In *The Writings of Abraham Lincoln,* ed. Arthur Brooks Lapsley (1905), there is a reconstruction, forty years later, of a speech to the first Republican state convention of Illinois, Bloomington, Illinois, May 29, 1856, in which this sentence appears: "Do not mistake that the ballot is stronger than the bullet" (vol. 2, p. 269). This lengthy reconstruction was not "worthy of serious consideration," in the opinion of Basler (*Collected Works,* vol. 2, p. 341).

1904 I believe that there are societies in which every man may safely be admitted to vote. . . . I say, sir, that there are countries in which the condition of the labouring-classes is such that they may safely be intrusted with the right of electing members of the Legislature. . . . Universal suffrage exists in the United States without producing any very frightful consequences.

THOMAS BABINGTON MACAULAY, speech in Parliament on parliamentary reform, March 2, 1831.—Macaulay, *Speeches, Parliamentary and Miscellaneous,* vol. 1, pp. 12–13 (1853).

1905 Bad officials are elected by good citizens who do not vote.

GEORGE JEAN NATHAN.—Clifton Fadiman, *The American Treasury, 1455–1955,* p. 344 (1955). Unverified in Nathan's works.

1906 The right of voting for representatives is the primary right by which other rights are protected. To take away this right is to reduce a man to slavery, for slavery consists in being subject to the will of another, and he that has not a vote in the election of representatives is in this case.

THOMAS PAINE, "Dissertation on First Principles of Government," *The Writings of Thomas Paine,* ed. Moncure D. Conway, vol. 3, p. 267 (1895). Originally published in 1795.

1907 Perhaps America will one day go fascist democratically, by popular vote.

WILLIAM L. SHIRER, as reported by *The New York Times,* December 29, 1969, p. 36.

1908 In times of stress and strain, people will vote.

Author unknown. Attributed to parliamentary debates, Great Britain, 1857. Unverified.

War

1909 In order for a war to be just, three things are necessary. First, the authority of the sovereign. . . . Secondly, a just cause. . . . Thirdly . . . a rightful intention.

ST. THOMAS AQUINAS, *Summa Theologica,* part II-II, question 40, article 1, pp. 1359-60 (1947). Written 1266–1273.

The three conditions are sometimes paraphrased as: public authority, just cause, right motive.

1910 Stout hearts, my laddies! If the row comes, REMEMBER THE MAINE, and show the world how American sailors can fight.

CLIFFORD K. BERRYMAN, caption under cartoon, *The Washington Post,* April 3, 1898, p. 1.

On February 15, 1898, the warship *Maine* blew up in the harbor at Havana, Cuba. Edward T. Folliard, correspondent and historian of *The Washington Post,* said of Berryman's cartoon: "Thus was born the slogan and battle cry of the Spanish-American War."—*The Washington Post,* September 24, 1972, *Potomac* magazine, special section, "The Washington Post, 1972," p. 8.

1911 I venture to say no war *can* be long carried on against the will of the people.

EDMUND BURKE, "Letters on a Regicide Peace," letter 1, 1796–1797, *The Works of the Right Honorable Edmund Burke,* vol. 5, p. 283 (1899).

1912 Let the officers and directors of our armament factories, our gun builders and munitions makers and shipbuilders all be conscripted—to get $30 a month, the same wage paid to the lads in the trenches. . . . Give capital thirty days to think it over and you will learn by that time that there will be no war. That will stop the racket—that and nothing else.

SMEDLEY D. BUTLER, "War Is a Racket," *The Forum and Century,* September 1934, p. 143.

1913 The eagle has ceased to scream, but the parrots will now begin to chatter. The war of the giants is over and the pigmies will now start to squabble.

WINSTON CHURCHILL, comment on May 7, 1945, after General Ismay, his wartime chief of staff, announced the news of V-E Day.—Kay Halle, *Irrepressible Churchill*, p. 249 (1966).

1914 To jaw-jaw is always better than to war-war.

WINSTON CHURCHILL, remarks at a White House luncheon, June 26, 1954. His exact words are not known, because the meetings and the luncheon that day were closed to reporters, but above is the commonly cited version.

His words are quoted as "It is 'better to jaw-jaw than to war-war,' " in the subheading on p. 1 of *The New York Times*, June 27, 1954, and as "To jaw-jaw always is better than to war-war" on p. 3.

The Washington Post in its June 27 issue, p. 1, has "better to talk jaw to jaw than have war," and *The Star*, Washington, D.C., p. 1, a slight variation, "It is better to talk jaw to jaw than to have war."

1915 War is not merely a political act but a real political instrument, a continuation of political intercourse, a carrying out of the same by other means.

KARL VON CLAUSEWITZ, *On War*, trans. O. J. Matthijs Jolles, book 1, chapter 1, section 24, p. 16 (1943). Originally published in 1833.

1916 War is only caused through the political intercourse of governments and nations . . . war is nothing but a continuation of political intercourse with an admixture of other means.

KARL VON CLAUSEWITZ, *On War*, trans. O. J. Matthijs Jolles, book 8, chapter 6, p. 596 (1943). Originally published in 1833.

1917 War is regarded as *nothing but the continuation of state policy with other means*.

KARL VON CLAUSEWITZ, *On War*, trans. O. J. Matthijs Jolles, author's note, p. xxix (1943). Originally published in 1833.

1918 I say when you get into a war, you should win as quick as you can, because your losses become a function of the duration of the war. I believe when you get in a war, get everything you need and win it.

DWIGHT D. EISENHOWER, news conference, Indio, California, March 15, 1968, as reported in *The New York Times*, March 16, 1968, p. 15.

1919 Nations have recently been led to borrow billions for war; no nation has ever borrowed largely for education. Probably, no nation is rich enough to pay for both war and civilization. We must make our choice; we cannot have both.

ABRAHAM FLEXNER, *Universities*, part 3, p. 302 (1930).

1920 All of us who served in one war or another know very well that all wars are the glory and the agony of the young.

President GERALD R. FORD, address to the 75th annual convention of the Veterans of Foreign Wars, August 19, 1974.—*Public Papers of the Presidents of the United States: Gerald R. Ford, 1974*, p. 25.

1921 Suffer not yourselves to be betrayed with a kiss. Ask yourselves how this gracious reception of our petition comports with those warlike preparations which cover our waters and darken our land. Are fleets and armies necessary to a work of love and reconciliation? Have we shown ourselves so unwilling to be reconciled, that force must be called in to win back our love? Let us not deceive ourselves, sir. These are the implements of war and subjugation—the last arguments to which kings resort.

PATRICK HENRY, speech to the Virginia Convention, Richmond, Virginia, March 23, 1775.—William Wirt, *Sketches of the Life and Character of Patrick Henry*, 9th ed., p. 139 (1836, reprinted 1970).

For information on the authenticity of the text of this speech, see the notes at No. 1061.

1922 *There is no longer any room for hope.* If we wish to be free—if we mean to preserve inviolate those inestimable privileges for which we have been so long contending—if we mean not basely to abandon the noble struggle in which we have been so long engaged, and which we have pledged ourselves never to abandon, until the glorious object of our contest shall be obtained—we must fight!—I repeat it, sir, we must fight!! An appeal to arms and to the God of Hosts, is all that is left us!

PATRICK HENRY, speech to the Virginia Convention, Richmond, Virginia, March 23, 1775.—William Wirt, *Sketches of the Life and Character of Patrick Henry*, 9th ed., p. 140 (1836, reprinted 1970).

For information on the authenticity of the text of this speech, see the notes at No. 1061.

1923 Older men declare war. But it is youth that must fight and die. And it is youth who must inherit the tribulation, the sorrow and the triumphs that are the aftermath of war.

HERBERT HOOVER, address to the 23d Republican national convention, Chicago, Illinois, June 27, 1944.—*Official Report of the Proceedings of the Twenty-third Republican National Convention*, p. 166 (1944).

1924 You have not been mistaken in supposing my views and feeling to be in favor of the abolition of war. Of my dispos[i]tion to maintain peace until its condition shall be made less tolerable than that of war itself, the world has had proofs, and more, perhaps, than it has approved. I hope it is practicable, by improving the mind and morals of society, to lessen the dispos[i]tion to war; but of its abolition I despair.

THOMAS JEFFERSON, letter to Noah Worcester, November 26, 1817.—*The Writings of Thomas Jefferson*, ed. Andrew A. Lipscomb, vol. 18, p. 298 (1903).

1925 Among the calamities of war, may be justly numbered the diminution of the love of truth, by the falsehoods which interest dictates, and credulity encourages.

SAMUEL JOHNSON, *The Idler*, no. 30, November 11, 1758.

A more succinct version is: "The first casualty when war comes is truth," attributed to Senator Hiram Johnson, remarks in the Senate, 1918.—*The Macmillan Book of Proverbs, Maxims, and Famous Phrases*, ed. Burton Stevenson, p. 2445 (1948). Unverified.

1926 War is itself a political act with primarily political objects and under the American form of government political officials must necessarily direct its general course.

Captain DUDLEY W. KNOX, *A History of the United States Navy*, chapter 24, final paragraph, p. 274 (1936).

1927 The struggles waged by the different peoples against U.S. imperialism reinforce each other and merge into a torrential worldwide tide of opposition to U.S. imperialism. . . . It can be split up and defeated. The peoples of Asia, Africa, Latin America, and other regions can destroy it piece by piece, some striking at its head and others at its feet. That is why the greatest fear of U.S. imperialism is that people's wars will be launched in different parts of the world . . . and why it regards people's war as a mortal danger.

LIN PIAO, minister of defense, People's Republic of China. Text released September 2, 1965.—Samuel B. Griffith, *Peking and People's Wars,* p. 102 (1966).

1928 Thus, if there is anyone who is confident that he can advise me as to the best advantage of the state in this campaign which I am about to conduct, let him not refuse his services to the state, but come with me into Macedonia. I will furnish him with his sea-passage, with a horse, a tent, and even travel-funds. If anyone is reluctant to do this and prefers the leisure of the city to the hardships of campaigning, let him not steer the ship from on shore.

LIVY, book 44, chapter 22.—*Livy*, trans. Alfred C. Schlesinger, vol. 13, p. 161 (1951). Lucius Aemilius Paulus is addressing the people at a public meeting.

President Franklin Roosevelt attacked armchair generals by citing this and preceding passages at his press conference, March 17, 1942: "Being of an historical turn of mind, [I figured] that probably some poor devil had gone through this process of annoyance in past years, some previous time in history, so I went quite far back and I found [Lucius Aemilius] . . . it sounds as if it were written in 1942."—*The Public Papers and Addresses of Franklin D. Roosevelt, 1942,* p. 166 (1950).

See also No. 1941.

1929 Once blood is shed in a national quarrel reason and right are swept aside by the rage of angry men.

DAVID LLOYD GEORGE, *War Memoirs,* vol. 2, chapter 81, p. 1815 (1942).

1930 That's the way it is in war. You win or lose, live or die—and the difference is just an eyelash.

DOUGLAS MACARTHUR, *Reminiscences,* p. 145 (1964).

1931 The constitution supposes, what the History of all Governments demonstrates, that the Executive is the branch of power most interested in war, & most prone to it. It has accordingly with studied care, vested the question of war in the Legislature. But the Doctrines lately advanced strike at the root of all these provisions, and will deposit the peace of the Country in that Department which the Constitution distrusts as most ready without cause to renounce it. For if the opinion of the President not the facts & proofs themselves are to sway the judgment of Congress, in declaring war, and if the President in the recess of Congress create a foreign mission, appoint the minister, & negociate a War Treaty, without the possibility of a check even from the Senate, untill the measures present alternatives overruling the freedom of its judgment; if again a Treaty when made obliges the Legislature to declare war contrary to its judgment, and in pursuance of the same doctrine, a law declaring war, imposes a like moral obligation, to grant the requisite supplies until it be formally repealed with the consent of the President & Senate, it is evident that the people are cheated out of the best ingredients in their Government, the safeguards of peace which is the greatest of their blessings.

JAMES MADISON, letter to Thomas Jefferson, April 2, 1798.—*The Writings of James Madison,* ed. Gaillard Hunt, vol. 6, pp. 312–13 (1906).

1932 War contains so much folly, as well as wickedness, that much is to be hoped from the progress of reason; and if any thing is to be hoped, every thing ought to be tried.

JAMES MADISON, "Universal Peace," *National Gazette*, February 2, 1792.—*The Writings of James Madison*, ed. Gaillard Hunt, vol. 6, pp. 88–89 (1906).

These words are inscribed in the Madison Memorial Hall, Library of Congress James Madison Memorial Building.

1933 The enemy advances, we retreat; the enemy camps, we harass; the enemy tires, we attack; the enemy retreats, we pursue.

MAO TSE-TUNG, letter, January 5, 1930.—*Selected Military Writings of Mao Tse-Tung*, p. 72 (1966).

Mao was quoting from a letter from the Front Committee to the Central Committee, on guerrilla tactics.

1934 War is an ugly thing, but not the ugliest of things: the decayed and degraded state of moral and patriotic feeling which thinks nothing *worth* a war, is worse. When a people are used as mere human instruments for firing cannon or thrusting bayonets, in the service and for the selfish purposes of a master, such war degrades a people. A war to protect other human beings against tyrannical injustice; a war to give victory to their own ideas of right and good, and which is their own war, carried on for an honest purpose by their free choice,—is often the means of their regeneration. A man who has nothing which he is willing to fight for, nothing which he cares more about than he does about his personal safety, is a miserable creature who has no chance of being free, unless made and kept so by the exertions of better men than himself. As long as justice and injustice have not terminated *their* ever-renewing fight for ascendancy in the affairs of mankind, human beings must be willing, when need is, to do battle for the one against the other.

JOHN STUART MILL, "The Contest in America," *Dissertations and Discussions*, vol. 1, p. 26 (1868). First published in *Fraser's Magazine*, February 1862.

1935 War challenges virtually every other institution of society—the justice and equity of its economy, the adequacy of its political systems, the energy of its productive plant, the bases, wisdom and purposes of its foreign policy.

WALTER MILLIS, *The Faith of an American*, p. 27 (1941).

1936 There is a time for all things, a time to preach and a time to pray, but those times have passed away. There is a time to fight, and that time has now come.

PETER MUHLENBERG.—The precise text of this Lutheran clergyman's sermon in Woodstock, Virginia, in January 1776, does not exist. The quotation above is from Edward W. Hocker, *The Fighting Parson of the American Revolution*, p. 61 (1936).

Muhlenberg served in Congress 1789–1791, 1793–1795, and 1799–1801.

1937 We have to go along a road covered with blood. We have no other alternative. For us it is a matter of life or death, a matter of living or existing. We have to be ready to face the challenges that await us.

GAMAL ABDEL NASSER, speech to Egypt's National Assembly, Cairo, November 6, 1969, as reported by *The Washington Post*, November 7, 1969, p. 1.

1938 I seriously doubt if we will ever have another war. This is probably the very last one.

President RICHARD M. NIXON, on-the-record interview with C. L. Sulzberger, March 8, 1971.—*The New York Times*, March 10, 1971, p. 14.

1939 A riot is a spontaneous outburst. A war is subject to advance planning.

RICHARD M. NIXON, address before the National Association of Manufacturers, New York City, December 8, 1967.—James J. Kilpatrick quoted a transcript in his syndicated column in *The Evening Star*, Washington, D.C., December 26, 1967, p. A13. Nixon's topic was "the war in our cities."

1940 Stand your ground. Don't fire unless fired upon, but if they mean to have a war, let it begin here.

JOHN PARKER.—George Stimpson, *A Book About American History*, p. 109 (1950).

Captain Parker said this to his Minutemen troops at Lexington, Massachusetts, on April 19, 1775, as they prepared to meet the British in battle. Inscription on a marker at Lexington green.

1941 Paulus Aemilius, on taking command of the forces in Macedonia, and finding them talkative and impertinently busy, as though they were all commanders, issued out his orders that they should have only ready hands and keen swords, and leave the rest to him.

PLUTARCH, *Plutarch's Lives*, trans. John Dryden, rev. A. H. Clough, life of Galba, vol. 5, p. 456 (1859).

See also No. 1928.

1942 I want to stand by my country, but I cannot vote for war. I vote no.

Representative JEANETTE RANKIN, casting her vote against the United States entering World War I, in the early hours of April 6, 1917, as reported by *The New York Times*, April 6, 1917, p. 1.

Jeanette Rankin of Montana was the first woman elected to Congress, where she served 1917–1919 and 1941–1943. Not only did she vote against World War I, she was the only member of Congress to oppose declaring war on Japan in December 1941.

1943 I have always said that a conference was held for one reason only, to give everybody a chance to get sore at everybody else. Sometimes it takes two or three conferences to scare up a war, but generally one will do it.

WILL ROGERS, syndicated column, July 5, 1933.—*The New York Times*, July 6, 1933, p. 23.

Disraeli is another who had an unsanguine view of conferences: "The Conference lasted six weeks. It wasted six weeks. It lasted as long as a Carnival, and, like a Carnival, it was an affair of masks and mystification. Our Ministers went to it as men in distressed circumstances go to a place of amusement—to while away the time, with a consciousness of impending failure."—Speech in the House of Commons on Denmark and Germany, vote of censure, July 4, 1864, *Hansard's Parliamentary Debates*, 3d series, vol. 176, col. 743.

1944 I originated a remark many years ago that I think has been copied more than any little thing that I've every said, and I used it in the FOLLIES of 1922. I said America has a unique record. *We never lost a war and we never won a conference* in our lives. I believe that we could without any degree of egotism, single-handed lick any nation in the world. But we can't confer with Costa Rica and come home with our shirts on.

WILL ROGERS.—Paula McSpadden Love, *The Will Rogers Book*, p. 177 (1972).

The author was a niece of Will Rogers's and curator of the Will Rogers Memorial in Claremore, Oklahoma.

1945 And while I am talking to you mothers and fathers, I give you one more assurance. I have said this before, but I shall say it again and again and again: Your boys are not going to be sent into any foreign wars.

President FRANKLIN D. ROOSEVELT, campaign speech, Boston, Massachusetts, October 30, 1940.—*The Public Papers and Addresses of Franklin D. Roosevelt, 1940*, p. 517 (1941).

1946 Sometime they'll give a war and nobody will come.

CARL SANDBURG, "The People, Yes," stanza 23, line 23, *The Complete Poems of Carl Sandburg*, rev. and expanded ed., p. 464 (1970). First published in 1936 in *The People, Yes.*

1947 For God's sake, do not drag me into another war! I am worn down, and worn out, with crusading and defending Europe, and protecting mankind; I *must* think a little of myself.

SYDNEY SMITH, letter to the Countess Grey, February 19, 1823.—*A Memoir of the Rev. Sydney Smith by His Daughter Lady Holland*, p. 434 (1874).

1948 Be convinced that to be happy means to be free and that to be free means to be brave. Therefore do not take lightly the perils of war.

THUCYDIDES, "The Funeral Speech," *The Speeches of Pericles*, trans. H. G. Edinger, p. 39 (1979).

1949 They said we were soft, that we would not fight, that we could not win. We are not a warlike nation. We do not go to war for gain or for territory; we go to war for principles, and we produce young men like these. I think I told every one of them that I would rather have that medal, the Congressional Medal of Honor, than to be President of the United States.

President HARRY S. TRUMAN, remarks at presentation of the Congressional Medal of Honor to fourteen members of the Navy and Marine Corps, October 5, 1945.—*Public Papers of the Presidents of the United States: Harry S. Truman, 1945*, p. 375.

1950 When you have prayed for victory you have prayed for many unmentioned results which follow victory—*must* follow it, cannot help but follow it. Upon the listening spirit of God the Father fell also the unspoken part of the prayer. He commandeth me to put it into words. Listen!

"O Lord our Father, our young patriots, idols of our hearts, go forth to battle—be Thou near them! With them—in spirit—we also go forth from the sweet peace of our beloved firesides to smite the foe. O Lord our God, help us to tear their soldiers to bloody shreds with our shells; help us to cover their smiling fields with the pale forms of their patriot dead; help us to drown the thunder of the guns with the shrieks of their wounded, writhing in pain; help us to lay waste their humble homes with a hurricane of fire; help us to wring the hearts of their unoffending widows with anavailing grief; help us to turn them out roofless with their little children to wander unfriended the wastes of their desolated land in rags and hunger and thirst, sports of the sun flames of summer and the icy winds of winter, broken in spirit, worn with travail, imploring Thee for the refuge of the grave and denied it—for our sakes who adore Thee, Lord, blast their hopes, blight their lives, protract their bitter pilgrimage, make heavy their steps, water their way with their tears, stain the white snow with the blood of their wounded feet! We ask it, in the spirit of love, of Him Who is the Source of Love, and Who is the ever-faithful refuge and friend of all that are sore beset and seek His aid with humble and contrite hearts. Amen."

MARK TWAIN (Samuel L. Clemens), "The War Prayer," *Europe and Elsewhere*, pp. 397–98 (1923). Dictated 1904–1905.

1951 . . . I saw these terrible things,
and took great part in them.
(. . . quaeque ipse miserrima vidi
et quorum pars magna fui.)

VIRGIL, *The Aeneid*, trans. James H. Mantinband, book 2, lines 5–6, p. 25 (1964).

This sentence has also been translated as: "All of which misery I saw, and a great part of which I was." Aeneas was describing the sack of Troy.

1952 The War That Will End War.

H. G. WELLS, book title, 1914.

While the phrase "The war to end war" is often associated with Woodrow Wilson, its authorship was claimed by Wells in an article in *Liberty*, December 29, 1934, p. 4. Bertrand Russell also credited Wells in *Portraits from Memory*, p. 83 (1956). A cynical version attributed to David Lloyd George is: "This war, like the next war, is a war to end war." See William Safire, *Safire's Political Dictionary*, p. 777 (1978), for contemporary uses of the phrase.

1953 A time will come when a politician who has wilfully made war and promoted international dissension will be as sure of the dock and much surer of the noose than a private homicide. It is not reasonable that those who gamble with men's lives should not stake their own.

H. G. WELLS, *The Salvaging of Civilization*, chapter 1, conclusion, p. 40 (1921).

1954 War is much too serious a matter to be entrusted to the military.

Attributed to various Frenchmen including Talleyrand, Clemenceau, and Briand. Unverified.

Often heard, ". . . entrusted to generals."

War and peace

1955 Croesus said to Cambyses; That peace was better than war; because in peace the sons did bury their fathers, but in wars the fathers did bury their sons.

FRANCIS BACON, *Apophthegms, New and Old* (vol. 13 of *The Works of Francis Bacon*), ed. James A. Spedding, Robert L. Ellis and Douglas D. Heath, no. 149, p. 359 (1860, reprinted 1969). First published 1625.

1956 And he shall judge among the nations, and shall rebuke many people: and they shall beat their swords into plowshares, and their spears into pruninghooks: nation shall not lift up sword against nation, neither shall they learn war any more.

The Bible, Isaiah 2:4.

1957 An analysis of the history of mankind shows that from the year 1496 B.C. to the year 1861 of our era, that is, in a cycle of 3357 years, were but 227 years of peace and 3130 years of war: in other words, were thirteen years of war for every year of peace. Considered thus, the history of the lives of peoples presents a picture of uninterrupted struggle. War, it would appear, is a normal attribute to human life.

JEAN DE BLOCH, *The Future of War,* trans. R. C. Long, p. lxv (1903).

1958 In War: Resolution
In Defeat: Defiance
In Victory: Magnanimity
In Peace: Good Will

WINSTON CHURCHILL, *The Second World War,* p. viii (1948–1954). This motto, the "moral of the work," appeared on p. viii of each of the six volumes in this work.

1959 War is an invention of the human mind. The human mind can invent peace with justice.

NORMAN COUSINS, *Who Speaks for Man?*, p. 318 (1953).

1960 Such subtle Covenants shall be made,
Till Peace it self is War in Masquerade.

JOHN DRYDEN, *Absalom and Achitophel,* part 2, lines 268–69, p. 9 (1682, reprinted 1970).

A variant of the second part, "And Peace it self is War in Masquerade," appears earlier in the poem, part 1, line 752, p. 23.

1961 Peace will never be won if men reserve for war their greatest efforts, Peace, too, requires well-directed and sustained sacrificial endeavor. Given that, we can, I believe, achieve the great goal of our foreign policy, that of enabling our people to enjoy in peace the blessings of liberty.

JOHN FOSTER DULLES, secretary of state, news conference statement, December 31, 1954.—*Department of State Bulletin,* January 10, 1955, p. 44.

1962 WAR IS PEACE
FREEDOM IS SLAVERY
IGNORANCE IS STRENGTH.

GEORGE ORWELL, *Nineteen Eighty-Four,* p. 5 (1949).
These three slogans of the Party were engraved on the Ministry of Truth building.

1963 You bring me the deepest joy that can be felt by a man whose invincible belief is that Science and Peace will triumph over Ignorance and War, that nations will unite, not to destroy, but to build, and that the future will belong to those who will have done most for suffering humanity.

LOUIS PASTEUR, speech at celebration honoring his seventieth birthday, the Sorbonne, Paris, France, December 27, 1892. Pasteur's son read the speech of thanks because of the weakness of his father's voice.—René Vallery-Radot, *The Life of Pasteur,* trans. Mrs. R. L. Devonshire, vol. 2, p. 297 (1902).

On his 1956 Christmas card, Adlai E. Stevenson used a version of this passage which varies slightly from the arrangement and translation given above: "Not to destroy but to construct, / I hold the unconquerable belief / that science and peace will triumph over ignorance and war / that nations will come together / not to destroy but to construct / and that the future belongs to those / who accomplish most for humanity."

1964 Pile the bodies high at Austerlitz and Waterloo.
Shovel them under and let me work—
I am the grass; I cover all.

And pile them high at Gettysburg
And pile them high at Ypres and Verdun.
Shovel them under and let me work.
Two years, ten years, and passengers ask the conductor:
What place is this?
Where are we now?

I am the grass.
Let me work.

CARL SANDBURG, "Grass," *The Complete Poems of Carl Sandburg*, rev. and expanded ed., p. 136 (1970). First published in 1918 in *Cornhuskers*.

1965 Wars are, of course, as a rule to be avoided; but they are far better than certain kinds of peace.

THEODORE ROOSEVELT, *Thomas Hart Benton*, chapter 12, p. 289 (1897, reprinted 1968).

1966 Since wars begin in the minds of men, it is in the minds of men that the defences of peace must be constructed.

Author unknown. Preamble to the constitution of UNESCO, the United Nations Educational, Scientific and Cultural Organization.—U.S. National Commission for UNESCO, *UNESCO: Basic Documents*, 7th ed., p. 9 (1965).

The UNESCO office in Washington, D.C., has identified the author of this sentence both as Clement Richard Attlee, prime minister of Great Britain, and more recently as Archibald MacLeish, chairman of the American delegation to the London conference to draw up the UNESCO constitution, which was adopted in London on November 16, 1945.

War in Asia

1967 I am under no illusion that our present strategy of using means short of total war to achieve our ends and oppose communism is a guarantee that a world war will not be thrust upon us. But a policy of patience and determination without provoking a world war, while we improve our military power, is one which we believe we must continue to follow. . . .

Under present circumstances, we have recommended against enlarging the war from Korea to also include Red China. The course of action often described as a "limited war" with Red China would increase the risk we are taking by engaging too much of our power in an area that is not the critical strategic prize.

Red China is not the powerful nation seeking to dominate the world. Frankly, in the opinion of the Joint Chiefs of Staff, this strategy would involve us in the wrong war, at the wrong place, at the wrong time, and with the wrong enemy.

General OMAR N. BRADLEY, chairman of the Joint Chiefs of Staff, testimony before the Senate Committees on Armed Services and Foreign Relations, May 15, 1951.—*Military Situation in the Far East*, hearings, 82d Congress, 1st session, part 2, p. 732 (1951).

On p. 753, Bradley repeats his conviction that it is "a wrong war at the wrong place and against a wrong enemy."

1968 While no man in his right mind would advocate sending our ground forces into continental China and such was never given a thought, the new situation [Korea] did urgently demand a drastic revision of strategic planning if our political aim was to defeat this new enemy as we had defeated the old.

General DOUGLAS MACARTHUR, address to a joint session of Congress, April 19, 1951.—*Congressional Record*, vol. 97, p. 4124.

Washington, D.C.

1969 Too small to be a state but too large to be an asylum for the mentally deranged.

ANNE M. BURFORD, characterizing the District of Columbia, remarks to a Colorado state convention of wool growers, Vail, Colorado, July 27, 1984, as reported by *The Washington Post*, July 29, 1984, p. 1.

Burford was a former administrator of the Environmental Protection Agency. Her remark is reminiscent of one reportedly made by James L. Petigru during Christmas week, 1860, in Charleston, South Carolina, when he was asked by Robert Barnwell Rhett, a leader of the secessionists, if he were with them: "South Carolina is too small for a republic and too large for an insane asylum."—Earl Schenck Miers, *The Great Rebellion*, p. 50 (1958).

1970 If I wanted to go crazy I would do it in Washington because it would not be noticed.

Attributed to IRWIN S. COBB. Unverified.

1971 Washington is full of famous men and the women they married when they were young.

FANNY DIXWELL HOLMES, remark to President Theodore Roosevelt at the reception preceding a dinner at the White House in honor of her husband, Supreme Court Justice Oliver Wendell Holmes, January 8, 1903.—Catherine Drinker Bowen, *Yankee from Olympus*, p. 362 (1944).

1972 Somebody once said that Washington was a city of Northern charm and Southern efficiency.

President JOHN F. KENNEDY, remarks to the trustees and advisory committee of the national cultural center, November 14, 1961.—*Public Papers of the Presidents of the United States: John F. Kennedy, 1961*, p. 719.

1973 So I came to Washington, where I knew I would be farther away from America than I could be on some foreign shore; not that I do not respect this as a good part of America but in its general routine the heart of America is felt less here than at any place I have ever been.

Senator HUEY LONG, remarks in the Senate, May 17, 1932, *Congressional Record*, vol. 75, p. 10393.

1974 [George] Washington intended this to be a Federal city, and it is a Federal city, and it tingles down to the feet of every man, whether he comes from Washington State, or Los Angeles, or Texas, when he comes and walks these city streets and begins to feel that "this is my city; I own a part of this Capital, and I envy for the time being those who are able to spend their time here." I quite admit that there are defects in the system of government by which Congress is bound to look after the government of the District of Columbia. It could not be otherwise under such a system, but I submit to the judgment of history that the result vindicates the foresight of the fathers.

President WILLIAM HOWARD TAFT, address at a banquet given in his honor by the Board of Trade and Chamber of Commerce of Washington, D.C., May 8, 1909.—*Presidential Addresses and State Papers of William Howard Taft*, vol. 1, chapter 7, pp. 82–83 (1910).

1975 Now, I am opposed to the franchise in the District [of Columbia]; I am opposed, and not because I yield to any one in my support and belief in the principles of self-government; but principles are applicable generally, and then, unless you make exceptions to the application of these principles, you will find that they will carry you to very illogical and absurd results. This was taken out of the application of the principle of self-government in the very Constitution that was intended to put that in force in every other part of the country, and it was done because it was intended to have the representatives of all the people in the country control this one city, and to prevent its being controlled by the parochial spirit that would necessarily govern men who did not look beyond the city to the grandeur of the nation, and this as the representative of that nation.

President WILLIAM HOWARD TAFT, address at a banquet given in his honor by the Board of Trade and Chamber of Commerce of Washington, D.C., May 8, 1909.—*Presidential Addresses and State Papers of William Howard Taft*, vol. 1, chapter 7, p. 83 (1910).

Washington, George (1732–1799)

1976 And as to you, Sir, treacherous in private friendship (for so you have been to me, and that in the day of danger) and a hypocrite in public life, the world will be puzzled to decide whether you are an apostate or an impostor; whether you have abandoned good principles, or whether you ever had any.

THOMAS PAINE, letter to George Washington, July 30, 1796.—*The Writings of Thomas Paine*, ed. Moncure D. Conway, vol. 3, p. 252 (1895).

1977 Gentlemen, the character of Washington is among the most cherished contemplations of my life. It is a fixed star in the firmament of great names, shining without twinkling or obscuration, with clear, steady, beneficent light.

DANIEL WEBSTER, secretary of state, letter to the New York Committee for the Celebration of the Birthday of Washington, February 20, 1851.—*The Writings and Speeches of Daniel Webster*, vol. 12, p. 261 (1903).

Webster served in Congress as a representative from New Hampshire, 1813–1817, and from Massachusetts, 1823–1827, and as a senator from Massachusetts, 1827–1841 and 1845–1850.

Water

1978 Mr. Toastmaster, Gentlemen: I feel highly honored indeed to be one of the chosen to say a few words this evening. I am requested to respond to the toast: "Water, the purest and most wonderful thing that was ever created." You, as well as I, have seen it glistening in small globular teardrops on the eyelids of troubled sweethearts and peevish infants, as well as go rushing in torrents down the wrinkled cheeks of the aged ones. And in the early morning I have seen it glistening and sparkling like so many diamonds on the grass blades and the flowers. I have seen it rushing like some wild thing down the rapids of the river, only to flow quietly and lazily where the river widens. I have heard it roar and rumble as it dashed down some steep precipice. And what I have seen—I have seen—Gentlemen, what I want to say is, that as a *beverage,* it's a failure.

Author unknown.—Arthur Leroy Kaser, *Good Toasts and Funny Stories,* p. 98 (1923). This quotation was submitted to the Queries column of *The New York Times Book Review* in 1971. One response to the query attributed this toast to a Colonel Bob Maxe at an annual dinner of the Bar Association of North Arkansas. The wording varied, and the attribution has not been verified in a published source.

A more succinct version found its way into Congressional Research Service files: "Gentlemen—I have seen water in all of its majesty, pouring in torrents over great falls, rushing madly through deep gorges, and tossing wildly as waves of the oceans. I have seen it in the frozen stillness of a winter pond, in the flower-like crystals of snow flakes. I have seen it as the soft morning dew, and as the gentle teardrop in the eye of a beautiful lady—But gentlemen, as a beverage, it is a damn failure!"

Watergate affair

1979 We must maintain the integrity of the White House, and that integrity must be real, not transparent. There can be no whitewash at the White House.

President RICHARD M. NIXON, address to the nation about the Watergate investigations, April 30, 1973.—*Public Papers of the Presidents of the United States: Richard Nixon, 1973,* p. 332.

1980 There are these and other great causes that we were elected overwhelmingly to carry forward in November of 1972. And what we were elected to do, we are going to do, and let others wallow in Watergate, we are going to do our job.

President RICHARD M. NIXON, remarks to members of the White House staff on returning from Bethesda Naval Hospital, July 20, 1973.—*Public Papers of the Presidents of the United States: Richard Nixon, 1973,* p. 657.

1981 Maybe this [Watergate] is like the Old Testament. It was visited upon us and maybe we're going to benefit from it.

NELSON A. ROCKEFELLER, governor of New York, speech to the State Broadcasters Association, Cooperstown, New York, July 17, 1973, as reported by *The New York Times,* July 18, 1973, p. 20.

Weather

1982 Everybody talks about the weather, but nobody does anything about it.

Generally, but perhaps mistakenly, attributed to MARK TWAIN. It has never been verified in his writings.

Many quotation dictionaries credit Charles Dudley Warner, a friend of Twain's, with this remark. But what Warner actually wrote, in an editorial in the *Hartford* (Connecticut)

Courant, August 27, 1897, p. 8, was: "A well known American writer said once that, while everybody talked about the weather, nobody seemed to do anything about it."

Later, Robert U. Johnson, in his autobiography, *Remembered Yesterdays*, p. 322 (1923), says, "Nor have I ever seen in print Mark's saying about the weather, 'We all grumble about the weather, but—but—but nothing is *done* about it.' "

The true author remains a debatable subject, and the quotation remains a popular one.

Welfare

1983 Doing for people what they can and ought to do for themselves is a dangerous experiment. In the last analysis the welfare of the workers depends upon their own initiative. Whatever is done under the guise of philanthropy or social morality which in any way lessens initiative is the greatest crime that can be committed against the toilers. Let social busy-bodies and professional "public morals experts" in their fads reflect upon the perils they rashly invite under this pretense of social welfare.

SAMUEL GOMPERS, "The Shorter Workday—Its Philosophy," *Eight Hours*, pp. 36–37 (191?).

1984 We have here a human as well as an economic problem. When humane considerations are concerned, Americans give them precedence. The lessons of history, confirmed by the evidence immediately before me, show conclusively that continued dependence upon relief induces a spiritual and moral disintegration fundamentally destructive to the national fibre. To dole out relief in this way is to administer a narcotic, a subtle destroyer of the human spirit.

President FRANKLIN D. ROOSEVELT, annual message to the Congress, January 4, 1935.—*The Public Papers and Addresses of Franklin D. Roosevelt, 1935*, p. 19 (1938).

Westward movement

1985 Our well-founded claim, grounded on continuity, has greatly strengthened, during the same period, by the rapid advance of our population toward the territory—its great increase, especially in the valley of the Mississippi—as well as the greatly increased facility of passing to the territory by more accessible routes, and the far stronger and rapidly-swelling tide of population that has recently commenced flowing into it.

JOHN C. CALHOUN, secretary of state, letter to Richard Pakenham, British minister to the United States, September 3, 1844, concerning the boundary dispute between the two countries.—*Congressional Globe*, December 2, 1845, vol. 15, Appendix, p. 26.

When the dispute was settled in 1846, the United States was given all the land south of the forty-ninth parallel except Vancouver Island. The area included the modern states of Oregon, Idaho, and Washington, as well as parts of Montana and Wyoming.

Calhoun served in Congress 1811–1817, 1832–1843, and 1845–1850. He was vice president 1825–1832.

1986 What do we want with this vast, worthless area? This region of savages and wild beasts, of deserts of shifting sands and whirlwinds of dust, of cactus and prairie dogs? To what use could we ever hope to put these great deserts, or those endless mountain ranges, impenetrable and covered to their very base with eternal snow? What can we ever hope to do with the western coast, a coast of three thousand miles, rock-bound, cheerless, uninviting, and not a harbor on it? What use have we for this country?

Westward movement

Attributed to DANIEL WEBSTER, supposedly from a speech in the Senate.—Benjamin Perley Poore, *Perley's Reminiscences*, vol. 1, chapter 15, pp. 213–14 (1886).

The same quotation, with slight word variation, appears in Edmund J. Carpenter, *The American Advance*, p. 216 (1903), with the additional sentence, "Mr. President, I will never vote one cent from the public treasury to place the Pacific coast one inch nearer to Boston than it is now."

These remarks have never been verified in the speeches or writings of Webster, and are probably spurious. T. C. Elliott, *The Outlook*, August 15, 1908, p. 869, said, "It is safe to say he never uttered it."

Webster served in Congress as a representative from New Hampshire 1813–1817, and from Massachusetts, 1823–1827, and as a senator from Massachusetts, 1827–1841 and 1845–1850.

Winning

1987 I will not only give 'em battle, I will lick 'em!

Lieutenant RICHARD W. (DICK) DOWLING, purported remark to a Confederate council of war urging him not to fight.—May M. Pray, *Dick Dowling's Battle*, chapter 10, p. 108 (1936). Unverified.

During the Battle of Sabine Pass, September 8, 1863, the Confederates at Fort Griffin did defeat the Union forces trying to occupy southeast Texas. In forty-five minutes, Dowling and his forty-six men captured 350 prisoners, cannon, and two gunboats, while crippling a third, without suffering any casualties.

1988 Whoever can surprize well must Conquer.

JOHN PAUL JONES, letter to the American commissioners to France, February 10, 1778.—Papers of Benjamin Franklin, American Philosophical Society, Philadelphia, Pennsylvania. Reproduced courtesy of the APS Library.

This appears as "Who can surprise well must conquer" in *John Paul Jones, Fighter for Freedom and Glory* by Lincoln Lorenz, p. xiii (1943).

1989 Whether you like it or not, history is on our side. We will bury you.

NIKITA S. KHRUSHCHEV, remark at a Polish embassy reception following the signing of a Moscow-Warsaw joint declaration in Moscow, November 18, 1956.—*The Washington Post*, November 19, 1956, p. 1.

Khrushchev later explained what he had meant in response to a question at the National Press Club, Washington, D.C., September 16, 1959: "The expression I used was distorted, and on purpose, because what was meant was not the physical burial of any people but the question of the historical force of development. It is well known that at the present time no one social or economic system is dominant throughout the world, but that there are different systems, social systems in different countries. And those systems change. At one time the most widespread system of society in the world was feudalism. Then capitalism took its place. . . . We believe that Karl Marx, Engels and Lenin gave scientific proof of the fact that the system, the social system of socialism, would take the place of capitalism . . . that is why I said that looking at the matter from the historical point of view, socialism, communism, would take the place of capitalism and capitalism thereby would be, so to speak, buried."—Transcript of Khrushchev's address and subsequent question-and-answer session (simultaneous translation), *The New York Times*, September 17, 1959, p. 18, col. 8.

Winning

1990 Winning isn't everything, it's the only thing.

RED SANDERS, Vanderbilt University football coach, c. 1948. —Leo Green, *Sportswit*, p. 57 (1984). Verified by Scoop Hudgins, Vanderbilt's sports information director 1946–1948, and Fred Russell, retired sports editor of the Nashville, Tennessee, *Banner* and a friend of Sanders's, who quoted this phrase in his columns at the time.

This remark has been widely attributed to football coach Vince Lombardi. In *Vince Lombardi on Football*, ed. George L. Flynn, vol. 1, chapter 1, p. 16 (1973), Lombardi is quoted, "I have been quoted as saying, 'Winning is the only thing.' That's a little out of context. What I said is that 'Winning is not everything—but making the effort to win is.' "

Not everyone agrees. *Time*, September 14, 1970, p. 61, attributed this remark to Lombardi and called it his creed. Bob Rubin, *Green Bay's Packers*, p. 84 (1973), quotes this from Lombardi's opening talk on the first day of training camp in 1959.

Winning and losing

1991 If we win, nobody will care. If we lose, there will be nobody to care.

Prime Minister WINSTON CHURCHILL, secret session, House of Commons, June 25, 1941.—*Winston S. Churchill: His Complete Speeches, 1897–1963*, ed. Robert Rhodes James, vol. 6, p. 6438 (1974).

1992 You make your own luck, Gig.
You know what makes a good loser? Practice.

ERNEST HEMINGWAY, speaking to his son.—Gregory H. Hemingway, *Papa, a Personal Memoir*, p. 4 (1976).

1993 For when the One Great Scorer comes to mark against your name,
He writes—not that you won or lost—but how you played the Game.

GRANTLAND RICE, "Alumnus Football," last two lines, *Only the Brave and Other Poems*, p. 144 (1941).

1994 I would rather lose in a cause that will some day win, than win in a cause that will some day lose!

Attributed to WOODROW WILSON.—Hugh A. Bone, *American Politics and the Party System*, p. 482 (1949). Not verified in the writings of Wilson.

Wisdom

1995 Drop, drop—in our sleep, upon the heart
sorrow falls, memory's pain,
and to us, though against our very will,
even in our own despite,
comes wisdom
by the awful grace of God.

AESCHYLUS, *Agamemnon*. The above lines are from Edith Hamilton, trans., *Three Greek Plays*, p. 170 (1937). Other translations of this passage from Aeschylus vary.

Robert F. Kennedy, delivering an extemporaneous eulogy to Martin Luther King, Jr., the evening of April 4, 1968, in Indianapolis, Indiana, said, "Aeschylus wrote: 'In our sleep, pain that cannot forget falls drop by drop upon the heart and in our own despair, against our will, comes wisdom through the awful grace of God.' "

These words, lacking "own," have been used as one of the inscriptions at the Robert F. Kennedy gravesite in Arlington National Cemetery.

1996 [The argument of Alcidamas:] Everyone honours the wise. Thus the Parians have honoured Archilochus, in spite of his bitter tongue; the Chians Homer, though he was not their countryman; the Mytilenaeans Sappho, though she was a woman; the Lacedaemonians actually made Chilon a member of their senate, though they are the least literary of men; the inhabitants of Lampsacus gave public burial to Anaxagoras, though he was an alien, and honour him even to this day.

ARISTOTLE, *Rhetoric,* book 2, *The Complete Works of Aristotle,* rev. Oxford trans., ed. Jonathan Barnes, vol. 2, pp. 2228–29 (1984).

1997 Ask counsel of both times—of the ancient time what is best, and of the latter time what is fittest.

FRANCIS BACON, "Of Great Place," *The Essays, or Counsels Civil & Moral of Francis Bacon,* p. 48 (1905). Based on the 1625 edition but with modernized spelling.

1998 Wisdom too often never comes, and so one ought not to reject it merely because it comes late.

Justice FELIX FRANKFURTER, dissenting, *Henslee* v. *Union Planters Bank,* 335 U.S. 600 (1948).

1999 Standing in this presence, mindful of the solemnity of this occasion, feeling the emotions which no one may know until he senses the great weight of responsibility for himself, I must utter my belief in the divine inspiration of the founding fathers.

President WARREN G. HARDING, inaugural address, March 4, 1921.—*Inaugural Addresses of the Presidents of the United States from George Washington, 1789, to Richard Milhous Nixon, 1969,* p. 207 (1969). House Doc. 91-142.

Harding is credited with originating the phrase *founding fathers.* Senator Harding's remarks before the Sons and Daughters of the Revolution, Washington, D.C., February 22, 1918, included this sentence: "It is good to meet and drink at the fountains of wisdom inherited from the founding fathers of the Republic."—*Address on Washington's Birthday,* p. 3 (1918). Senate Doc. 65-180. He also used the phrase in his speech on being officially notified of his nomination for the presidency, Marion, Ohio, July 22, 1920.

According to "Of Deathless Remarks . . . ," *American Heritage,* June 1970, p. 57, his 1918 remarks were "the first use of the phrase that the combined efforts of the experts at the Library of Congress have been able to find."

2000 The poet's aim is either to profit or to please, or to blend in one the delightful and the useful. Whatever the lesson you would convey, be brief, that your hearers may catch quickly what is said and faithfully retain it. Every superfluous word is spilled from the too-full memory.

HORACE, *Ars Poetica,* lines 333–37.—Edward Henry Blakeney, *Horace on the Art of Poetry,* p. 54 (1928, reprinted 1970).

Horace's message is often condensed to "Whatever advice you give, be brief." (Quidquid praecipies, esto brevis.)—line 335.

Wisdom

2001 That which seems the height of absurdity in one generation often becomes the height of wisdom in the next.

Attributed to JOHN STUART MILL.—Adlai E. Stevenson, *Call to Greatness*, p. 102 (1954). Unverified.

2002 Pain makes man think. Thought makes man wise. Wisdom makes life endurable.

JOHN PATRICK, *The Teahouse of the August Moon*, act I, scene i, p. 6 (1957).

These words are spoken by Sakini, an Okinawan, to the audience. They are repeated in act III, scene iii, and at the conclusion of the play.

2003 When I was a boy of 14, my father was so ignorant I could hardly stand to have the old man around. But when I got to be 21, I was astonished at how much the old man had learned in seven years.

Attributed to MARK TWAIN (Samuel L. Clemens).—*The Reader's Digest*, September 1939, p. 22. Unverified.

This has been widely reprinted and attributed to Twain, but has never been found in his works, though various Twain groups and the Twain Papers staff have searched for it.

Wives

2004 *Lady Nancy Astor:* If I were your wife I'd put poison in your coffee.
Winston Churchill: If I were your husband I'd drink it.

Exchange described as a false story by George Thayer in a review of a book about Churchill.—*The Washington Post*, April 27, 1971, p. B6.

Thayer spent a year as research assistant to Randolph Churchill on the biography of his father, Sir Winston Churchill. Another story Thayer declared false has Lady Astor reproaching Churchill, "Winston, you are drunk," to which he replied, "Indeed, Madam, and you are ugly—but tomorrow *I'll* be sober."

2005 Rich widows are the only secondhand goods that sell at first-class prices.

Attributed to BENJAMIN FRANKLIN.—*The Home Book of Humorous Quotations*, ed. A. K. Adams, p. 378 (1969). Unverified.

2006 Gentlemen, to the lady without whom I should never have survived for eighty, nor sixty, nor yet thirty years. Her smile has been my lyric, her understanding, the rhythm of the stanza. She has been the spring wherefrom I have drawn the power to write the words. She is the poem of my life.

Attributed to Justice OLIVER WENDELL HOLMES.

Not verified in works about him nor in *Magnificent Yankee*, the film about him. He expressed a similar sentiment in a letter to Sir Frederick Pollock, May 24, 1929: "For sixty years she made life poetry for me."—*Holmes-Pollock Letters*, ed. Mark De Wolfe Howe, vol. 2, p. 243 (1941).

2007 I do not think it altogether inappropriate to introduce myself to this audience. I am the man who accompanied Jacqueline Kennedy to Paris, and I have enjoyed it.

President JOHN F. KENNEDY, remarks at a press luncheon, Paris, France, June 2, 1961.—*Public Papers of the Presidents of the United States: John F. Kennedy, 1961*, p. 429.

Wives

2008 An incautious congressman playfully ran his hand over Nick's shiny scalp and commented, "It feels just like my wife's backside." Nick instantly repeated the gesture. "So it does," he replied.

Representative NICHOLAS LONGWORTH.—This episode was recounted in James Brough, *Princess Alice,* p. 273 (1975). A slightly different version is repeated in an article by E. Raymond Lewis in *Capitol Studies,* fall 1975, p. 125, and still later in R. B. and L. V. Cheney, *Kings of the Hill,* p. 157 (1983).

2009 Look you, *Amanda,* you may build Castles in the Air, and fume, and fret, and grow thin and lean, and pale and ugly, if you please. But I tell you, no Man worth having is true to his Wife, or can be true to his Wife, or ever was, or ever will be so.

SIR JOHN VANBRUGH, "The Relapse; or, Virtue in Danger," act III, scene ii, *Plays,* p. 56 (1759). Berinthia is speaking.

Women

2010 If perticuliar care and attention is not paid to the Laidies we are determined to foment a Rebelion, and will not hold ourselves bound by any Laws in which we have no voice, or Representation.

ABIGAIL ADAMS, letter to John Adams, March 31, 1776.—*Adams Family Correspondence,* ed. L. H. Butterfield, vol. 1, p. 370 (1963).

2011 Next to God, we are indebted to women, first for life itself, and then for making it worth having.

C. NESTELL BOVEE, *Thoughts, Feelings, and Fancies,* p. 308 (1857).

2012 They talk about a woman's sphere as though it had a limit;
There's not a place in Earth or Heaven,
There's not a task to mankind given,
There's not a blessing or a woe,
There's not a whispered yes or no,
There's not a life, or death, or birth,
That has a feather's weight or worth—
Without a woman in it.

C. E. BOWMAN, "The Sphere of Woman."—Joseph M. Chapple, *Heart Throbs in Prose and Verse,* p. 343 (1905).

A similar version:
They talk about a 'woman's sphere'
As though it has a limit;
There's not a spot on sea or shore,
In sanctum, office, shop or store,
Without a woman in it.

Author unknown.—Jennie Day Haines, *Sovereign Woman Versus Mere Man,* p. 50 (1905).

2013 I confess that I do not understand the principle on which the power to fix a minimum for the wages of women can be denied by those who admit the power to fix a maximum for their hours of work. I fully assent to the proposition that here as elsewhere the distinctions of the law are distinctions of degree, but I perceive no difference in the kind or degree of interference with liberty, the only matter with which we have any concern, between the one case and the other. The bargain is equally affected whichever half you regulate. . . . It will need more than the Nineteenth Amendment to convince me that there are no differences between men and women, or that legislation cannot take those differences into account.

Justice OLIVER WENDELL HOLMES, dissenting, *Adkins, et al., Constituting the Minimum Wage Board of the District of Columbia,* v. *Children's Hospital of the District of Columbia; Same* v. *Lyons,* 261 U.S. 569–70 (1923).

2014 A Nation spoke to a Nation,
A Queen sent word to a Throne:
'Daughter am I in my mother's house,
But mistress in my own.
The gates are mine to open,
As the gates are mine to close,
And I set my house in order,'
Said our Lady of the Snows.

RUDYARD KIPLING, "Our Lady of the Snows," stanza 1, *The Collected Works of Rudyard Kipling: The Seven Seas, The Five Nations, The Years Between,* vol. 26, p. 227 (1941, reprinted 1970).

The poem is about the Canadian preferential tariff of 1897.

2015 On one issue, at least, men and women agree: they both distrust women.

H. L. MENCKEN, *A Little Book in C Major,* p. 59 (1916).

2016 Patience makes a woman beautiful in middle age.

Attributed to ELLIOT PAUL. Unverified.

2017 And behind every man who's a *failure* there's a woman, too!

JOHN RUGE, cartoon caption, *Playboy,* March 1967, p. 138.

2018 One should never trust a woman who tells one her real age. A woman who would tell one that would tell one anything.

OSCAR WILDE, *A Woman of No Importance,* act I, in *The Complete Works of Oscar Wilde,* vol. 7, p. 197 (1923). Lord Illingworth is speaking.

Words

2019 "When *I* use a word," Humpty Dumpty said, in rather a scornful tone, "it means just what I choose it to mean—neither more nor less." "The question is," said Alice, "whether you *can* make words mean so many different things." "The question is," said Humpty Dumpty, "which is to be master—that's all."

LEWIS CARROLL (Charles L. Dodgson), *Through the Looking-Glass,* chapter 6, p. 205 (1934). First published in 1872.

Words

2020 A word is not a crystal, transparent and unchanged, it is the skin of a living thought and may vary greatly in color and content according to the circumstances and the time in which it is used.

Justice OLIVER WENDELL HOLMES, *Towne* v. *Eisner*, 245 U.S. 425 (1918).

2021 In *Words*, as *Fashions*, the same Rule will hold;
Alike Fantastick, if *too New*, or *Old;*
Be not the *first* by whom the *New* are try'd,
Nor yet the *last* to lay the *Old* aside.

ALEXANDER POPE, "An Essay on Criticism," *Poems of Alexander Pope*, ed. E. Audra and Aubrey Williams, vol. 1, p. 276, lines 333–36 (1961).

Work

2022 The day is short, the labor long, the workers are idle, and reward is great, and the Master is urgent.

Aboth, 2:15, saying of Rabbi Tarfon. Pirkay Avot, often known in English as the "Chapters of the Fathers," is the best known of the books of the Mishnah, first part of the Talmud. Translations vary; that above is from *A Treasury of Jewish Quotations*, ed. Joseph L. Baron, p. 277 (1956).

2023 Nothing is really work unless you would rather be doing something else.

Attributed to SIR JAMES M. BARRIE.—*The International Encyclopedia of Quotations*, comp. John P. Bradley, Leo F. Daniels, and Thomas C. Jones, p. 781 (1978). Unverified.

2024 The most unhappy of all men is the man who cannot tell what he is going to do, who has got no work cut-out for him in the world, and does not go into it. For work is the grand cure of all the maladies and miseries that ever beset mankind,—honest work, which you intend getting done.

THOMAS CARLYLE, inaugural address as rector of the University of Edinburgh, Edinburgh, Scotland, April 2, 1866.—Carlyle, *Critical and Miscellaneous Essays*, vol. 6 (vol. 29 of *The Works of Thomas Carlyle*), p. 455 (1899, reprinted 1969).

2025 Do the day's work. If it be to protect the rights of the weak, whoever objects, do it. If it be to help a powerful corporation better to serve the people, whatever the opposition, do that. Expect to be called a stand-patter, but don't be a stand-patter. Expect to be called a demagogue, but don't be a demagogue. Don't hesitate to be as revolutionary as science. Don't hesitate to be as reactionary as the multiplication table. Don't expect to build up the weak by pulling down the strong. Don't hurry to legislate. Give administration a chance to catch up with legislation.

CALVIN COOLIDGE, speech to the Massachusetts state Senate on being elected its president, Boston, Massachusetts, January 7, 1914.—Coolidge, *Have Faith in Massachusetts*, pp. 7–8 (1919).

2026 Our greatest weariness comes from work not done.

ERIC HOFFER, "Thoughts of Eric Hoffer, Including: 'Absolute Faith Corrupts Absolutely,' " *The New York Times Magazine*, April 25, 1971, p. 55.

2027 If you work for a man, in heaven's name work for him!
If he pays you wages that supply you your bread and butter, work for him—speak well of him, think well of him, stand by him and stand by the institution he represents.
I think if I worked for a man I would work for him. I would not work for him a part of the time, and the rest of the time work against him. I would give an undivided service or none. If put to the pinch, an ounce of loyalty is worth a pound of cleverness.

ELBERT HUBBARD, "Get Out or Get in Line," *Selected Writings of Elbert Hubbard,* pp. 59-60 (1928).

2028 In the Great Society, work shall be an outlet for man's interests and desires. Each individual shall have full opportunity to use his capacities in employment which satisfies personally and contributes generally to the quality of the Nation's life.

President LYNDON B. JOHNSON, Manpower Report of the President, March 5, 1965.—*Public Papers of the Presidents of the United States: Lyndon B. Johnson, 1965,* book 1, p. 262.

2029 I long to accomplish a great and noble task, but it is my chief duty to accomplish humble tasks as though they were great and noble. The world is moved along, not only by the mighty shoves of its heroes, but also by the aggregate of the tiny pushes of each honest worker.

Attributed to HELEN KELLER.—Charles L. Wallis, *The Treasure Chest,* p. 240 (1983). Unverified.

2030 As good play for nothing, you know, as work for nothing.

SIR WALTER SCOTT, letter to Charles Kirkpatrick Sharpe, December 30, 1808.—John Gibson Lockhart, *The Life of Sir Walter Scott,* vol. 3, p. 144 (1902, reprinted 1983).

Another use of this proverb was attributed, in an obituary, to Sir Alexander Cockburn, Lord Chief Justice of England. "He subsequently acquired a large practice in London in railway and election cases. Although he did his best for his clients, he was careful that they should do their duty by him, and the story is told that on one occasion, when an election committee met, Mr. Cockburn, the counsel for one of the parties, was absent because his fee had not accompanied the brief, and the only message left was that he had gone to the Derby, with the remark that 'a man might as well play for nothing as work for nothing.' "—*Canada Law Journal,* January 1, 1881, p. 11.

2031 You must obey this now for a Law, that he that will not worke shall not eate (except by sicknesse he be disabled:) for the labours of thirtie or fortie honest and industrious men shall not be consumed to maintaine an hundred and fiftie idle loyterers.

Captain JOHN SMITH, advice to his company when he was governor of Jamestown Colony, Virginia, 1608.—Smith, *The Generall Historie of Virginia, New England & The Summer Isles,* vol. 1, chapter 10, p. 174 (1907).

The preceding paragraph notes that "six houres each day was spent in worke, the rest in Pastime and merry exercises, but the untowardnesse of the greatest number caused the President [to] advise as followeth."

2032 Drive a nail home and clinch it so faithfully that you can wake up in the night and think of your work with satisfaction,—a work at which you would not be ashamed to invoke the Muse.

Work

HENRY DAVID THOREAU, *Walden*, chapter 18, p. 436 (1966). Originally published in 1854.

World

2033 Give me matter, and I will construct a world out of it!

IMMANUEL KANT, "Universal Natural History and Theory of the Heavens," Preface, *Kant's Cosmogony*, trans. W. Hastie, p. 29 (1900).

2034 The world is large, when its weary leagues two loving hearts divide;
But the world is small, when your enemy is loose on the other side.

JOHN BOYLE O'REILLY, "Distance," *Watchwords from John Boyle O'Reilly*, ed. Katherine E. Conway, p. 16 (1892).

These lines were quoted by Senator John F. Kennedy in a speech at the Al Smith Memorial Dinner in New York City, October 19, 1960, and, as president, to the Irish Parliament, Dublin, Ireland, June 28, 1963.

2035 We have it in our power to begin the world over again.

THOMAS PAINE, "Common Sense," conclusion, *The Complete Writings of Thomas Paine*, ed. Philip S. Foner, vol. 1, p. 45 (1945). Originally published in 1776.

President Ronald Reagan quoted these words in a televised presidential campaign debate with Walter F. Mondale, October 7, 1984.

2036 The world of the future will not flourish behind walls—no matter who builds them and no matter what their purpose. A world divided economically must inevitably be a world divided politically. As Secretary of State, I cannot contemplate that prospect with anything but deep disquiet.

WILLIAM P. ROGERS, secretary of state, address before the Chamber of Commerce of the United States, Washington, D.C., May 1, 1972.—*The Washington Post*, May 22, 1972, p. A20.

2037 Physicists and astronomers see their own implications in the world being round, but to me it means that only one-third of the world is asleep at any given time and the other two-thirds is up to something.

DEAN RUSK, secretary of state, speech to the American Bar Association, Atlanta, Georgia, October 22, 1964, as reported by *The Atlanta Constitution*, October 23, 1964, p. 10.

2038 For I dipt into the future, far as human eye could see,
Saw the Vision of the world, and all the wonder that would be;

Saw the heavens fill with commerce, argosies of magic sails,
Pilots of the purple twilight, dropping down with costly bales;

Heard the heavens fill with shouting, and there rain'd a ghastly dew
From the nations' airy navies grappling in the central blue;

Far along the world-wide whisper of the south-wind rushing warm,
With the standards of the peoples plunging thro' the thunder-storm;

Till the war-drums throbb'd, no longer, and the battle-flags were furl'd
In the Parliament of man, the Federation of the world.

There the common sense of most shall hold a fretful realm in awe,
And the kindly earth shall slumber, lapt in universal law.

ALFRED, LORD TENNYSON, "Locksley Hall," verses 60–65, *The Poetical Works of Alfred, Lord Tennyson*, p. 111 (1897).

World domination

2039 The United States, delighting in her resources, feeling that she no longer had within herself sufficient scope for her energies, wishing to help those who were in misery or bondage the world over, yielded in her turn to that taste for intervention in which the instinct for domination cloaked itself.

CHARLES DE GAULLE, *The War Memoirs of Charles de Gaulle*, trans. Richard Howard, vol. 2, p. 88 (1959).

2040 Since World War II, U.S. imperialism has stepped into the shoes of German, Japanese, and Italian fascism and has been trying to build a great American empire by dominating and enslaving the whole world. It is actively fostering Japanese and West German militarism as its chief accomplices in unleashing a world war. Like a vicious wolf, it is bullying and enslaving various peoples, plundering their wealth, encroaching upon their countries' sovereignty, and interfering in their internal affairs. It is the most rabid aggressor in human history and the most ferocious common enemy of the people of the world.

LIN PIAO, minister of defense, People's Republic of China. Text released September 2, 1965.—Samuel B. Griffith, *Peking and People's Wars*, p. 99 (1966).

2041 When our Statesmen are in conversation with the defeated enemy, some airy cherub should whisper to them from time to time this saying:
Who rules East Europe commands the Heartland:
Who rules the Heartland commands the World-Island:
Who rules the World-Island commands the World.

SIR HALFORD JOHN MACKINDER, *Democratic Ideals and Reality: A Study in the Politics of Reconstruction*, p. 186 (1919).

2042 Nothing has changed in Russia's policy. . . . Her methods, her tactics, her maneuvers may change, but the pole star—world domination—is immutable.

KARL MARX, speech delivered in London, January 22, 1867.—*On the First International* (vol. 3 of *The Karl Marx Library*), ed. and trans. Saul K. Padover, p. 84 (1972).

2043 Red China and Russia are having their differences. But we cannot take too much comfort in the fact that what they are debating about is not how to beat each other but how to beat us. They are simply arguing about what kind of a shovel they should use to dig the grave of the United States.

RICHARD M. NIXON, speech to the American Society of Newspaper Editors, Washington, D.C., April 20, 1963.—"American Policy Abroad," *Vital Speeches of the Day*, June 1, 1963, p. 487.

2044 For whosoever commands the sea commands the trade; whosoever commands the trade of the world commands the riches of the world, and consequently the world itself.

SIR WALTER RALEIGH, "A Discourse of the Invention of Ships, Anchors, Compass, &c.," *The Works of Sir Walter Ralegh, Kt.*, vol. 8, p. 325 (1829, reprinted 1965).

2045 There are now two great nations in the world which, starting from different points, seem to be advancing toward the same goal: the Russians and the Anglo-Americans. Both have grown in obscurity, and while the world's attention was occupied elsewhere, they have suddenly taken their place among the leading nations, making the world take note of their birth and of their greatness almost at the same instant. All other peoples seem to have nearly reached their natural limits and to need nothing but to preserve them; but these two are growing. . . . The American fights against natural obstacles; the Russian is at grips with men. The former combats the wilderness and barbarism; the latter, civilization with all its arms. America's conquests are made with the plowshare, Russia's with the sword. To attain their aims, the former relies on personal interest and gives free scope to the unguided strength and common sense of individuals. The latter in a sense concentrates the whole power of society in one man. One has freedom as the principal means of action; the other has servitude. Their point of departure is different and their paths diverse; nevertheless, each seems called by some secret desire of Providence one day to hold in its hands the destinies of half the world.

ALEXIS DE TOCQUEVILLE, *Democracy in America*, ed. J. P. Mayer, trans. George Lawrence, vol. 1, part 2, Conclusion, final paragraphs, pp. 412–13 (1969). Originally published in 1835–1840.

World War I (1914–1918)

2046 If you hadn't entered the World War we would have made peace with Germany early in 1917. Had we made peace then there would have been no collapse in Russia followed by communism, no break-down in Italy followed by fascism, and Germany would not have signed the Versailles Treaty, which has enthroned nazi-ism in Germany. In other words, if America had stayed out of the war all of these "isms" wouldn't today be sweeping the Continent of Europe and breaking down parliamentary government, and if England had made peace early in 1917, it would have saved over 1,000,000 British, French, American, and other lives.

Attributed to WINSTON CHURCHILL, but denied by him.—William Griffin, sworn statement, September 8, 1939, reprinted in the *Congressional Record*, October 21, 1939, vol. 84, p. 686.

Griffin, publisher of the *New York Enquirer*, said the conversation had taken place in London during August 1936. Griffin brought a $1,000,000 libel suit against Churchill in October 1939, but the charges were dismissed on October 21, 1942, when Griffin or his lawyers failed to appear when the case was called. At that time Griffin was under indictment in Washington, D.C., on charges of conspiring to lower the morale of the armed forces of this country.

In his answer to the suit, Churchill admitted the 1936 interview, but denied the statement.—*The New York Times*, October 22, 1942, p. 13. The proceedings against Griffin were later quashed after a hearing in federal court on January 26, 1944.

2047 Nothing will bring American sympathy along with us so much as American blood shed in the field.

WINSTON CHURCHILL, first lord of the Admiralty, memorandum to Prime Minister Sir Edward Grey and Lord Kitchener, September 5, 1914.—Winston S. Churchill, *The World Crisis, 1911–1914*, 2d ed., vol. 1, p. 272 (1923).

2048 In Flanders fields the poppies blow
Between the crosses, row on row,
That mark our place; and in the sky
The larks, still bravely singing, fly
Scarce heard amid the guns below.

We are the Dead. Short day ago
We lived, felt dawn, saw sunset glow,
Loved and were loved, and now we lie,
In Flanders fields.

Take up our quarrel with the foe:
To you from failing hands we throw
The torch; be yours to hold it high.
If ye break faith with us who die
We shall not sleep, though poppies grow
In Flanders fields.

JOHN MCCRAE, "In Flanders Fields," *In Flanders Fields and Other Poems*, p. 3 (1919).

2049 It is a fearful thing to lead this great peaceful people into war, into the most terrible and disastrous of all wars, civilization itself seeming to be in the balance. But the right is more precious than peace, and we shall fight for the things which we have always carried nearest our hearts, for democracy, for the right of those who submit to authority to have a voice in their own governments, for the rights and liberties of small nations, for a universal dominion of right by such a concert of free peoples as shall bring peace and safety to all nations and make the world itself at last free. To such a task we can dedicate our lives and our fortunes, everything that we are and everything that we have, with the pride of those who know that the day has come when America is privileged to spend her blood and her might for the principles that gave her birth and happiness and the peace which she has treasured. God helping her, she can do no other.

President WOODROW WILSON, address to a joint session of Congress recommending that Germany's course be declared war against the United States, April 2, 1917.—*The Messages and Papers of Woodrow Wilson*, ed. Albert Shaw, vol. 1, pp. 382–83 (1924).

World War II (1939–1945)

2050 How horrible, fantastic, incredible it is that we should be digging trenches and trying on gas masks here because of a quarrel in a far-away country between people of whom we know nothing. It seems still more impossible that a quarrel which has already been settled in principle should be the subject of war.

NEVILLE CHAMBERLAIN, national broadcast, London, September 27, 1938.—Chamberlain, *In Search of Peace*, p. 174 (1939). He was prime minister at the time.

2051 Give us the tools, and we will finish the job.

Prime Minister WINSTON CHURCHILL, radio broadcast, London, February 9, 1941.—*Winston S. Churchill: His Complete Speeches, 1897–1963*, ed. Robert Rhodes James, vol. 6, p. 6350 (1974).

2052 The gratitude of every home in our Island, in our Empire, and indeed throughout the world, except in the abodes of the guilty, goes out to the British airmen who, undaunted by odds, unwearied in their constant challenge and mortal danger, are turning the tide of the World War by their prowess and by their devotion. Never in the field of human conflict was so much owed by so many to so few.

Prime Minister WINSTON CHURCHILL, speech during the Battle of Britain, House of Commons, August 20, 1940.—*Winston S. Churchill: His Complete Speeches, 1897-1963,* ed. Robert Rhodes James, vol. 6, p. 6266 (1974).

2053 There is a hush over all Europe, nay, over all the world. . . . Alas! it is the hush of suspense, and in many lands it is the hush of fear. Listen! No, listen carefully, I think I hear something—yes, there it was quite clear. Don't you hear it? It is the tramp of armies crunching the gravel of the paradegrounds, splashing through rain-soaked fields, the tramp of two million German soldiers and more than a million Italians—"going on maneuvers"—yes, only on maneuvers!

WINSTON CHURCHILL, "A Hush over Europe," broadcast to the United States from London, August 8, 1939.—*Winston S. Churchill: His Complete Speeches, 1897-1963,* ed. Robert Rhodes James, vol. 6, p. 6150 (1974).

2054 Thus, by every device from the stick to the carrot, the emaciated Austrian donkey is made to pull the Nazi barrow up an ever-steepening hill.

WINSTON CHURCHILL, "The Rape of Austria," letter, July 6, 1938.—Churchill, *Step by Step, 1936-1939,* p. 262 (1939).

This volume is a compilation of the fortnightly letters he wrote from 1936-1939, mainly on foreign policy and defense.

2055 What General Weygand called the Battle of France is over. I expect that the Battle of Britain is about to begin. Upon this battle depends the survival of Christian civilization. Upon it depends our own British life, and the long continuity of our institutions and our Empire. The whole fury and might of the enemy must very soon be turned on us. Hitler knows that he will have to break us in this Island or lose the war. If we can stand up to him, all Europe may be free and the life of the world may move forward into broad, sunlit uplands. But if we fail, then the whole world, including the United States, including all that we have known and cared for, will sink into the abyss of a new Dark Age made more sinister, and perhaps more protracted, by the lights of perverted science. Let us therefore brace ourselves to our duties, and so bear ourselves that, if the British Empire and its Commonwealth last for a thousand years, men will still say, "This was their finest hour."

Prime Minister WINSTON CHURCHILL, speech, House of Commons, June 18, 1940.—*Winston S. Churchill: His Complete Speeches, 1897-1963,* ed. Robert Rhodes James, vol. 6, p. 6238 (1974).

2056 When I warned them [the French] that Britain would fight on alone whatever they did, their generals told their Prime Minister and his divided Cabinet, "In three weeks England will have her neck wrung like a chicken." Some chicken! Some neck!

Prime Minister WINSTON CHURCHILL, speech to a joint session of the Canadian Parliament, Ottawa, Canada, December 30, 1941.—*Winston S. Churchill: His Complete Speeches, 1897-1963,* ed. Robert Rhodes James, vol. 6, p. 6544 (1974).

2057 Once Japan is destroyed as an aggressive force, we know of no other challenging power that can appear in the Pacific. . . . Japan is the one enemy, and the only enemy, of the peaceful peoples whose shores overlook the Pacific Ocean.

JOSEPH C. GREW, address for United China Relief, Carnegie Hall, New York City, October 10, 1942.—*The Department of State Bulletin,* October 10, 1942, p. 798. Grew was the U.S. ambassador to Japan, 1932–1941.

2058 Bataan is like a child in a family who dies. It lives in our hearts.

General DOUGLAS MACARTHUR, reflection on the first anniversary of the fall of Bataan, April 9, 1942, as reported by *The New York Times,* April 9, 1943, p. 9, which added, "It was the first time General MacArthur had mentioned the name Bataan publicly" since the day after the fall.

2059 I shall return.

General DOUGLAS MACARTHUR. After leaving the Philippines March 12, 1942, he later arrived in Australia. When he was pressed by reporters, General MacArthur issued the following statement: "The President of the United States ordered me to break through the Japanese lines and proceed from Corregidor to Australia for the purpose, as I understand it, of organizing the American offensive against Japan, a primary object of which is the relief of the Philippines. I came through and I shall return."—*Representative Speeches of General of the Army Douglas MacArthur,* p. vi (1964). Senate Doc. 88-95.

See also his *Reminiscences,* p. 145 (1964).

2060 No army has ever done so much with so little.

General DOUGLAS MACARTHUR, as reported by *The New York Times,* April 11, 1942, p. 1.

He referred to the fall of Bataan.

2061 People of the Philippines: I have returned. By the grace of Almighty God, our forces stand again on Philippine soil. . . . The hour of your redemption is here. . . . Rally to me. . . . As the lines of battle roll forward to bring you within the zone of operations, rise and strike. Strike at every favorable opportunity. For your homes and hearths, strike! For future generations of your sons and daughters, strike! In the name of your sacred dead, strike! Let no heart be faint. Let every arm be steeled. The guidance of Divine God points the way. Follow in His name to the Holy Grail of righteous victory.

General DOUGLAS MACARTHUR, speech to the people of the Philippines, on Leyte, October 17, 1944.—MacArthur, *Reminiscences,* pp. 216–17 (1964).

2062 The time has come when we must proceed with the business of carrying the war to the enemy, not permitting the greater portion of our armed forces and our valuable material to be immobilized within the continental United States.

General GEORGE C. MARSHALL, Army chief of staff, as reported by the Washington, D.C., *Times-Herald,* March 3, 1942, p. 1.

2063 Our spirit of enjoyment was stronger than our spirit of sacrifice. We wanted to have more than we wanted to give. We tried to spare effort, and met disaster.

Marshal HENRI PETAIN.—Attributed to him in a caption, which said, "Frenchmen . . . heard Marshal Petain pronounce this requiem over a lost France." The caption accompanies an article, "Danger: Men *Not* at Work!" by Hatton W. Summers, *Nation's Business*, May 1941, p. 15.

2064 The frontier of America is on the Rhine.

Attributed to President FRANKLIN D. ROOSEVELT, by a member or members of the Senate Committee on Military Affairs, meeting in executive session at the White House, January 31, 1939.—Whitney H. Shepardson and William O. Scroggs, *The United States in World Affairs*, p. 104 (1940).

Reports of this remark caused an outcry by American isolationists and in the German press, while they gave courage to the British and French. Roosevelt vehemently denied the remark, calling it a "deliberate lie" at his press conference on February 3.—*The Public Papers and Addresses of Franklin D. Roosevelt, 1939*, p. 113 (1941).

Representative John A. Martin referred to this in remarks in the House during a discussion of building military airplanes: "A controversy has been raging over an alleged private remark of the President that the frontier of America is on the Rhine. Whether he said it or not, the frontier of America has been on the Rhine, and beyond. An American Army has trod the soil of Germany. The American frontier has been on the coasts of Europe, of Africa, and of Asia, when those coasts were vastly more distant from ours than they are today."—*Congressional Record*, February 14, 1939, vol. 84, p. 1394.

2065 In time of this grave national danger, when all excess income should go to win the war, no American citizen ought to have a net income, after he has paid his taxes, of more than $25,000 a year.

President FRANKLIN D. ROOSEVELT, message to Congress, April 27, 1942.—*The Public Papers and Addresses of Franklin D. Roosevelt, 1942*, p. 221 (1950).

2066 Yesterday, December 7, 1941—a date which will live in infamy—the United States of America was suddenly and deliberately attacked by naval and air forces of the Empire of Japan.

President FRANKLIN D. ROOSEVELT, address to a joint session of Congress asking that a state of war be declared between the United States and Japan, December 8, 1941.—*The Public Papers and Addresses of Franklin D. Roosevelt, 1941*, p. 514 (1950).

2067 There is no doubt that the absence of a second front in Europe considerably relieves the position of the German Army, nor can there be any doubt that the appearance of a second front on the Continent of Europe—and undoubtedly this will appear in the near future—will essentially relieve the position of our armies to the detriment of the German Army.

JOSEPH STALIN, radio address from Moscow, November 6, 1941.—*Vital Speeches of the Day*, December 1, 1941, p. 102.

2068 What place does the possibility of a second front occupy in the Soviet estimates of the current situation? A most important place; one might say a place of first-rate importance.

JOSEPH STALIN, letter to Henry C. Cassidy, representative of The Associated Press in Moscow, October 4, 1942.—*The New York Times*, October 5, 1942, p. 1.

2069 I fear all we have done is to awaken a sleeping giant and fill him with a terrible resolve.

Attributed to ISOROKU YAMAMOTO, a Japanese admiral in World War II, in the motion picture *Tora, Tora, Tora.*—Twentieth Century Fox, *Tora, Tora, Tora; Dialogue and Cutting Continuity,* reel 18, p. 16 (1970).

The screenplay was written by Gordon W. Prange, based on his unpublished material, and by Ladislas Farago, who had published his *The Broken Seal* in 1967. The sentence is not in Farago's book, nor did it appear later in Prange's book, *At Dawn We Slept,* published posthumously in 1981.

No evidence exists that these words were Yamamoto's. However, in a letter to Ogata Taketora, dated January 9, 1942, Yamamoto wrote, "A military man can scarcely pride himself on having 'smitten a sleeping enemy'; in fact, to have it pointed out is more a matter of shame."—Hirosuki Asawa, *The Reluctant Admiral,* trans. John Bester, p. 285 (1979).

2070 There are two kinds of mines; one is the personnel mine and the other is the vehicular mine. When we come to a mine field our infantry attacks exactly as if it were not there. The losses we get from personnel mines we consider only equal to those we would have gotten from machine guns and artillery if the Germans had chosen to defend that particular area with strong bodies of troops instead of with mine fields. The attacking infantry does not set off the vehicular mines, so after they have penetrated to the far side of the field they form a bridgehead, after which the engineers come up and dig out channels through which our vehicles can go.

GEORGY K. ZHUKOV.—Dwight D. Eisenhower attributes this statement to the Russian marshal in *Crusade in Europe,* pp. 467–68 (1948), and adds, "I had a vivid picture of what would happen to any American or British commander if he pursued such tactics, and I had an even more vivid picture of what the men in any one of our divisions would have had to say about the matter had we attempted to make such a practice a part of our tactical doctrine. Americans assess the cost of war in terms of human lives, the Russians in the over-all drain on the nation."

Worth

2071 When I was a child of seven years old, my friends, on a holiday, filled my pocket with coppers. I went directly to a shop where they sold toys for children; and, being charmed with the sound of a *whistle,* that I met by the way in the hands of another boy, I voluntarily offered and gave all my money for one. I then came home, and went whistling all over the house, much pleased with my *whistle,* but disturbing all the family. My brothers, and sisters, and cousins, understanding the bargain I had made, told me I had given four times as much for it as it was worth; put me in mind what good things I might have bought with the rest of the money; and laughed at me so much for my folly, that I cried with vexation; and the reflection gave me more chagrin than the *whistle* gave me pleasure. This however was afterwards of use to me, the impression continuing on my mind; so that often, when I was tempted to buy some unnecessary thing, I said to myself, *Don't give too much for the whistle;* and I saved my money.

BENJAMIN FRANKLIN, letter to Madame Brillon, November 10, 1779.—*The Works of Benjamin Franklin,* ed. Jared Sparks, vol. 2, p. 181 (1836).

Worth

2072 Earth gets its price for what Earth gives us;
The beggar is taxed for a corner to die in,
The priest hath his fee who comes and shrives us,
We bargain for the graves we lie in;
At the Devil's booth are all things sold,
Each ounce of dross costs its ounce of gold;
For a cap and bells our lives we pay,
Bubbles we buy with a whole soul's tasking:
'T is heaven alone that is given away,
'T is only God may be had for the asking;
No price is set on the lavish summer;
June may be had by the poorest comer.
And what is so rare as a day in June?
Then, if ever, come perfect days;
Then Heaven tries the earth if it be in tune,
And over it softly her warm ear lays:
Whether we look, or whether we listen,
We hear life murmur, or see it glisten.

JAMES RUSSELL LOWELL, "The Vision of Sir Launfal," prelude to part 1, lines 21–38, *The Vision of Sir Launfal and Other Poems*, p. 4–5 (1887).

2073 Anything worth doing is worth 10%.

KONOSUKE MATSUSHITA.—*Business Week*, August 21, 1965, p. 80, says this is the highly successful Japanese businessman's "expressed philosophy."

Writers and writing

2074 When that passage was written only God and Robert Browning understood it. Now only God understands it.

RUDOLF BESIER, *The Barretts of Wimpole Street*, act II, p. 66 (1932). Robert Browning is speaking.

2075 The original style is not the style which never borrows of any one, but that which no other person is capable of reproducing.

(L'écrivain original n'est pas celui qui n'imite personne, mais celui que personne ne peut imiter.)

FRANÇOIS RENÉ DE CHATEAUBRIAND, *The Genius of Christianity (Génie du Christianisme)*, trans. Charles I. White, part 2, book 1, chapter 3, p. 221 (1856, reprinted 1976).

This sentence has also been translated as: "The original writer is not he who refrains from imitating others, but he who can be imitated by none."—*The Oxford Dictionary of Quotations*, 3d ed., p. 141 (1979).

2076 If I let my fingers wander idly over the keys of a typewriter it *might* happen that my screed made an intelligible sentence. If an army of monkeys were strumming on typewriters they *might* write all the books in the British Museum.

ARTHUR S. EDDINGTON, *The Nature of the Physical World*, chapter 4, p. 72 (1928). Eddington calls this "a rather classical illustration" of chance.

A discussion of this concept is in William Ralph Bennett, *Scientific and Engineering Problem-solving with the Computer*, chapter 4, p. 105 (1976).

A similar quotation was attributed, apparently incorrectly, to [Thomas Henry?] Huxley by Sir James Jeans, *The Mysterious Universe*, p. 4 (1931).

2077 If you steal from one author, it's plagiarism. If you steal from two, it's research.

WILSON MIZNER.—John Burke (Richard O'Connor), *Rogue's Progress: The Fabulous Adventures of Wilson Mizner,* chapter 9, p. 167 (1975).

2078 The present letter is a very long one, simply because I had no leisure to make it shorter.

BLAISE PASCAL, *Pensées, The Provincial Letters,* provincial letter 16, p. 571 (1941). See also No. 1288.

2079 Fine writers should split hairs together, and sit side by side, like friendly apes, to pick the fleas from each other's fur.

LOGAN PEARSALL SMITH, "Afterthoughts," *All Trivia: Trivia, More Trivia, Afterthoughts, Last Words,* p. 150 (1933).

2080 Originality is nothing but judicious imitation. The most original writers borrowed one from another. The instruction we find in books is like fire. We fetch it from our neighbor's, kindle it at home, communicate it to others, and it becomes the property of all.

Attributed to VOLTAIRE (François Marie Arouet).—Tryon Edwards, *Dictionary of Thoughts,* p. 392 (1891). Unverified.

2081 I am more or less familiar with the works of the members of this Institute. I have worked in the same field. I have felt that quick comradeship of letters which is a very real comradeship, because it is a comradeship of thought and of principle.

WOODROW WILSON, "That Quick Comradeship of Letters," address at the Institute of France, Paris, France, May 10, 1919.—*The Public Papers of Woodrow Wilson,* ed. Ray Stannard Baker and William E. Dodd, vol. 5, p. 482 (1927).

2082 The imaginative artist willy-nilly influences his time. If he understands his responsibility and acts on it—taking the art seriously always, himself never quite—he can make a contribution equal to, if different from, that of the scientist, the politician, and the jurist. The anarchic artist so much in vogue now—asserting with vehemence and violence that he writes only for himself, grubbing in the worst seams of life—can do damage. But he can also be so useful in breaking up obsolete molds, exposing shams, and crying out the truth, that the broadest freedom of art seems to me necessary to a country worth living in.

HERMAN WOUK.—Kirk Polking. "An Exclusive Interview with Herman Wouk," *Writer's Digest,* September 1966, p. 50.

Youth

2083 I pray for no more youth
To perish before its prime;
That Revenge and iron-heated War
May fade with all that has gone before
Into the night of time.

AESCHYLUS.—John Lewin, *The House of Atreus,* p. 110 (1966). This modern version is an adaptation of the *Oresteia;* the lines above are from *Eumenides (The Furies).*

Senator Edward Kennedy quoted this passage in testimony before the Commission on Campus Unrest, July 15, 1970.—*Congressional Record,* vol. 116, p. 24309.

2084 Young men are fitter to invent, than to judge; fitter for execution than for counsel; and fitter for new projects than for settled business; . . . Young men, in the conduct and manage of actions, embrace more than they can hold; stir more than they can quiet; fly to the end, without consideration of the means and degrees; pursue some few principles which they have chanced upon absurdly; care not to innovate, which draws unknown inconveniences; use extreme remedies at first; and that, which doubleth all errors, will not acknowledge or retract them, like an unruly horse, that will neither stop nor turn. Men of age object too much, consult too long, adventure too little, repent too soon, and seldom drive business home to the full period, but content themselves with a mediocrity of success.

FRANCIS BACON, "Of Youth and Age," essay 42, *The Works of Francis Bacon,* ed. Basil Montagu, vol. 1, p. 48 (1844). Based on the 1625 edition but with modernized spelling.

2085 I'm youth, I'm joy, I'm a little bird that has broken out of the egg.

SIR JAMES M. BARRIE, *Peter Pan,* act V, scene i, p. 143 (1928). Peter Pan is speaking.

2086 Tell me what are the prevailing sentiments that occupy the minds of your young men, and I will tell you what is to be the character of the next generation.

Attributed to EDMUND BURKE.—John P. Bradley, Leo F. Daniels, and Thomas C. Jones, *The International Encyclopedia of Quotations,* p. 791 (1978). Unverified.

2087 The young leading the young, is like the blind leading the blind; "they will both fall into the ditch."

LORD CHESTERFIELD, letter to Philip Stanhope, his natural son, November 24, 1747.—*The Letters of Philip Dormer Stanhope, 4th Earl of Chesterfield,* vol. 3, p. 1057 (1932).

The second part of the sentence quotes the Bible, Matthew 15:14.

In a later letter to his son, January 15, 1753, Lord Chesterfield remarked that "Young men are as apt to think themselves wise enough, as drunken men are to think themselves sober enough."—*Letters,* vol. 5, pp. 1994–95.

2088 Twenty to twenty-five! These are the years! Don't be content with things as they are. . . . Don't take No for an answer. Never submit to failure. Do not be fobbed off with mere personal success or acceptance. You will make all kinds of mistakes; but as long as you are generous and true, and also fierce, you cannot hurt the world or even seriously distress her. She was made to be wooed and won by youth. She has lived and thrived only by repeated subjugations.

WINSTON CHURCHILL, *A Roving Commission,* chapter 4, p. 60 (1930).

2089 We have all seen with a sense of nausea the abject, squalid, shameless avowal made in the Oxford Union. We are told that we ought not to treat it seriously. *The Times* talked of "the children's hour." I disagree. It is a very disquieting and disgusting symptom. One can almost feel the curl of contempt upon the lips of the manhood of Germany, Italy, and France when they read the message sent out by Oxford University in the name of Young England.

Let them be assured that it is not the last word. But before they blame, as blame they should, these callow ill-tutored youths, they must be sure that they have not been set a bad example by people much older and much higher up.

WINSTON CHURCHILL, extract of address, Anti-Socialist and Anti-Communist Union meeting, London, February 17, 1933.—*Winston S. Churchill: His Complete Speeches, 1897–1963*, ed. Robert Rhodes James, vol. 5, p. 5220 (1974).

On February 9, undergraduates at the Oxford Union had approved the resolution, "That this House refuses in any circumstances to fight for King and Country" by a vote of 275 to 153. The editorial in *The Times* (London) appeared February 13, p. 13. See Martin Gilbert, *Winston S. Churchill*, vol. 5, p. 456 (1976) for a slightly varied version of Churchill's speech.

2090 That we may live to see England once more possess a free Monarchy and a privileged and prosperous People, is my Prayer; that these great consequences can only be brought about by the energy and devotion of our Youth is my persuasion. We live in an age when to be young and to be indifferent can be no longer synonymous. We must prepare for the coming hour. The claims of the Future are represented by suffering millions; and the Youth of a Nation are the trustees of Posterity.

BENJAMIN DISRAELI, *Sybil*, final sentence, p. 497 (1980). First published 1845.

2091 Through our great good fortune, in our youth our hearts were touched with fire. It was given to us to learn at the outset that life is a profound and passionate thing.

OLIVER WENDELL HOLMES, associate justice, supreme court of Massachusetts, address before John Sedgwick Post No. 4, Grand Army of the Republic, Keene, New Hampshire, May 30, 1884.—*Speeches of Oliver Wendell Holmes*, p. 11 (1934).

2092 Thou know'st the o'er-eager vehemence of youth,
How quick in temper, and in judgement weak.

Homer, *The Iliad*, book 23, lines 677–78, trans. Edward, Earl of Derby, ed. 5, vol. 2, pp. 372–73 (1865).

The many translations of these lines of Homer's vary: *The Iliad of Homer*, trans. into blank verse by William Cullen Bryant, vol. 4, p. 139 (1905),

"Thou dost know
The faults to which the young are ever prone;
The will is quick to act, the judgment weak";

Robert Graves, *The Anger of Achilles*, p. 364 (1959), "It is easy for a youngster to go wrong from hastiness and lack of thought"; and Robert Fitzgerald, p. 553, lines 588–89 (1974), "You know a young man may go out of bounds: / his wits are nimble, but his judgment slight."

2093 Into my heart an air that kills
From yon far country blows:
What are those blue remembered hills,
What spires, what farms are those?

That is the land of lost content,
I see it shining plain,
The happy highways where I went
And cannot come again.

A. E. HOUSMAN, "Into my heart an air that kills," *A Shropshire Lad*, verse 40, p. 72 (1932).

2094 It is very natural for young men to be vehement, acrimonious and severe. For as they seldom comprehend at once all the consequences of a position, or perceive the difficulties by which cooler and more experienced reasoners are restrained from confidence, they form their conclusions with great precipitance. Seeing nothing that can darken or embarrass the question, they expect to find their own opinion universally prevalent, and are inclined to impute uncertainty and hesitation to want of honesty, rather than of knowledge.

SAMUEL JOHNSON, *The Rambler,* no. 121, May 14, 1751.—*The Rambler; A Periodical Paper, Published 1750, 1751, 1752,* p. 210 (1825).

2095 Our answer is the world's hope; it is to rely on youth. The cruelties and obstacles of this swiftly changing planet will not yield to obsolete dogmas and outworn slogans. It cannot be moved by those who cling to a present which is already dying, who prefer the illusion of security to the excitement of danger. It demands the qualities of youth: not a time of life but a state of mind, a temper of the will, a quality of the imagination, a predominance of courage over timidity, of the appetite for adventure over the love of ease.

Senator ROBERT F. KENNEDY, "Day of Affirmation," address delivered at the University of Capetown, South Africa, June 6, 1966.—*Congressional Record,* June 6, 1966, vol. 112, p. 12430.

Kennedy was quoting Samuel Ullman's description of youth; see No. 2099.

2096 Nothing matters more to the future of this Nation than insuring that our young men and women learn to believe in themselves and believe in their dreams, and that they develop this capacity—that you develop this capacity, so that you keep it all of your lives. . . . I believe one of America's most priceless assets is the idealism which motivates the young people of America. My generation has invested all that it has, not only its love but its hope and faith, in yours.

President RICHARD M. NIXON, remarks at the University of Nebraska, Lincoln, Nebraska, January 14, 1971.—*Public Papers of the Presidents of the United States: Richard Nixon, 1971,* pp. 31, 33.

2097 Youth is a wonderful thing. What a crime to waste it on children.

Attributed to GEORGE BERNARD SHAW.—Franklin P. Adams, *FPA Book of Quotations,* p. 883 (1952).

Archibald Henderson, in his third biography of Shaw, *George Bernard Shaw: Man of the Century,* chapter 62, p. 845 (1956), included this statement (using "sin" instead of "crime") in a section of anecdotes. He had not included this in earlier biographies of 1911 and 1932.

The anecdote apparently was first told in the 1930s, since it is one which appears in Lewis and Faye Copeland, *10,000 Jokes, Toasts, & Stories,* p. 555 (1939, 1940). It was also used in *Reader's Digest,* April 1940, p. 84. Sometimes heard ". . . waste it on the young."

Dr. Stanley Weintraub, author and editor of books on Shaw, believes this is incorrectly attributed to Shaw and that it actually belongs to Oscar Wilde, since Shaw often took quotations from Wilde and inverted them for his own use.

2098 Youth, which is forgiven everything, forgives itself nothing: age, which forgives itself everything, is forgiven nothing.

GEORGE BERNARD SHAW, "Maxims for Revolutionists," appendix 2 to *Man and Superman,* in his *Selected Plays with Prefaces,* vol. 3, p. 742 (1948).

2099 Youth is not a time of life—it is a state of mind. It is not a matter of red cheeks, red lips and supple knees. It is a temper of the will; a quality of the imagination; a vigor of the emotions; it is a freshness of the deep springs of life. Youth means a tempermental predominance of courage over timidity, of the appetite for adventure over a life of ease. This often exists in a man of fifty, more than in a boy of twenty. Nobody grows old by merely living a number of years; people grow old by deserting their ideals.

Years may wrinkle the skin, but to give up enthusiasm wrinkles the soul. Worry, doubt, self-distrust, fear and despair—these are the long, long years that bow the head and turn the growing spirit back to dust.

Whether seventy or sixteen, there is in every being's heart a love of wonder; the sweet amazement at the stars and starlike things and thoughts; the undaunted challenge of events, the unfailing childlike appetite for what comes next, and the joy in the game of life.

You are as young as your faith, as old as your doubt; as young as your self-confidence, as old as your fear, as young as your hope, as old as your despair.

In the central place of your heart there is a wireless station. So long as it receives messages of beauty, hope, cheer, grandeur, courage, and power from the earth, from men and from the Infinite—so long are you young. When the wires are all down and the central places of your heart are covered with the snows of pessimism and the ice of cynicism, then are you grown old, indeed!

SAMUEL ULLMAN, "Youth."—Jane Manner, *The Silver Treasury, Prose and Verse for Every Mood,* pp. 323–24 (1934). This version is longer and also has minor variations in wording and punctuation from that in a privately printed edition of Ullman's poems, *From the Summit of Years, Four Score* (n.d.). The oft-quoted "you are as young as your faith, as old as your doubt," etc., is missing in *From the Summit of Years* . . . fourth paragraph:

> Whether sixty or sixteen, there is in every human being's heart the lure of wonder, the unfailing child-like appetite of what's next, and the joy of the game of living. In the center of your heart and my heart there is a wireless station; so long as it receives messages of beauty, hope, cheer, courage and power from men and from the Infinite, so long are you young.

General Douglas MacArthur quoted the entire poem without attribution on his seventy-fifth birthday, in a speech to the Los Angeles County Council, American Legion, Los Angeles, California, January 26, 1955.—*Representative Speeches of General of the Army Douglas MacArthur,* p. 85 (1964). Senate Doc. 88–95.

MacArthur had this framed over his desk when visited in Manila by war correspondent Colonel Frederick Palmer, according to an article in *This Week Magazine* condensed in the December 1945 issue of *The Reader's Digest,* p. 1, which said, "The General has had it in sight ever since it was given to him some years ago . . . it is based on a poem written by the late Samuel Ullman of Birmingham, Ala."

Speaker of the House Sam Rayburn's seventy-eighth birthday fell upon the opening day of the second session of the 86th Congress. "During the January 6 [1960] ceremonies someone remembered what General Douglas MacArthur had said on his own seventy-fifth birthday and thought it applied quite well to Rayburn."—C. Dwight Dorough, *Mr. Sam,* chapter 22, p. 546 (1962). There followed an excerpt of this poem, but it is not to be found in the *Congressional Record* account of the day, so perhaps the remembrance was an informal one.

2100 The most conservative persons I ever met are college undergraduates. The radicals are the men past middle life.

WOODROW WILSON, president of Princeton, speech to the Inter-Church Conference on Federation, New York City, November 19, 1905, as reported by *The New York Times* next day.—*The Papers of Woodrow Wilson,* ed. Arthur S. Link, vol. 16, p. 228.

Author Index

This index includes the names and dates of all the authors whose quotations appear in this book and of recipients of letters. Authors are listed under their pseudonyms, generally, with a reference from the real name. Samuel Langhorne Clemens is listed under Mark Twain, for example, with a reference under Clemens.

Quotations whose author is not known are listed under Author unknown, and subarranged by the subject under which they are listed. The reference in each case is to the **entry number** of the quotation, not the page number.

Some of the authors have also been written about and have been characters in plays. References to them as characters in plays are under their names in this index, but other people's writings about them are to be found in the Keyword and Subject Index. Under George Washington, for example, in this index are references to his writings and to him as a character in a play, and in the Keyword and Subject Index are references to others' writings about him.

A

Aboth, 1673, 2022
Acton, John Emerich Edward Dalberg-Acton, Lord (1834–1902), 1443–1444, 1668
Adams, Abigail (1744–1818)
  letter to John Adams, 2010
  letters from John Adams, 44, 392, 481, 896, 1462, 1581
Adams, Henry Brooks (1838–1918), 287, 297, 1409
Adams, James Truslow (1878–1949), 43, 1018
Adams, John (1735–1826), 259, 273
  (character in musical play, *1776*), 991, 1669
  letter from Abigail Adams, 2010
  letters to:
    Adams, Abigail, 44, 392, 481, 896, 1462, 1581
    Jefferson, Thomas, 1200, 1619
    McKean, Thomas, 1620
    Taylor, John, 413
Adams, John Quincy (1767–1848), 613, 876, 1710
Adams, Samuel (1722–1803), 1621
  letter from Arthur Lee, 1067
Addison, Joseph (1672–1719), 1304
AE (*pseudonym of* George William Russell). *See* Russell, George William.
Aeschylus (525–456 B.C.), 945, 1864, 1995, 2083
Aesop (fl. c. 550 B.C.), 1859
Agathon (c. 445–400 B.C.), 1291
Agnew, Spiro Theodore (1918–), 153–154, 441, 1042, 1330, 1389, 1553, 1876
Aiken, George (1892–1984), 888
Alcoholics Anonymous, 1472
Alderman, Edwin Anderson (1861–1931), 238
Alexander II, King of Russia (1818–1881), 1698
Alfange, Dean (1900–), 71

B

C

D

E

F

Flexner, Abraham (1866–1959), 1919
Forbes, Malcolm S. (1919–), quoting Socrates, 195
Ford, Gerald Rudolph (1913–), 74, 255, 264, 282, 404, 527, 543, 714–715, 761, 889, 1302, 1490–1492, 1831, 1863, 1880, 1920
quoting Thomas Henry Huxley, 263
Foss, Sam Walter (1858–1911), 685
Foullon, Joseph François (1717–1789), 1347
France, Anatole (*pseudonym of* Jacques Anatole François Thibault, 1844–1924), 487
Francis, Saint, of Assisi (c. 1181–1226), 1466
Francis, James Allan (1864–1928), 916
Frankfurter, Felix (1882–1965), 551, 1005, 1998
Franklin, Benjamin (1706–1790), 265, 321–323, 395, 674, 703, 716, 890–891, 967, 1036, 1056–1057, 1146, 1240, 1460, 1593, 2005
letters to:
Brillon, Madame, 2071
Galloway, Joseph, 1560
Hartley, David, 347
Mecom, Mrs. Jane, 1551
Vaughan, Benjamin, 608, 953
Washington, George, 59
Friedman, Milton (1912–), 143
Frohman, Charles (1860–1915), quoting Sir James Matthew Barrie, 988
Fromm, Erich (1900–1980), 933
Frost, Holloway Halstead (1889–1935), 1769
Frost, Robert (1874–1963), 475, 860
Fulbright, James William (1905–), 50, 125, 433, 580, 1030, 1170, 1281, 1868
quoting Erasmus, 451
Fuller, Margaret, Marchioness Ossoli (1810–1850), 1680
Fuller, Melville Weston (1833–1910), 717

G

Gallatin, Albert (1761–1849), 1202
Galloway, Joseph (c. 1731–1803), letter from Benjamin Franklin, 1560
Galsworthy, John (1867–1933), 4
Gandhi, Indira (1917–1984), 1303
Gandhi, Mohandas Karamchand, Mahatma (1869–1948), 1021
memorial inscription of "The Seven Sins," 1697
García Lorca, Federico (1898–1936), 14
Gardner, John William (1912–), 16–17, 568, 1025
Garfield, James Abram (1831–1881), 718, 1666, 1824
letter to William Babcock Hazen, 510
Gascoyne-Cecil, Robert Arthur Talbot. *See* Salisbury, Robert Arthur Talbot Gascoyne-Cecil, 3d Marquis of.
Gautier, Théophile (1811–1872), 173
Gay, John (1688–1732), 1871
Gellius, Aulus (c. 123–c. 165), 1832
Genêt, Edmond-Charles-Édouard (1763–1834), letter from Thomas Jefferson, 1809
George, David Lloyd. *See* Lloyd George, David.
Gérard, Rosemonde (1871–1953), 1130
Gerry, Elbridge (1744–1814), letters from Thomas Jefferson, 382, 1493
Gibbon, Edward (1737–1794), 324, 1647
Gibran, Kahlil (1883–1931), 642, 766, 836, 968, 1131, 1229, 1366, 1833
Gilliam, Shelton, letter from Thomas Jefferson, 802
Giovanni, Fra, 1467
Gladstone, William Ewart (1809–1898), 290, 325, 363, 530, 954, 1294, 1790
Goethe, Johann Wolfgang von (1749–1832), 666, 719, 877, 1813
Goggan, John Patrick. *See* Patrick, John.
Goldwater, Barry Morris (1909–), 581
Gompers, Samuel (1850–1924), 982–983, 1983
telegram from Calvin Coolidge, 1775
Grant, Ulysses Simpson (1822–1885), 467, 1687
Graves, Robert (1895–1985), 2092
Gray, Thomas (1716–1771), 1216
Greeley, Horace (1811–1872), 1594
Green, Thomas Jefferson (1801–1863), 32
Greene, Graham (1904–), 1656
Greenspan, Alan (1926–), 144
Grenville, George (1712–1770), 720
Grew, Joseph Clark (1880–1965), 2057
Grey, Mary Elizabeth, Countess (177?–1861), letter from Sydney Smith, 1947
Grey de Wilton, Arthur Edward Holland Grey Grosvenor, Viscount (1833–1885), letter from Benjamin Disraeli, 713
Griffin, William (1897–1949), 2046
Grimes, James Wilson (1816–1872), letter from Abraham Lincoln, 511
Griswold, Alfred Whitney (1906–1963), 168, 898
Gromyko, Andrei (1909–), 1708
Guest, Edgar Albert (1881–1959), 1841
Guren, David. *See* Ben-Gurion, David.

H

Haile Selassie, Emperor of Ethiopia (1891–1975), 1721
Hale, Edward Everett (1822–1909), 289, 899, 1434
Hale, Nathan (1755–1776), 1304, 1561
Halsey, William Frederick, Jr. (1882–1959), 819
Hamilton, Alexander (1755–1804), 762, 865, 1058, 1334, 1395
The Federalist, 468 (no. 71); 615 (no. 75); 721 (no. 85); 1348 (no. 85); 1446 (no. 73); 1791 (no. 30)
letter from George Washington, 1192
Hamilton, Edith (1867–1963), 643, 1087
Hammarskjöld, Dag (1905–1961), 1857
Hammond, Charles, letter from Thomas Jefferson, 941, 1246
Hand, Learned (1872–1961), 258, 1059
Harding, David, letter from Thomas Jefferson, 1283
Harding, Warren Gamaliel (1865–1923), 767
inaugural address (1921), 1999
letter from Will Rogers, 1385
Harington, Sir John (1561–1612), 1826
Harlan, John Marshall (1883–1911), 326
Harper, Robert Goodloe (1765–1825), 804
Harrington, James (1611–1677), 991
Harris, Sidney Justin (1917–1986), 868
Harrison, William Henry (1773–1841), 763

I

J

K

L

M

N

S

T

U

V

W

Y

Z

Keyword and Subject Index

This index is the key to the quotations. It includes all the subject headings (printed in boldface) and a comprehensive listing of the keywords and phrases to be found in the quotations. In addition to the principal words of a quotation, an effort has been made to include the unusual words and phrases by which a quotation might be remembered. Even so, memory is sometimes faulty, and not every word could be indexed, so readers are urged to try synonyms and other possibilities in searching for a quotation not found on the first try. The List of Subjects at the front of this book with its cross-references can be helpful.

Subject headings are followed by the entry numbers (both in boldface) of the quotations listed together in that category. Subject headings are often keywords as well, both for the quotations listed under the heading and for quotations from other headings. When a quotation contains the word that is the subject, it is not always listed under that word in this index. And some quotations do not contain the word that is the subject. To find everything on a topic, readers should turn to the quotations in the particular category as well as examining the entries under the keyword. For example, there are three quotations listed under the subject Belief, numbers 105–107, and four other quotations are listed under that keyword. To see everything, the reader should look at all the entries, as well as those under related words: *beliefs, believable, believe,* and *believes.*

This index follows alphabetical order. Names of individuals are listed when they are subjects.

To aid in finding quotations, a number of subindexes are included:

Congress—Members of

Names of individuals who were Members of Congress at the time of the words or writings quoted

Geographic names

Cities, countries, continents, and geographic features, most of which will also be found under their names in the index

Hearings, congressional

Inaugural addresses, presidential

Inscriptions

Poems

Spurious quotations

Supreme Court opinions

Arranged by justice and including the subject under which the quotation is listed, which may be quite different from the topic of the opinion as a whole

"A great deal of care has been spent on the index and the compilers look at it with some pride," a sentiment expressed by the compilers of *The Oxford Dictionary of Quotations*, 2d ed., p. ix (1953), is true also for this book. Even without referring to the quotations, a perusal of this index can prove "fruitfull and delightsome."

A

Abolition of slavery. *See* **Slavery.**
Abortions, 1085
Abraham
children of the Stock of A., 670
Absolute
faith corrupts as absolutely as a. power, 1448
power corrupts absolutely, 1443
Absurdity
height of a. in one generation, 2001
Abundance
restless in the midst of a., 86
to selfishness, 1238
Abuse
dies in a day, 672
Abyss
of the human species, 213
sink into the a. of a new Dark Age, 2055
Acceptance
of every consequence of living and dying, 1127
Accident
prominence not through luck or by mere a., 281
Accidents
judge . . . by its general tendency, not by happy a., 736
Account
authentic moderately conceivable a., 1035
Accountable
individual is not a. to society, 649
Accusation
guilty who justifies himself before a., 837
Accuses
who excuses himself, a. himself, 837
Achieve
I asked God for strength, that I might a., 1477
political power and do big things, 1361
seek to a. good in their own small corner of the world, 1361
Achievement
in public life, 97
jail sentence is no longer a dishonor but a proud a., 221
love and a., 845
reward a. in the arts as we reward a. in business or statecraft, 96
triumph of high a., 10
Achievements
Enjoy your a. as well as your plans, 1114
noble deeds and high a., 502
Achilles
see the great A., 575
Acres of Diamonds speech, 817, 1201
Act
as you breathe, 2
character of every a. depends upon the circumstances, 675
from honest motives purely, 1126
Man is . . . born to a., 869
not only for the moment but for our time, 1815
only according to that maxim, 1010
promptly, 6
quick to a., 2092
to a. is to affirm the worth of an end, 869
to the best of my judgment, 300
unless they a., 1
unwillingness to a., 854
Action, 1–14
freedom as the principal means of a., 2045
is a lack of balance, 3
justice is truth in a., 952
liberty of thought and a., 671
Life is a., 1115
life is a. and passion, 1088
life of a., 11
man of a., 2–3
of the enemy is judged by one standard, 933
vital necessity of a. today, 1772
what is meant by a., 3
would be simple and effective, 854
See also **Doing**
Actions
my a. did belie my tongue, 1019
not accountable to society for his a., 649
Activism
generation before us was inspired by an a., 697
Acts
of God, 701
to improve the lot of others, 8
Adam
another A. and Eve, 1259
Adams, John (1735–1826), 1018
Adams, Samuel (1722–1803), 1630
Addict
The Psalm of the A., 852
Administer
the affairs of government, 1683
Administering
the government, 1670
Administration
a chance to catch up with legislation, 2025
Art of Legislation and A., 481
Bad a., to be sure, can destroy good policy, 1372
good a. can never save bad policy, 1372
government is distinctive from a., 734
no a., . . . can very seriously injure the government in the short space of four years, 735
oppose the particular principles and methods of a., 734
will be remembered in spite of ourselves, 1701
Administrative
power of a. bodies, 582
Adultery
Do not a. commit, 1805
Thou shalt not commit a., 1804
Advancement
of the arts, 1532
Adventure
life and death are parts of the same Great A., 1121
Life for him was an a., 1087
spirit of enterprise and a., 658
To die will be an awfully big a., 988
Adventures
bold a. abroad and witch hunts at home, 580
Adversity
partners in a., 1667
Advertisements
vulgarizing charming landscapes with hideous a., 313
Advice
about the main matter, 1269
pass on to this Congress a., 888
to your children, 197
whatever a. you give, be brief, 2000
Advise
he can a. me . . . but [let him] come with me into Macedonia, 1928
no one to send his child where the Holy Scriptures are not supreme, 239
Aemilius Paulus, Lucius (229?–160 B.C.) 1928, 1941
Aerodynamics
theory of a., 604
Aeschylus (525–456 B.C.), 1087
Affluence, 15–18
Affluent
less livable as it becomes more a., 16
misery, 17
most a. slum on earth, 18
society, 18, 1896
Africa, 1609

is a fabulous country, 69
is a great, and in many respects a blessed and hopeful phenomenon, 45
is a great, unwieldy Body, 44
is better than every other country, 1308
is great because she is good, 829
is no better than any other country, 1308
is open to receive not only the Opulent and respectable Stranger, 884
is privileged to spend her blood and her might for the principles that gave her birth, 2049
is the only idealistic nation in the world, 871
is the paradise of lawyers, 1014
like a young phoenix, 1067
lost here in A., 67
might become the dictatress of the world, 613
nation of hucksters, 226
nation of many nationalities, many races, many religions, 1482
needs new immigrants, 881
not for A. alone, 56
not only the problems of A., 621
now is stumbling through the darkness of hatred and divisiveness, 1302
people of A. believe in American institutions, 73
percentage of fools in this country, 606
plague A. with misery in the name of liberty, 1047
promise of A., 68
proud of what A. has meant to himself and to the world, 54
secret of atomic energy does not belong to A., 1254
there will her heart, her benedictions and her prayers be, 613
to remain master of her power, 1311
turning A. into a prison house of the spirit, 18
virtues that made A., 58
voice of A., 66, 74
what A. means, 349
what are you [America] going to do with all these things, 51
when A. was the most powerful nation in the world, 1140
where religious intolerance will someday end, 669
which commands respect throughout the world, 96
which will not be afraid of grace and beauty, 104
wilds of A., 88
will enter its third century, 1617
will one day go fascist democratically, 1907
will rise full plumed and glorious from her mother's ashes, 1067
would be the first to claim, 1346
would involve herself . . . in all the wars of interest and intrigue, 613
young people of A., 2096
zealous in the cause of A., 1620
See also United States

American
as cherry pie, 1889
as great an A. as ever lived, 830
average A., 83
blood shed in the field, 2047
boys 9 or 10,000 miles away from home, 1881
built, American owned, and American manned, 1687
by his mother he [Churchill] is A., 1352
cannot be an A. solution to every world problem, 1735
city, 210
divergence of A. life from its starting point, 1018
Dream, 463
duty to give him the full rights of an A., 883
fights against natural obstacles, 2045
first President to preside over an A. defeat, 1885
free man first and an A. second, 1396
make, 617
my country is the great A. Republic, 1641
name of A., 1312
no. A. is held down by race or color, 1343
society is covered with a layer of democratic paint, 64
solution to every world problem, 1735
sympathy, 2047
values upon which our [A.] system is built, 1868
wants to preserve his dignity and his equality, 1671
what it means to be an A., 71
What then is the A., 48
will build a house in which to pass his old age and sell it, 86

American Constitution. *See* **Constitution of the United States.**

American people, 71–88
are a very generous people, 84
business of the A. p. is business, 140
compatible with the mission of the A. p., 796
energy will test the character of the A. p., 526
forgive almost any weakness, with the possible exception of stupidity, 84
glory of the people of America, 82
into one common mass, 1762
long-term common sense of the A. p., 1489
not what I intend to offer the A. p., but what I intend to ask of them, 769
talk sense to the A. p., 52, 85
what we are and what we hope to be, 418
will prove themselves, 1641
See also Americans; **People**

American Revolution. *See* **Revolutionary war (1775–1783).**

Americanism
basic principles of A., 61
means the virtues of courage, honor, justice . . ., 58
shout the loudest about A., 61

Americans
all that A. want is security, 1671
are appalled by the ravages of industrial progress, 16
assess the cost of war in terms of human lives, 2070
cleave to the things of this world, 86
combine to give fetes, found seminaries, build churches, 99
dreams of these earlier generations of A., 621
feel threatened by runaway technology, 16
generation of A. has a rendezvous with destiny, 1607
hurry after some new delight, 86
I want them [Adam and Eve] to be A., 1259
little A., 72
most creative statesmen in modern history, 1622
never quit, 80
Put none but A. on guard tonight, 1629

recipients of the choicest bounties of Heaven, 53
truths to the Americans' attention, 362
[unwillingness] to identify themselves with something as vast as the United States, 50
We [England] do not intend to part from the A., 531
when they die, go to Paris, 75
whether A. are to be, Freemen, or Slaves, 1627
America's
conquests are made with the plowshare, 2045
everlasting, living dream, 67
finest hours, 1884
One of A. most priceless assets is . . . idealism, 2096
Amnesty
Thou Shalt Demand A. for Them, 441
Amplification
is the vice of modern oratory, 1283
Anarchy
is anarchy, 1895
is loosed upon the world, 454
where does a. exist, 1623
Ancestors
barbarous a., 178
never boast, 121
remember your a., 1732
toils, and sufferings, and blood of their a., 63
Anchor
sail, and not drift, not lie at a., 5
Your constitution is all sail and no a., 334
Angel
mother, 1225
of light compared to that of man, 1457
Angels
If a. were to govern men, 739
If men were a., 739
ten a. swearing I was right would make no difference, 110, 1490
Angle
of vision, 1086
Anglo-Americans
two great nations in the world . . . the Russians and the A., 2045
Angry
refuse to become frustrated and a., 524
When a., count ten, before you speak, 1116
Animal
political a., 1390
soft spot in their heart for an a., 90
Animals, 89–90
all a. are equal, but some a. are more equal than others, 553
Animosity
pretext for still deeper hatred and a., 224
Annihilation
triumph of scientific a., 1258
Anno Domini, 1569
Annoying
to be honest to no purpose, 862
Answer
comes from the graves of our fathers, 506
What is the a., 989
Antarctic
some men are stationed in the A., 1092
Antarctica
"off limits" to military preparations, 1739
Antichrist
is he who turns the wine of an original idea into the water of mediocrity, 874
Anti-Semitism, 166
Anvil
be an a.—or a hammer, 494
Apathy
to dependence, 1238
Apes
like friendly a., . . . pick the fleas from each other's fur, 2079
Appeal
no successful a. from the ballot to the bullet, 1903
Appears
to have appeared to me then, 1263
Appointed
course with all speed, 1439
swift completion of their a. rounds, 1439
Appointments
cabinet a., chargeships and foreign missions, 1313
do not promise to consider race or religion in my a., 1577
short duration of their a., 765
Appomattox Court House, inscription, 223
Appropriation
of public money is always perfectly lovely until some one is asked to pay the bill, 797
Appropriations
votes for all a., 299
Approve
I do not at present a., but I am not sure I shall never a., 321
Archers
prudent a., . . . take an aim much higher than their mark, 825
Architect
of decay, 184
would you consent to be the a. on those conditions?, 432
Architects
of consummate skill and fidelity, 63
one of the greatest of English a., 458
Architecture, 91–94
aims at eternity, 93
has its Political use, 93
worth great attention, 92
Are
begin where you a., 817
By how much we know, so much we a., 1086
conjecture where we now a., 1286
If we could first know where we a., 936
what we a. and what we hope to be, 418
what we a. is what becomes of us, 1676
what you a. stands over you, 186
Arena
Bullfight critics row on row / Crowd the vast a. full, 14
Caesar and Christ had met in the a., 206
cattle of the political a., 1566
for men from the West and men from the East, 1366
man . . . in the a., 10
met upon the a., 1019
of life one may meet the challenge of courage, 355
political a., 494, 1566
Aristocracy
monied a., 101
Aristocrat
in morals as in mind, 188
Aristocratic
colors breaking through, 64
Arizona
When I come back to A., 298
Arlington National Cemetery, inscriptions
Kennedy, John Fitzgerald, 7, 77, 516, 661, 769–770, 1066
Kennedy, Robert Francis, 8, 1864, 1995
Tomb of the Unknown Soldier, 1734
Arm
yourselves, 402
Armament
must be adequate to the needs, 409
tremendously deadly a., 1538

Armaments
deplore expenditure on a., 784
world-wide reduction of a., 655
Armchair generals, 1928
Armed
might is worthless if we lack the brain power to build a world of peace, 493
Armies
All the armies of Europe, Asia, and Africa combined, 406
number itself in a. importeth not much, 1176
Arms
clash of resounding a., 1061
not as a call to bear a., though a. we need, 516
not willing to bear a., 1191
world in a. is not spending money alone, 403
Army
attend to all the details of the a., 1180
Courage and Conduct of this a., 1627
discipline, more than numbers, 1182
general was doing more for victory by writing a poem than . . . by commanding an a., 1589
General Officers of this a., . . . [make me] tremble, 1184
it won't be a bit like the A., 1514
No a. has ever done so much with so little, 2060
of monkeys, 2076
only difference between a mob and a trained a. is organization, 1375
trusted for their defence to a mercenary a., 1647
See also **Military affairs; Military service; Soldiers**
Aroma
is mixed with the grosser air, 1228
Art
minimal the a., 95
of politics, 1422
of self-government, 1425
processes and fulfillments of a., 98
study the works of a. and literature, 658
Artist
imaginative a., 2082
Artistic
standards of a. accomplishment, 96
Arts, 95–98
advancement of the a., 1532
[architecture] among the most important a., 92
progress in the a., 97
reward achievement in the a., 96
Ashamed
doing something he is a. of, 472
Ashes
burn my body to a., 1638
mother's a., 1067
new national life springs greenly, luxuriantly, from their a., 1594
Asia
All the armies of Europe, A., and Africa, 406
American frontier has been on the coasts of . . . A., 2064
cultures of A., 182
if we lose the war to communism in A., 247
In A., the masses now count for something, 1618
land war in A., 1887
peoples of A. . . . can destroy it piece by piece, 1927
See also **Vietnam Conflict**
Asian
Western nations and the A. peoples, 235
Ask
counsel of both times, 1997
Life . . . gives you what you a., 1099
not just what government will do for me, 771
not what I intend to offer . . . what I intend to a., 769
not what your country can do for you, 769
ourselves what we can do for our country, 768
What can I do for my city, 767
what can I do for myself, 771
what you can do for your country, 769
Asleep
one-third of the world is a. at any given time, 2037
See also **Sleep;** Sleeping
Asphalt
You could cover the whole world with a., 542
Ass
law is a a., 1002
Assassination
recourse was had to a., 891
Assateague Island, 308
Assets
one of America's most priceless a. is . . . idealism, 2096
Assistance
to foreign lands should be curtailed, 795
Association
in the United States you are sure to find an a., 99
Associations, 99
Astor, Nancy Witcher (Langhorne) (1879–1964), 2004
Asylum
too large to be an a., 1969
Atavistic
barbaric and a. forces will stand in awe, 1861
Atheist
could not be as great a military leader, 1729
Athenian
citizen does not neglect the state, 1552
not an a. . . . , but a citizen of the world, 216
Athenian Oath, 100
Athenians, 1404
Athens
greatest and richest of all cities, 1022
possessed of great wealth and riches in which all citizens had a right to share, 643
there will not be different laws at Rome and at A., 1000
Atlanta Journal, 1244
Atom
beginning to imagine the force and composition of the a., 111
Atomic
brink of a. war, 1657
Effect of the A. Bomb, 125
first a. bomb, 123
hydrogen bomb releases a greater amount of energy, 126
powerful [a.] bombs of a new type, 124
secret of a. energy does not belong to America, 1254
worst is a. war, 403
See also **Bombs and bombing**
Atrophy
slow a. of a life, 183
Attitude
awareness of the public a., 1406
in an American citizen, 1507
Attlee, Clement Richard, Earl (1883–1967), 1276
Auntie Mame, 1094
Australia
from Corregidor to A., 2059
Authority
bow to no a., 1748
corruption by a., 1443
Dress'd in a little brief a., 1159
struggle between Liberty and A., 1071
Autobiographies
Great nations write their a., 1236

Autocracy
save the people from a., 789
Automaton
Man is about to be an a., 1144
Automobiles, 108
Average
American, 83
Avowal
abject, squalid, shameless a., 2089
Awaken
a sleeping giant, 2069
Away
this, too, shall pass a., 1221

B

Babies
If a legislature decided that all blue-eyed b. should be murdered, 1040
Baby
is God's opinion that life should go on, 1100
Back
All that we send . . . comes b. into our own [lives], 136
struck it [dagger] into the b., 113
Bacon, Sir Francis (1561–1626), 119
Bad
administration, to be sure, can destroy good policy, 1372
from b. to worse, 177
good administration can never save b. policy, 1372
growing old . . . a b. habit, 25
if men be b., let government be never so good, 745
Let men be good, and the government cannot be b., 745
nothing so b. or so good that you will not find an Englishman doing it, 535
When b. men combine, 560
Balance-wheel
of the social machinery, 498
Balanced
budget, 379, 795, 801, 1411
Ballot
is stronger than the bullet, 1903
Band
begins to play, 1723
Bank
mania, 101
robbers to work in a b., 1588
Bankruptcy
and ruin were as remote as ever, 387
and ruin were at hand, 387
put the Nation into b., 388
road to b., 809
Banks and banking, 101
Banned
Books won't stay b., 168
Banner
mongrel b. invented for a league, 1026
Bao Dai (1913–), 1878
Baptists
Catholics can go to Heaven, so can B., 897
Barbaric
and atavistic forces will stand in awe, 1861
Barbarism
from b. to degeneration, 47
Barbarous
relic, 1205
Bare
stripped b. by the curse of plenty, 15
Bargain
for the graves we lie in, 2072
I had made, 2071
Bataan, 2060
is like a child in a family who dies, 2058
Battle
as you go into b., 1732
care for him who shall have borne the b., 1325
died gloriously on the field of b., 370
give 'em b., 1987
Grant us fair weather for b., 1473
is not to the strong alone, 1061
Battle of Britain, 2055
Bay of Pigs invasion, 1872
Bayonet
glittering b., 222
Be
To be. what no one ever was, 659
Beacon
of hope to the world, 65
[let] your b. [be] beauty, 1360
Beacons
Shine for us, dear b., 1474
Bear
any burden, 1066
the burden, 89
Beast
save both man and b., 89
Your people sir, is nothing but a great b., 1334
Beasts
humble b., who with us bear the burden, 89
Beat
If you can't b. 'em, 257
Beaten
nation . . . does not get b., 660
The Beatitudes, 102
Beautiful
Patience makes a woman b., 2016
Beauty, 103–104
America which will not be afraid of b., 104
Faded the shape of b., 1219
Faded the sight of b., 1219
[let] your beacon [be] b., 1360
Because
it is there, 1741
Become
such as she [the land] would b., 475
Bed-fellows
Politics makes strange b., 1431
Bedlam
We commit honest maniacs to B., 926
Bedrooms
of the nation, 1685
Bee
is on the wing, 470
Beef, beef, beef, 277
Beer
[British] are like their own b., 536
Beggar
is taxed for a corner to die in, 2072
Beggars
millionaire and many b., 39
Begin
the world over again, 2035
with a single step, 1533
Belief, 105–107
epoch of b., 1818
strongest b. was in democracy, 414
that the only thing we have to fear is fear itself, 599
that the real sin is taking a loss, 138
Beliefs
revolutions in an individual's b., 1837
Believable
we must make government b., 715
Believe
Do not b. what your teacher tells you, 105
don't b. in God, 1743
don't b. in labels, 1396
in a fate, 1
in action before acting, 2
in man, 1743
in their dreams, 2096
in themselves, 2096
nothing, O monks, 105
that grave modifications of the policy . . . may be voted in or out, 1004
that truth is the glue that holds government together, 255, 1831

that we are lost here in America, 67
we shall be found, 67
young civilians who b. that the laws make the city, 1004
Believes
to be true, 1677
Bell
for whom the b. tolls, 134
like a fire b. in the night, 1700
tolls for thee, 134
Belly
how much fire you have in your b., 1089
Bend
to the collective will of their peoples, 1767
Beneficence
comprehensive b. of the founder, 1710
Benign
neglect, 1579
Benso, Camillo, Conte di Cavour. *See* Cavour.
Bequeath
deprive them of benefits which it was in our power to b., 1608
Berlin
citizens of B., 215
Bermuda, 108
Berliner
Ich bin ein B., 215
Best, 109–112
do his b. and be his b., 1081
do the very b. I know how, 110
does the b. he can, 1515
done my b., 513
done the b. you can, 109
for the b., 112
generation of mankind in the history of the world, 545
of all possible worlds, 112
of times, it was the worst of times, 1818
picture has not yet been painted, 111
to be expected, 403
vote fer th' b. man, 1899
Betray
a jay will b., 305
flatter the people in order to b. them, 63
Betrayal, 113–114
Betrayed
with a kiss, 1921
Better
a thousand-fold abuse of speech than a denial of free speech, 672
I would he were b., 1392
100 guilty Persons should escape, 953
perhaps a little b., 1679
that ten guilty persons escape, 953
Wars are . . . far b. than certain kinds of peace, 1965
Beverage
[Water] as a b., it's a failure, 1978
Beware
of Greeks bearing gifts, 118
Bible
ghosted you up a swell story, too, / Called it B., 917
of democracy, 1247
See also Bible in author index
Bicentennial of American Independence, 65
See also **Revolutionary war (1775–1783)**
Big
achieve political power and do b. things, 1361
Bigger
cars, bigger parking lots, bigger . . ., 50
Bigness
against b. and greatness in all their forms, 822
impressed by your b., 51
is still the curse, 137
Bigotry
gives to b. no sanction, 670
Bill of Rights, 132, 394, 1389
Billion
dollars of navy, half a billion of farm relief, 797
here, a billion there, 800
Billions
borrow b. for war, 1919
Bind
up the nation's wounds, 1325
Bipartisan
foreign policy, 634
Bipartisanship
meant consultation in advance, 1386
Bird
I call that b. a duck, 1278
little b. that has broken out of the egg, 2085
that walks like a duck, 1278
Birminghams
Manchesters and B., 1847
Birth
parents who merely gave them b., 482
Bite
the hand that feeds them, 906
Black
lawyers for blacks, 1015
let the word . . . "b." be stricken, 119
night of despair, 59
power, 116
woman for a slave, 1702
Black, Hugo La Fayette (1886–1971), eulogy, 376
Black Panthers, 117
Blackguard
a coward, and a liar, 1447
Blacklist, 115
Blackmail
Laws . . . are made by a process of b. and intimidation, 1039
Blacks, 116–119
Blame
him when he does wrong, 1507
Bleeding
hearts, 445
Blessed
act of oblivion, 1294
are the meek, 102
are the merciful, 102
are the peacemakers, 102
are the poor in spirit, 102
are the pure in heart, 102
are they that mourn, 102
are they which are persecuted, 102
are they which do hunger and thirst after righteousness, 102
are those among nations, 1233
are ye, when men shall revile you, 102
is the man . . . abstains from giving us wordy evidence, 1692
Blessing
on This House, 1462
Blessings
of freedom, 663–664
on our deliberations, 703
to all the peoples and powers of earth, 1470
were produced by some superior wisdom and virtue of our own, 53
Blind
leading the blind, 2087
let us not be b. to our differences, 436
Religion without science is b., 1662
until we see, 1149
veneration for antiquity, 82
with the lust for money, 832
Bliss
of Dante has been lost in our civilization, 1093
Blondin, Charles (*Originally* Jean-François Gravelet) (1824–1897), 731
Blood, 120–121
all of one b., 1481
American b. shed in the field, 2047
and sweat and tears, 57
expence of so much time, b., and treasure, 525

Brevity
sentensious b., which, using not a word to spare, 1283
Bricks
when they throw b. at me, 1523
Bridge
double-cross that b. when he comes to it, 1399
is love, 1136
[politicians] build a b. even where there is no river, 1398
Bridges
are America's cathedrals, 94
Brief
be b., 2000
Britain
always wins one battle—the last, 529
British
and American peoples, 41
are like their own beer, 536
democracy approves the principles of movable party heads and unwaggable national tails, 201
government . . . [has] a just and friendly disposition towards us, 618
lament the fall of B. liberty, 1067
mandate came to an end, 914
nation will find it very hard to look up to leaders who are detected in that somewhat ungainly posture, 1554
prevent the B. from invading us, 1495
See also **England**; Great Britain
British Empire
liquidation of the B. E., 528
British Museum, 2076
Britons
would rather take the risk of civilizing communism, 532
Broils
To share in the b. of none, 619
Brother
call him b. still, 135
Brotherhood, 134–136
of man, 1117
Brothers
destiny that makes us b., 136
Like my three b. before me, 1299
on that bright loveliness in the unending night, 1742
who see now they are truly b., 1742
Browning, Robert (1812–1889), 2074
"Bryan's Ten Rules for the New Voter," 776, 1573
Buchenwald
generation of B., 1093
Buck
stops here, 1490, 1610
Budget
balanced, 379, 795, 801, 1411
slashes in their [budget] estimates, 1178
See also **Government spending**
Bugaboo
Communist b., 250
Build
a house in which to pass his old age and sell it, 86
a way of life, 56
a world of peace, 493
helping . . . b. a beautiful cathedral, 458
In vain we b. the world, unless / The builder also grows, 1149
me a son, O Lord, 1469
to b. and not to destroy, 526
when we b. they b., 400
when we cut they b., 400
Builders
stone which the b. refused, 91
Buildings
publick B. being the ornament of a country, 93
Bullet
ballot is stronger than the b., 1903
Bullfight
critics row on row, 14
Bully
pulpit, 1508
Bulwark
of continuing liberty, 750
of our own liberty, 1069
Bumblebee
is unable to fly, 604
Bums
blowing up the campuses, 156
Bunker Hill
Battle of, 150th anniversary, 645
Monument, 13
Burden
bear any b., 1066
bear the b., 89
carry his b., however hard, until nightfall, 1104
free from the b. of a life that was self-dependent, 643
of a long twilight struggle, 516
Burdened
with the heavy curse on those who come afterwards, 697
Bureau
immortality on earth is a government b., 709
Bureaucracy
giant power wielded by pigmies, 706
of the corporation state and of government, 1613
patronizing favor of swollen b., 708
shifting corruption is better than a permanent b., 1595
Bureaucratic
despotism, 1646
Burn
down your cities, 27
my body to ashes, 1638
Burnes, James Nelson (1827–1889), eulogy by John James Ingalls, 368
Bury
We will b. you, 1989
Business, 137–147
abolition of b., 147
America can no more survive and grow without big b. than it can . . . without small b., 142
corrupts everything it touches, 158
credit is the lifeblood of b., 357
government being the people's b., 1573
happiest b. in all the world is that of making friends, 684
of America is business, 140
of government, 781
of the American people is business, 140
People are not an interruption of our b., 1345
People are our b., 1345
prevent Trouble in B., 146
principles, 535
responsibilities in their b. activities, 143
reward achievement in b. or statecraft, 96
Buy
never b. what you do not want, because it is cheap, 1116
Buying
nothing without the money in our pockets to pay for it, 358

C

Cabbage
rose smells better than a c., 870
tomatoes [can still be distinguished] from the c., 49
Cabbages
of c.—and kings, 1811
Cabinet
not going to promise a C. post, 1577
of eight millionaires and one plumber, 1510
officers of this present administration, 1342
Caesar
and Christ had met in the arena, 206

Charm
Northern c. and Southern efficiency, 1972
that conquers the enemy, 1131
Chase, Salmon Portland (1808–1873), 1270
Cheap
never buy what you do not want, because it is c.: it will be dear to you, 1116
what we obtain too c., we esteem too lightly, 1845
Chesapeake Bay, 189
Chicken
England will have her neck wrung like a c., 2056
Some c.! Some neck!, 2056
Chicory
lettuce can still be distinguished from the c., 49
Chief
I am their c., 1021
Ye call me c., 1019
Child
Average American is just like the c. in the family, 83
cry of a single hungry c., 811
develop the c. into a man, 501
Give me a c. for the first seven years, 199
Give us the c. for 8 years, 194
has its fairy godmother in its soul, 196
Know you what it is to be a c.?, 196
Monday's c. is fair of face, 200
of seven years old, 2071
of the House of Comons, 1333
spoiled and eventually a very weak individual, 83
to remain always a c., 191
Children, 190–200
a right to study Painting, 481
advice to your c., 197
are now tyrants, 195
begin by loving their parents, 198
contradict their parents, 195
crime to waste it [youth] on c., 2097
devise to c., 192
for our children's c., to live in a world of peace, 54
from their parents, 1193
hopes of its c., 403
leave to c. the long, long days to be merry in, 192
let the c. and childbearers toil, 1695
My clients are the c., 698
no longer obey their parents, 456
now love luxury, 195
those who are in the dawn of life, 724
tortured c., 190
transmit that Freedom to their C., 644
vagabond, ignorant, and ungoverned, 46
Children's
for our c. children, to live in a world of peace, 54
hour, 2089
China, 201–204
ambitious and aggressive C., 1881
is a sea that salts all the waters, 201
land war against Red China, 1887
limited war with Red China, 1967
no man in his right mind would advocate sending our ground forces into continental C., 1968
Red China and Russia are having their differences, 2043
tail of C. is large and will not be wagged, 201
war with C., 202
Chinese
No dogs or C. allowed, 204
Choice, 205
We have a c., 391
We must make our c., 1919
Choose
between life in the Soviet Union and life in the U.S.A., 1656
what you have, 205
Christ
Caesar and C. had met in the arena, and C. had won, 206
Goodbye C., 917
Religion of C., 207
See also **Jesus Christ**
Christianity, 206–207
persecutes C., 1653
Christians
peace, not just for C., 1877
Christmas
at this C. time, I greet you, 1467
child that's born on a C. day, 200
night of the nativity of the young Lord Jesus, 921
See also **Santa Claus**
Church
is not the master or servant of the state, 1759
[is] the conscience of the state, 1759
separation of c. and state is absolute, 669
Churches
of America, 829
You have despoiled c., 1368
Churchill, Sir Winston Leonard Spencer (1874–1965), 2004
dismissal, 1419
introduction by Mark Twain, 1352
Cigar, 208
a really good 5-cent c., 208
Circumstances
make c. fit those plans, 1362
Cities, 209–213
are the abyss of the human species, 213
Burn down your c., 27
When they get piled upon one another in large c., 726
will spring up again as if by magic, 27
Citizen
American c. [of German blood required] to give up all allegiance to Germany, 883
Athenian c. does not neglect the state, 1552
attitude in an American c., 1507
character earns him as an American c., 1343
every person . . . can[not] be made into a productive c., 1330
humble station of a private c., 778
not a good c. unless he also takes thought of the state, 628
of the world, 216
Politics ought to be the part-time profession of every c., 1420
private c. without wrong, 820
reproach against any American c. should be that he is not a politician, 1425
Roman c., 215
when a c. is in any way distinguished, 1568
who enjoys the protection of a free government, 1192
without concerned c. action . . . we shall look in vain for progress, 866
you are a subject and not a c., 671
See also **Government—citizen participation**
Citizenry
alert and knowledgeable c. can compel, 1177
Citizens
Bad officials are elected by good c. who do not vote, 1905
incline the hearts of the C., 1476
most valuable c., 29

Rule of C., 452
rules of c., that are commands to the citizen, 793
shock us with unaccustomed c., 258
supported or opposed exactly to the degree which is warranted by his good c. or bad c., 1507
Conference
affair of masks and mystification, 1943
lasted six weeks . . . wasted six weeks, 1943
to arrange the matter [deciding that they would disarm], 440
was held for one reason only, 1943
we [America] never won a c., 1944
Conferences
takes two or three c. to scare up a war, 1943
Confidence
abuse of c., 1246
assure to us the c. of mankind, 1082
considered in c., 1669
Public c. in the integrity of Government, 752
Confidentiality
of their sources, 1522
Confinement
deteriorated by c., 1526
Conflict
between giant organized system, 224
Conformity, 258
Congress, 259–278
ability of the President and the C. to govern this Nation, 526
and this administration will be remembered in spite of ourselves, 1701
As long as C. does not revise its priorities, 806
can be remembered for its opening the way to a new A.nerican revolution, 1617
cannot authorize the payment . . . of any other debts but those due to the United States, 1202
coequal role of the C. in our constitutional process, 264
critics of, 263, 269, 296
decided whether or not to declare a state of war exists with North Vietnam, 1879
drawbacks of being in C., 302
every time they make a joke it's a law, 271
every time they make a law it's a joke, 271
finest c. money can buy, 274
[greatness not] in her democratic C., 829
I am your man, 1491
I have been in C. two months and haven't done it, 302
if the President in the recess of C. [acts] . . . without the possibility of a check, 1931
in declaring war, 1931
in its committee-rooms is Congress at work, 276
in session is Congress on public exhibition, 276
inquiries being conducted by committees of the C., 893
is bound to look after the government of the District of Columbia, 1974
is so strange, 266
jeopardized any moment C. decides to do so, 214
just and lawful wars authorized by C., 55
kid C. and the Senate, dont scold em, 270
let C. jargon as it will, 711
most enlightened body of men in the world, 262
motto toward the C., 264
negroes' temporary farewell to the American C., 119
no distinctly native American criminal class except C., 275
no need to learn how C. speaks for the people, 74
on public exhibition, 276
pass on to this C. advice, 888
plead their cause before C., 1516
power to interpret the people's will, 1711
principle of free debate, inside or outside the halls of C., 678
propriety of having a C., 1496
provided an appropriation for the . . . expenses of each of the great national parties, 152
sometimes the C. has won, 272
substantive evils that C. has a right to prevent, 675
three or more [useless men], 273
through their C. [the people] decide how far they wish to go, 797
urge this C. . . . to join me in that effort [war on poverty], 1440
war-making power to C., 1495
Congress—House of Representatives, 279–286, 762, 1824
advice to freshmen, 284
honesty and plain sense, in a H.R., 259
I love the H.R., 264
an impeachable offense is whatever a majority of the H.R. considers [it] to be, 889
is composed of very good men, not shining, but honest, 279
is the most peculiar assemblage in the world, 281
know its idiosyncracies, 281
length of service is what gives influence, 285
no great respect for the lower house, 297
People's House, 282
power of impeachment is . . . solely entrusted . . . to the H.R., 893
right in the H.R. to demand . . . all the Papers respecting a negotiation with a foreign power, 792
vs. House of Commons, 279
Congress—Members of
are chosen with that great end in view, 1376
are fully possessed of their contents, 1669
as good as anybody else, 303
elect m. of C. who believe in that [prohibition], 37
personal discussions with M. of C., 1128
Here are entered the words and writings of individuals while they were Members of Congress
Adams, John Quincy, 1710
Aiken, George, 888
Ames, Fisher, 279
Anderson, John B., 1411
Ashurst, Henry F., 298, 1391
Bailey, Joseph W., 1392
Barkley, Alben W., 699
Benton, Thomas Hart, 304
Boggs, Thomas Hale, quoting, 279
Borah, William E., 72, 671
Brownlow, Walter P., 299
Calhoun, John C., 300
Cannon, Clarence, quoting, 277
Cannon, Joseph G., 115, 251, 260, 281, 308, 932, 1084, 1137, 1373, 1418, 1437
Choate, Rufus, 160
Clark, Champ, 261, 301
Clay, Henry, 267, 614
Cockrell, Francis Marion, 261
Crockett, David (Davy), 262
Danielson, George E., 1394
Depew, Chauncey, 1387
Dirksen, Everett M., 288, 800
Douglas, Stephen A., 1378
Ervin, Sam, quoting Shakespeare, 705

spirit which prizes liberty, 1069
machines of d., 409
Millions for d., but not one cent for tribute, 804
owes not only a portion of his property, but even his personal services to the d. of it [free Government], 1192
power of d., 412
slashes in their [defense budget] estimates, 1178
strong d. is the surest way to peace, 404
trusted for their d. to a mercenary army, 1647
Defenses
enemy d., 407
Defensive
weapons, 440
Deficit
defeat through d., 52
Mr. Roosevelt apologized for each annual d., 379
Deficits
continues to pile up d., 809
Deflation, 1204
Degree
of civilization, 1527
to which justice is carried out, 957
Dehumanization
instruments of d., 1448
Deity
Perfect happiness . . . was never intended by the D., 841
See also **God**
Delay
till to-morrow what ought to be done to-day, 1290
without undue d., 1758
Deliberate
all d. speed, 1758
Delicate
extremely d. matters, 40
Delights
the Eye . . . of every observing Traveller, 59
Delightsome
fruitfull and d. land, 189
Demagogue
Expect to be called a d., 2025
Democracy, 413–426
always collapses over loose fiscal policy, 424
an attitude of mind, a spiritual testament, and not an economic structure or a political machine, 414
be ready to die for it [d.], 1340
cannot exist as a permanent form of government, 424
collisions and conflict that tear d. apart, 154
cure for the evils of d. is more d., 422
in order to have a revolution, 416
is baffled, 1170
is cumbersome, slow and inefficient, 426
is the theory that the common people know what they want, 423
is the worst form of Government except all those other forms, 417
make real the promise of d., 1693
means freeing intelligence for independent effectiveness, 639
must prove its capacity to act, 678
never lasts long, 413
no man has the right to strangle d. with a single set of vocal cords, 678
No one pretends that d. is perfect or all-wise, 417
of the dead, 368
pure and perfect d. is a thing not attainable by man, 425
revolution in order to establish a d., 416
soon wastes, exhausts, and murders itself, 413
unsatisfied cannot long survive, 418
we are called a d., 1568
Were our State a pure d., 1591
which economically was largely socialist, 414
will prevail when men believe the vote of Judas as good as that of Jesus Christ, 415
Democracy's
opportunity, 419
Democrat
I am not a member of any organized party—I am a D., 429
might almost be suspected of being a D., 1385
public servant third and a D. fourth, 1396
resist the concentration of power, 1458
You've got to be [an] optimist to be a D., 431
Democratic
government is the only one in which those who vote for a tax can escape the obligation to pay it, 1797
institutions purely d. must, sooner or later, destroy liberty, 420
Legal process is an essential part of the d. process, 1005
no. D. or Republican way of cleaning the streets, 1383
paint, 64
politicians rarely feel they can afford the luxury of telling the whole truth, 1563
purely d. government, 421
society is outraged, 1170
Democratic party, 427–431
ain't on speakin' terms with itsilf, 427
however bad the Republican party was, the D. p. was much worse, 1600
Democrats
southern D. are in the saddle, 428
stop telling lies about the D., 1387
tell the truth about the Democrats, 1387
Denial
slays the life of the people, 672
Denounce
them for things that we ourselves do every day, 1509
Depart
I say; and let us have done with you, 1035
Dependence
back again to bondage, 1238
Depravity
Law cannot give to d. the rewards of virtue, 783
Depression, 15
that will curl your hair, 1795
Deputies
Two d., one of whom is a radical, 1031
Descendants
remember your d., 1732
who boast of ancestors, 121
Desert
convert it [a garden] into a d., 1550
Nor d. my comrade, 100
oasis in the d., 766
those who make the d. bloom, 912
Deserts
civilization always results in d., 833
"Desiderata," 1114
Desire
deep within the soul, 1229
to do right, 1307
Despair
as old as your d., 2099
black night of d., 59
hope in the midst of d., 863
never d., 1357
winter of d., 1818
Desperate
From the d. city you go into the d. country, 1124

Desperation
men lead lives of quiet d., 1124
Despotic
reality of universal suffrage, 1595
Despotism
arrested the course of d., 676
bureaucratic d., 1646
can only end in d., . . . when the people become corrupted, 322
Commerce between master and slave is d., 1062
not a government of laws, 756
of ill health, 1615
protection against political d., 652
seeds of d., 1069
Destinies
just God who presides over the d. of nations, 1061
of half the world, 2045
of the world, 488
Destiny, 432–433
by d. rather than choice, 662
fabric of human d., 432
face to face with our d., 11
grow towards the stars of my greater d., 1480
if we are to achieve our d., 132
of the state is in the hands of the many, 912
our d., with the aid of God, remains in our own hands, 433
rendezvous with d., 1607
There is a d. that makes us brothers, 136
where the meaning of our lives matches the products of our labor, 691
Destroy
begetting the very thing it seeks to d., 1893
necessary to d. the town to save it, 1888
power to tax is not the power to d., 1792
power to tax is the power to d., 1798
we exercise the right to d. him [the president], 1509
Destroyer
subtle d. of the human spirit, 1984
Destruction
If d. be our lot we must ourselves be its author and finisher, 522
seem'd to be threaten'd with absolute d., 59
Detente
Strength makes d. attainable, 404
Determination
to make the right things happen, 1636
Developing
help the d. nations of the world, 611
Devil, 434–435
benefit of law, 434
courage to treat with the d. in person, 435
from the d. himself, if he wore a crown, 614
himself cannot make him say yes, 1272
Devil's
brew, 38
Devils
doctrines of d., 1457
Devise
to boys, 192
to children, 192
To lovers I d., 192
Dew
Covers Dixie like the d., 1244
Diamonds
are only chunks of coal, 1356
Dice
casting of the d. of death and birth, 1542
Dictator
only d. that freemen acknowledge, 1196
Dictatorial
not bow his neck to any d. government, 1671
Dictators
people reach for d., 1774
Dictatorship
of ignorance, 1615
Dictatorships
do not grow out of strong and successful governments, 750
Dictatress
of the world, 613
Die
Be ashamed to d., 1875
be ready to d. for it [democracy], 1340
but once to serve our country, 1304
danger that he may d., 1105
for one's country, 367
for our country, 367
happy, 1655
Old soldiers never d., 1727
on the gallows or of the pox, 372
so it [my epitaph] can be carved, 1155
taught us how to d., 1222
time to be born, and a time to d., 1810
To d. will be an awfully big adventure, 988
when we come to d. even the undertaker will be sorry, 1125
who are not afraid to d., 1121
who do not fear to d., 1121
Who lets his country d., lets all things d., 348
who've no retreat, 1871
without a vision, 43
without hard practical sense, 43
Died
foolish and wrong to mourn the men who d., 1730
gloriously on the field of battle, 370
Let me not mourn for the men who have d., 1730
Dies
anyone who d. for his country is a fortunate man, 1721
never d. the dream, 457
nobody d. to get it [liberty], 1045
the same, 1223
when a great man d., 371
Difference
of opinion is not a difference of principle, 1596
Differences, 436
between men and women, 2013
let us not be blind to our d., 436
Different
laws, 1631
manners, 1631
prudent without having my mind closed to anything that is new or d., 1396
right to be d., 645
[tasks] from those which our fathers faced, 697
Difficult
if it is only d., it is done, 1183
we do at once, 1183
we do immediately, 1183
Difficulties
A man's worst d. begin when he is able to do as he likes, 646
Dig
the grave of the United States, 2043
Dignified
quiet and d. simplicity, 108
Dignity
assaults upon human d., 85
each person respects the feelings and the d. . . . of his neighbor, 54
inferior in eloquence, science, and d., 279
solid rock of human d., 1693
Diminished
rights of every man are d., 219
Diplomacy, 437–439

patriotic art of lying for one's country, 437
qualities of an ideal d., 439
shall proceed always frankly and in the public view, 1027
Diplomatic
definition of d. life—Protocol, alcohol, and Geritol, 1858
relations are merely practical conveniences, 627
Diplomatist
qualities of my ideal d., 439
Disagrees
then everybody d., 266
Disarm
Once upon a time all the animals in the Zoo decided that they would d., 440
Disarmament, 128, 440
Disaster
tried to spare effort, and met d., 2063
Discipline
more than number, gives one army the superiority, 1182
neglect of d., 1182
one's habits and efforts and wishes, 1289
Discords
free from ruinous d., 915
Discrimination
equal justice, equal opportunity, equal dignity without d., 866
racial d., 117
without d. because of sex, 550
Disease
combating the d., 847
enemies of man: tyranny, poverty, d., 516
Diseases
Publicity is . . . a remedy for social and industrial d., 1572
Disenthrall
ourselves, 1300
Disgrace
not d. my sacred arms, 100
Dish-watery
utterances, 1487
Disobey
our inner selves that hurt us when we d. it [truth], 1833
Disparaged
[Senate has been] unreasonably d., 296
Dissent, 441–445
men who do not respect d., 444
we witness is a reaffirmation of faith in man, 1144
Dissenters
suppress the d., 1613
Dissents
series of protests and d., 1717
Disservices
One of the greatest d. you can do a man, 385
Dissidents
demands that d. are making of the universities, 153
Dissolution
germ of d. of our federal government, 941
then will begin the rot and d., 60
Dissolve
this Union, 1267
Dissolved
in a universal confusion, 1097
District
that is best represented, 283
District of Columbia.
See Washington, D.C.
Diversity
make the world safe for d., 436
Divide
and conquer, 634
Divided
we ever have been, 1620
world d., 2036
Divine
human form d., 1464
Divinest
music has not been conceived, 111
Divinity
written . . . by the hand of the d. itself, 865
See also **God**
Dixie
Covers D. like the dew, 1244
Dixiecrats, 811
Do
all the good you can, 452
ask not just what government will do for me, 771
Ask not what your country can do for you, 769
ask what you can do for your country, 769
being constrained to do what we ought not to will, 1055
difficulties begin when he is able to do as he likes, 646
don't do it in the streets and frighten the horses, 895
for a community of people whatever they need to have done, 780
for my city, 767
justly, and to love mercy, 947
nothing, 560
Presidency . . . offers a chance to *do* something, 1501
so much for so many on so little, 449
something, 899
State, has a right to do exactly as it pleases, 1761
that which befits a king, 956
that which is just, 956
to ourselves what we have done unto others, 1612
To see what is right and not to do it, 1635
the very best I know how, 110
watch what we do instead of what we say, 9
well if well done by, 79
what are you going to do with all these things, 51
what can I do for myself, 771
what we can do for our country in return, 768
What we do belongs to what we are, 1676
what you can do for your country, 766
what your country can do for you, 766
your own thing, 447
Dr. Facts (Bernard M. Baruch), 1262
Doctrine
that d. believe and cling to, 105
Does
He who can, d., 1800
Dog, 446
rather be a d. and bay at the moon than stay in the Senate, 295
stands highest as man's friend, 90
Dogmas
obsolete d., 2095
of the quiet past, 1300
Dogs
as true of men as of d., 1129
No d. or Chinese allowed, 204
Sichaun d. bark at the sun, 203
Dogwood
never again shall the d. tree grow large enough to be used as a cross [legend of d.], 918
Doing, 447–449
Be not weary in well d., 450
for people what they can and ought to do for themselves is a dangerous experiment, 1983
for them what they could and should do for themselves, 1117
instrument of d., 1679
Joy's soul lies in the d., 12
Doing good, 450–453
Dollar
man before the d., 1068
Nothing can happen to the almighty d., 811
Dominating
and enslaving the whole world, 2040
Domination
cloaked itself, 2039
See also **World domination**

Domitian (Titus Flavius Augustus) (51-96 A.D.), 1457
Done
  the best you can, 109
  do to ourselves what we have d. unto others, 1612
  gets things d. he wants d., 1400
  a hundred things / You have not dreamed of, 603
  if it is only difficult, it is d., 1183
  it couldn't be d., 1841
  it ourselves, 1020
  make undone whatever hath been d., 1291
  so much with so little, 2060
  tackled the thing / That couldn't be d., 1841
  they would have been d. by others, 1679
  Things won are d., 12
  what in hell have you d. for me lately, 1897
  what our country has d. for each of us, 768
  what we have d. for others and the world remains, 887
  What we have d. for ourselves alone dies with us, 887
Donkey
  emaciated Austrian d., 2054
Don't
  give up the ship, 990
  take No for an answer, 2088
Doomed
  race which does not value trained intelligence is d., 505
Doomsday, 454–456
Doones
  are in the valley, 515
Dorothy Q., 1090
Double
  our numbers every 20 years, 92
Double-cross
  that bridge when he comes to it, 1399
Douglas, Stephen Arnold (1813–1861), 1110, 1313
Douglas, William Orville (1898–1980), impeachment resolution, 893
Drachma
  not make his estate a single d. greater, 1022
Draft. *See* **Military service.**
Drag
  my soul down to the regions of darkness and despair, 1638
Dream
  American D., 463
  America's everlasting, living d., 67
  dare to d., 54
  fade like a d., 1220
  freedom of man and mind, is nothing but a d., 463
  I have a d., 462
  never dies the d., 457
  Nothing happens unless first a d., 464
  Out of a misty d., 460
  realization of the American d., 220
  republic is a d., 464
  that one day this nation will rise up, 462
  then [our path] closes / Within a d., 460
  things that never were; and I say "Why not?" 465
  to d. the impossible d., 459
  What happens to a d. deferred?, 461
Dreamed
  I have always d. of a country, 267
Dreamer
  The d. dies, but never dies the dream, 457
Dreams, 457–466
  believe in their d., 2096
  confluence of d., 1866
  live his d.—not in fear, but in hope, 54
  of these earlier generations of Americans, 621
  Say nevermore / That d. are fragile things, 457
  will begin to take on flesh and reality, 621
Dregs
  at bottom, 536
Dreyfus, Alfred (1859-1935), 958
Drinks
  wine d. the man, 34
Drum
  hear the farthest d., 811
  hear the most distant d., 811
  you can muffle the d., 642
Drum case, 446
Drummer
  he hears a different d., 905
Drunk
  My mother, d. or sober, 345
  Winston, you are d., 2004
Drunkards
  habitual d. as a class, 36
Drunken
  men are [as apt] to think themselves sober enough, 2087
Duck
  bird that walks like a d., 1278
Due
  to the lack of experienced trumpeters, 455
Dumb
  people are too damned d., 76
  people criticize something they do not understand, 76
Dungeon
  Himself is his own d., 563
Duration
  of power, 765
Durkin, Martin Patrick (1894–1955), 1510
Dust
  dry d., secure of change, 377
  earthly frame has crumbled into d., 1752
  long years that . . . turn the growing spirit back to d., 2099
  of centuries, 1753
Duties
  and responsibilities of citizenship, 57
  of life, 1098
  one of the high d. of a good citizen, 1009
  public d., 1764
  teach new d., 1838
Duty, 467–474
  And to my d. haste, 470
  Do your d. in all things, 469
  he always declares that it is his d., 472
  his [the President's] d. to do anything that the needs of the Nation demanded, 1505
  is to preserve what the past has had to say for itself, 1295
  know our d. better than we discharge it, 471
  neglected in its season, 1830
  of being happy, 473
  of government to make its citizens happy, 786
  of governments, 776
  of the persons whom they have appointed, 468
  of those serving the people in public place, 796
  performing a public d., 467
  Science of Government it is my d. to study, 481
  strenuous performance of d., 11
  then is the sublimest word in our language, 469
  to accomplish humble tasks, 2029
  to find ourselves, 474
  to give him the full rights of an American, 883
  to make money and still more money, 1207
  to oppose him [the President] when he serves it badly, 1506
  to sacrifice his repose, his pleasure, his satisfactions, to theirs [constituents], 280
  to support him [the President] when he serves the United States well, 1506

to tell the truth about the President, 1506
which you must fulfill, 1605
writer's d. is to write about these things, 1145
Duty-first, 58
Dwarf
add to the stature of a d., 142
Dwelling
make this thy d. place, 955
Dying Words. *See* **Last Words.**

E

E, is for her eyes, 1226
E pluribus unum, 1867
Eagle
flies in the air as well as a little gnat, 1744
has ceased to scream, 1913
not the oyster, is the emblem of America, 70
Eagle
has landed, 1737
Early
and provident fear, 595
Earn
Now you must e. them [the good things] again, 1605
over again for yourselves or it will not be yours, 666
Earned
everything I have got, 1564
Ears
having e., hear not, 1834
Earth, 475–478
as it truly is, 1742
as we now see it, 1742
belongs as much to those who are to come after us, 1608
belongs in usufruct to the living, 1298
but cloaks your heaven, 1467
Cultivators of the e., 29
gets its price for what E. gives us, 2072
God has lent us the e. for our life, 1608
is a great entail, 1608
is degenerate in these latter days, 456
is heaven, and we are gods, 1132
last, best hope of e., 1701
make room upon the e. for honest men, 665
materials of wealth in the e., 478
no security on this e., 1672
on e. peace, 1315
our fragile craft, 477
peace on e., good will toward men, 662
people who know about the e., 541
riders on the e. together, 1742
shall slumber, lapt in universal law, 2038
slipped the surly bonds of e., 603
uses up the fat and greenery of the e., 833
Earth Day (1970), 543
Earth Day (1971), 521
East
no E., no West, no North, no South, 267
Eastward
I go only by force, 657
to realize history, 658
Easy
You have lived the e. way, 1605
Eat
he that will not work shall not e., 2031
People don't e. in the long run, 1336
Eaten
We never repent of having e. too little, 1116
Economic
forgotten man at the bottom of the e. pyramid, 1154
infantry of our e. army, 1154
national e. problem, 1763
one e. lesson, 142
social and e. experiments without risk, 1755
Economies
simplicity and prudential e., 796
Economists
American wage earner and the American housewife are a lot better e., 714
Economy, 479–480
among the first and most important of republican virtues, 383
and liberty, 381
favor the policy of e. . . . to save people, 798
is idealism in its most practical form, 798
justice and equity of its [society's] e., 1935
must be conservative, 801
of the United States could well be destroyed, 811
reduce the government to the practice of a rigorous e., 803
See also Budget; **Government spending**
Edison, Thomas (1847–1931), 65
Educate
a man in mind and not morals, 500
a menace to society, 500
most folks e. their prejudices, 1266
Educated
world is full of e. derelicts, 1355
Educating
long, slow process of e. mind and character, 783
the young generation along the right lines, 488
Education, 481–505
benefits of e. and of useful knowledge, 489
has for its object the formation of character, 501
is a good thing generally, 1266
is the cheap defence of nations, 483
is the great equalizer, 498
isn't how much you have committed to memory, 486
liberal e., 168
military instruction a regular part of collegiate e., 1187
need e. in the obvious, 925
no nation has ever borrowed largely for e., 1919
race between e. and catastrophe, 858
shall forever be encouraged, 55
Upon the e. of the people of this country the fate of this country depends, 485
Educational
national e. needs, 50
Effete
corps of impudent snobs, 1876
Efficiency
model of horrible e., 1372
Northern charm and Southern e., 1972
Effort
inevitable comes to pass . . . through e., 1842
no e. without error and shortcoming, 10
We tried to spare e., 2063
Efforts
Extremes that fence all e. in, 659
Egg
little bird that has broken out of the e., 2085
Egghead
The way of the e. is hard, 503
Egocentric
quality, 1406
Eighteenth
amendment, 37
Einstein, Albert (1879–1955), 65
Eisenhower, Dwight David (1890–1969), 1510, 1514

distorted way of looking at things produced, . . . such incalculable e., 1231
good End cannot sanctifie e. Means, 564
indifference to public affairs is to be ruled by e. men, 565
Instead of diminishing e., it multiplies it, 1893
nor must we ever do E., that Good may come of it, 564
only thing necessary for the triumph of e., 560
sin to believe e. of others, but seldom a mistake, 562
That which one believes of others, 562
There are few things wholly e. or wholly good, 561
thousand hacking at the branches of e. to one who is striking at the root, 566
whether it have more of e. than of good, 561

Evils
cure for the e. of democracy, 422
it is too feeble to overthrow, 1237
of city life, 212
of superficiality, 1097
of war are great in their endurance, 840
substantive e. that Congress has a right to prevent, 675
we cannot abolish all the e. in this world by statute, 783
which have never happened, 1116

Exaggerate
I don't even have to e., 748

Exaggerated
report of my death has been . . . e., 378

Example
do not copy our neighbors, but are an e. to them, 1568
encouragement of a great e., 99

Excellence, 567–569
claim of e. is also recognised, 1568
conformity with e. or virtue, 567
four-squared e., 569
full use of your powers along lines of e., 567
of what is in their hands, 880
society which scorns e. in plumbing, 568

Excess
of the opposite virtue, 826
virtue like valour when it is pushed to e., 826

Excuses
who e. himself, accuses himself, 837

Excusing
of a fault / Doth make the fault the worse by excuse, 837

Executive
as necessary to good Government as a single E., 1036
discretion of the E., 1447
interpretation of e. power, 1505
legislative power is nominated by the e., 324
power, 1078
provide in the Constitution for the regular punishment of the e., 891
rescue Liberty from the grasp of e. power, 1078

Executive Branch
head, heart, and hand, 282
is clearly obligated . . . to supply relevant information to the Legislative Branch, 893
is the branch of power most interested in war, 1931
Under the Constitution, I now belong to the e. b., 282

Executives
have given inspiration and push to the advancement of human society, 1030
have played a powerful role in the development of civilization, 1030

Exercise
active e. of his soul's faculties, 567
our strength with wisdom and restraint, 662
preclude the e. of arbitrary power, 789

Exercises
should be devoted to it [health] in preference to every other pursuit, 851

Exhortation
of the Dawn, 1106

Exigency
of the times, 1357

Exile
honorable e., 842

Exits
and their entrances, 1158

Expand
tangible and the functional e., 50

Expectations
revolution of rising e., 182, 1618

Expected
Of other generations much is e., 1607

Expenditure
annual e. twenty pounds ought and six, result misery, 380
on armaments as conflicting with the requirements of the social services, 784
poor cannot hope for much economy in public e., 812

Expenditures
cutting e., 801
defense e., 400
limit public e. to the actual needs of the government, 796

Expense
of so much time, blood, and treasure, 525

Expensive
immoral, illegal, fattening, or too e., 846

Experience, 570–577
all e. is an arch wherethro' / Gleams that untravell'd world whose margin fades, 575
analogy of e., 573
eye may be opened by e., 1002
get out of an e. only the wisdom that is in it, 576
how incapable must Man be of learning from e., 574
instinct has learned nothing from e., 1292
lamp of e., 571
lessons of their own e., 82
may . . . bring certain truths to the Americans' attention, 362
teaching which e. offers in history, 570
triumph of hope over e., 1167
which is going on around me, 1102

Experiment
Doing for people . . . is a dangerous e., 1983

Experimentation
country demands bold, persistent e., 1843

Experiments
without risk to the rest of the country, 1755

Experts, 578
as many opinions as there are e., 1273
I've known better than to depend on the e., 578

Explain
never complain and never e., 1113
Never e.; your friends do not need it, 686

Explanation
maximum the e., 95

Exploration, 579
We shall not cease from e., 579

Expositions
timekeepers of progress, 1537

Exposure
of folly, 681

nothing chills pretense like e., 610
Ex-Presidents
What shall be done with our e., 1488
Extravagance
no e. of anticipation, 1710
public e. begets e., 796
Extravagant
and sporting set, 108
Extreme
valour and e. benevolence, 826
Extremes
that fence all efforts in, 659
Extremism, 580–581
in the defense of liberty is no vice, 581
Extremist
splinter groups, 524
Extremists
who are advocating a soft approach, 580
Extremity
We do not display our greatness by placing ourselves at one e., 826
Exuberance
bursting and sprouting out in wonderful e., 1313
Eye
delights the e. . . . of every observing Traveller, 59
Eyelash
difference is just an e., 1930
Eyes
having e., see not, 1834
of all people are upon us, 1611

F

Fable
of the Snake, 265
on disarmament, 440
Fabulous
country, the only f. country, 69
Face
fair in f., 200
round, jolly, fruitful f., 1313
Fact
finding of f., 582
marries old opinion to new f., 1837
merely marks the point where we have agreed to let investigation cease, 585
Sit down before f. as a little child, 263, 583
wordy evidence of the f., 1692
Factories
walk alone in huge f., 987
Facts, 582–585
Dr. F. (Bernard M. Baruch), 1262
for the people of my country, 582
have a cruel way of substituting themselves for fancies, 584
imagination for his f., 1175
Practical politics consists in ignoring f., 1409
report the f., 748
right to be wrong in his f., 1262
state the f. as they really occurred, 1748
subject all f. to a prefabricated set of interpretations, 1268
Trust them [the people] with the f., 1343
tyranny of f., 585
What are f. but compromises?, 585
when he states his f. that you admire the flights of his imagination, 1175
Fade
like a dream, 1220
they [old soldiers] just f. away, 1727
Faded
the flower, 1219
the shape of beauty, 1219
the sight of beauty, 1219
Fail
hard to f., 589
no use for men who f., 588
shall not f., 688
to meet [challenges], 229
With public sentiment, nothing can f., 1557
With that assistance, I cannot f., 1497
Failed
A man's life is interesting primarily when he has f., 586
Failings
reading about one's f. in the daily papers, 1522
Fails
while daring greatly, 10
Failure, 586–590
Ambition is the last refuge of the f., 590
behind every man who's a f. there's a woman, too, 2017
cause of their f. is no business of mine, 588
consequences of f., 1784
Never submit to f., 2088
Not f., but low aim, is crime, 587
sign that he tried to surpass himself, 586
throw the stone of malice when f. settles its cloud upon our heads, 446
[Water] as a beverage, it's a failure, 1978
Fair
determine to be adult and f., 524
for me and foul for another, 115
many things in life that are not f., 1085
we have as leaders an obligation to be f., 418
Fairies
not believe in f., 1660
Fairness
of the trial, 117
Faith, 591–592
absolute f. corrupts absolutely, 1448
as a grain of mustard seed, 592
as young as your f., 2099
form may survive the substance of the f., 717
grant us a common f., 1463
in democracy, 752
is not primarily in these machines of defense but in ourselves, 409
Let us move forward with strong and active f., 695
lost f. in everything we fight and spend for, 752
sign and symbol of a man without f., 863
Some will lose f. in them [rulers], 1020
triumphant result of f. in human kind, 514
utmost good f. shall always be observed towards the Indians, 55
what f. [leads us], 107
When I examined my political f., 414
Fall
both f. into the ditch, 2087
if these columns f., 755
of British liberty, 1067
unless we stand for something, we shall f. for anything, 106
False
canst not then be f. to any man, 1675
witness, 1804-1805
Falsehoods
which interest dictates, and credulity encourages, 1925
Fame, 593–594
air was f., 1686
lived for ends more durable than f., 549
of the brave outlives him, 886
precarious f., 376
true f. . . . is to be acquired only by noble deeds, 502
Fame's
proud cliff, 593

Family
Average American is just like the child in the f., 83
bind together all the branches of the human f., 1536
happiest moments of my life have been [spent] in the bosom of my f., 842
harmful to my f., 1606
honorable exile from one's f., 842
rather start a f. than finish one, 121
useful to my f. and not to my country, 1606
Fancy
in his narratives, 1175
Farce
[in history the] second time as f., 856
Farms
destroy our f., 27
leave our f., 27
Fascism
break-down in Italy followed by f., 2046
Fascist
America will one day go f. democratically, 1907
Fashions, 2021
Fat
opera ain't over till the f. lady sings, 1817
Fatal
great deal of it [sincerity] is absolutely f., 1696
Fate
book of f., 1576
Concern for the man himself and his f., 1661
finger of f., 505
is Freedom / Grace and Surprise, 1856
Nothing is more certainly written in the book of f., 1062
of this country depends [on education], 485
of unborn Millions, 1627
starveling of F. forgets himself into immortality, 1110
terror of overhanging f., 51
that falls on men, 1
Father
Honor thy f. and thy mother, 1804
One f. is enough to governe one hundred sons, 193
[to] a boy of 14, my f. was so ignorant, 2003
Fatherland
transmit my f. not diminished, 100
Father's
brought up in my f. house to believe in democracy, 1333
Fathers
founding f., 1999
in wars the f. did bury their sons, 1955
result vindicates the foresight of the f., 1974
victory has 100 f., 1872
we confront tasks . . . [different] . . . from those which our f. faced, 697
Fatigue
terrors of f., 1097
Fatigues
of supporting it [freedom], 664
Fattening
immoral, illegal, or f., 846
Fault
excusing of a f. / Doth make the f. the worse by excuse, 837
Faults
admitted of peaceable and legal remedies, 737
are not in our Constitution, but in ourselves, 318
Constitution, with all its f., 322
knowledge of her f., 1460
Fear, 595–600
as old as your f., 2099
brave man is not he who feels no f., 353
do not f. to die, 1121
early and provident f. is the mother of safety, 595
free every man from f., 785
freedom from f., 655
frivolous f., 1082
let us never f. to negotiate, 598
Let us never negotiate out of f., 598
mind is shackled or made impotent through f., 671
need not f. to say it, 169
never strike sail to a f., 597
not in f., but in hope, 54
not to f. the young, 19
Nothing is so much to be feared as f., 600
only thing we have to f. is f. itself, 599
result not of caution but of f., 596
singing in the dark does not dispel f., 1836
was translated into doctrines, 925
Feared
public debt as the greatest of the dangers to be f., 383
worst to be f., 403
Fearless
historian should be f. and incorruptible, 1748
Federal
city, 1974
district, 512
Federal Constitution. *See* Amendment; Constitution; **Constitution of the United States.**
Federalists
We are f., 1596
Federation
of the world, 2038
Feed
him for a lifetime, 484
Feeds
bite the hand that f. them, 906
Feet
man who had no f., 1682
of clay, 248
were bare, 1682
Felicity
which always escapes him, 86
Feline
delinquency, 163
Fellow
immigrants, 882
revolutionaries, 1615
Female
Commend her among her f. acquaintances, 1460
Fence
Extremes that f. all efforts in, 659
Fermi, Enrico (1901–1954), 124
Few
prejudices of the f., 314
so f. have been asked to do so much for so many on so little, 449
so much owed by so many to so f., 2052
Fictitious
value of money, 1203
Field
like a ripe f. of wheat where once drove plough, 915
Fields
of friendly strife, 1874
Fierce
women in combat might be too f., 1190
Fifth
Column, 408
Fifty
At f., chides his infamous delay, 1223
Fig
calls f. a f., 1748
Fight
for his rights, 1191
for the right, 1634
for the things which we have always carried nearest to our hearts, 2049
for things sacred / And things profane, 100
I have not yet begun to f., 1625
in the fields and in the streets, 1354
in the hills, 1354
not to enslave, 665

nothing which he is willing to f. for, 1934
on the beaches, 1354
on the landing grounds, 1354
rearm in order to f., 401
their way to many a liberty, 1076
time to f., and that time has now come, 1936
war with arms while the diplomats . . . f. it with words, 247
we must f., 1922
when there is no hope of victory, 1634
Fighter
born f. . . . who can dispense with success, 1087
Fighting
aggressive f. for the right, 1637
Fights
you on patriotic principles, 535
Finest
America's f. hours, 1884
hour, 2055
Finger
of fate, 505
Finish
the work we are in, 1325
Fire
count on us [America] to furnish the [f.] hose and water, 626
Don't f. unless fired upon, 1940
for the second time in the history of the world, man will have discovered f., 1134
glow from that f. can truly light the world, 770
hearts were touched with f., 2091
how much f. you have in your belly, 1089
instruction we find in books is like f., 2080
like a f. bell in the night, 1700
not light that is needed, but f., 1575
of genius, in the discovery and production of new and useful things, 1535
of genius was extinguished, 1647
a single shot, 1657
Firebrands
wars have been precipitated by f., 253
Fires
of freedom . . . burn low, 654
Fireside chats, 56, 379, 750
Firmness
in the right, 1325
First
Amendment, 167, 1015
by whom the New are tried, 2021
free man f. and an American second, 1396
is but a splendid misery, 1493
Fiscal
rocks of loose f. policy, 480
Fish
Give a man a f. and you feed him for a day, 484
Teach a man to f. and you feed him for a lifetime, 484
Fixed
star in our constitutional constellation, 647
Flag, 601–602
behold the gorgeous ensign of the republic, 1855
loved but one f., 1026
our standard, Old Glory, a symbol of freedom, 1364
pledge allegiance to the F. of the United States, 1363
Rally round the f., boys, 601
Your f. and my f., 602
Flags
[blue battle-flag inscribed] Don't give up the ship, 990
tattered f. of the tented field, 778
Flame
pulpits f. with righteousness, 829
Which naught but tears can drown, 844
Flanders Fields, 65, 2048
Flash
of the day, 1028
Flatter
fawn and f. to avoid a sneer, 656
the people in order to betray them, 63
Flattery
he should spread it on, not in thin layers, 1391
to give or to receive f., 1459
Unseduced by F., 549
unwarranted f., 1403
Fleas
like friendly apes, to pick the f. from each other's fur, 2079
Fleeing
from himself and denying his human nature, 1000
Fleet
sailing under Convoy, 44
the works of men, 1220
Flies
He who f. proves himself guilty, 835
Flights
of the human mind, 1195
Float
before we f. farther on the waves of this debate, 1286
Flower
Faded the f., 1219
Flowers
give them the f. now, 1218
Flying, 603–604
chariot in which a man may sit, 1744
Foe
go forth from the sweet peace of our beloved firesides to smite the f., 1950
oppose any f., 1066
without hate, 820
See also **Enemies**; Enemy
Folger Shakespeare Library, inscriptions, 1686
Follow
as the night the day, 1675
I must f. them, for I am their leader, 1021
know how to f., too, 1023
State must f. and not lead the character and progress of the citizen, 1004
Folly
by the exposure of folly . . . it is defeated, 681
going underground to escape the consequences of his own f., 125
three things which are real: God, human f., and laughter, 1095
war contains so much f., 1932
words of delusion and f., 1855
Fool
all of the people all of the time, 609
all of the people some of the time, 609
an assembly of great men is the greatest f. upon earth, 608
At thirty man suspects himself a f., 1223
if a man is a f., . . . encourage him to advertise the fact by speaking, 681
keeps a f. at court, 1156
power to make a f. of himself, 1898
silence any friend of yours whom you know to be a f., 610
some of the people all the time, 609
whosoever shall say, Thou f., shall be in danger of hell fire, 605
Foolish
consistency is the hobgoblin of little minds, 1194
he [Abraham Lincoln] was, 1110
more f., 23

Foolishness
age of f., 1818
Fools, 605–610
old men know young men are f., 607
[patriotism] is the first, last and middle range of f., 1306
percentage of f. in this country, 606
Twenty-seven millions, mostly f., 606
young men think old men are f., 607
For
what counts now is . . . what we are f., 107
whom the bell tolls, 134
Force
use of f. should not be excluded, 253
Forebears
hold fast to the cliches of our f., 1268
Forefathers
moved on to triumph, 57
Foreign
article of f. manufacture, 617
assistance to f. lands should be curtailed, 795
interests in the hands of the President and the Senate, 632
Foreign aid, 611–612
Foreign policy, 613–634
bipartisan f. p., 634
finding a balance between means and ends that is the heart of f. p., 631
great goal of our f. p., 1961
it conducts f. p. in order to live, 620
meet it [communism] with every instrumentality of f. p., 580
Our greatest f. p. problem is our divisions at home, 624
political society does not live to conduct f. p., 620
purpose of f. p., 622
Soviet f. p., 1657
whimpering isolationism in f. p., 1042
wisdom and purposes of its f. p., 1935
Foreign Secretary
is always faced with this cruel dilemma, 438
Forget
never f. what you have said, 1839
Forgets
where she [America] came from, 60
Forgive
almost any weakness, . . . [except] stupidity, 84
never f. one who did so [shot him] accidentally, 1231
rarely if ever do they f. them, 198
Forgiven
age is f. nothing, 2098
should not be forgotten nor f., 139
Youth, which is f. everything, 2098
Forgiveness, 635
God, at least, has a degree of f., 1408
Thou Shalt Not Ask F. for Thy Transgressions, 441
Forgives
youth f. itself nothing, 2098
Forgiveth
he who f., and is reconciled unto his enemy, 517
Forgotten
man at the bottom of the economic pyramid, 1154
should not be f. or forgiven, 139
Fork
in the political road, 62
Forlorn
standard-bearer of this f. hope, 863
Forlornness
imbecile candle in the heart of that almighty f., 863
Form
may survive the substance of the faith, 717
Fortune, 636–638
hostages have I given to f., 638
hostages to f., 1163
suffers not the same man to prosper for ever, 637
that with malicious joy, 636
vicissitudes of f., 1682
Fortunes
men's f. are on a wheel, 637
Forty
knows it [he is a fool] at f., 1223
views at f., 26
Forum
mad racket and the hazards of the f., 376
Forward
and not back, 1434
go f. now together, 1863
move f. with strong and active faith, 695
Foster, Stephen (1826–1864), 65
Foul
fair for me and f. for another, 115
Found
was lost, and is f., 635
we shall be f., 67
Foundations
put the f. under them, 466
Founding
fathers, 1999
fathers of our country gave balanced representation, 1592
Four
essential human freedoms, 655
things a man must learn to do, 1126
things greater than all things are, 824
4-H Club, 1553
Fourteen Points, 1027
Fourth
estate, 1520
I was a . . . Democrat f., 1396
Fourth of July. *See* **Independence Day.**
Foxes
have a sincere interest in prolonging the lives of the poultry, 509
France
[American Independence Day] is celebrated with more . . . fervor . . . in F., 897
arrangement was made between F. and Holland, 890
contempt upon the lips of the manhood of . . . F., 2089
Every man has two countries, his own and F., 343
military hospital in F., 1897
ordered armies of the United States, to the soil of F., 698
When F. has a cold, all Europe sneezes, 559
Frankenstein
to destroy both sides, 1258
Franklin, Benjamin (1706–1790), 65
Fraud
and prevarication our servile vices, 1082
prosecution of f., 467
Frederick the Great, King of Prussia (1712–1786), 820
Free
assemblage, 1711
at last, 547
disappearance of f. enterprise, 141
dicussion, 414
expression of thought, 1642
from ruinous discords, 915
government is . . . what the people think, 774
Happy are all f. peoples, 1233
hope for the salvation of f. government, 506
huddled masses yearning to breathe f., 1770
let me live f. from solicitude, 376
limitations placed upon the right of f. speech, 673

judging its g. by their covering, cast them away, 1467
Give
have more than we wanted to g., 2063
in the same measure as I have received, 1603
light and the people will find their own way, 971
me a child for the first seven years, 199
me liberty, or g. me death, 1061
me matter, and I will construct a world out of it, 2033
me my roses now, 1217
me your tired, your poor, 1770
Never g. in, 1353
the public what it wants, 1803
them the flowers now, 1218
us courage and gaiety and the quiet mind, 1475
us the tools, 2051
you are called upon to g. much, 1102
Give-and-take policy, 257
Given
to some generations much is g., 1607
to whom much is g., 1604
Gives
who g. in friendship's name shall reap what he has spent, 684
Glad
be g. that such heroes have lived, 1730
Gladness
not in sorrow, but in g. of heart, 843
See also **Happiness; Joy**
Gloat
isn't right to g. over the dead, 365
Global
conquest, 247
Globaloney, 625
Gloom
of the world is but a shadow, 1467
Glorious
it is to die for our country, 367
Gloriously
died g. on the field of battle, 370
Glory
Boasting of g. does not make g., 1836
glimpses of his Fathers g. shine, 919
greatest G. of a free-born People, 644
my g. was I had such friends, 690
of the people of America, 82
Old G., 1364
paths of g. lead but to the grave, 1216
rest in honored g., 1734
to God in the highest, 1315
Vain pomp and g. of this world, I hate ye, 1103
wars are the g. and the agony of the young, 1920
Glow
from that fire can truly light the world, 770
her g. has warmed the world, 448
Glows
world-wide welcome, 1770
Glue
that holds government together, 255, 1831
Go
desired them to go away, 1035
forward and give us victories, 1873
forward now together, 1863
In the name of God,—go, 1035
on or go under, 1340
placidly amid the noise and the haste, 1114
to Hell, 327
Goal
is nearer than / It seems to a faint and faltering man, 1358
riders in a race do not stop short when they reach the g., 1115
walk consciously only part way toward our g., 1786
Gold
crucify mankind upon a cross of g., 27
standard, 27
God, 699–705
acknowledgement of G. in Christ, 700
As the Will of G. is in Heaven, 402
at least, has a degree of forgiveness, 1408
be at peace with G., whatever you conceive Him to be, 1114
bless us every one, 1465
chance is the pseudonym of G., 173
divine spark leaps from the finger of G. to the finger of Adam, 898
event is in the hand of G., 340
for in thee do I put my trust, 1827
fresh from the burning, creative hand of G., 59
fulfils himself in many ways, 181
give me the serenity to accept things which cannot be changed, 1472
governs in the affairs of men, 703
grants liberty only to those who love it, 1079
Had I but serv'd my G., 705
hath created the mind free, 667
higher Power, by whatever name we honor Him, 761
hold you in the palm of His hand, 1478
human folly, and laughter, 1095
I know there is a G., 907
is forgotten, 1731
is living there [in space], 1743
is the author of this law, 1000
jealous G., 1804
just G. who presides over the destinies of nations, 1061
love of liberty which G. has planted in our bosoms, 1069
made the oyster, 70
not even G. can change the past, 1291
not even G. can do, 1291
of the hidden purpose, 1474
One Great Scorer, 1993
only G. and Robert Browning understood it, 2074
our destiny, with the aid of G., remains in our own hands, 433
Our shelter and our shield is G., 1721
Perfect happiness . . . was never intended by the Diety, 841
power to make money is a gift from G., 1207
Put out my hand, and touched the face of G., 603
receive his reward from G., 517
reigns and the government at Washington still lives, 718
reigns over you, 978
rules over the universe, 87
solves for thee / All questions in the earth and out of it, 700
Standeth G. within the shadow, 1838
Thou shalt have one G. only, 1805
'T is only G. may be had for the asking, 2072
under a just G., cannot long retain it [freedom], 648
was tired when He made it, 33
we have forgotten G., 53
When God made the oyster, 70
who gave us life gave us liberty, 1062
See also Lord
God's
forgotten, 1731
if you can accept it [poverty] as G. will yourself, 1441
Man, created to G. image and likeness, 1152

opinion that life should go on, 1100
proof of G. omnipotence that he need not exist in order to save us, 702
pursue the study of G. word, 239
work must truly be our own, 7
Gods
how jealous are the g., 1781
no other g. before me, 1804
Gold
and silver that waits for them in West, 476
isn't all, 33
natural stability of g., 159
Not g. but only men, 1234
property turns sand to g., 1550
standard, 1205
vote for g., 159
Golden
Age, 309
door, 1770
shining, g. opportunity, 68
Silence is g., 1691
Gompers, Samuel (1850-1924), 115
Good
achieve g. in their own small corner of the world, 1361
administration can never save bad policy, 1372
America is great because she is g., 829
Bad administration, to be sure, can destroy g. policy, 1372
churches, 217
conducive to the g., 105
consists in maintaining, promoting, and enhancing life, 1214
Do all the g. you can, 452
few things wholly evil or wholly g., 561
For every g. that you wish to preserve, 1605
greatest g. for the greatest number, 119
If a g. deed I may do, 453
if men be bad, let the government be never so g., 745
Let men be g., and the government cannot be bad, 745
men to do nothing, 560
more power than any g. man should want, 1447
most g. things are produced by labor, 977
must associate; else they fall one by one, 560
no g. man would deserve, 1447
nor must we ever do Evil, that G. may come of it, 564
not even for the general g. of the whole community, 997
nothing so bad or so g. that you will not find an Englishman doing it, 535
of those who confer . . . the trust, 712
penalty g. men pay for indifference to public affairs, 565
pursuing our own g. in our own way, 650
rather do the g. that is straight under our noses, 1361
roads, 217
schools, 217
took the g. things for granted, 1605
what was g. for our country was g. for General Motors, 352
whether it have more of evil than of g., 561
will toward men, 1315
Goodbye
Christ Jesus Lord God Jehova, 917
Goose
so plucking the g., 1788
Gorbachev, Mikhail Sergeyevich (1931-), 1708
Govern
ability of the President and the Congress to g. this Nation, 526
heard by those who g., 1747
Here, sir, the people g., 762
One father is enough to g. one hundred sons, 193
only legitimate right to g., 763
People who own the country ought to g. it, 764
representatives chosen by the people to g., 1364
teaches us to g. ourselves, 719
Governed
by different laws, 1631
by God, 746
consent of the g., 760
express grant of power from the g., 763
one of the g. instead, 1566
that country is best g., which is least g., 723
to be g. is to be watched over, 747
Governing
class is composed of the strong men, 1566
forfeit your right to be considered one of the g., 1566
great art of g., 744
not g. too much, 751
[United States] can do without g., 711
Government, 706–759
administration of g., like a guardianship, 712
aim of g. is liberty, 785
aim of g. is not to rule, 785
are carrying an immense weight, 731
are very keen on amassing statistics, 1768
art of g., 751
at all levels was refreshed and renewed and made truly responsive, 1617
at Washington still lives, 718
bad g. has grown out of too much g., 758
becomes a lawbreaker, 707
being the people's business, 1573
best g. is that which governs least, 753
big enough to give you everything you want, 714
big enough to take from you everything you have, 714
boards of control, 1588
business of g., 781
by the people, 760–765
called a republic, 425
cannot choose between party g. and Parliamentary g., 1377
cannot endure permanently half slave and half free, 1851
cannot expect perfect g., 1351
citizen participation, 766–772
contribute to his G., 1794
corporation we may all well dread, 722
critics of, 731
definition of, 773–775
democracy is the worst form of G. except all those other forms, 417
duty of g. to make its citizens happy, 786
essence of g., 729
essence of G. is power, 1450
Every country has the g. it deserves, 740
faults of a G., 749
folly or the wickedness of g., 1193
form may survive the substance of the faith, 717
free system of g., 738
freest g. . . . would not be long acceptable, 1549
functions do not include the support of the people, 777
functions of the general g. on which you have a right to call, 405
God-given right to kick the g. around, 743

Creative ideas do not spring from g., 898
Growing
old, 25
Guaranteed
existence, 71
Guard
and defend it [liberty], 1079
on our g. to protect liberty, 1048
Put none but Americans on g. tonight, 1629
with jealous attention the public liberty, 1060
Guardian
genius of Democracy, 1196
of our freedom, 1030
Guardians
of the liberties and welfare of the people, 1037
of those interests, 468
Guardianship
administration of government, like a g., 712
Guideposts
Great men are the g., 816
Guilt, 835–837
punishment of his g., 1054
Guilty
better 100 g. Persons should escape, 953
He declares himself g. who justifies himself before accusation, 837
He who flies proves himself g., 835
Let no g. man escape if it can be avoided, 467
of despicable actions, 849
Gun
every g. that is made, 403
Political power grows out of the barrel of a g., 1451
Guns
train your g. a little lower, 515
Gyre
Turning and turning in the widening g., 454

H

H, is for her heart of purest gold, 1226
Had
I but serv'd my God with half the zeal / I serv'd my king, 705
Haiti, 838
is going to be written on my heart, 838
Hale, Nathan (1755–1776), 65
Half
a loaf is better than a whole loaf, 252
a loaf was better than no bread, 252
Hamilton, Alexander, (1755–1804) 43, 813, 1018
epitaph, 830
Hamlet
Could *H.* have been written by a committee, 898
Hammarskjöld, Dag (1905-1961), 1324
Hammer
be an anvil—or a h., 494
Hand
bite the h. that feeds them, 906
invisible h., 1344
Lend a H., 1434
that held the dagger, 113
Handicapped, 724
Handle
Take things always by their smooth h., 1116
Hands
Don't know what good they hold in their h., 880
excellence of what is in their h., 880
ready h. and keen swords, 1941
Hang
him with them, 908
sell us the rope to h. them with, 246
separately, 395
something in them which will h. him, 908
We must all h. together, 395
Hanged
[if] I was being h., the crowd would be twice as big, 1277
when a man knows he is to be h. in a fortnight, it concentrates his mind wonderfully, 369
Hanging
of some working people by other working people, 980
Hanks, Nancy. *See* Lincoln, Nancy (Hanks).
Happen
make the right things h., 1636
What has once happened will invariably h. again, 855
Happiest
moments of my life have been the few which I have past at home in the bosom of my family, 842
Happiness, 839–846
care of human life and h., 778
comes from humans through fellowship, 923
distraction from his h., 86
Greek definition of h., 567
health, without which there is no h., 851
in his knowledge that man has found his . . . h., 972
Joy is not the same as pleasure or h., 923
lend its [legislature's] weight to the cause of virtue and h., 786
of man, 779
of mankind, 55
of mankind is best promoted by the useful pursuits of peace, 840
of society, 782
private rights and public h., 82
public employment contributes neither to advantage nor h., 842
pursuit of h., 396–397
right to the pursuit of h., 776
two roads that lead to something like human h., 845
who gave it [life] for h., 1091
Happy
accidents, 736
are all free peoples, 1233
die h., 1655
duty of being h., 473
highways where I went, 2093
incidents of the federal system, 1755
means to be free, 1948
mind is contented and h., 487
till all are h., 1350
to be h. oneself . . . make at least one other person h., 845
Union of these States is a wonder, 1854
Happy Home Recipe, 844
Hard
as rock, 1109
Hardihood
virtues of courage, honor, . . . and h., 58
Harm, 847–848
help, or at least do no h., 847
Persecution cannot h. him who stands by Truth, 1833
Harm's
in h. way, 848
Harness
for God the energies of love, 1134
Harnessing
the ether, the winds, the tides, gravitation, 1134
Hasty
thousand h. counsels, 937
Hate, 849–850
cannot drive out h., 1893
I could never h. anyone I knew, 850
a man because he was born in another country, 1481
murder the hater, but you do not murder the h., 1893

nobody can h. America as much as native Americans, 881
time to love, and a time to h., 1810
trick their hearts with h., 457
Violence merely increases h., 1893
Hating
practice to avoid h. anyone, 849
we are turned to h., 1580
Hatred
and animosity, 224
any h., 225
Where there is h., let me bring love, 1466
Have
can't h. what you choose, 205
eat your cake and have it too, 1335
more than we wanted to give, 2063
Havens
men are not made for save h., 1087
Hawaii, 65
See also Pearl Harbor
Hawthorne, Nathaniel (1804–1864), 1272
Hay
let them eat h., 1347
Hazards
fullness of life is in the h. of life, 1087
Head
empties his purse into his h., 967
stone, 91
Heads
turn our h. the other way, 1746
Heal
time to kill, and a time to h., 1810
Health, 851
every American's h., 801
without which there is no happiness, 851
Hear
the farthest drum, 811
the most distant drum, 811
Hearings, congressional
Army-McCarthy, on decency, 1171
Brown, Harold, on defense spending, 400
Danielson, George E., on Watergate, 1394
Ervin, Sam, on Watergate, 705
Ford, Gerald R. on compromise, 255
Kennedy, Robert F., on black power, 116
MacArthur, Douglas, on communism, 247
Reischauer, Edwin O., on communism, 248
Rusk, Dean, on foreign aid, 612
Sandler, Bernice, on prejudice, 1483
Willkie, Wendell, on oratory, 1287
Wilson, Charles E., nomination of, 352
Hears
step to the music which he h., 905
Heart
and hand / To love, and serve, and keep the land, 1239
Calais lying in my h., 838
Haiti is going to be written on my h., 838
inaudible language of the h., 922
not in sorrow, but in gladness of h., 843
perverseness is one of the primitive impulses of the human h., 1359
shines like a great star in his breast, 921
stone of the h., 1659
to help, 959
Hearthstone
bright and dear, 1239
Hearts
deceitfulness of our h., 53
weary leagues two loving h. divide, 2034
were touched with fire, 2091
Heat
can't stand the h., get out of the kitchen, 1513
snow, nor rain, nor h., nor gloom of night, 1439
thing to be supplied is light, not h., 937
Heaven
and earth never agreed better, 189
Catholics can go to H., 897
choicest bounties of H., 53
going direct to H., 1818
if you wish to go to H., 897
precious boon of H., 1075
what's a h. for, 1840
Height
of absurdity in one generation, 2001
of wisdom in the next, 2001
Hell
gate of h., 1771
go to h., 327
going direct the other way, 1818
hottest places in h., 1211
if my fellow citizens want to go to H. I will help them, 327
is truth seen too late, 1830
road to h. is paved with them [good intentions], 291
Tyranny, like h., is not easily conquered, 1845
what in h. have you done for me lately, 1897
whosoever shall say, Thou fool, shall be in danger of h. fire, 605
Help
them help themselves, 623
Hemisphere
government in the Western h., 243
situated in the Western h., 630
States in a h. then unknown, 1867
Henry IV, King of England (1366–1413), 1007
Henry VIII, King of England (1491–1547), 1103
Henry, Patrick (1736–1799), 65
Here
the people rule, 761
sir, the people govern, 762
Heroes
are created by popular demand, 1556
glad that such h. have lived, 1730
mighty shoves of its h., 2029
Heroin, 852
King H. is my shepherd, 852
Hesitate
Don't h. to be as revolutionary as science, 2025
Hesitation
impute uncertainty and h. to want of honesty, 2094
Plains of H., 1823
Hide
But he can't h., 1651
High
and lonely office, 1494
privileges of h. office, 1522
Highways
happy h., 2093
Historian
should be fearless and incorruptible, 1748
History, 853–858
analysis of the h. of mankind, 1957
becomes more and more a race between education and catastrophe, 858
cannot escape h., 1701
comes, after they [underdogs] are long dead, and puts them on top, 822
eastward to realize h., 658
Emerson recedes grandly into h., 1297
endless repetition of h., 854
the final judge of our deeds, 7
Final judgment upon them can only be recorded by h., 253
for models of government, 716
furnishes one example only, 891

I

Ice
of cynicism, 2099
Ich bin ein Berliner, 215
Idea
no i. so uplifting as the i. of the service of humanity, 1570
of progress, 182
one i.,—and that was wrong, 872
which commands his own, 873
wine of an original i. into the water of mediocrity, 874
Ideal
institution which proposes the i., 1456
stands up for an i., 8
Idealism
Economy is i. in its most practical form, 798
from intelligent self-interest into pure i., 1084
which motivates the young people of America, 2096
Idealist
believes the short run doesn't count, 868
is one who, on noticing that a rose smells better than a cabbage, 870
Man is born a predestined i., 869
Sometimes people call me an i., 871
Idealistic
nation in the world, 871
Idealists, 868–871
Ideals
loyalty to high i., 363
of a Joan of Arc, 1400
our successors may decide to switch i., 1361
people grow old by deserting their i., 2099
Ideas, 872–875
better i., 168
Creative i. do not spring from groups, 898
difficulty lies, not in the new i., but in escaping from the old ones, 875
free trade in i., 1835
freedom of expression and of i., 169
jeweled i., 129
weapon against bad i. is better i., 168
won't go to jail, 168
Idiosyncrasies
fully know its [House of Representatives'] i., 281
Idiosyncratic
condition of things so strictly i., 570
Idle
Why stand we here i., 1061
Idleness, 876
is sweet, and its consequences are cruel, 876
Ignorance, 877–880
dictatorship of i., 1615
is strength, 1962
Knowledge will forever govern i., 969
Mr. Kremlin himself was distinguished for i., 872
Nothing is worse than active i., 877
of the natural rights of mankind, 1058
of the nature of coin, credit, and circulation, 1200
protective shell of i., 1156
Rail on in utter i., 879
Ignorant
and free, 492
freedom is fragile if citizens are i., 493
irresponsible class, 46
men / Don't know what good they hold in their hands, 880
of moral principle, 46
of what occurred before you were born, 191
person makes a fuss about something which he alone finds strange, 203
Ill
meet them well or i., 827
Illegal
immoral, i., or fattening, 846
Illinois
agricultural products, 149
public policy of I., 163
Illusion
of progress, 1539
political power is primarily an i., 1415
I'm
youth, I'm joy, 2085
Image
graven i., 1804
Images
graven i., 1805
Imagination
flights of his i., 1175
for his facts, 1175
quality of the i., 2095
Imaginative
artist willy-nilly influences his time, 2082
Imitate
those who have been especially admirable, 825
Imitated
he who can be i. by none, 2075
Imitating
he who refrains from i. others, 2075
Imitation
Originality is nothing but judicious i., 2080
Immigrants, 881–884
America needs new i. to love and cherish it, 881
descended from i. and revolutionists, 882
my fellow i., 882
Immigration
from overcrowded Europe, 476
Immoral
illegal, or fattening, 846
Immortal
Change alone is eternal, perpetual, i., 180
indestructible [spirit], 1751
men's i. minds, 1198
thinks himself i., 1223
what we have done for others and the world remains and is i., 887
Immortality, 885–887, 1360
[America] has been reared for i., 63
forget himself into i., 1110
his portion is i., 886
on earth is a government bureau, 709
Impassible
gulf divided the Rich from the Poor, 1631
Impeach
Either i. him [Nixon] or get off his back, 888
power to i. and remove the President, 894
Impeachable
[if] i., a regular and peaceful inquiry would have taken place, 890
offense is whatever a majority of the House of Representatives considers [it] to be, 889
Impeachment, 888–894
is scarcely a scare-crow, 941
power of i., 893
subject him to i. himself, 1500
your presumptuous i., 72
Impeachments
which are the groans of the people, 892
Imperative
categorical i., 1010
Imperfect
man, 1348
We are all i., 1351
Imperial
principles, 535
Imperialism
American i., 1657
may obstruct the paths to international peace, 910

struggles waged by the different peoples against U.S. i., 1927
U.S. i. has stepped into the shoes of German, Japanese, and Italian fascism, 2040
See also **Capitalism**
Importance
all we have left is i., 1681
Impossible
nothing shall be i. unto you, 592
readiness to attempt the i., 1448
takes a bit longer, 1183
takes a little longer, 1183
we do at once, 1183
Impropriety, 895
constitutional i., 1512
In
harm's way, 848
Inactivity
wise and masterly i., 1038
Inalienable
endowed by their creator with certain i. rights, 397
right to make their own mistakes, 1618
rights inherent & i., 396
rights of the individual, 776
Inaugural addresses, presidential
Cleveland, Grover (1885), 796; (1893), 777
Coolidge, Calvin (1925), 798
Davis, Jefferson (1861), 760
Harding, Warren G. (1921), 1999
Harrison, William Henry (1841), 763
Hayes, Rutherford B. (1877), 1380
Jefferson, Thomas (1801), 619, 1267, 1596
Kennedy, John F. (1961), 7, 77, 516, 598, 623, 661, 769–770, 1066; reading by Robert Frost, 475
Lincoln, Abraham (1861), 735, 944; (1865), 1325
Nixon, Richard M. (1973), 771
Reagan, Ronald (1985), official invitation quoting Madison, 82
Roosevelt, Franklin Delano (1933), 599
Washington, George (1789), 1344
Income
annual i. twenty pounds, 380
Incomes
have gone down the most, 144
Incorruptible
historian should be fearless and i., 1748
Increase
and diffusion of knowledge among men, 1710
Incredulity
epoch of i., 1818
Independence
courage which is nourished by the love of i., 1647
of the will of the nation is a solecism, 943
preserve their i., 381
too much attached to savage i., 742
Independence Day, 65, 613 **896–897**
Independent
always be drastically i., 1249
country shall be i., 1621
India
rather starve than sell our national honor, 1303
revolution in I., 202
young man in I., 1768
Indian Ocean, 1526
Indians
their lands and property shall never be taken, 55
white man took our lands, 1545
Indifference
of private life, 1647
to public affairs is to be ruled by evil men, 565
Indifferent
to be young and to be i., can be no longer synonymous, 2090
Indispensable
no i. man, 1153
Individual, 898–905
enlargement of liberty for i. human beings, 901
feels he should do those things which only can and should be done by the many, 912
inalienable rights of the i., 776
increase respect for the creative i., 98
independence, 652
is naturally entitled to do as he pleases with himself, 1761
is not accountable to society for his actions, 649
is sovereign, 651
spoiled and eventually a very weak i., 83
submergence of the i. in the impersonal corporation, 141
too much i. privilege . . . was selfish license, 759
Individuality
free development of i., 904
society has now fairly got the better of i., 903
Individuals
They [creative ideas] spring from i., 898
worth of a state . . . is the worth of the i. composing it, 1760
Indivisible
incapable of being divided, 1364
Indolence
from i. . . . they are unequal to the exertions necessary for preserving it [free government], 741
Indolent
fate of the i., 1054
Industrialization, 621
Industry
encouragement to i. and enterprize, 1547
Inequality
no greater i. than equal treatment of unequals, 551
Inequity
in life, 1092
Inevitable
[being drafted] is i. if you don't [enlist], 1186
change . . . is i., 176
comes to pass is through effort, 1842
fall of Europe is i., 247
Infamy
date which will live in i., 2066
Infantry
attacks exactly as if it [mine field] were not there, 2070
he [Napoleon] forgot his i., 1154
of our economic army, 1154
Inflation
first by i., 1204
hurt by i., 144
Influence
and not authority, 1443
good i. of our conduct, 451
guard against the acquisition of unwarranted i., 1177
high i. to protect them, 467
under the i. of none, 619
Influences
imaginative artist willy-nilly i. his time, 2082
Information
how to use the i. you get, 486
I have no disposition to withhold any i. which the duty of my station will permit, 792
popular Government, without popular i., . . . [is] . . . a Farce or a Tragedy, 969
Ingratitude, 906
Inherit
youth must i. the tribulation, . . . and the triumphs . . . of war, 1923

Inheritance
all but squandered this i., 1605
all the I. I can give, 207
gift of a common tongue is a priceless i., 537
noble i., 63
Inherited
We i. freedom, 666
What you have i. from your fathers, earn over again, 666
Initiative
concentration of power . . . precedes the destruction of human i., 1458
Injustice, 907–909
and frustration, 1894
any i., 225
He [God] hates i., 907
quicksand of racial i., 1693
a single i., 958
strikes out against i., 8
Innocent
if i., restored to the confidence of the public, 890
six sentences written by the most i. of men, 908
than that one i. Person should suffer, 953
Innovate
young men . . . care not to i., 2084
Innovations
numerous i. displayed on the American theatre, 82
Innuendo
land of sly i., 62
Insane
to act you must be somewhat i., 3
Inscriptions
Alamo, 32
Appomattox Court House, 223
Arlington National Cemetery
Kennedy, John Fitzgerald, 7, 77, 516, 661, 769–770, 1066
Kennedy, Robert Francis, 8, 1864, 1995
Tomb of the Unknown Soldier, 1734
Boone County Court House, Missouri, 955
Capitol Building, Washington, D.C., 13, 56, 225, 310, 490, 674, 763, 1048, 1827
Folger Shakespeare Library, 1686
Jefferson Memorial, 178, 397, 667, 1062, 1844
John F. Kennedy Center for the Performing Arts, 96–98, 104, 1632, 1753
John F. Kennedy International Airport, 1770
Kean College of New Jersey, 1799
Lexington Green marker, Massachusetts, 1940
Liberty Bell, Philadelphia, 1046
Library of Congress, 1251
James Madison Memorial Building, Madison Memorial Hall, 496, 552, 738, 782, 1450, 1548, 1854, 1932
main entrance, 497, 969
Lincoln Memorial, 1107
National Archives Building, 1296
National Museum of American History, 972, 1663, 1710
New York University, Hall of Fame, Robert E. Lee's bust, 469
Newark State College, 1799
Normandy Chapel, 1733
Oise-Aisne Cemetery, 1733
Old South Meeting House, Boston, 1630
Post Office Building, New York City, 1439
Post Office Building, Washington, D.C., 1438
Seabees Memorial, Arlington, Virginia, 1183
Statue of Liberty, 641, 655, 779, 1046, 1056, 1069, 1081, 1770
Union Station, Washington, D.C., 1252
U.S. Department of Justice Building, 963
U.S. Military Academy, West Point, 1874
University of Virginia, 238
Veterans Administration Building, Washington, D.C., 1325
White House, State Dining Room, 1462
World's Columbian Exposition, Chicago (1893), Transportation Building, 815, 1536
See also **Epitaphs**
Inside
want to get out, 1426
Institution
which proposes the ideal, 1456
Institutions
all such i. must be sacrificed, 782
Learned I., 496
model i. and constitutions, 45
must advance also to keep pace with the times, 178
political i. aim, 782
purely democratic must, sooner or later, destroy liberty, 420
will be fairly brought to the test, 1847
will provide it [the state] with great men, 1151
Instrument
of doing, 1679
of thy peace, 1466
Insult
If we desire to avoid i., 410
Intangible
and the beautiful shrink, 50
Integrity
of my heart, 1626
were we truly men of i., 1604
Intellect
awakens the human i., 1663
no i. comparable to my own, 1680
Intellectual
and moral progress, 1663
Intellectually
superior to all men, 1349
Intellectuals
snobs who characterize themselves as i., 1876
Intelligence
best human i. is still decidedly barbarous, 1156
Intelligent
man known to history flourishes within a dullard, 1156
Intention
rightful i., 1909
Intentions
good i., 291, 297
One never expected from a Congressman more than good i., 297
peaceful i., 440
plea of good i., 1231
Interest
citizens themselves display in the affairs of state, 772
maintained your i., against your opinions, 1028
Means devoured by i., 386
pays the best i., 967
public good and the national i., 1604
public i., 1511
serve the national i., 1381
to pay i. on it [the national debt] they will pay that i. to themselves, 388
views of private i., 1551
Interests
are eternal and perpetual, 42
of men, 1456
special i., 1567
vigilant protection of all their varied i., 1670
Internal
graver threats today are i., 1896
International
capacity to keep peace, 1324
order, 624

organizations for peacekeeping, 1326
war's . . . a medium for the practical settlement of i. differences, 1258
International Platform Association (IPA), 218
Interstate commerce
horse-and-buggy definition of i. c., 1763
Interstate Commerce Commission, 1588
Intervention
in which the instinct for domination cloaked itself, 2039
Intolerance
eternal truths of the past are threatened by i., 654
Intoxicated
with unbroken success, 53
Invent
Young men are fitter to i., than to judge, 2084
Inventions
are wont to be pretty toys, 1540
which abridge distance have done most for civilization, 1536
Inventor
had no special advantage from his own invention, 1535
Investment
in knowledge, 967
IPA. *See* International Platform Association.
Ireland
conduct of England towards I., 530
Irish
lawyers for Irish, 1015
"An Irish Blessing," 1478
Irish Rebellion of 1916, 1866
Iron
curtain has descended, 234
curtain is drawn down, 234
he's got i. teeth, 1708
ties which though light as air, are as strong as links of i., 694
Irony
of this involvement with size, 50
Irrecoverably
principles of a free constitution are i. lost, 324
Irrelevant
national preoccupation with the i., 50
Island
no man is an i., 134
"isms"
wouldn't be sweeping the Continent of Europe, 2046
Isolation
does not answer . . . in politics for nations, 911
Isolationism, 910–911
retreat to i., 910
whimpering i. in foreign policy, 1042
Isolement
no confidence in the system of i., 911
Israel, 912–914
was planning to proclaim a Jewish state at midnight that day, 914
Italy, 915
break-down in I. followed by fascism, 2046
contempt upon the lips of the manhood of . . . I., 2089
Her Brain, her Soul, her Sword, 915
is doing everything possible to disunite us, 1721
I've
been to the other side of the mountain, 577
heard the owl, 577
looked over and I've seen the promised land, 572
seen the elephant, 577
See also I *and* I'm

J

Jackass
can kick a barn down, 268
impertinent letters from a j. like you, 302
Jail
sentence is no longer a dishonor, 221
Japan
is the one enemy, 2057
United States . . . was suddenly and deliberately attacked by . . . J., 2066
Jaw-Jaw
to j. is always better than to war-war, 1914
Jaws
of that which feeds them, 942
Jay
hasn't got any more principle than a Congressman, 305
Jay, John (1745–1829), 930
Jay Treaty, 792
Jealous
are the gods, 1781
Jefferson Day, 695
Jefferson Memorial, Washington, D.C.
inscriptions, 178, 397, 667, 1062, 1844
Jefferson, Thomas (1743–1826), 43, 65, 823, 1719
epitaph, 546
Statute of Virginia for Religious Freedom, 546, 669
Jenkins Hill, Washington, D.C., 161
Jeopardy
If the government is in j., 442
Jests
indebted to his memory for his j., 1175
Jesus Christ, 916–921, 1059
life and death of J. are those of a god, 920
nativity of the young Lord J., 921
when men believe the vote of Judas as good as that of J. C., 415
Jewel
give us that precious j. [liberty], and you may take every thing else, 1060
in the world comparable to learning, 1001
Jeweled
ideas, 129
Jewish
lawyers for Jews, 1015
Jews
Hitler attacked the J., 1749
Joan of Arc, Saint (c. 1412–1431), 1400
Job
we will finish the j., 2051
Jobs
stuck to their j., 1356
Jocund
vein of j. malice, 24
John F. Kennedy Center for the Performing Arts, inscriptions, 96–98, 104, 1632, 1753
John F. Kennedy International Airport, inscription, 1770
Johnson, Lyndon Baines (1908–1973), 1517–1518
Johnston, Sarah Bush. *See* Lincoln, Sarah Bush (Johnston).
Join
If you can't lick 'em, j. 'em, 257
Joint Chiefs of Staff, 1967
Joke
every time they make a j. it's a law, 271
every time they make a law it's a j., 271
Jokes
of Congress, 278
when he makes j., 1175

Jones, John Paul (1747-1792), 65
  funeral, 886
Journalism
  in America, the President reigns . . . and J. governs, 1524
  probing j., 1522
Journey
  of a thousand miles, 1533
Jove
  birth of Minerva from the brain of J., 813
Joy, 922–923
  comes from loving God and neighbor, 923
  deepest j. that can be felt by man, 1963
  I'm youth, I'm j., 2085
  is not the same as pleasure or happiness, 923
  is steady and abiding, like a fixed star, 923
  Love . . . changes worthless things to j., 1132
Joy's
  soul lies in doing, 12
Judas Iscariot
  men believe the vote of J. as good as that of Jesus Christ, 415
  was nothing but a low, mean premature Congressman, 306
Judge
  among the nations, 1956
  [historian should be] an impartial j., 1748
  history the final j. of our deeds, 7
  of a form of government by its general tendency, not by happy accidents, 736
  what to do, and how to do it, 936
  Young men are fitter to invent, than to j., 2084
Judged
  being j. not to have lived, 1088
  by one standard, 933
  society can be j. by entering its prisons, 1527
Judges, 924–930
  after they are seventy, 928
  are apt to be naif, simple-minded men, 925
  Constitution is what the j. say it is, 328
  English j. look like rats peeping through bunches of oakum, 927
  like people, may be divided roughly into four classes, 929
  should be withdrawn from their bench, 926
  who possess both head and a heart, 929
  with head but no heart, 929
  with heart but no head, 929
Judging
  its gifts by their covering, cast them away, 1467
Judgment, 931–937
  act to the best of my j., 300
  danger of the j., 605
  Final j. upon them can only be recorded by history, 253
  form a correct j. between them, 935
  high court of history sits in j., 1604
  historical j. upon a man, 1231
  in j. weak, 2092
  In the last analysis sound j. will prevail, 932
  let j. run down as waters, 931
  not measures of moral j., 627
  of death, 934
  on wrong conduct, 934
  One cool j., 937
  owes you, not his industry only, but his j., 280
  slight, 2092
  truly men of j., 1604
  vote as my conscience and j. dictates, 262
  which will then be pronounced on the uneducated, 505
Judicial
  sooner or later turn into a j. one, 1429
Judiciary, 938–944
  bodies were supposed to be the most helpless and harmless members of the government, 940
  constitution . . . is a mere thing of wax in the hands of the j., 330
  constitution of the federal j., 941
  great object of my fear is the federal j., 942
  independent of a king or executive alone, is a good thing, 943
  is the safeguard of our liberty and of our property, 328
  of the United States is the subtle corps of sappers and miners, 943
June
  what is so rare as a day in J., 2072
Juries
  can censor, suppress, and punish, 167
Just
  cause, 1909
  do that which is j., 956
  God who presides over the destinies of nations, 1061
Justice, 945–963
  among nations might prevail, 1733
  And then the j., / In fair round belly, 1158
  blow against freedom and decency and j., 1746
  cannot sleep forever, 1062
  cruelty, not j., 959
  degree to which j. is carried out, 957
  delayed is j. denied, 954
  deviate nothing from j., 956
  even-handed j. to all, 961
  God's j. cannot sleep forever, 1062
  in the life and conduct of the State, 963
  is itself the great standing policy of civil society, 948
  is never given; it is exacted, 960
  is truth in action, 952
  law secures equal j. to all alike, 1568
  make this thy dwelling place, 955
  Moderation in the pursuit of j. is no virtue, 581
  no republic where there is no j., 946
  no right where there is no j., 946
  principle or quality of dealing fairly with others, 1364
  single wrong to j., 958
  though her dome [doom] she does prolong, 962
  time will do us j., 1560
  virtues of courage, honor, j., 58
  voiceless, unseen, seeth thee when thou sleepest, 945
  when expelled from other habitations, 955
  without mercy if I fail to show mercy, 1490
Justice Department. *See* United States, Department of Justice.
Justly
  Do j., and to love mercy, 947

K

Kaiser Wilhelm. *See* Wilhelm II.
Katydid
  apostrophe to a k., 631
Kean College of New Jersey, inscription, 1799
Kennedy Center. *See* John F. Kennedy Center for the Performing Arts.

Kennedy International Airport. *See* John F. Kennedy International Airport.
Kennedy, Jacqueline (1929–), 2007
Kennedy, John Fitzgerald (1917–1963), 900
  presidential election debates, 508
Kennedy, Joseph Patrick (1888–1969), eulogy, 109
Kentucky, 964
  first rate land in K., 554
  like that boy in K., who stubbed his toe, 399
  politics—the damnedest in K., 964
Kick
  the government around, 743
Kicks
  lick the boot that k. them, 906
Kill
  let's k. all the lawyers, 1017
  Thou shalt not k., 1804–1805
  time to k., and a time to heal, 1810
Kills
  it [truth] k. us when we betray it, 1833
"Kind Words Can Never Die" (gospel hymn), 1727
King
  acknowledge no k., 1748
  conspiracies against their country or k., 1690
  do that which befits a k., 956
  half the zeal I serv'd my k., 705
  Heroin is my shepherd, 852
  refuses in any circumstances to fight for K. and Country, 2089
  strangle the last k. with the guts of the last priest, 965
King, Martin Luther, Jr. (1929–1968), 65
  eulogy by Robert F. Kennedy, 1864, 1995
Kingcraft, 1703
Kings, 965
  arguments that k. have made for enslaving the people, 1703
  had always been involving and impoverishing their people in wars, 1495
  having cut off the head of one of their k., 1598
  last arguments to which k. resort, 1921
  no rope to strangle k., 965
  of cabbages—and k., 1811
  of the earth, 1361
  power of K., 1453
  where k. have always stood, 1495
Kiss
  betrayed with a k., 1921
Kitchen
  can't stand the heat, get out of the k., 1513
Knew
  I k. something useful, 1606
Knot
  cut the k. rather than unravel it, 1448
Know
  all the people worth knowing in America, 1680
  better to k. nothing, 966
  not what he doesn't k. that bothers me, 966
  so much that ain't so, 966
  what you do k. and what you don't, 486
  where we are, 936
  wisdom to k. what we did not k., 1604
Knowing
  court doubt and darkness as the cost of k., 1127
  his limitations, 1097
  how to use the information you get, 486
  is the measure of man, 1086
  less that is false, 966
  more that is new, 966
Knowledge, 966–974
  being necessary to good government, 55
  Benefits of education and of useful k., 489
  catharsis of k. and conviction, 67
  comes, but wisdom lingers, 973
  establishment for the increase and diffusion of k., 972
  follow k. like a sinking star, 575
  in his k. that man has found his greatness and his happiness, 972
  increase and diffusion of k. among men, 1710
  investment in k., 967
  men who have neither the right nor the k., 747
  no learning so excellent . . . as k. of laws, 1001
  of her faults, 1460
  Perplexity is the beginning of k., 968
  rather than [want] of k., 2094
  should not be viewed as existing in isolated parts, 1663
  subtracting from the sum of human k., 970
  true k. is achieved, 1317
  will forever govern ignorance, 969
  without character, 1697
Knows
  what he k. for sure just ain't so, 966
Korea, 65, 1968

L

La Bruyère, Jean de (1645–1696), 362
Labels
  I don't believe in l., 1396
Labor, 975–981
  -doing machines, 981
  grace to l. for, 1471
  is prior to, and independent of, capital, 979
  is the superior of capital, 979
  long, 2022
  press down upon the brow of l. this crown of thorns, 27
  productive l., which is what gives money its value, 1203
  quid pro quo for l., 986
  robs l. of its bread, 1209
  -saving machines, 981
  system of l. where there can be a strike, 1776
  understand what American l. means, 987
  U.S. commissioner, 1541
Labor unions, 982–987
  have meant new dignity and pride to millions, 987
Labor's
  sheltered in l. house, 985
  supped at l. table, 985
Labors
  of thirtie or fortie honest and industrious men, 2031
  prevent the government from wasting the l. of the people, 727
  under coercion to satisfy another's desires, 1705
Lady
  without whom I should never have survived, 2006
Lafayette, Marie-Joseph-Paul-Yves-Roch-Gilbert du Motier de, 897
Laissez faire, 147, 414
Lamar, Lucius Quintus Cincinnatus (1825–1893), 1447
Lame
  Science without religion is l., 1662
Lamp
  I have . . . but one l. by which my feet are guided, 571
  I lift my l. beside the golden door, 1770
  of experience, 571
  one l. lights another, 1251
Lance
  lay a l. in rest, 4
Land

vast restructuring of our l. is essential, 442
which protect life, 994
Lawyers, 1014–1017
America is the paradise of l., 1014
are apt to speak as though the legislature were omnipotent, 1040
let's kill all the l., 1017
Men are men before they are l., 1150
produce good l. for Americans, 1015
Lazy
[rules are] for the l. to hide behind, 1649
Lead
State must follow and not l., 1004
their country by a short route to chaos, 1764
Leader
atheist could not be as great a military l., 1729
follow the people for I am their l., 1021
must help create that [moral] tide, 1025
Leaders
appear sporadically, 1030
great Presidents were l. of thought, 1504
[have] an obligation to be fair and keep in perspective what we are and what we hope to be, 418
of the republic, 1018
political l. replacing moral imperatives with a Southern strategy, 444
should keep their ears to the ground, 1554
who are detected in that somewhat ungainly posture, 1554
Leadership, 1018–1025
place of moral l., 1504
Leads
man who l., 1024
who l. us is less important than what l. us, 107
League of Nations
72, 871, **1026–1027**, 1346
Leagues
two loving hearts divide, 2034
Leap
in the dark to our success, 1786
one giant l. for mankind, 1738
Learn
give up every preconceived notion . . . or you shall l. nothing, 583
never cease to l., 1799
some men l. quicker than others, 301
Learned
Institutions, 496
Learning
how incapable must Man be of l. from experience, 574
Liberty and L., each leaning on the other, 497
no jewel in the world comparable to l., 1001
seats of l., 66
Lebanon
I have my L. and its people, 1366
You have your L. and its people, 1366
Lee, Robert Edward (1807-1870), 65, 223, 820
Left
criminal l., 154
nondemocratic l., 153
Legal
Men's indignation . . . is more excited by l. wrong than by violent wrong, 909
plunder, 993
process is an essential part of the democratic process, 1005
revised l. structures [are necessary], 147
victims of l. prostitution, 1210
Legend of the Dogwood, 918
Legislate
Don't hurry to l., 2025
be in a better temper to l., 510
Legislation
Art of L., 481
cash on the barrel for every piece of l., 986
committee will not permit doubts as to constitutionality . . . to block the suggested l., 337
foolish l. is a rope of sand, 1004
Give administration a chance to catch up with l., 2025
In l. we all do a lot of "swapping tobacco across the lines," 260
is a series of compromises, 257
is the result of compromise, 251
to apply the principle of equal pay for equal work, 550
we pour l. into the senatorial saucer to cool it, 294
Legislative
greatest l. body in the world, 261
no longer listened to in the l. halls, 222
power, 324
power to the executive, at the expense of the l. branch, 1044
Legislator
best l. is the one who votes for all appropriations and against all taxes, 299
is an indispensable guardian of our freedom, 1030
people is the true l., 1029
understands that no measure of importance could be passed without this give-and-take policy, 257
who has given stability and continuity, 1030
See also Politician
Legislators, 1028–1032
are elected by voters, 1032
represent people, 1032
wisdom of patriots and l., 839
See also **Politicians**
Legislature, 1033–1041
[is the] creature of pressure groups, 1039
[is the] creature of the people, 1039
may . . . lend its potential weight to the cause of virtue and happiness, 786
No man's life, liberty or property are safe while the L. is in session, 1041
plural l. is as necessary to good Government as a single Executive, 1036
right of electing members of the L., 1904
should be divided, 1036
vested the question of war in the L., 1931
were omnipotent, 1040
Wisdom is the specific Quality of the L., 1036
Legislatures
are ultimate guardians of the liberties and welfare of the people, 1037
some l. that bring higher prices, 274
Legitimate
government, 779
object of government, 780
Lend
a Hand, 1434
him money that he can't pay back, 385
Length
of service, 285, 301
Lenin, Vladimir Ilyich (Ulyanov) (1870-1924), 244, 917
Less
government which is likely to perform l., 781
you are entitled to no l., 513
You should never wish to do l., 469
Let
them eat cake, 1347

Like
  All the things I l. to do are either immoral, illegal, or fattening, 846
  being cheated by an equal, 909
  being compelled by a superior, 909
  a big baby, 775
  a fire bell in the night, 1700
  a fixed star, 923
  a flash of lightning, 923
  never met a man I dident l., 1155
  People l. Government, 710
Likes
  do as he l., 646
Limit
  woman's sphere as though it had a l., 2012
Limited
  war with Red China, 1967
Lincoln, Abraham (1809–1865), 65, 801, 1024, **1107–1110**, 1425, 1487, 1853
  death of, 718
Lincoln, Nancy (Hanks) (1783–1818), 1225
Lincoln, Sarah Bush (Johnston), 1225
Lincoln Memorial, Washington, D.C., 1853
  inscription, 1107
Link
  one rusted l., 1695
Lion
  heart, 1276
Listen
  to the Exhortation of the Dawn, 1106
Listens
  Nobody l., 266
  to the deniers and mockers, 60
Literati
  battle between the l. and the Philistines, 167
Literature
  liberal views exclude no branch of science or l., 1663
  ransack the l. of all countries, 530
  study the works of art and l., 658
Little
  Americans, 72
  do so much for so many on so l., 449
  done so much with so l., 2060
"Little American" speech, 72
Littlefield, Charles (1851–1915), 115
Liturgy
  opening accents of a grand new l., 379
Live
  by bread only, 1112
  henceforth, you will l. the hard way, 1605
  his dreams—not in fear, but in hope, 54
  how to l., 1222
  in infamy, 2066
  not to exist, 1118
  Only those are fit to l., 1121
  skim milk, 111
  sweetly, patiently, lovingly, purely, till the sun goes down, 1104
  that when we come to die even the undertaker will be sorry, 1125
  together for a period, and then go our separate ways, 1520
  underground with the moles, 125
  without our lives, 1293
Lived
  being judged not to have l., 1088
  not l. in vain, 1323, 1469
  whether my country is the better for my having l., 1679
  you have l. the easy way, 1605
Lives
  Every one l. by selling something, 1123
  of others, 136
  those who gamble with men's l. should not stake their own, 1953
Living, 1111–1127
  from the dead, 482
  land of the l., 1136
  like drunken sailors, 309
  partnership . . . between those who are l., 1715
  process of l. is the process of having stress, 1122
  will envy the dead, 1257
Livy (Titus Livius) (59 B.C.–A.D. 17), 1283
Loaf
  half a l. is better than a whole l., 252
  half a l. was better than no bread, 252
Lobbyist, 1128
  President is the only l., 1516
Lobbyists, 1128
  are in many cases expert technicians, 1128
Loiterers
  idle l., 2031
London
  wiping out the whole of L., 864
Loneliness, 1129
  that makes the loudest noise, 1129
Lonesome
  place against the sky, 1108
Long run, 1367
  human rights and property rights are . . . in the l. r. identical, 867
  in the l. r. every Government, 710
  l. r. doesn't matter, 868
  l. r. is a misleading guide to current affairs, 693
  People don't eat in the l. r.,—they eat every day, 1336
  people, in the l. r. . . . do more to promote peace than our governments, 1321
  worth of a state, in the l. r., is the worth of the individuals composing it, 1760
Longer
  I live, the more convincing proofs I see of this truth, 703
Longevity
  has its place, 572
Longfellow, Henry Wadsworth (1807–1882), 65
Look
  up and not down, . . . forward and not back . . . out and not in, 1434
Lord
  is always on the side of the right, 704
  make me a channel of your peace, 1466
  make me an instrument of thy peace, 1466
  What doth the L. require of thee, 947
  See also **God**
Lorna Doone, 515
Los Angeles, California, 1974
Lose
  how to l., 1222
  If we l., there will be nobody to care, 1991
  rather l. in a cause that will some day win, 1994
Loser
  what makes a good l.? Practice, 1992
Loss
  real sin is taxing a l., 138
Lost
  as much as we gained by prying into that matter, 974
  because its [liberty's] possessors failed to stretch forth a saving hand, 1077
  here in America, 67
  Horse was l., 1240
  not that you won or l., 1993
  Rider was l., 1240
  Shoe was l., 1240
  was l., and is found, 635

going underground to escape the consequences of his own folly, 125
has only a thin layer of soil between himself and starvation, 31
he seems / In all his lineaments, 919
his strength, his possibilities, his reason, 1743
human nature in m., 1148
I joked about every prominent m. of my time, 1155
If m. could be crossed with the cat it would improve the m., 164
indebted to no m., 1492
is a born predestined idealist, 869
is a piece of the continent, 134
is a social animal, 911
is about to be an automaton, 1144
is also, and pre-eminently, intelligent and free, 1152
is by nature a political animal, 1390
is not made for defeat, 398
is not made to be trusted for life, 940
is the touchstone of value, 901
let no more be heard of confidence in m., 331
must first care for his own household before he can be of use to the state, 628
my own m., 1491
neither m. nor nation can prosper unless . . . thought is . . . taken for the future, 312
never met a m. I dident like, 1155
no indispensable m., 1153
no m. is an island, 134
no M. worth having is true to his Wife, 2009
No particular m. is necessary to the state, 1151
nothing better becomes a well-bred m. than agriculture, 28
Nothing is worth the making if / It does not make the m., 1149
of action, 2–3
one small step for a m., 1738
one useless m. is called a disgrace, 273
only m. is vile, 1147
people's m., 1491
proper function of m. is to live, not to exist, 1118
proud m., 1159
Remember, thou, too, art a m., 1224
shall know bread and peace, 1463
tame the savageness of m., 1864
This was a m., 1160
Treat him as a m., 119
What then is the American, this new m.?, 48
who fights the bull, 14
who had no feet, 1682
who is actually in the arena, 10
who leads a great, free, democratic nation, 1024
who rises to power / From one suspender, 1452
who spends himself in a worthy cause, 10
who was tarred and feathered and carried out of town on a rail, 1498
whose . . . statue [should be] placed in every college, 6
will not merely endure: he will prevail, 1145
wine drinks the m., 34
your m., 1491

Manchesters
and Birminghams, 1847

Maneuvers
going on m.—yes, only on m., 2053

Manhood
begins when we have in any way made truce with Necessity, 1143

Mania
bank m., 101

Maniacs
we commit honest m. to Bedlam, 926

Mankind
blessing and not a curse to m., 1661
chief end of human effort . . . should be usefulness to m., 502
I am involved in m., 134
it [atomic energy] belongs to all m., 1254
might enjoy freedom and inherit peace, 1733
natural rights of m., 1058
not for America alone, but for all m., 56
one giant leap for m., 1738
sacred rights of m., 865
which began in a cave, 1162

Manners
were their own business, 81

Man's
any m. death diminishes me, 134
house is his castle, 859

Manufacturers
Men are men before they are . . . m., 1150

Many
appeal to the passions of the m., 314
do so much for so m. on so little, 449
so much owed to so m., 2052

Marble
If we work upon m., it will perish, 1198

March
triumphal, 220
we are on the m., 218

Marching
our God is m. on, 220

Margin
is narrow, 1902

Market
America is a free m. for people who have something to say, 169
get itself accepted in the competition of the m., 1835
limited patterns which the m. offers, 258

Marriage, 1163–1169
I want a good m., 74
triumph of hope over experience, 1167
young man not yet, 1163

Married
famous men and the women they m. when they were young, 1971

Marry
elderly man [should] not [m.] at all, 1163
every woman should m., and no man, 1164
men m. because they are tired, 1169
when a man should m., 1163
women [m.] because they are curious, 1169

Marshall, John (1755–1835), 939

Martial
virtues must be the enduring cement, 526

Martyrdom
opportunities for m., 1579
spirit should be ready to devote itself to m., 676

Marx, Karl (1818–1883), 242, 244, 917

Marxist
I am not a M., 242

Masks
affair of m. and mystification, 1943

Masochism
spirit of national m. prevails, 1876

Masquerade
Peace itself is War in M., 1960

Mass
bonds of m. misery, 623
great m. of the people, 1620

Merit
ready appreciation of m. and character, 281
Message to Garcia, 6
Messenger
There's the King's M., 950
a very well paid m. boy doing your errands, 298
who brings bad news, 1243
Metal
sleeping in the mountainside, 1542
Metaphor
of the melting pot, 49
Meteor
superb m., every atom . . . in magnificent glow, 1118
Meter
electrical energy too cheap to m., 1256
Method
goes far to prevent Trouble, 146
Mexican War (1845–1848), 734
Middle
age, 2016
excellent, 536
Mighty
sit in the seats of the m., 699
Military
instruction a regular part of collegiate education, 1187
leader, 1729
manliness to which the m. mind so faithfully clings, 526
order and property would be saved by a strong m. government, 421
preparedness, 493
rejects include tomorrow's hard core unemployed, 1189
spirit evaporated, 1647
War is much too serious a matter to be entrusted to the m., 1954
Military affairs, 1176–1185
Military-industrial complex, 1177
Military service, 1186–1193
Millionaire
one m. and many beggars, 39
Millionaires
eight m. and one plumber, 1510
Millions
fate of unborn M., 1627
for defense, 804
yet unborn, 1630
Milton, John (1608–1674), 1574
Mimesis
withdrawal of m. on the part of the majority, 227
Mind, 1194–1198
Almighty God hath created the m. free, 667
aristocrat in morals as in m., 188
at work for itself, 1282
can invent peace with justice, 1959
creations of our m., 1661
cultivated m. is the guardian genius of Democracy, 1196
emancipation of m., 639
he who can alter my state of m., 818
improving the m. and morals of society, 1924
is contented and happy, 487
is shackled or made impotent through fear, 671
it [hanging] concentrates his m. wonderfully, 369
Let them m. their own affairs, 1008
light over the public m., 496
military m., 526
of man is never satisfied, 1195
progress of the human m., 178
state of m., 1436
To educate a man in m. and not in morals, 500
to preserve the freedom of the human m., 676
tyranny over the m. of man, 1844
War is an invention of the human m., 1959
[Youth] is a state of m., 2099
Minds
business of little m. to shrink, 356
chance favors only those m. which are prepared, 174
curiosity of young m., 487
hobgoblin of little m., 1194
men's immortal m., 1198
narrow m., 1663
of your young men, 2086
wars begin in the m. of men, 1966
Mine
personnel m., 2070
vehicular m., 2070
Minerva
birth of M. from the brain of Jove, 813
Minimal
more m. the art, 95
Minimum
for the wages of women, 2013
of jolt, 1837
Minister
from the devil himself, if he wore a crown, we should receive a m., 614
Ministers
business of m. . . . to consult . . . the people, 794
Minority
failure of creative power in the m., 227
Hates a m., 1141
rich, who are always a m., 1139
should be ready to yield to a majority, 414
To protect the weak and the m., 786
Miracles
happen all the time, 69
Miraculous
takes a little longer, 1183
Mirrors
and blue smoke, 1415
blue smoke and m., 1415
only way you can do that is with m., 1411
Mischievous
position on almost every public question was . . . m., 1274
Misery
affluent m., 17
annual expenditure twenty pounds ought six, result m., 380
bonds of mass m., 623
first is but a splendid m., 1493
I saw, and a great part of which I was, 1951
of old age, 21
Physical m. is great everywhere out here [Africa], 1609
plague America with m. in the name of liberty, 1047
produce that m. which he strives in vain to relieve, 566
sumptuous m., 16
trafficking in human m., 832
Misfortune
Success is the necessary m. of life, 1785
Misfortunes
strength to endure the m. of others, 1773
Missiles, 407
Mississippi, 1985
Mistake
Biggest damfool m. I ever made, 924
sin to believe evil of others, but it is seldom a m., 562
Mistakes
face reality and our past m., 1836
Mistress
in my own [house], 2014
Mistresses
your Lordship's principles, or your Lordship's m., 372
Mitchell, John Newton (1913–   ), 1394
Mob
are called to suppress the free expression of thought, 1642
infuriated and degraded m., 46

only difference between a m. and a trained army is organization, 1375
Mobs
of great cities, 1337
should . . . not depend on government, 795
Mock
patriotism, 1641
Mocked
power which dominates in the United States does not understand being m., 362
Mockery
a sham, a pretense—the sheerest m., 671
of a trial, 916
Mocking bird speech, 295
Moderately
good is not so good as it ought to be, 1199
Moderation, 1199
in principle, is a species of vice, 1199
in temper, is always a virtue, 1199
in the pursuit of justice is no virtue, 581
Modernization
see the processes of m. in motion, 182
Moles
force us to live underground with the m., 125
Molière (*pseudonym of* Jean Baptiste Poquelin, 1622–1673), 362
Moments
of unutterable fulfillment, 922
Mona Lisa
painted by a club, 898
Monarchy
abuses of m., 1597
everything republican which was not m., 1597
gradually transforms itself into a republic, 1598
Republic or a M., 1593
virtually and substantially a m., 425
Mondale, Walter F. (1928–), 1611
Monday's
child is fair in face, 200
Money, 1200–1209
appropriation of public m. always is perfectly lovely until some one is asked to pay the bill, 797
blind with the lust for m., 832
buying nothing without the m. in our pockets to pay for it, 358
Credit is to m. what m. is to articles of merchandise, 359
duty to make m. and still more m., 1207
I saved my m., 2071
is power, 1201
patronage of m., 803
paying our own m. for unexplained projects, 802
people's m., 801
power to make m., 1207
pretty soon you're talking about real m., 800
spending other people's m., 805
spending the public m., 799
value of m., 1203
we do spend on Government, 807
Money's
get their m. worth, except for these [taxes], 1789
Moneys
dispensation of the public m., 802
Mongrel
banner invented for a league, 1026
Monied
aristocracy, 101
Monkeys
might write all the books in the British Museum, 2076
Monogamists
who don't monog, 1168
Monroe Doctrine, 629–630
Monument
pedestal waiting for a m., 161
The Republic is his m., 830
Monuments
of man's pride, 822
Moon
first radio message from, 1737
first words spoken on, 1738
landing a man on the m., 1740
means invented of journeying to the m., 1744
See also **Space exploration**
Moral
chains upon their own appetites, 1051
complaisance, 258
courage to enter the m. conflict, 1212
dependence upon relief induces a spiritual and m. disintegration, 1984
equivalent of war, 526
factor involved, 1085
imagination is missing, 442
imperatives with a Southern strategy, 444
invisible molecular m. forces, 822
not measures of m. judgment, 627
period of m. crisis, 1211
place of m. leadership. 1504
power is to physical as three parts out of four, 1213
progress, 1663
sanction and support wherever she thinks that justice is, 533
standards and values, 1018
standards of our society, 1802
test of government, 724
This struggle may be a m. one, 443
tide of the moment, 1025
till all are m., 1350
Morale
is to material as is the ratio of three to one, 1213
Morality, 1210–1214
and knowledge, being necessary to good government, 55
commerce without m., 1697
fundamental principle of m., 1214
I know but one code of m. for men, 667
Morally
and intellectually superior to all men, 1349
no matter how m. wrong he may be, 982
not progressed m., 1538
treasonable, 1507
wrong, 1640
Morals
aristocrat in m., 188
have need of the laws, 1011
improving the mind and m. of society, 1924
Rome's decline lay in her . . . m., 1646
To educate a man in mind and not in m., 500
More
government which attempts m., 781
No man can do m., 513
will sometimes be demanded of you than is reasonable, 1119
You cannot do m., 469
Mormons, 1168
Morning
day is a perpetual m., 1808
shall always come, 1517
Mortal
all men m. but themselves, 1223
power, 865
remember that thou art m., 1224
Mortality, 1215–1224
Mortifying
Every proceeding respecting myself has been so thoroughly m., 1626
Mother
fear is the m. of safety, 595

Honor thy father and thy m., 1804
My m., drunk or sober, 345
of Exiles, 1770
owe to my angel m., 1225
a word that means the world to me, 1226
Mother-power
sheer waste of m., 1165
Mother's
ashes, 1067
Mothers, 1225–1226
Motive
right m., 1909
which impels them, 1307
Motives, 1227–1231
not inquire too curiously into m., 1228
value world sets upon m., 1230
Motto
E pluribus unum, 1867
I heartily accept the m., 753
Liberty and Union, now and for ever, one and inseparable, 1855
toward the Congress, 264
Mottos
Atlanta Journal, 1244
Christopher Society, 448
Lend a Hand Society, 1434
Scripps-Howard newspapers, 971
U.S. Army Corps of Engineers, 1183
Mount Everest, 1741
Mountain
He's allowed me to go up to the m., 572
I've been to the other side of the m., 577
Mountains
From the big dizzy m., 33
Mourn
foolish and wrong to m. the men who have died, 1730
Let me not m. for the men who have died, 1730
time to m., 1810
Mourning
Don't waste any time m., 984
Mouse-trap
make a better m., 1780
Movements
many of the world's great m. . . . have flowed from the work of a single man, 902
Movie
stars, 1406
Much
do so m. for so many on so little, 449
done so m. with so little, 2060
so m. owed by so many to so few, 2052
tho' m. is taken, m. abides, 575
Mulish
obstructionism in domestic policy, 1042
Multiply
we m. whenever we are mown down, 1065
Multitude
vicious, reckless m., 46
Murphy's Law, 1232
Muses
may the "sweet M." . . . bear me away, 376
Music
divinest m. has not been conceived, 111
of our own opinions, 678
step to the m. which he hears, 905
Mussolini, Benito Amilcare Andrea (1883–1945), 1372
Mustard
faith as a grain of m. seed, 592
Myself
If I am not for m., 1673
if I am only for m., 1673
Mysteries
love for the m. of nature, 1664
of the future, 41
Mystery
and concealment, 1670
inside an enigma, 1652
of sex, 1684
Mystification
affair of masks and m., 1943

N

Nabobs
nattering n. of negativism, 1553
Nail
Drive a n. home, 2032
a drop of water to the wall, 1394
want of a n., 1240
Naked
to mine enemies, 705
Name
I am become a n., 575
of the Lord thy God in vain, 1804
Napoleon I (Napoleon Bonaparte) (1769–1821), 334, 406, 820, 1154, 1559
Narratives
fancy in his n., 1175
Nation, 1233–1239
accept the first defeat in its [America's] proud 190-year history, 1885
bedrooms of the n., 1685
can [not] prosper unless . . . thought is . . . taken for the future, 312
character of an independent n., 1344
claim to be a great n., 628
Cleanse the body of this n., 1235
conscience of the n. must be roused, 1575
distress that has infested this entire N., 1342
future of this N., 2096
hope to be a happy N., 1476
hypocrisy of the n. must be exposed, 1575
I am the n., 65
is burdened with the heavy curse on those who come afterwards, 697
is living within its income, 809
keep a n. strong and free, 1239
meaning, so blessed by God, 1364
necessities of a n. . . . equal to its resources, 1791
never a n. great until it came to the knowledge that it had nowhere in the world to go for help, 831
new in spirit, 1617
no n. is rich enough to pay for both war and civilization, 1919
of employees cannot be free, 1081
of many nationalities, many races, many religions, 1482
of mere hucksters, 226
one N. under God, 1363
one's own n. stands for everything that is good and noble, 933
organizing a n. in the midst of war and crisis, 1622
political parties . . . serve the interests of the whole n., 1376
propriety of the n. must be startled, 1575
shall not lift up sword against n., 1956
spoke to a N., 2014
territory does not make a n., 51
that cannot preserve itself ought to die, 1237
that loves liberty, 1081
This N. was founded, 219
three things which make a n. great, 815
way the n. is moving, 658
which attacks and occupies foreign territory, 913
which makes the final sacrifice for life and freedom, 660
will not only of Parliament but of the whole n., 1276

O

O, means only that she's growing old, 1226
Oak
nourishing the mighty o., 1437
Oakland, California, 148
Oasis
in the desert, 766
Oath
Athenian Ephebic o., 100
Oath of Office, 1260
Object
of good government, 778
of government, 780, 785
Objection
every imaginable o. seems to be obviated, 512
Objectivity
lack of o., 933
Objects
at which all political institutions aim, 782
of all legitimate government, 779
Oblivion
blessed act of o., 1294
Obloquy
lurid glare of o., 258
Obscenity, 1261
definition of o., 1261
Obstructionism
mulish o. in domestic policy, 1042
Ocean
part of the heaving surface of the o., 1102
without the awful roar of its many waters, 443
Offense
to our friends and Allies, 40
Office
not man [seek] the o., 1571
perpetual o. seekers, 1563
sanctifies the holder of it, 1444
should seek the man, 1571
stay in o. too long, 1569
Official
limits of my o. capacity, 117
no o. . . . can prescribe what shall be orthodox in politics, 647
nobody counts for anything except . . . an o., 1716
Officialdom
arrogance of o. should be tempered, 795
Officials
Bad o. are elected by good citizens who do not vote, 1905
elective o. shall not lead but merely register the popular will, 1018
political o. must necessarily direct its [war's] general course, 1926
See also **Government officials**
Ohio
a mistake has been made in recent years, 285
Oise-Aisne Cemetery, inscription, 1733
Old
age isn't so bad, 20
as your despair, 2099
as your doubt, 2099
as your fear, 2099
disreputable, vigorous, unhonoured, and disorderly o. age, 24
girl called Anno Domini, 1569
growing o., 25
house in which to pass his o. age, 86
last to lay the o. aside, 2021
man had learned in seven years, 2003
men know young men are fools, 607
men plant trees they will never sit under, 694
misery of o. age, 21
not letting men grow o. in their jobs, 744
order standing, 1837
people grow o. by deserting their ideals, 2099
possible for o. people not to fear the young, 19
systems and the Word, 1838
too o. to cry, but it hurt too much to laugh, 399
young men think o. men are fools, 607
"Old Soldiers Never Die" (song), 1727
Old Testament
[Watergate] is like the O. T., 1981
See also Bible
Older
bad example by people much o., 2089
men declare war, 1923
one becomes wiser and more foolish, 23
order changeth, 181
Olney Corollary, 630
Olympic games, 80
Once
upon a time all the animals in the Zoo decided that they would disarm, 440
What has o. happened will invariably happen again, 855
One
All for o., 1862
blaze of blinding light, 1866
cool judgment, 937
for all, 1862
giant leap for mankind, 1738
great poem of New England, 1241
I am only o., 899
man can make a difference, 900
man with courage makes a majority, 900
nothing o. man or o. woman can do, 902
river born of many streams, 1866
small step for a man, 1738
Solitary Life, 916
useless man is called a disgrace, 273
with the law is a majority, 1138
One-party
government, 1489
One-third
of the world is asleep, 2037
struggle with the o., 1620
Only
freedom which deserves the name, 650
I am o. one, 899
those are fit to live, 1121
Open
My life has been as an o. book, 519
Opera
ain't over till the fat lady sings, 1817
Opinion
absence of debate unrestricted utterance leads to the degradation of o., 677
difference of o. is not a difference of principle, 1596
error of o. may be tolerated, 1267
foolish and the dead alone never change their o., 1271
God's o. that life should go on, 1100
legitimate interference of collective o., 652
marries old o. to new fact, 1837
matters of o., 647
of the people, 1245
own o. universally prevalent, 2094
public o. polls to tell me what is right, 1490
right to his o., 1262
sacrifices it to your o., 280
that all who can should vote, 1900
Unawed by O., 549
unbiased o., 280
voicing your o., 1747
Opinions, 1262–1275
as many o. as there are experts, 1273
as you and I must have five years hence, 1028
change o. even on important subjects, which I once

Oyster
When God made the o., 70

P

Pabulum
every man's hand is out for p., 708
Pace
not keep p. with his companions, 905
that all may keep an even P., 44
Pacific Ocean, 2057
Pacifists
talk against war, 1642
Paid
sign that he expects to be p. for it, 1309
Pain
accept p. as a condition of existence, 1127
makes man think, 2002
Paine, Thomas (1737–1809), 65
Palestine, 914
Pamper
him and cater to him too much, 83
Pan-American Exposition, Buffalo, New York (1901), 1470, 1537
Panama
here, P. and its poverty, 834
Pantheon, 1248
Paradigm
Let music for peace / Be the p., 1856
Paradise
what would be left for p., 1084
Paradox
What a p. if our own cleverness in science should force us to live underground, 125
Parasite
I won't be a p., 656
living on the flesh of others, 766
you are a p., 766
Pardon
a man who shot him on purpose, 1231
Parent
aim of p. and teacher, 501
Parents
Children begin by loving their p., 198
take . . . p. from their children, 1193
who merely gave them birth, 482
Paris
Bostonians, when they die, if they are good, go to P., 75
Good Americans, when they die, go to P., 75
In P. they just simply opened their eyes and stared, 88
man who accompanied Jacqueline Kennedy to P., 2007
Parley
rearm in order to p., 401
Parliament
by its very nature cannot do work, 1034
can do talk only, 1034
he is going to stand for P., 1397
hear . . . unlimited quantities of foolish talk, 1033
not fit they should sit as a p. any longer, 1035
of man, 2038
parties in P., 175
there all the Lords must judge, 892
when a member [of P.] resumes his seat, 1280
will not only of P., 1276
will train you to talk, 1033
Parliamentarism
British p., 414
Parliamentary
majestic p. phrase, 678
party government and P. government, 1377
Parliaments
all the p. that ever sat, 916
give it [power] to the p., 1044
We assemble p. . . . to have the benefit of their collected wisdom, 608
Parricide
lift its p. hands against freedom and science, 676
Parrots
will now begin to chatter, 1913
Part
of all that I have met, 575
of the main, 134
of which I was, 1951
with him when he goes wrong, 1639
Parties
both major p. today seek to serve the national interest, 1381
common interests of the p., 618
Congress provided an appropriation for the . . . expense of each of the great national p., 152
do not maintain themselves, 73
in Parliament, 175
two great political p. in this country, 1378
two great political p. of the nation, 1376
two p. which divide the state, 1379
See also **Political parties**
Partners
in adversity, 1667
in prosperity, 1667
stronger we are, the better p. we shall be, 531
Partnership
by definition, serves both partners, 1667
Society is a p., 1715
Party
anxious politicians of his p., 1313
chance for this p. to have been of service, 419
come to the aid of the p., 1388
government and Parliamentary government, 1377
I am not a member of any organized p.—I am a Democrat, 429
influenced by p. feeling, 519
leader, 1512
militant p. wedded to a principle, 107
necessary to have p. organization, 1375
never intend to belong to any other p., 1599
of Conservatism and that of Innovation, 1379
of freedom and progress, 1599
opinions, 1900
prejudice, 119
responsibility we owe not to our p., 1381
serves his p. best who serves his country best, 1380
Sometimes p. loyalty asks too much, 1382
stick to your p., 1373
that is out of Power, 1385
that wants to see an America in which people can still get rich, 1384
we can make this thing into a P., instead of a Memory, 430
which gives the best promise, 1670
without the yoke of any p. on me, 262
zealous labors of a political p., 1380
See also **Political parties**
Pass
from this body to another, 1752
I shall not p. this way again, 453
this, too, shall p. away, 1221
Passed
away, and are nowhere, 1301
Passengers
on a little space ship, 477
Passion

is the measure of the holder's lack of rational conviction, 1275
life is action and p., 1088
opinions that are held with p., 1275
Passions
and interests of men, 1456
forge their fetters, 1051
intentionally to arouse and inflame p., 524
interesting too strongly the public p., 335
love of our country soar above all minor p., 1305
Passive
non-elastic sand-bag, 1119
Past, 1291–1293
cannot remember the p. are condemned to repeat it, 1292
dogmas of the quiet p., 1300
future he [Emerson] predicted becomes a p., 1297
glory of his p., 1145
horrors of the p., 1294
How will we know it's us without our p., 1293
injuries of the p., 1294
judgment of the future as well as the p., 1604
may rob the present of much joy and much mystery, 1093
no way of judging the future but by the p., 571
not even God can change the p., 1291
preserve what the p. has had to say for itself, 1295
reformer who does not remember the p. will find himself condemned to repeat it, 853
what's p. is prologue, 1296
Past and future, 571, **1294–1297,** 1838
Past and present, 1093, **1298–1301**
Past's
blood-rusted key, 1838
Patent
system, 1535
Patents
U.S. commissioner, 1532
Paternalism
lessons of p. ought to be unlearned, 777
Path
Our p. emerges for a while, 460
world will make a beaten p. to his door, 1780
Paths
of glory, 1216
to international peace, 910
Patience
makes a woman beautiful, 2016
Patriot
devoted p., 766
good p., 1765
sunshine p., 1821
volunteer, 1722
Patriotic
art of lying for one's country, 437
feeling which thinks nothing worth a war, 1934
principles, 535
Patriotism, 1302–1312
exalt the just pride of P., 1312
from the standpoint of American p. one is as important as the other, 883
is the first, last and middle range of fools, 1306
is the first [resort of a scoundrel], 1306
is the last refuge of a scoundrel, 1306
mock p., 1641
sometimes requires of men to act exactly contrary, 1307
that puts country ahead of self, 1311
that stands for love of country, 1302
that stands for love of people, 1302
watchword of true p., 1641
which is not short, frenzied outbursts of emotion, 1311
Patriots
wisdom of p. and legislators, 839
Patronage, 1313–1314
for my constituents, 298
of money, 803
Search out some powerful p., 656
Paul
robs Peter to pay P., 1796
stoned for the sake of Truth, 1833
Paulus, Lucius Aemilius (229?-160 B.C.), 1928, 1941
Pay
any price, bear any burden, 1066
Pays
the best interest, 967
Peace, 1315–1329
alleged imperfections of the p., 910
-at-any-price, 58
blessings of p., 1324
build a world of p., 493
Can say p. / When we mean war, 1856
commerce, and honest friendship with all nations, 619
cultivate p. and friendship with all nations, 618
giving them p. and rest at last, 432
good will toward men, 1315
great step towards p., 440
honorable p., 1624
the human dress, 1464
If we desire to secure p., 410
In P.: Good Will, 1958
in p. the sons did bury their fathers, 1955
in the minds of men that . . . p. must be constructed, 1966
in this world, 1317
in war as well as in p., 1367
inherit p., 1733
instrument of thy p., 1466
international capacity to keep p., 1324
is a virtue that springs from force of character, 1328
is an unstable equilibrium, 1320
is not mere absence of war, 1328
itself is War in Masquerade, 1960
just and lasting p. among ourselves, and with all nations, 1325
keep the p. outside its own borders, 1326
last hopes for p. and freedom, 1140
Let music for p. / Be the paradigm, 1856
life so dear, or p. so sweet, 1061
man shall know bread and p., 1463
may obstruct the paths to international p., 910
means of preserving p., 411
no p. lies in the future which is not hidden in this present little instant, 1467
not enough just to be for p., 1327
not just for Christians but for the whole of humanity, 1877
of the world, 233
of the world has been preserved, not by statesmen, but by capitalists, 1319
on earth, good will toward men, 662
on earth p., good will toward men, 1315
Only a p. between equals can last, 1329
Open covenants of p., 1027
p.,—but there is no p., 1061
p.; when there is no p., 1316
people are going to do more to promote p., 1321
people want p. so much that one of these days governments had better get out of the way, 1321

politicians . . . swear eternal devotion to the ends of p. and security, 631
possible for our children, . . . to live in a world of p., 54
program of the world's p., 1027
restless p. that's shadowed by the threat of violence, 558
right is more precious than p., 2049
safeguards of p., 1931
safety, and concord, 1323
Science and P. will triumph over Ignorance and War, 1963
side by side in majesty, in justice and in p., 41
Sleep sweetly, tender heart, in p., 377
strong defense is the surest way to p., 404
they [wars] are far better than certain kinds of p., 1965
time of war, and a time of p., 1810
Universal p. is declared, 509
unspeakable and perfect, 1109
until its condition shall be made less tolerable than that of war itself, 1924
useful pursuits of p., 840
was better than war, 1955
will never be won if men reserve for war their greatest efforts, 1961
will not be kept, 1861
with all nations, . . . our object, 1322
with Germany in 1917, 2046
with justice, 1959
years of war for every year of p., 1957
See also **War and peace**

Peaceful
economic competition, 1713
intentions, 440

Pearl Harbor, attack on (1941), 65, 2066

Peculiar
something p. in the temper of the House, 1824

Pecuniary reward, 1561

Pedestal
waiting for a monument, 161

Peerless
We are p., 1349

Pen
earned my living by p. and tongue, 1276

Pendulum
will swing back, 1418

Pennsylvania, 65, 1620

Penny
I bargained with Life for a p., 1099
no; no; not a p., 804

People, 1330–1347
are calling us, 1342
are cheated out of the best ingredients in their Government, 1931
are going to do more to promote peace than our governments, 1321
are not an interruption of our business, 1345
are our business, 1345
are responsible for the acts of their government, 1346
are the natural, lawful and competent judges of this matter [a free government], 774
are to be free, 1576
are too damned dumb, 76
ask other p. to follow you, 1023
bestrode the necks of the p., 1703
can not be all, and always, well informed, 1623
committed to them in trust from the P., 1453
common p. know what they want, 423
common-looking p., 1339
consult the inclinations of the p., 794
deserve to get it [what they want] good and hard, 423
don't eat in the long run, 1336
dumb p. criticize something they do not understand, 76
enthusiasm of the p., 757
favor the policy of economy . . . to save p., 798
follow the p., for I am their leader, 1021
go with the moral tide of the moment, 1025
Government is the exact symbol of its P., 710
government responsive to the p., 715
great mass of the p., 1620
groans of the p., 892
Here the p. rule, 761
in our society who should be separated and discarded, 1330
is of weak courage, 1176
is the true legislator, 1029
keepers [of the constitution], 63
know all the p. worth knowing in America, 1680
Legislators represent p., 1032
Like P. like Government, 710
long-term common sense of the American p., 1489
manners and spirit of a p., 1337
may safely be trusted to hear everything true and false, 935
must either go on or go under, 1340
needs of the p., 1670
No P. can be bound to acknowledge and adore the invisible hand, 1344
no safe deposit for these but with the p. themselves, 492
of America believe in American institutions, 73
of ill will have used time much more effectively, 1693
of this nation—they will ever do well if well done by, 79
of those foreign countries, 88
opportunity to be of service to the p., 419
power in the p., 1454
power was turned back to the p., 1617
reign over the American political world, 87
retain their virtue and vigilance, 735
rising p., full of potential force, 119
safe depository of the ultimate powers of the society, 491
shackles for the liberties of the p., 1455
should be writhing under oppression and injury, 1747
should patriotically and cheerfully support their Government, 777
silence of the good p., 1693
strong enough and well enough informed to maintain its sovereign control, 750
tell p. what they want to hear, 1391
There go the p., 1021
they can be trusted with their own government, 1338
They [the Americans] were a P., 81
tribune of the p., 1499
Trust the p., 1333, 1343
voice of the p., 1341
voice of the p. will be heard, 426
want respect, 1618
we come from the p. and we are of the p., 279
We have done it ourselves, 1020
we ought not to succeed unless we do have the p. with us, 1332
were better off for being ridden, 1703
wherever the p. are well-informed, 1338
Where there is no vision, the p. perish, 1331

Justice is itself the great standing p. of civil society, 948
like all organic entities is always in the making, 1370
mulish obstructionism in domestic p., 1042
national p. from the quicksand of racial injustice, 1693
no such thing as a fixed p., 1370
of confiscation, 1368
rocks of loose fiscal p., 480
should be settled by free discussion, 414
war is . . . the continuation of state p., 1917
which is devised for a nation, 1367
See also **Foreign policy**

Polish
lawyers for Poles, 1015

Politburo
prisoner of the P., 1658

Politic
unless the bodies p. will exert themselves, 525

Political
achieve p. power and do big things, 1361
activity prevailing in the United States, 1428
adequacy of its p. systems, 1935
aim was to defeat this new enemy, 1968
always on trial for their p. lives, 1563
ambition, 1604
animal, 1390
applicability, 1231
architecture has its p. Use, 93
arena, 494
career brings out the basest qualities in human nature, 1416
cattle of the p. arena, 1566
cowardice, 1199
dangerous to the p. process, 150
deprived of p. strength or union, 1647
domesticated p. and social creature, 1423
dreamer, 1762
enemies, 519
Fable of the Snake, 265
fork in the p. road, 62
gods, 1642
hazards, 1567
if instead of making a p. speech I was being hanged, 1277
law of my p. life, 723
leaders replacing moral imperatives with a Southern strategy, 444
machine, 414
mediocre p. talents, 1401
novice in p. economy, 786
objects at which all p. institutions aim, 782
only one thing I want to say . . . that has a p. tinge, 285
Our present p. position has been achieved in a manner unprecedented, 760
people reign over the American p. world as God rules over the universe, 87
philosophy, 1343
power grows out of the barrel of a gun, 1451
power is primarily an illusion, 1415
preservation of our p. system, 894
prowess of an Adam Clayton Powell, 1400
punishes p. opinions, 1653
puppets, 1455
question in the United States, 1429
recipe for p. success, 1391
regeneration, 1613
rights, 1653
society does not live to conduct foreign policy, 620
to live under the American Constitution is the greatest p. privilege, 320
turn their decisions to p. purposes, 944
vocal at all times on p. matters, 1747
War is a p. act, 1926
War is not merely a p. act, 1915
what kills p. writing, 1248
When I examined my p. faith, 414
wisdom, 716

Political parties, 152, **1373–1388,** 1489
See also **Campaign funds**

Politically
right, 1640

Politician
asking what your country can do for you, 766
contribution equal to . . . the p., 2082
eel in the fundamental mud upon which the superstructure of organized society is reared, 1393
garden . . . [is a] refuge of a disappointed p., 1395
He'll double-cross that bridge when he comes to it, 1399
is a man who understands government, 1405
must always tell the people what they want to hear, 1391
no p. can afford to admit this, 1445
no such thing as a nonpolitical speech by a p., 1402
nobody counts for anything except a p., 1716
not a p., 1425
not a p. and my other habits air good, 1407
of monumental littleness, 1403
proud that I'm a p., 1405
sound p., 1271
suffers the disadvantage of being alive, 1393
Tax reduction has an almost irresistible appeal to the p., 17
too honest a man to be a p. and live, 1404
true p., 1765
who has willfully made war, 1953
See also Legislators

Politicians, 1389–1408
and movie actors and movie executives are similar in more ways than they're different, 1406
anxious p. of his party, 1313
are the same all over, 1398
God and the p. willing, 1318
if more p. knew poetry, 1397
in this country, in their feverish search for group acceptance, 1389
keep my promises to other p. than to God, 1408
of the United States are not so fastidious as some gentlemen, 1314
rarely feel they can afford the luxury of telling the whole truth, 1563
swear eternal devotion to the ends of peace and security, 631
when p. go to Hollywood, they're absolutely fascinated by the movie stars, 1406
whole Race of P. put together, 30
See also **Legislators**

Politics, 1409–1432
aim of practical p., 1421
and the pulpit are terms that have little agreement, 1417
art of p., 1422
awareness that we are all human beings together has become lost in war and through p., 1157
[business] corrupts p., sports, 158
consists in directing rationally

Properties
  which belong to honorable men, 185
Property, 1547–1550
  as its prey and plunder, 1549
  banks and corporations . . . will deprive the people of all their p., 1204
  belongs to man and not man to p., 867
  destruction of p., 46
  free to acquire p., 1633
  hard money represents p., 359
  helplessness of p. holders, 46
  in few hands, 1549
  in his rights, 1548
  inequality of p., 1549
  is the fruit of labor, 1547
  judiciary is the safeguard of our liberty and of our p., 328
  magic of p. turns sand to gold, 1550
  man's p., . . . is surely that which is the result of his mental activity, 1197
  may be regulated to a certain extent, 1586
  men of some p., 1629
  no dangers to the value of p., 46
  No man's life, liberty or p. are safe while the Legislature is in session, 1041
  of all, 2080
  [pollution] reduces p. values, 544
  preserve p., 314
  regard of the law for private p., 997
  right of p., 1068
  rights are fundamentally and in the long run, identical, 867
  rights must be carefully safeguarded, 867
  rights of p., 1549
  their lands and p. shall never be taken from them [the Indians], 55
  Without p. of any kind he cannot educate himself, 1698
  would be saved by a strong military government, 421
Prophets
  persecuted they the p., 102
Proportion
  inverse p. to our creative capacity, 1681
Propriety
  decency and p. of conduct, 884
  of having a Congress, 1496
  of the nation must be startled, 1575
  See also **Impropriety**
Prosper
  [Fortune] suffers not the same man to p. for ever, 637
  neither man nor nation can p. unless . . . thought is . . . taken for the future, 312
Prosperity
  -at-any-price, 58
  general p., 1644
  instruments of our rising p., 410
  on these alone a stable p. can be founded, 840
  partners in p., 1667
  plain way of life . . . promotes thrift and p., 796
  time of p., 1468
  will rise upward . . . through the ranks, 479
Prostitution
  victims of legal p., 1210
Protect
  the people, 292
Protest
  against living under rules and prejudices and attitudes that produce the extremes of wealth and poverty, 1144
  human race / Has climbed on p., 1695
  only effective p., 1890
  politics of p. is shutting out the process of thought, 441
  Ten Commandments of P., 441
Protestant
  Hitler attacked me and the P. church, 1749
Protests
  series of p., 1717
Protocol
  alcohol, and Geritol, 1858
Proud
  and unbending in honest defeat, 1469
  man, / Dress'd in a little brief authority, 1159
  men asking / Not to be safe, but free, 1474
  men compete for nameless graves, 1110
  of his community, proud of his country, proud of what America has meant, 54
  that I was a free man first, 1396
  that I'm a politician, 1405
  too p. to pray, 53
  undying thought in man, 593
Providence
  consequences with P., 1551
  playing P., 1361
  some secret design of P., 2045
  task for which P. has chosen me, 821
  trust from P., 280
  unwilling to leave anything to P., 1361
  will put a speedy end to the acts of God under which we have been laboring, 701
Providential
  token of p. agency, 1344
Prudence
  [forbids] . . . paying our own money for unexplained projects, 802
  there is also a false, reptile p., 596
Prudent
  archers . . . take aim much higher than their mark, 825
  progressive who is p., 1396
  without having my mind closed to anything that is new or different, 1396
Prying
  lost as much as we gained by p. into that matter, 974
Psalm of brotherhood, 1693
"The Psalm of the Addict," 852
Psychology
  [has not yet found] a sensible soul, 111
Public
  authority, just cause, right motive, 1909
  awareness of the p. attitude, 1406
  chore, 1423
  consider himself as p. property, 1562
  courage to resist p. presure, 1604
  Credit, 813
  danger of disturbing the p. tranquillity, 335
  discover in the p. felicity the latent causes of decay, 1647
  duties, 1764
  emploiment contributes neither to advantage nor happiness, 842
  expenditure, 812
  good, 1561, 1604, 1643
  Honour and Gain of p. Posts, 1565
  interest, 1511, 1567
  married and endowed the p., 1163
  men have no sure tenure, 1563
  money, 799
  no right to strike against the p. safety, 1775
  officer without vices, 820
  passions, 335
  private rights and p. happiness, 82
  sentiment is everything, 1557
  servant third, 1396
  starving the p. sector, 17
  taste, 1803

Q

R

nothing is more r. than the passions and interests of men, 1456
Received
give in the same measure as I have r., 1603
Recipe
for political success, 1391
Happy Home R., 844
Reciprocity
of affection, 1406
Reclamation
of arid public lands, 311
Recollection
for his wit, 1175
Red
[better] R. than dead, 128
Red China. *See* **China**
Redeeming
social importance, 1261
social value, 1261
Reelects
him year after year, 283
Reflection
more cool and sedate r., 468
Reform, 1583–1585
haven for r. movements, 326
that you may preserve, 1584
Reform Bill of 1867, 176
Reformed
by showing him a new idea, 873
Reformer
thinks he was ilicted because he was a r., 1583
who does not remember the past will find himself condemned to repeat it, 853
Reformers
best r. the world has ever seen are those who commence on themselves, 1585
Refuge
of a scoundrel, 1306
Refusal
point blank r., 1543
prefer a false promise to a flat r., 1543
Refuse
if you r. you are sure to offend many, 1543
Regardless
of color, creed, ancestry, sex or age, 729
Region
of savages and wild beasts, 1986
Regret
that I have but one life, 1304
Regulate
that which it subsidizes, 1587
Regulation, 1586–1588
goes too far it will be recognized as a taking, 1586
Reigns
in America the President r. . . . and Journalism governs, 1524
Rejoice
in it [our national life], 768
Relevance, 1589
negative r., 1589
Relief
dependence upon r. induces a spiritual and moral disintegration, 1984
Religion
and virtue alike lend their sanctions to meekness and humility, 253
free to profess and by argument maintain, their opinions in matters of r., 667
morality, and knowledge, being necessary to good government, 55
of Christ, 207
opinions in politics and r., 1275
set one r. against another, 1482
without science is blind, 1662
See also **Freedom of religion**
Religions
nation of many nationalities, many races, many r., 1482
oppressed and persecuted of all Nations and R., 884
Religious
highest act of r. teaching—sacrifice, 1728
hot discussion on the merits of r. sects, 897
Religious freedom. *See* **Freedom of religion**
Remember
the Alamo, the Maine, and Pearl Harbor, 65
don't have to r. what you have said, 1839
the Maine, 1910
minutely and precisely only the things which never really happened to us, 1174
reformer who does not r. the past, 853
the sabbath day, 1804
We must r., 225
Remembered
in spite of ourselves, 1701
not for victories or defeats, 1753
perform something worthy to be r., 13
Remorseless
nothing more r., . . . than truth, 584
Rendezvous
with death, 373
with destiny, 1607
Reorganizing
meet any new situation by r., 1539
Repeat
who cannot remember the past are condemned to r. it, 1292
Repeats
history r. itself, 574
Report
of my death has been greatly exaggerated, 378
Reporters
should ever lose the right to protect the confidentiality of their sources, 1522
Represent
elected spokesmen r. the Establishment, 1891
Representation, 1590–1592
equal r. in one House, 1592
equal r. then proposed, 1597
is based on geographical boundaries, 1128
no voice, or R., 2010
proportionate r. based upon population, 1592
rights of r., 1590
Representative
choosing a r., 1428
happiness and glory of a r., 280
a man must learn to be a R., 301
of the people, 1496
of the people as a sentinel on the watch-tower of liberty, 307
of the whole society, 1757
value of the R. or Senator increases in proportion to his length of service, 301
worthy of you ought to be a person of stability, 1028
See also **Congress;** Legislator
Representatives
chosen by the people to govern, 1364
here they act by their immediate r., 762
no special r., 1516
of all the people in the country control this one city, 1975
right of voting for r., 1906
See also **Congress; Legislators**
Represented
district that is best r., 283
Repression
force and r. have made the wrecks in the world, 680
people of America are ready to support r., 444
Reproach
him with the very defect or vice . . . you feel . . . in yourself, 520
Republic, 1593–1598
falls under one man's yoke, 1598
for which it stands, 1363
government called a r., 425

if you can keep it, 1593
is a dream, 464
is his monument, 830
is in danger, 155
is the weal of the people, 946
leaders of the r., 1018
mass will hold together under the forms of a r., 1595
Model R., 45
monarchy gradually transforms itself into a r., 1598
needed to be passed through chastening . . . fires, 1594
no r. where there is no justice, 946
of the grave, 368
or a Monarchy, 1593
preserve a r. in vigor, 1337
saves the r., which is the first and supreme law, 926
a state in which sovereign power is invested in representatives, 1364
they died to save, 370
too small for a r., 1969
Republican
black, dyed in the wool R., 1599
change its [the Union's] r. form, 1267
economy among the first and most important of r. virtues, 383
everything r. which was not monarchy, 1597
I will not be a R., 1385
no Democratic or R. way of cleaning the streets, 1383
proposition to my R. friends, 1387
such a good statement of the R. case that he wished it were his, 1386
Republican party, 1599–1602
as the sheet anchor of the colored man's political hopes, 1601
however bad the R. p., 1600
refrain from telling any lies about the R. p., 1387
Republicans
are for both the man and the dollar, 1068
come forward with programs, 801
some R. I would trust with anything, 1602
stop telling the truth about them, 1387
We are all r., 1596
Republicans (Club), 682
Republics
are created by the virtue, public spirit, and intelligence of the citizens, 63
are not in and of themselves better than other forms of government, 671
fall, when the wise are banished, 63
which, having been formed with seeds of their own dissolution, now no longer exist, 716
Reputation
are not above attacking methods and possibly my official r., 519
damage his r., 520
falls to pieces, 446
make a bonfire of your r., 1745
Seeking the bubble r., 1158
Required
much is r., 1604
Re-rat
certain amount of ingenuity to r., 1374
Research
steal from two, it's r., 2077
Resistance
history of r., 1080
Resources
[America's] material r., 51
equal to its r., 1791
He smote the rock of the national r., 813
of our land, 13
steadily decreasing r., 811
See also Natural resources
Responsibilities
in their business activities, 143
men aware of their grave trust and their great r., 1611
to the state, 1604
wake from slumber and face our r., 1609
Responsibility, 1603–1611
give him some r. and he is going to amount to something, 83
I do not shrink from this r.—I welcome it, 661
in an ever-widening sphere for all that lives, 1101
is clear, 1902
Liberty means r., 1074
standard of r. which no government can possibly meet, 783
was the price every man must pay for freedom, 643
we owe not to our party or even to our constitutents but to our individual consciences, 1381
what we mean is a sense of national r., 1311
worthy of our power and r., 662
Responsible
for their conduct, 1500
people are r. for the acts of their government, 1346
Restless
in the midst of abundance, 86
Restructuring
vast r. of our society is needed, 1717
Resurrection City, 1442
Resurrections
countless deaths and r., 1752
three thousand r., 1752
Retirement
compulsory r., 1569
merit in calm r., 295
Retreat
convert r. into advance, 599
enemy advances, we r., 1933
know when to r., 1185
No r., 1871
Retreats
enemy r., we pursue, 1933
Retribution, 1612
Return
I shall r., 2059
not knowing when or whether ever I may r., 1497
Returned
I have r., 2061
Returning
were as tedious as go o'er, 114
Revelations
first dreadful r., 46
Revenue
streams of r. gushed forth, 813
Revere, Paul (1735–1818), 65
Revision
fearlessness of r., 183
Revolt
enough spark left in me to lead a mighty good r., 1892
Revolution, 1613–1618
as profound, as far-reaching, as exciting as that first r., 1617
democracy in order to have a r., 416
era of r., 1618
greatest r. of all, 182
in India, 202
in order to establish a democracy, 416
in the nature of an explosive political regeneration, 1613
new American r., 1617
of rising expectations, 182, 1618
peaceful r., 1617
peaceful r. impossible, 1616
redress, honored in tradition, is also r., 1614
support r. as long as it is done with a cultured voice and a handsome profile, 1389
violent r. inevitable, 1616
was in the minds of the people, 1619
Revolutionaries
salute you as fellow r., 1615
Revolutionary
as science, 2025

become a prey to the active, 1054
civil r. movement, 116
duty to give him the full r. of an American, 883
endowed by their creator with certain inalienable r., 397
fight for his r., 1191
inherent & inalienable, 396
natural r. of mankind, 1058
of every man, 219
of Man, 347, 394
of nations, 864
of one man, 219
of property, 1549
of the States, 1849
other man's r., 1761
political r., 1653
private r. and public happiness, 82
protection of every individual's private r., 1643
sacred r. of mankind, 865
Rights of man. *See* **Human rights.**
Riot
is a spontaneous outburst, 1939
Riots
more r. that come on college campuses, the better world for tomorrow, 157
Ripple
of hope, 8
Rise
Great nations r. and fall, 1238
without his [God's] aid, 703
Rising
expectations, 182, 1618
sun fresh from the burning, 59
tide lifts all the boats, 1667
Risk
of wearing out, 11
reach out to the r. of living with both arms, 1127
Risks
man sits as many r. as he runs, 1105
River, 1645
build a bridge even where there is no r., 1398
is more than an amenity, 1645
One r. born of many streams, 1866
our magnificent r. system, 311
Rivers
turn our r. and streams into sewers, 313
Road
ahead is not altogether smooth, 220
covered with blood, 1937
Fork in the political r., 62
in search not merely of its r. but even of its direction, 474
rise to meet you, 1478
to hell is paved with them [good intentions], 291
to success, 1777
Roads
Good r., 217
two r. that lead to something like human happiness, 845
Roar
called upon to give the r., 1276
Robbers
don't put r. to work in a bank, 1588
Robs
Peter to pay Paul, 1796
you on business principles, 535
Rochambeau, Jean-Baptiste-Donatien de Vimeur, Comte de (1725–1807), 897
Rock
of the national resources, 813
solid r. of human dignity, 1693
upon which states are built, 526
Rockets
rattle their r., 1881
Rocking chair
sit here in our r. c. . . . and let the Communists, 243
Rocky Mountains, 476
Rogers, Will (1879–1935), 65, 966
Roman
citizen, 215
Emperors, 1653
Empire, 334
noblest R. of them all, 1160
Republic, 1867
Romantic
life is a r. business, 1089
Rome, 1071, **1646–1648**
Empire of R., 1019
lest R. become bankrupt, 795
more glorious edifice than Greece or R., 755
strongest state that history has known, 206
there will not be different laws at R. and at Athens, 1000
Rome's
decline lay in her people, 1646
liberties were not auctioned off in a day, 1648
Roosevelt, Anna Eleanor (1884–1962)
tribute by Adlai E. Stevenson, 448
Roosevelt, Franklin Delano (1882–1945), 249, 379, 986, 1463, 1499, 1512
Roosevelt, Theodore (1858–1919), 1392, 1488
Root
tap r. of civilization, 1437
Rope
of sand, 1004
sell us the r. to hang them with, 246
Rose
more nourishing than a cabbage, 870
smells better than a cabbage, 870
Roses
days of wine and r., 460
Don't strew me with r. after I'm dead, 1217
give me my r. now, 1217
Ross, Betsy (1752–1836), 65
Rot
and dissolution, 60
Route
short r. to chaos, 1764
Ruin
inevitable r. must follow, 525
Ruinous
always descreditable, and sometimes r., 713
free / From r. discords, 915
Ruins
disease-soaked r. of a slum, 1162
Rule
Here the people r., 761
under This Roof, 1462
Wars are, of course, as a r. to be avoided, 1965
which has been made by the legislature, 1040
Ruled
by tyrants, 746
Rulers
not let our r. load us with perpetual debt, 381
Of the best r., 1020
protect the people against their r., 292
Rules, 1649
are mostly made to be broken, 1649
by terror, 1653
for campus conduct, 153
governing the relations between members of the same society, 1013
Who r. East Europe, 2041
Who r. the Heartland, 2041
Who r. the World-Island, 2041
Run
He can r. But he can't hide, 1651
Running, 1650-1651
all the r. you can do, to keep in the same place, 1650
Runs
man sits as many risks as he r., 1105
Rural-life
policies, 312

Rush, Richard (1780–1859), 1172
Russia, 1652–1658
collapse in R. followed by communism, 2046
has lost the cold war, 236
is one of the worst tyrannies, 1653
is threatening us with her might, 155
Red China and R. are having their differences, 2043
riddle wrapped in a mystery inside an enigma, 1652
runs from Dantzic or perhaps Stettin to Trieste, 1654
So you've been over into R., 696
world's troubles are not due just to R., 1618
Russian
comedy, everybody dies, 1655
is at grips with men, 2045
national interest, 1652
serf, 1698
tragedy, everybody dies, 1655
Russians
I want them to be Americans and not R., 1259
in the over all drain on the nation, 2070
two great nations in the world . . . the R. and the Anglo-Americans, 2045
Russia's
[conquests are made] with the sword, 2045
policy, 2042
Rust
unburnish'd, not to shine in use, 575
Rusting
out, 11

S

Sabbath
Remember the s. day, 1804
Sacred
cause half so s. as the cause of a people, 1570
fight for things s., 100
not disgrace my s. arms, 100
rights of mankind, 865
trust, 1604
Sacrifice, 1659
final s. for life and freedom, 660
highest act of religious teaching, 1728
his enlightened conscience, he ought not to s., 280
Too long a s., 1659
unpitied s. in a contemptible struggle, 560
worship without s., 1697
Sacrifices
it [unbiased opinion] to your opinion, 280
Sacrificing
absurdly s. the end to the means, 1009
Safe
deposit of these but with the people themselves, 492
depository of the ultimate powers of the society, 491
where shall a man be s., if it be not in his house, 859
Safeguard
of our liberties, 333
Safer
to be wrong before it has become fashionable to be right, 1563
Safety
clamorous to be led to s., 1421
deserve neither Liberty nor S., 1056
fear is the mother of s., 595
sit in s. under his own vine and fig-tree, 670
to obtain a little s., 1056
to purchase a little temporary S., 1056
Safety-first, 58
Safire, William (1929–), 1553
Said
what I meant and meant what I s., 513
what is s. against me, 110
Sail
and not drift, not lie at anchor, 5
For what avail the plough or s., . . . if freedom fail?, 641
never strike s. to fear, 597
no connexion with any ship that does not s. fast, 848
sometimes with the wind and sometimes against it, 5
with God the seas, 597
Your constitution is all s. and no anchor, 334
Sailing
farther than Ulysses even dreamed of, 129
Fleet s. under Convoy, 44
Sailors
fleetest S. must wait for the dullest and slowest, 44
Saint
I am not a s., 1491
Saint Louis. *See* Louis IX, King of France.
Salad
bowl, 49
describing an Italian s., 1867
preparation of a s., 1867
Salk, Jonas (1914–), 65
Sallust (Gaius Sallustius Crispus) (86–34 B.C.), 1283
Salutation of the Dawn, 1106
Salvation
for a race, nation, or class must come from within, 960
San Domingo, annexation, 1484
San Francisco
some [men] are stationed in S. F., 1092
Sand
magic of property turns s. to gold, 1550
see a world in a grain of s., 196
sketches in the s., 1248
wrote my name upon the s., 1215
Sans
teeth, s. eyes, s. taste, s. everything, 1158
Santa Claus, 1660
Yes, Virginia, there is a S.C., 1660
See also Christmas
Sappho (fl. c. 600 B.C.)
though she was a woman [was honored], 1996
Sat
long enough, 1035
too long here for any good you have been doing lately, 1035
Satellites
we [England] do not intend to be satellites, 531
Satire
is this on government, 1789
Satirize
the political gods, 1642
Satisfaction
one great universal s., 1227
think of your work with s., 2032
Saturday Evening Post, 917
Saturday's
child works hard for its living, 200
Saucer
we pour legislation into the senatorial s. to cool it, 294
Sausages
laws and s., 996
Savage
chief of still more s. men, 1019
lonely s., 839
Savageness
tame the s. of man, 1864
Save
he [God] need not exist in order to s. us, 702
Saved
I s. my money, 2071
Savior
of Europe, 534
Say
Don't s. things, 186

having nothing to s., 1692
I am not going to s. anything I do not think, 673
I didn't s. that I didn't s. it, 232
kindly of him what is, chiefly, true, 135
need not fear to s. it, 169
watch what we do instead of what we s., 9
what the critics s., 110
Says
speak and s. nothing, 266
Say'st
Thou s. an undisputed thing / In such a solemn way, 631
Scalp
ran his hand over Nick's shiny s., 2008
Scandals
corruption and injustice in our nation's history, 1522
Scapegoats
people are looking for s., 524
Scare
land of slander and s., 62
Scarecrow
impeachment is scarcely a s., 941
Scared
be s. of a coward the same as a brave man has got to be, 354
Scenery
Not one cent for s., 308
Schoolmaster
and remain fit for anything else, 287
Schools
and the means of education, 55
Science, 1661–1665
and Peace will triumph over Ignorance and War, 1963
lights of perverted s., 2055
main objects of all s., 779
Modern civilization depends on s., 1663
of Government it is my Duty to study, 481
our own cleverness in s., 125
will have moved forward yet one more step, 505
without humanity, 1697
without religion is lame, 1662
Scientific
and technological achievements, 1134
triumph of s. annihilation, 1258
truth, 1665
Scientist
What is a s., 1664
Scorpions
two s. in a bottle, 237
Scotland
first rate land in . . . S., 554
Scoundrel
refuge of a s., 1306
Scratch
another's back if he'll s. mine, 656
Scriptures
advise no one to send his child where the Holy S. are not supreme, 239
Sea, 1666–1667
from which all heights and depths are measured, 1666
Had washed my feeble lines away, 1215
lashed into fury, 1666
that salts all the waters that flow into it [China], 201
thy s. is so great, 1479
why the s. is boiling hot, 1811
will wash away, 1248
Sealing-wax, 1811
Sea-shore
three geographical miles from the s., 1809
Season
duty neglected in its s., 1830
it was the s. of light, it was the s. of darkness, 1818
of suffering, 220
To every thing there is a s., 1810
Second
free man first and an American s., 1396
front in Europe, 2067
office of this government is honorable and easy, 1493
What place does the possibility of a s. front occupy, 2068
Secrecy, 1668–1670
Secret
Everything s. degenerates, 1668
neither have I gained office by any s. promises, 1492
of success 1779
you have not chosen me by s. ballot, 1492
Secrets
no s. from government, 1529
Security, 1671–1672
abandon altogether the search for s., 1127
absolute economic and social s., 70
against crafty and dangerous encroachments on the public liberty, 496
Americans want is s., 1671
Decency, s. and liberty alike demand, 793
greatest s. of the people, 1052
light . . . is the best s., 496
live in all possible s., 785
Nation's s. is at stake, 1530
no s. on this earth, 1672
only s. which freemen desire, 1196
politicians . . . swear eternal devotion to the ends of peace and s., 631
prefer the illusion of s. to the excitement of danger, 2095
seek opportunity—not s., 71
Seduction
"temperate and moderate," are words [of] s., 1199
See
content to wait and s. what will happen, 1636
the light, 1665
to s., we have only to look, 1467
what is right and not to do it, 1635
Seed
faith as a grain of mustard s., 592
Seeds
of despotism, 1069
Seeker
this, s., is the promise of America, 68
Seen
from the s. to the unseen, 1229
Self, 1673–1676
to thine own s. be true, 1675
Self-confidence
as young as your s., 2099
Self-deception, 1677
nothing is easier than self-deceit, 1677
Self-esteem, 1680
Self-examination, 1678–1679
Self-forgotting, 845
Self-government
art of s., 1425
principles of s., 1975
qualifications for s. in society are not innate, 725
Self-importance, 1680–1681
Self-interest
predominant principle of s., 425
Self-pity, 1682
Self-preservation
strikes its jarring gong, 854
Self-realization, 1674
Self-respect, 1683
man can draw the breath of s., 350
Self-righteousness, 224
Self-sacrifice, 1674
Self-seeking, 845
Selfish
license, 759
Selling
Every one lives by s. something, 1123
Senate
representation in our State S., 1592
See also **Congress—Senate**

is golden, 1691
is of Eternity, 1691
Keep s., and we'll get you safe across, 731
of the good people, 1693
remember what peace there may be in s., 1114
sin be s., 1695
that is better, 1691
time to keep s., and a time to speak, 1810
Silent
Be s., even when you are misrepresented, 1119
dumb and s. we may be led, like sheep, to the Slaughter, 679
majority of my fellow Americans, 1140
remain s. and look wise, 681
Silk
purse out of a sow's ear, 1084
Silly
flat, and dish-watery utterances, 1487
Silvern
Speech is s., 1691
Simplicity
quiet and dignified s., 108
Sin
by silence, 1695
making a profit is a s., 138
real s. is taking a loss, 138
to believe evil of others, but seldom a mistake, 562
to waste it [youth] on children, 2097
Sincerity, 1696
little s. is a dangerous thing, 1696
virtues of courage, honor, justice, truth, s., 58
Singing
in the dark, 1836
Single
injustice, a s. crime, a s. illegality, 958
work of a s. man, 902
Sins, 1697
of the cold-blooded and the s. of the warm-hearted, 749
seven s. are wealth without works, 1697
Sits
man s. as many risks as he runs, 1105
Six
[America is] like a Coach and s., 44
lines written by the hand of the most honest of men, 908
Size
involvement with s., 50
is not grandeur, 51
Sketches
in the sand, 1248
Skim
pray cream, and live s. milk, 1111
Sky
is the limit, 70
lonesome place against the s., 1108
Skylark
who shall command the s. not to sing?, 642
Slain
not right to glory in the s., 365
Slander
land of s. and scare, 62
Slaughter
led, like sheep, to the S., 679
Slave
black woman for a s., 1702
Commerce between master and s. is despotism, 1062
economic s. pulling an oar in the galley of the state, 1756
freedom to the s., 1701
half s. and half free, 1851
he who would be no s. must consent to have no s., 648
negro woman for a s., 1702
no land free, that holds one fettered s., 1695
of the lash, 164
That which fundamentally distinguishes the s., 1705
without tools to work out his salvation, 1698
Slavery, 1698–1706
arguing for s., 1704
consists in being subject to the will of another, 1906
He [God] hates injustice and s., 907
impulse to see it [slavery] tried on him personally, 1704
not to speak one's thought, 1699
rooting out of s., 1706
socialism involves s., 1705
Slaves
from whom the unfortunate state of things with us takes away the right of will and of property, 1591
in breeding compared with freemen, 1016
perish than live as s., 1634
Sleep, 1707
each night a little better, 1517
snore and you s. alone, 1707
sweetly, tender heart, in peace, 377
Sleeping
enemy, 2069
giant, 2069
Slip
of the tongue, 1509
Slogan
"press on," 1355
Thou Shalt Not Write Anything Longer than a S., 441
Slogans
outworn s., 2095
strength is but a matter of s., 52
Slow
me down Lord, 1480
Slum
conditions, 1892
disease-soaked ruins of a s., 1162
Sly
land of s. innuendo, 62
Small
with s. men no great thing can really be accomplished, 1760
Smash
land of s. and grab, 62
Smile, 1708–1709
in trouble, 356
is genuine, 244
nice s., but . . . iron teeth, 1708
Soviet delegates s., 244
When you call me that, s., 1709
when you say that, partner, 1709
Smiles
beside my grave . . . all s. and garlands, 376
Smithson, James (1765–1829), 1663
Smithsonian Institution, 1710
establishment for the increase and diffusion of knowledge, 972
Smoke
blue s. and mirrors, 1415
Smoot, Reed (1862–1941), 1168
Smote
the rock of the national resources, 813
Snake
died with thirst, 265
Fable of the S., 265
Sneeze
do not s. when Mr. Calhoun takes snuff, 559
Sneezes
all Europe s., 559
Snobs
effete corps of impudent s., 1876
Snore
and you sleep alone, 1707
Snow
nor rain, nor heat, nor gloom of night, 1439
Snows
Lady of the S., 2014

Spend
a little more than it earns, 808
Never s. your money before you have it, 1116
tax and tax, and s. and s., and elect and elect, 1793
Spending
more than your income, 1117
no sacrifice at all in s., 809
other people's money, 805
the public money, 799
Soviet s. has shown no response to U.S. restraint, 400
the sweat of its laborers . . . the hopes of its children, 403
was no longer the rock of unsound finance, 379
See also **Government spending**
Sphere
woman's s., 2012
Spiral
it [violence] is a descending s., 1893
Spirit, 1750–1754
[America] no longer ruler of her own s., 613
conquers forever, 1750
contribution to the human s., 1753
crisis of the s., 806
Great S. placed me and my people on this land poor and naked, 1545
long years that . . . turn the growing s. back to dust, 2099
of enjoyment was stronger, 2063
of enterprise and adventure, 658
of liberty, 1059
of Liberty constantly awake, 1052
of man be unable to pass from this body to another, 1752
of sacrifice, 2063
preserve the freedom of the human s., 676
prison house of the s., 18
shall cease to be never, 1751
should be ready to devote itself to martyrdom, 676
subtle destroyer of the human s., 1984
Unrest of s., 1096
which prizes liberty, 1069
"The Spirit of Liberty" speech, 1059
Spirits
Does he use ardent s., 35
from the vasty deep, 1754
Spiritual
dependence upon relief induces a s. and moral disintegration, 1984
Spiritually
poor, 1632
redeemed s., 230
Spoiled
and eventually a very weak individual, 83
Spoils
to the victor belong the s., 1314
Spoilt
we civilised people have been s., 1609
Sponge
nor friends to s., 1407
Sport
it's [politics] the only s. for grownups, 1432
noblest s. the world affords, 1637
Spring
of hope, 1818
Spurious quotations
Aeschylus, 945
Author unknown, stone tablet, 456
Churchill, Winston, 2004
Cicero, Marcus Tullius 795
Emerson, Ralph Waldo, 1528
Hitler, Adolf, 155
Jefferson, Thomas, 35, 1204
Lee, Robert E., 469
Lenin, Vladimir Ilich (Ulyanov), 246
Lincoln, Abraham, 1117
Socrates, 195
Thoreau, Henry David, 1528
Webster, Daniel, 1986
Squandered
all but s. this inheritance, 1605
Squanderers
of planetary capital, 309
Squandering
the capital of metallic ores and fossil fuels, 309
Stage
All the world's a s., 1158
Stagecoach
travelling in a s., 177
Stalin, Joseph (1879–1953), 917, 1658
Stand
fast and suffer long, 1234
firm, 688
for something, [or] . . . fall for anything, 106
great thing in this world is not so much where we s., 5
the heat, get out of the kitchen, 1513
take a s. on any issue, 38
up for them [rights and interests], 1644
what to s. for, 106
where to s., 106
with anybody that stands right, 1639
with him while he is right, 1639
your ground, 1940
Standard
Every action of the enemy is judged by one s., 933
Let us raise a s. to which the wise and the honest can repair, 340
of freedom and independence has been or shall be unfurled, 613
pick up a fallen s., 1299
Standard-bearer
of this forlorn hope, 863
Standards
integrity of their own intellectual and moral s., 1018
Laws can embody s., 1746
Stand-patter
Expect to be called a s., 2025
Stands
one's own nation s. for everything that is good and noble, 933
up for an ideal, 8
Star
fixed s. in our constitutional constellation, 647
fixed s. in the firmament of great names, 1977
follow knowledge like a sinking s., 575
Joy is . . . like a fixed s., 923
quenched on high, 371
Stars
above our cornfields, 1474
and Stripes, 601
In my s. I am above thee, 828
night already devoid of s., 1893
Started
end of all our exploring / Will be to arrive where we s., 579
Starvation
only a thin layer of soil between himself and s., 31
Starve
rather s. than sell our national honor, 1303
Starving
to death, 1094
State, 1755–1760
Athenian citizen does not neglect the s., 1552
cannot be expected to move with the celerity of a private business man, 1758
chief power in the S., 1419
[church] is not the master or the servant of the s., 1759
[church is] the conscience of the s., 1759
comes into existence . . . for the sake of a good life, 209

Streams
of revenue gushed forth, 813
Streets
no Democratic or Republican way of cleaning the s., 1383
of our country are in turmoil, 155
won't buy him clean s., 17
Strength, 1772–1774
action today to ensure our s. tomorrow, 1772
exercise our s. with wisdom and restraint, 662
I asked God for s., 1477
In Union there is s., 1859
is but a matter of slogans, 52
makes detente attainable, 404
of the general government, 405
of the Pack is the Wolf, 1865
of the Wolf is the Pack, 1865
righteousness of our cause must always underlie our s., 662
to endure the misfortunes of others, 1773
today, 1772
Stress
process of living is the process of having s., 1122
time of s. and strain, 1908
Strike, 1775–1776
at every favorable opportunity, 2061
For future generations of your sons and daughters, s., 2061
For your homes and hearths, s., 2061
In the name of your sacred dead, s., 2061
laborer can s. if he wants to, 1776
no right to s. against the public safety by anybody, anywhere, any time, 1775
Stripes
for ever gleam, 602
Stars and S., 601
Striving
mightily, 11
Strong
and successful governments, 750
battle . . . is not to the strong alone, 1061
be s. for the rest, 1233
enough to know when he is weak, 1469
in will to strive, to seek, to find, and not to yield, 575
make a people great and s., 1234
man stumbles, 10
only the productive can be s., 1774
Only the s. can be free, 1774
too s. for the liberties of the people, 733
weakening the s., 1117
Stronger
than its weakest think, 1807
we are, the better partners we shall be, 531
Struggle
against a powerful and resourceful enemy, 580
against the common enemies of man, 516
between Liberty and Authority, 1071
burden of a long twilight s., 516
history . . . presents a picture of uninterrupted s., 1957
If there is no s. there is no progress, 443
in which we have been so long engaged, 1922
long, patient, costly s. . . . over the great enemies of man, 85
this book has been for the author of long s. of escape, 875
unpitied sacrifice in a contemptible s., 560
Struggler
has given up / When he might have captured the victor's cup, 1358
Struggling
to maintain the government, not to overthrow it, 732
Stuck
to their jobs, 1356
Students
have not tried to overthrow the Government, 221
rebelling and rioting, 155
Study
Politicks and War that my sons may have liberty to s., 481
Stupefied
for a score of years, 26
Stupid
when a s. man is doing something he is ashamed of, 472
Stupidity
forgive almost any weakness, with the possible exception of s., 84
Style
original s., 2075
which never borrows of any one, 2075
Sublimest
word in our language [duty], 469
Subsistence
mobs should . . . not depend on government for s., 795
Succeed
If it does not s., 110
If it does s., 110
it is worse never to have tried to s., 589
proposed operation likely to s., 1784
we ought not to s. unless we do have the people with us, 1332
without it, nothing can s., 1557
Without the assistance of that Divine Being who ever attended him, I cannot s., 1497
Succeeded
difficult task and we s., 1884
Success, 1777–1786
begins with a fellow's will, 1436
born fighter . . . who can dispense with s., 1087
Do not be fobbed off with mere personal s., 2088
do us honor when s. is with us, 446
in modern war requires . . . careful preparation, 1726
in modern war requires something more than courage, 1726
intoxicated with unbroken s., 53
is the necessary misfortune of life, 1785
is won / By any chance, 656
leap in the dark to our s., 1786
mediocrity of s., 2084
only one s., 1783
Push. One of two things mainly conducive to s., 1412
road to s., 1777
secret of s., 1779
we deserved, 139
without having to fire a single shot, 1657
Successes
against all big s., 822
I like not these great s. of yours, 1781
Successful
I want s. men as my associates, 588
Suez Crisis, 913
Suffering
season of s., 220
shall follow vice, 783
Sufferings
endure the most terrible s., though medical science could avert them, 1609
Suffrage
despotic reality of universal s., 1595

for one-eighth of the entire population, 119
Universal s. . . . could not long exist, 1549
Universal s. exists in the United States without producing any frightful consequences, 1904
Suicide
germs of double s., 1258
never was a democracy yet that did not commit s., 413
we must live through all time, or die by s., 522
Sum
of the whole matter, 230
Summer
soldier and sunshine patriot, 1821
Sumptuous
misery, 16
Sun
and not the moon, 1222
behold for the last time the s., 1855
In Sichuan dogs bark at the s., 203
it is a rising, and not a setting s., 323
keeps pace with the s., 1808
no new thing under the s., 1301
nothing new under the s., 1301
rising s. fresh from the burning, 59
setting s. of a black night, 59
The Sun
If you see it in *The Sun* it's so, 1660
Sunday
one great poem of New England is her S., 1241
Sunlight
is said to be the best of disinfectants, 1572
Suns
radiance of a thousand s., 123
Sunshine
keep your face to the s., 1435
of life, 687
patriot, 1821
Superior
like being compelled by a s., 909
position assigned to the white race, 1578
to all men, 1349
wisdom and virtue of our own, 53
Support
any friend, 1066
Governments do not and cannot s. the people, 781
of the people, 777
their Government, 777
Suppress
the free expression of thought, 1642
Suppresses
free speech, 1653
Supreme Court, 938–939, 944, 1763
appointment of Earl Warren, 924
has even ruled that I am the executive branch, 282
nor should this Court . . . be thought of as a general haven for reform movements, 326
See also **Judiciary**
Supreme Court opinions
Black, Hugo L.
on citizenship, 214
Brandeis, Louis D.
on government, 707
on government—separation of powers, 789
on government officials, 793
on liberty, 1048–1049
on the state, 1755
Brennan, William J., Jr.
on obscenity, 1261
Douglas, William O.
on censorship, 167
on lawyers, 1015
on privacy, 1529
Frankfurter, Felix
on equality, 551
on law, 1005
on wisdom, 1998
Fuller, Melville Weston
on government, 717
Harlan, John Marshall
on the Constitution, 326
Holmes, Oliver Wendell
on freedom of speech, 675
on legislature, 1037
on regulation, 1586
on rivers, 1645
on taxation, 1792
on the state, 1758
on truth, 1835
on women, 2013
on words, 2020
Jackson, Robert H.
on freedom, 647
on regulation, 1587
Marshall, John
comments by Andrew Jackson, 939
on states rights, 1762
on taxation, 1798
Sutherland, George
on liberty, 1077
Warren, Earl
on legislators, 1032
Sure
of the dock and much surer of the noose, 1953
thing, 172
what he knows for s. just ain't so, 966
Surprise
Whoever can s. well must conquer, 1988
Surrender
we shall never s., 1354
Surveillance
everyone is open to s., 1529
Survival
On their resolution depends the s. of us all, 477
Suspender
rises to power / From one s., 1452
Swapping
tobacco across the lines, 260
Swear
not at all, 1805
Sweat
In the s. of thy face shalt thou eat bread, 977
Sweet
and fitting to die for one's country, 367
Swindlers
enough [fools] to fatten the s., 606
Sword
arbitrament of the s., 222
conquered for a while, 1750
nation shall not lift up s. against nation, 1956
Russia's [conquests are made] with the s., 2045
Swords
beat their s. into plowshares, 1956
ready hands and keen s., 1941
Symbol
of union for [the United] States, 1867
Symbols
reverence to their s., 183
System
is the best that the present views and circumstances of the country will permit, 721
lost faith in the s., 752
Systems
adequacy of its political s., 1935
giant organized s., 224
Szechwan
dogs bark at the sun, 203
Szilard, Leo (1898–1964), 124

T

T, is for the tears she shed to save me, 1226
Table
supped at labor's t., 985
Tacitus, Publius Cornelius (c. 55–c. 117), 1283
Tail
of China is large and will not be wagged, 201

envious of the good t. that is coming to us, 24
fade . . . into the night of t., 2083
for all things, 1936
has come, the Walrus said, 1811
has come when we must proceed with the business of carrying the war to the enemy, 2062
has upset many fighting faiths, 1835
I shall use my t., 1118
If well made at the right t. it is effective, 1824
imaginative artist willy-nilly influences his t., 2082
is always ripe to do right, 1693
know what to do with it, 1820
latter t. what is fittest, 1997
like all times, is a very good one, 1820
look at its operation for a considerable t., 1367
makes ancient good uncouth, 1838
most valuable and the most perishable of all our possessions, 1816
night of t., 2083
no t. like the old t., 1814
no t. to lose, plant it this afternoon, 1815
not a t. of life, 2095, 2099
Now is the t. for all good men, 1388
of peace, 1810
of war, 1810
orderly arrangement of his t., 1290
people of ill will have used t. much more effectively, 1693
saves abundance of T., 146
something which no t. can efface, 1198
Speech is of T., 1691
speech is shallow as T., 1691
study the right t., 1824
to be born, and a t. to die, 1810
to embrace, 1810
to every purpose under the heaven, 1810
to fight, and that t. has now come, 1936
to keep silence, and a t. to speak, 1810
to kill, and a t. to heal, 1810
to love, and a t. to hate, 1810
to plant, and a t. to pluck up that which is planted, 1810
to preach and a t. to pray, 1936
to weep, and a t. to laugh, 1810
Truth the daughter of T., 1832
wheels of t., 1290
will do us justice, 1560

Times, 1818–1822
all t. are essentially alike, 1819
All t. I have enjoy'd / Greatly, have suffer'd greatly, 575
It was the best of t., it was the worst of t., 1818
keep pace with the t., 178
law is behind the t., 1006
most turbulent and tormented t. in the history of this nation, 418
no t. like the old t., 1814
of ours are serious and full of calamity, 1819
of stress and strain, 1908
that try men's souls, 1821
those t. have passed away, 1936

Timing, 1823–1824

Tiny Tim, 1465

Tiresome
repetition of inadequate catch words, 1282

Tithe
contribute to his Government, not the scriptural t., 1794

Tobacco
swapping t. across the lines, 260

Today, 1825
action t. to ensure our strength tomorrow, 1772
deed . . . we t. call weakness, will appear tomorrow as . . . essential, 836
How queer everything is t., 1678
is the first day of the rest of your life, 1825
only limits to our realization of tomorrow will be our doubts of t., 695
well lived, 1106
what ought to be done t., 1290
what you can do t., 1116

Together
go forward now t., 1863

Toil
and Blood and Treasure, 392

Told
all who t. it, added something new, 594

Tolls
for whom the bell t., 134
if t. for thee, 134

Tomatoes
[can still be distinguished] from the cabbage, 49

Tomb of the Unknown Soldier, 1734

Tombstone, Arizona, 1515

Tommy
Oh, it's T. this, 1723

Tomorrow
action today to ensure our strength t., 1772
deed . . . we today call weakness, will appear t. as . . . essential, 836
delay till t., 1290
every T. a Vision of Hope, 1106
is only a Vision, 1106
less than t., 1130
might be better, 182
Never put off till t., 1116
only limit to our realization of t. will be our doubts of today, 695
was not worse than today, 182

Tongue
earned my living by pen and t., 1276
my actions did belie my t., 1019
on ev'ry T. it grew, 594
Presidential slip of the t., 1509
two-edged t., 1284

Tools
Give us the t., and we will finish the job, 2051

Top
of the greasy pole, 1778

Torch
has been passed, 77
to light the way, 1302
woman with a t., 1770

Torture
to death only one tiny creature, 432

Totalitarian
Thou Shalt Not Revere Any But T. Heroes, 441

Totalitarianism
and anarchy will threaten free nations, 1886
business also corrupts and undermines monolithic t., 158
peace and freedom . . . suffocated by the forces of t., 1140
wishy-washy imitation of t., 708

Touched
I am deeply t., 151
not as deeply t. as you, 151

Town
necessary to destroy the t. to save it, 1888

Town-meetings
that ushered in the Revolution, 1630

Townshend, Charles (1725-1767), 1787

Trade
election of intelligent, honest, earnest t. unionists, 983

Trades
and deals among the senators, 257

are not of a sinister nature, 257
Tradition
Approves all forms of competition, 1805
men . . . whose names have become a splendid t., 281
Traditional
because it is t., 105
Traditions
when to adhere to them, 1766
when to depart from t., 1766
Tragedy
first time as t., 856
government without . . . information . . . [is] a Farce or a T., 969
Russian t., everybody dies, 1655
Tranquil
and steady dedication of a lifetime, 1311
Tranquility
at my age, is the supreme good of life, 1246
Transportation Building. *See* World's Columbian Exposition, Chicago (1893).
Traveling
up and down the vast territories of the United States, 86
Treason, 1826
doth never prosper, 1826
none dare call it t., 1826
Treasure
river is more than an amenity, it is a t., 1645
Treasury
of the world, 476
Treaties
mode of making t., 792
Treaty
reject the t., 1332
Tree
of liberty, 1065
plant it this afternoon, 1815
Trees
old men plant t. they will never sit under, 694
Trembles
I only hope . . . the enemy . . . t. as I do, 1184
Trial
deny others a fair t., 1170
fairness of the t., 117
Trickle
down theory, 479
Tried
if any thing is to be hoped, every thing ought to be t., 1932
See also Try; **Trying**
Trieste, 234, 1654
Triumph
because its opponents eventually die, 1665
magnificent mixture of t. and tragedy, 355
of high achievement, 10
our forefathers moved on to t., 57
over the great enemies of man, 85
Posterity will t., 392
Science and Peace will t., 1963
Triumphs
the sorrow and the t. that are the aftermath of war, 1923
Trojan
governmental citadel of a T. horse, 633
Trophies
will never be envied, 778
Trouble
day of t., 1468
take the t. to do the work of government, 1566
Troy, 1951
Far on the ringing plains of windy T., 575
Truant
Deal with him as a t., 135
Truce
to terror, 1324
Truckle
to the people, 1018
True
believes to be t., 1677
danger is when liberty is nibbled away, 1053
knowledge is achieved, 1317
liberty consists only in the power of doing what we ought to will, 1055
no Man . . . is t. to his wife, 2009
to thine own self be t., 1675
Truer
than if they had really happened, 131
Trumpeters
Due to the lack of experienced t., 455
Trust, 1827–1828
committed to them in t. from the People, 1453
divert from fulfillment of our sacred t., 1604
don't t. anybody over 30, 1828
good of those who confer, not of those who receive the t., 712
in God and Heaven securely, 1126
in thee [O God] do I put my t., 1827
never t. a woman who tells her real age, 2018
nothing to the enthusiasm of the people, 757
the people, 1333, 1343
Republicans I would t. with anything— . . . except public office, 1602
should be placed not in a few, but in a number of hands, 765
them [the people] with the facts, 1343
Thou Shalt Not T. Anybody Over Thirty, 441
Trusted
for their defence to a mercenary army, 1647
man is not made to be t. for life, 940
they [the people] can be t. with their own government, 1338
Trustees
of Posterity, 2090
Trusting
to your works to defend you, 1119
Trusts
and combinations, 139
Truth, 1829–1839
best test of t., 1835
crushed to earth, shall rise again, 1829
the daughter of time, 1832
diminution of love of t., 1925
discernment they [the people] have manifested between t. and falsehood, 935
do not be vexed with me for telling the t., 1404
duty . . . to tell the t. about the President, 1506
enemy of the t., 1268
even more important to tell the t. . . . about him [the President], 1507
Every Communist must grasp the t., 1451
first casualty when war comes is t., 1925
forever on the scaffold, 1838
full liberty to tell the t. about his [the President's] acts, 1507
Hell is t. seen too late, 1830
in favor of the eternal forces of t., 822
is being more and more realized by the public, 301
is the glue that holds the government together, 255, 1831
is the only ground upon which their wishes safely can be carried out, 1835
justice is t. in action, 952
know the whole t., 1834
let me go down linked with the t., 1851
light of t., 238

loving frankness and t., 1748
new t. is always a go-between, 1837
nothing more remorseless, just as there is nothing more helpful, than t., 584
Persecution cannot harm him who stands by T., 1833
politicians rarely feel they can afford the luxury of telling the whole t., 1563
save in the cases where to tell the t. at the moment would benefit the public enemy, 1506
scientific t., 1665
search out the deep t. of life, 1664
shut our eyes against a painful t., 1834
simply tell the t., 1839
sting of t. turns it fierce, 362
stop telling the t. about them [Republicans], 1387
tell the t. about the Democrats, 1387
to the knowledge of nations, 738
universal t. and applicability, 1644
virtues of courage . . . t., 58
without free speech no search for t. is possible, 672

Truths
being faced with cruel t., 556
eternal t. of the past, 654
We hold these t. to be sacred & undeniable, 396
We hold these t. to be self-evident, 397, 462

Try
above all, t. something, 1843
harder than anyone else, 109

Trying, 1840–1843
no such thing as half-t., 109

Tuesday's
child is full of grace, 200

Tunis
bey of T., 614

Turmoil
streets of our country are in t., 155

Turning
and t. in the widening gyre, 454

Turnip
Boiled t. will a roasted pullet be, 1682

TVA. *See* Tennessee Valley Authority.

Twain, Mark (*pseudonym of* Samuel Langhorne Clemens, 1835–1910), 108

Twenty
God forbid we should ever be 20 years without such a rebellion, 1623
same views at forty as we held at t., 26
to twenty-five! These are the years, 2088

Twenty-one
when I got to be 21, I was astonished at how much the old man had learned, 2003

Two
roads that lead to something like human happiness, 845

Two-thirds
of the people, 1620
[of the world] is up to something, 2037

Tyler, John (1747–1813), 1403

Tyrannical
In all t. governments, 788

Tyrannies
Russia is one of the worst t., 1653

Tyranny, 1844–1845
and oppressions of body and mind will vanish, 490
definition of t., 790
enemies of man: t., poverty and disease and war itself, 516
enemies of man—war, poverty, and t., 85
in our fair land, 1069
like hell, is not easily conquered, 1845
of poverty, 1615
over the mind of man, 1844
rid the world of the t. of facts, 585
That means first chaos, then t., 1005
two different and incompatable names—liberty and t., 1070

Tyrant
freedom cannot be served by the devices of the t., 640

Tyrants
children are now t., 195
ruled by t., 746

U

Ugliness
man-made u., 16

Ugly
you are u.—but tomorrow I'll be sober, 2004

Ultraliberalism
today translates into a whimpering isolationism, 1042

Ulysses
I am a part of all that I have met, 575
sailing farther than U. even dreamed of, 129

Un-American
most u. thing in America, 286

Unborn
fate of u. Millions, 1627
millions yet u., 1630
service to human kind yet u., 267

Uncertainty
no such u. as a sure thing, 172

Uncle Sam
over a barrel of oil, 527

Uncommon
right to be u., 71

Undecided
highly intelligent and well informed just to be u. about them [problems], 390

Underdogs
always, till history comes, after they are long dead, and puts them on top, 822

Underground
going u. to escape consequences of his own folly, 125
live u. with the moles, 125

Understanding
imperfection of human u., 716

Undisputed
thing, 631

Unemployment, 1846–1847
When a great many people are unable to find work, 1846

Unesco. *See* United Nations Educational, Scientific and Cultural Organization.

Unfair
Life is u., 1092

Union, 1848–1855
benefits and burdens of the U., 1849
But I'm a U. man, 1407
the Constitution, and the liberties of the people shall be perpetuated, 1852
dissolve this U., 1267
Emancipates the U., 1853
existence of our u., 1706
happy U. of these States, 1854
how stands the U., 1848
In u. there is strength, 1859
know how to save the U., 1701
Liberty first and U. afterwards, 1855
My allegiance is to this U. and to my State, 267
next to our liberty, most dear, 1849
now and forever, one and inseparable, 1855
of the English-speaking peoples, 499
Our U.—it must be preserved, 1849
saves the U. and the dream goes on, 1853

shall go on, 162
stands as she stood, rock-bottomed and copper-sheathed, one and indivisible, 1848
symbol of u. for [the United] States, 1867
that can only be maintained by swords and bayonets, 1850
While the U. lasts, 1855
would be imperiled, 938
Union Station, Washington, D.C.
inscription, 1252
Unions
Hitler attacked the u., 1749
penetrate the trade u., 245
Unitarians, 897
Unite
mankind u. together, 1861
nations will u., 1963
United
that means that we have all come together, 1364
United Mine Workers, 986
United Nations, 449, 477, 914, 1324, **1856–1858**
United Nations Educational, Scientific and Cultural Organization
preamble to the constitution, 1966
"United Nations Prayer," 1463
United States
acts like a pitiful, helpless giant, 1886
appear to be destined by Providence, 1047
can declare peace upon the world, 1318
creeping socialism spreading in the U.S., 1712
dig the grave of the U.S., 2043
drained, ditched, and damned the U.S. in three years, 1519
enemy of the people of the world, 2040
greatest fear of U.S. imperialism, 1927
if you incorporate those tropical countries with the Republic of the U.S., 1484
imperialism, 1927
is neither omnipotent or omniscient, 1735
is not just an old cow, 612
Is the U.S. going to decide, 1763
keep the U.S. free from political connexions, 619
not permitting . . . our armed forces and our valuable material to be immobilized within the continental U.S., 2062
Our loyalty is due entirely to the U.S., 1506
political activity prevailing in the U.S., 1428
property of the U.S. illegally transferred or leased, 951
recognition by the U.S. of the provisional government of Israel, 914
students from the U.S., 499
symbol of union for [the U.] S., 1867
take an affirmative position in outer space, 1740
traveling up and down the vast territories of the U.S., 86
Universal suffrage exists in the U.S. without producing any frightful consequences, 1904
unlettered pot-bellied money magnates of the U.S., 532
was suddenly and deliberately attacked by . . . Japan, 2066
we turn our rivers and streams into sewers, 313
will sink into the abyss of a new Dark Age, 2055
would [not] come to an end, 938
yielded in her turn to that taste for intervention, 2039
See also **America; American People; People**
United States Capitol. *See* **Capitol building, Washington, D.C.**
United States Department of Justice
inscription, 963
it is a problem for the Department of Justice, 154
should be kept most free from any suspicion of improper action, 961
United States Military Academy, West Point
inscription, 1874
Unity, 1859–1867
brethren to dwell together in u., 1860
frank cooperation and free debate are indispensable to ultimate u., 634
loss of social u., 227
of freedom and equality, 1482
Universal
satisfaction, 1227
suffrage exists in the United States without producing any frightful consequences, 1904
truth and applicability, 1644
Universities
are filled with students rebelling and rioting, 155
are wide gates to hell, 239
demands that dissidents are making of the u., 153
if . . . do not breed men who riot, 157
University
Do these murmurs come into the corridors of the u.?, 66
modern u., 504
University of Virginia
Father of the U. of V. [Thomas Jefferson's epitaph], 546
"Good Old Song," 1812
inscription, 238
University of Washington, 1015
Unjust
grossly u., 1230
Unlettered
pot-bellied money magnates of the United States, 532
Unpatriotically
to speak u. [of America], 45
Unrest
there must be created an adult u., 442
young people's u., 442
Untrue
could argue it u., 1284
Unwanted
woman is still doomed to lead a solitary life, 1165
Unwieldy
America is a great, u. Body, 44
Up
and not down, 1434
with which I will not put, 538
Uranium
may be turned into a new and important source of energy, 124
Urbanization, 621
haphazard u., 1896
Use
I shall u. my time, 1118
what u. is it, 1790
Useful
I knew something u., 1606
Usurpations
violent and sudden u., 523
Utopia
look for a different u., 1361
Utterances
silly, flat and dishwatery u., 1487
Utterly
without redeeming social importance, 1261
without redeeming social value, 1261

V

Vacations
art of taking minute v., 1480

Vagabond
class of v., ignorant, and ungoverned children, 46
Vain
did not live, or die, in v., 1324
erect no v. memorial, 376
I have not lived in v., 1323, 1469
life is v. unless one can act through the central government, 1361
name of the Lord thy God in v., 1804
pomp and glory of this world, 1103
Valleys
to the deep, deathlike v., 33
Valor
be ye men of v., 402
extreme v. and extreme benevolence, 826
virtue like v., 826
Valuable
Time is at once the most v. . . . of our possessions, 1816
Value
dearness only that gives everything its v., 1845
individual man . . . is the touchstone of v., 901
no dangers to the v. of property, 46
of government to the people it serves, 772
of money, 1203
the world sets upon motives, 1230
Values, 1868
and moral standards of our society, 1802
depart from these v. . . . at our peril, 1868
destroying the traditional v. of a civilization, 621
life's enduring v., 1480
moral standards and v., 1018
upon which our system is built, 1868
Vanity, 103
Vehemence
of youth, 2092
Vehement
young men to be v., 2094
Vehicular
mine, 2070
Velvet
man . . . who is both steel and v., 1109
Veneration
blind v. for antiquity, 82
Verdict
Sentence first—v. afterwards, 949
Vermin
I fear the v. that shall undermine, 293
Vermont, 65, 1848
Vermonter
advice which I received recently from a fellow V., 888
Versailles Treaty, 2046
Vertebrae
stiffening of the v., 6
Veterans Administration Building, Washington, D.C., inscription, 1325
Vice
blame him for the very v. which you feel in yourself, 520
contending elements of v. and virtue, 425
Extremism in the defense of liberty is no v., 581
moderation in principle, is a species of v., 1199
reproach him with the very defect or v. . . . you feel . . . in yourself, 520
suffering shall follow v., 783
Vice-Presidency
honorable and easy, 1493
Vices
and absurdities of contemporaries, 362
Fraud and prevarication are servile v., 1082
Victim
without murmuring, 820
Victor
to the v. belong the spoils, 1314
without oppression, 820
Victories
go forward and give us v., 1873
Victorious
people who remained v., 1869
Victor's
cup, 1358
Victory, 1869–1875
bear the fruits of v., 1874
Dawn of V., sat down to wait, and waiting—died, 1823
fight when there is no hope of v., 1634
Follow in His name to the Holy Grail of righteous v., 2061
general was doing more for v. by writing a poem, 1589
has 100 fathers, 1872
however long and hard the road may be, 1870
humble and gentle in v., 1469
in spite of all terror, 1870
In V.: Magnanimity, 1958
is liberty, 601
is sure to come, 688
that in us which can turn defeat into v., 1087
There is no substitute for v., 247
to the right, 1903
unmentioned results which follow v., 1950
v. at all costs, 1870
will be sure and not too costly, 1634
won some v. for humanity, 1875
Vietnam
freedom of South V. vital to our [United States] interests, 1880
people of V., against the Communists, 1882
state of war exists with North V., 1879
steaming jungle of V., 65
We cannot remain silent on V., 1877
Vietnam War, 110, 127, 169, 1140, **1876–1888**
Vietnamese
had nothing to fight for, 1878
View
of human life, 1574
of the universe, 1365
open to public v., 1573
Views
at forty, 26
felt in public affairs, 221
not limit our v. to . . . a single year, 1367
Vigilance
eternal v., 1054, 1073
people retain their virtue and v., 735
Vigilant
battle . . . is to the v., 1061
Be specially v., 467
be v. in its [freedom's] preservation, 663
protection of all their varied interests, 1670
Vim
youthful v. and vigor, 157
Vimeur, Jean-Baptiste-Donatien de, Comte de Rochambeau. *See* Rochambeau, Jean-Baptiste-Donatien deVimeur, Comte de.
Vinci, Leonardo da (1452–1519), 97
Vindicates
result v. the foresight of the fathers, 1974
Vindicating
opportunity of v. his character, 891
Violence, 1889-1896
apostles of v., 1894
as an instrument of persuasion, 1890
has no constitutional sanction, 1891
is as American as cherry pie, 1889

W